First Workshop on Natural Language Processing for Indigenous Languages of the Americas (AmericasNLP 2021)

Online
11 June 2021

ISBN: 978-1-7138-3015-3

Printed from e-media with permission by:

Curran Associates, Inc.
57 Morehouse Lane
Red Hook, NY 12571

Some format issues inherent in the e-media version may also appear in this print version.

Printed with permission by Curran Associates, Inc. (2021)

For permission requests, please contact the Association for Computational Linguistics at the address below.

Association for Computational Linguistics
209 N. Eighth Street
Stroudsburg, Pennsylvania 18360

Phone: 1-570-476-8006
Fax: 1-570-476-0860

acl@aclweb.org

Additional copies of this publication are available from:

Curran Associates, Inc.
57 Morehouse Lane
Red Hook, NY 12571 USA
Phone: 845-758-0400
Fax: 845-758-2633
Email: curran@proceedings.com
Web: www.proceedings.com

NAACL-HLT 2021

Natural Language Processing for Indigenous Languages of the Americas (AmericasNLP)

Proceedings of the First Workshop

June 11, 2021

Preface

This area is in all probability unmatched, anywhere in the world, in its linguistic multiplicity and diversity. A couple of thousand languages and dialects, at present divided into 17 large families and 38 small ones, with several hundred unclassified single languages, are on record. In one small portion of the area, in Mexico just north of the Isthmus of Tehuantepec, one finds a diversity of linguistic type hard to match on an entire continent in the Old World.
—McQuown (1955)

Workshop Organizers:

Manuel Mager
Arturo Oncevay
Annette Rios
Ivan Vladimir Meza Ruiz
Alexis Palmer
Graham Neubig
Katharina Kann

Shared Task Organizers:

Manuel Mager
Arturo Oncevay
Abteen Ebrahimi
John Ortega
Annette Rios
Angela Fan
Ximena Gutierrez-Vasques
Luis Chiruzzo
Gustavo A. Giménez-Lugo
Ricardo Ramos
Ivan Vladimir Meza Ruiz
Rolando Coto-Solano
Alexis Palmer
Elisabeth Mager
Vishrav Chaudhary
Graham Neubig
Ngoc Thang Vu
Katharina Kann

Program Committee:

Abhilasha Ravichander
Abteen Ebrahimi
Adam Wiemerslage
Alexandra Birch
Alfonso Medina-Urrea
Annette Rios
Antonios Anastasopoulos
Arturo Oncevay
Barry Haddow
Candace Ross
Cynthia Montaño
Daan van Esch
Ekaterina Vylomova
Emily M. Bender
Emily Prud'hommeaux
Eneko Agirre
Fernando Alva-Manchego
Francis Tyers
Gerardo Sierra Martínez
Ivan Vulić

John Miller
Judith Klavans
Luke Gessler
Manuel Mager
Marco Antonio Sobrevilla Cabezudo
Nickil Maveli
Pavel Denisov
Rico Sennrich
Robert Pugh
Roberto Zariquiey
Ronald Cardenas
Sarah Moeller
Shruti Rijhwani
Taraka Rama
William Abbott Lane
Ximena Gutierrez-Vasques
Yoshinari Fujinuma
Zoey Liu

Table of Contents

Workshop Program

June 11, 2021

June 11, 2021 (continued)

Leveraging English Word Embeddings for Semi-Automatic Semantic Classification in Nêhiyawêwin (Plains Cree)
Atticus Harrigan and Antti Arppe

Restoring the Sister: Reconstructing a Lexicon from Sister Languages using Neural Machine Translation
Remo Nitschke

Expanding Universal Dependencies for Polysynthetic Languages: A Case of St. Lawrence Island Yupik
Hyunji Park, Lane Schwartz and Francis Tyers

The More Detail, the Better? – Investigating the Effects of Semantic Ontology Specificity on Vector Semantic Classification with a Plains Cree / nêhiyawêwin Dictionary
Daniel Dacanay, Atticus Harrigan, Arok Wolvengrey and Antti Arppe

Experiments on a Guarani Corpus of News and Social Media
Santiago Góngora, Nicolás Giossa and Luis Chiruzzo

Towards a First Automatic Unsupervised Morphological Segmentation for Inuinnaqtun
Ngoc Tan Le and Fatiha Sadat

Toward Creation of Ancash Lexical Resources from OCR
Johanna CORDOVA and Damien Nouvel

Ayuuk-Spanish Neural Machine Translator
Delfino Zacarías Márquez and Ivan Vladimir Meza Ruiz

Explicit Tone Transcription Improves ASR Performance in Extremely Low-Resource Languages: A Case Study in Bribri
Rolando Coto-Solano

Towards a morphological transducer and orthography converter for Western Tlacolula Valley Zapotec
Jonathan Washington, Felipe Lopez and Brook Lillehaugen

Peru is Multilingual, Its Machine Translation Should Be Too?
Arturo Oncevay

Findings of the AmericasNLP 2021 Shared Task on Open Machine Translation for Indigenous Languages of the Americas
Manuel Mager, Arturo Oncevay, Abteen Ebrahimi, John Ortega, Annette Rios, Angela Fan, Ximena Gutierrez-Vasques, Luis Chiruzzo, Gustavo Giménez-Lugo, Ricardo Ramos, Ivan Vladimir Meza Ruiz, Rolando Coto-Solano, Alexis Palmer, Elisabeth Mager-Hois, Vishrav Chaudhary, Graham Neubig, Ngoc Thang Vu and Katharina Kann

June 11, 2021 (continued)

June 11, 2021 (continued)

qxoRef 1.0: A coreference corpus and mention-pair baseline for coreference resolution in Conchucos Quechua

Elizabeth Pankratz
Department of Linguistics, Universität Potsdam
14476 Potsdam, Germany
`pankratz1@uni-potsdam.de`

Abstract

This paper introduces qxoRef 1.0, the first coreference corpus to be developed for a Quechuan language, and describes a baseline mention-pair coreference resolution system developed for this corpus. The evaluation of this system will illustrate that earlier steps in the NLP pipeline, in particular syntactic parsing, should be in place before a complex task like coreference resolution can truly succeed. qxoRef 1.0 is freely available under a CC-BY-NC-SA 4.0 license.

1 Introduction

Coreference resolution is the task of identifying and grouping the phrases in a text that refer to the same real-life object, or in other words, grouping the mentions in a text—the phrases that refer to real-life objects—together into entities: clusters which represent those real-life objects (Ng, 2010; Jurafsky and Martin, 2020).

Coreference resolution has been an important area of focus in NLP for the last thirty years. It is often used as one component of an NLP pipeline: it builds on information gained through tools like syntactic parsers and semantic word embeddings, yielding clusters of mentions that can be useful for further NLP tasks like question answering and sentiment analysis (Pradhan et al., 2012).

To succeed at coreference resolution requires the synthesis of both linguistic and contextual (world) knowledge. Current state-of-the-art coreference systems accomplish this using deep learning (Lee et al., 2018) and are trained on large coreference corpora in majority languages like English, Chinese, and Arabic (Weischedel et al., 2011). Although the aims of the present paper are more modest, it still makes two important contributions to the field of coreference resolution for low-resource languages.

The first contribution is qxoRef 1.0, the first coreference corpus to be developed for a Quechuan language. The name reflects the variety of Quechua that appears in the corpus, namely (Southern) Conchucos Quechua (ISO 639-3 code `qxo`). qxoRef 1.0 is freely available under a Creative Commons CC-BY-NC-SA 4.0 license.[1] The second contribution is a baseline coreference resolution system trained on this corpus.

The term "Quechua" is generally used to refer to the Quechuan language family, a large group of related local varieties spoken widely in South America (Adelaar and Muysken, 2004; Sánchez, 2010). The number of speakers of Quechuan languages around the turn of the millennium was estimated at about eight million (Adelaar and Muysken, 2004), so it is not a small language family. However, it contains two branches of different sizes. According to the classification of Torero (1964), the smaller "Quechua I" is spoken in the Peruvian Highlands, while the much larger "Quechua II" is spoken throughout central and southern Peru as well as in parts of Ecuador (Adelaar and Muysken, 2004). The two branches differ lexically, morphologically, and orthographically.

The variety of Quechua appearing in qxoRef is spoken in Conchucos, a district within the department of Ancash in the Peruvian Highlands, and it belongs to Quechua I. (An alternative division of the language family is offered by Parker 1963, who labels Quechuan varieties with A or B. In that schema, Conchucos Quechua belongs to Quechua B.)

One challenge of having chosen a Quechua I variety to work with is the limited number of resources for that branch of the family tree. Quechua II, being much larger, has a handful of NLP tools already, including a toolknit developed by Rios (2015). This paper thus presents an exploratory illustration of how to develop a coreference corpus and baseline coreference system for a morphologically complex language in a low-resource situation.

[1] `https://github.com/epankratz/qxoRef`

Proceedings of the First Workshop on Natural Language Processing for Indigenous Languages of the Americas, pages 1–9
June 11, 2021. ©2021 Association for Computational Linguistics

Most coreference corpora are created for morphologically simple languages like English, but this project shows that the standard format for modern coreference corpora (the CoNLL-2012 shared task tabular format; Pradhan et al., 2012) can also easily accommodate a morphologically complex language like Quechua.

The paper will first discuss the creation of qxoRef in Section 2, and then move on to the baseline mention-pair system developed for it in Section 3. In the evaluation of this system in Section 4, we will see the consequences of not having earlier steps of the NLP pipeline in place before constructing a coreference resolution system. While surface features may passably substitute for some parts of a deeper linguistic analysis (Durrett and Klein, 2013) and are often the only type of feature that is available in a low-resource language, we will see that the data in qxoRef would still benefit significantly from linguistic analysis before the coreference resolution step takes place.

However, before turning to these details, a few words on Quechuan grammar are in order.

1.1 Quechua Grammar

Quechuan languages can be described as agglutinative (Sánchez, 2010, 10): words are morphologically complex, and one morpheme generally encodes a single meaning, although a handful of syncretic morphemes also exist (e.g., *-shayki* in (1) below).

A relevant feature of Quechua for the coreference resolution task is the use of null arguments (Sánchez, 2010, 12); in other words, Quechua is a pro-drop language. Consider the sentence in (1).

(1) cuenta-ri-shayki huk cuento-ta
tell-ITER-1.SUB>2.OBJ.FUT one story-ACC
'I will tell you a story.' (KP04, 2–7)[2]

Nothing explicitly fills the role of subject (*I*) or indirect object (*you*) in this sentence. The suffix *-shayki*, like all personal reference markers on Quechua verbs, only indicates agreement and has no pronominal function (Sánchez, 2010, 21). Ideally, we would want to include null arguments in the mention annotation, as other coreference corpora of pro-drop languages do. However, as we will see in the next section, no resources for Conchucos Quechua exist that would make this possible.

[2]Examples from qxoRef will be referred to using the document identifier, here KP04, and the range of indices in that document that the example spans, here 2 to 7 (inclusive).

2 qxoRef 1.0

This section presents qxoRef 1.0, a coreference corpus for Conchucos Quechua and, to the author's knowledge, the first such resource developed for a Quechuan language. The section first explores how earlier coreference corpora in other pro-drop languages are structured (Section 2.1). It then moves on to the data that qxoRef is based on (Section 2.2), how the mentions in this data were annotated (Section 2.3), and some remaining limitations of the present version of the corpus (Section 2.4).

2.1 Coreference corpora for pro-drop languages

Three pro-drop languages for which coreference corpora have been developed are Czech, Spanish, and Catalan. Corpora in these languages—PCEDT 2.0 (Nedoluzhko et al., 2016) for Czech, AnCora (Recasens and Martí, 2010) for Spanish and Catalan—incorporate null subjects by way of syntactic annotation. All sentences in the corpora receive syntactic parses, and crucially, the parser introduces nodes that correspond to the null arguments, so that those nodes can then be annotated for coreference (Recasens and Martí, 2010, 319; Nedoluzhko et al., 2016, 173).

Unlike many other Indigenous languages, Quechua does have an NLP toolkit that includes a dependency parser (Rios, 2015). Unfortunately, two features of this toolkit make it inapplicable to the current project. For one, it was developed for Cuzco Quechua, a Quechua II variety, and Cuzco Quechua differs enough from Conchucos Quechua (Quechua I) that significant intervention would be needed in order to apply the parser to the present data. For another, while the parser does insert dummy elements for phenomena like omitted copulas, verb ellipsis in coordinations, and internally headed relative clauses, it does not insert anything for null arguments (Rios, 2015, 62). Thus, even if the parser were adapted for Conchucos Quechua, it would not supply the null argument nodes that would be needed for coreference annotation. We are therefore forced to rely on the information already provided in the data. We turn to this next.

2.2 The data

The data in qxoRef consists of transcribed recordings of stories told by native Quechua speakers in Huari, Peru in 2015 (Bendezú Araujo et al., 2019). The recordings are a subset of a larger audio cor-

Orthography	huk	runa	oshqu	ñawiwan	tinkuskiyaan
Segmentation	huk	runa	oshqu	ñawi-wan	tinku-ski-yaa-n
Glosses (Sp.)	uno	persona	azul	ojo-INST	encontrar-ITER-PL-3
Glosses (En.)	one	person	blue	eye-INST	find-ITER-PL-3
Translation (Sp.)	se encuentra con una persona de ojos azules				
Translation (En.)	he meets a person with blue eyes				

Table 1: A representation of the data's original multi-tier annotation format

pus of Quechua speakers participating in various experimental tasks.[3] The chosen subset consists of the "cuento" task, which mimics the children's game "telephone": the experimenters first told the Quechua speakers an invented story, and the speakers were recorded while recounting this story to one another in pairs. The "cuento" task was chosen because the format of a story, with repeated references to recurring entities, provides the most suitable data for coreference resolution. qxoRef contains the stories told by twelve participants, resulting in twelve documents.

The contents of the stories are somewhat surreal: one focuses on a healer's journey to search for medicinal plants, and the other is about a corpse's encounter with two woodpeckers. The unusual content is due to the goals of the original research project. The project studied Quechua prosody and phonology, so the stories were built around words chosen for their metrical properties in Quechua. English translations of each of these stories are given in Appendix A.

As Table 1 illustrates, the documents in their original forms consist of a transcription of the audio data, morphological segmentation and glossing, and translations into English and Spanish. The transcriptions, morphological segmentation and glossing, and translations into Spanish were done by hand by Quechua speakers in Huaraz and Lima, Peru. Further postprocessing, including normalising the orthography, unifying the morphological analyses and glosses, and translating into English, was done by the original researchers. The documents in this corpus are provided as `.eaf` files that can be processed using the annotation software ELAN (Sloetjes and Wittenburg, 2008).

[3]This corpus is provided under a CC-BY-NC-SA 4.0 licence at `https://refubium.fu-berlin.de/handle/fub188/25747`, and its documentation, including details about the "cuento" task used in qxoRef, can be found at `https://www.geisteswissenschaften.fu-berlin.de/en/we05/forschung/drittmittelprojekte/Einzelprojekte/DFG-projekt-zweisprachige-Prosodie/index.html`.

Before converting these files to the standard CoNLL-2012 shared task format (Pradhan et al., 2012), problematic artefacts of speech data (filled pauses within noun phrases, false starts, and utterances marked as unintelligible) were removed. The stems were also POS-tagged, the sentences divided, and the (non-null) mentions manually annotated by the author. The mention annotation will be the focus of the next section.

Table 2 gives the number of words, morphemes, and mentions in each of the documents in qxoRef 1.0, as well as the story that each document contains, and Table 3 shows the same phrase from Table 1 in the CoNLL format. The CoNLL-U guidelines[4] define how morphologically complex units can be split into smaller sub-word elements. The indexing of these elements is done by sub-word unit, with morphologically complex elements indexed with the integer range of the elements they contain. And as Table 3 illustrates, the gloss of each morpheme is always attached to that morpheme, rather than to the stem, for clarity and for easier access to individual tags.

2.3 Mentions in qxoRef

The mentions in qxoRef 1.0 belong to two classes: nouns and pronouns. The nominal mentions involve nouns that may or may not host case endings, that stand alone or next to other nouns, that are preceded by numerals or demonstratives, or that belong to complex phrases with modifying elements.

Two types of pronouns appear in qxoRef: personal pronouns and demonstrative pronouns. Personal pronouns are rare, since they are generally dropped; in fact, in all of qxoRef, there is only one instance each of the first and third person pronouns, *nuqa* and *pay* respectively, and a handful more of the second person, *qam*.

There are two types of demonstrative pronouns: proximal *kay* and distal *tsay*. *Tsay* is a multifunctional element: it may be used as a determiner, and it can also act as a deictic element in space and time

[4]`https://universaldependencies.org/format.html#words-tokens-and-empty-nodes`

Doc. ID	Story	Wd.	Morph.	Ment.
Training set				
AZ23	H	121	294	22
HA30	W	42	90	12
KP04	H	197	420	52
QF16	H	151	305	35
SG15	H	79	176	14
XQ33	W	69	164	16
XU31	H	201	452	51
ZR29	W	146	309	38
Test set				
LC34	W	82	190	24
OA32	H	105	224	26
TP03	H	136	334	27
ZZ24	H	84	179	15
	Σ train	1006	2210	240
	Σ test	407	927	92
	Σ total	1413	3137	332

Table 2: The number of words, morphemes, and mentions in each document in qxoRef, along with the train/test split and which story each document contains (H: the healer's journey; W: an encounter with woodpeckers)

as in *tsay-chaw* 'there' (lit. DEM.DIST-LOC(ative); AZ23, 55–56) and *tsay-shi* 'then' (lit. DEM.DIST-REP(ortative); XU31, 8–9). Occasionally it is also used as a filler in speech. Only the demonstrative pronouns that are clearly referential (identifiable by the case marking) are annotated as mentions.

In addition to the unambiguously referential pronouns, all nominal phrases were annotated as mentions. The mentions spanned all morphemes contained in those phrases so that the classifiers could potentially use the case and number information to establish coreference.

The annotation process was straightforward. It was possible to annotate mentions at the lexical level because Quechua has no referential sub-word elements. (The agreement marking on verbs would be the closest candidate, but as mentioned above, they are only markers and not incorporated pronouns, so they should not be considered mentions.) In any cases where a pronoun could refer to multiple available entities, the English and Spanish translations were used as a guideline for selecting the correct antecedent.

2.4 Limitations of qxoRef 1.0

One limitation of the present version of the corpus has already been discussed: since the data has not been syntactically parsed to produce slots in the sentences where the null arguments would be, those arguments are not annotated as mentions.

The second limitation also concerns the mention annotation. Since the project was fairly limited in scope, the annotation was done only by the author. Annotating only nouns and pronouns does not involve as many degrees of freedom as the annotation of a larger corpus like OntoNotes, which contains many classes of coreference (cf. Pradhan et al., 2012), but the mention annotation in qxoRef 1.0 is still potentially idiosyncratic. And because reliable annotation is crucial for creating robust coreference systems that can be depended on in downstream applications (Pradhan et al., 2012, 1–2), in future iterations of this corpus, multiple annotators should be involved.

3 A mention-pair baseline for Conchucos Quechua

The data in qxoRef 1.0 was used to train a baseline coreference resolution system for Conchucos Quechua. How that system was implemented will be the focus of the present section; afterward, Section 4 will discuss its performance with an illustrative error analysis.

3.1 The mention-pair approach to coreference resolution

The idea behind the mention-pair approach is simple: given a pair of mentions—a candidate anaphor and a candidate antecedent—a binary classifier is trained to predict whether that pair is coreferential (Ng, 2010; Jurafsky and Martin, 2020).

This method has been influential in the field of coreference resolution since the earliest days, and the motivation to apply it again here, despite the availability of modern deep-learning-based methods, is twofold. For one, binary classification is a simple task, and much less data is needed to train a binary classifier than would be required for state-of-the-art deep learning methods. For another, training a classifier using an interpretable algorithm like a random forest (Breiman, 2001) can tell us which features are important for establishing coreference in the available data: helpful information for conducting an error analysis and determining how to improve the system.

138	huk	P1	one	NUM	(12
139	runa	P1	person	NOUN	-
140	oshqu	P1	blue	ADJ	-
141-142	ñawiwan	P1		_	-
141	ñawi	P1	eye	NOUN	-
142	-wan	P1		INST	12)
143-146	tinkuskiyaan	P1		_	-
143	tinku	P1	find	VERB	-
144	-ski	P1		ITER	-
145	-yaa	P1		PL	-
146	-n	P1		3	-

Table 3: A sample sentence from qxoRef (AZ23, 138–146; 'He meets a person with blue eyes') in the CoNLL format. Note that the null arguments are not annotated; there is no mention corresponding to the third-person subject of *tinkuskiyaan*. (Columns: morpheme index, Quechua text, speaker ID, English translations of the stems, POS tags of stems/glosses for each morpheme, coreference annotation)

3.2 Features

The coreference classifier was trained using 28 features generated for every mention pair in the training data (see Section 3.3). These features included information about each mention in the pair as well as the relationship between them. The features can be divided into three classes: string-based features, grammatical features, and discourse features.

The **string-based features** include the Levenshtein edit distance between the two mention strings, the length of the longest common substring, whether the anaphor string contains the antecedent string and vice versa, and whether or not the anaphor is longer than the antecedent.

Next, the **grammatical features** have to do with characteristics like the plurality of individual mentions; the type of individual mentions (whether they are nouns or pronouns); and how many stems, grammatical morphemes, and morphemes overall they share.

Finally, the **discourse features** include the number of sentences between the two mentions in the pair, the number of other mentions between the mention pair, and whether or not the mentions were produced by the same speaker.

Further classes of features are known to be important for establishing coreference (Ng, 2010), such as syntactic features (e.g., what role the mention plays in the sentence) and semantic features (e.g., cosine similarity between embedding representations of the head word). Here again, we feel the effects of the lack of resources. If we had a syntactic parser, we could to include syntactic features, and if we had embeddings, we could include semantic ones.[5] Nevertheless, surface features have been shown to pick up on some linguistically relevant information (Durrett and Klein, 2013), and we will see below that the present selection does an adequate job.

3.3 Creating training data

In order to learn whether two mentions are coreferential, the classifier was trained on a dataset in which a pair of mentions is represented as an instance. In general, creating training data by simply taking all ordered pairs of mentions in a document is not recommended, because then the data will contain far more negative instances than positive instances (i.e., many more non-coreferential pairs than coreferential ones), and a skewed class distribution in the training data will lead to poorer performance on the test data (Soon et al., 2001).

Therefore, the literature proposes several different heuristics for creating training datasets for mention-pair systems. For the sake of exploration, this project used three of these heuristics to create three different training sets, train one classifier on each of these, and compare the performance of the three classifiers. Will a larger training set lead to better performance because there is simply more data, or will a more selectively-chosen set lead to better performance?

The first heuristic is the most common one in the literature, proposed by Soon et al. (2001). This method creates training instances by pairing each mention with every preceding mention up to and including the closest coreferential one, that is, up to and including the closest true antecedent of the given anaphor. Thus, for each mention, there is one positive instance and some number of negative instances (possibly zero).

[5]Sub-word embeddings for a Quechua II variety do exist (Heinzerling and Strube, 2018), but as with the toolkit developed by Rios (2015), the differences between Quechua I and Quechua II make those embeddings inapplicable here.

Heuristic	Inst.	Neg. inst.	Prop.
Soon et al.	1358	1214	89.4%
Ng & Cardie	1194	1060	88.8%
Bengtson & Roth	3922	3463	88.3%

Table 4: Properties of the three training sets: the number of instances, the number of negative instances, and the proportion of negative instances

The next heuristic is an adaptation to Soon et al.'s method by Ng and Cardie (2002). They refine this algorithm by excluding any mention pairs in which the candidate anaphor is a noun and the candidate antecedent a pronoun, because "it is not easy for a human, much less a machine learner, to learn from a positive instance where the antecedent of a non-pronominal NP is a pronoun" (Ng, 2010, 1398). Like the method of Soon et al., this heuristic yields one positive instance and zero or more negative instances for each mention.

The final heuristic was proposed by Bengtson and Roth (2008) and is more liberal than the previous two. This method simply uses all ordered pairs of mentions going back to the beginning of the document, but maintaining Ng and Cardie's stipulation that nouns not refer back to pronouns. This heuristic yields multiple negative instances and potentially multiple positive instances for each mention.

The train/test split, shown in Table 2 above, is approximately 70/30 in the number of words, morphemes, and mentions. Table 4 shows some properties of the three training datasets created from the eight training documents using the heuristics from Soon et al., Ng and Cardie, and Bengtson and Roth. The proportion of negative instances to positive ones is comparable in all three cases, but the size of the datasets ranges widely.

Finally, it should be noted that for all documents, singleton mentions—those referring to entities that are only mentioned once—were removed before generating both training and test sets (in line with the OntoNotes corpus, which does not annotate singletons at all).

3.4 Creating test data

The mentions used in the test data are the original gold mentions (rather than, say, those proposed by a mention detection algorithm). Using gold mentions is more appropriate for a baseline, since it keeps the focus on the performance of the system, and comparing mentions that have the same boundaries also makes the evaluation more straightforward (Ng, 2010, 1403).

Each of the four test documents was converted into a test dataset following the method outlined by Soon et al. (2001, 528): each mention serves as a candidate anaphor, and each candidate anaphor is paired with every mention that precedes it in the given document.

3.5 The coreference classifier

As mentioned above, the coreference classifier used in the present system was a random forest, continuing the tradition of the widespread use of decision-tree-based systems in coreference resolution (Ng, 2010). Random forests are ensemble learning methods that reduce error rates by taking the majority vote from many individual decision trees trained on random subsets of the data. A great strength of random forests is their interpretability: we can ascertain how important individual features are for the classification decision based, roughly speaking, on how high they appear in the decision trees used in the ensemble (cf. Breiman, 2001).

The random forest was implemented in Python using the machine learning library `scikit-learn` (Pedregosa et al., 2011). After training, the top-ranking features for all three classifiers were both indicators of string similarity: the Levenshtein edit distance and the length of the longest common substring. This result is unsurprising, considering the kinds of mentions that were included in qxoRef 1.0: mostly nouns (88% of all mentions), a handful of pronouns (12%), and no null arguments. Thus, coreferential mentions are generally similar to one another at the level of the string. Mentions that would require grammatical or discourse-based information (pronouns and null arguments) are rare or non-existent.

3.6 Clustering

The final step of the coreference resolution procedure was to apply the trained classifiers to the test data to predict which mention pairs contained in those documents are coreferential. This was done using the method used in Soon et al. (2001) that was later called "closest-first clustering" (Ng, 2010; Jurafsky and Martin, 2020).

This algorithm iterates through the test data one anaphor at a time, looking at the pair that anaphor makes with every mention that precedes it in the document. The classifier is applied to each of these

	MUC			B^3			$CEAF_e$			
Heur.	**Rec.**	**Prec.**	**F1**	**Rec.**	**Prec.**	**F1**	**Rec.**	**Prec.**	**F1**	**Avg. F1**
SO	55.51	88.82	68.2	47.43	**91.53**	62.3	64.98	67.45	65.75	65.41
NC	**60.56**	**91.26**	**72.79**	**51.13**	90.98	**65.42**	**68.26**	**68.43**	**67.33**	**68.51**
BR	58.73	86.9	70.04	49.48	86.84	62.93	60.9	63.76	61.08	64.68

Table 5: Evaluation results for the three training data creation heuristics (SO: Soon et al.; NC: Ng & Cardie; BR: Bengtson & Roth)

mention pairs until a positive classification occurs. Then, the algorithm skips the rest of the pairs containing the current anaphor and moves on to the next one. Importantly, if there is never a positive classification decision, then the anaphor is not classified as coreferential with anything and is ignored.

This clustering algorithm was applied to predict all the mention pairs in the test documents. Then, to arrive at the representations of the entities in each document, the transitive closure of all of the predicted mention pairs was computed. The next section compares the performances of the three classifiers and analyses the errors that they made.

4 Evaluation and error analysis

The evaluation of each classifier's performance used the standard three coreference metrics—MUC, B^3, and $CEAF_e$—as implemented in the scoring scripts from the CoNLL-2012 shared task (Pradhan et al., 2012). The results are given in Table 5.

Strikingly, although the proportion of positive to negative instances in the training data is nearly identical (see Table 4), the resulting classifiers performed quite differently. Even though the heuristic from Ng and Cardie (2002) produced the smallest amount of training data, it performed best—far better, in fact, than the heuristic that produces the largest amount of training data, Bengtson and Roth (2008). By removing pronouns as antecedents, Ng and Cardie's algorithm was likely more faithful to the actual imbalanced proportion of nouns to pronouns in the data.

The general pattern, at least in the MUC and B^3 metrics, is high precision and low recall. In other words, when the mentions were classified as coreferential, this was generally done correctly. However, the clustering procedure often failed to identify coreference links between anaphors and their true antecedents, leading to that anaphor's omission from the final entity representations. The error analysis in the next section will explore why this might have been the case.

4.1 Error analysis

The interpretability of random forests serves us well in trying to understand the results of the evaluation. For example, we can see that, because the classifiers favoured string and morpheme similarity, they fell short when dealing with coreferential mentions whose surface forms diverge.

For instance, *hampi ashiq runaqa* 'person searching for medicine' (TP03, 316–320) is the same person as *tsay hampikuq runa* 'that healer person' (TP03, 213–215), and although the strings do contain some overlap (*runa* 'person' and *hampi* 'medicine' appear in both), they are dissimilar enough that none of the classifiers recognised these two mentions as coreferential.

For the same reason, the classifiers also frequently failed to identify an antecedent for demonstrative pronouns, since often, the only commonality between the string of a demonstrative pronoun and the antecedent was the case marking (and sometimes not even that). For example, *tsayqa* 'that one' (ZZ24, 25–26) was not recognised by any of the classifiers as coreferential with *hampikuq runa* 'healer person' (ZZ24, 3–4) because the strings have very little in common.

Further, the corpus contains cataphoric constructions like *tsayqa, tsay, huk runaqa* 'that one, that, a person' (OA32, 147–152) in which *tsayqa* and *huk runaqa* are coreferential (and the middle *tsay* acts as a filled pause). None of the classifiers successfully identified the coreference there—not even the Soon et al. classifier, which was the only one to have seen pronouns as antecedents in its training data.

These examples show that the classifiers all failed on certain kinds of mention pairs. But were there any systematic differences between the classifiers?

The feature importance scores of the classifiers indicated that the importance of grammatical features was, on average, higher for the Bengtson and Roth classifier than for the other two. One might therefore expect this classifier to be better at identifying coreference involving pronouns. However, this prediction is not borne out; all classifiers seemed to deal with pronouns equally poorly.

In sum, the low recall is probably due to the nature of the mentions in qxoRef 1.0. The dominance of explicit nominal mentions rewarded string matching over grammatical knowledge, meaning that connections between superficially dissimilar mentions were often overlooked. If null arguments were also included, however, the classifiers would have to base their decisions on more broadly applicable grammatical features. This would be a more accurate representation of what is really involved in the coreference resolution task.

5 Conclusion and outlook

This paper introduced qxoRef 1.0, a new coreference corpus for Conchucos Quechua, and presented a mention-pair baseline for coreference resolution with this corpus that obtains an average F1 score of 68.51.

Several directions for future work are clear. First, the coreference corpus should be improved. A more reliable dataset should be created by having mentions annotated by multiple annotators and computing the inter-annotator agreement.

Further, the sentences should be syntactically parsed. Not only would this allow a more sophisticated feature representation for use in the classifier, it would also allow null arguments to be annotated as mentions. This should lead to higher recall, since fewer mentions will be discarded because the coreference connections are missed. (And until a parser for Conchucos Quechua becomes available, an interim measure of introducing empty slots where the null arguments would be would already likely lead to a more robust system, even without the underlying syntactic structure.)

Additionally, other avenues for improving the feature representations should be explored. For example, embeddings for a compatible variety of Quechua are not out of reach. Ancash Quechua is a variety that subsumes Conchucos Quechua, and a collection of texts in this variety is available on the Ancash Quechua wikimedia page. This material could be used to create sub-word embeddings, for example following the procedure laid out in Heinzerling and Strube (2018), that could then be used to encode semantic information about the mentions for use in the classifier.

Overall, this project has highlighted some of the issues involved in NLP for low-resource languages. To succeed at complex NLP tasks like coreference resolution, certain steps in the text processing pipeline should already have been achieved, syntactic parsing being a prominent example. Improving the basic NLP toolkits for low-resource languages will lead to greater success on tasks like coreference resolution, which is in turn important for even more complex downstream tasks. Our focus should therefore first be on developing basic tools and extending existing ones, and then we can work upward from there.

References

Willem F. H. Adelaar and Pieter Muysken. 2004. *The Languages of the Andes*. Cambridge Language Surveys. Cambridge University Press, Cambridge/New York.

Raúl Bendezú Araujo, Timo Buchholz, and Uli Reich. 2019. *Corpora Amerikanischer Sprachen: Interaktive Sprachspiele Aus Dem Mehrsprachigen Lateinamerika (Quechua 1)*. Refubium, Freie Universität Berlin, Berlin.

Eric Bengtson and Dan Roth. 2008. Understanding the Value of Features for Coreference Resolution. In *Proceedings of the 2008 Conference on Empirical Methods in Natural Language Processing*, pages 294–303, Honolulu, Hawaii. Association for Computational Linguistics.

Leo Breiman. 2001. Random forests. *Machine learning*, 45(1):5–32.

Greg Durrett and Dan Klein. 2013. Easy Victories and Uphill Battles in Coreference Resolution. In *Proceedings of the 2013 Conference on Empirical Methods in Natural Language Processing*, pages 1971–1982, Seattle, Washington, USA. Association for Computational Linguistics.

Benjamin Heinzerling and Michael Strube. 2018. BPEmb: Tokenization-free Pre-trained Subword Embeddings in 275 Languages. In *Proceedings of the Eleventh International Conference on Language Resources and Evaluation (LREC 2018)*, pages 2989–2993.

Daniel Jurafsky and James H. Martin. 2020. *Speech and Language Processing: An Introduction to Natural Language Processing, Computational Linguistics, and Speech Recognition*, 3rd ed. draft edition.

Kenton Lee, Luheng He, and Luke Zettlemoyer. 2018. Higher-Order Coreference Resolution with Coarse-to-Fine Inference. In *Proceedings of the 2018 Conference of the North American Chapter of the Association for Computational Linguistics: Human Language Technologies, Volume 2 (Short Papers)*, pages 687–692, New Orleans, Louisiana. Association for Computational Linguistics.

Anna Nedoluzhko, Michal Novak, Silvie Cinkova, Marie Mikulova, and Jiři Mırovsky. 2016. Coreference in Prague Czech-English Dependency Treebank. In *Proceedings of LREC 2016*, pages 169–176.

Vincent Ng. 2010. Supervised Noun Phrase Coreference Research: The First Fifteen Years. In *Proceedings of the 48th Annual Meeting of the Association for Computational Linguistics*, pages 1396–1411, Uppsala, Sweden. Association for Computational Linguistics.

Vincent Ng and Claire Cardie. 2002. Improving Machine Learning Approaches to Coreference Resolution. In *Proceedings of the 40th Annual Meeting of the Association for Computational Linguistics*, pages 104–111, Philadelphia, Pennsylvania, USA. Association for Computational Linguistics.

Gary J. Parker. 1963. Clasificacion genetica de los dialectos quechuas. *Revista del Museo Nacional*, 32:241–252.

F. Pedregosa, G. Varoquaux, A. Gramfort, V. Michel, B. Thirion, O. Grisel, M. Blondel, P. Prettenhofer, R. Weiss, V. Dubourg, J. Vanderplas, A. Passos, D. Cournapeau, M. Brucher, M. Perrot, and E. Duchesnay. 2011. Scikit-learn: Machine learning in Python. *Journal of Machine Learning Research*, 12:2825–2830.

Sameer Pradhan, Alessandro Moschitti, Nianwen Xue, Olga Uryupina, and Yuchen Zhang. 2012. CoNLL-2012 Shared Task: Modeling multilingual unrestricted coreference in OntoNotes. In *Joint Conference on EMNLP and CoNLL - Shared Task*, pages 1–40, Jeju Island, Korea. Association for Computational Linguistics.

Marta Recasens and M. Antònia Martí. 2010. AnCora-CO: Coreferentially annotated corpora for Spanish and Catalan. *Language Resources and Evaluation*, 44(4):315–345.

Annette Rios. 2015. *A Basic Language Technology Toolkit for Quechua*. PhD thesis, University of Zurich.

Liliana Sánchez. 2010. *The Morphology and Syntax of Topic and Focus: Minimalist Inquiries in the Quechua Periphery*. Number v. 169 in Linguistik Aktuell/Linguistics Today (LA). John Benjamins Pub. Co, Amsterdam/Philadelphia.

Han Sloetjes and Peter Wittenburg. 2008. Annotation by category - ELAN and ISO DCR. In *Proceedings of the 6th International Conference on Language Resources and Evaluation (LREC 2008)*.

Wee Meng Soon, Hwee Tou Ng, and Daniel Chung Yong Lim. 2001. A Machine Learning Approach to Coreference Resolution of Noun Phrases. *Computational Linguistics*, 27(4):521–544.

Alfredo Torero. 1964. Los dialectos quechuas. *Anales Científicos de la Universidad Agraria*, 2(4):446–478.

Ralph Weischedel, Eduard Hovy, Mitchell Marcus, Martha Palmer, Robert Belvin, Sameer Pradhan, Lance Ramshaw, and Nianwen Xue. 2011. OntoNotes: A large training corpus for enhanced processing. In Joseph Olive, Caitlin Christianson, and John McCary, editors, *Handbook of Natural Language Processing and Machine Translation*, pages 54–63. Springer.

A Story translations

An encounter with woodpeckers (adapted from ZR29): "They say a corpse met some woodpeckers. When they met, the woodpeckers were below an alder. Those woodpeckers were the children of a healer. They were eating some lice. When they met the corpse, the corpse asked the woodpeckers, 'Is there a healer here? You are the children of the healer. I believe I am sick, I want to be healed.' When he said this, the woodpeckers laughed and said, 'How will we do that for you? You want to be healed. But you are already dead.'"

The healer's journey (adapted from TP03): "It's said that once upon a time, a healer went looking for medicine. It was already afternoon when he left, and while he was going, night came. He finished his meal: only corn and a little meat. While he walked and it got dark, he got very cold, and having nothing more to eat, he ate six flies that had come to him. When it got dark, he stayed where he was. Early the next day, he left and met a squinty-eyed [or sometimes blue-eyed -EP] man. This man was sitting on top of a chuchura plant. The healer asked the man, 'Where could I find medicinal plants?' The one sitting on the chuchura said, 'If you give me your soul, I will tell you.' The healer was clever, so he gave him the souls of the six flies instead. When he gave them to him, the other man was suspicious that he was being cheated, but he told him where to go anyway to find the medicinal plants. The healer got there quickly and laughed a lot."

A corpus of K'iche' annotated for morphosyntactic structure

Francis M. Tyers
Department of Linguistics
Indiana University
ftyers@iu.edu

Robert Henderson
Department of Linguistics
University of Arizona
rhenderson@arizona.edu

Abstract

This article describes a collection of sentences in K'iche' annotated for morphology and syntax. K'iche' is a language in the Mayan language family, spoken in Guatemala. The annotation is done according to the guidelines of the Universal Dependencies project. The corpus consists of a total of 1,433 sentences containing approximately 10,000 tokens and is released under a free/open-source licence. We present a comparison of parsing systems for K'iche' using this corpus and describe how it can be used for mining linguistic examples.

1 Introduction

For some time, one of the fundamental resources for language technology has been a part-of-speech tagged (or morphologically annotated and disambiguated) corpus. Creating these resources has traditionally been a lengthy process, from defining an annotation scheme to collecting texts, training annotators and performing the annotation. Recently however advances in annotation schemes and end-to-end linguistic processing pipelines mean that the development of a single resource, a treebank can enable a whole pipeline of language analysis tools from tokenisation to dependency parsing from a single resource.

In this paper we describe the annotation of such a corpus for K'iche', a Mayan language of Guatemala and outline how the corpus can be used to train systems for linguistic annotation.

The remainder of the paper is laid out as follows: Section 2 gives a brief grammatical overview of K'iche'; Section 3 gives an overview of related work on K'iche' syntax; Section 4 describes the corpus and preprocessing steps; Section 5 describes the annotation process; Section 6 describes a range of syntactic constructions in K'iche' and how they were annotated. We evaluate parsing performance using the corpus in Section 7 and show how models trained on the corpus can be used in finding linguistic examples. Finally, we describe some future work (Section 8) and present some concluding remarks (Section 9).

2 K'iche'

K'iche' (ISO-639-3: `quc`, also *K'ichee'*, previously *Quiché*) is a language within the Quichean-Mamean branch of the Mayan language family. As of the 2018 Guatemalan census, it is documented to have over 1.5 million native speakers, however the number is likely higher now and does not account for speakers in the diaspora. There are roughly 23 variants of K'iche' spoken throughout southwestern Guatemala.

K'iche' is a language with ergative-absolutive alignment, basic verb-initial order of constituents, and prefixes for agreement. The language is both prefixing (for inflection) and suffixing (for derivation and some inflection). Neither subject nor object need be overtly expressed when recoverable from context.

An important part of the K'iche' grammatical system are the sets of agreement markers. These are traditionally split into set A and set B. Set A, or the ergative (ERG) markers, are used on nouns to cross-reference, that is, agree with, their possessors and on verbs to indicate a transitive subject. Set B markers, or the absolutive (ABS) markers, are used to cross-reference the transitive object or intransitive subject. Table 1 shows the markers.

K'iche' verbal morpho-syntax, like other Mayan languages, is organised around transitivity. Root verbs, i.e., verbs of the form CVC, and their derived non-CVC counterparts are classified as either transitive or intransitive, and this classification has implications for the kinds of morphology the verb can take. It controls the distribution of Set A and Set B morphology that we have already seen, but it also constrains what kinds of nominalisations a verb stem allows (Can Pixabaj, 2009), a well as which 'Status Suffixes' a verb stem takes (see section 6.9

Proceedings of the First Workshop on Natural Language Processing for Indigenous Languages of the Americas, pages 10–20
June 11, 2021.

Person	Set A (ERG)		Set B (ABS)
	_ C	_ V	_
SG1	*nu-*	*inw-*	*in-*
SG2	*a-*	*aw-*	*at-*
SG3	*u-*	*r-*	*ø-*
PL1	*qa-*	*q-*	*oj-*
PL2	*i-*	*iw-*	*ix-*
PL3	*ki-*	*k-*	*e-*

Table 1: The Set A and Set B person and number agreement markers for K'iche'. Set A markers are used on nouns to indicate possession and on verbs to indicate a transitive subject, and Set B markers are used on nouns for predication and on verbs for transitive object or intransitive subject. The third person singular Set B marker is null. The Set A markers have phonological variants before consonants, C and vowels, V. There are also formal forms which appear as a combination of one of the prefixes with a following particle, *lal* or *alaj*. The Set B first person plural morph may also be *uj-*.

for more discussion of this unique aspect of Mayan morphology).

While the basic word of K'iche' is VOS, all possible word orders are attested, conditioned by discourse factors, the most important of which are topic and focus. Focus involves marking the focused expression with a focus particle, and then preposing it to a position before the verb. Topicalisation involves morphologically unmarked preposing of the topicalised expression before the verb. If a clause contains both topicalised and focused expressions, the topic comes before the focus.

3 Related work

Broadly, this work is a corpus of K'iche' sentences, morphosyntactically analysed and annotated in a way to support downstream natural language processing tasks like machine translation, relation extraction, etc. While there are annotated corpora of K'iche', like the K'iche' segment of the *Oxlajuuj Keej Maya' Ajtz'iib'* Mayan Languages Collection (Oxlajuuj Keej Maya' Ajtz'iib', 2021) of Telma Can Pixabaj's 2018 annotated collection of ceremonial discourse in K'iche', these are not in easily parsable formats that can be fed directly into existing NLP pipelines. The nearest analogs to the work presented here are Sachse's 2016 XML standard for morphological annotations of Mayan languages, including K'iche', and Palmer's 2010 IGT-XML corpus of the related language Uspanteko. While parseable, and annotated with grammatical information like part-of-speech, these are not treebanks like the present work. In fact, ours is the first treebank of any Mayan language.

4 Corpus

The corpus is composed of sentences from a range of text types. Around two thirds are example sentences either from a published dictionary (Medrano Rojas, 2004) or from linguistic research (Can Pixabaj, 2015; Henderson, 2012). To this we added some language learning materials (Romero et al., 2018), and religious, medical and legal texts (Wycliffe Bible Translators, 2011; Wikimedia Incubator, 2017; Méndez López, 2020; Gobierno de Guatemala, 2009). The remainder was from a collection of folk tales (Ministerio de Educación, 2016a,b). The majority of the texts came with a translation either in Spanish or in English. Some texts, such as the linguistic examples additionally came with interlinear glosses. For the texts that did not have translations, we performed a rough-and-ready glossing into Spanish with the aid of a prototype machine translation system.[1]

The texts were chosen for their availability and for the range of linguistic phenomena they exhibited, as one of the aims of the work was to create annotation guidelines that can be used in further annotation and adapted to other Mayan languages, this was an important consideration.

4.1 Preprocessing

The texts were preprocessed using a freely-available finite-state morphological analyser (Richardson and Tyers, 2021). The morphological analyser returned, for each token the set of possible morphological analyses, including multiple output tokens in the case of contractions. These analyses were then disambiguated by hand, and missing analyses added.

This disambiguated output was then converted to the ten-column CoNLL-U format.[2] Morphological tags were converted to Feature=Value pairs by using a deterministic maximum-set-overlap matching algorithm.

5 Annotation process

The annotation guidelines are based on Universal Dependencies (Nivre et al., 2020), an international

[1] `apertium-quc-spa: https://github.com/apertium/apertium-quc-spa`

[2] `https://universaldependencies.org/format.html`

Source	Description	Sentences	Words	Avg. length
Medrano Rojas (2004)	Dictionary examples	657	4081	6.21
Romero et al. (2018)	Language learning material	301	1838	6.11
Can Pixabaj (2015)	Linguistic examples	268	1612	6.01
Ministerio de Educación (2016a,b)	Folk tales	104	1525	14.66
Henderson (2012)	Linguistic examples	57	286	5.02
Wycliffe Bible Translators (2011)	Religious scripture	16	211	13.19
Wikimedia Incubator (2017)	Encyclopaedic text	12	213	17.75
Gobierno de Guatemala (2009)	Legal text	7	113	16.14
Méndez López (2020)	Medical guidance	6	87	14.50
Total:		1433	10002	6.97

Table 2: Composition of the corpus. It is notable, but unsurprising that the example sentences and learning materials are around three-times shorter than the other texts.

collaborative project to make cross-linguistically consistent treebanks available for a wide variety of languages. At time of writing, data for over 111 languages is available through the project in a standardised format and with a standardised annotation scheme.

We chose the UD scheme for the annotation as it provides pre-defined recommendations on which to base annotation guidelines. This reduces the amount of time needed to develop annotation guidelines for a given language, as where the existing universal guidelines are adequate, they can be imported wholesale into the language-specific guidelines.

The treebank was annotated by the first author and difficult cases were determined by discussion between the first author and the second author.

6 Constructions

In the following subsections we describe some particular features of K'iche' that are interesting or novel with respect to the Universal Dependencies annotation scheme, and our approach to annotating them. Inline examples are given on three lines, with the original text, a segmentation showing the inflectional morphs, and an approximate translation in English. Glosses are provided when necessary for explaining some particular feature or construction.[3] Where contractions are split, the split is indicated with a hyphen on the both sides of the split, so for example *ch-* followed by *-we* should be read *chwe*.

[3]The following is a list of glossing tags: Question particle QST, Passive PASS, Perfective PERF – also called completive, Imperfective IMPF – also called non-completive, Negative NEG, Classifier CLF, Relative REL, Relational noun RELN, Active ACT, Antipassive AP, Status suffix SS, Directional DIR.

The focus is primarily on the relation between syntactic words, so for example constructions such as the morphological expression and annotation of agreement, tense-aspect-mood prefixes, incorporated movement, and possessive prefixes are not outlined here. It suffices to say that these are encoded with Feature=Value pairs.

6.1 Relational nouns

K'iche' has two prepositions with locative meaning *chi* 'in' and *pa* 'in, at, on, to, towards, from'. Following the guidelines these are attached using the `case` relation to their complement, as in (1).

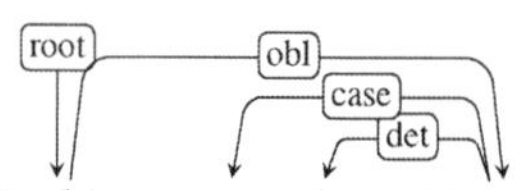

	Kinch'aw	*pa*	*le*	*ch'aweb'al.*
(1)	K-in-ch'aw	pa	le	ch'aweb'al.
	I speak	on	the	telephone.

All other adpositional phrases are made using either relational nouns or combinations of relational nouns with these two prepositions.[4] For readers familiar with Indo-European languages, these relational nouns are similar in function to nouns of the

[4]The fact that we can have relational nouns co-occurring with prepositions — cf. (4) overleaf — is a strong argument that they should not be treated as sharing the category preposition. Instead, bona fide prepositions take nouns as complements, including this special subclass of relational nouns which must bear agreement. Another argument for keeping prepositions and relational nouns separate concerns their behaviour under questioning. Relational nouns can undergo pied-piping with inversion—i.e., the question *ruk' jachin* 'with whom' can also be *jachin ruk'* lit. *whom with*. This inversion is impossible with simple prepositions, which is unexpected if they were structurally equivalent. We direct the reader to Svenonius (2006) for a crosslinguistic survey of preposition-like expressions that are not, in fact, prepositions.

type *front, top, side* in English or *frente* 'front', *cima* 'top', *lado* 'side' in Spanish (e.g. *al* ***lado*** *de la casa* 'at the **side** of the house'). However, they are more extensive, used for encoding relations that in Indo-European languages are encoded with prepositions, such as *with, by, of*, etc. or even determiners or pronouns, e.g. *-onojel* 'all'.

Relational nouns agree with their complements using possessive markers (set B affixes) and may have an complement or not. For example, in (2) the relational noun *-uk'* 'with' is used with a complement *le nunan* 'my mother'.

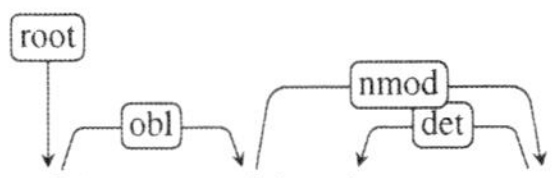

	Kinch'aw	*ruk'*	*le*	*nunan.*
(2)	K-in-ch'aw	r-uk'	le	nu-nan.
	I speak	with	the	my mother.

In (3) the same relational noun *-uk'* 'with' is used without a nominal complement.

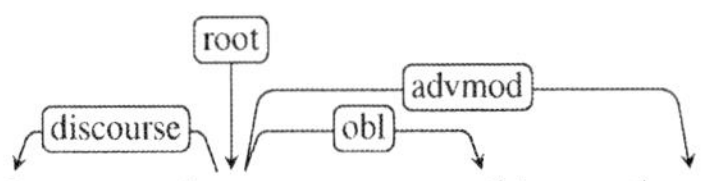

	¿La	*katpe*	*quk'*	*chwe'q?*
(3)	La	k-at-pe	q-uk'	chwe'q
	QST	will you come	with us	tomorrow

To maintain language-internal consistency these are annotated with the relational noun as the head of the construction, attached to predicates with the `obl` oblique relation and to nominals with the `nmod` relation.

It is worth noting that relational nouns can also be used in conjunction with the true prepositions, as in for example (4).

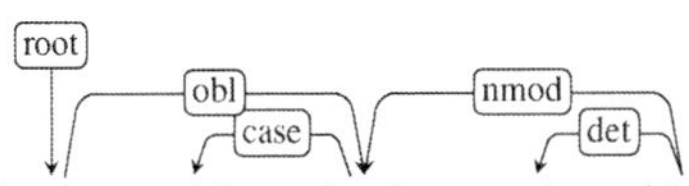

	...	*kyajon*	*chi*	*kech*	*ri*	*ak'alab'.*
(4)	...	k-yajon	chi	k-ech	ri	ak'al-ab'.
	...	tells off	PR	B3PL-RELN	the	children.

In this sentence, *[Ri ajtij,] kyajon chi kech ri ak'alab'.* "[The teacher,] tells off the children." (4), the relational noun *-ech* is introduced by the true preposition *chi*.

6.2 Nominal possession

In terms of nominal possession, K'iche' is a head marking language. The schema for possession is a noun with a possessive prefix followed by the possessor, POS-N_1 N_2 = N_2 of N_1. For example, *utzij ri ajq'ij* "the daykeeper's word" (lit. "his word the daykeeper".

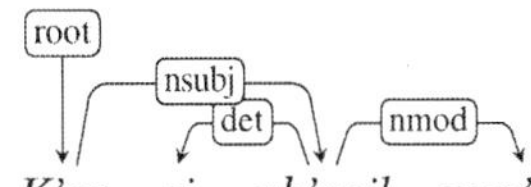

	K'ax	*ri*	*ub'aqil*	*nuq'ab'.*
(5)	K'ax	ri	u-b'aqil	nu-q'ab'.
	Bad	the	its bone	my arm.

Possession can also be expressed on multiple nouns in series, as in the sentence *K'ax ri ub'aqil nuq'ab'.* "The bones of my arms hurt" (5).

6.3 Relative clauses

Following Can Pixabaj (2021), relative clauses in K'iche' are post-nominal and come in two broad types, headed (6) and headless (7). For the headed example we can examine the sentence *[Osea pa taq wa' le] komunidades jawi e k'ow le winaq* "[That is to say that in these] communities where these people are in..." (Can Pixabaj, 2021, ex. 31).

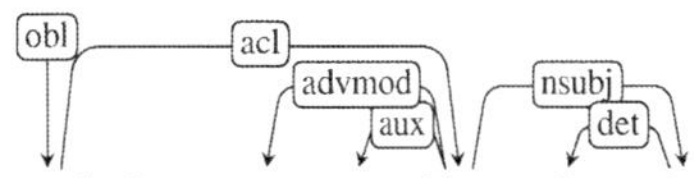

	...	*komunidades*	*jawi*	*e*	*k'ow*	*le*	*winaq*
(6)	...	komunidad-es	jawi	e	k'o-w	le	winaq

In headless relatives, the head becomes the relative itself and the verb is attached to it as an adnominal clause, as in the sentence *Kojtzalijoq jawi ri xojkanaj wi kan [junab'iir].* "Let's go back where we stayed [last year]." (Can Pixabaj, 2021, ex. 39)

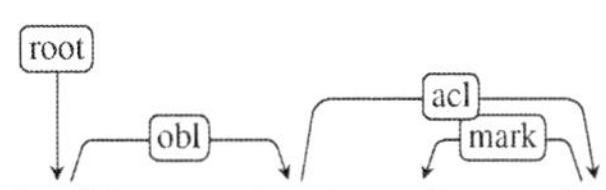

	Kojtzalijoq	*jawi*	*ri*	*xojkanaj*	...
(7)	K-oj-tzalij-oq	jawi	ri	x-oj-kanaj	...
	Let's return	where	that	we stayed	...

Relative clauses embedded under a head nominal, like (6), can be further split into those that contain an interrogative relative pronoun and those that contain a determiner acting as a subordinating conjunction. The reason for treating the latter as a subordinating conjunction and not a relative pronoun, pointed out by Bridges Velleman (2014), is that the two can co-occur, as in (8).

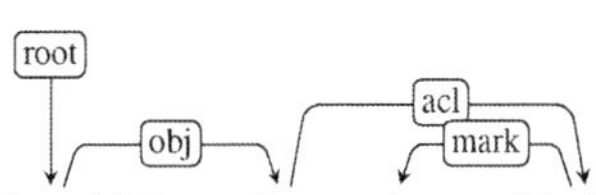

	Chitatab'ej	*jas*	*le*	*kimb'ij.*
(8)	Ch-ø-i-tatab'ej	jas	le	k-ø-im-b'ij.
	Listen	what	that	I say.

In (8), the relative clause *jas le kimb'ij*, lit. "what that I'm saying" is introduced by the interrogative relative pronoun *jas* which is given the relation of `object`. It is then followed by a relative clause complementiser we give the `mark` relation. The predicate in the relative clause is then attached to the nominal it modifies with the relation `acl`, adnominal clausal modifier.

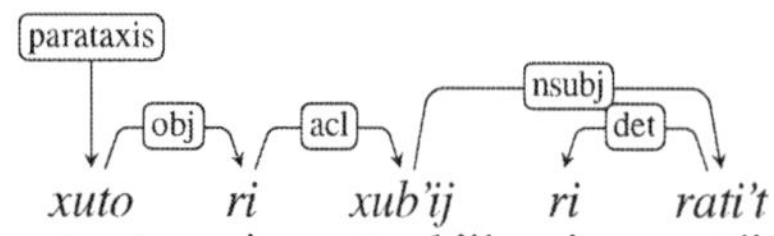

... *xuto ri xub'ij ri rati't*
(9) ... x-ø-u-to ri x-ø-u-b'ij ri r-ati't
... listen the say it the her mum

In addition to headed and headless relatives, Can Pixabaj (2021) also discusses so-called light-headed relatives. In these, the noun head is usually modified by relative not expressed, leaving only a determiner. As shown in (9), in this case we promote the determiner as head of the construction, and treat the light-headed relative as adnominal clause modification (namely `acl`).

6.4 Non-verbal predicates

In non-verbal predication, for example with nouns or adjectives, the predicate is the root, and the subject, as the example *B'ixonel ri a Lu'* "Lu' is a singer" (10) and *K'ax le kib'e ri winaq.* "The road of the people is difficult" (11).

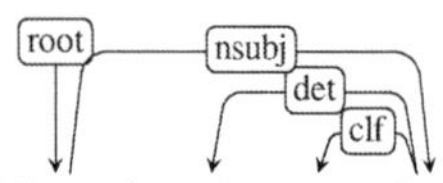

B'ixonel ri a Lu'.
(10) B'ixonel ri a Lu'
Singer the CLF Lu'

Note that there are three definite determiners in K'iche', *ri*, *le* and *we*. They are distinguished by degree of definiteness and familiarity and proximity/visibility to the speaker (Can Pixabaj, 2015).

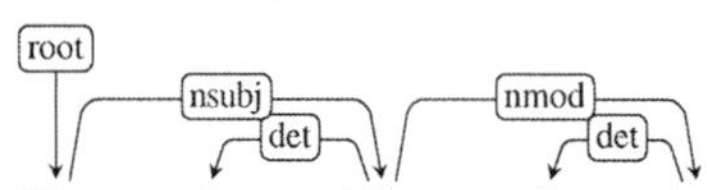

K'ax le kib'e le winaq.
(11) K'ax le ki-b'e ri winaq.
Difficult the their road the people.

For existential sentences in the affirmative and in the negative, two non-inflecting words are used *k'o* in the case of existence and *maj* in the case of non-existence. In these constructions, the non-inflecting word is the head and the thing existing is the subject, as in *K'o jun tz'i' pa b'e.* "There is a dog in the street." (12)

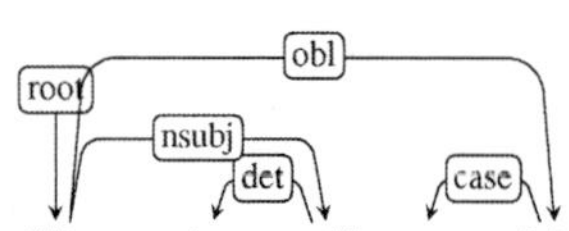

K'o jun tz'i' pa b'e.
(12) K'o jun tz'i' pa b'e.
There is a dog in street.

Another set of non-verbal predicates involve forms such as *rajawaxik* 'necessary', *k'ax* 'difficult' with verbal subjects. These are analysed as nominals (nouns or adjectives), and the complement is an embedded clausal subject.

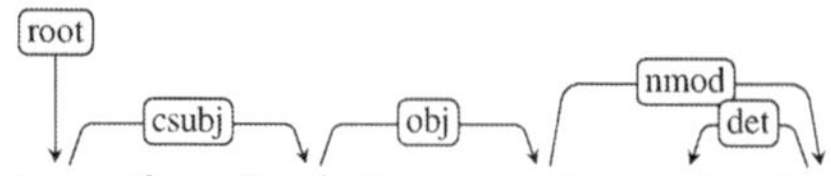

Rajawaxik kqakoj utzij ri Ajq'ij.
(13) Rajawaxik k-ø-qa-koj u-tzij ri Ajq'ij.
Necessary we listen his word the Ajq'ij.

In this example *Rajawaxik kqakoj utzij ri Ajq'ij.* "We need to listen to the Ajq'ij."[5] (13) we see a non-verbal predict with a single argument which is itself a predicate.

6.5 Complement clauses

Our analysis of complement clauses is based on research done by Can Pixabaj (2015), whose thesis gives a thorough treatment of the topic. This section is based on Chapter 3 of (Can Pixabaj, 2015, p.85). In K'iche', complements can be split into three subcategories: finite with complementiser, finite without complementiser and non-finite.

In UD, the distinction in complements is between those with obligatory control, `xcomp` and those without control, `ccomp`. Each of the three types defined in K'iche' may have control or not. In (14) the subordinate clause is introduced by a subordinator, while in (15) there is no subordinator.

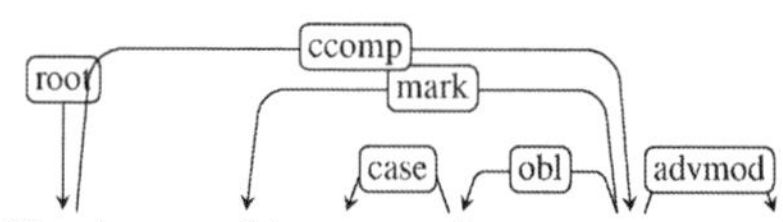

Weta'm chi p- -ulew xwar wi.
(14) Ø-w-eta'm chi pa ulew x-war wi
I know that on floor he slept

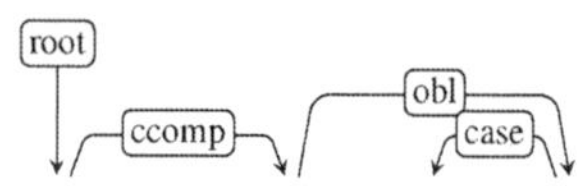

Kawaj kimb'e pa tinamit.
(15) Ka-ø-w-aj k-im-b'e pa tinamit
I want I go to village

Although in (15) the subjects happen to agree, the fact that this is not a control construction can be seen in (16) where the subordinate clause has a subject not controlled by the matrix clause.

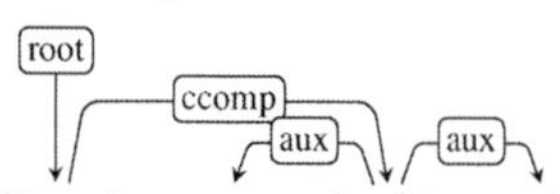

Kawaj na katb'e taj .
(16) Ka-ø-w-aj na k-at-b'e taj
I want NEG you go NEG

[5] *Ajq'ij*, sometimes translated as 'daykeeper', a Maya spiritual guide or shaman-priest.

In (17) and (18) we see examples of obligatory control.

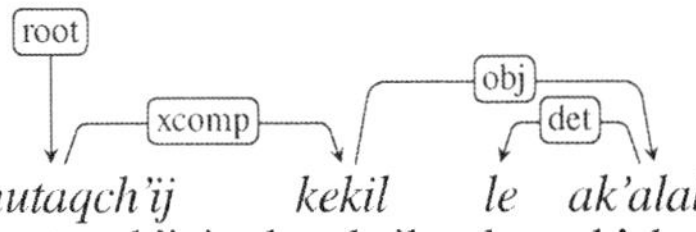

Xenutaqch'ij *kekil* *le* *ak'alab'.*
(17) X-e-nu-taqch'i-j k-e-k-il le ak'al-ab'
I forced them take care the children

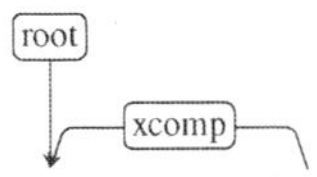

Xuchap *nukunaxik.*
(18) X-u-chap nu-kuna-x-ik
She began to cure me

6.6 Adverbial clauses

There are a number of types of adverbial clauses in K'iche', including those introduced using word order, by a subordinator (e.g. *we* 'if' or *are taq* 'when'), and using a relational noun (e.g. *-umal* 'because', *-ech* 'in order to').

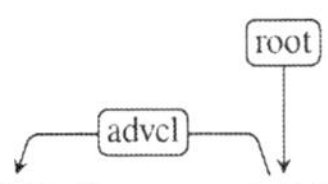

Kinb'inik *xin'ek.*
(19) K-in-b'in-ik x-in-'e-k.
I was walking I left.

In (19) a manner clause *k-in-b'in-ik* 'IMPF-B3S-walk-SS' precedes its main clause. This ordering is mandatory for manner clauses as is the lack of subordinator.

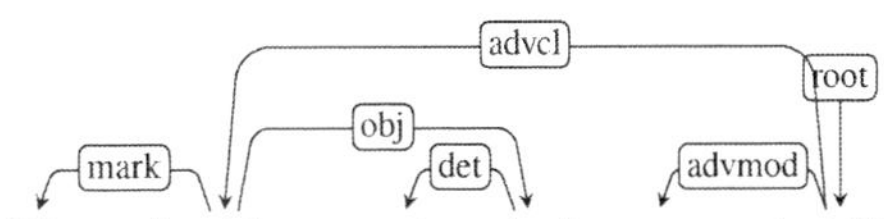

We *keqb'an* *ri* *q'uch* *utz* *kujelik.*
(20) We k-e-q-b'an ri q'uch utz k-uj-el-ik.
If we practice the *q'uch* well we come.

Other kinds of adverbial clauses may precede or follow the main clause. In *We keqb'an ri q'uch utz kujelik.* 'If we practice q'uch[6] it will be good for us.' (20) the conditional clause introduced by the subordinator *we* 'if' appears before the main clause.

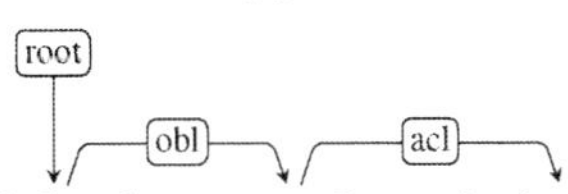

Xinkosik *rumal* *xinchakunik.*
(21) X-in-kos-ik r-umal x-in-chakun-ik.
I am tired because I worked.

Adverbial clauses can also be introduced by relational nouns, as in (21) where the relational noun *-umal* 'by' has the function of `obl` standing in for a manner oblique and the clause is dependent on it as a adnominal clause.

[6] *Q'uch*, mutual aid, or a group of persons who agree to help each other at certain times

6.7 Valency changing

Transitive verbs in K'iche' are subject to two main valency changing operations, the passive and the antipassive. These are morphological processes which involve suffixation. For the passive, either the final vowel is lengthened, or the suffix *-x* is added. For the antipassive the suffixed morpheme is *-Vn* or *-n*.

In the passive, the subject is omitted and the object promoted to subject position. This can be seen in the comparison between the sentence *Xkikunaj le ali ri ixoqib'.* "The women cured the girl." (22) where the verb *x-ø-ki-kuna-j* 'PERF-B3S-A3P-cure-ACT' has agreement for both subject and object and the sentence *Xkunax le ali kumal ri ixoqib'.* "The girl was cured by the women." (23) where the verb *x-ø-kuna-x* 'PERF-B3S-cure-PASS' agrees only for the subject (previously object) and the subject is demoted to oblique using the relational noun *-umal* 'by'.

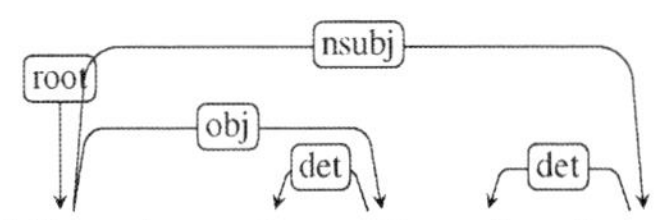

Xkikunaj *le* *ali* *ri* *ixoqib'.*
(22) X-ø-ki-kuna-j le ali ri ixoq-ib'.
Cured the girl the women.

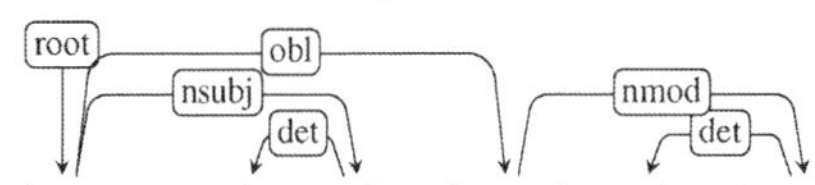

Xkunax *le* *ali* *kumal* *ri* *ixoqib'.*
(23) X-ø-kuna-x le ali k-umal ri ixoq-ib'.
Was cured the girl by the women.

In the antipassive, the subject is retained, but encoded with the absolutive, and the object is demoted to oblique status using the preposition *chi* 'to' and the relational noun *-e(ch)*.

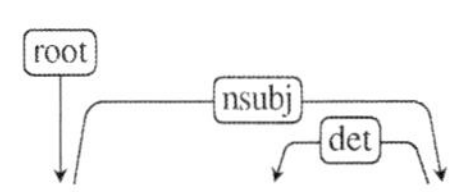

Kinuloq'oj *le* *nutat.*
(24) K-in-u-loq'o-j le nu-tat.
He loves me the my father

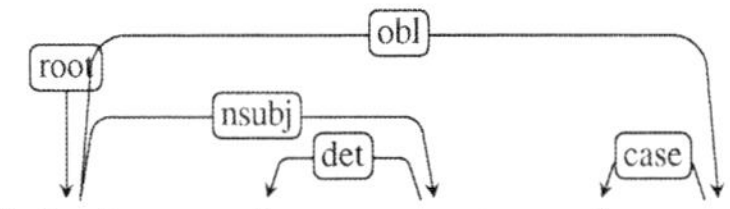

Kaloq'on *le* *nutat* *ch-* *-we.*
(25) Ka-ø-loq'o-n le nu-tat chi we.
He loves the my father to me

Compare the transitive sentence *Kinuloq'oj le nutat.* 'My father loves me.' (24) where the verb *k-in-u-loq'o-j* 'IMPF-B1S-A3S-love-ACT' has agreement for both subject and object with the antipassive version in (25) which exhibits agreement only for the subject, *ka-ø-loq'o-n* 'IMPF-B3S-love-AP'.

6.8 Directionals

In Mayan languages there is a category of words called directionals, which are grammaticalised forms of intransitive verbs of motion (Can Pixabaj, 2017). Some examples are *b'i(k)* < *-b'e* 'go', *qaj(oj)* < *-qaj* 'go down', and *kan(oq)* < *-kan* 'stay'. The part in parentheses after the directional is the status suffix (see §6.9). They usually follow verbs and other predicates to express movement, deictic or aspectual information and are related to the incorporated movement prefixes *e'-* < *b'e* 'go' and *ul-* < *ul* 'arrive'. Despite being derived from verbs, these are not full predicates, being either modifiers or co-predicates. We analyse them as adverbial modifiers and provide a feature `AdvType=Dir` for linguists interested in querying the corpus for this phenomenon.

6.9 Status suffixes

Status suffixes are a particular feature of the Mayan languages. These are suffixes that appear on verbs (and directionals which historically come from verbs). The particular status suffix a verb bears is conditioned by an amalgamation of morphosyntactic facts about the clause, including the transitivity of the verb, whether the verb is a root verb (i.e., CVC form) or has undergone derivation, the tense-aspect-mood of the clause, and whether the clause is an independent or dependent clause. In K'iche' there are four status suffixes, *-ik*, *-oq*, *-u* ~ *-o* (with vowel harmony) and *-u'* ~ *-a'* ~ *-o'* (with vowel harmony).[7]

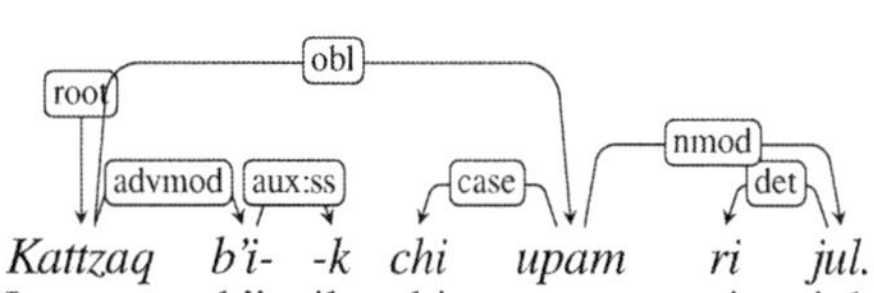

	Kattzaq	*b'i-*	*-k*	*chi*	*upam*	*ri*	*jul.*
(26)	K-at-tzaq	b'i	ik	chi	u-pam	ri	jul.
	Fall	DIR	SS	in	its inside	the	hole.

In this example, the directional, itself derived from a verb, bears the status suffix *-ik*, which indicates that the verb is intransitive and non-dependent. One might wonder why *tzaq* 'fall', the main verb does not bear its own status suffix. This is because, in K'iche', these suffixes only appear at the edges of certain prosodic phrases (Henderson, 2012). These is no such phrase break between the verb and directional, and so only the latter bears the status suffix.

[7]Some linguists, e.g., Kaufman (1986) also treat the suffix verbs bear in the perfect as a status suffix. We do not do so here, instead treating these suffixes as deriving stative predicates.

We have chosen to link status suffixes to their verbs with a flavour of the `aux` relation. The reason is that status suffixes are function words accompanying the verb that express aspect and mood information like verbal auxiliaries do in more familiar languages. For instance, swapping the *-ik* and *-oq* status suffixes on an intransitive verb (in certain aspects) is enough to change the interpretation from conditional mood to imperative mood.

7 Experiments

Here we present two experiments using the corpus. The first is an evaluation of three different parsing pipelines and the second is an experiment in using automatic parsing for mining linguistic examples.

7.1 Automatic parsing

In order to test the usage of the corpus for automatic parsing, performed three experiments using three off-the-shelf natural-language processing pipelines: UDPipe 1.2 (Straka et al., 2016), UDPipe 2.0 (Straka, 2018) and UDify (Kondratyuk and Straka, 2019). Version 1.2 (Straka et al., 2016) of UDPipe is a pipeline-based model where tokenisation is performed by a BiLSTM, morphological analysis and part-of-speech tagging are performed using an averaged perceptron model and dependency parsing uses a transition-based non-projective parser, where transitions are predicted by a neural network. Version 2.0 (Straka, 2018) is a complete rewrite of the UDPipe parser. It implements a joint model for part-of-speech tagging, morphological analysis, lemmatisation and parsing. The parsing model is graph-based using the Chu-Liu/Edmonds algorithm for decoding. Finally, UDify (Kondratyuk and Straka, 2019) is a multilingual model that supports parsing 75 languages. This is also a joint model, with a shared BERT representation for all 75 languages. The pre-trained model can be fine-tuned on language data from a new language, and we provide the results for fine-tuning on K'iche'. All parsers were trained with default hyperparameters.

As there was not enough data to maintain a held out test set of sufficient size, we performed ten-fold cross validation. Table 3 presents the results of the comparison. The evaluation was carried out using the official evaluation script from the 2017 *CoNLL Shared Task* (Zeman et al., 2017).

As can be seen from the results in Table 3, UDPipe 2.0 performs significantly better than UDPipe 1.2 and UDify for all of the tasks. This comes at a

	Straka et al. (2016)	Straka (2018)	Kondratyuk and Straka (2019)
Training time	20:22 ± 00:32	636:19 ± 28:56	618:27 ± 18:49
Model size	2.3M	64M	760M
Tokens	**99.8** ± 0.3	—	—
Words	**97.6** ± 0.4	—	—
Lemmas	88.3 ± 1.1	**94.9** ± 0.5	88.3 ± 0.9
UPOS	91.4 ± 1.4	**96.5** ± 0.7	94.2 ± 1.1
Features	92.0 ± 1.2	**96.6** ± 0.8	93.5 ± 0.7
UAS	82.8 ± 1.9	**91.1** ± 2.0	85.2 ± 2.8
LAS	76.7 ± 2.5	**86.5** ± 2.4	78.9 ± 2.5

Table 3: Results on tasks from tokenisation to dependency parsing. Standard deviation is obtained by running ten-fold cross validation. The columns are F_1 score: **Tokens** tokenisation; **Words** splitting syntactic words (e.g. contractions); **Lemmas** lemmatisation; **UPOS** universal part-of-speech tags; **Feats** morphological features; **UAS** unlabelled attachment score (dependency heads); **LAS** labelled attachment score (dependency heads and relations). Model size is in megabytes, training time is in mm:ss, as run on a consumer-grade laptop.

substantial increase in model size and training time compared to UDPipe 1.0, but results in a model that is still tractable on a consumer-grade laptop.

7.2 Linguistic example mining

Using corpora of under-resourced languages to test predictions pertinent to linguistic theory is often difficult. The reason is that the predictions are usually highly structurally dependent, making it hard, or even impossible, to search for relevant examples via string matching. We show the utility of the present treebank through a case study probing the distribution of phrase-final status suffixes (see section 6.9). Henderson (2012) proposes that the status suffixes that only appear phrase-finally are sensitive to intonational phrase boundaries, which roughly map onto clause boundaries. The generalisation is that a phrase final status suffix should only appear if the verb / directional bearing it is (i) utterance final, (ii) directly before an embedded clause, (iii) directly before a functional head that itself embeds a clause. Notice that to find counterexamples to this generalisation, one must search for sentences that do not satisfy a structural description—e.g., give me sentences containing a status suffix that is not directly followed by an embedded clause. This is impossible to do without a treebank. It is not even possible to do via string matching over a corpus with grammatical annotations like part-of-speech tags.

We used the corpus to test the generalization in Henderson (2012) against a larger set of K'iche' texts. In order to produce a larger corpus of examples, we took all of the texts we had available from the sources mentioned in Section 4 and to that added the *Crúbadán* corpus of K'iche' (Scannell, 2007) and processed them with the UDPipe 2.0 model described in the previous section.

We used the *Grew* (Guillaume, 2019) corpus query language to extract all sentences where a verb had both a dependent that was an auxiliary with the relation of `aux:ss` and a noun with the relation `obj`. The query can be seen schematically in (27).

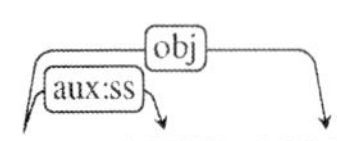

(27) VERB AUX NOUN

This lead to a total of 16,196 sentences containing 352,509 tokens. Note that the annotation for these sentences was not hand annotated, but simply the output of the data-driven parser. Although the output contained errors, the number of false positives due to errors in the parse tree was unexpectedly low.

The result is that we discovered a series of examples with structures that have not yet been considered in the literature on status suffixes, including direct counterexamples to Henderson (2012). For instance, we see in the following example a directional bearing the phrase-final dependent status suffix *-oq*. Yet, the directional is not at clause boundary or before a functional head that embeds a clause. Instead, it occurs before a reflexive pronoun, which in K'iche' is a relational noun construction.

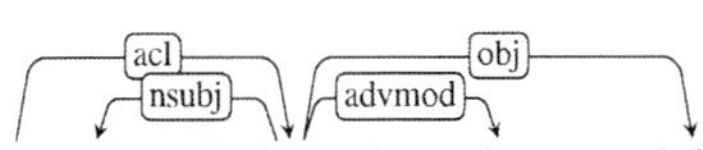

	...	*e*	*kakimiq'*	*ukoq*	*kib'.*
(28)	...	e	ka-ø-ki-miq'	uk-**oq**	k-ib'.
	...	B3PL	they warm	DIR-SS	themselves.

An example like *Kekanaj kan kuk' chila' [e kakimiq' ukoq kib'].* "They remained over there with those [that were warming themselves]." (28) is intriguing because while a counterexample, there are plausible stories one could tell. For instance, these reflexives are prosodic clitics. Perhaps the requirement that the status suffix be phrase final ignores expressions that are prosodically deficient because they do not count as independent phonological words. While arguing for this account would take more work, the fact that we have very quickly found a theoretically interesting counterexample to a prominent generalisation in literature shows the utility of the treebank for example mining.

8 Future work

We would like to investigate the use of *enhanced dependencies*[8] to provide a more semantics-oriented encoding of relational nouns. For example if we take example (23), we could envisage an enhanced `obl` link from the verb *Xkunax* 'was cured' to the semantic head of the agent phrase *ixoqib'* 'the women' (29) where we indicate the differences with respect to the basic tree in boldface. This would fall under *Case information* in the enhanced schema and would be an additional layer on top of the basic syntax. The process could be partially automated using the *Grew* tool.

(29)

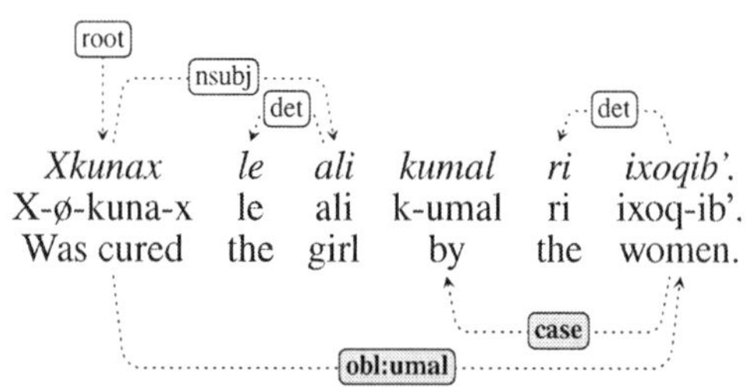

We also intend to expand the treebank and apply the lessons learnt and annotation solutions to other Mayan languages, this is a large group and we would like to start with languages related to K'iche' such as Uspanteko and Kaqchikel.

9 Concluding remarks

We have presented the first syntactically annotated corpus of sentences in K'iche'. Both the corpus and the documentation of the annotation scheme are freely available[9] through the Universal Dependencies project.[10] It is our hope that the work we describe here will facilitate the annotation of, and promote language technology for other Mayan languages.

Acknowledgements

We would like to thank Telma Can Pixabaj for the permission to use the examples from her PhD thesis. The Academia de las Lenguas Mayas de Guatemala kindly allowed us to use the example sentences from their K'iche'–Spanish dictionary. Dan Zeman provided helpful feedback on specific constructions at an early stage of the treebank, and Gus Hahn-Powell gave feedback on the pre-review manuscript. We would additionally like to thank the two anonymous reviewers for their kind comments and helpful suggestions. Any errors remain our own.

References

Leah Bridges Velleman. 2014. *Focus and movement in a variety of K'ichee'.* Ph.D. thesis, University of Texas at Austin.

Telma Angelina Can Pixabaj. 2009. Verbal nouns in K'iche'. Master's thesis, University of Texas at Austin.

Telma Angelina Can Pixabaj. 2015. *Complement and purpose clauses in K'iche'.* Ph.D. thesis, University of Texas at Austin.

Telma Angelina Can Pixabaj. 2017. K'iche'. In Judith Aissen, Nora C. England, and Roberto Zavala Maldonado, editors, *The Mayan Languages*. Routledge, Oxford.

Telma Angelina Can Pixabaj. 2018. Documentation of formal and ceremonial discourses in K'ichee'. London: SOAS University of London, Endangered Languages Archive. Handle: http://hdl.handle.net/2196/00-0000-0000-000F-B63F-4. Accessed on Feb 3, 2021.

Telma Angelina Can Pixabaj. 2021. Headless relative clauses in K'iche'. In Ivano Caponigro, Harold Torrence, and Roberto Zavala Maldonado, editors, *Headless Relative Clauses in Mesoamerican Languages*. Oxford University Press, Oxford.

Gobierno de Guatemala. 2009. Taqanik b'elejeb' junab' joq'o' (9-2009): Taqanik rech uq'atuxik ri eqelenik ruk' chuq'ab'il, ch'akow pwaq xuquje' ub'anik k'ax chi kech ri winaq. *[Decreto Número 9-2009: Ley contra la violencia sexual, explotación y trata de personas].*

Bruno Guillaume. 2019. Graph matching for corpora exploration. In *JLC 2019 - 10èmes Journées Internationales de la Linguistique de corpus*, Grenoble, France.

[8]`https://universaldependencies.org/u/overview/enhanced-syntax.html`

[9]`https://github.com/UniversalDependencies/UD_Kiche-IU`

[10]`https://universaldependencies.org`

Robert Henderson. 2012. Morphological alternations at the intonational phrase edge. *Natural Language & Linguistic Theory*, 30(3):741–789. Doi:10.1007/s11049-012-9170-8.

Terrence Kaufman. 1986. Some structural characteristics of the Mayan languages, with special reference to Quiché. *Unpublished ms., University of Pittsburgh.*

Dan Kondratyuk and Milan Straka. 2019. 75 languages, 1 model: Parsing universal dependencies universally. In *Proceedings of the 2019 Conference on Empirical Methods in Natural Language Processing and the 9th International Joint Conference on Natural Language Processing (EMNLP-IJCNLP)*, pages 2779–2795, Hong Kong, China. Association for Computational Linguistics.

José Miguel Medrano Rojas. 2004. *K'iche' choltzij: K'iche'-kaxl'an tzij, kaxl'an tzij-k'iche.* Academia de Lenguas Mayas de Guatemala, Guatemala. [Vocabulario k'iche'].

Ministerio de Educación. 2016a. *Tzijob'elil K'aslemal*, volume I. USAID Leer y Aprender. [Antología de cuentos: I].

Ministerio de Educación. 2016b. *Tzijob'elil K'aslemal*, volume II. USAID Leer y Aprender. [Antología de cuentos: II].

Tomás Alberto Méndez López. 2020. Tajin kraqpux le xk'ulmatajem pa uwi' le yab'il covid-19 (esam pa le oms). `https://covid-no-mb.org/?page_id=2009`.

Joakim Nivre, Marie-Catherine de Marneffe, Filip Ginter, Jan Hajič, Christopher D. Manning, Sampo Pyysalo, Sebastian Schuster, Francis M. Tyers, and Dan Zeman. 2020. Universal dependencies v2: An evergrowing multilingual treebank collection. In *Proceedings of the 12th Conference on Language Resources and Evaluation (LREC 2020)*, pages 4027–4036.

Oxlajuuj Keej Maya' Ajtz'iib'. 2021. Oxlajuuj Keej Maya' Ajtz'iib' Mayan languages collection. The Archive of the Indigenous Languages of Latin America, ailla.utexas.org. Access: public. PID ailla:124456. Accessed Feb 3, 2021.

Alexis Palmer, Taesun Moon, Jason Baldridge, Katrin Erk, Eric Campbell, and Telma Can. 2010. Computational strategies for reducing annotation effort in language documentation. *Linguistic Issues in Language Technology*, 3(4):1–42.

Ivy Richardson and Francis M. Tyers. 2021. A morphological analyser for K'iche'. *Procesamiento de Lenguaje Natural*, 66:99–109.

Sergio Romero, Ignacio Carvajal, Mareike Sattler, Juan Manuel Tahay Tzaj, Carl Blyth, Sarah Sweeney, Pat Kyle, Nathalie Steinfeld Childre, Diego Guarchaj Tambriz, Lorenzo Ernesto Tambriz, Maura Tahay, Lupita Tahay, Gaby Tahay, Jenny Tahay, Santiago Can, Elena Ixmata Xum, Enrique Guarchaj, Sergio Manuel Guarchaj Can, Catarina Marcela Tambriz Cotiy, Telma Can, Tara Kingsley, Charlotte Hayes, Christopher J. Walker, María Angelina Ixmatá Sohom, Jacob Sandler, Silveria Guarchaj Ixmatá, Manuela Petronila Tahay, and Susan Smythe Kung. 2018. Chqeta'maj le qach'ab'al K'iche'! `https://tzij.coerll.utexas.edu/`.

Frauke Sachse and Michael Dürr. 2016. Morphological glossing of Mayan languages under XML: Preliminary results. Working Paper 4, Nordrhein-Westfälische Akademie der Wissenschaften und der Künste.

Kevin Scannell. 2007. The Crúbadán Project: Corpus building for under-resourced languages. In *Proceedings of the 3rd Web as Corpus Workshop*, pages 5–15.

M. Straka, J. Hajič, and J. Straková. 2016. UDPipe: trainable pipeline for processing CoNLL-U files performing tokenization, morphological analysis, POS tagging and parsing. In *Proceedings of the Tenth International Conference on Language Resources and Evaluation (LREC'16)*, Paris, France. European Language Resources Association (ELRA).

Milan Straka. 2018. UDPipe 2.0 prototype at CoNLL 2018 UD shared task. In *Proceedings of the CoNLL 2018 Shared Task: Multilingual Parsing from Raw Text to Universal Dependencies*, pages 197–207, Brussels, Belgium. Association for Computational Linguistics.

Peter Svenonius. 2006. The emergence of axial parts. Working Paper 33.1, Universitetet i Tromsø.

Wikimedia Incubator. 2017. Wp/quc/tripanosomiasis africana — Wikimedia Incubator. `https://incubator.wikimedia.org/w/index.php?title=Wp/quc/Tripanosomiasis_africana`.

Wycliffe Bible Translators. 2011. *Ru Loq' Pixab' Ri Dios.* Wycliffe Bible Translators. `https://ebible.org/Scriptures/details.php?id=qucNNT`.

Daniel Zeman, Martin Popel, Milan Straka, Jan Hajič, Joakim Nivre, Filip Ginter, Juhani Luotolahti, Sampo Pyysalo, Slav Petrov, Martin Potthast, Francis Tyers, Elena Badmaeva, Memduh Gökırmak, Anna Nedoluzhko, Silvie Cinková, Jan Hajič jr., Jaroslava Hlaváčová, Václava Kettnerová, Zdeňka Urešová, Jenna Kanerva, Stina Ojala, Anna Missilä, Christopher Manning, Sebastian Schuster, Siva Reddy, Dima Taji, Nizar Habash, Herman Leung, Marie-Catherine de Marneffe, Manuela Sanguinetti, Maria Simi, Hiroshi Kanayama, Valeria de Paiva, Kira Droganova, Héctor Martínez Alonso, Çağrı Çöltekin, Umut Sulubacak, Hans Uszkoreit, Vivien Macketanz, Aljoscha Burchardt, Kim Harris, Katrin Marheinecke, Georg Rehm, Tolga Kayadelen, Mohammed Attia, Ali Elkahky, Zhuoran Yu, Emily Pitler, Saran Lertpradit, Michael Mandl, Jesse Kirchner, Hector Fernandez Alcalde, Jana Strnadova, Esha

Banerjee, Ruli Manurung, Antonio Stella, Atsuko Shimada, Sookyoung Kwak, Gustavo Mendonça, Tatiana Lando, Rattima Nitisaroj, and Josie Li. 2017. CoNLL 2017 Shared Task: Multilingual Parsing from Raw Text to Universal Dependencies. In *Proceedings of the CoNLL 2017 Shared Task: Multilingual Parsing from Raw Text to Universal Dependencies*, pages 1–19, Vancouver, Canada. Association for Computational Linguistics.

Investigating variation in written forms of Nahuatl using character-based language models

Robert Pugh and **Francis M. Tyers**
Department of Linguistics, Indiana University, Bloomington, IN
{pughrob,ftyers}@iu.edu

Abstract

We describe experiments with character-based language modeling for written variants of Nahuatl. Using a standard LSTM model and publicly available Bible translations, we explore how character language models can be applied to the tasks of estimating mutual intelligibility, identifying genetic similarity, and distinguishing written variants. We demonstrate that these simple language models are able to capture similarities and differences that have been described in the linguistic literature.[1]

1 Introduction

The diversity of language variants[2] in a linguistic continuum presents an interesting challenge to the development of language technology. For marginalized and endangered languages, the general lack of resources in the language as a whole exacerbates this challenge.

Character-level features have been shown to be effective for a wide range of textual NLP tasks, including language identification (Dunning, 1994; Veena et al., 2018), native language detection (Kulmizev et al., 2017), and machine translation (Lee et al., 2017; Chen et al., 2018). Furthermore, they offer the advantage of requiring little-to-no preprocessing or linguistic engineering (e.g. word tokenization, morphological segmentation, etc.) other than possibly orthographic normalization[3].

In this paper we investigate the usefulness of character language models in addressing questions about variation within a linguistic continuum. Specifically, we examine the extent to which these simple surface-level features of written language correspond to structural phonological and grammatical differences between different variants of Nahuatl. We examine three tasks: variant identification, linguistic sub-classification/genetic similarity, and the prediction of mutual intelligibility.

2 Background

In this section we give some background on the language, language modeling, and some relevant related work.

2.1 Nahuatl

Nahuatl is a polysynthetic, agglutinating Uto-Aztecan language continuum spoken throughout Mexico and Mesoamerica. The Mexican Government's *Instituto Nacional de Lenguas Indígenas* (INALI) recognises 30 distinct variants (INALI, 2009). These variants have highly-variable levels of intelligibility between them, and linguistic similarity and mutual intelligibility is not always correlated with geographic distance. Furthermore, the recognition and treatment of Nahuatl's linguistic diversity has far-reaching impacts on language activism and revitalization projects (Pharao Hansen, 2013).

Nahuatl variants can differ along lexical (*totoltetl* vs. *teksistli* 'egg'), phonological (common isoglosses include *t-tl-l* and *e-i*), and morphological (e.g. the presence or absence of word-initial *o-* for past tense verbs) dimensions, and orthography can vary within and across variants. Table 1 gives an example of these types of variation.

Computational modeling of Nahuatl variants is useful for many language technology applications. Automatic variant detection may be useful for grouping and categorizing texts in a large corpus such as the Axolotl corpus (Gutierrez-Vasques et al., 2016), where the provenance of the texts is not always known. For automated dialogue systems, variant modeling can be used to assess the degree to which a generated turn will be understood by a

[1] Code is available at `https://github.com/Lguyogiro/nahuatl-variant-charlms-americasnlp`

[2] We use the term *variants* to refer to instances of any kind of intra-language variation, including variation based on region (dialect), culture or ethnicity (ethnolect) etc. These may or may not be considered the same language or separate languages.

[3] Subword tokenization methods, such as Byte-Pair Encoding, also share this property. We leave the investigation of unsupervised subword tokenization for written Nahuatl for future experiments.

Proceedings of the First Workshop on Natural Language Processing for Indigenous Languages of the Americas, pages 21–27
June 11, 2021.

user. Finally, for applications that generate text on a user's behalf, such as predictive keyboards and spell-checking systems, it is vital to maintain consistency in both language variant and orthographic norms.

2.2 Language Modeling

Language models are probability distributions over sequences of vocabulary items with parameters learned from data. They are ubiquitous in Natural Language Processing in areas including machine translation, automatic speech recognition, and spelling correction, among others. Traditional n-gram language models estimate the conditional probability of each vocabulary item given contexts of preceding vocabulary items based on their frequency in the data. Neural language models represent each vocabulary item as a distributed feature vector, and learn the joint probability function of the sequence of feature vectors and the feature vectors themselves simultaneously (Bengio et al., 2000). We use the latter in the experiments presented in this paper.

$$\text{PP} = e^{-\frac{1}{N}\sum_{i=1}^{N} \ln p(x_i)} \quad (1)$$

A common metric for evaluating the performance of a language model is perplexity (1), or how "surprised" the model is when seeing a sequence of vocabulary items (the more surprised, the worse the model fits the data).

We specifically focus on character-based language models for two reasons. First and foremost is the simplicity of character-based tokenization, which involves none of the assumptions about sequence groupings required by other tokenization methods. Secondly, there are a number of morphemes in Nahuatl that are written with a single character, such as the past-tense prefix *o:-*[4], some realizations of the third-person singular object prefix *k-*, and the singular-subject future tense suffix *-s*. Since these single-character morphemes are linguistically important, and subword tokenization methods risk merging them with arbitrary adjacent characters, character tokenization is more appropriate.

2.3 Related Work

There has been a great deal of research into computational approaches for assessing similarity/intelligibility between related languages and language variants, most notably highlighted in the *Workshop on NLP for Similar Languages, Varieties and Dialects* (VarDial) (Gaman et al., 2020). Particularly relevant to the work presented in this paper, Gamallo et al. (2017) describe a method for discriminating between similar languages using word and character n-gram language model perplexity. Character language models have also been shown to be effective in distinguishing between dialects of written Arabic (Sadat et al., 2014; Malmasi et al., 2015).

With respect to Nahuatl, Farfan (2019) analyzed contemporary written Nahuatl variants for points of convergence using a finite-state morphological analyzer built from a grammar of Classical Nahuatl. Other efforts in developing language technology for Nahuatl include a large parallel Nahuatl-Spanish text corpus (Gutierrez-Vasques et al., 2016), and a morphological analyzer for the Western Sierra (`nhi`) variant (Pugh et al., 2021).

3 Data

The most widely available corpus of text in the variants of Nahuatl is the Bible. We used translations into 10 different Nahuatl variants available from `scriptureearth.org`[5]. The complete list of variants employed in this study is: `azz` *Highland Puebla*, `ngu` *Guerrero*, `nch` *Central Huasteca*, `nhe` *Eastern Huasteca*, `nhy` *Northern Oaxaca*, `ncj` *Northern Puebla*, `nhi` *Western Sierra*, `nsu` *Sierra Negra*, `ncl` *Michoacán*, `nhw` *Western Huasteca*.

As translators merge verses differently in different languages, to maintain data parity for all of the variants being investigated we only included verses which were present in all variants (7,363 verses).

3.1 Orthography

Nahuatl is commonly written in a range of different orthographies. Phonemes /k/, /w/, and /h/ typically have variable graphemic representations in different orthographies. Vowel-length, which is phonemic in many Nahuatl variants but has a low functional load, can be written but is commonly ignored. See de la Cruz Cruz (2014) for a more in-depth discussion of Nahuatl orthography.

The different translations of the Bible do not adhere to a single orthographic norm, so we decided to normalize them to remove the choice of orthography as a confounding factor. Our normalization

[4]The *augment*, as it is often referred to in the literature, /o:/- is not morphologically a prefix, but is typically written attached to the verb. See Chapter 8.8 of Launey and Mackay (2011) for a detailed description of its morphological status and behavior.

[5]In fact, scriptureearth.org has translations in 11 variants, but due to an error during processing, we excluded Isthmus-Mecayapan Nahuatl (`nhx`). We plan to evaluate `nhx` in future work

Word	Segmentation	Gloss	Language Code
quinilij	∅-quin-ilij	s3SG-i3PL-tell	`azz`
oquiniluic	o-∅-quin-iluic	PST-s3SG-i3PL-tell	`ncj`
okinmilvi	o-∅-kinm-ilvi	PST-s3SG-i3PL-tell	`nsu`
oquimiluih	o-∅-quim-iluih	PST-s3SG-i3PL-tell	`nhi`

Table 1: The different forms of the ditransitive verb "to tell/say (s.t. to s.o.)" from 4 of the variants studied. Note the variation in the use of a past-marking *o-* prefix, verb stem and object prefix, and different orthographies. These forms came from Matthew 14:2, and correspond to the phrase 'said unto (his servants)' in the King James Bible: "And said unto his servants, This is John the Baptist;".

method makes the following changes to account for well-known orthographic variation in contemporary Nahuatl writing:

- Replaces *hu*, *uh*, and *w* with *u*;
- Replaces *qu* followed by front vowel and *c* followed by back vowel or consonant (except *h*) with *k*;
- Neutralizes vowel length.

3.2 Language codes

For two of our three case studies, we compare our system's analysis of Nahuatl variants with fieldwork. Since each Bible translation is associated with an ISO-639 code, and in many cases the mapping of towns/locales described in fieldwork to the variants indicated by ISO-639 codes is not clear-cut, we needed to match the ISO codes in our corpus to the variants described in the literature. To do this, we (1) consulted Ethnologue (Eberhard et al., 2021) for towns and municipalities associated with each ISO code, (2) searched for matching locations in the respective fieldwork descriptions, and (3) consulted a map to identify the closest matching place name in cases where there were no exact location matches. For more details, see Appendix A.

4 Methods

In order to analyze the three case studies described below, we evaluated the cross-variant perplexity of character language models for each Nahuatl variant in our corpus. Specifically, we split the data by verse into train (6,258 verses), dev (552 verses), and test (552 verses) partitions. For each variant, we trained a character language model on the training data for 50 epochs (this was manually verified to be sufficient for convergence). The epoch with the lowest perplexity on the dev set was selected, and the perplexity of the model at that epoch on the test set was calculated for all variants. We used PyTorch (Paszke et al., 2019) to train a unidirectional LSTM language model with 100-dimension character embeddings (with dropout) and a single recurrent layer with 1024 hidden units.

5 Case studies

In this section we present three case studies using character-based language models.

5.1 Variant identification

In order to test the usefulness of character language models for predicting the variant of a text, we combined the test set verses for all variants and calculated the perplexity for each variant's language model on the entire data set. To produce predictions, for each verse we simply chose the variant with the lowest perplexity.

This approach yields near-perfect results (accuracy=0.99). The few errors were confusions between the different Huasteca variants, (`nhw`, `nhe`, and `nch`). This is unsurprising given their high similarity. In fact many of the verses our system incorrectly identified were identical to the same verse in the correct variant. The near-perfect performance is likely due to the restricted domain of our corpus, and the fact that the same translator(s) produced all of the verses for a given variant. Thus, it is likely that many of the patterns exploited by the language models are not language-specific (e.g. presence or absence of the *o-* prefix in the preterite) but author/document/domain specific (e.g. stylistic decisions such as word choice).

5.2 Sub-classification and genetic similarity

There are a number of different systems for subclassification of Nahuan languages. Lastra (1986), in an analysis based on synchronic lexical and grammatical similarities in 93 surveyed locations, suggests grouping Nahuatl variants into four groups: "Central", "Huasteca", "Western Periphery" and "Eastern Periphery".

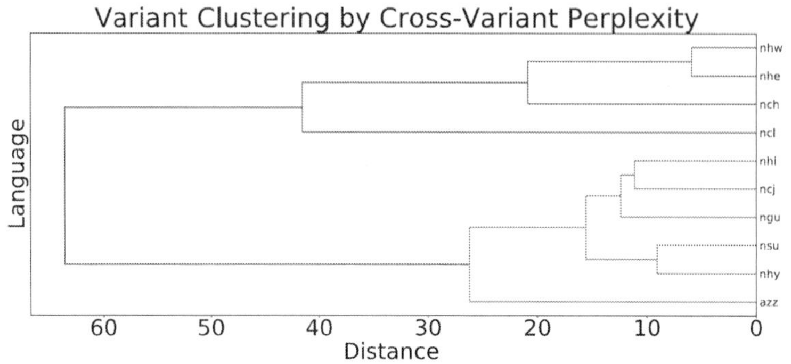

Figure 1: A dendrogram showing the variants studied, hierarchically clustered by relative perplexity. Our character language-modeling approach appears to be quite well-suited for capturing synchronic linguistic similarities between Nahuatl variants, but is less effective at identifying historical, genetic variant relationships.

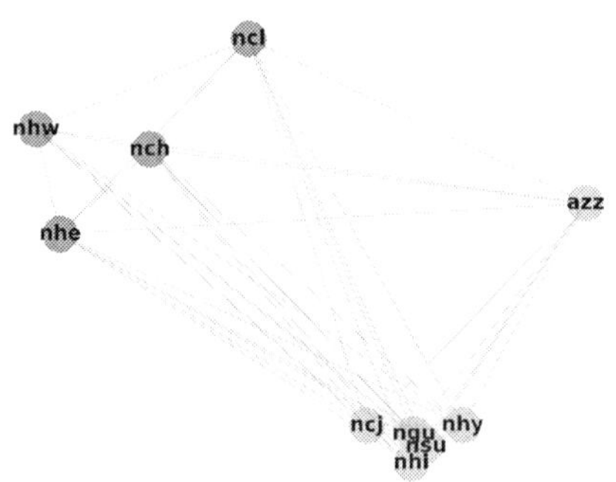

Figure 2: A force atlas diagram showing relative perplexity. Longer edges indicate higher perplexity. Node color corresponds to the clusters in Figure 1

The "East-West Split" (Canger and Dakin, 1985; Canger, 1988; Pharao Hansen, 2014) is a widely-held grouping of Nahuatl variants based on historical evidence of two waves of migration of early Nahuatl-speakers to Mexico. The first wave is thought to have resulted in what are known as the "Eastern" variants (the Huasteca and Highland Puebla variants among others), and the second in the "Western" variant group (including variants spoken near present-day Mexico City, Northern Sierra Puebla, Southeastern Puebla, and Michoacán). Importantly, many of the measurable indicators of similarity in the above two groupings, such as the existence of lexical cognates and phonological/morphological isoglosses, are often recoverable from the written form.

We grouped the variants by hierarchically clustering the vectors of cross-variant perplexity.

Central-Periphery Clustering based on the cross-variant perplexity shows a general correspondence to the Central-Periphery grouping of Lastra (1986), with some exceptions. Lastra's Central group is prominently represented in both Figure 1 (the orange lines, with the exception of the outermost `azz`) and Figure 2 (the cluster of nodes at the bottom right). The Huasteca group also stands out in our data as a cluster of three variants (`nhw`, `nhe`, `nch`) distinct from the Central group. In fact, of all variant-pairs in our data, Eastern Huasteca (`nhe`) and Western Huasteca (`nhw`) have the lowest cross-variant perplexity (clearly illustrated in Figure 1). The two Periphery groups, Western Periphery and Eastern Periphery, were not represented by any clear grouping in the cross-variant clustering, other than being separate from the *Central* group. This may be due to the lack of representation of these groups in our dataset, with only one variant from the Eastern Periphery (`azz`), and one from the Western Periphery (`ncl`).

East-West Split The distinction between Eastern and Western variants is less pronounced when clustering on cross-variant perplexity, though the distinction between the Huasteca variants and Central variants mentioned above does overlap substantially with the East-West split. The variants whose position in our grouping most contradicts the East-West sub-classification are `ngu`, `azz`, and `ncl`[6]. One possible explanation for a lack of clear distinction between the East and West groups is the fact that certain variants may tend to be more "innovative" than others, leading to new linguistic forms that set them

[6]As Pharao Hansen (2014) points out, the status of Guerrero variants within the "East-West" grouping remains unclear.

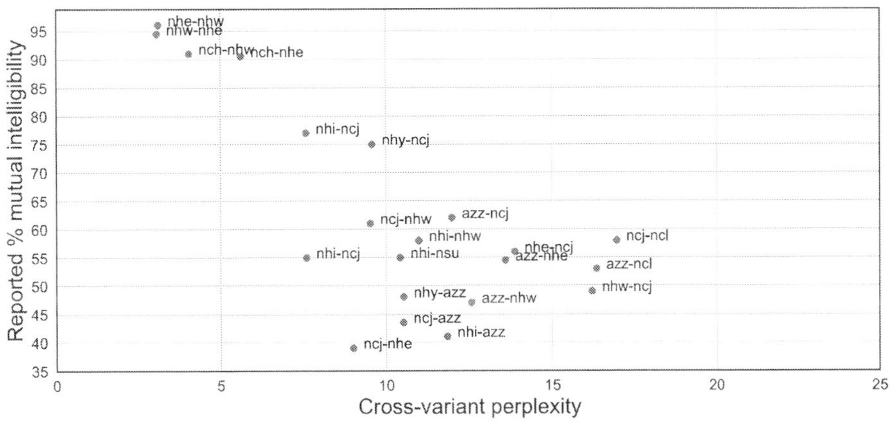

Figure 3: A plot of mutual intelligibility of variant-pairs and the corresponding cross-variant perplexity.

apart from otherwise related variants.

5.3 Mutual intelligibility

The primary systematic study of mutual intelligibility between Nahuatl varieties is Egland and Bartholomew (1978), which involved surveying speakers from 58 different communities throughout Mexico. Mutual intelligibility was assessed by playing a recording of a narrative by a speaker from a different community and asking the listener a series of comprehension questions. The results were adjusted and reported as percentages[7].

The resulting mutual intelligibility numbers are reported for community-pairs (e.g. "Tetlalpan-Xochiatipan: 99%"). In order to compare these numbers to our variant models, we assigned each community to an ISO-639 code as described in 3.2, giving us code pairs ("`nhw-nhe`: 99%").

To evaluate whether our character language models can tell us something about mutual intelligibility, we compared each available ISO code pair's mutual intelligibility percentages with the corresponding cross-variant perplexity. We essentially treat our language model as if it were a speaker, such that (in keeping with the above example) to compare the understanding of an `nhw` speaker listening to a narration from an `nhe` speaker, we take the language model trained on `nhw` Bible translation and evaluate its perplexity on `nhe` Bible translation. When a single language code contained multiple measurements, we used the average.

The results of this comparison, which includes all relevant measurements from Egland and Bartholomew (1978) as well as any additional reported intelligibility numbers from Ethnologue[8], are plotted in Figure 3. We found the reported mutual intelligibility between two variants and their cross-variant perplexity to be moderately negatively correlated in our data, r(19) = -0.734, p = .0002. The relationship is particularly strong for the variants with the lowest cross-variant perplexity (the Huasteca variants). However, this method is less effective at distinguishing between the mutual intelligibility of less similar variants as seen by the bunching in the center of the graph.

6 Concluding remarks

Our three case studies suggest that a simple character language model can capture a non-trivial amount of information about some of the linguistic properties, relationships, and similarities of written Nahuatl variants. The experiments also support existing literature on the utility of character features in the computational modeling of similar languages. We note the limitations of our data set, i.e. that each variant is represented by a parallel text published by the same organization (and likely by a single author per variant), and that our approach may not yield similar results on non-parallel or comparable text.

We are also interested in exploring language models under various tokenization schemes, such as unsupervised subword tokenization and morphological segmentation.

[7]We recommend consulting the first two sections of this work for details about arriving at the final percentages.

[8]Measurements reported with less than 5 speakers were excluded. Two of the measurements, `nhi-nsu` and `nhi-ncj`, were reported as "50-60%" in Ethnologue. For these data points we used 55%.

References

Yoshua Bengio, Réjean Ducharme, and Pascal Vincent. 2000. A neural probabilistic language model. In *Proceedings of the 13th International Conference on Neural Information Processing Systems*, pages 893–899.

Una Canger. 1988. Subgrupos de los dialectos nahuas. In J. Kathryn Josserand and Karen Dakin, editors, *Smoke and Mist: Mesoamerican Studies in Memory of Thelma D. Sullivan*, volume 402 of *BAR International*, pages 473–498. BAR, Oxford.

Una Canger and Karen Dakin. 1985. An inconspicuous basic split in nahuatl. *International Journal of American Linguistics*, 51(4):358–361.

Huadong Chen, Shujian Huang, David Chiang, Xinyu Dai, and Jiajun Chen. 2018. Combining character and word information in neural machine translation using a multi-level attention. In *Proceedings of the 2018 Conference of the North American Chapter of the Association for Computational Linguistics: Human Language Technologies, Volume 1 (Long Papers)*, pages 1284–1293, New Orleans, Louisiana. Association for Computational Linguistics.

Victoriano de la Cruz Cruz. 2014. La escritura náhuatl y los procesos de su revitalización. *Contribution in New World Archaeology*, 7:187–197.

Ted Dunning. 1994. Statistical identification of language. Technical Report 94-273, New Mexico State University.

David M. Eberhard, Gary F. Simons, and Charles D. Fennig, editors. 2021. *Ethnologue: Languages of the World. Twenty-fourth edition*. SIL International. Online version: `http://www.ethnologue.com`.

S. Egland and D. Bartholomew. 1978. La inteligibilidad inter-dialectal en mexico: Resultados de algunos sondeos. Technical report.

J.I.E. Farfan. 2019. *Nahuatl Contemporary Writing: Studying Convergence in the Absence of a Written Norm*. University of Sheffield.

Pablo Gamallo, José Ramom Pichel Campos, and Inaki Alegria. 2017. A perplexity-based method for similar languages discrimination. In *Proceedings of the fourth workshop on NLP for similar languages, varieties and dialects (VarDial)*, pages 109–114.

Mihaela Gaman, Dirk Hovy, Radu Tudor Ionescu, Heidi Jauhiainen, Tommi Jauhiainen, Krister Lindén, Nikola Ljubešić, Niko Partanen, Christoph Purschke, Yves Scherrer, et al. 2020. A report on the vardial evaluation campaign 2020. In *Proceedings of the 7th Workshop on NLP for Similar Languages, Varieties and Dialects*. International Committee on Computational Linguistics.

Ximena Gutierrez-Vasques, Gerardo Sierra, and Isaac Hernandez Pompa. 2016. Axolotl: a web accessible parallel corpus for spanish-nahuatl. In *Proceedings of the Tenth International Conference on Language Resources and Evaluation (LREC'16)*, pages 4210–4214.

INALI. 2009. *Catálogo De Las Lenguas Indígenas Nacionales: Variantes Lingüísticas De México Con Sus Autodenominaciones Y Referencias Geoestadísticas*. Instituto Nacional de Lenguas Indígenas, México, D.F.

Artur Kulmizev, Bo Blankers, Johannes Bjerva, Malvina Nissim, Gertjan van Noord, Barbara Plank, and Martijn Wieling. 2017. The power of character n-grams in native language identification. In *Proceedings of the 12th workshop on innovative use of NLP for building educational applications*, pages 382–389.

Yolanda Lastra. 1986. *Las areas dialectales del nahuatl moderno*. Universidad Nacional Autónoma de México, Instituto de Investigaciones Antropológicas.

M. Launey and C. Mackay. 2011. *An Introduction to Classical Nahuatl*. Cambridge University Press.

Jason Lee, Kyunghyun Cho, and Thomas Hofmann. 2017. Fully character-level neural machine translation without explicit segmentation. *Transactions of the Association for Computational Linguistics*, 5:365–378.

Shervin Malmasi, Eshrag Refaee, and Mark Dras. 2015. Arabic dialect identification using a parallel multidialectal corpus. In *Conference of the Pacific Association for Computational Linguistics*, pages 35–53. Springer.

Adam Paszke, Sam Gross, Francisco Massa, Adam Lerer, James Bradbury, Gregory Chanan, Trevor Killeen, Zeming Lin, Natalia Gimelshein, Luca Antiga, Alban Desmaison, Andreas Kopf, Edward Yang, Zachary DeVito, Martin Raison, Alykhan Tejani, Sasank Chilamkurthy, Benoit Steiner, Lu Fang, Junjie Bai, and Soumith Chintala. 2019. Pytorch: An imperative style, high-performance deep learning library. In H. Wallach, H. Larochelle, A. Beygelzimer, F. d'Alché-Buc, E. Fox, and R. Garnett, editors, *Advances in Neural Information Processing Systems 32*, pages 8024–8035. Curran Associates, Inc.

Magnus Pharao Hansen. 2013. Nahuatl in the plural: Dialectology and activism in Mexico. In *Proceedings of the American Anthropological Association, Annual Meeting*.

Magnus Pharao Hansen. 2014. The East-West split in Nahuan dialectology: Reviewing the evidence and consolidating the grouping. In *Friends of Uto-Aztecan Workshop*.

Robert Pugh, Francis Tyers, and Marivel Huerta Mendez. 2021. Towards and open source finite-state morphological analyzer for zacatlán-ahuacatlán-tepetzintla nahuatl. In *Proceedings of the Workshop on Computational Methods for Endangered Languages*, volume 1, pages 80–85.

Fatiha Sadat, Farzindar Kazemi, and Atefeh Farzindar. 2014. Automatic identification of arabic language varieties and dialects in social media. In *Proceedings of the Second Workshop on Natural Language Processing for Social Media (SocialNLP)*, pages 22–27.

PV Veena, M Anand Kumar, and KP Soman. 2018. Character embedding for language identification in hindi-english code-mixed social media text. *Computación y Sistemas*, 22(1):65–74.

A Language variants

In Table 2 we give the equivalences between ISO-639 language codes, variant names and locations where the variant is reported to be spoken.

Code	Variant	Locations
azz	Highland Puebla	Chichiquila Tatóscac Zacatipan Zautla
nch	Central Huasteca	Las Balsas
ncj	Northern Puebla	Cuaohueyalta Masacoatlán Tlaxpanaloya Xaltepuxtla
ncl	Michoacán	Pómaro
ngu	Guerrero	Copalillo Zitlala
nhe	Eastern Huasteca	Cuautenáhuatl Ixcatepec Jaltocan Xochiatipan Yahualica
nhi	Western Sierra	Tlalitzlipa
nhw	Western Huasteca	Casotipan Macuilocatl Tampacan Tetlalpan
nhy	Northern Oaxaca	—
nsu	Sierra Negra	—

Table 2: A listing of the locations tested for mutual intelligibility in Egland and Bartholomew (1978) as assigned to specific variants and language codes. The variants nhy and nsu did not appear in the report, but mutual intelligibility scores are available from Ethnologue (Eberhard et al., 2021).

Apurinã Universal Dependencies Treebank

Jack Rueter[1], Marília Fernanda Pereira de Freitas[2], Sidney da Silva Facundes[2], Mika Hämäläinen[1] and Niko Partanen[1]
[1]University of Helsinki
[2]Universidade Federal do Pará
[1]firstname.lastname@helsinki.fi
[2]{mfpf,sidi}@ufpa.br

Abstract

This paper presents and discusses the first Universal Dependencies treebank for the Apurinã language. The treebank contains 76 fully annotated sentences, applies 14 parts-of-speech, as well as seven augmented or new features – some of which are unique to Apurinã. The construction of the treebank has also served as an opportunity to develop finite-state description of the language and facilitate the transfer of open-source infrastructure possibilities to an endangered language of the Amazon. The source materials used in the initial treebank represent fieldwork practices where not all tokens of all sentences are equally annotated. For this reason, establishing regular annotation practices for the entire Apurinã treebank is an ongoing project.

1 Introduction

Apurinã (ISO code apu) is an endangered language spoken in the Amazon Basin. The language has around 2,000 native speakers and it is definitely endangered according to the UNESCO classification (Moseley, 2010). This paper is dedicated to describing the first ever Universal Dependencies (UD) treebank for Apurinã[1]. We describe how the treebank was created, and what exact decisions were made in different parts of the process.

The UD project (Zeman et al., 2020) has the goal of collecting syntactically annotated corpora containing information about lemmas, parts-of-speech, morphology and dependencies in such a fashion that the annotation conventions are shared across languages, although there may be inconsistencies between languages (see Rueter and Partanen 2019). As the number of South American languages represented in the Universal Dependencies project has grown rapidly in the last years (see i.e. Vasquez et al., 2018; Thomas, 2019), the descriptions of individual treebanks are thereby also a very valuable resource that helps to maintain consistency in the treebanks of this complex linguistic regions.

The advantage of UD treebanks is that they can be used directly in many neural NLP applications such as parsers (Qi et al., 2020) and part-of-speech taggers (Kim et al., 2017). Although the endangered languages have a very different starting point in comparison with large languages (Hämäläinen, 2021), there has been recent work (Lim et al., 2018; Ens et al., 2019; Hämäläinen and Wiechetek, 2020; Alnajjar, 2021) showcasing good results on a variety of tasks even for the few endangered languages that have a UD treebank.

The fact that UD treebanks can be used with neural models to build higher level NLP tools is one of the key motivations for us to build this resource for Apurinã. In addition to NLP research, UD treebanks have been used in many purely linguistically motivated research papers (Croft et al., 2017; Levshina, 2017, 2019; Sinnemäki and Haakana, 2020). We believe such developments will only grow stronger, and believe that easily available treebanks in the UD project, covering continuously better the world's linguistic diversity, will continue widening their role as suitable and valuable tools for both descriptive linguistic research and computational linguistics. This goal will be achievable only by creating an open discussion about the conventions and choices done in different treebanks, which can be adjusted and refined at the later stage. This study aims to provide such description about Apurinã treebank. An example of a UD annotated sentence in Apurinã can be seen in Figure 1.

2 Modelling the Apurinã Language in UD

The Apurinã language has a rich morphology with regular correlation between numerous formatives and semantic categories. One challenge in the conversion from fieldwork/typology style annotation to that used in the UD project is to choose what

[1]https://github.com/UniversalDependencies/UD_Apurina-UFPA

Proceedings of the First Workshop on Natural Language Processing for Indigenous Languages of the Americas, pages 28–33
June 11, 2021.

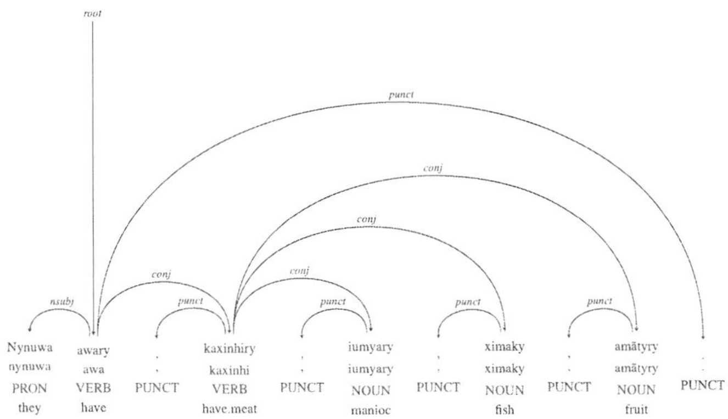

Figure 1: An example of a UD tree for an Apurinã sentence meaning *'They had it, had meat, manioc, fish, fruit'*.

features should or can be highlighted with specific transferability to other UD projects and which ones should only be represented as language specific morphology.

The task has also been contemplated from a finite-state perspective, where regular inflection plays a decisive role in determining lemma and regular inflection strategies. Finite-state description also entails the use of the open-source GiellaLT infrastructure (Norwegian Arctic University, Tromsø) (Moshagen et al., 2014), which introduces a large number of mutual tag definitions and practices that can be applied to Apurinã with ample analogy from the morphologically challenging Uralic and other languages of the Circum-Polar region.

Solutions for dealing with the categories of case, number, person and gender are available in the GiellaLT infrastructure. Extensions, however, have been required for Apurinã in the categories of number, person and gender. Unlike some Indo-European and Uralic languages, the category of gender must also be applied to the subjects and objects of verbs; subject and object marking for number (see Facundes et al. 2021) and person categories could have been adapted directly from description work in the Erzya (Rueter and Tyers, 2018) and Moksha (Rueter, 2018) UD treebanks.

2.1 Case

The Feature of CASE, for example, permeates many of the individual language projects, and some attempts are made to align case documentation with principles adapted in the Unimorph project (Kirov et al., 2018). In the instance of Apurinã, parallel case categories have been adapted with names familiar to those used in work with languages of the Uralic language family. This was done principally because the team involved in the annotation was most familiar with this language family: at the same time the Uralic UD annotations, especially for the minority languages, are already closely adapted to the UD project at large. Whether such generalizations work is also one test for the cross-linguistic suitability of the current annotation model.

The concept of case in Apurinã is most salient in oblique marking. While the subject, object and adposition complements show no special marking, there are at least six oblique marker to deal with (Facundes, 2000, 385–390). The labeling of these cases also underlines a problem not new to UD, namely, every language research tradition tends to apply its own terms for similar functions. Apurinã, as in the Uralic languages, shows evidence of case-like formatives associated not only with nominals but verbs, as well. In the first version of the Apurinã UD treebank, the formative case name pairs have been assigned as follows: *munhi* = Dat (dative, allative, goal), *kata* = Com (comitative, associative), *ã* = Loc (locative, instrumental), *Ø* = Nom (nominative). Subsequent work in the dataset will introduce the additional case formative *sawaky* = Temp (temporal), and show the extent of shared morphology across parts-of-speech.

2.2 Possession

One complexity of Apurinã morphology is encountered in the expression of possession. While the possessor of a noun may be indicated morphologically on the possessum, it is not obligatory. A preceding personal pronoun, for example, also serves as a marker of possession, to which the morphology of the possessum reacts and shows indication of being possessed. Hence, there are four basic categories that can be expressed on the possessum:

person, number and gender of the possessor, on the one hand, and indication of whether the entity is a possessum or not, on the other. These categories are expressed as feature and value pairs in the UD project:

- Gender[psor]=Masc|Fem
- Number[psor]=Plur|Sing
- Person[psor]=1|2|3
- Possessed=Yes|No

While matters of gender, number and person are directly attested in the morphology of the possessum, the feature POSSESSED identifies the individual noun as to whether there is or is not marking indicating that it is possessed. This particular issue of research is dealt with extensively in Freitas, 2017.

Apurinã nouns can be split into four groups on the basis of how their morphology is affected by possession. There are nouns that never take possession or possessive affixes. Such nouns include proper names (Freitas, 2017, 179–180). The remaining nouns, however, take possessive affixes, on the one hand, and additional marking to indicate whether the word is possessed or not. First, there are nouns, such as kinship terms, that virtually always appear with possessive affixes and no morphology to indicate that they are possessed. These nouns may only be construed as not possessed in some verbal incorporations where the noun is non-specific by nature. A formative *-txi* is present to indicate the noun is not possessed. Other words in this group, including terms for body parts and individual belongings, for example, take the *-txi* formative to indicate the item is not possessed more freely, e.g. *kywy* 'head (possessed)' vs *kywĩtxi* 'head (possessed)' (Freitas, 2017, 163-171; Facundes, 2000, 199-204,228-236). Second, there are noun categories that take the formatives *-ne*, *-te* and *-re1* to indicate the item is possessed, but they, in contrast, have no morphology to indicate that the item is not possessed. Third, there is group of nouns which actually mark both the possessed with the formative *-re2* and the non-possessed with the formative *-ry2*. This alternation is described in Facundes, 2000, and explicitly Freitas, 2017, (112-123) (see Table 1)

The Apurinã treebank solution has been to introduce the **possessed** feature with **Yes** and **No** values. Nouns that cannot be possessed are simply left without the feature Possessed.

	Possessed	Not Possessed	translation
body part	kywy	kywĩ-txi	'head'
person	sytu-re	sytu	'woman'
other	kuta-re2	kuta-ry2	'basket'

Table 1: Marking of possessed feature

2.3 Intransitive descriptive verbs

Apurinã verbs can bear morphology indicating subject and object, be that simultaneously or separately. What is interesting, however, is that a specific subclass of intransitive descriptive verbs attest to the use of object marking to indicate congruence with the subject (Facundes, 2000, 278–283). There are, in fact, certain verbs that distinguish object and subject marking strategies for the same intransitive verbs, such that subject marking indicates a short temporal frame, and object marking indicates permanency (cf. Chagas, 2007; Freitas, 2017, 70–71).

The solution here has been to refer to object-looking morphology with subject congruence as subject marking:

- Gender[subj]=Fem|Masc
- Number[subj]=Plur|Sing
- Person[subj]=1|2|3

To cope, an additional feature value set has been introduced to distinguish verbs of the intransitive descriptive (Vid) nature, and this subset is subsequently split on the on basis of whether the formative entails object-identical *Vido* or subject-identical marking *Vids*.

2.4 Derivations

Fieldwork annotations of certain derivational morphology are minimalistic, and their conversion in the UD treebank calls for more specific representation. Whereas some formatives have been referred to using the same terms, e.g. nominalizer, gerund, we have been obliged to elaborate. Only one feature has been provided for Derivation, Proprietive (*ka-*). The proprietive construction is one of many annotated as **atrib** in the fieldwork materials.

2.5 Lemmatization

The Apurinã language is spoken in 18 indigenous communities of the Purus basin (Lima Padovani et al., 2019). Grammar descriptions from Facundes, 2000 to Freitas, 2017 demonstrate a change in orthographic development, on the one hand, and actual variation in forms of the same words in relation to geographic location, on the other. Materials in the treebank alone show some vacillation with regard to stem-initial *h* and word-internal *e* vs *i*. Since the orthographic standard is still in a developmental state, lemma forms have been chosen on a basis of whether they occur in the manuscript dictionary (Lima-Padovani and Facundes, 2016) or not, and a preference for longer word forms, i.e., *h*-initial stems are forwarded, since it easier to drop a letter in the description than to automatically insert one. Thus the form *hãty* 'one' is given as a lemma instead of its variant *ãty* (as given in the dictionary), and *herãkatxi* (given as a variant) is forwarded as a lemma over both *erãkatxi* and *erẽkatxi* (given in the examples of the alphabet), *arẽkatxi*. The high vowel *i* is preferred over the middle *e* such that *tiwitxi* 'thing' is given as a lemma for the forms *teetxi* and *tiitxi*. Fortunately, work with Apurinã variation is continuing (Lima Padovani et al., 2019), and an updated version of the Apurinã-Portuguese dictionary is forthcoming.

3 Treebanks in figures

There were 76 valid and dependency-annotated sentences in the first release. Broken into figures, these sentences contain 574 tokens and a 454 word count, which can be further broken down into features, parts-of-speech and dependency relations.

The most salient features are *Case* (101), *Gender* (96), *Number* (73), but the newly introduced *Gender[obj]* (47) is also well attested. The *Case* feature owes its prominence to the presence of all nouns not marked for oblique cases, i.e. *Nom*; this leaves a total of 25 obliques (see Table 2).

Feature	№	Feature	№
AdvType=Tim	1	Number[obj]=Plur,Sing	1
Aspect=Prog	1	Number[obj]=Sing	51
Case=Com	4	Number[psor]=Sing	10
Case=Dat	7	Number[subj]=Plur	1
Case=Loc	11	Number[subj]=Sing	7
Case=Nom	76	Person=3	53
Case=Temp	3	Person[obj]=3	52
Derivation=Proprietive	2	Person[psor]=3	8
Gender=Fem	14	Person[subj]=3	8
Gender=Masc	82	Possessed=No	27
Gender[obj]=Masc	47	Possessed=Yes	8
Gender[psor]=Fem	3	PronType=Prs	53
Gender[psor]=Masc	11	VerbForm=Conv	2
Gender[subj]=Masc	8	VerbForm=Vnoun	9
Number=Plur	16	VerbType=Vido	2
Number=Sing	57		

Table 2: Features

The most prominent parts-of-speech the NOUN (170) and VERB (137) classes, followed by PRON (59) and ADV (39), whereas two instances of the same unknown word *pekana* outnumber the ADJ, CCONJ and PROPN, each at one (see Table 3).

PoS	№	PoS	№	PoS	№
ADJ	1	DET	11	PROPN	1
ADP	3	NOUN	170	SCONJ	3
ADV	39	NUM	9	VERB	137
AUX	6	PART	13	X	2
CCONJ	1	PRON	59		

Table 3: Part-of-speech Figures

An important dependency relation (*deprel*) is *nsubj* (83), which is made possible through the extensive use of the *conj* relation. Language-specific *deprels* have extensions such as: *lmod* = locative modifier, *neg* = negation, *poss* = possession, *relcl* = relative clause *tcl* = temporal clause and *tmod* = temporal modifier (see Table 4).

deprel	№	deprel	№	deprel	№
acl	10	mark	3	advmod:lmod	1
advcl	5	nmod	18	advmod:neg	13
advmod	22	nsubj	83	advmod:tmod	13
aux	5	nummod	9	nmod:poss	2
case	3	obj	63	nsubj:cop	2
cc	3	obl	15	obj:agent	1
conj	48	root	76	obl:lmod	19
dep	2	xcomp	1	obl:tmod	4
det	24	acl:relcl	5		
csubj	2	advcl:tcl	2		

Table 4: Dependency relations

4 Future work

Due to the size and orientation of the dataset some features of the Apurinã language have been neglected. It will also be a challenge to apply recent studies in noun incorporation annotation for UD in Tyers and Mishchenkova, 2020 to what Facundes and Freitas, 2015 describe for Apurinã noun and classifier incorporation.

Another obvious goal for further work is to make Apurinã treebank so large that it can be split into train, test and dev portions. The goal to expand the treebank is connected to the availability of resources. Currently the sentences used in the treebank come mainly from the grammatical descriptions. As a language documentation corpus exists[2], an important consideration is whether the treebank sentences could be more closely connected to audio and video recordings as well, and, of course, the main corpora in Belém, as multimodal resources are valuable in language documentation.

[2] https://elar.soas.ac.uk/Collection/MPI1029704

References

Khalid Alnajjar. 2021. When word embeddings become endangered. In Mika Hämäläinen, Niko Partanen, and Khalid Alnajjar, editors, *Multilingual Facilitation*. Rootroo Ltd.

Angela Fabíola Alves. Chagas. 2007. *Aspectos Semântico, Morfológicos e Morfossintáticos das Palavras Descritivas Apurinã*. Belém, Pará. Belém, Pará: Programa de Pós-graduação em Letras – Mestrado em Estudos Linguísticos da Universidade Federal do Pará (Dissertação de Mestrado), 2007.

W. Croft, D. Nordquist, Katherine Looney, and Michael Regan. 2017. Linguistic Typology meets Universal Dependencies. In *TLT*.

Jeff Ens, Mika Hämäläinen, Jack Rueter, and Philippe Pasquier. 2019. Morphosyntactic disambiguation in an endangered language setting. In *Proceedings of the 22nd Nordic Conference on Computational Linguistics*, pages 345–349.

Sidney da Silva Facundes. 2000. *The Language of the Apurinã People of Brazil (Maipure/Arawak)*. SUNY Buffalo, New York.

Sidney da Silva Facundes, Marília Fernanda Pereira de Freitas, and Bruna Fernanda Soares de Lima-Padovani. 2021. Number expression in apurinã (arawák). In Mika Hämäläinen, Niko Partanen, and Khalid Alnajjar, editors, *Multilingual Facilitation*. Rootroo Ltd.

Sidney da Silva Facundes and Marília Fernanda Pereira de Freitas. 2015. De compostos nominais produtivos a um sistema incipiente de classificação nominal em Apurinã (Aruák). *Revista Moara – Edição 43*, vol. 2 – jul - dez 2015, Estudos Linguísticos:23–50.

Marília Fernanda Pereira de Freitas. 2017. *A Posse em Apurinã: descrição de construções atributivas e predicativas em comparação com outras línguas Aruák*. Universidade Federal Do Pará Programa De Pós-Graduação Em Letras Curso De Doutorado Em Letras – Estudos Linguísticos.

Mika Hämäläinen and Linda Wiechetek. 2020. Morphological disambiguation of South Sámi with FSTs and neural networks. In *Proceedings of the 1st Joint Workshop on Spoken Language Technologies for Under-resourced languages (SLTU) and Collaboration and Computing for Under-Resourced Languages (CCURL)*, pages 36–40.

Mika Hämäläinen. 2021. Endangered languages are not low-resourced! In Mika Hämäläinen, Niko Partanen, and Khalid Alnajjar, editors, *Multilingual Facilitation*. Rootroo Ltd.

Joo-Kyung Kim, Young-Bum Kim, Ruhi Sarikaya, and Eric Fosler-Lussier. 2017. Cross-lingual transfer learning for POS tagging without cross-lingual resources. In *Proceedings of the 2017 Conference on Empirical Methods in Natural Language Processing*, pages 2832–2838, Copenhagen, Denmark. Association for Computational Linguistics.

Christo Kirov, Ryan Cotterell, John Sylak-Glassman, Géraldine Walther, Ekaterina Vylomova, Patrick Xia, Manaal Faruqui, Sabrina J Mielke, Arya D McCarthy, Sandra Kübler, et al. 2018. Unimorph 2.0: Universal morphology. In *Proceedings of the Eleventh International Conference on Language Resources and Evaluation (LREC 2018)*.

Natalia Levshina. 2017. Communicative efficiency and syntactic predictability: A cross-linguistic study based on the Universal Dependencies corpora. In *Proceedings of the NoDaLiDa 2017 Workshop on Universal Dependencies, 22 May, Gothenburg Sweden*, 135, pages 72–78. Linköping University Electronic Press.

Natalia Levshina. 2019. Token-based typology and word order entropy: A study based on Universal Dependencies. *Linguistic Typology*, 23(3):533–572.

KyungTae Lim, Niko Partanen, and Thierry Poibeau. 2018. Multilingual dependency parsing for low-resource languages: Case studies on North Saami and Komi-Zyrian. In *Proceedings of the Eleventh International Conference on Language Resources and Evaluation (LREC 2018)*.

Bruna Fernanda S. de Lima-Padovani and Sidi Facundes. 2016. *Dicionário pedagógico Apurinã-Português*. Amazonas – Manaus. Esta publicação foi produzida com recursos do FNDE em parceria com a UFPA, FOCIMP e CIMI Todos os direitos autorais são reservados às comunidades indígenas Apurinã.

Bruna Fernanda Soares de Lima Padovani, Rayssa Rodrigues da Silva, and Sidney da Silva Facundes. 2019. Levantamentos da variação linguística em três domínios do complexo dialetal Apurinã (ARÚAK). *Entreletras, Araguaína*, page 161–179.

Christopher Moseley, editor. 2010. *Atlas of the World's Languages in Danger*, 3rd edition. UNESCO Publishing. Online version: http://www.unesco.org/languages-atlas/.

Sjur Moshagen, Jack Rueter, Tommi Pirinen, Trond Trosterud, and Francis M. Tyers. 2014. Open-Source Infrastructures for Collaborative Work on Under-Resourced Languages. The LREC 2014 Workshop "CCURL 2014 - Collaboration and Computing for Under-Resourced Languages in the Linked Open Data Era".

Peng Qi, Yuhao Zhang, Yuhui Zhang, Jason Bolton, and Christopher D. Manning. 2020. Stanza: A Python natural language processing toolkit for many human languages. In *Proceedings of the 58th Annual Meeting of the Association for Computational Linguistics: System Demonstrations*.

Jack Rueter. 2018. rueter/erme-ud-moksha: Erme ud moksha v1.0. In *Zenodo*. 10.5281/zenodo.1156112.

Jack Rueter and Niko Partanen. 2019. Survey of Uralic Universal Dependencies development. In *Third Workshop on Universal Dependencies (UDW, SyntaxFest 2019)*, United States. The Association for Computational Linguistics.

Jack Michael Rueter and Francis M. Tyers. 2018. Towards an open-source universal-dependency treebank for Erzya. International Workshop for Computational Linguistics of Uralic Languages, IWCLUL ; Conference date: 08-01-2018 Through 09-01-2018.

Kaius Sinnemäki and Viljami Haakana. 2020. Variation in Universal Dependencies annotation: A token-based typological case study on adpossessive constructions. In *Proceedings of the Fourth Workshop on Universal Dependencies (UDW 2020)*, pages 158–167, Barcelona, Spain (Online). Association for Computational Linguistics.

Guillaume Thomas. 2019. Universal Dependencies for Mbyá Guaraní. In *Proceedings of the Third Workshop on Universal Dependencies (UDW, SyntaxFest 2019)*, pages 70–77.

Francis Tyers and Karina Mishchenkova. 2020. Dependency annotation of noun incorporation in polysynthetic languages. In *Proceedings of the Fourth Workshop on Universal Dependencies (UDW 2020)*, pages 195–204.

Alonso Vasquez, Renzo Ego Aguirre, Candy Angulo, John Miller, Claudia Villanueva, Željko Agić, Roberto Zariquiey, and Arturo Oncevay. 2018. Toward universal dependencies for Shipibo-Konibo. In *Proceedings of the Second Workshop on Universal Dependencies (UDW 2018)*, pages 151–161.

Daniel Zeman, Joakim Nivre, Mitchell Abrams, Elia Ackermann, Noëmi Aepli, Hamid Aghaei, Željko Agić, Amir Ahmadi, Ahrenberg, et al. 2020. Universal dependencies 2.7. LINDAT/CLARIAH-CZ digital library at the Institute of Formal and Applied Linguistics (ÚFAL), Faculty of Mathematics and Physics, Charles University.

Automatic Interlinear Glossing for Otomi language

Diego Barriga[1,3] **Victor Mijangos**[1,3] **Ximena Gutierrez-Vasques**[2,3]
[1]Universidad Nacional Autónoma de México (UNAM)
[2]URPP Language and Space, University of Zürich
[3]Comunidad Elotl
{dbarriga, vmijangosc}@ciencias.unam.mx ximena.gutierrezvasques@uzh.ch

Abstract

In linguistics, interlinear glossing is an essential procedure for analyzing the morphology of languages. This type of annotation is useful for language documentation, and it can also provide valuable data for NLP applications. We perform automatic glossing for Otomi, an under-resourced language. Our work also comprises the pre-processing and annotation of the corpus.

We implement different sequential labelers. CRF models represented an efficient and good solution for our task (accuracy above 90%). Two main observations emerged from our work: 1) models with a higher number of parameters (RNNs) performed worse in our low-resource scenario; and 2) the information encoded in the CRF feature function plays an important role in the prediction of labels; however, even in cases where POS tags are not available it is still possible to achieve competitive results.

1 Introduction

One of the important steps of linguistic documentation is to describe the grammar of a language. Morphological analysis constitutes one of the stages for building this description. Traditionally, this is done by means of interlinear glossing. This is an annotation task where linguists analyze sentences in a given language and they segment each word with the aim of annotating the morphosyntactic categories of the morphemes within this word (see example in Table 1).

Sentence	hí	tó=tsogí
Glossing	NEG	3.PRF=leave
Translation	'I have not left it'	

Table 1: Example of morpheme-by-morpheme glosses for Otomi

This type of linguistic annotated data is a valuable resource not only for documenting a language but it can also enable NLP technologies, e.g., by providing training data for automatic morphological analyzers, taggers, morphological segmentation, etc.

However, not all languages have this type of annotated corpora readily available. Glossing is a time consuming task that requires linguistic expertise. In particular, low-resource languages lack of documentation and language technologies (Mager et al., 2018).

Our aim is to successfully produce automatic glossing annotation in a low resource scenario. We focus on Otomi of Toluca, an indigenous language spoken in Mexico (Oto-Manguean family). This is a morphological rich language with fusional tendency. Moreover, it has scarcity of digital resources, e.g., monolingual and parallel corpora.

Our initial resource is a small corpus transcribed into a phonetic alphabet. We pre-process it and we perform manual glossing. Once we have this dataset, we use it for training an automatic glossing system for Otomi.

By using different variations of Conditional Random Fields (CRFs), we were able to achieve good accuracy in the automatic glossing task (above 90%), regardless the low-resource scenario. Furthermore, computationally more expensive methods, i.e., neural networks, did not perform as well.

We also performed an analysis of the results from the linguistics perspective. We explored the automatic glossing performance for a subset of labels to understand the errors that the model makes.

Our work can be a helpful tool for reducing the workload when manually glossing. This would have an impact on language documentation. It can also lead to an increment of annotated resources for Otomi, which could be a starting point for developing NLP technologies that nowadays are not yet available for this language.

Proceedings of the First Workshop on Natural Language Processing for Indigenous Languages of the Americas, pages 34–43
June 11, 2021.

2 Background

As we have mentioned before, glossing comprises describing the morphological structure of a sentence by associating every morpheme with a morphological label or gloss. In a linguistic gloss, there are usually three levels of analysis: a) the segmentation by morphemes; b) the glosses describing these morphemes; and c) the translation or lexical correspondences in a reference language.

Several works have tried to automatize this task by using computational methods. In Snoek et al. (2014), they use a rule-based approach (Finite State Transducer) to obtain glosses for Plains Cree, an Algonquian language. They focus only on the analysis of nouns. Samardzic et al. (2015) propose a method for glossing Chintang language; they divide the task into grammatical and lexical glossing. Grammatical glossing is approached as a supervised part-of-speech tagging, while for lexical glossing, they use a dictionary. A fully automatized procedure is not performed since word segmentation is not addressed.

Some other works have approached the whole pipeline of automatic glossing as a supervised tagging task using machine learning sequential models, and they have particularly focused on under-resourced languages (Moeller and Hulden, 2018; Anastasopoulos et al., 2018; Zhao et al., 2020). In Anastasopoulos et al. (2018), they make use of neural-based models with dual sources, they leverage easy-to-collect translations.

In Moeller and Hulden (2018), they perform automatic glossing for Lezgi (Nakh-Daghestanian family) under challenging low-resource conditions. They implement different methods, i.e., CRF, CRF+SVM, Seq2Seq neural network. The best results are obtained with a CRF model that leverages POS tags. The glossing is mainly focused on tagging grammatical (functional) morphemes. While the lexical items are tagged simply as stems.

This latter approach especially influences our work. In fact, Moeller and Hulden (2018) highlight the importance of testing these models on other languages, particularly polysynthetic languages with fusion and complex morphonology. Our case of study, Otomi, is precisely a language highly fusional with complex morphophonological patterns, as we will discuss on Section 3.

Finally, automatic glossing is not only crucial for aiding linguistic research and language documentation. This type of annotation is also a valuable source of morphological information for several NLP tasks. For instance, it could be used to train state-of-the-art morphological segmentation systems for low-resource languages (Kann and Schütze, 2018). The information contained in the glosses is also helpful for training morphological reinflection systems (Cotterell et al., 2016), this consists in predicting the inflected form of a word given its lemma. It also can help in the automatic generation of morphological paradigms (Moeller et al., 2020).

These morphological tools can then be used to build downstream applications, e.g., machine translation, text generation. It is noteworthy that these are language technologies that are not yet available for all languages, especially for under-resourced ones.

3 Methodology

3.1 Corpus

Otomi is considered a group of languages spoken in Mexico (around 300,000 speakers). It belongs to the Oto-Pamean branch of the Oto-Manguean family (Barrientos López, 2004). It is a morphologically rich language that shows particular phenomena (Baerman et al., 2019; Lastra, 2001):

- fusional patterns for the inflection of the verbs (it fuses person, aspect, tense and mood in a single affix);
- a complex system of inflectional classes;
- stem alternation, e.g., *dí=pädi* 'I know' and *bi=mbädi* 'He knew';
- complex morphophnological patterns, e.g., *dí=pädi* 'I know', *dí=pä-hu̱* 'We know';
- complex noun inflectional patterns.

Furthermore, digital resources are scarce for this language.

We focus on the Otomi of Toluca variety.[1] Our starting point is the corpus compiled by Lastra (1992), which is comprised of narrations and dialogues. The corpus was originally transcribed into a phonetic alphabet. We pre-processed this corpus, i.e., we performed digitization and orthographic

[1]An Otomi language spoken in the region of San Andrés Cuexcontitlán, Toluca, State of Mexico. Usually regarded as *ots* (iso639).

normalization.[2] We used the orthographic standard proposed by INALI (INALI, 2014), although we had problems in processing the appropriate UTF-8 representations for some of the vocals (Otomi has a wide range of vowels).

The corpus, then, was manually tagged,[3] i.e., interlinear glossing and Part Of Speech (POS). We followed the Leipzig glossing rules (Comrie et al., 2008).

Domain	Count
Narrative	32
Dialogues	4
Total sentences	1769
Total words (tokens)	8550

Table 2: General information about the Otomi corpus

In addition to this corpus, we included 81 extra short sentences that a linguist annotated; these examples contained particularly difficult phenomena, e.g., stem alternation, reduction of the stem and others. Table 2 contains general information about the final corpus size.

We also show in Table 3 the top ten most common POS tags and gloss labels in the corpus. We can see that the size of our corpus is small compared to the magnitude of resources usually used for doing in NLP in other languages.

POS tags	freq	Gloss	freq
V	2579	stem	7501
OBL	2443	DET	733
DET	973	3.CPL	444
CNJ	835	PSD	413
DEM	543	LIM	370
UNKWN	419	PRAG	357
NN	272	3.ICP	341
NEG	176	LIG	287
P.LOC	81	1.ICP	270
PRT	49	DET.PL	269

Table 3: More frequent POS tags and gloss in corpus

3.2 Automatic glossing

We focus on the two first levels of glossing, i.e., given an Otomi sentence, our system will be able to morphologically segment each word and gloss each of the morphemes within the words, as it is shown in the Example 1. Translation implies a different level of analysis and, due to the scarce digital resources, it is not addressed here.

Similar to previous works, we use a closed set of labels, i.e., we have labels for all the grammatical (functional) morphemes and a single label for all the lexical morphemes (*stem*). We can see in the Example 1 that morphemes like *tsogí* ('leave') are labeled as *stem*.

(1) hí tó=tsogí
NEG 3.PRF=stem

Once we have a gloss label associated to each morpheme, we prepare the training data, i.e., we pair each letter with a BIO-label. BIO-labeling consists on associating each original label with a Beginning-Inside-Outside (BIO) label. This means that each position of a morpheme is declared either as the beginning (B) or inside (I). We neglected O (outside). BIO-labels include the morpheme category (e.g. B-*stem*) or affix glosses (e.g. B-PST, for past tense). For example, the labeled representation of the word *tótsogí* would be as follows:

(2) t ó t s o g
B-3.PRF I-3.PRF B-stem I-stem I-stem I-stem
í
I-stem

As we can see, BIO-labels help to mark the boundaries of the morphemes within a word, and they also assign a gloss label to each morpheme. We followed this procedure from Moeller and Hulden (2018). Once we have this labeling, we can train a model, i.e., predict the labels that indicate the morphological segmentation and the associated gloss of each morpheme.

In this task, the input would be a string of characters $c_1, ..., c_N$ and the output is another string $g_1, ..., g_N$ which corresponds to a sequence of labels (from a finite set of labels), i.e., the glossing. In order to perform automatic glossing, we need to learn a mapping between the input and the output.

3.2.1 Conditional Random Fields

We approach the task of automatic glossing as a supervised structured prediction. We use CRFs for predicting the sequence of labels that represents the interlinear glossing. In particular, we used a linear-chain CRF.

The CRFs need to represent each of the characters from the input sentence as a vector. This is done by means of a feature function. In order

[2] The digitized corpus, without any type of annotation, can be consulted in `https://tsunkua.elotl.mx/`.

[3] The manual glossing of this corpus was part of a linguistics PhD dissertation (Mijangos, 2021).

to map the input sequence into vectors, the feature function need to take into account relevant information about the input and output sequences (features).

Feature functions play a major role in the performance of CRF models. In our case, we build these vectors by taking into account information about the current letter, the current, previous and next POS tags, beginning/end of words and sentences, letter position, and others (see Section 4.1).

Let $X = (c_1, ..., c_N)$ be a sequence of characters representing the input of our model (a sentence), and $Y = (g_1, ..., g_N)$ the output (a sequence of BIO-labels). The CRF model estimates the probability:

$$p(Y|X) = \frac{1}{Z}\prod_{i=1}^{N} exp\{w^T\phi(Y, X, i)\} \quad (1)$$

Here Z is the partition function and w is the weights vector. $\phi(Y, X, i)$ is the vector representing the ith element in the input sentence. This vector is extracted by the feature function ϕ.

The features taken into account by the feature function depend on the experimental settings, we specify them below (Section 4.1). Training the model consists in learn the weights contained in w.

Following Moeller and Hulden (2018), we used CRFsuite (Okazaki, 2007). This implementation uses the Limited-memory Broyden-Fletcher-Goldfarb-Shanno (L-BFGS) optimization algorithm in order to learn the parameters of the CRF. Elastic Net regularization (consisting of L_1 and L_2 regularization terms) were incorporated in the optimization procedure.

3.2.2 Other sequential models

We explored three additional sequential models: 1) a traditional Hidden Markov Model; 2) a vanilla Recurrent Neural Network (RNN); and 3) a biLSTM model.

Hidden Markov Model: A hidden Markov Model (HMM) (Baum and Petrie, 1966; Rabiner, 1989) is a classical generative graphical model which factorizes the joint distribution function into the product of connected components:

$$p(g_1, ..., g_N, c_1, ..., c_N) = \prod_{t=1}^{N} p(c_t|g_t)p(g_t|g_{t-1}) \quad (2)$$

This method calculates the probabilities using the Maximum Likelihood Estimation method. Likewise, the tagging of the test set is made with the Viterbi algorithm (Forney, 1973).[4]

Recurrent Neural Networks: In contrast with HMM, Recurrent Neural Networks are discriminative models which estimate the conditional probability $p(g_1, ..., g_N|c_1, ..., c_N)$ using recurrent layers. We used two types of recurrent networks:

1. Vanilla RNN: For the vanilla RNN (Elman, 1990) the recurrent layers were defined as:

   $$h^{(t)} = g(W[h^{(t-1)}; x^{(t)}] + b) \quad (3)$$

   Here, $x^{(t)}$ is the embedding vector representing the character c_t, $t = 1, ..., N$, in the sequence and $[h^{(t-1)}; x^{(t)}]$ is the concatenation of the previous recurrent layer with this embedding vector.

2. biLSTM RNN: The bidirectional LSTM (Hochreiter and Schmidhuber, 1997) or biLSTM uses different gates to process the recurrent information. However, it requires of a higher number of parameters to train. Each biLSTM layer is defined by:

   $$h^{(t)} = biLSTM(h^{(t-1)}, x^{(t)}) \quad (4)$$

   where $h^{(t-1)} = [\overrightarrow{h}^{(t-1)}; \overleftarrow{h}^{(t-1)}]$ is the concatenation of the forward and backward recurrent layers.

In each RNN model we used one embedding layer previous to the recurrent layers in order to obtain vector representations of the input characters.

4 Experiments

4.1 Experimental Setup

For CRFs we propose three different experimental settings.[5] Each setting varies in the type of features that are taken into account. We defined a general set of features that capture different type of information:

1. the current character in the input sentence;

[4] We used Natural Language Toolkit (NLTK) for the HMM model.

[5] The code is available on `https://github.com/umoqnier/otomi-morph-segmenter/`

2. indication if the character is the beginning/end of word;
3. indication if the word containing the character is the beginning/end of a sentence;
4. the position of the character in the word;
5. previous and next characters (character window);
6. the current word POS tag, and also the previous and the next one; and
7. a bias term.[6]

To sum up, the CRF takes the information of the current character as input; but in order to obtain contextual information, we also take into consideration the previous and next character. Grammatical information is provided by the POS tag of the word in which the character appears. In addition to this, we add the POS tag of the previous and next words. These are our CRF settings:

- **CRF**$_{linear}$: This setting considers all the information available, i.e., the features that we mentioned above.
- **CRF**$_{POSLess}$: In this setting we excluded the POS tags.
- **CRF**$_{HMMLike}$: This setting takes into account the minimum information, i.e. information about the current letter and the immediately preceding one. We use this name because this configuration contains similar information as the HMMs but using CRFs to build them.[7]

As previously mentioned, we included other sequential methods for the sake of comparison, i.e., a simple Hidden Markov Model, which can be see as the baseline since it is the simpler model, and two neural-based models: a basic vanilla RNN and a biLSTM model.

The embedding dimension was 100 units for both the vanilla RNN and the biLSTM models.[8] In both neural-based models we used one hidden, recurrent layer; the activation for the vanilla RNN was the hyperbolic tangent. The dimension of the vanilla and LSTM hidden layers was 200.[9]

The features used in the CRF settings are implicitly taken into account by the neural-based models. Except for the POS tags, we did not include that information in the neural settings. In this sense, these last neural methods contain the same information as the CRF$_{POSLess}$ setting.

4.2 Results

We evaluated our CRF-based automatic glossing models by using k-Fold Cross-Validation. We used $k = 3$ due to the small dataset size.

For the other sequential methods, we performed a hold-out evaluation.[10] In all cases we preserved the same proportion between training and test datasets (see Table 4).

	Instances (sentences)
Train	1180
Test	589

Table 4: Dataset information for every model

We report the accuracy, we also calculated the precision, recall and F1-score for every label in the corpus. Table 5 contains the results for all settings.

We can see that the CRF based models outperformed the other methods in the automatic glossing task. Among the CRF settings, CRF$_{HMMLike}$ was the one with the lowest accuracy (and also precision and recall), this CRF used the least information/features, i.e., the current character of the input sentence and the previous emitted label.

This is probably related to the fact that Otomi has a rich morphological system (with prefixes and suffixes), therefore, the lack of information about previous and subsequent characters affects the accuracy in the prediction of gloss labels.

The CRF settings CRF$_{POSLess}$ and the CRF$_{linear}$ are considerably better. The variations between these two settings is small, although the accuracy of CRF$_{linear}$ is higher. Interestingly, the lack of POS tags does not seem to affect the accuracy that much. If the glossing is still accurate (above 90%) after excluding POS tags, this could be convenient, especially in low-resource scenarios,

[6]The bias feature captures the proportion of a given label in the training set, i.e., it is a way to express that some labels are rare while others not.

[7]The maximum number of iterations in all cases was 50.

[8]Both RNN models were trained in similar environments: 150 iterations, with a learning rate of 0.1 and Stochastic Gradient Descent (SGD) as optimization method.

[9]The code for the neural-based models is available on `https://github.com/VMijangos/Glosado_neuronal`

[10]We took this decision due to computational cost.

	Accuracy	Precision (avg)	Recall (avg)	F1-score (avg)
CRF_{linear}	**0.962**	**0.910**	**0.880**	**0.870**
$\text{CRF}_{POSLess}$	0.948	0.909	0.838	0.856
$\text{CRF}_{HMMLike}$	0.880	0.790	0.791	0.754
HMM	0.878	0.877	0.851	0.858
Vanilla RNN	0.741	0.504	0.699	0.583
biLSTM	0.563	0.399	0.654	0.489

Table 5: Results for the different experimental setups

where this type of annotation may not always be available for training the model.

We do not know if this observation could be generalized to all languages. In the case of Otomi, the information encoded in the features could be good enough for capturing the morphological structure and word order that is important for predicting the correct label.

Additionally, we tried several variations on the hyperparameters of Elastic Net regularization (CRFs), however, we did not obtain significant improvements (see Appendix A).

The model that we took as the baseline, the HMM, obtained a lower performance compared to the CRF settings (0.878). However, if we take into consideration that HMM was the simpler model, its performance is surprisingly good.

The performance of $\text{CRF}_{HMMLike}$ is very similar to that of HMM. As we mentioned before, these two settings make use of the same information, but their approach is different: CRFs are discriminative while HMMs are generative.

The neural approaches that we implemented were not the most suitable for our task. They obtained the lowest accuracy, 0.741 for the vanilla RNN and 0.563 for the biLSTM. This result might seem striking, especially since neural approaches are by far the most popular nowadays in NLP.

5 Discussion

5.1 CRFs vs RNNs

We have several conjectures that could explain why neural approaches were not the most accurate for our particular task. For instance, we observed that the performance of the RNN models (vanilla and biLSTM) was highly sensitive to the frequency of the labels. Both neural models performed better for high frequency labels (such as *stem*).

In principle, the models that we used for automatic glossing have conceptual differences. HMMs are generative models, while CRFs and neural models are discriminative. This distinction, however, does not seem to influence the results. The HMM performed better than the neural-based models but it was outperformed by the CRFs.

CRFs and neural networks mainly in the way they process the input data. While CRFs depend on the initial features selected by an expert, neural networks process a simple representation of the input data (one-hot vectors) through a series of hidden layers which rely on a large number of parameters.

The number of parameters is a key factor in neural networks, they usually have a large number of parameters that allows them to generalize well in complex tasks. For example, the biLSTM model has the highest number of parameters, while the vanilla RNN has a considerably reduced number of parameters.

However, theoretically, a model with higher capacity will also require a larger number of examples to generalize adequately (Vapnik, 1998). The capacity on neural-based models depends on the number of parameters (Shalev-Shwartz and Ben-David, 2014). This could be problematic in terms of low-resource scenarios. In fact, in our experiments, the model with the highest number of parameters, the biLSTM, performed the worst. Models with fewer parameters, such as HMM and CRFs outperformed the neural-based models by a large margin.

It is worth mentioning that we are aware that hyperparameters and other factors can strongly influence neural model's performance. There could be variations that result in more suitable solutions for this task. However, overall, this would probably represent a more expensive solution than using CRFs (or even a HMM).

Our results seem consistent with previous works for the same task where neural approaches fail to outperform CRFs in low-resource scenarios (Moeller and Hulden, 2018).

Complex models with many parameters might not be the most efficient solution in these types of low-resource scenarios. However, we leave this as an interesting research question for the future.

Finally, our proposed models, CRF$_{linear}$ and the CRF$_{POSLess}$, seemed to be the best alternative for the task of automatic glossing of Otomi.

5.2 Linguistic perspective

In this section we focus on the results from a more qualitative point of view. We discuss some inguistic particularities of Otomi and how they affected the performance of the models. We also present an analysis of how the best evaluated method, i.e. CRF$_{linear}$, performed for a selected subset of gloss labels.

As we mentioned in previous sections, the information comprised in the features seems to be decisive in the performance of the CRF models. When some of these features were removed, performance tended to decay.

For the correct labeling of Otomi morphology, contextual information (previous and next characters in the sentence) did have an impact in performance. This may be attributed to the presence of both prefixes and affixes in Otomi words. Stem alternation, for example, is conditioned by the prefixes in the word. Stem reduction is conditioned by the suffixes. In order to correctly label both stem and affixes, the system must consider the previous and next elements.

There exist morphological or syntactic elements in the sentence that contributes to identify words category. For example, most of the nouns are preceded by a determiner (*ri*, singular, or *yi*, plural). This kind of information is captured in the features and can help in the performance of the automatic glossing task.

Frequency of labels is a factor that influence the performance of the models. Labels with high frequency are better evaluated. For the neural-based models the impact of frequency was more pronounced. However, despite of the low-resource scenario we were able to achieve good results with the CRFs (above 90%).

Languages exhibit a wide range of complexity in their morphological systems. Otomi has several phenomena that may seem difficult to capture by the automatic models. However, even when languages have complex morphological systems, there are frequent and informative patterns (e.g. inflectional affixes) that can help to the recognition of them. This hypothesis is reflected in the low entropy conjecture (Ackerman and Malouf, 2013), which concerns the organization of morphological patterns in order to make morphology learnable. This hypothesis points out that morphological organization seeks to reduce uncertainty.

Label	Precision	Recall	F1-score	Instances
DET	1	0.99	1	228
DET.PL	0.99	0.99	0.99	91
3.CPL	0.96	1	0.98	144
PRAG	0.97	0.99	0.98	116
stem	0.96	0.97	0.96	2396
CTRF	0.95	0.97	0.96	89
3.ICP	0.93	0.94	0.94	118
3.PLS	1	0.86	0.92	28
3.PSS	0.80	1	0.89	8
PRT	0.50	0.22	0.31	18

Table 6: Results from the CRF$_{linear}$ model on a subset of the glossing labels

Table 6 presents the evaluation results for a subset of the labels used for the automatic glossing. These labels are linguistically interesting as there is a contrast between productive and unproductive elements.

We can observe that labels like *stem*, 3.CPL (third person completive) or CTRF (counterfactual) were correctly labeled most of the time, as they were systematic and very frequent.

Items like PRT (particle) had lower frequency, a lower recall and lower precision. The lower recall could be attributed to the fact that PRT is not systematic, i.e. multiple forms can take the same label. Therefore, it is more difficult to discriminate.

PRAG (pragmatic mark) appears only in verbs, and always in the same position (at the end of the word), this probably made this mark more easy to discriminate, thus, more easy to predict by the model. It is interesting that this morpheme was relatively frequent but it did not bear semantic information as it only provided discursive nuances (it can be translated as the filler word 'well').

The 3.ICP (third person incompletive) label represents an aspect morpheme which is used very often since it is applied in the present tense and habitual situations. It always appears before the verb and in the same position, it seemed easier to predict. Therefore, this label has a high precision and recall.

The 3.PLS (third person pluscuamperfect) label also shows a systematic use before the verb; however, the latter did have a lower frequency on the corpus, what seems to have caused a lower recall.

Otomi has two determiner morphemes: one for singular number (DET) and one for plural number (DET.PL). The one for the plural is clearly distinguished from other morphemes as it has the form *yi̲*. However, for the singular number, the form is *ri̲* which is the same as the form for the third person possessive (3.PSS). We believe that this fact made the label 3.PSS more prone to be incorrectly labeled (it showed a lower precision). In some cases, the model tended to incorrectly label the form *ri̲* by preferring the most frequent label DET. This could explain the lower accuracy of 3.PSS compared to DET.

In general, productive affixes were correctly labeled by our automatic system. This may represent a significant advantage in terms of aiding linguistic manual annotation. Productive and frequent morphemes may represent a repetitive annotation task that can be easily substituted by an automatic glossing system.

Even in the understanding that the glossing system is not 100% accurate, it is probably easier for a human annotator to correct problematic mislabels than to do all the process from scratch. In this sense, automatic glossing can simplify the task of manually glossing, and, therefore, it can help in the process of language documentation.

6 Conclusion

We focused on the task of automatic glossing for Otomi of Toluca, an indigenous language with complex morphological phenomena. We faced a low-resource scenario where we had to digitize, normalize and annotate a corpus available for this language.

We applied a CRF based labeler with different variations in regard to the features that were taken into account by the model. Moreover, we included other sequential models, a HMM (baseline) and two RNN models.

CRFs outperfomed the baseline (HMM) but also the RNN models (Vanilla RNN and biLSTM). The CRF setting that took into account more information (encoded by the feature function) had the best performance. We also noticed that excluding POS tags do not seem to harm the system's performance that much. This could be an advantage since automatic POS tagging is a resource not always available for under resourced languages.

Furthermore, we provided a linguistically motivated insight of which labels were easier to predict by our system.

Our automatic glossing labeler was able to achieve an accuracy of 96.2% (and 94.8% without POS tags). This sounds promising for reducing the workload when manually glossing. This can represent a middle step not only for strengthen language documentation but also for facilitating the creation of language technologies that can be useful for the speakers of Otomi.

Acknowledgments

We thank the anonymous reviewers for their valuable comments. We also thank the members of Comunidad Elotl for supporting this work. This work has been partially supported by the SNSF grant no. 176305

References

Farrell Ackerman and Robert Malouf. 2013. Morphological organization: The low conditional entropy conjecture. *Language*, pages 429–464.

Antonios Anastasopoulos, Marika Lekakou, Josep Quer, Eleni Zimianiti, Justin DeBenedetto, and David Chiang. 2018. Part-of-speech tagging on an endangered language: a parallel Griko-Italian resource. In *Proceedings of the 27th International Conference on Computational Linguistics*, pages 2529–2539, Santa Fe, New Mexico, USA. Association for Computational Linguistics.

Matthew Baerman, Enrique Palancar, and Timothy Feist. 2019. Inflectional class complexity in the otomanguean languages. *Amerindia*, 41:1–18.

Guadalupe Barrientos López. 2004. *Otomíes del Estado de México*. Comisión Nacional para el Desarrollo de los Pueblos Indígenas.

Leonard E Baum and Ted Petrie. 1966. Statistical inference for probabilistic functions of finite state markov chains. *The annals of mathematical statistics*, 37(6):1554–1563.

Bernard Comrie, Martin Haspelmath, and Balthasar Bickel. 2008. The leipzig glossing rules: Conventions for interlinear morpheme-by-morpheme glosses. *Department of Linguistics of the Max Planck Institute for Evolutionary Anthropology & the Department of Linguistics of the University of Leipzig. Retrieved January*, 28:2010.

Ryan Cotterell, Christo Kirov, John Sylak-Glassman, David Yarowsky, Jason Eisner, and Mans Hulden. 2016. The SIGMORPHON 2016 shared Task—Morphological reinflection. In *Proceedings of the 14th SIGMORPHON Workshop on Computational*

Research in Phonetics, Phonology, and Morphology, pages 10–22, Berlin, Germany. Association for Computational Linguistics.

Jeffrey L Elman. 1990. Finding structure in time. *Cognitive science*, 14(2):179–211.

G David Forney. 1973. The viterbi algorithm. *Proceedings of the IEEE*, 61(3):268–278.

Sepp Hochreiter and Jürgen Schmidhuber. 1997. Long short-term memory. *Neural computation*, 9(8):1735–1780.

INALI. 2014. *Njaua nt'ot'i ra hñähñu. Norma de escritura de la lengua hñähñu (Otomí)*. INALI.

Katharina Kann and Hinrich Schütze. 2018. Neural transductive learning and beyond: Morphological generation in the minimal-resource setting. In *Proceedings of the 2018 Conference on Empirical Methods in Natural Language Processing*, pages 3254–3264, Brussels, Belgium. Association for Computational Linguistics.

Yolanda Lastra. 1992. *El otomí de Toluca*. Instituto de Investigaciones Antropológicas, UNAM.

Yolanda Lastra. 2001. *Unidad y Diversidad de la Lengua: Relatos otomíes*. UNAM.

Manuel Mager, Ximena Gutierrez-Vasques, Gerardo Sierra, and Ivan Meza-Ruiz. 2018. Challenges of language technologies for the indigenous languages of the Americas. In *Proceedings of the 27th International Conference on Computational Linguistics*, pages 55–69, Santa Fe, New Mexico, USA. Association for Computational Linguistics.

Víctor Mijangos. 2021. *Análisis de la flexión verbal del español y del otomí de Toluca a partir de un modelo implicacional de palabra y paradigma*. Ph.D. thesis, Instituto de Investigaciones Filológicas, UNAM, Mexico City.

Sarah Moeller and Mans Hulden. 2018. Automatic glossing in a low-resource setting for language documentation. In *Proceedings of the Workshop on Computational Modeling of Polysynthetic Languages*, pages 84–93.

Sarah Moeller, Ling Liu, Changbing Yang, Katharina Kann, and Mans Hulden. 2020. Igt2p: From interlinear glossed texts to paradigms. In *Proceedings of the 2020 Conference on Empirical Methods in Natural Language Processing (EMNLP)*, pages 5251–5262.

Naoaki Okazaki. 2007. Crfsuite: a fast implementation of conditional random fields (crfs).

Lawrence R Rabiner. 1989. A tutorial on hidden markov models and selected applications in speech recognition. *Proceedings of the IEEE*, 77(2):257–286.

Tanja Samardzic, Robert Schikowski, and Sabine Stoll. 2015. Automatic interlinear glossing as two-level sequence classification. In *Proceedings of the 9th SIGHUM Workshop on Language Technology for Cultural Heritage, Social Sciences, and Humanities (LaTeCH)*, pages 68–72.

Shai Shalev-Shwartz and Shai Ben-David. 2014. *Understanding machine learning: From theory to algorithms*. Cambridge university press.

Conor Snoek, Dorothy Thunder, Kaidi Loo, Antti Arppe, Jordan Lachler, Sjur Moshagen, and Trond Trosterud. 2014. Modeling the noun morphology of plains cree. In *Proceedings of the 2014 Workshop on the Use of Computational Methods in the Study of Endangered Languages*, pages 34–42.

Vladimir Vapnik. 1998. *Statistical Learning Theory*. John Wiley & Sons.

Xingyuan Zhao, Satoru Ozaki, Antonios Anastasopoulos, Graham Neubig, and Lori Levin. 2020. Automatic interlinear glossing for under-resourced languages leveraging translations. In *Proceedings of the 28th International Conference on Computational Linguistics*, pages 5397–5408.

A Appendix

The following are the detailed results of the three different settings for CRF models. We report average accuracy score. The prefixes in the model names mean whether regularization terms L_1 and/or L_2 were configured.

For example, the prefix *reg* means that both terms were present and conversely *noreg* means that no term is considered. Finally, *l1_zero* and *l2_zero* means if L_1 or L_2 term is equal to zero.

The variation of regularization parameters probed slight improvements between models of the same setting as can be showed in tables 7, 8 and 9.

	Accuracy
$CRF_{HMMLike}$_l2_zero	**0.8800**
$CRF_{HMMLike}$_reg	0.8760
$CRF_{HMMLike}$_noreg	0.8710
$CRF_{HMMLike}$_l1_zero	0.8707

Table 7: $CRF_{HMMLike}$ setting results

	Accuracy
$CRF_{POSLess}$_reg	**0.9482**
$CRF_{POSLess}$_l2_zero	0.9472
$CRF_{POSLess}$_l1_zero	0.9442
$CRF_{POSLess}$_noreg	0.9407

Table 8: $CRF_{POSLess}$ setting results

	Accuracy
CRF_{linear}_reg	**0.9624**
CRF_{linear}_l2_zero	0.9598
CRF_{linear}_l1_zero	0.9586
CRF_{linear}_noreg	0.9586

Table 9: CRF_{linear} setting results

A survey of part-of-speech tagging approaches applied to K'iche'

Francis Tyers[†◇]
† Department of Linguistics
Indiana University
Bloomington, IN
ftyers@iu.edu

Nick Howell[◇]
◇ School of Linguistics
HSE University
Moscow
nhowell@hse.ru

Abstract

We study the performance of several popular neural part-of-speech taggers from the Universal Dependencies ecosystem on Mayan languages using a small corpus of 1435 annotated K'iche' sentences consisting of approximately 10,000 tokens, with encouraging results: F_1 scores 93%+ on lemmatisation, part-of-speech and morphological feature assignment. The high performance motivates a cross-language part-of-speech tagging study, where K'iche'-trained models are evaluated on two other Mayan languages, Kaqchikel and Uspanteko: performance on Kaqchikel is good, 63-85%, and on Uspanteko modest, 60-71%. Supporting experiments lead us to conclude the relative diversity of morphological features as a plausible explanation for the limiting factors in cross-language tagging performance, providing some direction for future sentence annotation and collection work to support these and other Mayan languages.

1 Introduction

This paper presents a survey of approaches to part-of-speech tagging for K'iche', a Mayan language spoken principally in Guatemala. The Mayan languages are a group of related languages spoken throughout Mesoamerica. K'iche' belongs to the Eastern branch, which contains 14 other languages, including Kaqchikel in the Quichean subgroup and Uspanteko which belongs to its own subgroup.

Part-of-speech tagging has wide usage in corpus and computational linguistics and natural language processing, and is often considered part of a toolkit for basic natural language processing.

In the definition of part-of-speech tagging we subsume the tasks of determining the part of speech, morphological analysis and lemmatisation. That is, given a sentence such as in (1) part-of-speech tagging would return both the sequence of part-of-speech tags [`VERB, DET, NOUN`] but also the lemmata [`q'ojomaj, le, q'ojom`] and the set of feature value pairs for each of the forms.[1]

(1) Kinq'ojomaj le q'ojom.
k-∅-in-q'ojomaj le q'ojom.
IMP-B3SG-A1SG-play the marimba.

'I play the marimba.'

A brief reading guide: prior work, on Mayan and other languages of the Americas and on cross-language part-of-speech tagging, is reviewed in section 2. Our experimental design including the mathematical model used for analysing performance are given section 3. Universal dependencies annotation for K'iche' and the systems tested are described in section 4, and results are presented and analysed in section 5.

2 Prior work

Palmer et al. (2010) explore morphological segmentation and analysis for the purpose of generating interlinearly glossed texts. They work with Uspanteko, a language of the Greater Quichean branch, and the closest language to K'iche' we were able to identify with published studies of computational morphology. They explore several different systems: inducing morphology from parallel texts, an unsupervised segmentation+clustering strategy, and an interactive training strategy with a linguist.

In Sachse and Dürr (2016), a set of preliminary annotation conventions for Mayan languages in general, and K'iche' in particular, are proposed.

A maximum-entropy part-of-speech tagger is presented in Kuhn and Mateo-Toledo (2004) for Q'anjob'al, which, like K'iche', is a Mayan language of Guatemala. They work with a custom selection

[1] For example for the `VERB` it would return `Aspect=Imp, Number[obj]=Sing, Number[subj]=Sing, Person[obj]=3, Person[subj]=1, Subcat=Tran, VerbForm=Fin`.

Proceedings of the First Workshop on Natural Language Processing for Indigenous Languages of the Americas, pages 44–52
June 11, 2021.

of 60 tags, and trained on an annotated corpus of 4100 words (no lemmatisation is performed). In contrast to the systems we will study, Kuhn and Mateo-Toledo (2004) perform feature engineering and end up with F_1 scores between 63% and 78%, depending on the features chosen.

There is much work on part-of-speech tagging for languages of the Americas outside of the Mayan family: statistical lemmatisation and part-of-speech tagging systems are described by Pereira-Noriega et al. (2017) and a finite-state morphological analyser by Cardenas and Zeman (2018) for Shipibo-Konibo, a Panoan language of the Amazonian region of Peru.

In Rios (2010) and Rios (2015), respectively, finite-state morphology and support vector machine-based tagging+parsing systems are described for Quechua. The latter uses a corpus that comprises $2k$ sentences.

Cross-language part-of-speech tagging through parallel corpora, sometimes called annotation projection, is well-studied; in Mayan languages, Palmer et al. (2010) use a parallel corpus as a bridge to a higher-resourced language for which a part-of-speech tagger already exists.

In the absence of such a corpus, so-called "zero-shot" methods are created from other (presumably higher-resourced) languages and applied to the target language. The main balance to strike is between specificity of resources (how closely-related are the other languages) and quantity of resources (how much linguistic data is accessible). UDify of Kondratyuk and Straka (2019) is an example of preferring the latter: a deep neural architecture is trained on all of the Universal Dependencies treebanks. The former strategy can be seen in Huck et al. (2019), where in addition to annotation projection, authors attempt zero-shot tagging of Ukrainian with a model trained on Russian.

3 Methodology

We used a corpus of K'iche'[2] annotated with part-of-speech tags and morphological features (Tyers and Henderson, 2021). The corpus consisted of 1,435 sentences comprising approximately 10,000 tokens from a variety of text types and was annotated according to the guidelines of the Universal Dependencies (UD) project (Nivre et al., 2020). An example of a sentence from the corpus can be seen in Table 1.

We studied the performance of several popular part-of-speech taggers within the Universal Dependencies ecosystem; these are reviewed in section 4. Performance was computed as F_1 scores for lemmatisation, universal part-of-speech (UPOS), and universal morphological features (UFeats). We performed 10-fold cross validation to obtain mean and standard deviation of F_1. We also recorded training time and model size to compare the resource consumption of the models in the training process.

We selected the best-performing system and performed a convergence study (see section 5.3 for results). We decimated the training data of one of the test-train splits from the cross-validation, and plotted the performance of models trained on the decimations.

We make the following assumption about the performance: additional training data provides exponentially decreasing performance improvement. Under this assumption, we obtain the formula:

$$F_1(n) = F_1(\infty) - \Delta F_1 \cdot e^{-n/k}. \qquad (1)$$

Here $F_1(n)$ is the performance of a model trained on n tokens, $F_1(\infty)$ is the asymptotic performance, and ΔF_1 is the gap between $F_1(\infty)$ (estimated maximum performance) and $F_1(0)$ (zero-shot performance).

The parameter k is the *characteristic number of tokens*; each additional k tokens of training data causes the gap $\Delta F_1 = F_1(\infty) - F_1(n)$ to shrink by a factor of $1/e \approx 36\%$. This can be used to estimate the training data n required to meet a given performance target F_1^{target}:

$$n = k \cdot \log \frac{\Delta F_1}{F_1(\infty) - F_1^{\text{target}}} \qquad (2)$$

We fit this curve against our convergence data and estimate peak performance and characteristic number. Error propagation is used with the error in parameter estimation to compute the error bands in the graph:

$$(\delta F_1)^2 = \sum \left(\frac{\partial F_1}{\partial x} \delta x \right)^2 \qquad (3)$$

Here x runs over the parameters of $F_1(n)$: $F_1(\infty)$, ΔF_1 and k.

We also studied the best-performer in cross-language tagging on the related Kaqchikel and Uspanteko languages. The 10 models trained in

[2] https://github.com/UniversalDependencies/UD_Kiche-IU

cross-validation were all evaluated on small part-of-speech-tagged corpora of 157 (Kaqchikel) and 160 (Uspanteko) sentences. For results and overviews of the languages, see section 6.

4 Systems

We tested morphological analysis on three systems designed for Universal Dependencies treebanks: UDPipe (Straka et al., 2016), UDPipe 2 (Straka, 2018), and UDify (Kondratyuk and Straka, 2019). Of these, only UDPipe had a working tokeniser. For other taggers we trained, we trained the UDPipe tokeniser and other tagger together. We thus present combined tokeniser-tagger systems.

UDPipe (Straka et al., 2016) is a language-independent trainable tokeniser, lemmatiser, POS tagger, and dependency parser designed to train on and produce Universal Dependencies-format treebanks. It uses gated linear units for tokenisation, averaged perceptrons for part-of-speech tagging, and a neural network classifier for dependency parsing. It is the least resource-hungry model in our study by an order of magnitude or more, and we trained it from-scratch using the K'iche' corpus in section 3.

UDPipe 2 (Straka, 2018) is a Python prototype for a Tensorflow-based deep neural network POS-tagger, lemmatiser, and dependency parser. It won high rankings in the CoNLL 2018 shared task on multilingual parsing (Zeman et al., 2018), taking first place by one metric. Deep neural methods have achieved impressive performance results in recent years, but take considerable computational resources to train. We used UDPipe 2 without pretrained embeddings, and trained it from-scratch using the K'iche' corpus in section 3.

UDify (Kondratyuk and Straka, 2019) is a AllenNLP-based multilingual model using BERT pretrained embeddings and trained on the combined Universal Dependencies treebank collection; we fine-tuned this pretrained model on our K'iche' data. This was our most resource-intensive model, even though we only fine-tuned on K'iche'; our initialisation was the UDify-distributed BERT+UD model.

5 Results

5.1 Energy efficiency

Resource utilisation for the three systems is summarised in Table 2. Model production is reported in kilojoules for each of our systems; these were estimated by taking the reported runtime and multiplying it by the thermal design power (TDP) of the reported hardware. Error could be introduced into these estimates from many sources: only the reported device is considered, ignoring many other components of the machine; devices are assumed to run at their TDP the entire runtime; the UDify numbers as reported by Kondratyuk and Straka (2019) are approximate.

5.2 Task performance

We evaluated the performance of the models on five tasks: tokenisation (Tokens), word segmentation (Words), lemmatisation (Lemmas), part-of-speech tagging (UPOS) and morphological tagging (Features). The difference between tokenisation and word segmentation can be explained with reference to Table 1. The word *chqawach* 'to us' counts as a single token, but two syntactic words. So the performance of tokenisation is recovering the tokens, and the performance of word segmentation is recovering the words.

We performed 10-fold cross validation on the 1435 analysed sentences, with F_1 scores for lemmatisation, part-of-speech tagging, and morphological features computed using the evaluation scripts from Zeman et al. (2018), modified to not ignore language-specific morphological features. Results are summarised in Table 3; the winner is UDPipe2.

While both UDPipe 2 and UDify have deep neural architectures, it seems UDify is unable to overcome non-K'iche' biases from the BERT embeddings and initial training on Universal Dependencies releases; neither of these components incorporate Mayan languages. We speculate that training on data with a better representation of languages of the Americas would enable UDify to surpass UDPipe 2.

The original UDPipe makes an impressively resource-efficient performance: it obtains 95%, 97%, and 96% the performance of UDPipe 2 on lemmatisation, part-of-speech tagging, and feature assignment, all with 3.5% of the training time and 3.6% of the model size.

5.3 Convergence

We performed a convergence study on the best system, UDPipe 2. Results are shown in Figure 1. Asymptotic F_1 scores are $95.4\pm1.9\%$, $97.4\pm2.2\%$, and $95.7 \pm 2.1\%$ for lemmatisation, part-of-speech tagging, and feature assignment, respectively. Gaps at full use of the 1292 sentence-, 9559-token training set are 2.5%, 2.9%, and 3.8%, respectively, and

```
# sent_id = utexas:123.2
# text = Xuk'ut le K'iche' ch'ab'al le al Nela chqawach.
# text[spa] = Manuela nos enseñó el idioma k'iche'
# labels = tijonik-17 complete
1    Xuk'ut    k'ut      VERB   _  [...][1]                         _  _  _  _
2    le        le        DET    _  _                                _  _  _  _
3    K'iche'   k'iche'   ADJ    _  _                                _  _  _  _
4    ch'ab'al  ch'ab'al  NOUN   _  _                                _  _  _  _
5    le        le        DET    _  _                                _  _  _  _
6    al        ali       NOUN   _  Gender=Fem|NounType=Clf          _  _  _  _
7    Nela      Nela      PROPN  _  Gender=Fem                       _  _  _  _
8-9  chqawach  _         _      _  _                                _  _  _  _
8    ch        chi       ADP    _  _                                _  _  _  _
9    qawach    wach      NOUN   _  [...][2]                         _  _  _  _
10   .         .         PUNCT  _  _                                _  _  _  _
```

[1] Aspect=Perf|Number[obj]=Sing|Number[subj]=Sing|Person[obj]=3|Person[subj]=3|Valency=2|VerbForm=Fin
[2] NounType=Relat|Number[psor]=Plur|Person[psor]=1

Table 1: An example sentence from Romero et al. (2018) that has been included in the corpus. Here it is displayed annotated in 10-column CoNLL-U format. The sentence is *Xuk'ut le K'iche' ch'ab'al le al Nela chqawach.* "Manuela taught us the K'iche' language". This demonstrates: the treatment of contractions, e.g. *chqawach* 'to us' → *chi* + *qawach*, the lemmatisation and parts of speech and the morphological features.

Model	**Energy** (kJ) UD	K'iche'
UDPipe	0	50
UDPipe 2	0	1400
UDify	540000	1300

Table 2: Energy cost expended, per-source. K'iche' training costs are estimated as runtime × TDP of the processor, while UD training costs are runtime × TDP of the graphics card used in training.

characteristic numbers are 4700, 4800 and 4700 tokens. Using (2), we can use this to compute how much more training data would be required to close this gap; for example, to bring F_1 to within 1% of its maximum, we would need to annotate an additional 4400, 4500, and 5900 tokens, respectively.

6 Cross-language tagging

There are around 32 Mayan languages spoken in Mesoamerica, in the countries of Guatemala, Mexico, Honduras, El Salvador and Belize. Given the impressive performance of the best-performing system on K'iche' data, we decided to test it on two related languages spoken in Guatemala: Kaqchikel and Uspanteko. UDify is also reported as being suited to zero-shot inference, so we include two UDify-based models: fine-tuned on K'iche' (referred to as "UDify-FT") and the original UDify model (simply "UDify").

6.1 Kaqchikel

Kaqchikel (ISO-639: `cak`; previously Cakchiquel) is a Mayan language of the Quichean branch. It is spoken in Guatemala, to the south and east of the K'iche'-speaking area (see Figure 2) and has around 450,000 speakers. Some notable differences between Kaqchikel and K'iche' are the lack of status suffixes on verbs, no pied-piping inversion (Broadwell, 2005), and SVO order in declarative sentences (Watanabe, 2017).

For the Kaqchikel corpus, we extracted glossed example sentences from a number of published sources, including papers discussing topics in morphology and syntax (Henderson, 2007; Broadwell and Duncan, 2002; Broadwell, 2000) and grammar books (Garcia Matzar et al., 1999; Guaján, 2016). These sentences were then analysed with a morphological analyser (Richardson and Tyers, 2021) and manually disambiguated using the provided glosses.

6.2 Uspanteko

Uspanteko (ISO-639: `usp`; also referred to as *Uspantek*, or *Uspanteco*) is a Mayan language of the Greater Quichean branch. The language is spoken

	UDPipe	UDPipe 2	UDify
Training time	12.5 ± 0.1	356 ± 4	323 ± 2
Model size	2.3M	64M	760M
Tokens	99.7 ± 0.4	—	—
Words	98.6 ± 0.5	—	—
Lemmas	88.3 ± 1.1	$\mathbf{93.2 \pm 0.6}$	88.3 ± 0.9
UPOS	91.4 ± 1.4	$\mathbf{94.5 \pm 0.8}$	94.2 ± 1.1
Features	88.8 ± 1.1	$\mathbf{92.9 \pm 0.8}$	89.2 ± 1.2

Table 3: Results on tasks from tokenisation to morphological analysis. Standard deviation is obtained by running ten-fold cross validation. The columns are F_1 score: **Tokens** tokenisation; **Words** splitting syntactic words (e.g. contractions); **Lemmas** lemmatisation; **UPOS** universal part-of-speech tags; **Features** morphological features. Model size is in megabytes, training time is in mm:ss, as run on a machine with AMD Ryzen 7 1700 8-core CPU and 32GiB of memory.

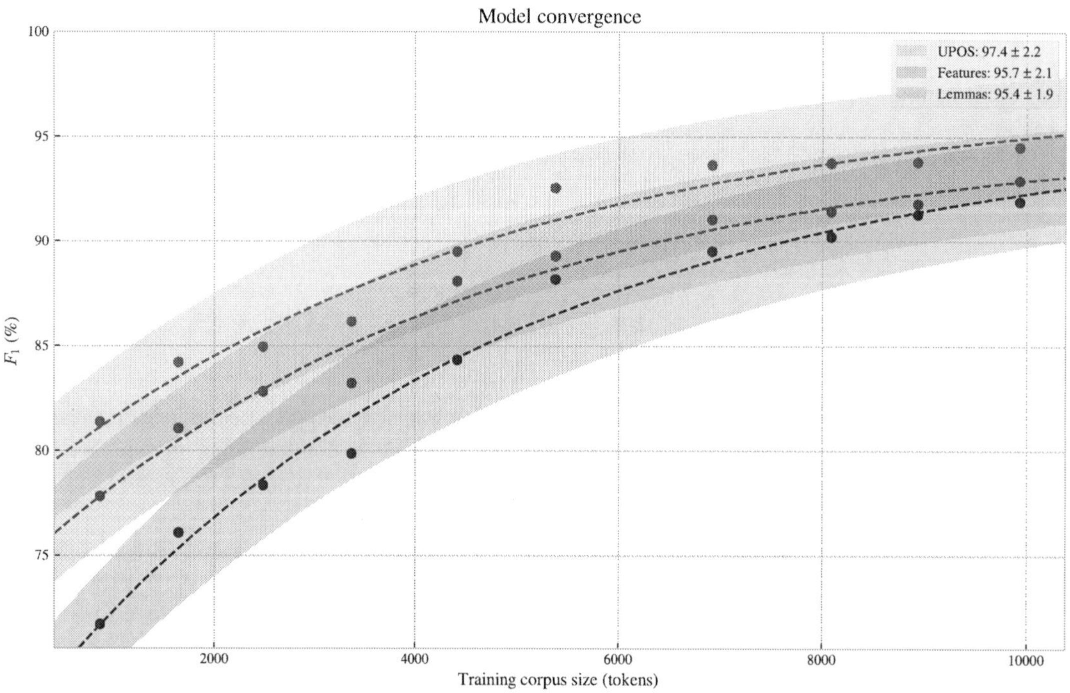

Figure 1: Convergence of the F_1 scores of the UDPipe 2 combined system for lemmas, universal part-of-speech, and universal feature tags, as a function of total number of tokens in training. The plotted points (p, s) are the decimation data: measurements of F_1 score p when given a training corpus of s tokens. Curves are obtained by constrained least-squares fitting of this data against (1). The shaded regions represent the propagation of the standard error (3) in the fit parameters through the curve; under hypothesis of the normal distribution, $\approx 68\%$ of observations are expected to lie within this region. The numbers in the legend are the asymptotic performance given by the fitting procedure; as more training data is supplied, model performance should converge to the asymptotic performance.

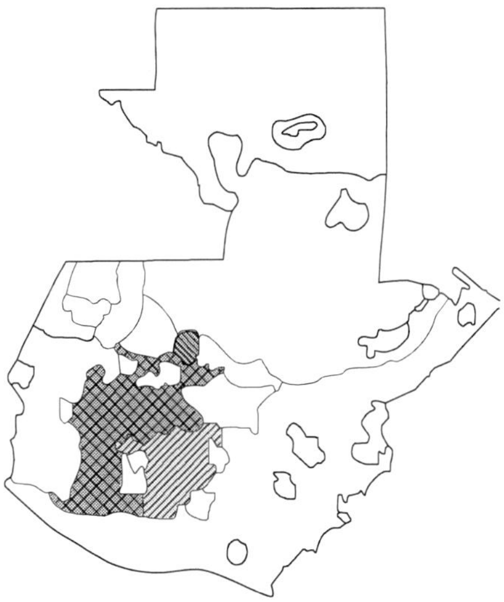

Figure 2: A map of Guatemala with approximate locations of speaker areas of Mayan languages. K'iche', Kaqchikel and Uspanteko are highlighted in purple (grid-hatched), green (forward slash-hatched), and red (backward slash-hatched), respectively.

Kaqchikel			
Sentences			157
Tokens			1091
	UDPipe 2	UDify-FT	UDify
UPOS	84.9 ± 0.4	**90.0** ± 0.4	34.3
Features	**63.4** ± 0.7	**63.4** ± 0.7	46.1
Lemmas	72.5 ± 0.5	**75.4** ± 0.5	3.2
Uspanteko			
Sentences			160
Tokens			1171
	UDPipe 2	UDify-FT	UDify
UPOS	60.8 ± 0.6	**64.7** ± 0.5	40.2
Features	**60.3** ± 0.9	59.1 ± 1.0	55.3
Lemmas	71.2 ± 0.5	**71.4** ± 0.4	6.3

Table 4: Results for cross-lingual tagging on Kaqchikel and Uspanteko, using our UDPipe 2, UDify, and UDify-FT systems for part-of-speech tagging. We evaluated on our corpora lemmatised and annotated for part-of-speech, morphological features. Performance for the K'iche'-trained systems are quoted as the average and standard deviation over the same 10 trained models used in cross-validation for K'iche' (see section 3).

in an area adjacent to the K'iche'-speaking area in Guatemala. It has around 2,000 speakers and is one of the few Mayan languages to have developed contrastive tone.

Palmer et al. (2010) present a large interlinearly-glossed corpus of Uspantek with approximately 3400 sentences and 27000 tokens. We selected 160 sentences from this corpus, totalling 1003 tokens and annotated them with part of speech, lemmas and morphological features. The lemmas were given by a morphological analyser[3] created from a lexicon provided by OKMA.

6.3 Results

The results of our cross-language tagging study are shown in Table 4; in general the winner is UDify-K'iche'; the original UDify model itself performs very poorly. UDPipe 2 manages nearly as good performance as UDify-FT, especially impressive considering its three orders of magnitude less energy consumption. For UDPipe 2 and UDify-FT, we used the ten models trained to provide the K'iche' tagging performance and confidence. The original UDify system is a single model, thus we are unable to provide confidence intervals.

We also studied convergence for the cross-language tagging task using our UDPipe 2 decimated K'iche' models; see figures 3a and 3b. We observe that for the given set of labels our models essentially have converged, with the exception of part-of-speech tagging for Uspanteko, which might benefit from additional examples of features already present in our K'iche' corpus.

In order to understand whether our K'iche' corpus covers a sufficient variety of labels (parts of speech, features, lemmatisation patterns), we selected two labels, one of high frequency and one of low frequency (see Table 5a), from our corpus with which to disable our model. For each label, new convergence runs where made using the 10%, 40%, and 70% subsets, omitting all sentences featuring the chosen label.

If our cross-language tagging models could not be improved by a more diverse K'iche' training corpus, we would expect these disabled datapoints to fall within error of the convergence trendlines. This is the case with the low-frequency label, "first-person". On the other hand, we see that the loss of the high-frequency label, perfective aspect, has

[3] `https://github.com/apertium/apertium-usp`

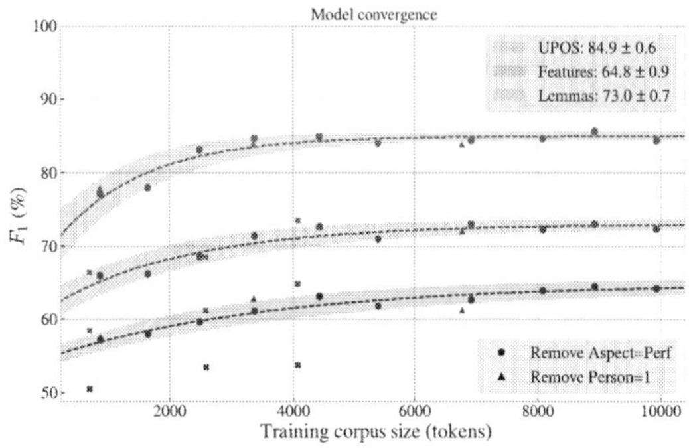

(a) Kaqchikel. Characteristic number of tokens of annotated K'iche' for these was 2200 (lemmatisation), 1400 (part-of-speech), and 3500 (features). At nearly 10000 tokens, all are essentially converged.

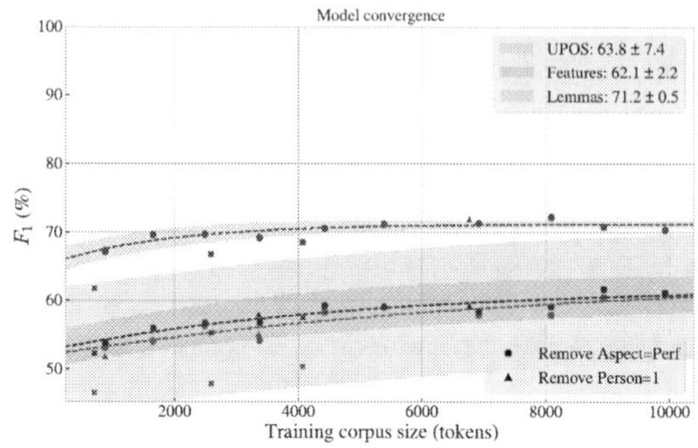

(b) Uspanteko. Characteristic number of tokens for these was 1900 (lemmatisation), 7900 (part-of-speech), and 4900 (features); part-of-speech tagging might see improvement from increased annotation of K'iche' data, but with such high uncertainty (over 10% in asymptotic performance) it is difficult to be sure.

Figure 3: Convergence of our UDPipe 2 on Kaqchikel (3a) and Uspanteko (3b). The legends show projected asymptotic performance for each of universal part-of-speech tagging, universal feature assignment, and lemmatisation.

a disproportionate impact on cross-tagging performance: removing this training data has caused the convergence curve to change parameters, lowering asymptotic performance.

This raises the possibility that we might improve the asymptotic performance of our cross-tagging models by locating labels which are high-frequency in our target language (Kaqchikel or Uspanteko) and extending our K'iche' corpus with sentences featuring those labels. See Table 5b for a sample of high-frequency labels which appear in our K'iche' corpus but not our cross-tagging evaluation corpus.

These all indicate that the small test corpora of Kaqchikel and Uspanteko we annotated are not as diverse in terms of text type as the K'iche' corpus. For example, the test corpora contain no infinitive forms (for example the morpheme *-ik* in K'iche'), although these certainly exist in both Kaqchikel — see §2.7.2.6 in Garcia Matzar et al. (1999) — and Uspanteko. Additionally they contain no examples of the imperative mood, relative clauses introduced by relative pronouns, the formal second person, or reflexives. All of these features certainly exist in the languages, but not in the selection of sentences we annotated.

7 Concluding remarks

We used an annotated corpus of 1435 part-of-speech tagged K'iche' sentences to to survey a number of neural part-of-speech tagging systems from that ecosystem. We found the best performance was generally with UDPipe 2, a deep neural system integrating lemmatisation, part-of-speech and morphological feature assignment. Our UDPipe 2-trained system achieved F_1 of 93% or better on all tasks, very encouraging results for a relatively small corpus.

Convergence studies showed that on corpora of similar morphological composition even better performance is attainable, but to close the gap to within 1% of projected optimal performance requires roughly half again the amount of training data.

The high performance on K'iche' led us to experiment using our model to perform cross-language tagging on the related languages of Kaqchikel and Uspanteko. Performance on the more closely-related language, Kaqchikel, was still respectable, with F_1 ranging from 63 to 85% on the tasks; on Uspanteko performance we observed more modest performance 60 − 71%. The K'iche' fine-tuned UDify model does show noticably better performance, but possibly not worth the energy expenditure.

Our results after disabling our cross-language tagger by withholding some labels during training imply that cross-language performance could be improved by annotating more data with similar features to the Kaqchikel and Uspanteko evaluation corpora, and suggest that cross-language tagging is a path forward to greater availability of part-of-speech annotation for Mayan languages.

Label	Frequency		Discrep.
	quc	evaluation	
Person=1	3%	1%	0.12σ
Aspect=Perf	49%	62%	$-3.5\ \sigma$

(a) The two labels chosen for the label diversity study for our cross-language taggers. We studied convergence of two additional models: training data alternately lacked first-person (Person=1), or perfective aspect (Aspect=Perf). Frequency is percentage of sentences in the corpus with the feature. We give the median discrepancy, computed as the performance gap between the disabled model and the prediction for a model trained on the same number of tokens, normalised by the uncertainty in that prediction σ. For the first-person label, we see a similar distribution with a very slight bias towards higher performance; perfective aspect seems to have an outsized effect, increasing the median discrepancy to 3.5σ.

Label	Frequency (% sents.)
VerbForm=Inf	6
Mood=Imp	3
Reflex=Yes	2
PronType=Rel	2
Polite=Form	2

(b) The results of our label diversity study. The top 20 labels for our K'iche' training corpus which do not appear in our Kaqchikel and Uspanteko evaluation corpora, along with their frequencies in the K'iche' corpus. See Table 5a for the impact missing high-frequency labels can have on cross-tagging performance.

Acknowledgements

We would like to thank the anonymous reviewers for their helpful comments. This article is an output of a research project implemented as part of the Basic Research Programme at the National Research University Higher School of Economics (HSE University).

References

George Aaron Broadwell. 2000. Word order and markedness in Kaqchikel. In *Proceedings of the LFG00 Conference*.

George Aaron Broadwell. 2005. Pied-piping and optimal order in Kiche (K'iche').

George Aaron Broadwell and Lachlan Duncan. 2002. A new passive in Kaqchikel. *Linguistic Discovery*, 1:26–43.

Ronald Cardenas and Daniel Zeman. 2018. A morphological analyzer for Shipibo-konibo. In *Proceedings of the Fifteenth Workshop on Computational Research in Phonetics, Phonology, and Morphology*, pages 131–139, Brussels, Belgium. Association for Computational Linguistics.

Pedro Oscar Garcia Matzar, Valerio Toj Cotzajay, and Domingo Coc Tuiz. 1999. *Gramática del idioma Kaqchikel*. PLFM.

Pakal B'alam Rodriguez Guaján. 2016. *Rutz'ib'axik ri Kaqchikel — Manual de Redacción Kaqchikel*. Editorial Maya' Wuj.

Robert Henderson. 2007. Observations on the syntax of adjunct extraction in Kaqchikel. In *Proceedings of the CILLA III Conference*.

Matthias Huck, Diana Dutka, and Alexander Fraser. 2019. Cross-lingual annotation projection is effective for neural part-of-speech tagging. In *Proceedings of the Sixth Workshop on NLP for Similar Languages, Varieties and Dialects*, pages 223–233, Ann Arbor, Michigan. Association for Computational Linguistics.

Dan Kondratyuk and Milan Straka. 2019. 75 languages, 1 model: Parsing universal dependencies universally. In *Proceedings of the 2019 Conference on Empirical Methods in Natural Language Processing and the 9th International Joint Conference on Natural Language Processing (EMNLP-IJCNLP)*, pages 2779–2795, Hong Kong, China. Association for Computational Linguistics.

Jonas Kuhn and B'alam Mateo-Toledo. 2004. Applying computational linguistic techniques in a documentary project for Q'anjob'al (Mayan, Guatemala). In *Proceedings of the 4th International Conference on Language Resources and Evaluation (LREC 2004)*, Lisboa, Portugal.

J. Nivre, M.-C. de Marneffe, F. Ginter, J. Hajič, C. D. Manning, S. Pyysalo, S. Schuster, F. Tyers, and D. Zeman. 2020. Universal dependencies v2: An evergrowing multilingual treebank collection. In *Proceedings of the 12th Conference on Language Resources and Evaluation (LREC 2020)*, pages 4027–4036.

Alexis Palmer, Taesun Moon, Jason Baldridge, Katrin Erk, Eric Campbell, and Telma Can. 2010. Computational strategies for reducing annotation effort in language documentation. *Linguistic Issues in Language Technology*, 3(4):1–42.

José Pereira-Noriega, Rodolfo Mercado-Gonzales, Andrés Melgar, Marco Sobrevilla-Cabezudo, and Arturo Oncevay-Marcos. 2017. Ship-LemmaTagger: Building an NLP toolkit for a Peruvian native language. In *International Conference on Text, Speech, and Dialogue*, pages 473–481. Springer.

Ivy Richardson and Francis M. Tyers. 2021. A morphological analyser for K'iche'. *Procesamiento de Lenguaje Natural*, 66:99–109.

Annette Rios. 2010. Applying finite-state techniques to a native American language: Quechua. Lizentiatsarbeit, Institut für Computerlinguistik, Universität Zürich.

Annette Rios. 2015. *A basic language technology toolkit for Quechua*. Ph.D. thesis, Institut für Computerlinguistik, Universität Zürich.

Sergio Romero, Ignacio Carvajal, Mareike Sattler, Juan Manuel Tahay Tzaj, Carl Blyth, Sarah Sweeney, Pat Kyle, Nathalie Steinfeld Childre, Diego Guarchaj Tambriz, Lorenzo Ernesto Tambriz, Maura Tahay, Lupita Tahay, Gaby Tahay, Jenny Tahay, Santiago Can, Elena Ixmata Xum, Enrique Guarchaj, Sergio Manuel Guarchaj Can, Catarina Marcela Tambriz Cotiy, Telma Can, Tara Kingsley, Charlotte Hayes, Christopher J. Walker, María Angelina Ixmatá Sohom, Jacob Sandler, Silveria Guarchaj Ixmatá, Manuela Petronila Tahay, and Susan Smythe Kung. 2018. Chqeta'maj le qach'ab'al K'iche'! `https://tzij.coerll.utexas.edu/`.

Frauke Sachse and Michael Dürr. 2016. Morphological glossing of Mayan languages under XML: Preliminary results. Working Paper 4, Nordrhein-Westfälische Akademie der Wissenschaften und der Künste.

M. Straka, J. Hajič, and J. Straková. 2016. UDPipe: trainable pipeline for processing CoNLL-U files performing tokenization, morphological analysis, POS tagging and parsing. In *Proceedings of the Tenth International Conference on Language Resources and Evaluation (LREC'16)*, Paris, France. European Language Resources Association (ELRA).

Milan Straka. 2018. UDPipe 2.0 prototype at CoNLL 2018 UD shared task. In *Proceedings of the CoNLL 2018 Shared Task: Multilingual Parsing from Raw Text to Universal Dependencies*, pages 197–207, Brussels, Belgium. Association for Computational Linguistics.

Francis M. Tyers and Robert Henderson. 2021. A corpus of K'iche' annotated for morphosyntactic structure. In *Proceedings of the First Workshop on NLP for Indigenous Languages of the Americas (AmericasNLP)*.

Akira Watanabe. 2017. The division of labor between syntax and morphology in the Kichean agent-focus construction. *Morphology*, 27:685–720.

Daniel Zeman, Jan Hajič, Martin Popel, Martin Potthast, Milan Straka, Filip Ginter, Joakim Nivre, and Slav Petrov. 2018. CoNLL 2018 shared task: Multilingual parsing from raw text to Universal Dependencies. In *Proceedings of the CoNLL 2018 Shared Task: Multilingual Parsing from Raw Text to Universal Dependencies*, pages 1–21, Brussels, Belgium. Association for Computational Linguistics.

Highland Puebla Nahuatl–Spanish Speech Translation Corpus for Endangered Language Documentation

Jiatong Shi
The Johns Hopkins University
jiatong_shi@jhu.edu

Jonathan D. Amith
Gettysburg College
jonamith@gmail.com

Xuankai Chang, Siddharth Dalmia, Brian Yan, and Shinji Watanabe
Carnegie Mellon University
shinjiw@ieee.org

Abstract

Documentation of endangered languages (ELs) has become increasingly urgent as thousands of languages are on the verge of disappearing by the end of the 21st century. One challenging aspect of documentation is to develop machine learning tools to automate the processing of EL audio via automatic speech recognition (ASR), machine translation (MT), or speech translation (ST). This paper presents an open-access speech translation corpus of Highland Puebla Nahuatl (glottocode high1278), an EL spoken in central Mexico. It then addresses machine learning contributions to endangered language documentation and argues for the importance of speech translation as a key element in the documentation process. In our experiments, we observed that state-of-the-art end-to-end ST models could outperform a cascaded ST (ASR > MT) pipeline when translating endangered language documentation materials.

1 Introduction

Due to the need for global communication, computational technologies such as automatic speech recognition (ASR), machine translation (MT: text-to-text), and speech translation (ST: speech-to-text) have focused their efforts on languages spoken by major population groups (Henrich et al., 2010). Many other languages that are spoken today will probably disappear by the end of the 21st century (Grenoble et al., 2011). For this reason, until very recently they have not been targeted for machine learning technologies. This is changing, however, as increasing attention has been paid to language loss and the need for preservation and, in best-case scenarios, revitalization of these languages.

This paper presents an open-access speech translation corpus from Highland Puebla Nahuatl to Spanish and discusses our initial effort on ST over the corresponding corpus. The following of this paper is organized as follows: in Section 2, we discuss the benefits of speech translation for EL documentation and pioneer-suggest it as the first step in the documentation process. In Section 3, we compare the strategies (i.e., cascaded model and end-to-end models) that can be used to automate ST for ELs. In Section 4 we introduce the Highland Puebla Nahuatl-to-Spanish corpus. Initial experimental efforts in building ST models are elaborated in Section 5. The conclusion is presented in in Section 6.

2 Benefits of speech-to-text translation as a first step in language documentation

The present article suggests that speech translation (ST) could be a viable and valuable tool for EL documentation efforts for three reasons (Anastasopoulos, 2019). First, the transcription of native language recordings may become particularly problematic and time-consuming (the "transcription bottleneck") when the remaining speakers are elderly, and the younger generation has at best a passive knowledge of the language, a common situation of ELs. Second, in many cases ST may be more accurate than MT for target language translation. Finally, many EL documentation projects suffer from a lack of human resources with the skills and time to transcribe and analyze recordings (for similar points about a "translation before transcription workflow", see Bird, 2020, section 2.2.2).

By beginning with ST, semi- and passive speakers can better contribute to EL documentation of their native languages with a level of effort far lower than needed for transcription and analysis. Bilingual native speakers or researchers with incomplete knowledge of the source language structure can quickly produce highly informative free translations even if the original text is never, or only much later, segmented and glossed. A free translation in audio and subsequent capture by typing or using ASR systems for the major target L2 lan-

Proceedings of the First Workshop on Natural Language Processing for Indigenous Languages of the Americas, pages 53–63
June 11, 2021.

guage (that are more accurate for major as opposed to minor and endangered languages) may take 4–5 hours of effort per hour of audio, whereas transcription (without analysis) may take 30–100 hours for the same unit. Starting with free translation, then, increases the pool of potential native speaker participants and quickly adds value to an audio corpus that may languish if the first step is always fixed as transcription and segmentation (morphological parsing and glossing).

In general, EL documentation proceeds in a fairly set sequence: (1) record; (2) transcribe in time-coded format; (3a) analyze by parsing (morphological segmentation) and glossing; and (3b) freely translate into a dominant, often colonial, language. It may be that some projects prioritize free translation (3b) over morphological segmentation and glossing. Given that each procedure adds a certain, often significant, amount of time to the processing pipeline, there is an increasing scarcity of resources as one proceeds from (1) to (3a/b). If the standard sequence is followed, there are invariably more recordings than transcriptions, more transcriptions than analyses, and (if the sequence is 3a > 3b) more analyses than free translations or (if the sequence is 3b > 3a) more free translations than analyses (see Bird, 2020, Table 3, p. 720).

The argument presented here is that the easiest data to obtain are the recordings followed by free translations into a major language. It may be beneficial to reorder the workflow so that an ST corpus, i.e., free translation of the recording, is prioritized. Only later would transcription and analysis (morphological segmentation and glossing) be inserted into the pipeline. To facilitate computational support for speech-to-text production, we would recommend a targeted number of recordings (e.g., 50 hours), followed by division into utterances with time stamps and free translation of the utterances into a major language. This corpus (or perhaps one even larger) would be used to train an end-to-end neural network in speech-to-text production. The trained ST system would then be used to process additional recordings, thus generating a very extensive freely translated corpus. Our hope would be that instead of basing ASR on an acoustic signal alone, using two coupled inputs—the speech signal and the free translation—might well lower ASR error rates from those obtained from the speech signal alone. The extent of improved accuracy is at this point simply a hypothesis. It would have to be empirically researched, something we hope to do in the near future (see Anastasopoulos, 2019, chap. 4). In this scenario for EL documentation, transcription and analysis proceed forward, but only after an extensive ST training/validation/test corpus has been developed. The resultant ST system would then be used to freely translate additional recordings as they are made.

Speech translation (ST) is very challenging, particularly for resource-scarce endangered languages. The degree of challenge might well be reduced if corpus creation focused from the beginning on translation without intermediate steps (transcription and analysis, which would take documentation in the direction of MT). Moreover, translation itself is a challenging art complicated by the lexical and morphosyntactic intricacies of languages and, more often than not, the discrepancies in vision and structure between source and target language (cf. Sapir, 1921, chap. 5). Extremely large corpora might smooth out the edges, but if free translations are created only after transcription, then the "transcription bottleneck" will also limit the availability of free translations. Limited EL free translation resources, in turn, creates the danger that idiosyncratic or literal translations might dominate the training set. This is another reason to position free translation directly from a recording *before* transcription and analysis.

Free translation and textual meaning: Even when a transcription has been produced and then morphologically segmented and glossed, free translations are beneficial, either generated from the transcription or directly from the speech signal. For example, although multiple sense glossing (i.e., choosing from multiple senses or functions in glossing a morpheme) clarifies ambiguous meanings, it is time-consuming for a human and challenging to automate. The semantic ambiguity of single morphemes will be mitigated if not resolved, however, if accompanied by free translations. Note the following interlinearization, in which, in isolation, the meaning of the gloss line is confusing. The free translations clarifies the meaning and offers a secondary sense to the verb root *koto:ni*.

Ko:koto:nis a:t komo a:mo kiowis.
0-ko:-koto:ni-s a:-t komo a:mo kiowi-s
3sgS-rdpl-to.snap-irreal.sg water-abs if not rain-irreal.sg

The stream will dry up into little ponds if it doesn't rain.

Note also that multi-word lemmas and idiomatic expressions are in many cases opaque in word-by-word (or, even more challenging, morpheme-by-morpheme) glossing. Again a gloss and parallel free translation preserve literal meaning while clarifying the actual meaning to target language speakers.

3 Strategies for automate speech-to-text translation: Cascaded model vs. end-to-end model

One intuitive solution to automating free translation is the cascaded model. But this is difficult to implement since it relies on a pipeline from automatic speech recognition (ASR) to machine translation (MT). Most ELs, however, lack the material and data necessary to robustly train both ASR and MT systems (Do et al., 2014; Matsuura et al., 2020; Shi et al., 2021).

End-to-end ST has received much attention from the NLP research community because of its simpler implementation and computational efficiency (Bérard et al., 2016; Weiss et al., 2017; Inaguma et al., 2019; Wu et al., 2020). In addition, it can also avoid propagating errors from ASR components by directly processing the speech signal. However, as with ASR and MT, ST also often suffers from limited training data and resultant difficulties in training a robust system, which makes the task challenging. There are few available examples of ST applied to endangered languages.

Indeed, most speech translation efforts are between major languages (Di Gangi et al., 2019a; Cattoni et al., 2021; Kocabiyikoglu et al., 2018; Salesky et al., 2021). In these corpora, both source and target languages usually have a standardized writing system and ample training data, a situation generally absent for ELs. A well-known low-resource ST corpus is the Mboshi-French corpus (Godard et al., 2018). However, it is based on the reading of written texts, which does not present the difficulties encountered in conversational speech scenarios. In EL documentation projects, it is these latter scenarios that are most common.

4 Corpus Description

4.1 Characteristics of Highland Puebla Nahuatl (glottocode high1278)

In this paper, we release a Highland Puebla Nahuatl (HPN; glottocode high1278) speech translation corpus for EL documentation. The corpus is governed by a Creative Commons BY-NC-SA 3.0 license and can be downloaded from `http://www.openslr.org/92`. We have analyzed the corpus and explored different ST models and corresponding open-source training recipes in ESPNet (Watanabe et al., 2018).

Nahuatl languages are polysynthetic, agglutinative, head-marking languages with relatively productive derivational morphology, reduplication, and noun incorporation. A rich set of affixes creates the basis for a high number of potential words from any given lemma. As illustrated in Table 1, a transitive verb may contain half a dozen affixes; up to eight in a single word is not uncommon. Suffixes (not represented in Table 1) include tense/aspect/mood markings as well as "associated motion" (*ti-cho:ka-ti-nemi-ya-h* 1plS-cry-ligature-walk-imperf-pl 'we used to go around crying' and directionals (*ti-mits-ih-ita-to-h* 1plS-2sgO-rdpl-see-extraverse.dir-pl 'we went to visit you').

Noun incorporation is not reflected in Table 1 as verbs with incorporated nouns may be treated as lexicalized stems with a compound internal structure. The function of the nominal stem can be highly varied (Tuggy, 1986) as it may lower valency (object incorporation) or leave valency unaffected, as with subject incorporation (not common), as well as both possessor raising (*ni-kone:-miki-k* 1sgS-child-die-perfective.sg 'My child died on me') and modification (*ni-kone:-tsahtsi-0* 1sgS-child-shout-pres.sg 'I shout like a child'). Though noun incorporation is not fully productive (Mithun, 1984), it does increase the number of lemmas. It complicates patterns and meaning of reduplication, which may be at the left edge of the compound (transitive *ma:teki* > *ma:ma:teki* 'to cut repeatedly on the arm') or stem internal (e.g., *ma:tehteki* 'to harvest by hand'). It also complicates automatic translation, particularly in the case of out of vocabulary compounds in which there is no precedent for any of the possible interpretations of the incorporated noun stem.

The main challenge to developing machine translation algorithms for HPN is its morphological complexity, large numbers of words with a low

A	B	C	D	E		F	G	H
subj.	referential obj.	directional prefix	reflexive	non-referential obj.		adverbials (na:l-, ye:k-)	redupli-cation	verb stem
				+human	-human			

Table 1: Transitional verb morphology: General overview of prefixation

Language	#Tokens	#Types	Ratio (Tokens/Type)	% Corpus in top 100 types
HPN	476,108	96,890	11.39	58.9
Yoloxóchitl Mixtec	955,602	26,445	36.14	59.0
English	783,555	9,601	81.61	63.0

Table 2: Comparative impact of morphological complexity on type-to-token ratios (the English statistics are from DARPA Transtac; the Mixtec statistics are from corpus presented in (Amith and García, 2020; Shi et al., 2021))

token-to-type ratio, and significant occurrences of both noun incorporation and reduplication accompanied by considerable variation in the semantic implications of incorporated noun stems and reduplicants. Table 2 lists type/token ratios in sample texts for three languages, including HPN. While the most frequent 100-word types cover roughly the same portion of text in all three languages, the remaining word types are represented in much lower frequency in HPN than in Yoloxóchitl Mixtec (glottologyolo1241, another EL spoken in Mexico) or English. As a corollary, this means that the remaining 41.1% of tokens (195,680) in the HPN corpus represents 41,718 types, a type-to-token ratio of 1:4.7. The equivalent ratio for English is 1:30.5.

Finally, HPN word order is relatively flexible, which may pose an additional challenge to free translation as neither case marking or word order unambiguously serves to indicate grammatical function. The degree to which MT or ST can handle this relative variability in word order, even with relatively abundant resources, It is not clear.

4.2 Corpus Transcription

Recording: The HPN corpus was developed with speakers from the municipality of Cuetzalan del Progreso, in the northeastern sierra of the state. Most speakers were from San Miguel Tzinacapan and neighboring communities. Recordings use a 48 kHz sampling rate at 16-bits. To facilitate transcription of overlapping speech, each speaker was miked separately into one of two channels with a head-worn Shure SM-10a dynamic mic. A total of 954 recordings were made in a variety of genres. The principal topic, with 591 separate conversations, was plant nomenclature, classification, and use.

Transcription: The workflow commenced with recording sessions in relatively isolated environments. The original transcription was done in Transcriber (Barras et al., 2001) by one of four native speaker members of the research team: Amelia Domínguez Alcántara, Hermelindo Salazar Osollo, Ceferino Salgado Castañeda, and Eleuterio Gorostiza Salazar. Amith then reviewed each transcription, checking any doubts with a native speaker, before importing the finalized Transcriber file into ELAN (Wittenburg et al., 2006). In import, each speaker was assigned a separate tier, and then an additional dependent tier for the free translation was created for each speaker.

Spanish influence: Endangered languages are often spoken in a (neo-)colonial context in which the impact of a dominant language (often but not always non-Indigenous) is felt in many spheres (McConvell and Meakins, 2005). HPN, particularly from the municipality of Cuetzalan, is striking for manifesting two perhaps contrary tendencies: (1) a puristic ideology that has motivated the creation of many neologisms along with (2) morphosyntactic shift under the subtle and covert influence of Spanish.[1] It is probably the case that neither neologisms nor morphosyntactic change poses much of a problem for machine translation; Spanish loans and code-switching into Spanish would undoubtedly be even less problematic. Indeed, it may well be that Spanish impact in many domains of HPN poses minimal problems for machine translation, particularly if the translation is text-to-text. One potential area of difficulty would be in speech translation, in which the Spanish translation is produced directly from a Nahuatl recording. In the conventions

[1] Details of two patterns are discussed in Appendix A.

for HPN transcription, a Spanish loan with distinct meanings in Spanish vs. Nahuatl contexts is distinguished orthographically. It might be difficult to disambiguate the two if the translation is direct from audio. Thus note the following: *āmo nikmati* como *tikchīwas* ('I don't know *how* you will do it') vs. *āmo nikmati komo tikchīwas* ('I don't know if you will do it'). Spanish *como* ('how') may retain its Spanish meaning in a Nahuatl narrative (in which case it is written as if Spanish), or it may be used as a conditional ('if'), in which case it is conventionally written in Nahuatl orthography (*komo*). Even though the decision to orthographically distinguish [komo] / <como> meaning 'how' from [komo] / <komo> meaning 'if' is a particular feature of HPN transcription conventions, the ambiguity in meaning (i.e., translation) would persist even if the orthographies of the two senses were to be different.

In sum, then, it may be that the Spanish impact on Nahuatl is less problematic for MT than for ASR. The most problematic situation for ST is when a Spanish word is used in a Nahuatl-speaking community with both its original Spanish meaning or an innovative Nahuatl meaning. In this case, working via MT from a written transcription may have an advantage if the orthography used for each different meaning (original Spanish vs. innovated) is represented differently based on orthographic convention (as with *como*). But in other cases of Spanish language impact, it is not clear that the cascaded ST (ASR > MT) pipeline enjoys advantages over the direct end-to-end ST system.

4.3 Standardized Splits

The HPN corpus includes corpora for two tasks: ASR and ST(MT). The statistics and the partition information are shown in Table 3. The ASR corpus contains high-quality speech with phone-level transcription. The ST corpus is a subset of the ASR corpus in that it comprises the subset of the ASR corpus that includes time-aligned free translation of the HPN transcription.

5 Experiments

In this section, we present our initial effort on building an automatic ST model for EL documentation. Following the discussion in Section 3, we compare the cascaded model with end-to-end models. To construct the cascaded model, we first conduct experiments on ASR and MT, respectively. Next, we compare different ST models. All the models are constructed with ESPNet, while all the training recipes are available at the ESPNet GitHub repository.[2]

Corpus	Subset	#Utts	Dur (h)
ASR	Train	96,890	123.67
	Validation	7,742	11.48
	Test	16,348	20.97
ST & MT	Train	30,414	36.17
	Validation	2,181	3.13
	Test	5,386	6.65

Table 3: Corpus partition for HPN-ASR and for HPN-ST/HPN-MT

5.1 Automatic Speech Recognition (ASR)

In many open-data tasks, end-to-end ASR compares favorably to traditional hidden Markov model–based ASR systems. The same trend is also shown in ASR for another endangered language, Yoloxóchitl Mixtec as presented in Shi et al. (2021), Table 2. Following a methodology similar to that used for ASR of Yoloxóchitl Mixtec, we have constructed a baseline system based on end-to-end ASR, specifically the transformer-based encoder-decoder architecture with hybrid CTC/attention loss (Watanabe et al., 2017; Karita et al., 2019). We have employed the exact same network configurations as the ESPNet MuST-C recipe.[3] The target of the system is 150 BPE units trained from the unigram language model. For decoding, we integrate the recurrent neural network language model with the ASR model. Specaugmentation is adopted for data augmentation (Park et al., 2019).

The results in character error rate (CER) and word error rate (WER) are shown in Table 4. The experiments show that ASR improves only slightly as the result of increasing the data size from 45 to 156 hours.

5.2 Machine Translation (MT)

The MT experiments are conducted over the ST corpus with ground truth HPN transcription by native-speaker transcribers. We also adopt ESPNet to train the MT model with encoder-decoder architecture (Inaguma et al., 2020). The settings

[2] https://github.com/espnet/espnet/tree/master/egs/puebla_nahuatl

[3] https://github.com/espnet/espnet/tree/master/egs/must_c/asr1

	% CER		% WER	
Corpus	dev	test	dev	test
ASR(156h)	8.8	8.5	23.9	22.4
ST (45h)	9.9	11.2	23.7	25.5

Table 4: ASR results for the HPN-ASR(156h) and HPN-ST(45h) corpora. ASR is directly used for cascaded model and applied for pre-training for end-to-end ST

Model	Val.	Test
MT	14.81	14.10
Cascaded-ST (ASR > MT)	14.72	13.26
E2E-ST w/ ASR-MTL	9.84	9.38
E2E-ST w/ ASR-SI	**15.22**	**15.41**

Table 5: MT and ST BLEU on different models: MTL is the system with multi-task learning; SI is the system with searchable intermediates.

exactly follow the settings for the ESPNet Must-C recipe.[4] The MT result on validation and test sets is shown in Table 5. As discussed in Section 3, the recordings are all of the conversational speech. For text-to-text machine translation the Nahuat inputs are native speaker transcriptions. For the cascading ST model, the Nahuat inputs are outputs from ASR, which have in built-in error rate. Due to the factor, the ASR transcription as a source text may not be an ideal candidate for cascaded ST translation, as it introduces additional noise from conversational transcription.

[4]https://github.com/espnet/espnet/tree/master/egs/must_c/asr1

Model	Val.	Test
E2E-ST w/ ASR-MTL	9.84	9.38
+ ASR encoder init.	14.77	14.05
+ MT decoder init.	11.06	11.03
+ ASR & MT init.	**15.08**	**14.24**

Table 6: Mitigating low resource ST by initializing encoders and decoders with pre-trained models. The ASR model is pre-trained using the 123.67 hours of HPN-ASR corpus, and the MT model is trained on the 30,414 text utterances from the HPN-ST corpus.

5.3 Speech Translation (ST)

While the traditional cascading approach to automating free translations (using two models, ASR and MT) shows strong results on many datasets, recent works have also shown competitive results using end-to-end systems that directly output translations from speech using a single model (Jan et al., 2019; Sperber and Paulik, 2020; Ansari et al., 2020). For low-resource settings, in particular, the data efficiencies of different methodologies become key performance factors (Bansal et al., 2018; Sperber et al., 2019). In this paper, we compare the performance of our dataset of both cascaded and single ST end-to-end systems. Both our cascaded and end-to-end systems are based on the encoder-decoder architecture (Bérard et al., 2016; Weiss et al., 2017) and the transformer-based model (Di Gangi et al., 2019b; Inaguma et al., 2019).

(a) Cascaded ST Model (ASR > MT Pipeline): The cascaded model consists of an ASR module and an MT module, each optimized separately during training. Each module is pre-trained with the same method as presented in Sections 5.1 and 5.2. During inference, the 1-best hypothesis from the ASR module is obtained via beam search with a beam size of 10, and this decoded transcription is passed to the subsequent MT module that finally outputs translated text. Results are shown in Table 5.

(b) End-to-end ST Model: In our experiments, we adopt the transformer-based encoder-decoder architecture with Specaugmentation. In addition, we default train the current system with the combination of ASR CTC-based loss from the encoder and ST translation loss from the decoder; this is referred to as E2E-ST with ASR-MTL. We also evaluate the Searchable Intermediates (SI) based ST model (E2E-ST with ASR-SI) introduced in Dalmia et al. (2021), where the ASR intermediates are found using the same decoding parameters as the ASR models of the cascade model. The detailed hyper-parameters follow the configuration of the ESPNet Must-C recipes.[5]

ST results are shown in Table 5. While the performance of the Cascaded-ST system is close to that of the MT system, the E2E-ST with ASR-MTL system shows a significantly worse result. Since E2E-ST with ASR-MTL jointly optimizes a speech

[5]https://github.com/espnet/espnet/tree/master/egs/must_c/asr1

encoder with an ASR decoder that is not included in the final inference network, this subnet waste is likely causing data inefficiency that is evident in our low-resource dataset (Sperber et al., 2019). In contrast, E2E-ST with SI actually outperforms both the MT and cascaded-ST systems, suggesting that it is less degraded by the low-resource constraint (Anastasopoulos and Chiang, 2018; Wang et al., 2020; Dalmia et al., 2021). Furthermore, this result shows that Nahuatl is more easily translated with a methodology that can consider both speech and transcript sequences as inputs.

(c) Pre-training for end-to-end ST: To investigate the pre-training effect for HPN, we adopt the models trained from Sections 5.1 and 5.2. The ASR model in Section 5.1 was used for initialization of the ST encoder, while the MT model in Section 5.2 was used for initialization of the ST decoder.

As shown in Table 6, the best performance is reached with initialization from both ASR encoder and MT decoder. Pre-training encoder and decoder could help better ST modeling, while using the pre-trained ASR encoder could contribute to more performance improvements.

Some examples with the best model in Table 6 are shown in Appendix B. Based on the analysis, it generally indicates that the current ST system can translate some essential information into Spanish. However, it still cannot fully replace the human effort on the task. And the translation still needs significant correction from a human annotator.

6 Conclusions

In this paper, we release the Highland Puebla Nahuatl corpus for ASR, MT, and ST tasks. The corpus, related baseline models, and training recipes are open source under the CC BY-NC-ND 3.0 license. We expect the corpus to facilitate all three tasks for EL documentation. We also discuss and present three specific reasons for prioritizing ST as an initial step in the endangered language documentation sequence after the recording has taken place. Finally, we explore different technologies for ST of Highland Puebla Nahuatl and compare these to results obtained by processing through the cascaded ST pipeline.

As discussed in Section 2, we suggest that prioritizing free translation as a first, not final, step in documentation should be considered as: (1) it can rapidly make a corpus valuable to potential users even if transcription, morphlogical segmentation, and morpheme glossing is incomplete; (2) it enables semi-, passive and heritage speakers to participate in documentation of their languages; (3) it provides an alternative process for ASR in which the ASR target is not a transcription but a translation into a Western language; and (4) it creates a scenario in which the acoustic signal and free translation may be coupled as inputs into an end-to-end ASR system. Therefore, our future works will focus on how the human effort could be reduced via ST models and on how to incorporate ST to improve the ASR performances.

Acknowledgements

The authors gratefully acknowledge the following support for documenting and studying Highland Puebla Nahuat: National Science Foundation, Documenting Endangered Languages (DEL): Awards 1401178, 0756536 (Amith, PI on both awards); National Endowment for the Humanities, Preservation and Access: PD-50031-14 (Amith, PI); Endangered Language Documentation Programme: Award MDP0272 (Amith, PI). The native speaker documentation team responsible for transcription and translation included Amelia Domínguez Alcántara. Ceferino Salgado Castañeda, Hermelindo Salazar Osollo, and Eleuterio Gorostiza Salazar. Yoloxóchitl Mixtec documentation was supported by the following grants: NSF-DEL: Awards 1761421, 1500595, 0966462 (Amith, PI on all three awards; the second was a collaborative project with SRI International, Award 1500738, Andreas Kathol, PI); Endangered Language Documentation Programme: Awards MDP0201, PPG0048 (Amith, PI on both awards). Rey Castillo García has been responsible for all transcriptions.

References

Jonathan D. Amith and Rey Castillo García. 2020. Audio corpus of Yoloxóchitl Mixtec with accompanying time-coded transcriptons in ELAN. http://www.openslr.org/89/. Accessed: 2021-03-05.

Antonios Anastasopoulos. 2019. *Computational tools for endangered language documentation*. Ph.D. thesis, University of Notre Dame, Computer Science and Engineering.

Antonios Anastasopoulos and David Chiang. 2018. Tied multitask learning for neural speech translation.

In *Proceedings of the 2018 Conference of the North American Chapter of the Association for Computational Linguistics: Human Language Technologies, Volume 1 (Long Papers)*, pages 82–91, New Orleans, Louisiana. Association for Computational Linguistics.

Ebrahim Ansari, Nguyen Bach, Ondřej Bojar, Roldano Cattoni, Fahim Dalvi, Nadir Durrani, Marcello Federico, Christian Federmann, Jiatao Gu, Fei Huang, et al. 2020. Findings of the IWSLT 2020 evaluation campaign. In *Proceedings of the 17th International Conference on Spoken Language Translation*, pages 1–34.

Sameer Bansal, Herman Kamper, Karen Livescu, Adam Lopez, and Sharon Goldwater. 2018. Low-resource speech-to-text translation. *Computing Research Repository (CoRR)*, abs/1803.09164.

Claude Barras, Edouard Geoffrois, Zhibiao Wu, and Mark Liberman. 2001. Transcriber: development and use of a tool for assisting speech corpora production. *Speech Communication*, 33(1-2):5–22.

Alexandre Bérard, Olivier Pietquin, Laurent Besacier, and Christophe Servan. 2016. Listen and translate: A proof of concept for end-to-end speech-to-text translation. In *NIPS Workshop on end-to-end learning for speech and audio processing*.

Steven Bird. 2020. Sparse transcription. *Computational Linguistics*, 46(4):713–744.

Roldano Cattoni, Mattia Antonino Di Gangi, Luisa Bentivogli, Matteo Negri, and Marco Turchi. 2021. MuST-C: A multilingual corpus for end-to-end speech translation. *Computer Speech & Language*, 66:101–155.

Siddharth Dalmia, Brian Yan, Vikas Raunak, Florian Metze, and Shinji Watanabe. 2021. Searchable hidden intermediates for end-to-end models of decomposable sequence tasks. In *Proceedings of Human Language Technologies: The Annual Conference of the North American Chapter of the Association for Computational Linguistics (NAACL-HLT)*.

Mattia A. Di Gangi, Roldano Cattoni, Luisa Bentivogli, Matteo Negri, and Marco Turchi. 2019a. MuST-C: A multilingual speech translation corpus. In *Proceedings of the 2019 Conference of the North American Chapter of the Association for Computational Linguistics: Human Language Technologies, Volume 1 (Long and Short Papers)*, pages 2012–2017, Minneapolis, Minnesota. Association for Computational Linguistics.

Mattia A Di Gangi, Matteo Negri, and Marco Turchi. 2019b. Adapting transformer to end-to-end spoken language translation. *Proc. Interspeech 2019*, pages 1133–1137.

Thi-Ngoc-Diep Do, Alexis Michaud, and Eric Castelli. 2014. Towards the automatic processing of Yongning Na (Sino-Tibetan): Developing a 'light' acoustic model of the target language and testing 'heavyweight' models from five national languages. In *Spoken Language Technologies for Under-Resourced Languages*.

P Godard, G Adda, Martine Adda-Decker, J Benjumea, Laurent Besacier, J Cooper-Leavitt, GN Kouarata, L Lamel, H Maynard, M Müller, et al. 2018. A very low resource language speech corpus for computational language documentation experiments. In *Language Resources and Evaluation Conference (LREC)*.

LA Grenoble, Peter K Austin, and Julia Sallabank. 2011. *Handbook of Endangered Languages*. Cambridge University Press.

Joseph Henrich, Steven J Heine, and Ara Norenzayan. 2010. Most people are not weird. *Nature*, 466(7302):29–29.

Hirofumi Inaguma, Kevin Duh, Tatsuya Kawahara, and Shinji Watanabe. 2019. Multilingual end-to-end speech translation. In *2019 IEEE Automatic Speech Recognition and Understanding Workshop (ASRU)*, pages 570–577. IEEE.

Hirofumi Inaguma, Shun Kiyono, Kevin Duh, Shigeki Karita, Nelson Yalta, Tomoki Hayashi, and Shinji Watanabe. 2020. ESPNet-ST: All-in-one speech translation toolkit. In *Proceedings of the 58th Annual Meeting of the Association for Computational Linguistics: System Demonstrations*, pages 302–311.

Niehues Jan, Roldano Cattoni, Stuker Sebastian, Matteo Negri, Marco Turchi, Salesky Elizabeth, Sanabria Ramon, Barrault Loic, Specia Lucia, and Marcello Federico. 2019. The IWSLT 2019 evaluation campaign. In *16th International Workshop on Spoken Language Translation 2019*.

Shigeki Karita, Nanxin Chen, Tomoki Hayashi, Takaaki Hori, Hirofumi Inaguma, Ziyan Jiang, Masao Someki, Nelson Enrique Yalta Soplin, Ryuichi Yamamoto, Xiaofei Wang, et al. 2019. A comparative study on transformer vs RNN in speech applications. In *2019 IEEE Automatic Speech Recognition and Understanding Workshop (ASRU)*, pages 449–456. IEEE.

Ali Can Kocabiyikoglu, Laurent Besacier, and Olivier Kraif. 2018. Augmenting LibriSpeech with French translations: A multimodal corpus for direct speech translation evaluation. In *Proceedings of the Eleventh International Conference on Language Resources and Evaluation (LREC 2018)*, Miyazaki, Japan. European Language Resources Association (ELRA).

Kohei Matsuura, Sei Ueno, Masato Mimura, Shinsuke Sakai, and Tatsuya Kawahara. 2020. Speech corpus of Ainu folklore and end-to-end speech recognition for the Ainu language. In *Proceedings of*

The 12th Language Resources and Evaluation Conference, pages 2622–2628.

Patrick McConvell and Felicity Meakins. 2005. Gurindji Kriol: A mixed language emerges from code-switching. *Australian Journal of Linguistics*, 25(1):9–30.

Marianne Mithun. 1984. The evolution of noun incorporation. *Language*, 60(4):847–894.

Daniel S Park, William Chan, Yu Zhang, Chung-Cheng Chiu, Barret Zoph, Ekin D Cubuk, and Quoc V Le. 2019. Specaugment: A simple data augmentation method for automatic speech recognition. *Proc. Interspeech 2019*, pages 2613–2617.

Elizabeth Salesky, Matthew Wiesner, Jacob Bremerman, Roldano Cattoni, Matteo Negri, Marco Turchi, Douglas W Oard, and Matt Post. 2021. The multilingual TEDx corpus for speech recognition and translation. *arXiv preprint arXiv:2102.01757*.

Edward Sapir. 1921. *An Introduction to the Study of Speech*. Harcourt, Brace & World, New York:.

Jiatong Shi, D Amith, Jonathan, Rey Castillo García, Esteban Guadalupe Sierra, Kevin Duh, and Shinji Watanabe. 2021. Leveraging end-to-end asr for endangered language documentation: An empirical study on Yoloxóchitl Mixtec. *arXiv preprint arXiv:2101.10877*.

Matthias Sperber, Graham Neubig, Jan Niehues, and Alex Waibel. 2019. Attention-passing models for robust and data-efficient end-to-end speech translation. *Transactions of the Association for Computational Linguistics*, 7:313–325.

Matthias Sperber and Matthias Paulik. 2020. Speech translation and the end-to-end promise: Taking stock of where we are. In *Proceedings of the 58th Annual Meeting of the Association for Computational Linguistics*, Online. Association for Computational Linguistics.

David Tuggy. 1986. Noun incorporations in nahuatl. In *Proceedings of the Annual Meeting of the Pacific Linguistics Conference*, volume 2, pages 455–470.

Chengyi Wang, Yu Wu, Shujie Liu, Zhenglu Yang, and Ming Zhou. 2020. Bridging the gap between pre-training and fine-tuning for end-to-end speech translation. In *Proceedings of the AAAI Conference on Artificial Intelligence*, volume 34, pages 9161–9168.

Shinji Watanabe, Takaaki Hori, Shigeki Karita, Tomoki Hayashi, Jiro Nishitoba, Yuya Unno, Nelson-Enrique Yalta Soplin, Jahn Heymann, Matthew Wiesner, Nanxin Chen, et al. 2018. ESPnet: End-to-end speech processing toolkit. *Proc. Interspeech 2018*, pages 2207–2211.

Shinji Watanabe, Takaaki Hori, Suyoun Kim, John R Hershey, and Tomoki Hayashi. 2017. Hybrid CTC/attention architecture for end-to-end speech recognition. *IEEE Journal of Selected Topics in Signal Processing*, 11(8):1240–1253.

Ron J Weiss, Jan Chorowski, Navdeep Jaitly, Yonghui Wu, and Zhifeng Chen. 2017. Sequence-to-sequence models can directly translate foreign speech. *Proc. Interspeech 2017*, pages 2625–2629.

Peter Wittenburg, Hennie Brugman, Albert Russel, Alex Klassmann, and Han Sloetjes. 2006. ELAN: A professional framework for multimodality research. In *5th International Conference on Language Resources and Evaluation (LREC 2006)*, pages 1556–1559.

Anne Wu, Changhan Wang, Juan Pino, and Jiatao Gu. 2020. Self-supervised representations improve end-to-end speech translation. *Proc. Interspeech 2020*, pages 1491–1495.

A Spanish language impact on Highland Puebla Nahuat

HPN, particularly from the municipality of Cuetzalan, is striking for manifesting two seemingly contrary tendencies: neologisms and morphosyntactic. The first is a puristic ideology that values the native language as an expression of Indigenous identity. The second is a very strong influence of Spanish syntax that has led to a significant number of calques that are not only direct translations of Spanish, but that yield expressions that violate basic grammatical constraints of Nahuatl. Puristic ideology motivates many neologisms, many of which are nouns, that provide an alternative to Spanish loans. Spanish impact on morphosyntax is also prevalent. For example, with very few exceptions, the valency of Nahuatl verbs is fixed as either intransitive, transitive, or ditransitive. Thus to accept an object, an intransitive must undergo valency increase through an overt morphological process. But Spanish influence has created situations in which intransitive Nahuat verbs mark two arguments (subject and object) on the erstwhile intransitive stem. Under Spanish influence, the intransitive verbs *kīsa* 'to emerge' (Spanish 'salir')' and *tikwi* 'to light up' (Spanish 'prenderse') manifest otherwise ungrammatical forms: (a) *āmo nēchkīsa* (*Ø-nēch-kīsa-Ø*; 3sgS-1sgO-to.emerge-pres.sg) is a calque from Spanish 'no me sale' ('it doesn't turn out right for me'); (b) *motikwi* (*Ø-mo-tikwi-Ø*; 'it lights up') uses an unnecessary and ungrammatical reflexive marker influenced by the reflexive Spanish term 'se prende'.

B Speech translation examples

This appendix shows five examples of our ST hypothesis (i.e., HYP) with speech transcription (i.e., HPN) and Spanish translation reference (i.e., REF). We indicate the corresponding utterance IDs in the parenthesis of each example.[6]

EG1 (AND308_2011-07-13-p-R_000105):
HPN: wa:n se: taman de n' kwaltia yo:n ista:k xo:no:t yo:n se: kehke:wa wa:n k..., se: kitsa:la:nwia
REF: y el segundo es el ista:k xo:no:t que se se puede usar este se le extrae la corteza se mete en un tronco partido a la mitad se jala con fuerza para separar la corteza con la fibra que es el jonote
HYP: y el otro tipo de árbol que se le puede extraer la fibra del jonote blanco se desprende la corteza y se jala con fuerza para separar la fibra
Notes: This is part of a recording about a tree called "jonote", which covers several species of *Heliocarpus*. The bark of one of these trees, the white jonote, is particularly good: It is stripped from the tree and then pulled through a wedge cut into the trunk so that the meaty part of the bark is stripped away and the fiber is left somewhat clean. The E2E translation captures the better quality of the white jonote and presents the process of stripping fiber. Note that the gist of the Nahuatl is accurately captured, from the fact that the narrator is now commenting on a second type of jonote (white) that is the most used, to the mechanism for cleaning the stripped bark. The word *kitsa:la:nwia* ('to put in the middle') is also correctly translated as the action of pulling the bark through a wedge to clean the fiber.

EG2 (AND308_2011-07-13-p-R_000133):
HPN: pero a:mo nochi kokotoka n' chi:chi:lxo:no:t
REF: pero no todo se revienta el chi:chi:lxo:no:t
HYP: pero no todos se revientan los frutos de chi:chi:lxo:no:t
Notes: Here the reference is to the red jonote, *chi:chi:lxo:no:t*, which is less commonly used than the white jonote. This is because the bark of the red jonote is more brittle and tends to snap into pieces as it is pulled off the trunk. Here, however, the narrator is commenting that not all red jonote trees have bark that pulls apart into pieces. The Nahuatl text, however, makes no mention of "fruit" ('fruto') as the computer generated translation suggests.

EG3 (AND308_2011-07-13-p-R_000186):
HPN: ke:mah wa:n no: kwali tine:chili:s compadrito de que
REF: sí y también puedes platicarme compadrito de que
HYP: sí y también puedes decirme compadrito que
Notes: The alternation between 'platicarme' and 'decirme' is basically a case of synonymy. The computer translation is accurate.

EG4 (AND308_2011-07-29-i-R_000077):
HPN: nextik ihkó:n pero yo:n a:mo
REF: es de color gris pero ésa planta no
HYP: es gris pero ese no
Notes: Here the computer translation is closer to the Nahuatl and fully understandable. The human translator inserted "color", which was not necessary to the understanding of 'grey' as a color.. The term *yo:n* is a pronoun, "that". The human translator added the anteceding referent, "flower", to make the text clearer. In English the difference would be: (1) it is a grey color, but that plant isn't" (Human) vs. (2) it is grey but that one isn't" (Computer). The computer translation is in fact closer to the original.

[6]The utterance IDs can be obtained from corresponding recipes at ESPNet

EG5 (RMM302_2011-07-27-l-L_000106):
HPN: oksé: no: n'neki nimitstahtani:s n' tehwa:tsi:n komo yehwa n' tein neh niki:mxattok ¿ke:niwki n' ixo:chiotsi:n
REF: otra coso quiero preguntarte si acaso sea el mismo que yo conozco ¿cómo es la flor
HYP: otra cosa que quiero preguntarte si es que yo conozco como es su flor
Notes: In the Nahuatl text the narrator is basically saying that he has another question to ask ('otra cosa que quiero preguntarte') and that this question is whether 'the flower that I know ..., what is its flower like?' (¿cómo es su flor?).

End-to-End Automatic Speech Recognition: Its Impact on the Workflow for Documenting Yoloxóchitl Mixtec

Jonathan D. Amith[1] **Jiatong Shi**[2] **Rey Castillo García**[3]
[1]Department of Anthropology, Gettysburg College, Gettysburg, Pennsylvania
[2]The Johns Hopkins University, Baltimore, Maryland
[3]Secretaría de Educación Pública, Estado de Guerrero, Mexico
(jonamith@gmail.com, jiatong_shi@jhu.edu, reyyoloxochitl@gmail.com)

Abstract

This paper describes three open access Yoloxóchitl Mixtec corpora and presents the results and implications of end-to-end automatic speech recognition for endangered language documentation. Two issues are addressed. First, the advantage for ASR accuracy of targeting informational (BPE) units in addition to, or in substitution of, linguistic units (word, morpheme, morae) and then using ROVER for system combination. BPE units consistently outperform linguistic units although the best results are obtained by system combination of different BPE targets. Second, a case is made that for endangered language documentation, ASR contributions should be evaluated according to extrinsic criteria (e.g., positive impact on downstream tasks) and not simply intrinsic metrics (e.g., CER and WER). The extrinsic metric chosen is the level of reduction in the human effort needed to produce high-quality transcriptions for permanent archiving.

1 Introduction: Endangered language documentation history and context

Endangered language (EL) documentation emerged as a field of linguistic activity in the 1990s, as reflected in several seminal moments. In 1991 the Linguistic Society of America held a symposium entitled “Endangered Languages and their Preservation"; in 1992 Hale et al. (1992) published a seminal article on endangered languages in *Language*, the LSA's flagship journal. In 1998, Himmelmann (1998) argued for the development of documentary linguistics as an endeavor separate from and complementary to descriptive linguistics. By the early years of the present millennium, infrastructure efforts were being developed: metadata standards and best practices for archiving (Bird and Simons, 2003); tools for lexicography and corpus developments such as Shoebox, Transcriber (Barras et al., 1998), and ELAN (Wittenburg et al., 2006), and financial support for endangered language documentation (the Volkswagen Foundation, the NSF Documenting Endangered Language Program, and the SOAS Endangered Language Documentation Programme). Recent retrospectives on the impact of Hale et al. (1992) and Himmelmann (1998) have been published by Seifart et al. (2018) and McDonnell et al. (2018). Within the last decade, the National Science Foundation supported a series of three workshops, under the acronym AARDVARC (Automatically Annotated Repository of Digital Audio and Video Resources Community) to bring together field linguists working on endangered languages and computational linguists working on automatic annotation—particularly automatic speech recognition (ASR)—to address the impact of what has been called the "transcription bottleneck" (Whalen and Damir, 2012). Interest in applying machine learning to endangered language documentation is also manifested in four biennial workshops on this topic, the first in 2014 (Good et al., 2021). Finally, articles directly referencing ASR of *endangered languages* have become increasingly common over the last five years (Adams et al., 2018, 2020; Ćavar et al., 2016; Foley et al., 2018, 2019; Gupta and Boulianne, 2020; Jimerson and Prud'hommeaux, 2018; Jimerson et al., 2018; Michaud et al., 2018; Mitra et al., 2016; Shi et al., 2021).

This article continues work on Yoloxóchitl Mixtec ASR (Mitra et al., 2016; Shi et al., 2021). The most recent efforts (2020 and 2021) have adopted the ESPNet toolkit for end-to-end automatic speech recognition (E2E ASR). This approach has proven to be very efficient in terms of time needed to develop the ASR recipe (Shi et al., 2021) and in yielding ASR hypotheses of an accuracy capable of significantly reducing the extent of human effort needed to finalize accurate transcribed audio for permanent archiving as here demonstrated. Section 2 discusses the Yoloxóchitl Mixtec corpora,

Proceedings of the First Workshop on Natural Language Processing for Indigenous Languages of the Americas, pages 64–80
June 11, 2021.

and Section 3 explores the general goals of EL documentation. Section 4 reviews the E2E ASR and corresponding results using ESPNet. The conclusion is offered in Section 5.

2 Yoloxóchitl Mixtec: Corpus characteristics and development

2.1 The language

Much work on computer-assisted EL documentation is closely related to work on low-resource languages, for the obvious reason that most ELs have limited resources, be they time-coded transcriptions, interlinearized texts, or corpora in parallel translation. The resources for Yoloxóchitl Mixtec, the language targeted in this present study, are, however, relatively abundant by EL standards (119.32 hours over three corpora), the result of over a decade of linguistic and anthropological research by Amith and Castillo García (2020).

Yoloxóchitl Mixtec (henceforth YM), an endangered Mixtecan language spoken in the municipality of San Luis Acatlán, Guerrero, Mexico, is one of some 50 languages in the Mixtec language family, which is within a larger unit, Otomanguean, that Suárez (1983) considers a hyper-family or stock. Mixtec languages (spoken in Oaxaca, Guerrero, and Puebla) are highly varied, the result of approximately 2,000 years of diversification. YM is spoken in four communities: Yoloxóchitl, Cuanacaxtitlan, Arroyo Cumiapa, and Buena Vista. Mutual intelligibility among the four communities is high despite differences in phonology, morphology, and syntax.

All villages have a simple common segmental inventory but apparently significant though still undocumented variation in tonal phonology; only Cuanacaxtitlan manifests tone sandhi. YMC (referring only to the Mixtec of the community of Yoloxóchitl [16.81602, -98.68597]) manifests 28 distinct tonal patterns on 1,451 to-date identified bimoraic lexical stems. The tonal patterns carry a significant functional load regarding the lexicon and inflection (Palancar et al., 2016). For example, 24 distinct tonal patterns on the bimoraic segmental sequence [nama] yield 30 words (including five homophones). The three principal aspectual forms (irrealis, incompletive, and completive) are almost invariably marked by a tonal variation on the first mora of the verbal stem (1 or 3 for the irrealis, 4 for the incompletive, and 13 for the completive; in addition 14 on the initial mora almost always indicates negation of the irrealis[1]). In a not-insignificant number of cases, suppletive stems exist, generally manifesting variation in a stem-initial consonant and often the stem-initial vowel.

The ample tonal inventory of YMC presents obstacles to native speaker literacy and an ASR system learning to convert an acoustic signal to text. It also complicates the construction of a language lexicon for HMM-based systems, a lexicon that is not required in E2E ASR. The phonological and morphological differences between YMC and the Mixtec of the three other YM communities create challenges for transcription and, by extension, for applying YMC ASR to speech recordings from these other villages. To accomplish this, it will be necessary first to learn the phonology and morphology of these variants and then use this as input into a transfer learning scenario. Intralanguage variation among distinct communities (see Hildebrandt et al., 2017b and other articles in Hildebrandt et al., 2017a) is an additional factor that can negatively impact computer-assisted EL documentation efforts in both intra- and intercommunity contexts.

2.2 The three corpora

YMC-Exp: The corpus originally available to develop E2E ASR, here titled YMC-Exp (Expert transcription), comprises 98.99 hours of time-coded transcription divided as follows for initial ASR development: Training: 92.46 hours (52,763 utterances); Validation: 4.01 hours (2,470 utterances); and Test: 2.52 hours (1,577 utterances).

The size of this initial YM corpus (505 files, 32 speakers, 98.99 hours) sets it apart from other ASR initiatives for endangered languages (Adams et al., 2018; Ćavar et al., 2016; Jimerson et al., 2018; Jimerson and Prud'hommeaux, 2018). This ample size has yielded lower character (CER) and word (WER) error rates than would usually occur with truly low-resource EL documentation projects.

Amith and Castillo García recorded the corpus at a 48KHz sampling rate and 16-bits (usually with a Marantz PMD 671 recorder, Shure SM-10a dynamic headset mics, and separate channels for each speaker). The entire corpus was transcribed by Castillo, a native speaker linguist (García, 2007).

YMC-FB: A second YMC corpus (YMC-FB; for 'field botany') was developed during ethno-

[1]Tones are V^1 low to V^4 high, with V^{13} and V^{14} indicating two of several contour tones; see also fn. 2.

botanical fieldwork. Kenia Velasco Gutiérrez (a Spanish-speaking botanist) and Esteban Guadalupe Sierra (a native speaker from Yoloxóchitl) led 105 days of fieldwork that yielded 888 distinct plant collections. A total of 584 recordings were made in all four YM communities; only 452 were in Yoloxóchitl, and of these, 435, totaling 15.17 hours with only three speakers, were used as a second test case for E2E ASR. Recordings were done outdoors at the plant collection site with a Zoom H4n hand-held digital recorder. The Zoom H4n internal mic was used; recordings were 48KHz, 16-bit, a single channel with one speaker talking after another (no overlap). Each recording has a short introduction by Velasco describing, in Spanish, the plant being collected. This Spanish section has not been factored into the duration of the YMC-FB corpus, nor has it been evaluated for character and word error rates at this time (pending future implementation of a multilingual model). The processing of the 435 recordings falls into two groups.

- 257 recordings (8.36 hours) were first transcribed by a novice trainee (Esteban Guadalupe) as part of transcription training. They were corrected in a separate ELAN tier by Castillo García and then the acoustic signals were processed by E2E ASR trained on the YMC-Exp corpus. The ASR CER and WER were obtained by comparing the ASR hypotheses to Castillo's transcriptions; Guadalupe's skill level (also measured in CER and WER) was obtained by comparing his transcription to that of Castillo. The results are discussed in Table 9 of Shi et al. (2021).
- 178 recordings (6.81 hours) were processed by E2E ASR, then corrected by Castillo. This set was not used to teach or evaluate novice trainee transcription skills but only to determine CER and WER for E2E ASR with the YMC-FB corpus.

No training or validation sets were created from this YMC-FB corpus, which for this present paper was used solely to test E2E ASR efficiency using the recipe developed from YMC-Exp corpus. CER and WER scores for YMC-FB were only produced after Castillo used the ELAN interface to correct the ASR hypotheses for this corpus (see Appendix A for an example ASR output).

YMC-VN: The final corpus is a set of 24 narratives made to provide background information and off-camera voice for a documentary video. The recordings involved some speakers not represented in the YMC-Exp corpus. All recordings (5.16 hours) were made at 44.1kHz, 16-bit with a boom-held microphone and a Tascam portable digital recorder in a hotel room. This environment may have introduced reverb or other effects that might have negatively affected ASR CER and WER.

Accessibility: All three corpora (119.32 hours) are available at the OpenSLR data portal (Amith and Castillo García, 2020)

3 Goals and challenges of corpora-based endangered language documentation

3.1 Overview

The oft-cited Boasian trilogy of grammar, dictionaries, and texts is a common foundation for EL documentation. Good (2018, p. 14) parallels this classic conception with a "Himmelmannian" trilogy of recordings, metadata, and annotations (see Himmelmann 2018). For the purpose of the definition proposed here, EL documentation is considered to be based on the Boasian trilogy of (1) corpus, (2) lexicon (in the sense of dictionary), and (3) grammar. In turn, each element in the trilogy is molded by a series of expectations and best practices. An audio corpus, for example, would best be presented interlinearized with (a) lines corresponding to the transcription (often in a practical orthography or IPA transcription), (b) morphological segmentation (often called a 'parse'), (c) parallel glossing of each morpheme, (d) a free translation into a target, often colonial language, and (e) metadata about recording conditions and participants. This is effectively the Himmelmannian trilogy referenced by Good. A dictionary should contain certain minimum fields (e.g., part of speech, etymology, illustrative sentences). Grammatical descriptions (books and articles) are more openly defined (e.g., a reference vs. a pedagogical grammar) and may treat only parts of the language (e.g., verb morphology).

In a best-case scenario, these three elements of the Boasian trilogy are interdependent. Corpus-based lexicography clearly requires ample interlinearized transcriptions (IGT) of natural speech that can be used to (a) develop concordances mapped to lemmas (not word forms); (b) enrich a dictionary by finding lemmas in the corpus that are absent from an extant set of dictionary headwords; and (c) discover patterns in the corpus suggestive of multiword lemmas (e.g., ku^3-na^3a^4 followed by i^3ni^2 (lit., 'darken heart' but meaning 'to faint'). A grammar will inform decisions about morphological segmentation used in the IGT as well as part-of-speech tags and other glosses. And a grammar itself would benefit greatly from a large set of annotated natural speech recordings not simply to provide examples of particular structures but to facilitate a statistical analysis of speech patterns (e.g., for YMC, the relative frequency of completive verbs marked solely by tone vs. those marked by the prefix ni^1-). This integration of elements into one "hypertextual" documentation effort is proposed by Musgrave and Thieberger (2021), who note the importance of spontaneous text (i.e., corpora, which they separate into two elements, media, and text) and comment that "all examples [in the dictionary and grammar] should come from the spontaneous text and should be viewed in context" (p. 6).

Documentation of YMC has proceeded on the assumption that the hypertextual integration suggested by Musgrave and Thieberger is central to effective endangered language documentation based on natural speech and that textual transcription of multimedia recordings of natural speech is, therefore, the foundation for a dictionary and grammar based on actual language use. End-to-end ASR is used to rapidly increase corpus size while offering the opportunity to target certain genres (such as expert conversations on the nomenclature, classification, and use of local flora and fauna; ritual discourse; material cultural production; techniques for fishing and hunting) that are of ethnographic interest but are often insufficiently covered in EL documentation projects that struggle to produce large and varied corpora. With the human effort–reducing advances in ASR for YMC presented in this paper, such extensive targeted recording of endangered cultural knowledge can now easily be included in the documentation effort.

The present paper focuses on end-to-end automatic speech recognition using the ESPNet toolkit (Guo et al., 2020; Shi et al., 2021; Watanabe et al., 2020, 2017, 2018). The basic goal is simple: To develop computational tools that reduce the amount of human effort required to produce accurate transcriptions in time-coded interlinearized format that will serve a wide range of potential stakeholders, from native and heritage speakers to specialized academics in institutions of higher learning, in the present and future generations. The evaluation metric, therefore, is not intrinsic (e.g., reduced CER and WER) but rather extrinsic: the impact of ASR on the downstream task of creating a large and varied corpus of Yoloxóchitl Mixtec.

3.2 Challenges to ASR of endangered languages

ASR for endangered languages is made difficult not simply because of limited resources for training a robust system but by a series of factors briefly discussed in this section.

Recording conditions: Noisy environments, including overlapping speech, reverberation in indoor recordings, natural sounds in outdoor recordings, less than optimal microphone placement (e.g., a boom mic in video recordings), and failure to separately mike speakers for multichannel recordings all negatively impact the accuracy of ASR output. Also to the point, field recordings are seldom made with an eye to seeding a corpus in ways that would specifically benefit ASR results (e.g., recording a large number of speakers for shorter durations, rather than fewer speakers for longer times). To date, then, processing a corpus through ASR techniques of any nature (HMM, end-to-end) has been more of an afterthought than planned at project beginning. Development of a corpus from the beginning with an eye to subsequent ASR potential would be immensely helpful to these computational efforts. It could, perhaps should, be increasingly considered in the initial project design. Indeed, just as funding agencies such as NSF require that projects address data management issues, it might be worth considering the suggested inclusion of how to make documentation materials more amenable to ASR and NLP processing as machine learning technologies are getting more robust.

Colonialization of language: Endangered languages do not die, to paraphrase Dorian (1978), with their "boots on." Rather, in the colonialized situation in which most ELs are immersed, there are multiple phonological, morphological, and syntactic influences from a dominant language. The incidence of a colonial language in native language recordings runs a gamut from multilanguage situations (e.g., each speaker using a distinct language, as often occurs in elicitation sessions: 'How would you translate ___ into Mixtec?'), to code-switching and borrowing or relexification in the speech of single individuals. In some languages (e.g., Nahuatl), a single word may easily combine stems from both native and colonial languages. Preliminary, though not quantified, CER analysis for YMC ASR suggests that "Spanish-origin" words provoke a significantly higher error rate than the YMC lexicon uninfluenced by Spanish. It is also not clear that a multilingual phone recognition system is the solution to character errors (such as ASR hypothesis 'cereso' for Spanish 'cerezo') that may derive from an orthographic system, such as that for Spanish, that is not designed, as many EL orthographies are, for consistency. Phonological shifts in borrowed terms also preclude the simple application of lexical tools to correct misspellings (as 'agustu' for the Spanish month 'agosto').

Orthographic conventions: The practical deep orthography developed by Amith and Castillo marks off boundaries of affixes (with a hyphen) and clitics (with an = sign). Tones are indicated by superscript numbers, from 1 low to 4 high, with five common rising and falling tones. Stem-final elided tones are enclosed in parentheses (e.g., underlying form $be'^{3}e^{(3)}{=}^{2}$; house=1sgPoss, 'my house'; surface form $be'^{3}e^{2}$). Tone-based inflectional morphology is not separated in any YMC transcriptions.[2]

The transcription strategy for YMC was unusual in that the practical orthography was a deep, underlying system that represented segmental morpheme boundaries and showed elided tones in parentheses. The original plans of Amith and Castillo were to use the transcribed audio as primary data for a corpus-based dictionary. A deep orthography facilitates discovery (without recourse to a morphological analyzer) of lemmas that may be altered in surface pronunciations by the effect of person-marking enclitics and certain common verbal prefixes (see Shi et al., 2021, §2.3).

Only after documentation (recording and time-coded transcriptions) was well advanced did work begin on a finite state transducer for the YMC corpus. this was made possible by collaboration with another NSF-DEL sponsored project.[3] The code was written by Jason Lilley in consultation with Amith and Castillo. As the FOMA FST was being built, FST output was repeatedly checked against expectations based on the morphological grammar until no discrepancies were noted. The FST, however, only generates surface forms consistent with Castillo's grammar. If speakers varied, for example, in the extent of vowel harmonization or regressive nasalization, the FST would yield only one surface form, that suggested by Castillo to be the most common. For example, underlying $be'^{3}e^{(3)}{=}an^{4}$ (house=3sgFem; 'her house') surfaces as $be'^{3}\tilde{a}^{4}$ even though for some speakers nasalization spreads to the stem initial vowel. Note, then, that the surface forms in the YMC-Exp corpus are based on FST generation from an underlying transcription as input and not from the direct transcription of the acoustic signal. It is occasionally the case that different speakers might extend vowel harmonization or nasalization leftward to different degrees. This could increase the CER and WER for ASR of surface forms, given that the reference for evaluation is not directly derived from the acoustic signal while the ASR hypothesis is so derived.

In an evaluation across the YMC-Exp development and test sets (total 6.53 hours) of the relative accuracy of ASR when using underlying versus surface orthography, it was found that training on underlying orthography produced slightly greater accuracy than training on surface forms: Underlying = 7.7/16.0 [CER/WER] compared to Surface = 7.8/16.5 [CER/WER] (Shi et al., 2021, see Table 4). The decision to use underlying representations in ASR training has, however, several more important advantages. First, for native speakers, the process of learning a deep practical orthography means that one learns segmental morphology as one learns to write. For the purposes of YMC language documentation, the ability of a neural network to directly learn segmental morphology as part of ASR training has resulted in a YMC ASR output across all three corpora with affixes and clitics separated and stem-final elided tones marked in parentheses. Semi- or un-supervised morphological learning as a separate NLP task is unnecessary when ASR training and testing was successfully carried out on a corpus with basic morphological segmentation. As the example in Appendix A demonstrates, ASR output includes basic segmentation at the morphological level.

[2]For example $ka'^{3}an^{4}$ 'to have faith (irrealis)'; $ka'^{14}an^{4}$ 'to not have faith (neg. irrealis)', $ka'^{4}an^{4}$ 'to have faith (incompletive)'; $ka'^{13}an^{4}$ 'to have faith (completive). For now, the tonal inflection on the first mora is not parsed out from stems such as $ka'^{3}an^{4}$; see also fn. 1

[3]Award #1360670 (Christian DiCanio, PI; Understanding Prosody and Tone Interactions through Documentation of Two Endangered Languages).

Corpus	Intrinsic		Extrinsic
	CER	WER	Correction Time
Reference	/	/	40 (estimated avg.)
Exp	7.6	14.7	(not measured)
FB	8.9	18.4	8.76
VN	6.1	15.8	10.28

Table 1: Intrinsic metrics vs. extrinsic metrics: Intrinsic metrics are based on Row I in Table 2. The extrinsic reference is the transcription time of an unaided human. The correction time for ASR output is measured in hours.

3.3 Intrinsic metrics: CER, WER, and consistency in transcriptions used as reference:

Although both CER and WER reference "error rate" in regards to character and word, respectively, the question of the accuracy of the *reference* itself is rarely explored (but cf. Saon et al., 2017). For YMC, only one speaker, Castillo García, is capable of accurate transcription, which in YMC is the sole gold standard for ASR training, validation, and testing. Thus there is a consistency to the transcription used as a reference.

In comparison, for Highland Puebla Nahuat (another language that the present team is exploring), the situation is distinct. Three native speaker experts have worked with Amith on transcription for over six years, but the reference for ASR development are native-speaker transcriptions carefully proofed by Amith, a process that both corrected simple errors and applied a single standard implemented by one researcher. When all three native speaker experts were asked to transcribe the same 90 minutes or recordings, and the results were compared, there was not an insignificant level of variation (9%).

The aforementioned scenario suggests the impact on ASR intrinsic metrics of variation in transcriptions across multiple annotators, or even inconsistencies of one skilled annotator in the context of incipient writing systems. This affects not only ASR output but also the evaluation of ASR accuracy via character and word error rates. It may be that rather than character and word *error* rate, it would be advisable to consider the character and word *discrepancy* rate a change in terminology that perhaps better communicates the idea that the differences between REF and HYP are often as much a matter of opinion as fact. The nature and value of utilizing intrinsic metrics (e.g., CER and WER) for evaluating ASR effectiveness for endangered language documentation merits rethinking.

An additional factor that has emerged in the YMC corpora, which contains very rapid speech, is what may be called "hypercorrection". This is not uncommon and may occur with lenited forms (e.g., writing $ndi^1ku^4chi^4$ when close examination of the acoustic signal reveals that the speaker used the fully acceptable lenited form $ndiu^{14}chi^4$) or when certain function words are reduced, at times effectively disappearing from the acoustic signal though not from the mind of a fluent speaker transcriber. In both cases, ASR "errors" might represent a more accurate representation of the acoustic signal than the transcription of even the most highly capable native speakers.

The above discussion also brings into question what it means to achieve human parity via an ASR system. Parity could perhaps best be considered as not based on CER and WER alone but on whether ASR output achieves a lower error rate in these two measurements as compared to what another skilled human transcriber might achieve.

3.4 Extrinsic metrics: Reduction of human effort as a goal for automatic speech recognition

Given the nature of EL documentation, which requires high levels of accuracy if the corpus is to be easily used for future linguistic research, it is essential that ASR-generated hypotheses be reviewed by an expert human annotator before permanent archiving. Certainly, audio can be archived with metadata alone or with unchecked ASR transcriptions (see Michaud et al., 2018, §4.3 and 4.4), but the workflow envisioned for YMC is to use ASR to reduce human effort while the archived corpus of audio and text maintains results equivalent to those that would be obtained by careful, and labor-intensive, expert transcription.

CER and WER were measured for YMC corpora with training sets of 10, 20, 50, and 92 hours. The CER/WER were as follows: 19.5/39.2 (10 hrs.), 12.7/26.2 (20 hrs.), 10.2/24.9 (50 hrs.), and 7.7/16.1 (92 hrs.); Table 5 in Shi et al. (2021). Measurement of human effort reduction suggests that with a corpus of 30–50 hours, even for a relatively challenging language such as YMC, E2E ASR can achieve the level of accuracy that allows a reduction of human effort by > 75 percent (e.g., from 40 to 10 hours, approximately).

Model	Unit	CER				WER			
		Exp(dev)	Exp(test)	FB	VN	Exp(dev)	Exp(test)	FB	VN
A	Morae	9.5	9.4	12.8	9.9	19.2	19.2	23.8	21.8
B	Morpheme	10.2	10.0	13.9	10.9	20.0	20.0	24.8	23.1
C	Word	12.0	11.9	14.0	11.4	19.3	19.3	21.2	20.2
D	BPE150	7.7	7.6	9.5	6.8	16.1	16.1	19.6	17.3
E	BPE500	7.6	7.7	9.3	6.6	15.8	16.0	19.1	16.7
F	BPE1000	7.9	7.7	9.8	6.8	16.1	15.9	19.5	16.9
G	BPE1500	7.9	7.8	10.1	6.9	16.3	16.1	19.8	16.9
H	ROVER (A-C)	9.2	9.2	12.5	9.4	21.8	22.0	27.0	23.6
I	ROVER(D-G)	7.5	7.6	**8.9**	**6.1**	14.6	**14.7**	**18.4**	**15.8**
J	ROVER(A-G)	**7.4**	**7.4**	9.0	**6.1**	**14.4**	14.8	18.6	15.9

Table 2: ASR results for different models with different units

Starting from the acoustic signal, Castillo García, a native speaker linguist, requires approximately 40 hours to transcribe 1 hour of YMC audio. Starting from initial ASR hypotheses incorporated into ELAN, this is reduced by approximately 75 percent to about 10 hours of effort to produce one finalized hour of time-coded transcription with marked segmentation of affixes and enclitics.

These totals are derived from measurements with the FB and VN corpora, the two corpora for which ASR provided the initial transcription, and Castillo subsequently corrected the output, keeping track of the time he spent. For the first corpus, Castillo required 58.20 hours to correct 6.65 hours of audio (from 173 of the 178 files that had not been first transcribed by a speaker trainee). This yields 8.76 hours of effort per hour of recording. The 5.16 hours (in 24 files) of the VN corpus required 53.07 hours to correct, a ratio of 10.28 hours of effort to finalize 1 hour of speech. Over the entire set of 197 files (11.81 hours), human effort was 111.27 hours, or 9.42 hours to correct 1 hour of audio. Given that the ASR system was trained on an underlying orthography, the final result of < 10 hours of human effort per hour of audio is a transcribed *and* partially parsed corpus. Table 3 presents an analysis of two lines of a recording that was first processed by E2E ASR and corrected by Castillo García. A fuller presentation and analysis are offered in the Appendix. This focus on extrinsic metrics reflects the realization that the ultimate goal of computational systems is not to achieve the lowest CER and WER but to help documentation initiatives more efficiently produce results that will benefit future stakeholders.

4 End-to-end ASR experiments

4.1 Experiment settings

Recently, E2E ASR has reached comparable or better performances than conventional Hidden-Markov-Model-based ASR (Graves and Jaitly, 2014; Chiu et al., 2018; Pham et al., 2019; Karita et al., 2019a; Shi et al., 2021). In practice, E2E ASR systems are less affected by linguistic constraints and are generally easier to train. The benefits of such systems are reflected in the recent trends of using end-to-end ASR for EL documentation (Adams et al., 2020; Thai et al., 2020; Matsuura et al., 2020; Hjortnaes et al., 2020; Shi et al., 2021).

In developing E2E ASR recipes for YMC, we have adopted transformer and conformer-based encoder-decoder networks with hybrid CTC/attention training (Karita et al., 2019b; Watanabe et al., 2017). We used the YMC-Exp (train-split) for training and other YMC corpora for evaluation. The hyper-parameters for the training and decoding follow Shi et al. (2021). Seven systems with different modeling units are examined in the experiments. Four systems employ the byte-pair encoding (BPE) method trained from unigram language models (Kudo and Richardson, 2018), with transcription alphabets limited to the 150, 500, 1000, and 1500 most frequent byte-pairs in the training set. The other three ASR systems adopt linguistic units, including word, morpheme, and mora. The YM word is defined as a stem with all prefixes (such as completetive ni^1-, causative sa^4-, and iterative nda^3-) separated from the stem by a hyphen; and all enclitics (particularly person markers for subjects, objects, and possessors, such as =yu^3, 1sg; =un^4, 2sg; =an^4, 3sgFem; =o^4, 1plIncl; as well as $=lu^3$, augmentive). Many vowel-initial enclitics have alternative vowels, and many encl-

ASR	yo'^{3}o^{4} xi^{13}i^{2} ba^{42} ndi^{4} ba'^{1}a^{3}=e^{2} ku^{3}-nu'^{3}ni^{2} tu^{3}tun^{4} kwi^{3}so$^{(3)}$=e^{4} mi^{4}i^{4} ti^{4} ba^{42} ko^{14}o^{3} yo'^{3}o^{4} kwa'^{1}an^{1} yo^{4}o^{4} xa^{14}ku'^{1}u^{1}
Exp	yo'^{3}o^{4} xi^{1}i^{32} ba^{42} ndi^{4} ba'^{1}a^{3}=e^{2} ku^{3}-nu'^{3}ni^{2} tu^{3}tun^{4} kwi^{3}so$^{(3)}$=e^{4} mi^{4}i^{4} ti^{4} ba^{42} ko^{14}o^{3} yo'^{3}o^{4} kwa'^{1}an^{1} ji'^{4}in$^{(4)}$=o^{4} xa^{14}ku'^{1}u^{1}
Note	ASR missed the word *ji'*^{4}*in*^{4} ('with', comitative) and as a result wrote the 1plInclusive as an independent pronoun and not an enclitic.
ASR	i^{3}ta$^{(2)}$=e^{2} ndi^{4} tan^{42} i^{4}in^{4} i^{3}ta^{2} tio^{3}o^{2} yu^{3}ku^{4} ya^{1} ba^{4}li^{4} coco nu^{14}u^{3} ñu'^{3}u^{4} sa^{3}kan^{4} i^{4}in^{4} i^{3}ta$^{(2)}$=e^{2}
Exp	i^{3}ta$^{(2)}$=e^{2} ndi^{4} tan^{42} i^{4}in^{4} i^{3}ta^{2} tio^{3}o^{2} yu^{3}ku^{4} ya^{1} ba^{4}li^{4} ko^{4}ko^{13} nu^{14}u^{3} ñu'^{3}u^{4} sa^{3}kan^{4} i^{4}in^{4} i^{3}ta$^{(2)}$=e^{2}
Note	ASR suggested Spanish 'coco' coconut for Mixtec *ko*^{4}*ko*^{13} ('to be abundant[plants]')

Table 3: Comparison of ASR and Expert transcription of two lines of recording (See Appendix A for full text).[4]

itics have alternative tones, depending on stem-final vowel and tone, respectively. Morphemes are stems, prefixes, and enclitics. The inflectional tone is not segmented out. The right boundary of a mora is a vowel or dipthong (with an optional <n> to indicate a nasalized vowel) followed by a tone. The left boundary is a preceding mora or word boundary. Thus the word ni^1-xa'^3nda^2=e^4 (completive-play(guitar)-1plIncl) would be divided into three morphemes ni^1-, xa'^3nda^2, =e^4 and into four morae given that xa'^3nda^2 would be segmented as xa'^3, nda^2.

We adopt recognizer output voting error reduction (ROVER) for the hypotheses combination (Fiscus, 1997). Three combinations have been evaluated: (1) ROVER among only linguistic units (i.e., morae, morpheme, and word), (2) ROVER among only sub-word units (in this case BPE); and (3) ROVER combination utilizing all seven systems.

4.2 Experimental results

Experimental results are presented in two subsections. The first addresses the performance of end-to-end ASR across three corpora, each with slightly different recording systems and content. As clear from the preceding discussion and illustrated in Table 2, in addition to training on the word unit, the YMC E2E ASR system was trained on six additional linguistic and informational sub-word units. ROVER was then used to produce composite systems in which the outputs of all seven systems were combined in three distinct manners. In all cases, ROVER combinations improved the result of any individual system, including the averages for either of the two types of units: linguistic and informational.

[4]Those interested in the recordings and associated ELAN files may visit Amith and Castillo García (2020).

ASR and ROVER across three YMC corpora: As evident in Table 2, across all corpora, informational units (BPE) are more efficient than linguistic units (word, morpheme, morae) in regards to ASR accuracy. The average CER/WER for linguistic units (rows A-C) was 10.4/19.5 (Exp[test]), 13.6/23.3 (FB), and 10.7/21.7 (VN). The corresponding figures for the BPE units (rows D–G) were 7.7/16.0 (Exp[test]), 9.7/19.5 (FB), and 6.8/16.8 (VN). In terms of percentage differences between the two types of units, the numbers are not insignificant. In regards to CER, performance improved from linguistic to informational units by 26.0, 28.7, and 36.4 percent across the Exp(Test), FB, and VN corpora. In regards to WER, performance improved by 17.9, 16.3, and 22.6 percent across the same three corpora.

The experiments also addressed two remaining questions: (1) does unweighted ROVER combination improve the accuracy of ASR results; (2) does adding linguistic unit performance units to the ROVER "voting pool" improve results over a combination of only BPE units. In regards to the first question: ROVER always improves results over any individual system (compare row H to rows A, B, and C, and row I to rows D, E, F, and G). The second question is addressed by comparing rows I (ROVER applied only to the four BPE results) to J (adding the ASR results for the three linguistic units into the combination). In only one of the six cases (CER of Exp[test]) does including word, morpheme, and morae lower the error rate from the results of a simple combination of the four BPE results (in this case from 7.6 [row I] to 7.4 [row J]). In one case, there is no change (CER for the VN corpus) and in four cases, including linguistic units slightly worsens the score from the combination of BPE units alone (row I with bold numbers). The implication of the preceding is that ASR using linguistic units yields significantly lower accuracy than ASR that uses informational (BPE) units. Combining the former with the latter in an unweighted ROVER system in most cases does not improve results. Whether a weighted combinatory system would do better is a question that will need to be explored.

5 Conclusion

A fundamental element of endangered language documentation is the creation of an extensive corpus of audio recordings accompanied by time-coded annotations in interlinear format. In the best of cases, such annotations include an accurate transcription aligned with morphological segmentation, glossing, and free translations. The degree to which such corpus creation is facilitated is the extrinsic metric by which ASR contributions to EL documentation should be considered. The project here discussed suggests a path to creating such corpora using end-to-end ASR technology to build up the resources (30–50 hours) necessary to train an ASR system with perhaps a 6–10 percent CER. Once this threshold is reached, it is unlikely that further improvement will significantly reduce the human effort needed to check the ASR output for accuracy. Indeed, even if there are no "errors" in the ASR output, confirmation of this through careful revision of the recording of the transcription would probably still take 3–4 hours. The effort reduction of 75 percent documented here for YMC is, therefore, approaching what may be considered the minimum amount of time to proofread transcription of natural speech in an endangered language.

This project has also demonstrated the advantage of using a practical orthography that separates affixes and clitics. In a relatively isolating language such as YM, such a system is not difficult for native speakers to write nor for ASR systems to learn. It has the advantage of creating a workflow in which parsed text is the direct output of E2E ASR. The error rate evaluations across the spectrum of corpora and CER/WER also demonstrate the advantage of using subword units such as BPE and subsequent processing by ROVER for system combination (see above and Table 2). The error rates could perhaps be lowered further as the corpus increases in size, as more care is placed on recording environments, and as normalization eliminates reported errors for minor discrepancies such as in transcription of back-channel cues. But such lower error rates will probably not significantly reduce the time for final revision.

A final question concerns additional steps once CER is reduced to 6–8 percent, and additional improvements to ASR would not significantly affect the human effort needed to produce a high-quality time-coded transcription and segmentation. Four topics are suggested: (1) address issues of noise, overlapping speech, and other challenging recording situations; (2) focus on transfer learning to related languages; (3) explore the impact of "colonialization" by a dominant language; and (4) focus additional ASR-supported corpus development on producing material for documentation of endangered cultural knowledge, a facet of documentation that is often absent from endangered language documentation projects.

Acknowledgments

The authors gratefully acknowledge the following support for documenting and studying Yoloxóchitl Mixtec: National Science Foundation, Documenting Endangered Languages (DEL): Awards 1761421, 1500595, 0966462 (Amith, PI on all three; the second was a collaborative project with SRI International, Award 1500738, Andreas Kathol, PI); Endangered Language Documentation Programme: Awards MDP0201, PPG0048 (Amith, PI on both). The following support is acknowledged for documenting and studying Highland Puebla Nahuat: NSF DEL: Awards: 1401178, 0756536 (Amith, PI on both awards); National Endowment for the Humanities, Preservation and Access: PD-50031-14 (Amith, PI); Endangered Language Documentation Programme: Award MDP0272 (Amith, PI); and the Comisión Nacional para el Conocimiento y Uso de la Biodiversidad, Mexico (Gerardo Salazar, PI; Amith, co-PI). The FOMA FST for Yoloxóchitl Mixtec was built by Jason Lilley, Amith, and Castillo with support from NSF DEL Award 1360670 (Christian DiCanio, PI).

Finally, the authors thank Shinji Watanabe both for his advice and guidance and for the key role he played in bringing together a field linguist, a native speaker, and a computational linguist for this project.

References

Oliver Adams, Trevor Cohn, Graham Neubig, Hilaria Cruz, Steven Bird, and Alexis Michaud. 2018. Evaluating phonemic transcription of low-resource tonal languages for language documentation. In *LREC 2018 (Language Resources and Evaluation Conference)*, pages 3356–3365.

Oliver Adams, Benjamin Galliot, Guillaume Wisniewski, Nicholas Lambourne, Ben Foley, Rahasya Sanders-Dwyer, Janet Wiles, Alexis Michaud, Séverine Guillaume, Laurent Besacier, et al. 2020. User-friendly automatic transcription of low-resource languages: Plugging ESPnet into Elpis. In *ComputEL-4: Fourth Workshop on the Use of Computational Methods in the Study of Endangered Languages*, pages 51–62.

Jonathan D. Amith and Rey Castillo García. 2020. Audio corpus of Yoloxóchitl Mixtec with accompanying time-coded transcriptons in ELAN. `http://www.openslr.org/89/`. Accessed: 2021-03-05.

Claude Barras, Edouard Geoffrois, Zhibiao Wu, and Mark Liberman. 1998. Transcriber: A free tool for segmenting, labeling and transcribing speech. In *First International Conference on Language Resources and Evaluation (LREC)*, pages 1373–1376.

Steven Bird and Gary Simons. 2003. Seven dimensions of portability for language documentation and description. *Language*, pages 557–582.

Malgorzata Ćavar, Damir Ćavar, and Hilaria Cruz. 2016. Endangered language documentation: Bootstrapping a Chatino speech corpus, forced aligner, ASR. In *Proceedings of the Tenth International Conference on Language Resources and Evaluation (LREC'16)*, pages 4004–4011.

Chung-Cheng Chiu, Tara N Sainath, Yonghui Wu, Rohit Prabhavalkar, Patrick Nguyen, Zhifeng Chen, Anjuli Kannan, Ron J Weiss, Kanishka Rao, Ekaterina Gonina, et al. 2018. State-of-the-art speech recognition with sequence-to-sequence models. In *2018 IEEE International Conference on Acoustics, Speech and Signal Processing (ICASSP)*, pages 4774–4778.

Nancy C Dorian. 1978. The fate of morphological complexity in language death: Evidence from East Sutherland Gaelic. *Language*, 54(3):590–609.

Jonathan G Fiscus. 1997. A post-processing system to yield reduced word error rates: Recognizer output voting error reduction (ROVER). In *1997 IEEE Workshop on Automatic Speech Recognition and Understanding Proceedings*, pages 347–354.

Ben Foley, Josh Arnold, Rolando Coto-Solano, Gautier Durantin, E Mark, Daan van Esch, Scott Heath, Frantisek Kratochvil, Zara Maxwell-Smith, David Nash, et al. 2018. Building speech recognition systems for language documentation: The CoEDL Endangered Language Pipeline and Inference System (ELPIS). *The 6th Intl. Workshop on Spoken Language Technologies for Under-Resourced Languages.*

Ben Foley, Alina Rakhi, Nicholas Lambourne, Nicholas Buckeridge, and Janet Wiles. 2019. ELPIS: An accessible speech-to-text tool. *Proc. Interspeech 2019*, pages 4624–4625.

Rey Castillo García. 2007. La fonología tonal del mixteco de Yoloxóchitl, Guerrero. Master's thesis, Centro de Investigaciones y Estudios Superiores en Antropología Social, Mexico City, Mexico. MA thesis in Lingüística Indoamericana.

Jeff Good. 2018. Reflections on the scope of language documentation. *Reflections on Language Documentation 20 Years after Himmelmann 1998. Language Documentation & Conservation, Special Publication 15*, pages 13–21.

Jeff Good, Julia Hirschberg, and Rambow Owen, editors. 2021. *Proceedings of the Workshop on Computational Methods for Endangered Languages*, volume 1-4.

Alex Graves and Navdeep Jaitly. 2014. Towards end-to-end speech recognition with recurrent neural networks. In *International Conference on Machine Learning*, pages 1764–1772.

Pengcheng Guo, Florian Boyer, Xuankai Chang, Tomoki Hayashi, Yosuke Higuchi, Hirofumi Inaguma, Naoyuki Kamo, Chenda Li, Daniel Garcia-Romero, Jiatong Shi, et al. 2020. Recent developments on ESPNet toolkit boosted by conformer. *arXiv preprint arXiv:2010.13956.*

Vishwa Gupta and Gilles Boulianne. 2020. Speech transcription challenges for resource constrained indigenous language Cree. In *Proceedings of the 1st Joint Workshop on Spoken Language Technologies for Under-resourced languages (SLTU) and Collaboration and Computing for Under-Resourced Languages (CCURL)*, pages 362–367.

Ken Hale, Michael Krauss, Lucille J Watahomigie, Akira Y Yamamoto, Colette Craig, LaVerne Masayesva Jeanne, and Nora C England. 1992. Endangered languages. *Language*, 68(1):1–42.

Kristine A Hildebrandt, Carmen Jany, and Wilson Silva. 2017a. *Documenting variation in endangered languages. Language Documentation & Conservation Special Publication 14.* University of Hawai'i Press.

Kristine A Hildebrandt, Carmen Jany, and Wilson Silva. 2017b. *Introduction: Documenting variation in endangered languages*, pages 1–7. University of Hawai'i Press.

Nikolaus P Himmelmann. 1998. Documentary and descriptive linguistics. *Linguistics*, 36:161–196.

Nikolaus P Himmelmann. 2018. Meeting the transcription challenge. *Reflections on Language Documentation 20 Years after Himmelmann 1998. Language Documentation & Conservation, Special Publication 15*, pages 33–40.

Nils Hjortnaes, Niko Partanen, Michael Rießler, and Francis M Tyers. 2020. Towards a speech recognizer for Komi: An endangered and low-resource Uralic language. In *Proceedings of the Sixth International Workshop on Computational Linguistics of Uralic Languages*, pages 31–37.

Robbie Jimerson and Emily Prud'hommeaux. 2018. ASR for documenting acutely under-resourced indigenous languages. In *Proceedings of the Eleventh International Conference on Language Resources and Evaluation (LREC 2018)*.

Robert Jimerson, Kruthika Simha, Ray Ptucha, and Emily Prud'hommeaux. 2018. Improving ASR output for endangered language documentation. In *The 6th Intl. Workshop on Spoken Language Technologies for Under-Resourced Languages*.

Shigeki Karita, Nanxin Chen, Tomoki Hayashi, Takaaki Hori, Hirofumi Inaguma, Ziyan Jiang, Masao Someki, Nelson Enrique Yalta Soplin, Ryuichi Yamamoto, Xiaofei Wang, et al. 2019a. A comparative study on transformer vs. RNN in speech applications. In *2019 IEEE Automatic Speech Recognition and Understanding Workshop (ASRU)*, pages 449–456.

Shigeki Karita, Nelson Enrique Yalta Soplin, Shinji Watanabe, Marc Delcroix, Atsunori Ogawa, and Tomohiro Nakatani. 2019b. Improving transformer-based end-to-end speech recognition with connectionist temporal classification and language model integration. *Proc. Interspeech 2019*, pages 1408–1412.

Taku Kudo and John Richardson. 2018. SentencePiece: A simple and language independent subword tokenizer and detokenizer for neural text processing. In *Proceedings of the 2018 Conference on Empirical Methods in Natural Language Processing: System Demonstrations*, pages 66–71.

Kohei Matsuura, Sei Ueno, Masato Mimura, Shinsuke Sakai, and Tatsuya Kawahara. 2020. Speech corpus of Ainu folklore and end-to-end speech recognition for Ainu language. In *Proceedings of The 12th Language Resources and Evaluation Conference*, pages 2622–2628.

Bradley McDonnell, Andrea L Berez-Kroeker, and Gary Holton. 2018. *Reflections on Language Documentation 20 Years after Himmelmann 1998. Language Documentation & Conservation, Special Publication 15*. University of Hawai'i Press.

Alexis Michaud, Oliver Adams, Trevor Anthony Cohn, Graham Neubig, and Séverine Guillaume. 2018. Integrating automatic transcription into the language documentation workflow: Experiments with Na data and the Persephone toolkit. *Language Documentation & Conservation*, 12.

Vikramjit Mitra, Andreas Kathol, Jonathan D Amith, and Rey Castillo García. 2016. Automatic speech transcription for low-resource languages: The case of Yoloxóchitl Mixtec (Mexico). In *Proc. Interspeech 2016*, pages 3076–3080.

Simon Musgrave and Nicholas Thieberger. 2021. The language documentation quartet. In *Proceedings of the Workshop on Computational Methods for Endangered Languages*, volume 1, pages 6–12.

Enrique L Palancar, Jonathan D Amith, and Rey Castillo García. 2016. Verbal inflection in Yoloxóchitl Mixtec. *Tone and inflection: New facts and new perspectives*, pages 295–336.

Ngoc-Quan Pham, Thai-Son Nguyen, Jan Niehues, Markus Müller, and Alex Waibel. 2019. Very deep self-attention networks for end-to-end speech recognition. *Proceedings of Interspeech 2019*, pages 66–70.

George Saon, Gakuto Kurata, Tom Sercu, Kartik Audhkhasi, Samuel Thomas, Dimitrios Dimitriadis, Xiaodong Cui, Bhuvana Ramabhadran, Michael Picheny, Lynn-Li Lim, et al. 2017. English conversational telephone speech recognition by humans and machines. *Proc. Interspeech 2017*, pages 132–136.

Frank Seifart, Nicholas Evans, Harald Hammarström, and Stephen C Levinson. 2018. Language documentation twenty-five years on. *Language*, 94(4):e324–e345.

Jiatong Shi, Jonathan D. Amith, Rey Castillo García, Esteban Guadalupe Sierra, Kevin Duh, and Shinji Watanabe. 2021. Leveraging end-to-end ASR for endangered language documentation: An empirical study on Yoloxóchitl Mixtec. *arXiv preprint arXiv:2101.10877*.

Jorge A Suárez. 1983. *The Mesoamerican Indian languages*. Cambridge University Press.

Bao Thai, Robert Jimerson, Raymond Ptucha, and Emily Prud'hommeaux. 2020. Fully convolutional ASR for less-resourced endangered languages. In *Proceedings of the 1st Joint Workshop on Spoken Language Technologies for Under-resourced languages (SLTU) and Collaboration and Computing for Under-Resourced Languages (CCURL)*, pages 126–130.

Shinji Watanabe, Florian Boyer, Xuankai Chang, Pengcheng Guo, Tomoki Hayashi, Yosuke Higuchi, Takaaki Hori, Wen-Chin Huang, Hirofumi Inaguma, Naoyuki Kamo, et al. 2020. The 2020 ESPNet update: New features, broadened applications, performance improvements, and future plans. *arXiv preprint arXiv:2012.13006*.

Shinji Watanabe, Takaaki Hori, Shigeki Karita, Tomoki Hayashi, Jiro Nishitoba, Yuya Unno, Nelson-Enrique Yalta Soplin, Jahn Heymann, Matthew Wiesner, Nanxin Chen, et al. 2018. ESPNet: End-to-end speech processing toolkit. *Proc. Interspeech 2018*, pages 2207–2211.

Shinji Watanabe, Takaaki Hori, Suyoun Kim, John R Hershey, and Tomoki Hayashi. 2017. Hybrid CTC/attention architecture for end-to-end speech recognition. *IEEE Journal of Selected Topics in Signal Processing*, 11(8):1240–1253.

Douglas Whalen and Ćavar Damir. 2012. Collaborative research: Automatically annotated repository of digital video and audio resources community (AARDVARC). https://nsf.gov/awardsearch/showAward?AWD_ID=1244713. Accessed: 2021-03-05.

Peter Wittenburg, Hennie Brugman, Albert Russel, Alex Klassmann, and Han Sloetjes. 2006. ELAN: A professional framework for multimodality research. In *5th International Conference on Language Resources and Evaluation (LREC 2006)*, pages 1556–1559.

A Analysis of ASR errors in one recording from the FB corpus

Unique identifier: 2017-12-01-b
Speakers: Constantino Teodoro Bautista and Esteban Guadalupe Sierra
Spanish: The first 13 seconds (3 segments) of the recording were of a Spanish speaker describing the plant being collected (*Passiflora biflora* Lam.) and have not been included below.
Note: A total 16 out of 33 segments/utterances are without ASR error. These are marked with an asterisk.
Original recording and ELAN file: Download at `http://www.balsas-nahuatl.org/NLP`

4*. 00:00:13.442 –> 00:00:17.105
ASR constantino teodoro bautista
Exp Constantino Teodoro Bautista.
Notes: ASR does not output caps or punctuation.

5*. 00:00:17.105 –> 00:00:19.477
ASR ya^{1} mi^{4}i^{4} tu^{1}tu’^{4}un^{4} ku^{3}rra^{42}
Exp Ya^{1} mi^{4}i^{4} tu^{1}tu’^{4}un^{4} ku^{3}rra^{42}
Notes: No errors in the ASR hypothesis.

6. 00:00:19.477 –> 00:00:23.688
ASR ta^{1} mas^{4}tru^{2} tela ya^{1} i^{3}chi^{4} ya^{3}tin^{3} ye’^{1}4e^{4} ku^{3}rra^{42} ndi^{4} covalentín yo’^{4}o^{4}
Exp ta^{1} mas^{4}tru^{2} Tele ya^{1} i^{3}chi^{4} ya^{3}tin^{3} ye’^{1}4e^{4} ku^{3}rra^{42} Nicu Valentín yo’^{4}o^{4},
Notes: ASR missed the proper name, Nicu Valentín (short for Nicolás Valentín) but did get the accent on Valentín, while mistaking the first name Nicu for *ndi*^{4} co[valentín]

7*. 00:00:23.688 –> 00:00:31.086
ASR ya^{1} i^{3}chi^{4} kwa’^{1}an$^{(1)}$=e^{4} tan^{3} xa^{1}a$^{(1)}$=e^{4} ku^{3}rra^{42} chi^{4}ñu^{3} ka^{4}chi^{2}=na^{1} ya^{1} kwa’^{1}an^{1} ni^{1}nu^{3} yo’^{4}o^{4} ju^{13}ta’^{3}an^{2}=ndu^{1} ya^{1} ko^{4}ndo^{3} kwi^{1}yo’^{1}o^{4} ndi^{3}ku’^{3}un^{3}
Exp ya^{1} i^{3}chi^{4} kwa’^{1}an$^{(1)}$=e^{4} tan^{3} xa^{1}a$^{(1)}$=e^{4} ku^{3}rra^{42} chi^{4}ñu^{3} ka^{4}chi^{2}=na^{1} ya^{1} kwa’^{1}an^{1} ni^{1}nu^{3} yo’^{4}o^{4} ju^{13}ta’^{3}an^{2}=ndu^{1} ya^{1} ko^{4}ndo^{3} kwi^{1}yo’^{1}o^{4} ndi^{3}ku’^{3}un^{3}
Notes: No errors in the ASR hypothesis.

8*. 00:00:31.086 –> 00:00:37.318
ASR kwi^{1}yo’^{1}o^{4} ndi^{3}ku’^{3}un^{3} kwi^{4}i^{24} ka^{4}chi^{2}=na^{1} yo’^{4}o^{4} ndi^{4} ya^{1} yo’^{4}o^{4} ndi^{4} xa’^{4}nu^{3} su^{4}kun^{1} mi^{4}i^{4} ti^{4} ba^{42} i^{4}yo$^{(2)}$=a^{2} mi^{4}i^{4} bi^{1}xin^{3} tan^{3}
Exp kwi^{1}yo’^{1}o^{4} ndi^{3}ku’^{3}un^{3} kwi^{4}i^{24} ka^{4}chi^{2}=na^{1} yo’^{4}o^{4} ndi^{4} ya^{1} yo’^{4}o^{4} ndi^{4} xa’^{4}nu^{3} su^{4}kun$^{(1)}$=a^{1} mi^{4}i^{4} ti^{4} ba^{42} i^{4}yo$^{(2)}$=a^{2} mi^{4}i^{4} bi^{1}xin^{3} tan^{3}
Notes: The ASR hypothesis missed the inanimate enclitic after the verb *su*^{4}*kun*^{1} and as a result failed to mark the elision of the stem-final low tone as would occur before a following low-tone enclitic.

9. 00:00:37.318 –> 00:00:42.959
ASR yo’^{3}o^{4} xi^{13}i^{2} ba^{42} ndi^{4} ba’^{1}a^{3}=e^{2} ku^{3}-nu’^{3}ni^{2} tu^{3}tun^{4} kwi^{3}so$^{(3)}$=e^{4} mi^{4}i^{4} ti^{4} ba^{42} ko^{14}o^{3} yo’^{3}o^{4} kwa’^{1}an^{1} yo^{4}o^{4} xa^{14}ku’^{1}u^{1}
Exp yo’^{3}o^{4} xi^{1}i^{32} ba^{42} ndi^{4} ba’^{1}a^{3}=e^{2} ku^{3}-nu’^{3}ni^{2} tu^{3}tun^{4} kwi^{3}so$^{(3)}$=e^{4} mi^{4}i^{4} ti^{4} ba^{42} ko^{14}o^{3} yo’^{3}o^{4} kwa’^{1}an^{1} ji’^{4}in$^{(4)}$=o^{4} xa^{14}ku’^{1}u^{1},
Notes: ASR missed the word *ji’*^{4}*in*^{4} (‘with’, comitative) and as a result wrote the 1plInclusive as an independent pronoun and not an enclitic.

10. 00:00:42.959 –> 00:00:49.142
ASR i^{3}ta$^{(2)}$=e^{2} ndi^{4} tan^{42} i^{4}in^{4} i^{3}ta^{2} tio^{3}o^{2} yu^{3}ku^{4} ya^{1} ba^{4}li^{4} coco nu^{14}u^{3} ñu’^{3}u^{4} sa^{3}kan^{4} i^{4}in^{4} i^{3}ta$^{(2)}$=e^{2}

Exp i^{3}ta$^{(2)}$=e^{2} ndi^{4} tan^{42} i^{4}in^{4} i^{3}ta^{2} tio^{3}o^{2} yu^{3}ku^{4} ya^{1} ba^{4}li^{4} ko^{4}ko^{13} nu^{14}u^{3} ñu'^{3}u^{4} sa^{3}kan^{4} i^{4}in^{4} i^{3}ta$^{(2)}$=e^{2},

Notes: ASR suggested Spanish 'coco' coconut for Mixtec *ko^{4}ko^{13}* ('to be abundant[plants]'). Note that 'coco' was spelled as it is in Spanish and no tones were included in the ASR output.

11. 00:00:49.142 –> 00:00:53.458

ASR la^{3}tun^{4}=ni^{42} ya^{3}a$^{(3)}$=e^{2} tan^{3} ti^{1}xin^{3}=a^{2} ndi^{4} ya^{1} nde'^{3}e^{4} ba^{42} tan^{3} o^{4}ra^{2} xi^{4}yo^{13} ndu^{1}u^{4}=a^{2} ndi^{4} ya^{1} kwi^{4}i^{24} ba^{43}

Exp la^{3}tun^{4}=ni^{42} ya^{3}a$^{(3)}$=e^{2} tan^{3} ti^{1}xin^{3}=a^{2} ndi^{4} ya^{1} nde'^{3}e^{4} ba^{42} tan^{3} o^{4}ra^{2} xi^{4}yo^{13} ndu^{1}u^{4}=a^{2} ndi^{4} ya^{1} kwi^{4}i^{24} ba^{42},

Notes: ASR missed tone 42, writing 43 instead. Note that the two tone patterns are alternate forms of the same word, the copula used in regards to objects.

12*. 00:00:53.458 –> 00:00:57.279

ASR tan^{3} o^{4}ra^{2} chi^{4}chi^{13}=a^{2} ndi^{4} ndu^{1}u^{4} nde'^{3}e^{4} ku^{4}u^{4} ndu^{1}u^{4}=a^{3}

Exp tan^{3} o^{4}ra^{2} chi^{4}chi^{13}=a^{2} ndi^{4} ndu^{1}u^{4} nde'^{3}e^{4} ku^{4}u^{4} ndu^{1}u^{4}=a^{3}.

Notes: No errors in the ASR hypothesis.

13*. 00:00:57.279 –> 00:01:02.728

ASR yu^{1}ku$^{(1)}$=a^{1} ndi^{4} tan^{42} i^{4}in$^{(4)}$=a^{2} ni^{1}-xa'^{3}nda^{2}=e^{4} tan^{42} i^{4}in^{4} yu^{1}ku^{1} tun^{4} si^{13}su^{2} kan^{4} sa^{3}kan^{4} i^{4}in^{4} yu^{1}ku$^{(1)}$=a^{1} tan^{3} ndi^{4}

Exp Yu^{1}ku$^{(1)}$=a^{1} ndi^{4} tan^{42} i^{4}in$^{(4)}$=a^{2} ni^{1}-xa'^{3}nda^{2}=e^{4} tan^{42} i^{4}in^{4} yu^{1}ku^{1} tun^{4} si^{13}su^{2} kan^{4} sa^{3}kan^{4} i^{4}in^{4} yu^{1}ku$^{(1)}$=a^{1} tan^{3} ndi^{4}

Notes: No errors in the ASR hypothesis.

14. 00:01:02.728 –> 00:01:06.296

ASR su^{14}u^{3} ya^{1} xa'^{4}nda^{2}=na^{1} ba^{42} ndi^{4} su^{14}u^{3} ki^{3}ti^{4} ja^{4}xi^{24}=ri^{4} sa^{3}kan^{4} i^{4}in^{4} yu^{1}ku^{1} mi^{4}i^{4} ba$^{(3)}$=e^{3}

Exp su^{14}u^{3} ya^{1} xa'^{4}nda^{2}=na^{1} ba^{42} tan^{3} ni^{4} su^{14}u^{3} ki^{3}ti^{4} ja^{4}xi^{24}=ri^{4}, sa^{3}kan^{4} i^{4}in^{4} yu^{1}ku^{1} mi^{4}i^{4} ba$^{(3)}$=e^{3},

Notes: ASR mistakenly proposed *ndi^{4}* for *tan^{3} ni^{4}*.

15*. 00:01:06.296 –> 00:01:10.981

ASR tan^{3} ya^{1} xa'^{4}nu^{3} su^{4}kun$^{(1)}$=a^{1} mi^{4}i^{4} ti^{4} ba^{42} sa^{3}ba^{3} xia^{4}an^{4} ku^{3}ta'^{3}an^{2}=e^{4}=e^{2} ndi^{4} xa'^{4}nu$^{(3)}$=a^{2} kwa^{1}nda^{3}a$^{(3)}$=e^{2} nda'^{3}a^{4} i^{3}tun^{4}

Exp tan^{3} ya^{1} xa'^{4}nu^{3} su^{4}kun$^{(1)}$=a^{1} mi^{4}i^{4} ti^{4} ba^{42} sa^{3}ba^{3} xia^{4}an^{4} ku^{3}ta'^{3}an^{2}=e^{4}=e^{2} ndi^{4} xa'^{4}nu$^{(3)}$=a^{2} kwa^{1}nda^{3}a$^{(3)}$=e^{2} nda'^{3}a^{4} i^{3}tun^{4}

Notes: No errors in the ASR hypothesis.

16. 00:01:10.981 –> 00:01:14.768

ASR u^{1}xi^{1} an^{4} nda^{1} xa'^{1}un^{1} metru ka^{1}a^{3} mi^{4}i^{4} i^{4}yo^{2} i^{3}tun^{4} ndo^{3}o^{3} tan^{3} ko^{4}ko^{13}=a^{2} kwa^{1}nde^{3}e^{3} ni^{1}nu^{3}

Exp u^{1}xi^{1} an^{4} nda^{1} xa'^{1}un^{1} metru ka^{1}a^{3} mi^{4}i^{4} i^{4}yo^{2} i^{3}tun^{4} ndo^{3}o^{3} tan^{3} ko^{4}ko^{13}=a^{2} kwa^{1}nda^{3}a$^{(3)}$=e^{2} ni^{1}nu^{3},

Notes: Not only did ASR recognize the Spanish *metru* borrowing but wrote it according to our conventions, without tone. Note that the correct underlying form *kwa^{1}nda^{3}a$^{(3)}$=e^{2}* (progressive of 'to climb [e.g., a vine]' with 3sg enclitic for inanimates =e^{2}) surfaces as *kwa^{1}nde^{3}e^{2}* quite close to the ASR hypothesis of *kwa^{1}nde^{3}e^{3}*, which exists, but as a distinct word (progressive of 'to enter[pl]').

17*. 00:01:14.768 –> 00:01:18.281

ASR mi^{4}i^{4} ba^{143} xa'^{4}nda^{2}=na$^{(1)}$=e^{1} ndi^{4} xa'^{4}nu^{3} su^{4}kun$^{(1)}$=a^{1}

Exp mi^{4}i^{4} ba^{143} xa'^{4}nda^{2}=na$^{(1)}$=e^{1} ndi^{4} xa'^{4}nu^{3} su^{4}kun$^{(1)}$=a^{1},

Notes: No errors in the ASR hypothesis.

18*. 00:01:18.281 –> 00:01:21.487
ASR ya^{1} kan^{4} ku^{4}u^{4} kwi^{1}yo'^{1}o^{4} ju^{13}ta'^{3}an^{2}=ndu^{1} i^{3}chi^{4} kwa'^{1}an^{1} ku^{3}rra^{42} chi^{4}ñu^{3} yo'^{4}o^{4}
Exp ya^{1} kan^{4} ku^{4}u^{4} kwi^{1}yo'^{1}o^{4} ju^{13}ta'^{3}an^{2}=ndu^{1} i^{3}chi^{4} kwa'^{1}an^{1} ku^{3}rra^{42} chi^{4}ñu^{3} yo'^{4}o^{4}.
Notes: No errors in the ASR hypothesis.

19*. 00:01:21.487 –> 00:01:24.658
ASR esteban guadalupe sierra
Exp Esteban Guadalupe Sierra.
Notes: ASR does not output caps or punctuation.

20. 00:01:24.658 –> 00:01:27.614
ASR ya^{1} ko^{4}ndo^{3} kwi^{1}yo'^{1}o^{4} ndi^{13}-kwi^{3}so^{3}=ndu^{2} ya^{1}
Exp ya^{1} ko^{4}ndo^{3} kwi^{1}yo'^{1}o^{4} ndi^{13}-kwi^{3}so^{3}=ndu^{2} ya^{1}
Notes: No errors in the ASR hypothesis.

21. 00:01:27.614 –> 00:01:33.096
ASR sa^{3}kan^{4} tan^{3} xa^{1}a$^{(1)}$=e^{4} ku^{3}rra^{42} chi^{4}ñu^{3} ya^{1} ja^{1}ta^{4} ku^{3}rra^{42} ta^{1} marspele yo'^{4}o^{4} ndi^{4}
Exp sa^{3}kan^{4} tan^{3} xa^{1}a$^{(1)}$=e^{4} ku^{3}rra^{42} chi^{4}ñu^{3} ya^{1} ja^{1}ta^{4} ku^{3}rra^{42} ta^{1} mas^{4}tru^{2} Tele yo'^{4}o^{4} ndi^{4}
Notes: ASR missed the Spanish *mas^{4}tru^{2}* Tele (teacher Tele(sforo)) and hypothesized a nonsense word in Spanish (note absence of tone as would be the case for Spanish loans).

22. 00:01:33.096 –> 00:01:39.611
ASR kwi^{1}yo'^{1}o^{4} ndi^{3}ku'^{3}un^{3} ba^{3} kwi^{1}yo'^{1}o^{4} ndi^{3}ku'^{3}un^{3} ka^{1}a^{3} ndi^{4} ko^{14}o^{3} u^{1}bi^{1} u^{1}ni^{1} nu^{14}u$^{(3)}$=a^{2} ña^{1}a^{4} ndi^{4} i^{3}nda^{14} nu^{14}u^{3} sa^{3}kan^{4} ba^{3} ba^{42}
Exp kwi^{1}yo'^{1}o^{4} ndi^{3}ku'^{3}un^{3} ba^{43}, kwi^{1}yo'^{1}o^{4} ndi^{3}ku'^{3}un^{3} ka^{1}a^{3} ndi^{4} ko^{14}o^{3} u^{1}bi^{1} u^{1}ni^{1} nu^{14}u$^{(3)}$=a^{2} ndi^{4} i^{3}nda^{14} nu^{14}u^{3} sa^{3}kan^{4} ba^{3} ba^{42},
Notes: ASR mistook the copula *ba^{43}* and instead hypothesized the modal *ba^{3}*. ASR also inserted a word not present in the signal, *ña^{1}a^{4}* ('over there').

23. 00:01:39.611 –> 00:01:43.781
ASR ya^{1} ka'^{4}an^{2}=na^{1} ji'^{4}in^{4} ku^{4}u^{4} kwi^{1}yo'^{1}o^{4} ndi^{3}ku'^{3}un^{3} kwi'^{4}i$^{2(4)}$=o^{4} tan^{3}
Exp ya^{1} ka'^{4}an^{2}=na^{1} ji'^{4}in^{4} ku^{4}u^{4} kwi^{1}yo'^{1}o^{4} ndi^{3}ku'^{3}un^{3} kwi'^{4}i^{24} yo'^{4}o^{4} tan^{3}
Notes: ASR mistook the adverbial *yo'^{4}o^{4}* ('here') as the enclitic *=o^{4}* (1plIncl) and as a result also hypothesized stem final tone elision (4).

24. 00:01:43.781 –> 00:01:49.347
ASR ba^{14}3 bi^{4}xi^{1} i^{4}in$^{(4)}$=a^{2} ndi^{4} kwi^{1}yo'^{1}o^{4} kwa^{1}nda^{3}a^{3} nda'^{3}a^{4} i^{3}tun^{4} ba^{3} tan^{3} kwi^{1}yo'^{1}o^{4}
Exp ba^{14}3 bi^{4}xi^{1} i^{4}in$^{(4)}$=a^{2} ndi^{4} kwi^{1}yo'^{1}o^{4} kwa^{1}nda^{3}a^{3} nda'^{3}a^{4} i^{3}tun^{4} ba^{42} tan^{3} kwi^{1}yo'^{1}o^{4}
Notes: As in segment #22 above, ASR mistook the copula, here *ba^{4}*, and instead hypothesized the modal *ba^{3}*.

25. 00:01:49.347 –> 00:01:55.001
ASR ndi^{3}i^{4} ba^{42} ko^{14}o^{3} tu^{4}mi^{4} ja^{1}ta^{4}=e^{2} ya^{1} kan^{4} ndi^{4} i^{4}yo^{2} i^{4}yo^{2} xi^{1}ki^{4}=a^{2} i^{4}in^{4} tan^{3}
Exp ndi^{3}i^{4} ba^{42} ko^{14}o^{3} tu^{4}mi^{4} ja^{1}ta^{4}=e^{2} tan^{3} ndi^{4} i^{4}yo^{2} i^{4}yo^{2} xi^{1}ki^{4}=a^{2} i^{4}in^{4} tan^{3}
Notes: ASR missed the conjunction *tan^{3}* ('and') and instead wrote *ya^{1} kan^{4}* ('that one').

26*. 00:01:55.001 –> 00:02:00.110
ASR ya^{1} ba'^{1}a^{3}=e^{2} ndi^{4} ba'^{1}a^{3}=e^{2} ju^{4}-nu'^{3}ni^{2} tu^{3}tun^{4} i^{4}xa^{3}=na^{2}
Exp ya^{1} ba'^{1}a^{3}=e^{2} ndi^{4} ba'^{1}a^{3}=e^{2} ju^{4}-nu'^{3}ni^{2} tu^{3}tun^{4} i^{4}xa^{3}=na^{2},
Notes: No errors in the ASR hypothesis.

27*. 00:02:00.110 –> 00:02:04.380
ASR na^{1}kwa^{4}chi^{3} tu^{3} ndi^{4} chi^{3}ñu^{3}=ni^{42}=na^{1} ka^{3}ya^{2}=na$^{(1)}$=e^{1} su^{4}-kwe^{1}kun^{1}=na^{1} i^{3}na^{2} ju^{4}si^{4}ki^{24} ba^{3}=na^{3}
Exp na^{1}kwa^{4}chi^{3} tu^{3} ndi^{4} chi^{3}ñu^{3}=ni^{42}=na^{1} ka^{3}ya^{2}=na$^{(1)}$=e^{1} su^{4}-kwe^{1}kun^{1}=na^{1} i^{3}na^{2} ju^{4}si^{4}ki^{24} ba^{3}=na^{3},
Notes: No errors in the ASR hypothesis.

28*. 00:02:04.380 –> 00:02:06.242
ASR a^{1}chi^{1} kwi^{1}yo'^{1}o^{4} nde^{3}e^{4} ba^{43}
Exp a^{1}chi^{1} kwi^{1}yo'^{1}o^{4} nde^{3}e^{4} ba^{43},
Notes: No errors in the ASR hypothesis.

29*. 00:02:06.242 –> 00:02:08.865
ASR tan^{42} ka'^{4}an^{2} ta^{1} ta^{4}u^{3}ni^{2} constantino yo'^{4}o^{4} ndi^{4}
Exp tan^{42} ka'^{4}an^{2} ta^{1} ta^{4}u^{3}ni^{2} Constantino yo'^{4}o^{4} ndi^{4}
Notes: No errors in the ASR hypothesis.

30*. 00:02:08.865 –> 00:02:13.473
ASR i^{3}ta$^{(2)}$=e^{2} ndi^{4} tan^{42} i^{4}in^{4} i^{3}ta^{2} ya^{1}kan^{3} kwi^{1}yo'^{1}o^{4} ya^{1} i^{3}ta^{2} tio^{3}o^{2} kan^{4} sa^{3}kan^{4} i^{4}in^{4} i^{3}ta$^{(2)}$=e^{2} tan^{3}
Exp i^{3}ta$^{(2)}$=e^{2} ndi^{4} tan^{42} i^{4}in^{4} i^{3}ta^{2}, ya^{1}kan^{3}, kwi^{1}yo'^{1}o^{4} ya^{1} i^{3}ta^{2} tio^{3}o^{2} kan^{4} sa^{3}kan^{4} i^{4}in^{4} i^{3}ta$^{(2)}$=e^{2} tan^{3}
Notes: No errors in the ASR hypothesis, the fifth consecutive annotation without an ASR error.

31. 00:02:13.473 –> 00:02:17.927
ASR xi^{4}yo^{13} a^{1}su^{3} tan^{42} i^{4}in^{4} tio^{1}o^{32} i^{4}in$^{(4)}$=a^{2} ba^{4}li^{4} ko^{4}ndo^{3} ndu'^{1}u^{4}=a^{2} ya^{1} kwi^{4}i^{24} ba^{42} na^{4}
Exp xi^{4}yo^{13} a^{1}su^{3} tan^{42} i^{4}in^{4} tio^{3}o^{2} i^{4}in$^{(4)}$=a^{2} ba^{4}li^{4} ko^{4}ndo^{3} ndu^{1}u^{4}=a^{2}, ya^{1} kwi^{4}i^{24} ba^{42} na^{4}
Notes: ASR missed a word, writing *tio*^{1}*o*^{32} (a word that does not exist) for *tio*^{3}*o*^{2} (the passion fruit, *Passiflora* sp.). It also miswrote *ndu*^{1}*u*^{4} (fruit) as *ndu'*^{1}*u*^{4} a verb ('to fall from an upright position').

32*. 00:02:17.927 –> 00:02:21.014
ASR i'^{4}i$^{(3)}$=a^{2} tan^{3} na^{4} chi^{4}chi^{13}=a^{2} ndi^{4} ya^{1} nde'^{3}e^{4} ba^{42}
Exp i'^{4}i$^{(3)}$=a^{2} tan^{3} na^{4} chi^{4}chi^{13}=a^{2} ndi^{4} ya^{1} nde'^{3}e^{4} ba^{42},
Notes: No errors in the ASR hypothesis.

33. 00:02:21.014 –> 00:02:25.181
ASR ya^{1} mi^{4}i^{4} bi^{1}xin^{3} ya^{3}tin^{3} yu'^{3}u^{4} yu^{3}bi^{2} kan^{4} ba^{42} xi^{4}yo$^{1(3)}$=a^{3}
Exp ya^{1} mi^{4}i^{4} bi^{1}xin^{3} ya^{3}tin^{3} yu'^{3}u^{4} yu^{3}bi^{2} i^{3}kan^{4} ba^{42} xi^{4}yo$^{1(3)}$=a^{3}.
Notes: ASR missed the initial *i*^{3} in *i*^{3}*kan*^{4} ('there'). It is to be noted that *kan*^{4} is an alternate form of *i*^{3}*kan*^{4}.

34*. 00:02:25.181 –> 00:02:27.790
ASR ya^{1} kan^{4} ba^{42} ndi^{13}-kwi^{3}so^{3}=ndu^{2} yo'^{4}o^{4}
Exp Ya^{1} kan^{4} ba^{42} ndi^{13}-kwi^{3}so^{3}=ndu^{2} yo'^{4}o^{4},
Notes: No errors in the ASR hypothesis.

35*. 00:02:27.790 –> 00:02:32.887
ASR tan^{3} ta^{1} ta^{4}u^{3}ni^{2} fernando yo'^{4}o^{4} ndi^{4} ji^{4}ni^{2}=ra$^{(1)}$=e^{1} ndi^{4} ji^{4}ni^{2}=ra$^{(1)}$=e^{1} ya^{1} sa^{3}kan^{4} i^{4}yo$^{(2)}$=a^{2} tan^{3}
Exp tan^{3} ta^{1} ta^{4}u^{3}ni^{2} Fernando yo'^{4}o^{4} ndi^{4} ji^{4}ni^{2}=ra$^{(1)}$=e^{1} ndi^{4} ji^{4}ni^{2}=ra$^{(1)}$=e^{1} ya^{1} sa^{3}kan^{4} i^{4}yo$^{(2)}$=a^{2} tan^{3}

Notes: No errors in the ASR hypothesis.

36. 00:02:32.887 –> 00:02:41.884
ASR ji^{14}ni^{2}=ra^{1} sa^{1}a^{3} na^{3}ni^{4}=a^{3} tan^{3} ni^{14}-ndi^{3}-kwi^{3}so^{3} ndu^{3}-ta^{1}chi^{4}=ra^{2} ji'^{4}in$^{(4)}$=a^{2} a^{1}chi^{1} ji^{14}ni^{2}=ra^{1} nda^{4}a$^{(2)}$=e^{2} ba'^{1}a$^{(3)}$=e^{3}
Exp ji^{14}ni^{2}=ra^{1} sa^{1}a^{3} na^{3}ni^{4}=a^{3}, tan^{3} ni^{14}-ndi^{3}-kwi^{3}so^{3}=ndu^{2} ta^{1}chi^{4}=ra^{2} ji'^{4}in$^{(4)}$=a^{2} a^{1}chi^{1} ji^{14}ni^{2}=ra^{1} nda^{4}a$^{(2)}$=e^{2} ba'^{1}a$^{(3)}$=e^{3}.
Notes: ASR hypothesized *ndu*^{3} as a verbal prefix instead of the correct interpretation as a person-marking enclitic (1plExcl) that is attached to the preceding verb.

A finite-state morphological analyser for Paraguayan Guaraní

Anastasia Kuznetsova[◇†]
◇ Department of Computer Science
Indiana University
Bloomington, IN
anakuzne@iu.edu

Francis M. Tyers[†]
† Department of Linguistics
Indiana University
Bloomington, IN
ftyers@iu.edu

Abstract

This article describes the development of morphological analyser for Paraguayan Guaraní, an agglutinative indigenous language spoken by nearly 6 million people in South America. The implementation of our analyser uses HFST (Helsiki Finite State Technology) to model morphotactics and phonological processes occurring in Guaraní. We assess the efficacy of the approach on publically available corpora and find that the naïve coverage of analyser is between 86% and 91%.

1 Introduction

Morphological modelling, under which we subsume both morphological analysis and morphological generation is one of the core tasks in the field of natural language processing. It is used in a wide variety of areas, including but not limited to: orthographic correction (Pirinen and Lindén, 2014), electronic dictionaries (Johnson et al., 2013), morphological segmentation for machine translation (Tiedemann et al., 2015; Forcada et al., 2011), as an additional knowledge source for parsing languages with non-trivial morphology (Gökırmak and Tyers, 2017; Tyers and Ravishankar, 2018), and in computer-assisted language-learning applications (Ledbetter and Dickinson, 2016).

In this article we describe a morphological analyser for Paraguayan Guaraní (in Guaraní: *Avañe'ẽ*, ISO-639: gn, grn), one of the official languages of Paraguay. Although Guaraní is an official language and spoken by over six million people throughout the South American continent (Eberhard et al., 2018), it does not benefit from a wide range of freely-available data and tools for building natural language processing systems. If we use Wikipedia as a proxy for viability of crowdsourcing linguistic data, as in (Moshagen et al., 2014), we see that although Guaraní has a large speaker population, the potential for crowdsourcing and big freely-available data is limited.[1]

The absence of large amounts of textual data means that data-driven approaches are hard to apply. In addition, supervised approaches, including neural networks which have become increasingly popular, require large amounts of annotated data to be trained. This in turn requires large numbers of trained annotators to annotate it. Given that neither of these are available, we apply tried-and-tested technique relying on formal linguistic description by means of finite-state transducers. Finite-state techniques have been widely applied to morphological modelling of many languages and are state of the art for many languages, especially those with non-trivial morphology such as languages described as agglutinative (Çöltekin, 2010; Pirinen, 2015) or polysynthetic (Schwartz et al., 2020; Andriyanets and Tyers, 2018).

The remainder of the article is laid out as follows: In Section 2 we give an overview of Guaraní, paying special attention to aspects of morphology and morphosyntax. Section 3 reviews the prior work, Section 4 describes the implementation of the analyser, including information about the linguistic data and tools used. We evaluate our analyser in Section 5, giving both a qualitative, quantitative and comparative evaluation. And finally in Section 6 we give some final remarks and comment on potential future work for Guaraní.

2 Language

Guaraní (Native name: *Avañe'ẽ*) is one of the most spoken indigenous languages of South America that belongs to Tupi-Guaraní stock. It is divided into dialects or even languages such as Paraguayan

[1]We note that the Guaraní *Vikipetã*, https://gn.wikipedia.org/ currently has a total of 3,767 articles (as of the 15th July 2020), while the English Wikipedia, http://en.wikipedia.org/ has 6,122,333 as of the same date. If we compare with a language with a similar number of speakers and official status, for example Catalan, we see that the Catalan *Viquipèdia* has vastly more articles 652,079.

Proceedings of the First Workshop on Natural Language Processing for Indigenous Languages of the Americas, pages 81–89

Guaraní, Bolivian Guaraní and some other dialects spoken in Brazil (Ava, Kaiowá, Nhandeva, Mbyá etc.). According to Ethnologue[2] population that speaks all the varieties of Guaraní is 6.162.840 people. The majority of Guaraní speaking population is located in Paraguay where Guaraní is considered the official language and consists of 5.850.000 monolinguals and bilinguals. See Figure 1 for Guaraní speaking area.

Guaraní is an agglutinative concatenative language. It's morphology has both derivational and inflectional traits: it uses suffixes, preffixes and circumfixes for word production. Roots (or stems) affect the phonology of affixes concatenated to the stem and vice-versa, mostly in cases of nasal harmonization or incorporation[3]. The majority of the words in Guaraní are oxytone with some exceptions when accentuation rules apply (Estigarribia, 2017).

Only recently Paraguayan institution *Academía de la Lengua Guaraní* approved current orthographic standard for written Guaraní (Sánchez, 2018). Thus in literature published before 2018 writing standards vary significantly. For example, postposition 'hag̃ua' or 'haguã' can be written with *g̃* or *ã* where nasalization is marked graphically by tilde. According to phonological rules, nasalization propagates over the entire syllable if there are any nasal phonemes in it (Krivoshein de Canese, 1983), therefore, both spellings are acceptable. In addition, tilde indicates the stress for nasal vowels and special nasality marking in *hag̃uã* may be considered excessive. In Wikipedia corpus some nasalized phonemes are also marked with diaeresis '¨' (ï, ÿ, ä, etc.). Our transducer handles all the spelling varieties and treats them as orthographic errors.

Despite Guaraní being one of the most spoken low-resource languages of South America grammars thoroughly describing the language are not abundant. Throughout this paper we mostly consult with (Krivoshein de Canese, 1983), (Estigarribia, 2017) and (Dietrich, 2017), although there are earlier reliable grammars available (Gregores and Suarez, 1967).

3 Prior work

Most of the existing computational resources for Guaraní so far are online dictionaries or translators supported by the community. They are based on aligned publicly avaliable corporas such as Wikipedia or Guaraní–Spanish Bible. For example, *iguarani.com* and *glosbe.com* are mostly supported by non-professionals i.e. native speakers or other enthusiasts. Glosbe even has its API (Application Programming Interface). But as textual sources for Guaraní are scarce these translators are not always reliable and lacking words.

At Indiana University Michael Gasser (Gasser, 2018) developed *Mainumby* translation system created mostly for Paraguayan translators with implementation of finite state morphological analyzer *ParaMorfo* embedded into translator. This analyser is very close to what we have done although is focused mostly on the form generation rather than morphological analysis. The analyser discussed in this paper and ParaMorfo were built independently and we will evaluate two transducers for comparison.

4 Development

Transducer-based morphology modelling is essentially the mapping between elementary morphological units (morphemes) to morphological (part of speech) tags or whole lexemes. This mapping reflects the combinatorics and morphological constraints of natural language i.e. which morphemes can combine into a lexeme and which morphemes are incompatible.

FST-based approaches use *continuation lexicons* term to denote the mapping as we will reference them throughout the paper. The implementation of continuation lexicons in our analyser is entirely built on dictionaries publicly available on the web. One of them is L3 project Guaraní dictionary[4] from the *hltdi-l3* GitHub repository.

Our two-level transducer uses two formalisms:

- `lexc` formalism which models morphotactics (morpheme combinatorics);
- `twol` formalism is used for implementing phonological rules.

Both of the formalism use specific syntax following HFST platform conventions. Our analyser is a part of Apertium[5] open-source platform and can be used freely and enhanced by any member of open-source community. In the paper it is referred as Apertium analyser.

[2] `https://www.ethnologue.com/language/grn`

[3] *Incorporation* is a type of word formation that comprises a compound from a verb and an object of that verb i.e. object is incorporated by a verb and becomes a sole lexeme.

[4] `https://github.com/LowResourceLanguages/hltdi-l3/blob/master/dicts/lustig_words_gn_es.txt`

[5] `https://github.com/apertium/apertium-grn`

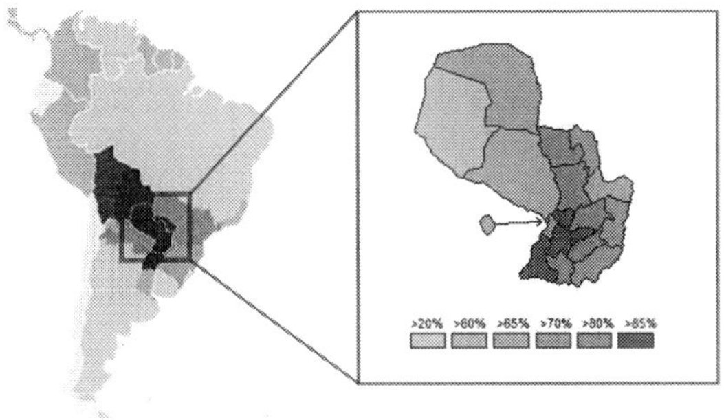

Figure 1: Areas where Guaraní is spoken in South America (including language varieties). The very dark green shows areas where the language has official status, dark green shows areas where there are a considerable number of speakers, while the light green shows areas where the language is official by virtue of its recognition by the Mercosur trade block. The box zooms in on Paraguay and shows the percentage of people having Guaraní as a native language by department according to the 2002 census.

```
LEXICON Nouns
achegety:achegety N ; ! "abecedario"
aguara:aguara N ; ! "zorro"
aguyjevete:aguyjevete N ; ! "gratitud"
ahoja:ahoja N ; ! "manta"
aho iha:aho iha N ; ! "carpa"
```

Figure 2: Lexicon for noun stems from `lexc` file. The first element before colon is an underlying form, the second element stands for surface form of the nouns adding further lexicons to the surface stem (N-lexicon). After exclamation mark follows the comment with translation to the word.

4.1 Morphotactics

4.1.1 Ambiguity of classes

The nature of stems in Guaraní is ambiguous. Those may pertain either to nominal or verbal classes. The same root may represent either a verb or a noun and even an adjective depending on the syntactic role, position in a sentence and morphological units attached to the root. Both nouns and verbs can serve as predicates. verbs express an action and nouns define qualities, states and notions (Dietrich, 2017). As a convention we group nouns, adjectives, adverbs as into a nominal class and refer to them as *nominals* and call verbal stems as *verbals*. Notably 'adjectives' and 'adverbs' are not always distinguished by the researchers in the literature. A lot of roots in these classes take comparative suffixes to form degree constructions at the same time verbs show similar behaviour so we cannot call them adjectives in its' full sense (Dietrich, 2017).

Because of the ambiguity the same stems appear in various basic lexicons (nouns, verbs, adjectives). In Table 1 we illustrate possible analyses for *arandu* root. As a noun *arandu* means 'intelligence' and as an adjective 'wise, educated'.

Our transducer consists of several lexicons: NOUNS (4455), VERBS, divided in two groups by transitivity (2537), ADJECTIVES (1668), ADVERBS (457) and other morphological categories including pronouns, determiners, toponyms, anthroponyms, barbarisms (in their majority Spanish loanwords), etc. In the following sections we discuss concrete linguistic phenomena in Guaraní as well as present our implementation decisions for them.

4.1.2 Nouns

Nouns in Guaraní can attach various suffixes and prefixes with pronominal, spacial, temporal meaning. They can serve as predicates and incorporate other nouns. Some nouns are so called multi-roots as they have several initial forms expressing different kinds of relations. Figure 2 shows an example of NOUNS lexicon. A simplified version of non-deterministic FST for noun derivation is shown on the Figure 3. The figure shows two branches of prefixing possible for nominal stems in Gurarani followed by case inflection, diverse types of derivation (pluralization, degree suffix attachment) and incorporation.

Case affixes Nouns in Guaraní can attach case affixes which sometimes behave as postpositions. The nouns and postpositions often times are written separately as the analysis of Wiki-corpus shows. Such behaviour of affixes is also described in grammar books (Estigarribia and Pinta, 2017). The exam-

Form	Translation
arandu<n>	'intelligence'
arandu<adj>	'wise, educated'

Table 1: Possible analyses for 'arandu'

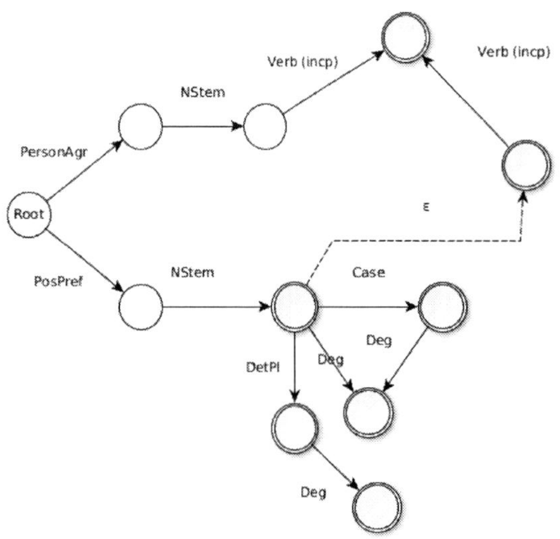

Figure 3: Reduced FST for Guaraní noun derivation/inflection. Labels used: *PersonAgr* for personal agreement prefixes, *PosPref* for possessive prefixes, *NStem* for nominal stems, *Verb* is used for marking incorporation of the noun by verb, *Deg* for degree, *DetPl* for plural determiner.

ples below illustrate the difference between usages of those segments. In (1), the suffix *-pe* (nasal variant of *-me*) expresses locative and in (2), the postposition *hağua* expresses direction.

(1) tetã-me
country-LOC

'in the country'

(2) *Ou* *o-mba'apo* *hağua.*
come-SG3 POSS.SG3-work to

'S/he comes to work'

The morphotactic transducer (*lexc* file) contains a `CASE` lexicon with postpositional tag `<post>` and inflects nominal lexicons.

Incorporation is a morphological process that fuses nouns into a verbal form as a direct object. Normally the object referring to a human being follows the verb. In case of incorporation the object is inserted between personal agreement marker and verbal stem. The verb itself remains intransitive while incorporating a noun. Compare examples (3) and (4) from (Dietrich, 2017).

(3) Iñirũ katu he'i ichupe.
3SG-friend but answer-3SG 3SG.DAT

'But his friend answered him.'

(4) a. *a-johéi*
SG1-wash

'I wash (it)'

b. *a-**py**-héi*
SG1-feet-wash

'I wash my feet.'

Noun incorporation in Guaraní transducer is modelled as follows: verbal stems are attached to stems in NOUNS lexicon.

Multi-form roots A challenging aspect of Guaraní nominals is that some of them have two or three initial forms (they are called biforms and triforms by Krivoshein and multiform roots by Estigarribia). They alter the first allomorph consonant of the word depending on the semantics a speaker wants to express. Most of these forms begin with /t-/ (biforms predominantly express the terms of kinship). Representations of biforms and triforms are distinguished by possessiveness. Absolute form generally begins with /t-/, the second form is relational where the possessor is not a 3P pronominal and starts with /r-/. The third form begins with /h-/ where there is a 3P pronominal possessor (see Table 2, examples are taken from (Estigarribia and Pinta, 2017)).

The transducer handles these allomorphs as determiners or possessive pronouns. The initial form marker /t-/ is eliminated by the rule and then triform nominal stems are appended to /r-/ and /h-/ initial segments (see Figure 4).

4.1.3 Verbs

Verbal classification The most complex part of morphological combinatorics is verbal modelling that could be completed in multiple ways depending on classification strategy. Verbal forms can be

Example	Gloss	Translation	Form
tembiapo	**t**embiapo	'work'	Absolute
Huã rembiapo	Huã **r**-embiapo	'Juan's work'	Relational
hembiapo	**h**-embiapo	'his/her work'	POSS.3-possessor

Table 2: Representations of *tembiapo* noun with it's three forms where the first form is absolute, second is relational with non-pronominal possessor and the third form with the pronominal possessor.

```
LEXICON DetTriformes
r%<det%>%+:r%{t%} Triformes ;
h%<prn%>%<pos%>%+:h{t%} Triformes ;
```

Figure 4: Lexicon defining triforms in `lexc` file. Special character `%{t%}` works here as archiphoneme and is a part of morphophonological module. It is always implied in underlying representation of the word and it actualizes on the surface only when 'r' or 'h' sounds are not around in the context i.e. in absolute forms.

divided by transitivity, areales a(i)reales and chendales. We give the definition for all the subclasses below.

According to (Estigarribia, 2017) *aireales* are the verbs that take /-i-/ sound between personal agreement suffixes and the root. /-i-/ vowel is a phonetic segment that does not carry any morphological load but it can significantly change semantics of the word. For example, areal verb *ke* "to enter" acquires a new meaning "to sleep" when /-i-/ is added. So *a-i-ke* means "I sleep" instead of *a-ke* "I enter".

Chendales is a subclass of verbal stems which attach possessive pronouns as prefixes. Possessive prefixes alter active verbs to states. The example below borrowed from (Estigarribia, 2017) shows the difference of active and stative forms:

(5) **a**-monda
SG1.ACT-steal

'I steal = I am stealing'

(6) **che**-monda
SG1.INACT-steal

'I steal=I am a thief'

Possessive prefixes in chendales behave like a subject of the predicate whereas can be interpreted as objects when attached to a(i)real verbs.

(7) Nde **che**-juhu.
SG2.NOMSG1.ACC-meet

'You meet me.'

Excessive splitting of verbal stems into separate verbal classes (transitive/intransitive, areales/aireales, chendales) can result in overgeneration of non-existing forms. Thus we segregate verbal stems in two lexicons by transitivity and then implement specific morphological alterations for each of the subclasses. For example, aireal verbs acquire /-i-/ phoneme between stem and prefix by using special character `%{i%}` called *archiphoneme* in HFST terminology. It allows to specify the context in the rule for a representation of a phoneme's underlying form. Archiphome is mapped to a set of surface representations of the sound and the context is specified for every surface form including 'zero sound'. Thus `%{i%}` appears as 'zero sound' in areal verbs and /-i-/ in aireales.

Verbal affixes Guaraní verbs undergo personal agreement (see example for verb *ke* – 'to enter' in Table 3) as well can attach tense, aspect and mood markers. A general model of verbal strategy can be found on Figure 5.

Tense, aspect and mood markers attach to the predicate but they are not obligatory unless mark future tense. In case a verb does not take any suffix it may be preceded by an adverbial or postpositional tense marker. Compare the two examples where *-akue* is a past tense marker and *va'ekue* is an adverb:

(8) Aha **va'ekue** nde rógape.
1SG-go ADV.PAST 2SG.POS house-LOC

'I went to your house.'

(9) Ou'**akue** che sy rógape.
Come-PAST 1SG.POS mother house-LOC.

'Came yesterday to my mother's house'.

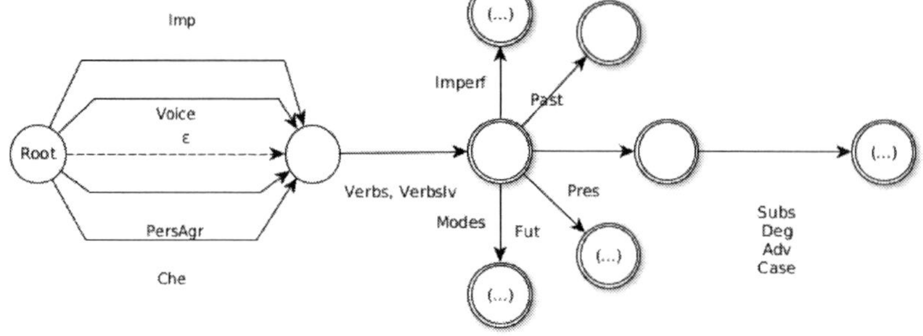

Figure 5: Reduced FST for Guaraní verb strategy. Labels used: *PersAgr* for personal agreement prefixes, *Che* for chendales, *Imp* for imperative, *Deg* for degree, *Imperf* for imperfect. Most of the finite states can be extended further by suffix combinations.

Form	Gloss	Translation
ake	`a<prn><p1><sg><nom>+ke`	I enter
reke	`re<prn><p2><sg><nom>+ke`	You enter
oke	`o<prn><p3><sg><nom>+ke`	S/he enters
jake	`ja<prn><p1><pl><nom>+ke`	We enter (inclusive)
roke	`ro<prn><p1><pl><nom>+ke`	We enter (exclusive)
peke	`pe<prn><p2><pl><nom>+ke`	You enter
oke	`o<prn><p3><pl><nom>+ke`	They enter

Table 3: Personal agreement for the verb *ke* (enter)

Orthographically there is no agreement in using some of tense markers as affixes or as adverbs. In literature and corpora we can find both interpretations so our analyzer handles it in both ways.

4.2 Morphophonology

Phonological aspects of Guaraní in Apertium analyser are modelled by HFST `twol` formalism and a set of archiphonemes in `lexc` file. `twol` file contains 30 rules that impose constraints on phonological alterations.

As we mentioned Guaraní is oxytone language i.e. the end of the word is always stressed. Accents are used for marking exceptions from this rule. Suffixes (or postpositions) that can attach to the stem may be tonal or atonal. As the stress is generally not marked it causes the shift of the accents in writing. If the suffix is tonal and it is attached to the root the stress should be removed from the stem and shifted to the tonal affix as in plural form of *óga* ('house') – *ogakuéra*. The case of tonal suffixes is solved by a phonological rule specifying contexts where the corresponding characters must change (Figure 6).

One more specific feature of Guaraní phonology is nasalization. Both vowels and consonants can be nasal/nasalized. A special character used for indicating nasalization is tilde. If a syllable contains nasal phoneme it automatically becomes nasal so there is no need to mark the rest of the phonemes of the syllable with the tilde. Although, if the word is a compound and/or incorporates two (or more) nasal roots both tildes remain. The same rule applies to nasal morphemes attached to the root as in examples below.

(10) akãperõ
akã-perõ

'bold-headed'

(11) omitãmohavõ
o-mitã-mohavõ
SG3-child-soap

'She soaps the child'

Nasalization affects suffixes and prefixes with a consonant adjacent to the root if the root is nasal. Consonants change to their nasal equivalents with the same place of articulation i.e. j → n, k → ng, etc. (see Figure 7).

```
"Change tonal vowel to atonal if tonal in affix"
Vt:Va <=> •:_ [Cns:|ArchiCns:|Nas:|VowsAton:|%>: ]+  VowsTon: ;
          •:_ [Cns:|%>:|ArchiCns:|Nas:|VowsAton:]+ %{E%}: ;
          •:_ [Cns:|%>:|ArchiCns:|Nas:|VowsAton:]+ [%{Y%}: g:u:a:] ;


"Delete ending -[i] before comparative -icha"
Vx:0 <=> _ %>: [ i: c: h: a: | %r%:0 i: ] ;
          where Vx in ( ĩ i í ) ;
```

Figure 6: The first `twol` rule handles alteration of tonal vowel (`Vt`) after a special character "•" that we added to each word form in `lexc` file containing accents to indicate tonal vowel if in the following context there are any tonal vowels (`VowsTon`). The second rule executes vowel deletion when preceding *icha* suffix or zero surface `%r%` suffix followed by `-i` which appears in negative circumfix if the stem ended in vowel.

```
•:0 ó:o g:g a:a >:0 {N}:0 {K}:k u:u é:ê r:r a:a
i:i r:r ũ:ũ >:0 {N}:n {K}:g u:u é:ê r:r a:a
```

Figure 7: Example of transducer's output for nasalization of *kuéra* plural suffix. Archiphonemes `{N}` and `{K}` actualize in a surface form preceded by nasal vowel ũ (> is a special symbol used for morpheme boundary).

Except nasalization our analyser handles phoneme deletion, vowel alteration, phoneme insertion (including glottal stop between two vowels). Transition of tonal vowel to atonal is showed on Figure 6. This rule applies to the words having a tonal vowel in the stem marked with tonal accent as in Spanish. Vowel 'é' in verb 'wash' 'johéi' changes to 'e' when suffix 'hína' indicating imperfect is added. As a result we receive `joheihína`. The other rule handles vowel deletion to avoid duplicate `i` sound on the morphemes' boundary. This can occur when comparative suffix *-icha* is added to a stem ending with `-i`. As in `morotĩ` 'white' underlying form would result in vowel duplication `morotĩ<adj>+icha<comp>` → `morotĩicha`. The rule deletes the duplicate `i` and we receive `moroticha` '(equally) white' on the surface.

5 Evaluation

To evaluate the analyser we estimate naive coverage metric and compare it to *ParaMorfo* system. *Naive coverage*[6] is the ratio of tokens that receive at least one morphological analysis to the total number of tokens in the corpus.

We estimate performance of our transducer on two publically available corpora: the Bible and the Guaraní Wikipedia. An example of a fully analysed Guaraní sentence is presented in Table 4. The asterisk, *, marks the example of erroneous output. Pronouns like *che* can serve as possessive and personal pronouns. The morphological analyser did not solve the case correctly, as we initially presumed that only personal pronouns will be written separately. Correct analysis of this lexeme is `che<prn><pos><p1><sg>`. Cases like this require enhancement so that any orthographical inconsistencies could be parsed. Table 5 shows the results of naive coverage evaluation as compared to *ParaMorfo*.

For fair comparison we ran Wikipedia texts and the Bible through Apertium analyser and dropped all the tokens that did not belong to open-class category because ParaMorfo does not recognize closed-class words (adverbs, conjunctions, numbers, etc.) and punctuation marks. ParaMorfo segments tokens differently than our analyser so at the end of processing we received different quantity of entry tokens for each analyser.

According to Table 5 the naive coverage of Apertium analyser is significantly higher than of ParaMorfo. One reason is that the latter does not cover Spanish barbarisms present in the corpora in increased proportion after closed class tokens are excluded. Moreover, ParaMorfo does not recognize proper names such as toponyms and anthroponyms.

We also evaluate conventional quality metrics for the analyser such as precision, recall and F-measure. To estimate precision, recall and F-measure we have annotated 8308 tokens from different sources where each tokens has a corresponding valid analysis in the context. Note that this estimate is only the approximation of the scores because in order to have true scores each form should be annotated with *all* valid

[6]The metric is called *naive* coverage because even if the word received an analysis it may not be grammatically correct e.g. in cases of over-generation or some grammatically correct analyses may not be delivered by the transducer.

Surface form	Analysis
Ojapo	o<prn><p3><pl><nom>+japo<v><tv><pres>
oréve	ore<adj>+ve<adj><dist>
guarã	guarã<post>
kuehe	kuehe<adv>
chipa	chipa<n>
che	*ché<prn><pers><p1><sg>
sy	sy<n>
.	.<sent>

Table 4: Example morphological analysis of Guaraní sentence with Apertium tag style. Note that morphological ambiguity in the example was manually solved for illustration purposes.

Corpus	Coverage	Tokens
Apertium:		
Wikipedia	0.86	375989
Bible	0.91	482941
ParaMorfo		
Wikipedia	0.54	379736
Bible	0.64	631724

Table 5: Naive coverage evaluation

analyses of the words instead of a single analysis per word. This is not an easy task to complete without a native speaker.

We define *true positives* as the list of the analyses present both in the gold standard and the transducer's output, *false positives* as those analyses in the transducer's output but not in the gold standard. Finally, *false negatives* are the analyses found in the gold standard but not the analyser's output. This evaluation method was previously used by Richardson and Tyers (2021). Apertium analyser yields the following scores: *precision* 0.30, *recall* 0.86 and *F1-score* 0.45.

Precision here reflects the likelihood of the form produced by the analyser to be in the gold standard, which is high in our case. Precision shows low score because the annotated data only contains one valid morphological analysis per word. Thus, overall we can conclude that the likelihood of the word being analysed correctly is fairly high. It does not possible to compare our results with *ParaMorfo* in this case because of the differences in morpheme mapping between the analysers, this way to do fair comparison additional effort is needed to annotate data using *ParaMorfo*'s tag convention.

Another metric we asses is *average ambiguity rate*, the average number of morphological analyses given by the transducer per word. Average ambiguity rate for Wikipedia corpus is 3.018 analyses per token and for Bible – 3.450 analyses. This fact gives us an interesting observation that Guaraní language is *moderately* polisynthetic as compared to other languages that according to (Estigarribia and Pinta, 2017) may have 5-6 analyses per word.

To briefly summarize our contributions in comparison with ParaMorfo analyser:

- Apertium analyser recognises closed class forms (adverbs, conjunctions, numerals) and punctuation;
- Handles Spanish barbarisms and Proper nouns;
- Flexible with orthographic variation.

6 Conclusions

We presented a finite-state morphological analyser for one of the indigenous polysynthetic languages of South America – Paraguayan Guaraní. Further work implies the expansion of the existing lexicons to reach most possible coverage mainly by adding more stems to continuation lexicons (verbs, nouns, proper names). Currently the analyser provides all possible analyses for a token and it requires further work on morphological disambiguation.

Acknowledgements

We would like to thank Michael Gasser, emeritus professor of Informatics and Computing at Indiana University, Dmitry Gerasimov, from the Institute for Linguistic Studies of the Russian Academy of Sciences, as well as the reviewers for the thorough evaluation of our work and suggestions.

References

Vasilisa Andriyanets and Francis M. Tyers. 2018. A prototype finite-state morphological analyser for Chukchi. In *Proceedings of the Workshop on Computational Modeling of Polysynthetic Languages*, pages 31–40, Santa Fe, New Mexico, USA. Association for Computational Linguistics.

Wolf Dietrich. 2017. Word classes and word class switching in Guaraní syntax. In *Guarani Linguistics in the 21st Century*, pages 101–137. Brill.

David M. Eberhard, Gary F. Simons, and Charles D. Fennig. 2018. Guaraní. `http://www.ethnologue.com`.

Bruno Estigarribia. 2017. A grammar sketch of Paraguayan Guarani. In *Guarani Linguistics in the 21st Century*, pages 7–85. Brill.

Bruno Estigarribia and Justin Pinta, editors. 2017. *Guarani Linguistics in the 21st Century*. Brill.

Mikel Forcada, Mireia Ginestí-Rosell, Jacob Nordfalk, Jim O'Regan, Sergio Ortiz-Rojas, Juan Antonio Pérez-Ortiz, Felipe Sánchez-Martínez, Gema Ramírez-Sánchez, and Francis M. Tyers. 2011. Apertium: a free/open-source platform for rule-based machine translation. *Machine Translation*, 25:127–144.

Michael Gasser. 2018. Mainumby: un ayudante para la traducción Castellano-Guaraní. In *Tercer Seminario International sobre Traducción, Terminología y Lenguas Minorizadas*.

Emma Gregores and Jorge Suarez, editors. 1967. *A Description of Colloquial Guaraní*. Mouton & Co.

M. Gökırmak and F. M. Tyers. 2017. A dependency treebank for kurmanji kurdish. In *Proceedings of the the International Conference on Dependency Linguistics, Depling 2017*.

Ryan Johnson, Lene Antonsen, and Trond Trosterud. 2013. Using finite state transducers for making efficient reading comprehension dictionaries. In *Proceedings of the 19th Nordic Conference of Computational Linguistics (NODALIDA 2013)*, volume 85, pages 59–71.

Natalia Krivoshein de Canese. 1983. *Gramática de la lengua guaraní*. Asunción.

Scott Ledbetter and Marcus Dickinson. 2016. Cost-effectiveness in building a low-resource morphological analyzer for learner language. In *Proceedings of the 11th Workshop on Innovative Use of NLP for Building Educational Applications*, pages 206–216.

S. Moshagen, T. Trosterud, J. Rueter, F. M. Tyers, and T. A. Pirinen. 2014. Open-source infrastructures for collaborative work on under-resourced languages. In *Proceedings of CCURL workshop 2014 organised in conjunction with LREC2014*.

Tommi A Pirinen. 2015. Development and use of computational morphology of Finnish in the open source and open science era: Notes on experiences with Omorfi development. *SKY Journal of Linguistics*, 28:381–393.

Tommi A. Pirinen and Krister Lindén. 2014. State-of-the-art in weighted finite-state spell-checking. In *Computational Linguistics and Intelligent Text Processing*, pages 519–532, Berlin, Heidelberg. Springer Berlin Heidelberg.

Ivy Richardson and Francis M. Tyers. 2021. A morphological analyser for k'iche'.

Lane Schwartz, Francis Tyers, Lori Levin, Christo Kirov, Patrick Littell, Chi kiu Lo, Emily Prud'hommeaux, Hyunji Hayley Park, Kenneth Steimel, Rebecca Knowles, Jeffrey Micher, Lonny Strunk, Han Liu, Coleman Haley, Katherine J. Zhang, Robbie Jimmerson, Vasilisa Andriyanets, Aldrian Obaja Muis, Naoki Otani, Jong Hyuk Park, and Zhisong Zhang. 2020. Neural polysynthetic language modelling.

Vidalia Sánchez, editor. 2018. *Guarani Ñe'ẽ Rerekuapavẽ*. Editorial Servilibro.

Jörg Tiedemann, Filip Ginter, and Jenna Kanerva. 2015. Morphological Segmentation and OPUS for Finnish-English Machine Translation. Technical report, University of Turku.

F. M. Tyers and V. Ravishankar. 2018. A prototype dependency treebank for breton. In *Actes de la conférence Traitement Automatique de la Langue Naturelle, TALN 2018*, pages 197–204.

Çağrı Çöltekin. 2010. A freely available morphological analyzer for Turkish. In *Proceedings of the 7th International Conference on Language Resources and Evaluation (LREC2010)*.

Morphological Segmentation for Seneca

Zoey Liu
Boston College
ying.liu.5@bc.edu

Robbie Jimerson
Rochester Institute of Technology
rcj2772@rit.edu

Emily Prud'hommeaux
Boston College
prudhome@bc.edu

Abstract

This study takes up the task of low-resource morphological segmentation for Seneca, a critically endangered and morphologically complex Native American language primarily spoken in what is now New York State and Ontario. The labeled data in our experiments comes from two sources: one digitized from a publicly available grammar book and the other collected from informal sources. We treat these two sources as distinct domains and investigate different evaluation designs for model selection. The first design abides by standard practices and evaluates models with the in-domain *development set*, while the second one carries out evaluation using a *development domain*, or the out-of-domain development set. Across a series of monolingual and cross-linguistic training settings, our results demonstrate the utility of neural encoder-decoder architecture when coupled with multi-task learning.

1 Introduction

A member of the Hodinöhšöni (Iroquoian) language family in North America, the Seneca language is spoken mainly in three reservations located in Western New York: Allegany, Cattaraugus and Tonawanda. Seneca is considered acutely endangered and is currently estimated to have fewer than 50 first-language speakers left, most of whom are elders. Motivated by the Seneca community's language reclamation and revitalization program, a few hundred children and adults are actively learning and speaking Seneca as a second language.

To further facilitate the documentation process of Seneca, recent years have witnessed the scholarly bridge between the language community and academic research, taking advantage of rapidly evolving technologies in natural language processing (NLP) (Neubig et al., 2020; Jimerson and Prud'hommeaux, 2018). In particular, ongoing work has mainly been devoted to developing automatic speech recognition (ASR) systems for Seneca (Thai et al., 2020, 2019). Their findings demonstrated that when combined with synthetic data augmentation and machine learning techniques, robust acoustic models could be built even with a very limited amount of recorded naturalistic speech. More importantly, the research output was incorporated into the Seneca people's documentation endeavors, illustrating the potential of collaborations between language communities and academic researchers.

The current study contributes to this line of research with the same ethical considerations (Meek, 2012). Specifically, we focus on morphological segmentation for Seneca, an area that has not yet been investigated thus far. Given a Seneca word, the task of morphological segmentation is to decompose it into individual morphemes (e.g., *hasgatgwë's* → *ha* + *sgatgwë'* + *s*).

With a series of in-domain, cross-domain and cross-linguistic experiments, the goal of our work is to build effective segmentation models that can support the community's ongoing language reclamation and revitalization efforts. Particularly for morphologically rich languages, it has been shown that morphological segmentation is a useful component in certain NLP tasks such as machine translation (Clifton and Sarkar, 2011), dependency parsing (Seeker and Çetinoğlu, 2015), keyword spotting (Narasimhan et al., 2014), and automatic speech recognition (ASR) (Afify et al., 2006). Given that Seneca is a highly polysynthetic language (see Section 2), good morphological segmentation models show promise for the development of other computational systems such as ASR, which would facilitate the documentation process of the language itself.

Another motivation for our experiments lies in the fact that previous research on morphological segmentation has mostly concentrated on

Proceedings of the First Workshop on Natural Language Processing for Indigenous Languages of the Americas, pages 90–101
June 11, 2021.

Indo-European languages in high-resource settings (Goldsmith, 2001; Goldwater et al., 2009; Cotterell et al., 2016b), sometimes relying on external large-scale corpora in order to derive morpheme or lexical frequency information (Cotterell et al., 2015; Ruokolainen et al., 2014; Lindén et al., 2009). By contrast, work on morphological segmentation of augmented low-resource settings or truly under-resourced languages is lacking in general (Kann et al., 2016). Hence demonstrations of what model architecture and training settings could be beneficial with data sets of very small size would be informative to other researchers whose work shares similar goals and ethical considerations as ours.

2 Data Statements

Following recently advocated scientific practices (Bender and Friedman, 2018; Gebru et al., 2018), we would like to first introduce the data of the indigenous languages to be explored.

The protagonist in our experiments is Seneca, the data of which came from three sources: the book *The Seneca Verb: Labeling the Ancient Voice* by Bardeau (2007) [1], informal transcriptions provided by members from the community, and a recently digitized Bible translated into Seneca. The grammar book provides morphological segmentation for only verbs and the morpheme boundaries were based on rules defined by grammarians. By contrast, the informal sources contain labeled segmentation for a mix of verbs and nouns conducted by community speakers. The Bible offers only unlabeled data.

One of the most distinct features of Seneca morphology is that it is highly polysynthetic. This means that a single word can consist of multiple morphemes and may contain more than one stem; and this single word is able to express the meaning of a whole phrase or even sentences at times (Aikhenvald et al., 2007; Greenberg, 1960). As a demonstration, consider the following example (the indicated morphological characteristics here abide by the annotation standards of Sylak-Glassman (2016)). Breaking the Seneca word into individual morphemes, *ye:nö* is the stem which has the verbal meaning of *grab* in present tense; the prefix *ke* denotes that *ye:nö* is a transitive action, with *I* being the subject and *her/them* being the object; the single apostrophe ' at the end marks the stative state.

(1) keyenö'

ke yenö '
I+her/them grab STAT

I've grabbed her/them.

A large number of words in Seneca have agglutinative morphological features, meaning when multiple morphemes are combined during word formation, their original forms remain unchanged. Consider the example presented above again. When the prefix and the stem are combined into the word, neither of them goes through any phonological and orthographic changes.

On the other hand, Seneca also has fusional properties; this means that during the formation of some words, the combining morphemes can undergo phonological (and orthographical) changes. As an illustration, consider the following word in Seneca. When combining the four morphemes together, the masculine singular subject *hra*, the verb stem *k* and the *s* that marks habitual state do not undergo any changes; whereas the initial *i* is replaced with í to make sure that the verbs or verb phrases have at least two syllables (Chafe, 2015).

(2) íhrakis

i hra k s
it he eat HAB

He eats it.

In addition to Seneca, we include four Mexican indigenous languages from the Yuto-Aztecan language family (Baker, 1997) for our crosslinguisitic training experiments: Mexicanero (888 words), Nahuatl (1,123 words), Wixarika (1,385 words), and Yorem Nokki (1,063 words). The data for these languages contains morphological segmentation that was initially digitized from the book collections of *Archive of Indigenous Language* (Mexicanero (Una, 2001), Nahuatl (de Suárez, 1980), Wixarika (Gómez and López, 1999), Yorem Nokki (Freeze, 1989)). The data collection was carried out by the authors of Kann et al. (2018) based on the descriptions in their work, and their preprocessed data sets are publicly available. The four Yuto-Aztecan languages are also polysynthetic.

3 Related Work

The task of morphological segmentation has been cast in distinct ways in previous work. One line of

[1] https://senecalanguage.com/wp-content/uploads/Verb-Book-Vol.1.pdf

Language	Location	N. of speakers	Domain	Train	Dev	Test	Total
Seneca	Western New York	50	Grammar book	2,278	1,139	2,277	5,694
	Ontario		Informal sources	2,168	1,084	2,167	5,419
			Bible	-	-	-	8,588

Table 1: Descriptive information of the Seneca language and data.

research focuses on *surface segmentation* (Ruokolainen et al., 2016), while the other attends to *canonical segmentation* (Cotterell et al., 2016b). Both involve correctly decomposing a given word into distinct morphemes, which also typically includes words that stand alone as free morphemes.

Nevertheless, the two tasks differ in one key aspect: whether the combination [2] of the segmented morpheme sequence stays true to the initial orthography of the word. For surface segmentation, the answer is yes (e.g., Indonnesian *dihapus* → *di+hapus*). On the other hand, canonical segmentation sometimes involves the addition and/or deletion of characters from the surface form of the initial word, in order to capture phonological or orthographic characteristics of the component morphemes when uncombined. For example, the word *measurable* in English would be segmented as *measure + able*, recovering the orthographic *e* that was lost during word formation.

For surface segmentation, both supervised and unsupervised approaches have gained in popularity over the years. Within the realm of supervised methods, a large number of experiments have developed rule-based finite-state transducers (FST) (Kaplan and Kay, 1994) with weights usually determined by rich linguistic feature sets. The high functionality of hand-crafted FST for morphological analyses has been demonstrated for languages such as Persian (Amtrup, 2003), Finnish (Lindén et al., 2009), Semitic languages such as Tigrinya (Gasser, 2009) and Arabic (Beesley, 1996; Shaalan and Attia, 2012), as well as various African languages (Gasser, 2011). Other work has shifted to more data-driven machine learning techniques, including but not limited to memory-based learning (van den Bosch and Daelemans, 1999; Marsi et al., 2005), conditional random field models (CRF) (Cotterell et al., 2015; Ruokolainen et al., 2013, 2014), and convolutional networks (Sorokin and Kravtsova, 2018; Sorokin, 2019).

Unsupervised methods have perhaps enjoyed a longer history (Harris, 1955), with earlier studies relying on information-theoretic measures as indexes of character-level predictability, which were then used to determine morpheme boundaries (Hafer and Weiss, 1974). Later work such as Linguistica (Goldsmith, 2001) and Morfessor (Creutz and Lagus, 2002) applied the analyses of Minimum Description Length for morpheme induction (Rissanen, 1998; Poon et al., 2009). Goldwater et al. (2009) developed Bayesian generative models that would also take into account the context of individual words, which were able to simulate the process of how children learn to segment words given child-directed speech.

In contrast to surface segmentation, the problem of *canonical* segmentation has mainly been addressed with supervised methods. Cotterell et al. (2016b) extended a previous semi-CRF (Cotterell et al., 2015) for surface segmentation to jointly predict morpheme boundaries and orthographic changes, leading to improved results for German and Indonesian. With the same datasets, Kann et al. (2016) adopted character-based neural sequence models coupled with a neural reranker, presenting further improvement from Cotterell et al. (2016b). There has, however, been some unsupervised induction of canonical segmentation (see Hammarström and Borin (2011) for a thorough review). For instance, Dasgupta and Ng (2007) showed that certain spelling rules (e.g. insertion, deletion) derived heuristically from corpus frequency were able to handle orthographic changes during word formation. In comparison, Naradowsky and Goldwater (2009) provided a Bayesian model that formulate spelling rules probabilistically with character-level contextual information; the simultaneous learning process of both the rules and morpheme boundaries in turn boosted segmentation performance.

Although Seneca has fusional morphological features, meaning that certain morpheme boundaries within words are not necessarily clear-cut, the Seneca morphological data currently does not provide labeled canonical segmentation. We therefore focus on the task of surface segmentation.

[2]Here we used the term *combination* instead of *concatenation*, because surface segmentation is applicable to words with concatenative morphology as well as those with non-concatenative morphology.

4 Experiments

4.1 Data preprocessing

As mentioned in Section 2, the labeled words for Seneca came from both the verbal paradigm book by Bardeau (2007) and informal sources. We treated the two sources as separate domains and constructed a dataset for each. The number of morphemes per word on average in the grammar book is 3.87 (95% confidence intervals: (3.86, 3.88); see Section 4.4), which is slightly lower than that in the informal sources (4.12 (4.10, 4.13)). On the other hand, the number of unique morphemes is much higher in the data from the informal sources (N = 1,641) than that in the grammar book (N = 631). This difference in the amount of morphological variation between the two domains raises the expectation that with the same model architecture, morphological segmentation of the words from the informal sources is possibly more challenging.

For each data set, to construct the low-resource settings, we set the train/dev/test ratio to be 2:1:2, then randomly generated five splits for every dataset with this ratio (Gorman and Bedrick, 2019). [3] We used the first random split of both domains for model evaluation as well as selection of training settings; the setting(s) eventually selected would then be applied to data from each of the five random splits to test the stability of the model performance.

4.2 Evaluation design

We took advantage of the fact that the two data sets for Seneca came from different domains by investigating two experimental designs: evaluating with a development set versus evaluating with a *development domain*. The former carried out the standard practices. When building models for morphological segmentation of a particular domain, only the in-domain training set would be (part of) the training data for the models, along with possible addition of training data from the other domain or indigenous languages. The development set from the same domain would be used to evaluate models and the one(s) with the best performance would be selected (e.g. segmentation for the grammar book data using the development set of the grammar book for evaluation).

However, realistically development sets are luxuries to critically endangered languages (Kann et al., 2019). To help with the documentation of these languages more effectively, one would want to use as much training data as possible, ideally from the same domain or language. Yet acquiring more data for languages like Seneca, whether with or without manual annotations, faces extreme difficulty. It requires not only extensive time and financial resources, but also expertise from the very few native speakers left, most of whom are elders.

To increase the utility of the already-limited data for Seneca, we experimented with a second design of using a development domain for model evaluation. That is, for morphological segmentation of a particular domain, the new in-domain training data would be the concatenation of the initial training set along with the development set from the same domain. This new combination would be (part of) the training data for the models. In this case the development set of the other domain would then be applied instead to evaluate model performance (e.g. segmentation for the grammar book using the development set of the informal sources for evaluation). Again, the model(s) with the best performance on the development domain would be selected.

Comparing the two designs, taking into account the different configurations of the training data, it is possible that evaluation with a development domain would lead to different model architectures/settings being selected. On the other hand, it is also possible that the same model architecture or setting would be favored regardless of the particular design. In addition, because using a development domain essentially means that there is more in-domain training data, it remains to be seen whether this evaluation design would achieve better results when testing the stability of the model setting.

4.3 Model training

We experimented with three general settings: in-domain training, cross-domain training, and cross-linguistic training. For all settings, we adopted character-based sequence-to-sequence (seq2seq) recurrent neural network (RNN) (Elman, 1990) trained with OpenNMT (Klein et al., 2017). This model architecture has been previously demonstrated to perform well for polysynthetic indigenous languages (Kann et al., 2018).

In cases where applicable, we also compared the performance of the neural seq2seq models to unsupervised Morfessor [4] (Creutz and Lagus, 2002). In

[3] Data, code, and models are available at `https://github.com/zoeyliu18/Seneca`.

[4] In preliminary experiments, semi-supervised Morfes-

what follows, we describe the details of the seq2seq models in each training setting.

4.3.1 In-domain training

Naive baseline Our first baseline applied the default parameters in OpenNMT — an encoder-decoder long-short term memory model (LSTM) (Hochreiter and Schmidhuber, 1997) with the attention mechanism from Luong et al. (2015). All embeddings have 500 dimensions. Both the encoder and the decoder contain two hidden layers with 500 hidden units in each layer. Training was performed with SGD (Robbins and Monro, 1951) and a batch size of 64.

Abiding by our experimental designs, for all the baseline models, when evaluating with the development set, the in-domain training data came from just the training set. By contrast, when evaluating with the development domain, the in-domain training data was the concatenation of the training and the development sets.

Less naive baseline Going beyond the default settings in the first baseline, our second baseline experimented with different combinations of parameter settings and attention mechanisms (Bahdanau et al., 2015):

- RNN type: LSTM / GRU
- embedding dimesions: {128, 300, 500}
- hidden layers: {1, 2}
- hidden units: {128, 300, 500}
- batch size: {16, 32, 64}
- optimizer: SGD / ADADELTA (Zeiler, 2012)

These models were trained and evaluated in the same way as the first baseline. Based on results from either the development set or the development domain (after statistical tests; see Section 4.4), the model architecture that was selected was an attention-based encoder-decoder (Bahdanau et al., 2015), where the encoder is composed of a bidirectional GRU while the decoder consists of a unidirectional GRU. Both the encoder and the decoder have two hidden layers with 100 hidden states in each layer. All embeddings have 300 dimensions. Training was performed with ADADELTA and a batch size of 16.

sor (Kohonen et al., 2010) was also explored; yet the performance was worse than the unsupervised method. Thus we eventually chose the unsupervised variant for systematic comparisons with the seq2seq models.

4.3.2 Cross-domain training

With the model architecture of our *less naive* baseline, we turned to our cross-domain training experiments using four different methods.

Self-training The first method utilized self-training (McClosky et al., 2008) and resorted to the unlabeled words from the Bible, which were first automatically segmented with the second baseline model from in-domain training. These words were then added to the in-domain training data given each of the two evaluation designs (Section 4.2).

Multi-task learning The second method applied multi-task learning (Kann et al., 2018). In this case, in addition to the task of morphological segmentation, we added a new task where the training objective is to generate output that is identical to the input. In the seq2seq model, the decoder does not always generate every character in the input sequence, which prevents accurate morphological segmentation of the full word. Thus the ulterior goal of this additional task is simple yet important: helping the model learn to *copy*.

In particular, words from the in-domain training data were used for the segmentation task, while words from the Bible were used for mapping input to output. Every word in the eventual training data was appended with a task-specific input symbol. For instance, let X represent the task of morphological segmentation, Y the task of mapping input to output, the goal of the model is to jointly perform the following :

- ëwënötgëh + X $\rightarrow$ ë + wën + ötgëh
- oiwa' + Y $\rightarrow$ oiwa'

Transfer learning The third method adopts domain transfer learning. Consider morphological segmentation of the grammar book as an example. When using a development set, the in-domain training data, which includes only the training set of the grammar book, would be combined with *all* data from the informal sources. On the other hand, when using a development domain, the in-domain training data, which includes the training and development sets of the grammar book, would be concatenated with just the training and test sets from the informal sources.

Fine-tuning With the model trained from transfer learning, we fine-tuned it further with in-domain training data.

One point to note is when evaluating with a development domain, we expected that the model trained with domain transfer learning (with fine-tuning) would yield the best results. However, these results would not be directly informative about whether this setting is indeed better than the others, the latter of which only included in-domain training data. Hence for this particular evaluation design, while we still carried out the domain transfer experiments for consistency, we selected models only based on the other training settings.

4.3.3 Cross-linguistic training

In order to examine whether data from other polysynthetic languages would improve model performance, we carried out cross-linguistic training with three different settings: multi-task learning, transfer learning (Kann et al., 2018), and fine-tuning. These settings are similar to those in cross-domain training, except that the data from the four Mexican languages was used as additional training data instead of the Bible or out-of-domain data.

4.4 Metrics

Three measures were computed as indexes of model performance (Cotterell et al., 2016a; van den Bosch and Daelemans, 1999): full form accuracy, morpheme F1, and average Levenshtein distance (Levenshtein, 1966). Significance testing of each metric was conducted with bootstrapping (Efron and Tibshirani, 1994). As an illustration, take full form accuracy as an example. After applying a model to the development set (or domain) with a total of N words, we: (1) randomly selected N words from the development set with replacement; (2) calculated the full form accuracy of the selected sample; (3) repeated step (1) and (2) for 10,000 iterations, which yielded an empirical distribution of full form accuracy; (4) measured the mean and the 95% confidence interval (CI) of the empirical distribution.

5 Results

5.1 Evaluation with development set

For evaluation, we considered a training setting to be better than another based on at least one of the three metrics calculated. As presented in Table 2, when evaluating with the development set, it appears that for the grammar book, the simple less naive baseline with careful parameter tuning is able to yield excellent performance, while other more complicated training configurations such as including additional out-of-domain data do not lead to further improvement (no significant differences in the results). Therefore we chose the less naive baseline from in-domain training for the final testing given its simplicity and average score for each of the three metrics.

By contrast, with the same training settings, the models show weaker performance for informal sources. This corresponds to our initial expectation that due to the higher number of unique morphemes in informal sources, accurately labeling the boundaries of these morphemes would be comparatively more challenging. Similar to results for the grammar book, none of the other training configurations seems to significantly surpass the two baselines. With that being said, we selected the cross-linguistic training with multi-task learning for the final testing, again because it has the best average score for each of the three measures.

5.2 Evaluation with development domain

On the other hand, when evaluating with the development domain, as shown in Table 3, almost all other training configurations appear to be better than the two baselines, a pattern that holds for data from the grammar book as well as that from the informal sources. When compared to the two baselines, while the other settings do not show significant improvement in terms of accuracy or F1 score, the average Levenshtein distance is shorter when the models are trained with multi-task learning and/or additional cross-linguistic data. Given the results, for both the grammar book and the informal sources, we selected cross-domain multi-task learning as the setting for final model testing.

Combining the results from Table 2 and Table 3 together, it appears that regardless of the particular evaluation design, in any of the settings where unsupervised Morfessor is applicable (Creutz and Lagus, 2002), the neural encoder-decoder models consistently yielded significantly better performance in relation to all three measures. This observation also speaks to previous findings from Kann et al. (2018), except that they adopted semi-supervised variants of Morfessor.

Comparing the segmentation results from the seq2seq models to those from Morfessor, overall there does not seem to be aspects where the latter systematically falls short, in the sense that the segmentation patterns by Morfessor are more or less "all over the place". One potential explanation lies in the fact that in both our data sets, the majority of

Grammar book	Models	Accuracy	F1	Avg. Distance	better than Morfessor?	Selected?
In-domain	*naive baseline*	86.03	93.10	0.39	Yes	
	less naive baseline	91.92	95.96	0.21	Yes	✓
Cross-domain	*self-training*	89.98	95.04	0.26	Yes	
	multi-task learning	91.38	95.78	0.21	Yes	
	transfer learning	86.02	92.54	0.39	Yes	
	fine-tuning	88.68	94.21	0.29		
Cross-linguistic	*multi-task learning*	91.06	95.50	0.22	Yes	
	transfer learning	90.00	95.15	0.24	Yes	
	fine-tuning	90.16	95.22	0.24		
Informal sources						
In-domain	*naive baseline*	69.99	84.47	0.96	Yes	
	less naive baseline	71.38	85.27	0.86	Yes	
Cross-domain	*self-training*	70.05	84.74	0.87	Yes	
	multi-task learning	72.04	85.38	0.83	Yes	
	transfer learning	67.42	82.50	0.98	Yes	
	fine-tuning	69.27	83.79	0.92		
Cross-linguistic	*multi-task learning*	73.51	86.04	0.78	Yes	✓
	transfer learning	70.95	85.19	0.83	Yes	
	fine-tuning	71.39	85.35	0.82		

Table 2: Model training and evaluation with **the development set**. The value of each metric for every model was compared to those of the two baselines; boldface indicates significant differences from **both baselines**, derived by comparing their respective 95% CI after bootstrapping. Selected training setting for model testing is checkmarked.

Grammar book	Models	Accuracy	F1	Avg. Distance	better than Morfessor?	Selected?
In-domain	*naive baseline*	11.43	40.32	5.90	Yes	
	less naive baseline	12.35	40.77	4.01	Yes	
Cross-domain	*self-training*	13.38	42.96	3.77	Yes	
	multi-task learning	14.66	42.97	**3.24**	Yes	✓
Cross-linguistic	*multi-task learning*	12.54	41.63	**3.28**	Yes	
	transfer learning	15.12	40.89	**3.40**	Yes	
	fine-tuning	15.52	41.15	**3.40**		
Informal sources						
In-domain	*naive baseline*	10.18	44.16	4.58	Yes	
	less naive baseline	12.97	45.38	3.66		
Cross-domain	*self-training*	12.92	45.08	**3.31**	Yes	
	multi-task learning	16.59	47.79	**2.97**	Yes	✓
Cross-linguistic	*multi-task learning*	14.65	45.91	**3.15**	Yes	
	transfer learning	13.61	45.07	**3.07**	Yes	
	fine-tuning	13.61	45.24	**3.06**		

Table 3: Model training and evaluation with **the development domain**. The value of each metric for every model was compared to those of the two baselines; boldface indicates significant differences from **both baselines**, derived by comparing their respective 95% CI after bootstrapping. Selected training setting for model testing is checkmarked.

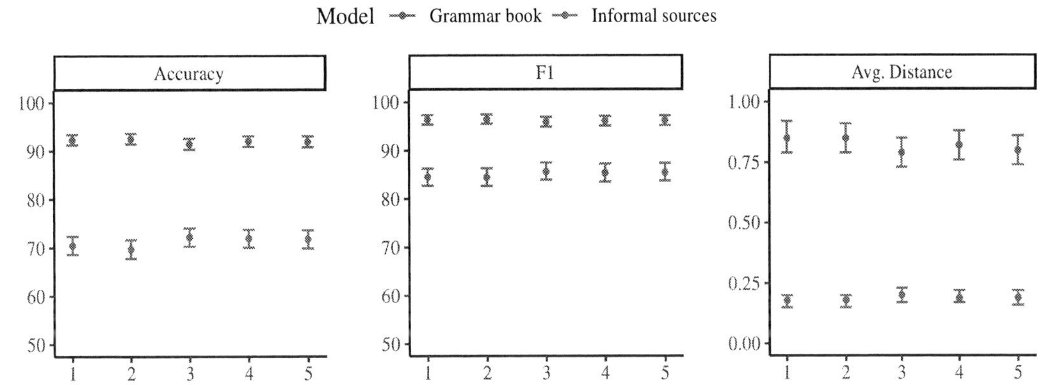

(a) using the development set for evaluation

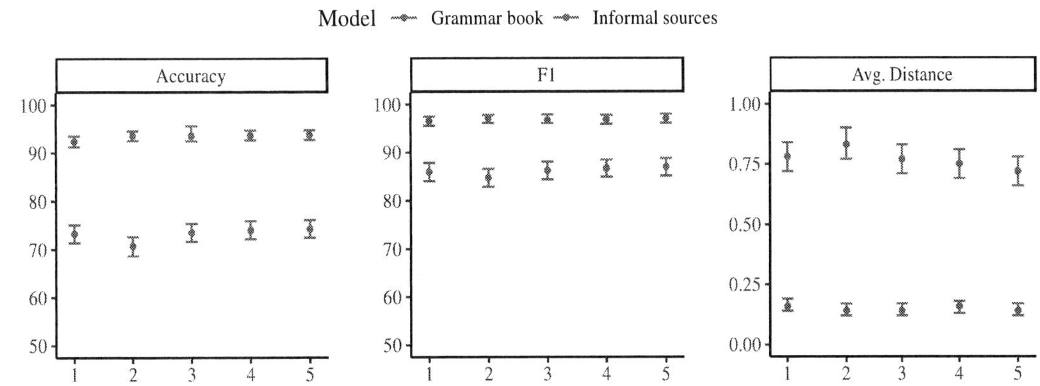

(b) using the development domain for evaluation

Figure 1: Model testing results given different evaluation designs; error bars indicate 95% CI after bootstrapping.

the words have a frequency of one (95.28% for the grammar book; 95.57% for the informal sources). On the other hand, successful segmentation by unsupervised Morfessor relies heavily on the frequency of a given word and accordingly the number of overlapping or common morphemes shared by different words, whether the occurrence frequency information was computed from the training data or from additional unlabeled data. In addition to the complex morphological features of Seneca and the high frequency of unique morphemes in the two data sets used in our experiments, the Bible dataset, despite containing more unlabeled words, is still relatively small (N = 8,588), and thus is not especially useful for deriving frequency estimates.

5.3 Testing

For both the grammar book and the informal sources, we tested the stability of the selected model settings across the five random splits (Section 4.1). With each random split, we trained a model following the selected setting for each of the evaluation designs; the model was then applied to the test set of the random split.

Based on Figure 1, within each evaluation design, the test performance of the model setting is stable across the random splits. Morphological segmentation of data from the grammar book was able to achieve consistently better results than that for the informal sources. Regardless of the data source, while there does not appear to be significant differences in model performance between the two evaluation designs, comparing to using a development set, evaluating with a development domain led to slight improvement of average scores for each of the three metrics.

6 Conclusions and Future Work

We have investigated morphological segmentation for Seneca, an indigenous Native American language with highly complex morphological characteristics. In a series of in-domain, cross-domain, and cross-linguistic training settings, the results demonstrate that neural seq2seq models are quite effective at correctly labeling morpheme boundaries, at least at the surface level. With the two evaluation designs explored here, the model settings were able to achieve above 96% F1 score for data from the grammar book, and above 85% for the informal sources.

Many of the languages indigenous to North America are as endangered as Seneca and have available resources comparable in both size and scope to those used in the current work. Our thorough investigation of how to effectively integrate these limited and varied resources can potentially serve as a model for other community-driven collaborations to document endangered languages for future generations, and to produce materials suitable for language immersion and revitalization. For our future work, in addition to refining and improving our models, we also plan to explore the utility of morphological segmentation for improving language modeling in ASR. This would be able to support transcription of both archival recordings and new recordings captured by community members involved in language revitalization projects.

Acknowledgements

We are grateful for the cooperation and support of the Seneca Nation of Indians. This material is based upon work supported by the National Science Foundation under Grant No. 1761562. Any opinions, findings, and conclusions or recommendations expressed in this material are those of the author(s) and do not necessarily reflect the views of the National Science Foundation.

References

Mohamed Afify, Ruhi Sarikaya, Hong-Kwang Jeff Kuo, Laurent Besacier, and Yuqing Gao. 2006. On the use of morphological analysis for dialectal arabic speech recognition. In *Ninth International Conference on Spoken Language Processing*.

Alexandra Y Aikhenvald et al. 2007. Typological distinctions in word-formation. *Language typology and syntactic description*, 3:1–65.

Jan W Amtrup. 2003. Morphology in machine translation systems: Efficient integration of finite state transducers and feature structure descriptions. *Machine Translation*, 18(3):217–238.

Dzmitry Bahdanau, Kyung Hyun Cho, and Yoshua Bengio. 2015. Neural machine translation by jointly learning to align and translate. In *3rd International Conference on Learning Representations, ICLR 2015*.

Mark C Baker. 1997. Complex predicates and agreement in polysynthetic languages. *Complex predicates*, pages 247–288.

Phyllis E. Wms. Bardeau. 2007. *The Seneca Verb: Labeling the Ancient Voice*. Seneca Nation Education Department, Cattaraugus Territory.

Kenneth R Beesley. 1996. Arabic finite-state morphological analysis and generation. In *COLING 1996 Volume 1: The 16th International Conference on Computational Linguistics*.

Emily M. Bender and Batya Friedman. 2018. Data statements for natural language processing: Toward mitigating system bias and enabling better science. *Transactions of the Association for Computational Linguistics*, 6:587–604.

Wallace L Chafe. 2015. *A Grammar of the Seneca Language*, volume 149. University of California Press.

Ann Clifton and Anoop Sarkar. 2011. Combining morpheme-based machine translation with post-processing morpheme prediction. In *Proceedings of the 49th Annual Meeting of the Association for Computational Linguistics: Human Language Technologies*, pages 32–42, Portland, Oregon, USA. Association for Computational Linguistics.

Ryan Cotterell, Arun Kumar, and Hinrich Schütze. 2016a. Morphological segmentation inside-out. In *Proceedings of the 2016 Conference on Empirical Methods in Natural Language Processing*, pages 2325–2330, Austin, Texas. Association for Computational Linguistics.

Ryan Cotterell, Thomas Müller, Alexander Fraser, and Hinrich Schütze. 2015. Labeled morphological segmentation with semi-Markov models. In *Proceedings of the Nineteenth Conference on Computational Natural Language Learning*, pages 164–174, Beijing, China. Association for Computational Linguistics.

Ryan Cotterell, Tim Vieira, and Hinrich Schütze. 2016b. A joint model of orthography and morphological segmentation. In *Proceedings of the 2016 Conference of the North American Chapter of the Association for Computational Linguistics: Human Language Technologies*, pages 664–669, San Diego, California. Association for Computational Linguistics.

Mathias Creutz and Krista Lagus. 2002. Unsupervised discovery of morphemes. In *Proceedings of the ACL-02 Workshop on Morphological and Phonological Learning*, pages 21–30. Association for Computational Linguistics.

Sajib Dasgupta and Vincent Ng. 2007. High-performance, language-independent morphological segmentation. In *Human Language Technologies 2007: The Conference of the North American Chapter of the Association for Computational Linguistics; Proceedings of the Main Conference*, pages 155–163, Rochester, New York. Association for Computational Linguistics.

Yolanda Lastra de Suárez. 1980. *Náhuatl de Acaxochitlán (Hidalgo)*. El Colegio de México.

Bradley Efron and Robert J Tibshirani. 1994. *An introduction to the bootstrap*. CRC press.

Jeffrey L Elman. 1990. Finding structure in time. *Cognitive science*, 14(2):179–211.

Ray A Freeze. 1989. *Mayo de Los Capomos, Sinaloa*. El Colegio de México.

Michael Gasser. 2009. Semitic morphological analysis and generation using finite state transducers with feature structures. In *Proceedings of the 12th Conference of the European Chapter of the ACL (EACL 2009)*, pages 309–317.

Michael Gasser. 2011. Hornmorpho: a system for morphological processing of amharic, oromo, and tigrinya. In *Conference on Human Language Technology for Development, Alexandria, Egypt*.

Timnit Gebru, Jamie Morgenstern, Briana Vecchione, Jennifer Wortman Vaughan, Hanna Wallach, Hal Daumé III, and Kate Crawford. 2018. Datasheets for datasets. In *Proceedings of the 5th Workshop on Fairness, Accountability, and Transparency in Machine Learning*.

John Goldsmith. 2001. Unsupervised learning of the morphology of a natural language. *Computational linguistics*, 27(2):153–198.

Sharon Goldwater, Thomas L Griffiths, and Mark Johnson. 2009. A bayesian framework for word segmentation: Exploring the effects of context. *Cognition*, 112(1):21–54.

Paula Gómez and Paula Gómez López. 1999. *Huichol de San Andrés Cohamiata, Jalisco*. El Colegio de México.

Kyle Gorman and Steven Bedrick. 2019. We need to talk about standard splits. In *Proceedings of the 57th Annual Meeting of the Association for Computational Linguistics*, pages 2786–2791, Florence, Italy. Association for Computational Linguistics.

Joseph H Greenberg. 1960. A quantitative approach to the morphological typology of language. *International journal of American linguistics*, 26(3):178–194.

Margaret A Hafer and Stephen F Weiss. 1974. Word segmentation by letter successor varieties. *Information storage and retrieval*, 10(11-12):371–385.

Harald Hammarström and Lars Borin. 2011. Unsupervised learning of morphology. *Computational Linguistics*, 37(2):309–350.

Zellig S Harris. 1955. From phoneme to morpheme. *Language*, 31(2):190–222.

Sepp Hochreiter and Jürgen Schmidhuber. 1997. Long short-term memory. *Neural computation*, 9(8):1735–1780.

Robbie Jimerson and Emily Prud'hommeaux. 2018. ASR for documenting acutely under-resourced indigenous languages. In *Proceedings of the Eleventh International Conference on Language Resources and Evaluation (LREC 2018)*, Miyazaki, Japan. European Language Resources Association (ELRA).

Katharina Kann, Kyunghyun Cho, and Samuel R. Bowman. 2019. Towards realistic practices in low-resource natural language processing: The development set. In *Proceedings of the 2019 Conference on Empirical Methods in Natural Language Processing and the 9th International Joint Conference on Natural Language Processing (EMNLP-IJCNLP)*, pages 3342–3349, Hong Kong, China. Association for Computational Linguistics.

Katharina Kann, Ryan Cotterell, and Hinrich Schütze. 2016. Neural morphological analysis: Encoding-decoding canonical segments. In *Proceedings of the 2016 Conference on Empirical Methods in Natural Language Processing*, pages 961–967, Austin, Texas. Association for Computational Linguistics.

Katharina Kann, Jesus Manuel Mager Hois, Ivan Vladimir Meza-Ruiz, and Hinrich Schütze. 2018. Fortification of neural morphological segmentation models for polysynthetic minimal-resource languages. In *Proceedings of the 2018 Conference of the North American Chapter of the Association for Computational Linguistics: Human Language Technologies, Volume 1 (Long Papers)*, pages 47–57, New Orleans, Louisiana. Association for Computational Linguistics.

Ronald M Kaplan and Martin Kay. 1994. Regular models of phonological rule systems. *Computational linguistics*, 20(3):331–378.

Guillaume Klein, Yoon Kim, Yuntian Deng, Jean Senellart, and Alexander Rush. 2017. OpenNMT: Open-source toolkit for neural machine translation. In *Proceedings of ACL 2017, System Demonstrations*, pages 67–72, Vancouver, Canada. Association for Computational Linguistics.

Oskar Kohonen, Sami Virpioja, and Krista Lagus. 2010. Semi-supervised learning of concatenative morphology. In *Proceedings of the 11th Meeting of the ACL Special Interest Group on Computational Morphology and Phonology*, pages 78–86.

Vladimir I Levenshtein. 1966. Binary codes capable of correcting deletions, insertions, and reversals. In *Soviet physics doklady*, volume 10, pages 707–710. Soviet Union.

Krister Lindén, Tommi Pirinen, et al. 2009. Weighted finite-state morphological analysis of Finnish compounding with hfst-lexc. In *NEALT Proceedings Series*.

Thang Luong, Hieu Pham, and Christopher D. Manning. 2015. Effective approaches to attention-based neural machine translation. In *Proceedings of the 2015 Conference on Empirical Methods in Natural Language Processing*, pages 1412–1421, Lisbon, Portugal. Association for Computational Linguistics.

Erwin Marsi, Antal van den Bosch, and Abdelhadi Soudi. 2005. Memory-based morphological analysis generation and part-of-speech tagging of Arabic. In *Proceedings of the ACL Workshop on Computational Approaches to Semitic Languages*, pages 1–8, Ann Arbor, Michigan. Association for Computational Linguistics.

David McClosky, Eugene Charniak, and Mark Johnson. 2008. When is self-training effective for parsing? In *Proceedings of the 22nd International Conference on Computational Linguistics (Coling 2008)*, pages 561–568, Manchester, UK. Coling 2008 Organizing Committee.

Barbra A Meek. 2012. *We are our language: An ethnography of language revitalization in a Northern Athabaskan community*. University of Arizona Press.

Jason Naradowsky and Sharon Goldwater. 2009. Improving morphology induction by learning spelling rules. In *Proceedings of the 21st international jont conference on Artifical intelligence*, pages 1531–1536.

Karthik Narasimhan, Damianos Karakos, Richard Schwartz, Stavros Tsakalidis, and Regina Barzilay. 2014. Morphological segmentation for keyword spotting. In *Proceedings of the 2014 Conference on Empirical Methods in Natural Language Processing (EMNLP)*, pages 880–885, Doha, Qatar. Association for Computational Linguistics.

Graham Neubig, Shruti Rijhwani, Alexis Palmer, Jordan MacKenzie, Hilaria Cruz, Xinjian Li, Matthew Lee, Aditi Chaudhary, Luke Gessler, Steven Abney, Shirley Anugrah Hayati, Antonios Anastasopoulos, Olga Zamaraeva, Emily Prud'hommeaux, Jennette Child, Sara Child, Rebecca Knowles, Sarah Moeller, Jeffrey Micher, Yiyuan Li, Sydney Zink, Mengzhou Xia, Roshan S Sharma, and Patrick Littell. 2020. A summary of the first workshop on language technology for language documentation and revitalization. In *Proceedings of the 1st Joint Workshop on Spoken Language Technologies for Under-resourced languages (SLTU) and Collaboration and Computing for Under-Resourced Languages (CCURL)*, pages 342–351, Marseille, France. European Language Resources association.

Hoifung Poon, Colin Cherry, and Kristina Toutanova. 2009. Unsupervised morphological segmentation with log-linear models. In *Proceedings of Human Language Technologies: The 2009 Annual Conference of the North American Chapter of the Association for Computational Linguistics*, pages 209–217.

Jorma Rissanen. 1998. *Stochastic complexity in statistical inquiry*, volume 15. World scientific.

Herbert Robbins and Sutton Monro. 1951. A stochastic approximation method. *The annals of mathematical statistics*, pages 400–407.

Teemu Ruokolainen, Oskar Kohonen, Kairit Sirts, Stig-Arne Grönroos, Mikko Kurimo, and Sami Virpioja. 2016. A comparative study of minimally supervised morphological segmentation. *Computational Linguistics*, 42(1):91–120.

Teemu Ruokolainen, Oskar Kohonen, Sami Virpioja, and Mikko Kurimo. 2013. Supervised morphological segmentation in a low-resource learning setting using conditional random fields. In *Proceedings of the Seventeenth Conference on Computational Natural Language Learning*, pages 29–37, Sofia, Bulgaria. Association for Computational Linguistics.

Teemu Ruokolainen, Oskar Kohonen, Sami Virpioja, and Mikko Kurimo. 2014. Painless semi-supervised morphological segmentation using conditional random fields. In *Proceedings of the 14th Conference of the European Chapter of the Association for Computational Linguistics, volume 2: Short Papers*, pages 84–89, Gothenburg, Sweden. Association for Computational Linguistics.

Wolfgang Seeker and Özlem Çetinoğlu. 2015. A graph-based lattice dependency parser for joint morphological segmentation and syntactic analysis. *Transactions of the Association for Computational Linguistics*, 3:359–373.

Khaled Shaalan and Mohammed Attia. 2012. Handling unknown words in Arabic FST morphology. In *Proceedings of the 10th International Workshop on Finite State Methods and Natural Language Processing*, pages 20–24, Donostia–San Sebastián. Association for Computational Linguistics.

Alexey Sorokin. 2019. Convolutional neural networks for low-resource morpheme segmentation: baseline or state-of-the-art? In *Proceedings of the 16th Workshop on Computational Research in Phonetics, Phonology, and Morphology*, pages 154–159.

Alexey Sorokin and Anastasia Kravtsova. 2018. Deep convolutional networks for supervised morpheme segmentation of Russian language. In *Conference on Artificial Intelligence and Natural Language*, pages 3–10. Springer.

John Sylak-Glassman. 2016. The composition and use of the universal morphological feature schema (unimorph schema). *Johns Hopkins University*.

Bao Thai, Robert Jimerson, Dominic Arcoraci, Emily Prud'hommeaux, and Raymond Ptucha. 2019. Synthetic data augmentation for improving low-resource asr. In *2019 IEEE Western New York Image and Signal Processing Workshop (WNYISPW)*, pages 1–9. IEEE.

Bao Thai, Robert Jimerson, Raymond Ptucha, and Emily Prud'hommeaux. 2020. Fully convolutional ASR for less-resourced endangered languages. In *Proceedings of the 1st Joint Workshop on Spoken Language Technologies for Under-resourced languages (SLTU) and Collaboration and Computing for Under-Resourced Languages (CCURL)*, pages 126–130, Marseille, France. European Language Resources association.

Canger Una. 2001. *Mexicanero de la sierra madre occidental.* El Colegio de México.

Antal van den Bosch and Walter Daelemans. 1999. Memory-based morphological analysis. In *Proceedings of the 37th Annual Meeting of the Association for Computational Linguistics*, pages 285–292, College Park, Maryland, USA. Association for Computational Linguistics.

Matthew D Zeiler. 2012. Adadelta: an adaptive learning rate method. *arXiv preprint arXiv:1212.5701*.

Representation of Yine (Arawak) Morphology by Finite State Transducer Formalism

Adriano M. Ingunza[2*] and **John E. Miller**[1*] and **Arturo Oncevay**[3] and **Roberto Zariquiey**[2]
[1] Artificial Intelligence/Engineering and [2] Linguistics/Humanities
Pontificia Universidad Católica del Perú, San Miguel, Lima, Peru
[3] School of Informatics, University of Edinburgh, Scotland

Abstract

We represent the complexity of Yine (Arawak) morphology with a finite state transducer (FST) based morphological analyzer. Yine is a low-resource indigenous polysynthetic Peruvian language spoken by approximately 3,000 people and is classified as 'definitely endangered' by UNESCO. We review Yine morphology focusing on morphophonology, possessive constructions and verbal predicates. Then we develop FSTs to model these components proposing techniques to solve challenging problems such as complex patterns of incorporating open and closed category arguments. This is a work in progress and we still have more to do in the development and verification of our analyzer. Our analyzer will serve both as a tool to better document the Yine language and as a component of natural language processing (NLP) applications such as spell checking and correction.

1 Introduction

Yine is a low resource indigenous polysynthetic Peruvian language of the Arawak family spoken by approximately 3,000 people living near the Ucayali and Madre de Dios rivers, tributary rivers of the Amazon. Yine is considered "definitely endangered" according to the UNESCO Atlas of the World's Languages in danger (Moseley, 2010).

As noted by Zariquiey et al. (2019), although Yine has a typologically oriented descriptive grammar, documentation and further study of several grammatical aspects are still urgently needed since the Yine language is at risk of entering into an obsolescent and consequently disappearing status. Therefore, such work is vital to not only adequately document the Yine language, but also to support its continued vitality through computer assisted tools such as spell-checkers and machine translators.

Formal and computational representation of morphology is considered a "solved problem" based on Beesley and Karttunen's work and seminal Finite State Morphology text (Beesley and Karttunen, 2003; Karttunen and Beesley, 2005). This does not mean that representing a language is either easy or fast, especially for the case of polysynthetic languages such as Yine.

Our goal is to construct a high coverage finite state transducer (FST) morphological analyzer both to document and preserve the Yine language, and to use it in NLP applications, such as spell checking and correction, that might promote language vitality. Our contributions at this point are: 1. a partial functioning morphological analyzer for nominal and verbal constructions including possessive constructions and verbal predicates, and 2. various project decisions and FST patterns employed so far in construction of the analyzer. Given the incomplete implementation, it is too early to report meaningful project results.

Representation of Yine morphology by a FST is a work in progress. This paper describes relevant morphological features of Yine, representation of these features by FST, particularly challenging representation problems, a preliminary evaluation, and our current and planned future states.

2 Related Work

Beesley and Karttunen (2003)'s Finite State Morphology text is a highly valuable resource for representing morphology by an FST. There are also numerous morphological analyses with FST representations available. Most relevant to this task are analyses performed for other indigenous Peruvian languages: Shipibo-Konibo (Cardenas and Zeman, 2018), Quechua (Rios, 2010) and pan-Ashaninka (Ortega et al., 2020; Castro Mamani, 2020). In particular, the last work includes applications of the FST to spell-checking and segmentation.

While we do not apply our work to spell checking in this paper, that is one of our planned goals.

*Authors contributed equally

Proceedings of the First Workshop on Natural Language Processing for Indigenous Languages of the Americas, pages 102–112
June 11, 2021. ©2021 Association for Computational Linguistics

Previously we had attempted to develop a HunSpell[1] based spell corrector, but found it too limiting given the polysynthetic nature of the Yine language. This is consistent with Pirinen and Lindén (2010, 2014), who found that FST correctors were essential to achieve performance on par with English for morphologically complex, and typically low resource, languages.

Software, tutorials, and examples for constructing FST morphology are available from the Finite State Morphology book website.[2] We use the Foma library[3] by Hulden (2009), compatible with FST Morphology, and available, along with some fine tutorials. Both applications offer a Python API, but neither is under active development. There is limited community support for Foma.

3 Linguistic Profile and Resources

Yine (ISO 639-3: *pib*) may be considered a morphosyntactically complex language due to its highly polysynthetic profile (mainly related to verbal structures). As noted by Aikhenvald (2020), Arawak languages are synthetic, predominantly head marking and suffixing, with a complex verbal morphology. Yine presents three open word classes: nouns, verbs, and adjectives (mostly by derivation); and four closed word classes: pronouns, adverbs, demonstratives and numerals. In this section, we will only discuss the pronominal system, and some features associated with the verbal and nominal morphology, since they are relevant to the current state of representation of Yine morphology by the FST formalism.

3.1 Morphological profile

As in almost all polysynthetic languages, Yine may express in just one word meanings that would require a whole sentence in other languages. This is illustrated by a complex predicative construction in (1), and a full possessive construction, in (2). Our morphological analysis is based on Hanson (2010)'s grammatical description; glosses have been adapted to the UniMorph schema (Kirov et al., 2018).

(1) niklokgimatanaktatkalu
ø-nikloka-gima-ta
ARGNO3SM-swallow-QUOT-LGSPEC1
-na-kta-tka-lu
-LGSPEC2-INDF-PFV-ARGAC3SM
'(The huge snake) swallowed him up somehow, reportedly.'

(2) ragmunateymana
r-gagmuna-te-yma-**na**
PSS3P-tree-PSSD-COM/INS-**PSS3P**
'With their trees'

Note that Yine's morphological complexity involves vowel deletion as seen in (1) and morphemes that may be accounted for as circumfixes, as is the case of possession marking in (2) where possessor indexation is achieved with two elements: prefix *r-* and the suffix *-na*. Its implications for FST expression are very interesting and will be discussed in §4 and §5. In the remaining subsections we present some of the mentioned features. Specifically, we present morphophonological rules, possessive constructions, verbal morphology aspects and argument indexing systems in relation with verbal predicates.

3.2 Morphophonological overview

Yine presents a rich set of morphophonological processes such as vowel deletion and rhotacism of liquid consonants. These processes are presented below.

Deletion between stem and suffix occurs when a specific group of suffixes trigger the deletion of the final vowel in the attached stem as shown in (3), where the frequentative suffix *-je* triggers the deletion of the stem's final vowel. However, this can only occur if vowel deletion does not generate a cluster of three consonants which is an overall restriction in the language as can be seen in (4), where the stem remains complete in its overt realization and avoids the sequence /mkj/.

(3) nnukjetlu
n-nuka-je-ta
ARGNO1S-eat-HAB-LGSPEC1
-lu
-ARGAC3SM
'I eat it (usually)'

(4) numkajetlu
n-gimka-je-ta
ARGNO1S-sleep-HAB-LGSPEC1
-lu
-ARGAC3SM
'I make you sleep (usually)'

Prefixing of possessive morphemes triggers other morphophonological processes that will be

[1] http://hunspell.github.io/
[2] http://www.fsmbook.com
[3] https://fomafst.github.io/

explained in §3.3. In (5) we see /l/ rhotacism, which occurs when an /l/ initial suffix mutates /l/ to /r/ when attached to a stem ending in *i, e, u* or *n*. Example (6) shows how the suffix behaves when attached to a different ending stem. Note that it also occurs an internal-boundary vowel deletion process triggered by the third person suffix.

(5) pnikanru
p-nika-ni-lu
ARGNO2S-eat-DED-ARGAC3SM
'You will eat it (masc)'

(6) piklu
p-nika-lu
ARGNO2S-eat-ARGAC3SM
'You eat it (masc)'

It is important to notice that the set of morphophonological rules developed by Hanson (2010) is neither exhaustive nor conclusive. The author mentions that a complete description of the morphological patterns of the language is still needed and leaves many issues open for further study. Thus, our application of them is based not only on the explicit description of Hanson (2010) but also in the examples presented by the author which entails some systematizable rules for our work. For example, examples (7) and (8) and how how the same 1PL object morpheme *wu* triggers vowel deletion in (7) and does not in (8) where it would create an identical consonant cluster *ww*. So, although vowel deletion seems to be lexically specified as mentioned by the author, phonological constraints seem to be highly relevant.

(7) yimaka giyolikletwuna
Ø-yimaka giyolika-le-ta
ARGNO3P-teach.hunt-COMP-LGSPEC1
-wu-na
-ARGAC1P-ARGNO3P
'They taught us (how) to hunt'.

(8) kaspukawawuna
Ø-kaspuka-**wa-wu**
ARGNO3P-let.go-**IMPFV-ARGAC1P**
-na
-ARGNO3P
'They are letting us go'.

There are other morphophonological rules applied in word formation which need to be studied in depth. Rules applied to prefixation processes, are presented in the next section.

3.3 Possessive constructions

Possessive constructions in Yine are formed by a possessor prefix (and if needed a linked possessor suffix), a possessed nominal root and, when needed, a 'possession status' suffix. Both morphological elements (i.e. the possessor prefix and the possession status suffixes) are determined by the semantics of the root they attach in terms of alienability. According to Hanson (2010) and Aikhenvald (2020), nominals are lexically specified for alienable versus inalienable possession.

Alienability is a category that makes a morphosyntactic distinction between possession that can be terminated (alienables) and possession that cannot (inalienable) (Payne, 2007). Of course, this is a language specific categorization. For example, in Yine, concepts such as *house* or *language*, are inalienable but a concept like *husband* is alienable. Nevertheless, concepts like *mother* or *hand* tend to be classified as inalienable in those languages that reflect this distinction in their grammar. Additionally, in Yine inalienable nouns present an internal sub-classification distinguishing between kinship terms (like *mother* or *son*) and non-kinship terms (like *hand* or *house*).

Depending on the noun root class and its initial consonant, Yine possessive constructions will use one of the three pronominal sets for possessor indexing.

Class 1 prefixes attach indistinctly to alienable or inalienable roots but only to those beginning with /g/. This consonant is always replaced by the pronoun. Additionally, if the first consonant is followed by a /u/, it mutates to a /i/ (this is always true with the exception of the 2PL prefix).

Class 2 prefixes attach also to alienable and inalienable roots with exception of non-kinship inalienable roots. Regarding morphophonology, this class does not attach to stems beginning with /g/ and does not replace the initial consonant of the stem. Classes 1 and 2 are almost identical, only differing in the 3rd person masculine/plural prefix: class 1 uses /r/ and class 2 uses a ø form.

Class 3 prefixes are attached only with those inalienable stems that do not begin with /g/. In the examples below we present the application of each pronominal class. The class 1 prefix pronoun for 1st person singular and its morphophonological effects on an alienable root is shown in (9), Class 2 prefix pronoun for 2nd person singular attached to an inalienable root is shown in (10), and Class

3 prefix pronoun for 3rd person plural is shown in (11). Finally, Class 3 forms for 3rd person plural are shown in (2) and (12).

(9) nutsrukate
n-gitsruka-te
PSS1S-ancestor-PSSD
'My ancestor'

(10) gmeknatjirne
g-meknatjir-ne
PSS2S-brother in law-PL
'Your brothers in law'

(11) gikamrurna
gi-kamruru-na
PSS3P-work-PSS3P
'Their work'

A last consequence of lexical specification of nominal stems is the usage of the so called 'possessed status suffixes'. These are affixed to alienable stems when possessor is expressed, as shown in (9) with *-te*, and to inalienable stems when possessor is not expressed as in (13) where *-chi* is used.

3.4 Verbal and verbal predicate morphology

Hanson (2010) treats morphological elements corresponding exclusively to the verbal stem separately from verbal predicate elements. She makes this separation to better leverage the commonality between verbal, nominal and adjectival predicates also attested to in Yine. Verbal stem morphology is exclusive to verbal stems, whereas predicative morphology may be applied to any predicate type.

Verbal stem morphology includes noun incorporants, oblique markers, evidentials, adverbial incorporants, aspect and subordination information, stem closure morphology, applicative suffixes and voice and mood morphemes.Verbal stem complexity is shown in (12). Notice that the example is not a simple stem but a predicate. Bolded morphemes correspond to what Hanson (2010) considers stem morphology.

(12) rustakatsyeggimatanrona
r-**gistaka-tsa-yegi-gima**
ARGNO3P-**cut-cord.of-PROX-QUOT**
-ta-na-
-LGSPEC1-LGSPEC2
-lo-na
-ARGAC3SF-ARGNO3P
'They cut the rope near her, reportedly'

Argument indexing and 'external aspect' specification do not correspond to the verbal stem but to the predicative morphology. Argument indexing is achieved by using prefixation for subjects and suffixation for objects. As for possessor indexing, 3PL forms are indexed by two morphological elements: prefix *r* and suffix *-na*. The pronominal forms are almost the same as the ones used for possessive constructions. The main distinction is that only classes 1 are 2 are used. Pronominal indexes are also classified in two classes and follow a regular pattern.

3.5 Available linguistic resources

Linguistic resources used for this paper such as analysis and corpora, come from three principal sources: Hanson (2010) which is a comprehensive typological oriented grammar, a Yine-Spanish/Spanish-Yine dictionary by Wise (1986) , and a theoretical guide developed by Zapata et al. (2017). Additionally, we used a Yine corpus by Bustamante et al. (2020) for evalution purposes (see §6).

4 Finite State Morphology

In the FST morphology formalism (Figure 1A), parallel language representations (tapes) are mapped one to the other, where by convention the upper tape corresponds to the morphological analysis and and lower tape corresponds to the word form. Each level accepts (generates) valid strings in their respective tape, and either level can be transduced to corresponding (possibly multiple) strings on the other level. FSTs can be stacked so that a lower or upper tape feeds into the corresponding tape of another FST. In summary: 1. words can be transduced to morphological analyses, 2. morphological analyses can be transduced to words, 3. only valid representations are accepted (generated) on either side, 4. a valid input representation may result in multiple output representations, and 5. transducers can be stacked to multiple levels.

Scripting for FST (see Figure 1B) includes an optional *Lexc* language for lexicons and an expansive *FST* language. While *Lexc* is a good fit for ordered concatenative morphology and is accessible for entering inventories of open category roots, it is not a natural fit for the highly agglutinative polysynthetic Yine language with its relatively free order of suffixes. Instead open category root inventories are edited in spreadsheets and exported via

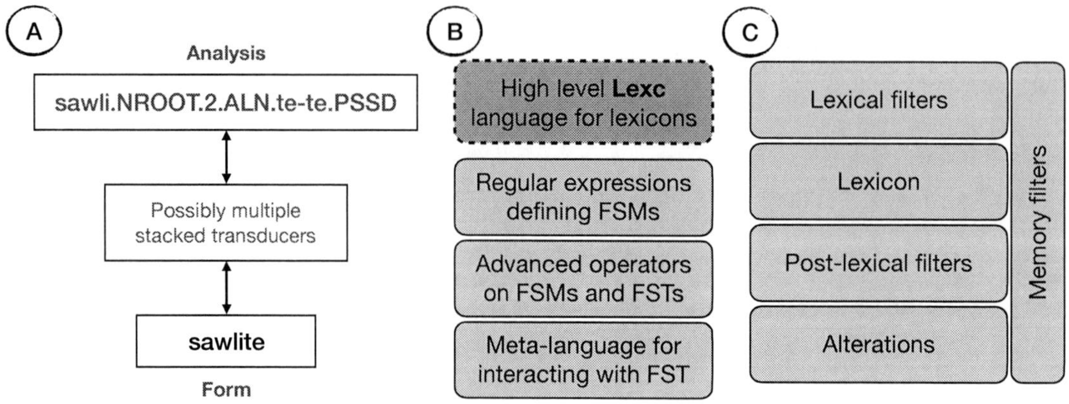

Figure 1: Language views: A) Upper analysis and lower form, B) By level/domain, C) By function.

Python scripts to FST source files. All morphological analysis is coded in *FST*, consistent with efforts by (Cardenas and Zeman, 2018; Ortega et al., 2020; Castro Mamani, 2020) for other Amazonian languages.

The *FST* language can be viewed as divided into regular expressions (defining finite state machines (FSMs)) typically used for string searching or pattern matching, advanced operators on FSMs or FSTs, and a meta-language for interacting with FSTs. Regular expressions largely suffice for the analysis tape; cross-product, rewrite rule, composition, and containment advanced operators are essential for operating on FSMs and FSTs; define, apply, file related, and virtual stack machine related meta-commands let us construct and interact with FSTs and the operating system.

FST components may also be grouped functionally as lexical, post-lexical and memory filters; lexicon; and alterations (Figure 1C). Filters which restrict lexical generation precede the lexicon; they serve to restrict the allowable combinations of constituent morphemes that might be generated by the lexicon. The lexicon, originates all constituent morphemes from both open and closed morpheme classes generating all possible valid (mostly) lexical sequences.

Sometimes it is difficult to prospectively generate only valid analyses, and so filters may be used to prevent over-generation. Similarly, some problems of over-generation (e.g., duplication) are more readily solved after generation with post-lexical filters. Phonological and morphophonological processing often imposes constraints on surface form realization of the morphological analyses, e.g., final vowel elision or rhotacism. Such constraints are implemented as alterations of the lexical analysis. Long range or discontinuous morphological relations are not readily handled by FSTs, but with use of limited memory based filters, with diacritic flags, even these problems can be resolved.

We chose to divide and conquer the analyzer project based on (Hanson, 2010)'s Yine Grammar structure. We define common terms, closed class morphemes, and open class roots, followed by higher level constructs expressible as single words: adjective, noun, noun phrase, verb, nominalization, predicate, and clause.

In the next section on morphological analysis we will see cogent examples combining language analysis from the previous section and finite state morphology described here.

5 Morphological analysis

We report several morphological analyses and snippets of corresponding FST code. FST is a multi-use term applying to simple definitions, regular expressions, filters, alterations, lexicon and the entire analyzer. All the terms beginning with /•/ are symbolic terms defined in file `common-u.foma`; their corresponding implementation specific and Unimorph terms are substituted on evaluation. Listing 1 shows a snippet of label definitions.

```
define •NRoot ".NROOT";
define •VRoot ".VROOT";
...
define •Quot ".QUOT";  # quote
define •Infer ".INFER";  # inference
```

Listing 1: Label definitions

```
define NRoot [
  [ {kamruru} [•NRoot •PossPfx3
    •Inalienable]:0 ]
| [ {gagmuna} [•NRoot •PossPfx1
    •Alienable •PossSfxte]:0 ]
];
```

Listing 2: Noun root snippet

5.1 Open word categories

Open word vocabulary is processed using Python scripts to construct root constituents with coded lexical information. The snippet in listing 2 defines noun roots, *kamruru* and *gagmuna* with form, alienability, and possessor prefix class. Inalienable nouns are further marked with `•Kin` when a kinship term. Alienable nouns are marked for their possessed suffix type. Possessor prefix class is largely determinable from alienability, kinship, and whether the initial sound segment is /g/, but it was more convenient, to index it directly. Note the use of `define` to define the FST of all noun roots and assign it to `NRoot`. The form `{kamruru}` is expanded to a string of characters and available on both the upper and lower tapes of this transducer. The regular expression `[•NRoot •PossPfx3 •Inalienable]:0` groups together the sequence of analysis terms on the upper tape as `.NROOT.3.NALN` and and maps them to ø on the lower tape via the `:` cross-product operation.

5.2 Noun root examples

Yine noun roots from the example just above are shown in (13) and (14). Inalienable nouns are preferentially possessed and are marked with the suffix *-chi* when unpossessed. Alienable nouns can readily occur without a possessor (unmarked) and are marked with their possessed suffix when possessed.[4]

(13) kamrurchi
kamruru-chi
work-UNPSSD

'(the unpossessed) work'

`kamruru.NROOT.3.NALN-chi.UNPSSD`

(14) gagmunate
gagmuna-te
tree-PSSD

'(a possessed) tree'

`gagmuna.NROOT.1.ALN.te-te.PSSD`

Listing 3 shows how noun possession is defined by FST. Inalienable unpossessed state is marked with *-chi* by selecting inalienable nouns, `$[•Inalienable]`, from noun roots, `NRoot`, writing the noun root and `-chi •Unposs` on the upper tape, and noun root and `^V chi` on the lower tape. `$[•Inalienable]` is a lexical filter which when composed, `.o.`, with noun roots from the lexicon selects only inalienable noun roots. The intermediate flag `^V` subsequently triggers a final vowel elision, defined by `VElision`.[5] Alienable possessed state is defined similarly except that for possessed suffix *-te* there is no final vowel elision.

```
define NounInalienUnposs $[•Inalienable]
    .o. [NRoot %-:"^V" {chi} •Unposs:0]
    .o. VElision;

define NounTe $[•Alienable •PossSfxte]
    .o. [NRoot %-:0 {te} •Poss:0];
```

Listing 3: Noun possession regexes

5.3 Nominal example

The noun shown in (15) is copied from (2) above. Word construction shows several phenomena taken into account by the FST: 1. possessor class 1 (stem with initial /g/), 2. comitative noun case, 3. elision alteration of initial /g/, 4. discontinuous dependency for possessor 3rd person plural.

(15) ragmunateymana
r-gagmuna-te-yma-na
PSS3P-tree-PSSD-COM/INS-PSS3P

'With their trees'

`r.PSS3P-gagmuna.NROOT.1.ALN.te`
`-te.PSSD-yma.COM/INS-na.PSS3P`

The snippet in listing 4 shows 3rd person singular and plural prefixes from possessor prefix class 1. For the singular case, `t •3SgFPssr -` is written to the upper tape, and `t ^g` to the lower tape. The intermediate flag `^g` subsequently triggers an alteration due to the initial /g/. The plural case adds complexity with a diacritic flag being set to positive by `@P.PSSR.3PL@` for both upper and lower tapes, in addition to writing `r •3PlPssr -` to the upper tape and `r ^g` to the lower tape. The diacritic flag with feature `PSSR` remembers its setting and permits completion of the word with the `PSS3P`

[4]The annotations shown in (13, 14) use standard four-line glossing format customary in contemporary grammatical description. Output from the FST morphological analyzer is added as a fifth line of the gloss.

[5]Intermediate flags are an essential technique for triggering alterations. See alteration rule examples in (Hulden, 2011).

suffix.[6]

```
define PronNPfxScl [
  ...
  | {t} [•3SgFPssr %-] : "^g"
  | "@P.PSSR.3PL@" {r} [•3PlPssr %-]:"^g"
];
```

Listing 4: Possessor paradigm 1 (initial 'g')

The snippet in listing 5 presents three mutually exclusive noun case alternatives of which comitative is matched in analysis; and so the comitative `-yma •Com` is written to the upper tape and `yma` to the lower tape. None of the cases trigger vowel elision.

```
define NounCase [
  %-:0 {yma} •Com:0
  | %-:0 {yegi} •Circ:0
  | %-:0 {ya} •Loc:0
];
```

Listing 5: Comitative noun case

The snippet in listing 6 decides whether or not to show the `PSS3P` suffix based on the `PSSR` diacritic flag setting. If the flag setting meets the `3PL` requirement, then `-na •3PlPssr` is written to the upper tape and `^Vu na` is written to the lower (intermediate) tape. The intermediate flag `^Vu` subsequently triggers an alteration of final vowel elision except for /u/. If the `PSSR` diacritic flag is not set then nothing is written to either tape; in this way the FST can accept the discontinuous 3rd person plural possessor.

```
define Pron3PlNSfx [
  %-:"^Vu" "@R.PSSR.3PL@" {na} •3PlPssr:0
  | "@D.PSSR@"
];
```

Listing 6: Possessor 3rd person plural suffix

The snippet in listing 7 generates the noun from optional possessor class 1 prefix, noun root, optional noun plural, optional noun case and diacritic flag determined 3rd person plural suffix. The alteration FSTs are composed with the lexical output to handle changes due to initial /g/, final vowel elision, or final vowel elision for vowels other than /u/.

```
define Nouns [•Noun:0 [
  (PronNPfxScl) NounPfxl (NounPlural)
  (NounCase) Pron3PlNSfx
  ...
  .o. gAlteration
  .o. VElision
  .o. VuElision;
```

Listing 7: Noun generation

[6]Diacritic flags are a powerful yet difficult to understand addition to FST. See (Hulden, 2011) for a brief introduction and (Beesley and Karttunen, 2003, pp 339-373) for an in depth explanation with examples.

The word *ragmunateymana* shows application of both the initial /g/ and final vowel elision except for /u/ alterations. The snippet in listing 8 shows how an initial *gi* is rewritten as /u/ or /g/ is rewritten as /ø/ after the `^g` intermediate flag in the lower tape; subsequently the flag itself is erased from the lower tape.

In *ragmunateymana* the initial /g/ of the noun root is elided and the /r/ of the pronoun prefix added. The case for final vowel other than /u/ elision is more complex, in that the vowel is not elided if it would result in a three consonant cluster. Such is the case here and so the final /a/ of *-yma* need not elide before *-na*. Since the three consonant cluster includes nasal consonants, the final /a/ could be elided resulting in the alternative valid word form *ragmunateymna* (Hanson, 2010).

```
define gAlteration [[g i -> u || "^g" _]
  .o. [g -> 0 || "^g" _ ]
  .o. ["^g" -> 0]
];
```

Listing 8: 'g' alteration

5.4 Verb predicate mega example

The verb predicate shown in (16) is not testified to by the Yine corpus, but rather is a *tour de force* act of word creation based on the grammar by Hanson, comparable to verb predicate phrase creation in non-polysynthetic languages. The analysis shown is based on the FST analysis and shows several important word generation features: 1. subject prefix class 1 (stem with initial /g/), 2. associate prefix *gim-*, 3. alteration due to initial /g/, 4. discontinuous dependency of form for 3rd person plural, 5. multiple incorporants for verb stem, 6. open category noun incorporant, 7. marker for closure of incorporants, 8. multiple incorporants for verb predicate, 9. vowel elision.

(16) rumustakasijnegimananjetyanupluna
r-gim-gustaka-siji-ne
ARGNO3P-LGSPEC3-cut-corn-PSSD
-gima-nanu-je-ta
-QUOT-EXTNS-HAB-LGSPEC1
-ya-nu-pa-lu-na
-APPL-DED-ALL-ARGAC3SM-ARGNO3P

'It is said that they, and someone else (usually) cut their (masc) corn during a specific time lapse'

```
r.ARGNO3P-gim.LGSPEC3-gustaka.VROOT.AMBI
-siji.NROOT.2.ALN.ne-ne.PSSD-gima.QUOT
-nanu.EXTNS-je.HAB-ta.LGSPEC1-ya.APPL
-nu.DED-pa.ALL-lu.ARGAC3SM-na.ARGNO3P
```

The subject pronoun prefix class 1 (with inital /g/) is similar to that of possessor prefix class 1 with nouns. Discontinuous behavior for `•Subj3Pl` is also similar to that for `•3PlPssr`, noun possessor 3rd person plural, with the obvious difference that the 3rd person plural subject suffix marker *-na* is now very distant from the prefix!

Adding the associative prefix *gim-* to the verb root triggers 'g' alteration for roots with initial /g/ similar to subject class 1. The FST, see listing 9, writes `gim •Assoc -` to the upper tape and `gim ^g` to the lower tape. The intermediate flag `^g` subsequently triggers 'g' alteration if the stem has initial /g/ as is the case here for the verb *gustaka*.

```
define VerbAssoc [{gim} [•Assoc %-]:"^g"];
```

Listing 9: 'g' alteration with *gim-*

A huge difference in relation nouns is that verbs and verb predicates can have several incorporated morphemes including open noun class morphemes. Individual closed form incorporants are similar in structure to NounCase (listing 5) and VerbAssoc (listing 9) above. With verb stems, multiple incorporants can appear, but each incorporant type only once, and according to Hanson (2010), the order of incorporants is flexible. The snippet in listing 10 shows forming the union of individual incorporants, and the snippet in listing 11 shows how this union is repeated over 1 to 9 iterations. While not obvious from the union (because everything is via definitions), the lexical form and analysis for each incorporant are written to the upper tape and the lexical form and a unique filter flag are written to the lower tape. The filter flags will be used to enforce the no more than one of each incorporant type rule. [7]

```
define VerbIncorporantsNoCoda [
    %-:0 NounAlienPoss 0:"^I.A"
    ...
    | VerbAspect2 0:"^I.H"
    | VerbAspect3 0:"^I.I" ];
```

Listing 10: Verb stem incorporant union

When verb stem incorporants are used, they must be followed by marking of incorporant list closure, or by a causative which also effects closure, `[VerbClosure | VerbCausative]`. While repetition for 1 to 9 iterations of the union of incorporants assures no more than 9 incorporants, it does not prevent repetition of some of the incorporants. This is where the filter flags, e.g., `"^I.H"`, are used. Composing `~[detectIncorporantDuplicates]` with the lower tape from verb incorporants excludes all cases where the same filter flag is repeated, thus eliminating repeated incorporants from the FST.

```
define VerbIncorporants
        [VerbIncorporantsNoCoda^{1,9}
        [VerbClosure | VerbCausative]]
    .o. ~[detectIncorporantDuplicates]
    .o. eraseIncorporantFlags;
```

Listing 11: Verb stem incorporants

Listing 12 shows a snippet for the FST of all duplicate filter flags. Each line such as `$["^I.A" ?* "^I.A"]` denotes the language containing that filter flag duplicated, and the union over all such flags denotes the union of languages with duplicate flags. Taking the complement of this results in all languages without duplicate flags, and composing this complement with the actual group of incorporants, excludes any cases where there are duplicate flags. This is a powerful operator!

```
define detectIncorporantDuplicates [
    $["^I.A" ?* "^I.A"]
    | $["^I.B" ?* "^I.B"]
    ...
    | $["^I.I" ?* "^I.I"]];
```

Listing 12: Incorporant test for duplicates

Alienable possessed nouns or inalienable nouns (possessed root form) can serve as incorporants. This augments the expressiveness of the verb stem dramatically in that the number of verb stem combinations now gets multiplied by the number of alienable nouns and by the number of inalienable nouns. Gloss (16) incorporates the possessed alienable noun *siji-ne*, 'corn'.

Elision processes are the same or similar for nouns and we don't repeat the FST code here. Note that with so many components in the word and multiple elision processes it is not obvious to the non-native speaker, how to derive the final word form with all applied elisions and other alterations.

5.5 Ambiguity

There may be multiple analyses for individual words of the language and similarly multiple word representations for the same analysis. This ambiguity can happen because: 1. elision of final vowels of morphemes so that forms are no longer distinct, 2. elision is optional so that inherently there are multiple forms, or 3. the same form is used across multiple morphemes. Language use is a constant

[7] Beesley and Karttunen (2003, pp 299-230) explains a lexical filter version of this. In our implementation, filter flags are written to the lower tape and post-lexical filters applied to eliminate duplicate incorporant types.

process of negotiation between ambiguity of expression and efficiency of communication.

6 Evaluation

For unit testing of noun, verb, and verb predicate analyses, we constructed forms for several distinct analyses each of 20 nouns sampled over possessor class and 20 verbs sampled over subject and object classes. Diverse analyses varied possessor/-subject/object person, number, and gender as well as noun or verb incorporants. While resulting derived forms were largely consistent with analyses, we discovered and corrected several cases of lexically specified vowel elision and rhotacism not covered in Hanson (2010)'s grammar.

For coverage on test data we sampled words matching on known root forms with 25 each of noun roots and verb roots sampled at random from a Yine corpus by Bustamante et al. (2020). This resulted in many out of vocabulary words from longer root forms than those used for selection. Yet, there remained numerous other words unrecognized (not covered) by the analyzer even though sharing the expected root. So we performed a detail error analysis from a sub-sample of 63 unrecognized words to diagnose errors and make model improvements.

The error analysis is reported in table 1. Some forms suffered from multiple errors and so error counts exceed the number of words sampled. For nouns major reasons for lack of coverage are: 1. morpheme not in FST vocabulary, 2. non-verbal predicate, 3. verbalizer changed category to verb, 4. noun root entry incorrect. For verbs major reasons for lack of coverage are: 1. morpheme not in FST vocabulary, 2. elision and rhotacism alterations, 3. nominalizer changed category to noun, 4. morpheme has more flexible order.

Corrections and improvements from easy to hard are: 1. Correct out of vocabulary, entry, and orthographic errors of roots on vocabulary spreadsheets. 2. Correct intermediate flags and alterations for elision and rhotacism. 3. Add missing suffixes and more flexible order for morpheme out of vocabulary and order errors. 4. Prioritize development of non-verbal predicate, nominalizer, and verbalizer functions to address non-verbal predicate and change of category errors.

Cardenas and Zeman (2018) obtained 78.9% average coverage over multiple domains on test data for a completed FST morphology of an Amazonian polysynthetic language. Our ≈15% coverage in a preliminary evaluation on multiple domain test data should be interpreted as a measure of the effort still to go on this project. Our goal remains a high coverage FST morphological analyzer.

Error	**Nouns**	**Verbs**
Root out of vocabulary	9	6
Morpheme out of vocabulary	7	10
Morpheme out of order	1	3
Elision incorrect	0	9
Rhotacism incorrect	0	6
Orthographic mismatch	0	2
Change of category	5	7
Non-verbal predicate	7	0
Root entry incorrect	5	1
Error counts	34	44
Sample size	30	33
Total words sampled	574	1292
Percentage recognized	11.3%	16.1%

Table 1: Lack of Coverage Reasons

7 Conclusion

We have shown our initial steps in developing noun, verb, verb predicate and pronoun categories for a morphological model of the Yine language, illustrating analyses performed and FST patterns used to solve challenging problems. Testing for analyzer coverage with real world data revealed several deficiencies, some expected (nominalizers, verbalizers, non-verbal predicate) and some surprises (unexpected elision, rhotacism, and missing morpheme errors). We will continue to improve the analyzer by fixing problems and adding major word categories and functions, now with added emphasis on testing with external data. Goals for the analyzer include both language documentation and use as a component of natural language processing (NLP) applications such as spell checking and low resource machine translation.

Acknowledgements

We are grateful to the bilingual teachers from NOPOKI Nimia Acho and Remigio Zapata. Similarly, we acknowledge the research grant of the "Consejo Nacional de Ciencia, Tecnología e Innovación Tecnológica" (CONCYTEC, Peru) under the contract 183-2018-FONDECYT-BM-IADT-MU.

References

Alexandra Aikhenvald. 2020. Morhology in arawakan languages. *Oxford Research Encyclopedia of Linguistics*.

Kenneth R. Beesley and Lauri Karttunen. 2003. *Finite State Morphology*. CSLI Studies in Computational Linguistics Online. CSLI publications, Stanford University, Stanford, CA, USA.

Gina Bustamante, Arturo Oncevay, and Roberto Zariquiey. 2020. No data to crawl? monolingual corpus creation from PDF files of truly low-resource languages in Peru. In *Proceedings of the 12th Language Resources and Evaluation Conference*, pages 2914–2923, Marseille, France. European Language Resources Association.

Ronald Cardenas and Daniel Zeman. 2018. A morphological analyzer for Shipibo-konibo. In *Proceedings of the Fifteenth Workshop on Computational Research in Phonetics, Phonology, and Morphology*, pages 131–139, Brussels, Belgium. Association for Computational Linguistics.

Richard Alexander Castro Mamani. 2020. Ashaninka-morph. github at https://github.com/hinantin/AshMorph.

Rebecca Hanson. 2010. *A Grammar of Yine (Piro)*. Ph.D. thesis, La Trobe University, Victoria, Australia.

Mans Hulden. 2009. Foma: a finite-state compiler and library. In *Proceedings of the 12th Conference of the European Chapter of the Association for Computational Linguistics*, pages 29–32. Association for Computational Linguistics.

Mans Hulden. 2011. Morphological analysis with fsts. Document in github: https://fomafst.github.io/morphtut.html.

Lauri Karttunen and Kenneth R. Beesley. 2005. Twenty-five years of finite-state morphology. In Antti Arppe, Lauri Carlson, Krister Lindén, Jussi Piitulainen, Mickael Suominen, Martti Vainio, Hanna Westerlund, and Anssi Yli-Jyrä, editors, *Inquiries into Words, Constraints and Contexts*. CSLI publications, Stanford University.

Christo Kirov, Ryan Cotterell, John Sylak-Glassman, Géraldine Walther, Ekaterina Vylomova, Patrick Xia, Manaal Faruqui, Arya D. McCarthy, Sandra Kübler, David Yarowsky, Jason Eisner, , and Mans Hulden. 2018. Unimorph 2.0: Universal morphology. In *Proceedings of the Eleventh International Conference on Language Resources and Evaluation (LREC 2018)*. European Language Resources Association (ELRA).

Christopher Moseley, editor. 2010. *Atlas of the world's languages in danger*, 3rd edition. UNESCO, Paris, France.

John Ortega, Richard Alexander Castro-Mamani, and Jaime Rafael Montoya Samame. 2020. Overcoming resistance: The normalization of an Amazonian tribal language. In *Proceedings of the 3rd Workshop on Technologies for MT of Low Resource Languages*, pages 1–13, Suzhou, China. Association for Computational Linguistics.

Thomas E Payne. 2007. *Describing Morphosyntax: A guide for field linguists*. Cambridge University Press.

Tommi A. Pirinen and Krister Lindén. 2010. Creating and weighting hunspell dictionaries as finite-state automata. *Investigationes Linguisticae*.

Tommi A. Pirinen and Krister Lindén. 2014. State-of-the-art in weighted finite-state spell-checking. In *Proceedings of the 15th International Conference on Computational Linguistics and Intelligent Text Processing*, CICLing 2014, pages 519–532, Berlin, Heidelberg. Springer-Verlag.

Annette Rios. 2010. *Applying Finite-State Techniques to a Native American Language: Quechua*. Ph.D. thesis, Universitaẗ Zuřich.

Mary Ruth Wise, editor. 1986. *Diccionario Piro*. Summer Institute of Linguistics, Yarinacocha, Perú.

Remigio Zapata, Nimia Acho, and Gerardo Zerdin. 2017. *Guía teórica del idioma yine*. Universidad Católica Sedes Sapientae.

Roberto Zariquiey, Harald Hammarström, Mónica Arakaki, Arturo Oncevay, John Miller, Aracelli García, and Adriano Ingunza. 2019. Obsolescencia lingüística, descripción gramatical y documentación de lenguas en el perú: hacia un estado de la cuestión. *Lexis*, 43(2):271–337.

Appendix: Unimorph and Hanson Grammar Terms Used in Paper

Unimorph	Hanson (2010)	Description
ALL	ELV	Allative / Ellative
APPL	APPL	Applicative
ARGNO1S	1SG	First person singular 'subject'
ARGNO2S	2SG	Second person singular 'subject'
ARGNO3P	3PL	Third person plural 'subject'
ARGNO3SM	3SGM	Third person masculine 'subject'
ARGAC1P	1PL	First person plural 'object'
ARGAC3SM	3SgM	Third person singular masculine 'object'
ARGAC3SF	3SgF	Third person singular feminine 'object'
COMP	SUBD	Comparative (subordination function)
COM/INS	COM	Commitative (and instrumental)
DED	SUBD	Deductive (subordination function)
EXTNS	EXTNS	Extensive aspect
HAB	CONTIN	Habitual / Continuative
INDF	GENZ	Indefinitness in time
IPFV	IMPFV	Imperfective aspect
LGSPEC1	VCL	Verb Stem Closure
LGSPEC2	CMPV	Completive aspect
LGSPEC3	ASSOC	Associative
PFV	PFV	Perfective aspect
PL	PL	Plural
PROX	VICIN	Proximative
PSSD	PSSD	Possessed noun
PSS1S	1SGPSSR	First person singular possessor
PSS2S	2SGPSSR	Second person singular possessor
PSS3P	3PLPSSR	Third person plural posessor
QUOT	QUOT	Quotative (epistemic marker)
UNPSSD	UNPSSD	Unpossessed noun

Table 2: FST Morphology - UniMorph categories with Hanson (2010)'s glossing equivalents.

Leveraging English Word Embeddings for Semi-Automatic Semantic Classification in Nêhiyawêwin (Plains Cree)

Atticus G. Harrigan
University of Alberta
4-32 Assiniboia Hall
University of Alberta, Edmonton
atticus.harrigan@ualberta.ca

Antti Arppe
University of Alberta
4-32 Assiniboia Hall
University of Alberta, Edmonton
arppe@ualberta.ca

Abstract

This paper details a semi-automatic method of word clustering for the Algonquian language, Nêhiyawêwin (Plains Cree). Although this method worked well, particularly for nouns, it required some amount of manual postprocessing. The main benefit of this approach over implementing an existing classification ontology is that this method approaches the language from an endogenous point of view, while performing classification quicker than in a fully manual context.

1 Introduction

Grouping words into semantic subclasses within a part of speech is a technique used widely throughout quantitative and predictive studies in the field of linguistics. Bresnan et al. (2007) use high level verb classes to predict the English dative alternation, Arppe et al. (2008) uses verb class as one of the feature sets to help predict the alternation of Finnish *think* verbs, and Yu et al. (2017) use polarity classifications (*good* vs *bad*) from pre-defined lexica such as WordNet (Miller, 1998). In many cases, classifications within word classes allow researchers to group words into smaller cohesive groups to allow for use as predictors in modelling. Rather than using thousands individual lexemes as predictors, one can use a word's class to generalize over the semantic features of individual lexemes to allow for significantly more statistical power.

While extensive ontologies of word classifications exist for majority languages like English (Miller, 1998), German (Hamp and Feldweg, 1997), and Chinese (Wang and Bond, 2013), minority languages, especially lesser resourced languages in North America generally do not boast such resources.[1] Where such ontologies do exist, for example in Innu-aimun (Eastern Cree) (Visitor et al., 2013), they are often manually created, an expensive process in terms of time. Alternatively, they may be based upon English ontologies such as WordNet. This opens the window to near-automatic ontology creation by associating definitions in a target language and English through a variety of methods. This is especially important, given the amount of time and effort that goes into manually classifying a lexicon through either an existing ontology (be it something like Rapidwords[2] or even Levin's like classes (Levin, 1993)). Moreover, there is a motivation based in understanding a language and its lexicalization process on its own terms, though how to do this with a lesser resourced language remains unclear.

2 Background

We begun word classification in preparation for modelling a morpho-syntactic alternation in Nêhiyawêwin verbs. One hypothesis we developed for this alternation, based on Arppe et al. (2008), is that the semantic classes of the verbs themselves as well as their nominal arguments would inform the verbal alternation. Due to constraints of time, we investigated methods to automatically classify both verbs and nouns in Nêhiyawêwin. Although statistical modelling remains the immediate motivator for the authors, semantic/thematic classifications have a wide range of benefits for language learners and revitalization, particularly in online lexicographic resources, where one may want to view all words to do with a theme, rather than simply finding translations of single English words.

In creating a framework for automatic semantic classification we make use of Word2vec (Mikolov et al., 2013a) word embeddings. Word embeddings are words represented by n-dimensional vectors. These vectors are ultimately derived from a word's

[1] There is one attempt at semantically classifying Nêhiyawêwin through automatic means found in Dacanay et al. (2021). This work makes use of similar techniques as desccribed in this paper, differing mainly in its mapping of Nêhiyawêwin words onto Wordnet classes.

[2] See http://rapidwords.net/

Proceedings of the First Workshop on Natural Language Processing for Indigenous Languages of the Americas, pages 113–121
June 11, 2021.

context in some corpus through the Word2vec algorithm. Unfortunately, the Word2vec method is sensitive to corpus size. We initially attempted to create basic word and feature co-occurrence matrices based on a 140,000 token Nêhiyawêwin corpus (Arppe et al., 2020) to create word vectors using Principal Components Analysis, but in the end found the results to be not practically useful. Similarly, an attempt at both tf-idf and Word2Vec using only the Nêhiyawêwin dictionary produces mostly ill-formed groupings, though in these cases preprocessing by splitting verbs and nouns was not performed. Regardless, the poor performance was most certainly due simply to the paucity of data. Although the available corpora are small, Nêhiyawêwin does have several English-to-Nêhiyawêwin dictionaries, the largest being Wolvengrey (2001). Although a bilingual Nêhiyawêwin-English dictionary, it is one formed from an Indigenous point of view, based on vocabulary from previous dictionaries, some of which have been compiled by Nêhiyawêwin communities from their own perspectives, or gleaned from a number of texts collections rather than attempting to find Nêhiyawêwin word matches for a pre-defined set of English words. This results in dictionary entries such as `sakapwêw: it roasts over a fire (by hanging, with string on stick)`. Definitions such as this take into account the nuanced cultural understanding reflected in the word's morphology.

3 Methodology

To address the issue of corpus size, we attempted to bootstrap our classification scheme with pre-trained English vectors in the form of the 3 million word Google News Corpus, which represents every word with a 300-dimensional vector.[3] We make use of the English definitions (sometimes also referred to as glosses) provided in Wolvengrey (2001) and fit to each word its respective Google News Corpus vector. This dictionary makes use of lemmas as headwords, and contains 21,717 entries. The presumption is that the real-world referents (at least in terms of denotation) of English and Nêhiyawêwin words are approximately comparable, in particular when taking the entire set of words in an English definition. Stop words were removed, and where content words were present in definitions in Wolvengrey (2001) but *not* available in the Google News Corpus, synonyms were used (one such example might be the word *mitêwin*, which is unavailable in the corpus and thus would replaced with something like *medicine lodge* or deleted if a synonym was given in the definition as well). Because the Google News Corpus is based in American spelling, while Wolvengrey (2001) is based in Canadian spelling, American forms (e.g. *color, gray*) were converted into Canadian forms (e.g. *colour, grey*). If such preprocessing is not performed, these words are simply unavailable for clustering, as they lack a matching vector.[4] Where a Nêhiyawêwin word had more than one word sense, each sense was given a separate entry and the second entry was marked with a unique identifier. Finally, where needed, words in the Nêhiyawêwin definitions were lemmatized.

Once every word in Wolvengrey (2001) definitions matched an entry in the Google News Corpus, we associated each word in a Nêhiyawêwin definition with its respective Google News Vector. That is, given a definition such as `awâsisihkânis: small doll`, the resulting structure would be:

$$\texttt{awâsisihkânis} = \begin{bmatrix} 0.159 \\ 0.096 \\ -0.125 \\ \vdots \end{bmatrix} \begin{bmatrix} 0.108 \\ 0.031 \\ -0.034 \\ \vdots \end{bmatrix}$$

Because all word-vectors in the Google News Corpus are of the same dimensionality, we then took the resulting definition and averaged, per dimension, the values of all its constituent word-vectors. This produced a single 300-dimensional vector that acts as a sort of naive sentence vector for each of the English glosses/definitions:

$$\texttt{awâsisihkânis} = \begin{bmatrix} 0.134 \\ 0.064 \\ -0.080 \\ \vdots \end{bmatrix}$$

Mikolov et al. (2013b) mention this sort of naive representation and suggests the use of phrase vectors instead of word vectors to address the representation of non-compositional idioms; however,

[3]This corpus was trained on a large corpus of 100 billion words. Available at `https://code.google.com/archive/p/word2vec/`

[4]In reality, there were only a handful of cases where words occurred in the dictionary but not in the Google News Corpus. Because there are so few examples of this, even simply leaving these items out would not substantiqally change clustering results.

given the way Wolvengrey (2001)'s definitions are written (e.g. with few idiomatic or metaphorical constructions), and for reasons of computational simplicity, we opted to use the above naive implementation in this paper.

After creating the sentence (or English definition) vectors, we proceeded to cluster definitions with similar vectors together. To achieve this, we created a Euclidean distance matrix from the sentence vectors and made use of the `hclust` package in R (R Core Team, 2017) to preform hierarchical agglomerative clustering using the Ward method (based on the experience of (Arppe et al., 2008) in using the method to produce multiple levels of smaller, spherical clusters). This form of clustering is essentially a bottom-up approach where groupings are made by starting with individual labels with the shortest distance, then iteratively at a higher level making use of the clusters that result from the previous step or remaining individual levels; this second step is repeated until there is a single cluster containing all labels. This method of clustering creates a cluster tree that can be cut at any specified level after the analysis has been completed to select different numbers of clusters, allowing researchers some degree of flexibility without needing to rerun the clustering. This method is very similar to what has been done by both Arppe et al. (2008), Bresnan et al. (2007), and Divjak and Gries (2006). The choice of what number of clusters was made based on an evaluation of the effectiveness of the clusters, based on an impressionistic overview by the authors.

For our purposes, we focused on the semantic classification of Nêhiyawêwin nouns and verbs. Nêhiyawêwin verbs are naturally morphosemantically divided into four separate classes: Intransitive verbs with a single inanimate argument (VII), Intransitive verbs with a single animate argument (VAI), transitive verbs with an animate actor[5] and an inanimate goal (VTI), and verbs with animate actors and goal (VTA). For verbs, clustering took place within each of these proto-classes. Among the VIIs, 10 classes proved optimal, VAIs had 25 classes, VTIs with 15 classes, and VTAs with 20 classes. The choice to preprocess verbs into these four classes was as not doing so resulted in a clustering pattern that focused mainly on the difference between transitivity and the animacy of arguments. Any more or fewer classes and HAC clusters were far less cohesive with obvious semantic units being dispersed among many classes or split into multiple classes with no obvious differentiation. Similarly, verbs were split from nouns in this process because definitions in Wolvengrey (2001) vary significantly between verbs and nouns.

Nouns are naturally divided into two main classes in Nêhiyawêwin: animate and inanimate.[6] For our purposes we divide these further within each class between independent (i.e. alienable) and dependent (i.e. inalienable) nouns to create four main classes: Independent Animate Nouns (NA), Dependent Animate Nouns (NDA), Independent inanimate Nouns (NI), and Dependent Inanimate Nouns (NDI). The reason for this further division is due to the morphosemantic differences between independent and dependent nouns in Nêhiyawêwin. While independent nouns can stand on their own and represent a variety of entities, they are semantically and morphologically dependent on some possessor. We opted to pre-split NDIs and NDAs into their own classes, so as not to have the clustering focus on alienablity as the most major difference.[7]

4 Results

In all cases, clusters produced by this procedure needed some amount of post-processing. For nouns, this post-processing was minimal and mostly took the form of adjustments to the produced clusters: moving some items from one class to another, splitting a class that had clear semantic divisions, etc. For the verbs, this processing was often more complex, especially for the VAI and VTA classes. Items were determined to not belong in one class or another based on it's central meaning of the action or entity. If the majority of group members pertained to smoking (a cigarette), a word describing smokiing meat (as food preparation) would not be placed in this group, as the essence of the action and its intended purpose diverged significantly from the rest of the group.

[5]As discussed in Wolvengrey (2005), Nêhiyawêwin sentences are devoid subject and objects in the usual sense. Instead, syntactic roles are defined by verbal direction alignment. For this reason, we use the terms *actor* and *goal* instead of *subject* and *object*.

[6]Although this gender dichotomy is *mostly* semantically motivated (e.g. nouns that are semantically inanimate are part of the inanimate gender) this is not always the case as in the word *pahkwêsikan*, 'bread', a grammatically animate word.

[7]Preliminary results for words not seperated by their conjugation class or declension did, in fact, create clusters based around these obvious differences. This likely due to the way definitions were phrased (e.g. dependent nouns would have a possessive determiner or pronoun).

Although most clusters produced somewhat cohesive semantic units, the largest clusters for the VAI and VTA classes acted as, essentially, catch-all clusters. Although computationally they seemed to have similar vector semantics, the relationship between items was not obvious to the human eye. Postprocessing for these clusters took substantial amounts of time and essentially comprised of using more cohesive clusters as a scaffold to fit words from these catch-all clusters into. In most cases, this resulted in slightly more clusters after postprocessing, though for VAIs this number was significantly higher, and for the NDIs it was slightly lower. Table 1 lists the number of cluster directly from HAC and from postprocessing.

Postprocessing grouped together words based on the most core semantic property of the word class: nouns were generally grouped based on the entity or state they represented, and verbs were generally grouped based on the most basic form action they represented. This is why, for example, `AI-cover` includes words for both covering and uncovering. In some cases a final class may seem like something that could be subsumed under another (e.g. `AI-pray` or `AI-cooking` might be understood as subsets of `AI-action`); however, in these cases, the subsumed class was judged to be sufficiently separate (e.g. *cooking* is an action of transforming resources into food for the purposes of nourishment, while verbs of `AI-action` are more manipulative, direct actions done for their own sake. Further, the automatic classification already grouped words in these ways, further justifying their separation. Finally, some grouping seem more morphosyntactic (e.g. `AI-reflexive`), though we argue that reflexivity, performing an action inwards, is in and of itself a salient semantic feature, and the inclusion of these terms into Wolvengrey (2001) indicates their lexicalization and distinction from the non-reflexive forms.

The actual quality of clustering varied form class to class. In general, nouns resulted in much more cohesive clusters out-of-the-box and required far less postprocessing. For example, nearly all of the HAC class NI_{14} items referred to parts of human bodies (and those that did not fit this description were terms clearly related to body parts like *aspatâskwahpisowin*, 'back rest'), NI_{13} was made up of trapping/hunting words and words for nests/animals.

The NA classes produced through HAC were similarly straightforward: NI_9 was made up of words for trees, poles, sticks, and plants; NI_8 was made up entirely of words form beasts of burden, carts, wheels, etc.; while much of NA_3 and NA_7, and nearly all of NA_2 referred to other animals. Once manually postprocessed, the NA lexemes settled into 8 classes: `NA-persons`, `NA-beast-of-burden`, `NA-food`, `NA-celestial`, `NA-body-part`, `NA-religion`, `NA-money/count`, and `NA-shield`.

The NDI and NDA classes required almost no postprocessing: NDA_1 and NDA_3 were each made up of various family and non-family based relationships, while NDA_2 was made up of words for body parts and clothing. The resulting classes for these were: `NDA-Relations`, `NDA-Body`, and `NDA-Clothing`.

The NDI lexemes basically took two classes: the vast majority of NDI forms referred to bodies and body parts while two lexemes referred to the concept of a house, resulting in only two classes: `NDI-body`, and `NDI-house`.

Verbs, on the other hand, required quite a deal more postprocessing. VIIs showed the best clustering results without postprocessing. For example, VII_6 was entirely made up of taste/smell lexemes, VII_7 was almost entirely weather-related, VII_8 contained verbs that only take plural subjects, VII_9 had only lexemes referring to sound and sight, and VII_10 had only nominal-like verbs (e.g. *mîsiyâpiskâw* '(it is) rust(y)'). Despite these well formed clusters, VII_1 through VII_5 were less cohesive and required manual clustering. In the end, distinct classes were identified: `II-natural-land`, `II-weather-time`, `II-sensory-attitude`, `II-plural`, `II-move`, `II-time`, and `II-named`.[8] Although postprocessing was required, this was not too substantial in scope or time.

The VAIs required significantly more work. Some classes were well defined, such as VAI_{23} whose members all described some sort of flight, but VAI_{12} contains verbs of expectoration, singing, dancing, and even

[8]The concepts of *weather* and *time* were combined here as many of the Nêhiyawêwin words for specific times also contain some concept of weather (e.g. the term for 'day' is *kîsikâw*, clearly related to the word for 'sky/heavens', *kîsik*; similarly, the word for 'night' is *tipiskâw*, which is the same word used for the night sky. Additionally, words like *pipon*, 'winter' and *sîkwan* 'spring' are obviously related to both time and weather.

	HAC classes	Manually Adjusted Classes	Lexemes
VII	10	6	581
VAI	25	13	5254
VTI	15	6	1825
VTA	20	7	1781
NI	15	13	3650
NDI	3	2	245
NA	10	8	1676
NDA	3	3	191

Table 1: HAC built cluster counts vs. counts after postprocessing

painting. The HAC classes were consolidated into 13 classes: `AI-state`, `AI-action`, `AI-reflexive`, `AI-cooking`, `AI-speech`, `AI-collective`, `AI-care`, `AI-heat/fire`, `AI-money/count`, `AI-pray`, `AI-childcare`, `AI-canine`, and `AI-cover`.

The VTIs similarly required manual postprocessing after HAC clustering. Although some classes such as VTI_{11} (entirely to do with cutting or breaking) or VTI_{14} (entirely to do with pulling) were very well formed, the majority of the classes needed further subdivision (though significantly less so than with the VAIs, resulting in the following 6 classes: `TI-action`, `TI-nonaction`, `TI-speech`, `TI-money/counter`, `TI-fit`, and `TI-food`.

Finally, the VTAs required a similar amount of postpreocessing as the VAIs. Although a few classes were well formed (such as VTA_4 which was entirely made up of verbs for 'causing' something), the vast majority of HAC classes contained two or more clear semantic groupings. Through manual postprocessing, the following set of classes were defined: `VTA_allow`, `VTA_alter`, `VTA_body-position`, `VTA_care-for`, `VTA_cause`, `VTA_clothes`, `VTA_cognition`, `VTA_create`, `VTA_deceive`, `VTA_do`, `VTA_existential`, `VTA_food`, `VTA_hunt`, `VTA_miss/err`, `VTA_money`, `VTA_move`, `VTA_play`, `VTA_restrain`, `VTA_religious`, `VTA_seek`, `VTA_sense`, `VTA_speech`, `VTA_teach`, `VTA_tire`, `VTA_treat-a-way`, `VTA_(un)cover`

4.1 Evaluation

In addition the above evaluation in the description of the manual scrutiny and adjustment of HAC results, which is in and of itself an evaluation of the technique presented in this paper (with single-subject experimentation proposed as a rapid path to data for less-resourced languages such as Vietnamese (Pham and Baayen, 2015)), we present a preliminary quantitative evaluation of this technique. This evaluation allows us to judge how useful these classes are in practical terms, providing an indirect measure of the informational value of the clusters. We make use of the mixed effects modelling that initially motivated automatic semantic clustering, focusing on a morphological alternation called Nêhiyawêwin Order, wherein a verb may take the form *ninipân* (the *Independent*) or *ê-nipâyân* (the *ê-Conjunct*), both of which may be translated as 'I sleep.' The exact details of this alternation remain unclear, though there appears to be some syntactic and pragmatic motivation (Cook, 2014). Using R (R Core Team, 2017) and the `lme4` package (Bates et al., 2015), we ran a logistic regression to predict alternation using verbal semantic classes as categorical variables. In order to isolate the effect of semantic class, no other effects were used. The semantic classes were included as random effects. To assess the effectiveness of semantic class in this context, we assess the pseudo-R^2 value, a measure of Goodness-of-Fit. Unlike a regular R^2 measure, the pseudo-R^2 can not be interpreted as a direct measure of how much a model explains variance, and generally "good" pseudo-R^2 value are comparatively smaller (McFadden et al., 1973), though a higher value still represents a better fit. As a general rule, a pseudo-R^2 of 0.20 to 0.40 represents a well fit model. (McFadden,

	Manual	HAC-Only
VII	0.18	0.19
VAI	0.13	0.09
VTI	0.04	0.01
VTA	0.06	0.06

Table 2: pseudo-R^2 Values for Modelling Independent vs. ê-Conjunct Order Choice Based on Manual and Automatic Clustering Evaluation

1977)[9] Models were fit for each of the four conjugation classes for both classes produced directly from the Hierarchical Agglomerative Clustering as well those manually adjusted. We used a subset of the Ahenakew-Wolfart Corpus (Arppe et al., 2020), containing 10,764 verb tokens observed in either the Independent or ê-Conjunct forms. The resulting pseudo-R^2 scores represent the way in which automatic and semi-manual clusters can explain the Nêhiyawêwin Order alternation.

Table 2 presents the result of these analyses. the *Manual* column represents clusters that were manually adjusted, while the *HAC-Only* column represents the result of the logistic model that used only the fully automatic HAC-produced clusters. The manually adjusted and HAC-only classes performed similarly, especially for VTAs, though manual adjustment had a slightly worse fit for the VIIs, and conversely the VAI and VTI has somewhat significantly better fits using the manually adjusted classes. Although it appears that manual adjustment produced classes that were somewhat better able to explain this alternation, both manually adjusted and HAC-only clusters appear to explain a non-negligible degree of this alternation phenomenon in the above models. This is significant, because it shows that the result of the clustering techniques presented in this paper produce a tangible and useful product for linguistic analysis. Further, it suggests that, although manual classification was sometimes more useful, automatic classes more or less performed as well, allowing for researchers to determine if the added effort is worth the small increase in informational value. Nevertheless, alternative methods of evaluation, such as evaluating clusters based on speaker input, particularly through visual meas as described in Majewska et al. (2020) should be considered.[10]

5 Discussion

In general, the best clustering was seen in classes with fewer items. The VAI and NI lexemes required the most postprocessing, with each having roughly double the number of items as the next most numerous verb/noun class. Verb classes in general seemed to produce less cohesive classes through HAC. Although the exact cause of this discrepancy in unknown, it could perhaps be due to the way words are defined in Wolvengrey (2001). In this dictionary, verb definitions almost always contain more words than noun definitions. Almost every single verb definition will have at least two words, owing to the fact that Nêhiyawêwin verbs are defined by an inflected lexeme. This means that if one looks up a word like *walk*, it would appear as: `pimohtêw: s/he walks, s/he walks along; s/he goes along.` Meanwhile, nouns tend to have shorter definitions. The definition for the act of walking, a nominalized form of the verb for walk, is written as: `pimohtêwin: walk, stroll; sidewalk`. This difference is exacerbated by the fact that definitions are often translated fairly literally. Something like *pêyakwêyimisow* might be translated simply as 's/he is selfish,' but contains morphemes meaning *one*, *think*, *reflexive*, and *s/he*. A gloss of this word is seen in (1). Rather than simply defining the word as 's/he is selfish,' (Wolvengrey, 2001) has opted to provide a more nuanced definition: `pêyakwêyimisow: s/he thinks only of him/herself, s/he is selfish, s/he is self-centered.`

(1) pêyakwêyimisow
pêyakw-êyi-m-iso-w
one-think-VTA-RFLX-3SG
's/he thinks only of him/herself'

The result of this complex form of defining is that words are defined more in line with how they are understood within the Nêhiyawêwin culture, which is indeed often manifested in the derivational morphological composition of these words. This is central to the motivation for this method of semi-automatic clustering, but produces verbs with relatively long definitions. An alternative explanation for why Nêhiyawêwin lexemes with English definitions consisting of more numerous parts of speech were more difficult to classify is that these divisions simply have significantly more variation in

[9] One can also compare the results in this paper with results from a similar alternation study in Arppe et al. (2008).

[10] It is worth noting that previous attempts at such experimentation via Nêhiyawêwin communities with which we have good relationships have been poorly received by speakers.

meaning for whatever reason. Further investigation into this is needed.

Also worth noting is the relative distributions of each of the postprocessed classes mentioned above. Table 3 details each of the postprocessed noun classes sorted by their size.

Perhaps unsurprisingly, the distribution of lexemes into different classes followed a sort of Zipfian distribution. The `NA-person` and `NA-other-animals` accounted for the vast majority of noun lexemes for animate nouns. Just under half of all NI lexemes were nominalized verbs, and roughly a quarter were smaller object-like items (e.g. tools, dishes, etc.). The NDAs were almost entirely dominated by words for family, while all but three NDIs were body part lexemes. Some categories such as `NI-scent`, `NI-days`, and `NA-shield` have extremely low membership counts, but were substantially different from other categories that they were not grouped into another class. Most interestingly, there appeared to be three NI lexemes that referred to persons, something usually reserved for NAs only. These lexemes were *okitahamâkêw* 'one who forbids,' *owiyasiwêwikimâw* 'magistrate,' and *mihkokwayawêw* 'red neck.' In all three cases, the lexemes seem to be deverbal nouns (from *kitahamâkêw* 's/he forbids,' *wiyasiwêw* 's/he makes laws,' and *mihkokwayawêw* 's/he has a red neck.'

Verbs showed a similar distribution. Table 4 details the distribution of words within each of semantic classes for verbs. With the exception of VII and VAIs, verbs were dominated by classes for action, which subsumes most volitional actions (e.g. *kîskihkwêpisiwêw* 's/he rips the face off of people,' *kâsîpayiw* 's/he deletes'), and nonaction which includes most verbs of thought, emotion, judgment, or sensory action (e.g *koskowihêw*, 's/he startles someone,' *nôcîhkawêw* 's/he seduces someone'). Other classes may include action verbs, such as `AI-cooking` and `TI-speech`. Although these verbs could be classified in one of the two previously mentioned systems, their automatic classification and semantics unify them in a way that is unique to other items in these larger classes.

Overall, verb forms, especially the most numerous classes of VAI and VTA, required a large degree of manual postprocessing. Because this approach assumes no underlying ontology, but rather attempts to work bottom-up (cf. Hanks (1996)), the time taken to postprocess VAI and VTA classes is likely not too far from what it would take to manually classify these words based off a prebuilt ontology; however, the appeal of a bottom-up classification should not be overlooked, however. As an example, many ontologies place concepts like *thinking*, and *being happy* into separate classes; however, in our classification these words were combined into a single class of *cognition*. This is done because emotion words like *môcikêyihtam*, 's/he is happy (because of something)' (in addition to being verbs and not adjectives) contain a morpheme, {-êyi-}, meaning 'thought.' For these reasons, such emotion words are often translated as having to do specifically with thought and cognition: *môcikêyihtam*, 's/he thinks happily (because of something).' (Wolvengrey, 2001) uses these sorts of definitions, and so unsurprisingly the majority of such emotion words were classified in the proposed scheme together with words of thought. Where this was not the case, manual postprocessing from a bottom-up approach allows us to maintain the cultural understanding of emotions as directly related to cognition. Furthermore, from the experiential standpoint of one of the authors, the use of semi-automatic clustering produces a kick-start that greatly aids to the starting of a semantic classification task, especially for non-native speakers.

6 Conclusion

This paper describes an attempt at, for the first time, semi-automatically classifying Nêhiyawêwin verbs and nouns. The process used in this paper is easily applied to any language that makes use of a bilingual dictionary with definitions written in a more resourced language. Resulting clusters of Nêhiyawêwin words are freely available on the online. Although the technique worked quite well with nouns, which required very little manual adjustment, verbs required more directed attention. Despite this, the technique presented in this paper offers a bottom-up, data-driven approach that takes the language on its own terms, without resorting to ontologies created primarily for other languages. If, however, one wishes to use a pre-defined ontology, the basis for this work (representing word definitions using pre-trained English word vectors) could be used in conjunction with existing ontologies to expedite the classification process. For example, Dacanay et al. (2021) compare the naive definition vectors for Wolvengrey (2001) with the same for the English WordNet word senses; word senses

NI (N)	NDI (N)	NA (N)	NDA (N)
NI-nominal (1783)	NDI-body (243)	NA-persons (720)	NDA-relations (143)
NI-object (902)	NDI-house (2)	NA-beast-of-burden (512)	NDA-body (45)
NI-natural-Force (283)		NA-food (325)	NDA-clothing (4)
NI-place (228)		NA-celestial (45)	
NI-nature-plants (198)		NA-body-part (37)	
NI-body-part (78)		NA-religion (23)	
NI-hunt-trap (60)		NA-money/count (12)	
NI-animal-product (48)		NA-shield (2)	
NI-religion (36)			
NI-alteration (23)			
NI-scent (4)			
NI-days (4)			
NI-persons (3)			

Table 3: Manually Adjusted Noun Classes

VII (N)	VAI (N)	VTI (N)	VTA (N)
II-natural-land (256)	AI-state (2083)	TI-action (1409)	TA-action (1013)
II-weather-time (103)	AI-action (1982)	TI-nonaction (293)	TA-nonaction (574)
II-sensory/attitude (92)	AI-reflexive (542)	TI-speech (80)	TA-speech (103)
II-plural (73)	AI-cooking (172)	TI-money/count	TA-food (54)
II-move (35)	AI-speech (131)	TI-fit (10)	TA-money/count (23)
II-named (3)	AI-collective (97)	TI-food (8)	TA-religion (9)
	AI-care (81)		TA-allow (5)
	AI-heat/fire (55)		
	AI-money/count (34)		
	AI-pray (29)		
	AI-childcare (17)		
	AI-canine (16)		
	AI-cover (15)		

Table 4: Manually Adjusted Verb Classes

whose vectors bear a strong correlation with the Nêhiyawêwin definitions can then be assumed to be semantically similar with a Nêhiyawêwin word, and the latter can take the WordNet classification of the former. Further research should investigate more sophisticated methods of creating embeddings, especially the use of true sentence vectors. Additionally, one could consider using weights for English words in the definitions of *Nêhiyawêwin* words based on measures like tf-idf. Over all, this technique provided promising results. Regardless of the language or particular implementation, this technique of bootstrapping under-resourced language data with pre-trained majority language vectors (for which very large corpora exist), should not be restricted by the sizes of dictionaries in the under-resourced language, as the underlying vectors are trained on a 100 million word English corpus.

Acknowledgements

We would like to thank the Social Sciences and Humanities Research Council of Canada for funding this research. We would also like to thank Dr. Arok Wolvengrey for providing his dictionary source for this study.

References

Antti Arppe, Katherine Schmirler, Atticus G Harrigan, and Arok Wolvengrey. 2020. A morphosyntactically tagged corpus for plains cree. In *Papers of the Forty-*

Ninth Algonquian Conference. Michigan State University Press.

Antti Arppe et al. 2008. Univariate, bivariate, and multivariate methods in corpus-based lexicography: A study of synonymy.

Douglas Bates, Martin Mächler, Ben Bolker, and Steve Walker. 2015. Fitting linear mixed-effects models using lme4. *Journal of Statistical Software*, 67(1):1–48.

Joan Bresnan, Anna Cueni, Tatiana Nikitina, and R Harald Baayen. 2007. Predicting the dative alternation. In *Cognitive foundations of interpretation*, pages 69–94. KNAW.

Clare Cook. 2014. *The clause-typing system of Plains Cree: Indexicality, anaphoricity, and contrast*, volume 2. OUP Oxford.

Daniel Dacanay, Antti Arppe, and Atticus Harrigan. 2021. Computational Analysis versus Human Intuition: A Critical Comparison of Vector Semantics with Manual Semantic Classification in the Context of Plains Cree. In *Proceedings of the 4th Workshop on the Use of Computational Methods in the Study of Endangered Languages*, volume 1, pages 33–43.

Dagmar Divjak and Stefan Th Gries. 2006. Ways of trying in russian: Clustering behavioral profiles. *Corpus linguistics and linguistic theory*, 2(1):23–60.

Birgit Hamp and Helmut Feldweg. 1997. Germanet-a lexical-semantic net for german. In *Automatic information extraction and building of lexical semantic resources for NLP applications*.

Patrick Hanks. 1996. Contextual dependency and lexical sets. *International journal of corpus linguistics*, 1(1):75–98.

Beth Levin. 1993. *English verb classes and alternations: A preliminary investigation*. University of Chicago press.

Olga Majewska, Ivan Vulić, Diana McCarthy, and Anna Korhonen. 2020. Manual clustering and spatial arrangement of verbs for multilingual evaluation and typology analysis. In *Proceedings of the 28th International Conference on Computational Linguistics*, pages 4810–4824.

Daniel McFadden. 1977. Quantitative Methods for Analyzing Travel Behaviour of Individuals: Some Recent Developments. Technical report.

Daniel McFadden et al. 1973. Conditional logit analysis of qualitative choice behavior.

Tomas Mikolov, Kai Chen, Greg Corrado, and Jeffrey Dean. 2013a. Efficient estimation of word representations in vector space. *arXiv preprint arXiv:1301.3781*.

Tomas Mikolov, Ilya Sutskever, Kai Chen, Greg S Corrado, and Jeff Dean. 2013b. Distributed representations of words and phrases and their compositionality. In *Advances in neural information processing systems*, pages 3111–3119.

George A Miller. 1998. *WordNet: An electronic lexical database*. MIT press.

Hien Pham and Harald Baayen. 2015. Vietnamese compounds show an anti-frequency effect in visual lexical decision. *Language, Cognition and Neuroscience*, 30(9):1077–1095.

R Core Team. 2017. *R: A Language and Environment for Statistical Computing*. R Foundation for Statistical Computing, Vienna, Austria.

Linda Visitor, Marie-Odile Junker, and Mimie Neacappo. 2013. Eastern james bay cree thematic dictionary (southern dialect). *Chisasibi: Cree School Board*.

Shan Wang and Francis Bond. 2013. Building the chinese open wordnet (cow): Starting from core synsets. In *Proceedings of the 11th Workshop on Asian Language Resources*, pages 10–18.

Arok Wolvengrey. 2001. *Nēhiyawēwin: itwēwina = Cree: words*. University of Regina press.

Arok Wolvengrey. 2005. Inversion and the absence of grammatical relations in plains cree. *Morphosyntactic expression in functional grammar*, 27.

Liang-Chih Yu, Jin Wang, K Robert Lai, and Xuejie Zhang. 2017. Refining word embeddings for sentiment analysis. In *Proceedings of the 2017 conference on empirical methods in natural language processing*, pages 534–539.

Restoring the Sister: Reconstructing a Lexicon from Sister Languages using Neural Machine Translation

Remo Nitschke
The University of Arizona
nitschke@email.arizona.edu

Abstract

The historical comparative method has a long history in historical linguists. It describes a process by which historical linguists aim to reverse-engineer the historical developments of language families in order to reconstruct proto-forms and familial relations between languages. In recent years, there have been multiple attempts to replicate this process through machine learning, especially in the realm of cognate detection (List et al., 2016; Ciobanu and Dinu, 2014; Rama et al., 2018). So far, most of these experiments aimed at actual reconstruction have attempted the prediction of a proto-form from the forms of the daughter languages (Ciobanu and Dinu, 2018; Meloni et al., 2019). Here, we propose a reimplementation that uses modern related languages, or sisters, instead, to reconstruct the vocabulary of a target language. In particular, we show that we can reconstruct vocabulary of a target language by using a fairly small data set of parallel cognates from different sister languages, using a neural machine translation (NMT) architecture with a standard encoder-decoder setup. This effort is directly in furtherance of the goal to use machine learning tools to help under-served language communities in their efforts at reclaiming, preserving, or reconstructing their own languages.

1 Introduction

Historical linguistics has long employed the historical comparative method to establish familial connections between languages and to reconstruct proto-forms (cf. Klein et al., 2017b; Meillet, 1967). More recently, the comparative method has been employed by revitalization projects for lexical reconstruction of lost lexical items (cf. Delgado et al., 2019). In the particular case of Delgado et al. (2019), lost lexical items of the target language are reconstructed by using equivalent cognates of still-spoken modern sister languages, i.e., languages in the same language family that share some established common ancestor language and a significant amount of cognates with the target language. By reverse-engineering the historical phonological processes that happened between the target language and the sister-languages, one can predict what the lexical item in the target language should be. This is essentially a twist on the comparative method, using the same principles, but to reconstruct a modern sister, as opposed to a proto-antecedent.

While neural net systems have been used to emulate the historical comparative method[1] to reconstruct proto-forms (Meloni et al., 2019; Ciobanu and Dinu, 2018) and for cognate detection (List et al., 2016; Ciobanu and Dinu, 2014; Rama et al., 2018), there have not, to the best of our knowledge, been any attempts to use neural nets to predict/reconstruct lexical items of a sister language for revitalization/reconstruction purposes.

Meloni et al. (2019) report success for a similar task (reconstructing Latin proto-forms) by using cognate pattern lists as a training input. Instead of reconstructing Latin proto-forms from only Italian roots, they use Italian, Spanish, Portuguese, Romanian and French cognates of Latin, i.e., mapping from many languages to one. As our intended use-case (see section 1.1) is one that suffers from data sparsity, we explicitly explore the degree to which expanding the list of sister-languages in the many-to-one mapping can compensate for fewer available data-points. Since the long-term goal of this project is to aid language revitalization efforts, the question of available data is of utmost importance. Machine learning often requires vast amounts of data, and languages which are undergoing revitalization usually have very sparse amounts of data available. Hence, the goal for a machine learning approach

[1] Due to the nature of neural nets we do not know whether these systems actually emulate the historical comparative method or not. What is meant here is that they were used for the same tasks.

Proceedings of the First Workshop on Natural Language Processing for Indigenous Languages of the Americas, pages 122–130
June 11, 2021.

here is not necessarily the highest possible accuracy, but rather the ability to operate with as little data as possible, while still retaining a reasonable amount of accuracy.

Our particular contributions are:

1. We demonstrate an approach for reframing the historical comparative method to reconstruct a target language from its sisters using a neural machine translation framework. We show that this can be done with easily accessible open source frameworks such as OpenNMT (Klein et al., 2017a).

2. We provide a detailed analysis of the degree to which inputs from additional sister languages can overcome issues of data sparsity. We find that adding more related languages allows for higher accuracy with fewer data points. However, we also find that blindly adding languages to the input stream does not always yield said higher accuracy. The results suggest that there needs to be a significant amount of cognates with the added input language and the target language.

1.1 Intended Use-Case and Considerations

This experiment was designed with a specific use-case in mind: Lexical reconstruction for language revitalization projects. Specifically, the situation where this type of model may be most applicable would be a *language reclamation* project in the definition of Leonhard (2007) or a *language revival* process in the definition of McCarty and Nicholas (2014). In essence, a language where there is some need to *recover or reconstruct* a lexicon. An example of such a case might be the Wampanoag language reclamation project (`https://www.wlrp.org/`), or comparable projects using the methods outlined in Delgado et al. (2019).

As this is a proof-of-concept, we use the Romance language family, specifically the non-endangered languages of French, Spanish, Italian, Portuguese and Romanian, and operate under assumption that these results can inform how one can use this approach with other languages of interest. However, we are aware that the Romance language morphology may be radically different from some of the languages that may be in the scope of this use case, such as agglutinative and polysynthetic languages, and that we cannot fully predict the performance of this type of system for such languages from the Romance example. Regardless of this, some insights gained here will still be applicable in those cases, such as the question of compensating lack of data by using multiple languages.

Languages that are the focus of language revitalization projects are typically not targets for deep learning projects. One of the reasons for this is the fact that these languages usually do not have large amounts of data available for training state of the art neural approaches. These systems need large amounts of data, and Neural Machine Translation systems, as the one used in this project, are no exception. For example, Cho et al. (2014) use data sets varying between 5.5million and 348million words. However, the task of proto-form reconstruction, which is really a task of cognate prediction, can be achieved with fairly small datasets, if parallel language input is used. This was shown by Meloni et al. (2019), whose system predicted 84% within an edit distance of 1, meaning that 84% of the predictions were so accurate that only one or 0 edits were necessary to achieve the true target. For example, if the target output is "grazie", the machine might predict "grazia" (one edit) or "grazie" (0 edits). Within a language revitalization context, this level of accuracy would actually be a very good outcome. In this scenario, a linguist or speaker familiar with the language would vet the output regardless, so small edit distances should not pose a big problem. Further, all members of a language revitalization project or language community would ultimately vet the output, as they would make a decision on whether to accept or reject the output as a lexical item of the language.

This begs the question of why a language revitalization project would want to go through the trouble of using such an algorithm in the first place, if they have someone available to vet the output, then that person may as well do the reconstructive work themselves, as proposed in Delgado et al. (2019). This all depends on two factors: First, how high is the volume of lexical items that need to be reconstructed or predicted? The effort may not be worth it for 10 or even a 100 lexical items, but beyond this an neural machine translation model can potentially outperform the manual labor. Once trained, the model can make thousands of predictions in minutes, as long as input data is available.

Second, and potentially more important, it will depend on how well the historical phonological relationships between the languages are understood.

	Spanish	French	Portuguese	Romanian	Italian (target)	status
1	-	-esque	-e:scere	-	-	*removed, no target*
2	mosto	moût	mosto	must	mosto	
3	-	-	-	-	lugano	*removed, no input*
4	párrafo	-	-	-	paragrafo	
5	-edad	-	-idade	-itate	-ità	

Table 1: Examples of data patterns, including types of data removed during cleanup (e.g., rows 1 and 3).

For a family like Romance, we have a very good understanding of the historical genesis of the languages and the different phonological processes they underwent, see for example Maiden et al. (2013). However, there are many language families in the world where these relationships and histories are less than clear. In such situations, a machine learning approach would be beneficial, because the algorithm learns[2] the relationships for us and gives predictions that just need to be vetted.

Under this perspective, the best model might not necessarily be the one that produces the most accurate output, but perhaps the one that produces the fewest incorrigible mistakes. An incorrigible mistake here would be the algorithm predicting an item that is completely unrelated to the target root e.g., predicting "cinque" for a target of "grazie"). Further, ease of usability and accessibility will be another factor for this kind of use-case, as not every project of this type will have a computational linguist to call on. Hence, another aim should be a low-threshold for reproducability and the utilization of easy to use open-source frameworks. In the spirit of the latter, all data and code necessary to reproduce the results are open-source and freely available. This paper is intended for computational linguists and linguists and/or community members who are involved with projects surrounding languages which might benefit from this approach. As such, it is written with both audiences in mind, with Section 6 ("Warning Labels for Interested Linguists") specifically aimed at linguists and community members interested in a potential application of this method.

2 The Dataset

The data set used for this experiment was provided by Shauli Rafvogel of Meloni et al. (2019). The initial set consisted of 5420 lines of cognate sextuples of the Romance language family, specifically: Ro-

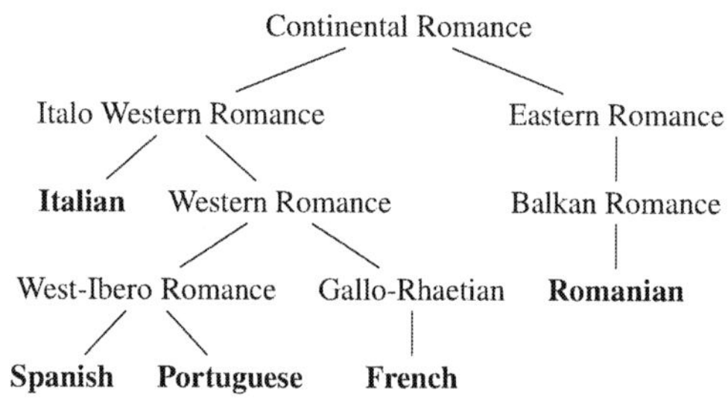

Figure 1: An abridged family tree of the relevant Romance languages. Adapted from glottolog (Hammarström et al., 2020).

manian, French, Spanish, Portuguese, Italian and Latin. As the aim for this experiment was to reconstruct from sister languages to a sister language, the Latin items were removed from the set and instead Italian was chosen to be the target language for the experiment, since it had the most complete pattern with respect to the other languages in the set. Table 1 illustrates the types of lines present in the initial dataset.

Lines with no target and lines with no input were removed. Lines where there was a target but no input (row 3) were also removed, as well as lines where there was input but no target (line 1). After the removal of all lines which lead to empty patterns in the Italian set, and all lines which were empty patterns in the input, 3527 remained. From these, 2466 lines were taken as training data, 345 were taken for validation, and 717 were set aside for testing.

Meloni et al. (2019) use both an orthographic and an IPA data set, and show that the orthographic set yielded more accurate results. Here, we use only orthographic representations, which we prefer not for accuracy, but because orthographic datasets are more easily acquired for most languages, particularly those of interest in language reclamation projects. If both an IPA set and an orthographic set are available, one may attempt using both to boost the accuracy of the results. Chen (2018) showed

[2]Or, rather, it interprets.

that this is possible with glossing data in the case of sentence level neural machine translation. We will discuss this implementation in Section 5.2.

See Figure 1 for a very *simplified* phylogenetic tree representation of the familial relations of the Romance languages used in this dataset. This tree was constructed using data from glottolog (Hammarström et al., 2020), and is included just for illustrative purposes and not as a statement about the phylogeny of Romance languages.[3]

3 Experimental Setup

This experiment was run using the OpenNMT-pytorch neural machine translation (Klein et al., 2017a) framework, using the default settings (a 2-layer LSTM with 500 hidden units on both the encoder and decoder). The opennmt-py default setup was chosen intentionally; the envisioned use-case requires an easily reproducable approach for interested users or communities who might profit from using this method for their own purposes, but who don't necessarily have deep expertise in machine learning or tuning neural models. A publicly available toolkit, like opennmt, and a no-configuration setup helps lower the bar to entry for these parties.

Neural machine translation (NMT) frameworks are designed to translate sentences from one language to another, but they can be used for a number of sequential data tasks (Neubig, 2017). One such task is the prediction of a cognate from a set of input words, as used here. These frameworks are typically an encoder-decoder setup, where both the encoder and decoder are often implemented as LSTM (Long Short-Term Memory) networks (Hochreiter and Schmidhuber, 1997), which have the advantage of effectively capturing long-distance dependencies (Neubig, 2017). In an encoder-decoder setup, the encoder reads in the character based input representation and transforms it into a vector representation. The decoder takes this vector representation and transforms it into a character based output representation (Cho et al., 2014).

NMT frameworks also employ a "vocabulary" set, which contains vocabulary of the language that is being translated from and vocabulary of the language that is being translated to. The size of this vocabulary is often an issue for the effectiveness of NMT models (Hirschmann et al., 2016). In our case, the source vocabulary simply contains all of the characters that occur in all the input language examples and the target vocabulary contains the characters that occur in the target language example. To illustrate: if this task was about predicting English words, then the target vocabulary would contain all the letters of the English alphabet.

3.1 Input Concatenation

Since the input in our case is a list of cognates from different languages, we need to consider how we feed this input to the machine. There are two obvious options for this task. We can either feed the cognates one by one, or we can merge the cognates first, before feeding them to the machine. In this experiment, we merge the words character by character to construct the input lines. This means that for every line in the input, the first character of each word was concatenated, then the second character of each word was concatenated, and so on. For an illustration:

(1) patterns in the input: aille, alha, al, aie

(2) target patterns: aglia

(3) *input*: aaaaillilhelae

(4) *target*: aglia

This merging delivered marginally better results than simple concatenation in early testing, which is why it was selected. It is unclear as to why this is the case. We suspect that the merged input makes it easier for the model to recognize if the same characters appear in the same position of the input, as is the case with "a" in the initial position in the above example. However, we are cautious to recommend this input representation in general, because different morphologies may be better represented in a concatenation.

3.2 Different Training Setups

To determine the performance gains from simply having more data versus having data from more languages, we create several training scenarios. In each, we use the same aforementioned 2-layer LSTM. To understand the benefit of additional language, we first train with the entire training set with all four languages, then successively remove languages from the input set until only one remains. Next, to compare this to the impact of simply having fewer data points, but from all languages, we generate several impoverished versions of the data set. For these impoverished versions, lines were

[3]We also acknowledge that tree representations are not necessarily the most accurate way to represent these relationships (Kaylan and François, 2019).

removed randomly[4] from the set reducing the data by 70%, 50%, 30% and 10% respectively.

4 Evaluation Measures

Machine translation is usually evaluated using the BLEU (Papineni et al., 2002) score, but BLEU is designed with sentence level translations in mind. We instead evaluate the output according to edit distance in the style of Meloni et al. (2019) by calculating the percentage of the output which is within a given edit distance. In addition to this metric, we also use a custom evaluation metric designed to emphasize the *usability* of the output for the intended use-case, i.e., as predictions to be vetted by an expert to save time over doing the entire analysis manually. In order to calculate this score, we calculate the Damerau-Levenshtein edit distance to the target for each word and assign weights to them by their edit distance. That is:

$$score = (a + b * .9 + c * .8 + d * .7 + e * .6)/t$$

where a is number of predictions with distance 0, b is the number with distance 1, c is the number with distance 2, d is the number with distance 3, e the number with distance 4, and t is the total number of predictions. As an example, consider a scenario where there are three predicted cognates. If system 1 produces 3 output patterns within an edit distance of 2, it would receive a score of 0.8. If system 2 produces two output patterns with edit distance 0 and one within a distance of 5, this would result in a score of 0.67.

The logic behind this metric is that any prediction with an edit distance larger than 4 edits is essentially useless for the proposed task. Since such a large edit distance essentially constitutes an incorrigible mistake as mentioned in (Section 1.1). The edit distance of 4 constitutes an arbitrary cut-off to a degree, but it allows us a simple and informative evaluation metric for our use case. This metric will rank a model that has a large number of items in a and a large number of items beyond 4 edits lower than a model with items mostly in the b-d range. Presumably, the latter is more useful to the task, as small errors can be adjusted by linguists or language users.

Using this metric, we can rank different input combinations according to their assumed usefulness to the task of lexical reconstruction for revitalization purposes.

5 Results

Table 2 shows the edit distance percentages and scores of different runs at 10,000 steps of training.[5] We can compare the difference in outcome between using fewer languages in the input versus using less input lines overall. This addresses the question of whether adding multiple languages to the input helps compensate for fewer data points (cognate pairs). The runs with successively reduced numbers of languages (top half of the table), are all trained with all available input lines (2466) but excluding specific columns/languages. The "reduced input" runs (bottom half of the table), on the other hand, are done with all four languages but with fewer cognates, by excluding rows. These runs had the following amount of training input lines: 10%: 2220 lines of input, 30%: 1793 lines of input, 50%: 1345 lines of input, 70%: 896 lines of input (recall that the total number of input lines available for training was 2466). All runs were tested on the same testing data target.

In Table 2 (see following page), we can observe that, unsurprisingly, the training sample with the most languages and data (Span-Fre-Port-Ro) performs best. 44.6% within edit distance 0 means that almost half the predictions the machine makes are correct. In terms of accuracy, this is not incredible, Meloni et al. (2019) report 64.1% within edit distance 0. However, considering that we are using a data set approximately a third the size of theirs for training (2466 cognates compared with 7038), the performance is surprisingly good. The more important measure for the intended use-case is the fact that over 80% of items are within an edit distance of 3, meaning that of the output produced, 80% need only three edits or fewer to meet the target.

We can also observe that the performance successively drops as we remove languages, with the Spanish only[6] performing worst. However, the way in which this performance drops is not entirely transparent. It appears that in terms of scoring, the Spanish-French (Spa-Fre) sample actu-

[4]This was done by simply removing every n^{th} line depending on how much reduction was needed.

[5]One step of training means that the algorithm has gone through one batch of input lines. The default batch-size for opennmt is 64.

[6]Spanish only was only trained for 5000 steps, as the model plateaus around 1000 steps. The performance of the Spanish only model was measured every 500 steps for Figure 2.

Edit Distance	0	≤1	≤ 2	≤3	≤4	score
Span-Fre-Port-Ro	44.63%	57.74%	69.6%	80.33%	88.42%	0.82
Span-Fre-Port	42.68%	53.27%	68.34%	77.68%	84.94%	0.78
Span-Port-Ro	42.54%	53.28%	66.39%	74.76%	81.59%	0.75
Span-Fre	39.9%	50.9%	63.88%	74.62%	83.4%	0.76
Spanish only	35.6%	47.98%	60.25%	69.03%	74.76%	0.68
10% Reduced Input	40.17%	54.25%	69.6%	81.31%	87.59%	0.8
30% Reduced Input	39.75%	50.91%	66.11%	73.36%	83.12%	0.77
50% Reduced Input	33.19%	45.61%	60.95%	71.27%	82.4%	0.75
70% Reduced Input	17.02%	26.08%	41%	50.77%	65.97%	0.59

Table 2: Edit distance percentiles at 10,000 training steps. Shown are the results from using all data points with different combinations of languages (top), as well as using all languages but with random downsampling of the data from each (bottom). All scores are calculated from the testing data.

ally performs better than the Spanish-Portuguese-Romanian sample. Further, while Span-Port-Ro has significantly better values in the 0-2 edit range, it is outperformed by Span-Fre in terms of score because Span-Fre has more items in the ≤ 4 edit range.

The noticeable difference between Span-Fre-Port and Span-Port-Ro is surprising and warrants some examination. The likely explanation is twofold. First, The Romanian set is the one with the most empty patterns. The Romanian training data only includes 930 filled patterns, in comparison, Portuguese includes 1905 patterns, French includes 1790, and Spanish has 2125. It may be the case that the Romanian data is too small in comparison with the others to have a significant impact on the outcome. The other factor may be that Romanian is phylogenetically the most distant from the target language (Italian) (Figure 1).

This becomes even more apparent in Figure 2, which. shows the performance of different models over time.[7] Here we can observe that there is hardly any difference between the performance of Span-Fre-Port-Ro and Span-Fre-Port over time, and it is only at 10,000 steps that they start to diverge. This divergence at the 10,000 step mark is likely random, the graph suggest that their overall performance is almost identical in regards to scoring. Another point in this direction are the seemingly convergent graphs of Span-Fre and Span-Port-Ro, suggesting that there is no difference between using 2 or 3 languages as input if the third language

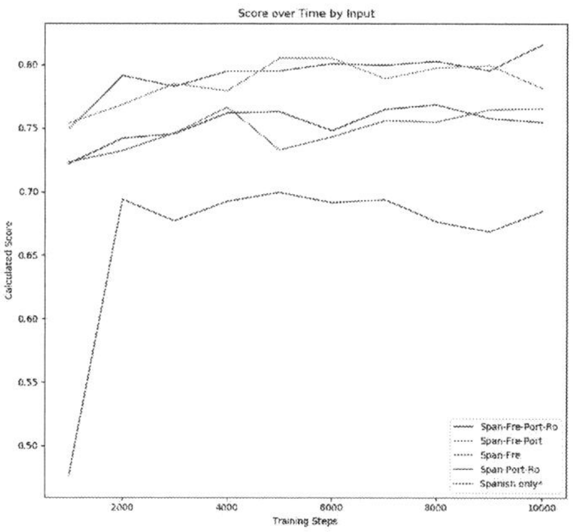

Figure 2: Performance at different training steps for models with different combinations of input languages, plotted by custom score. All scores are calculated from the testing data.

is Romanian.

Discounting the performance of the exclusion/inclusion of Romanian, we can observe that performance overall tends to increase with each parallel language added. This is especially evident with the obvious drop-off in performance of the Spanish only input. If we assume that Romanian has no impact, then we can see that 3 languages (blue and orange) perform similarly and two languages (red and green) perform similarly, and there is an obvious drop-off between those two patterns. This suggests that using parallel language input can compensate smaller datasets.

Due to the small dataset, the scores plateau fairly early, around the 3000 epoch mark for most. This

[7]This can give a better representation of the performance, because a neural net constantly adjusts its weights, so looking at just one point in time can be deceiving.

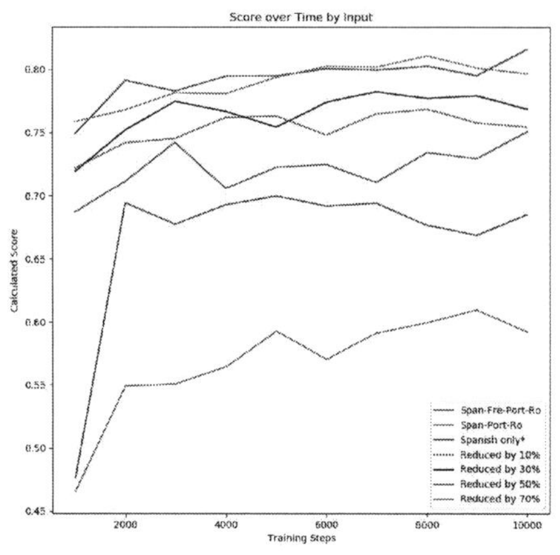

Figure 3: Performance of models trained on all four languages, but with varying levels of downsampled data. Included for comparison are models trained with all data on different language combinations. Plotted is the custom score over steps. Scores are calculated every 1000 training steps. All models were run on OpenNMT-py default parameters.

suggests that it would be sufficient to run these models at 3000 epochs, which would save some time on low-end hardware. However, with these small datasets, training time should rarely exceed 5 hours on consumer grade PCs.[8]

5.1 Parallel Languages vs Input Reduction

Let us now consider the second question of this paper: Can parallel language input compensate for small dataset size? We know that performance reduces if we reduce the number of languages in the input mix. Now we compare this drop-off to the reduction in performance caused by reducing the overall amount of input data. This can be seen in Figure 3, which shows the performance at different training steps for models trained on decreasing amounts of data. Included for comparison are models trained on all data using all four (Span-Fra-Port-Ro), three (Span-Port-Ro), and one (Span) input language.[9]

First, we observe that a 10% reduction in training data (grey) does not seem to have a strong impact, as this performs mostly equal to Span-Fre-Port-Ro. Further, we can see is that the 30% reduced case performs marginally better than Span-Port-Ro. This is a good result, as it suggests that we can compensate for a fair amount of data by using additional languages. Essentially, in this case we can observe that removing a language from the input can be equivalent to removing 30% of the input or more. Even the 50% reduced case (brown) still performs better than using just one language (Spanish only).

The extreme fall-off between the 50% reduction and the 70% reduction suggests that there is some point beyond which even multiple languages cannot compensate for lack of data points. Where this fall-off point is exactly, will likely fluctuate depending on the data set.

5.2 Potential Improvements

Chen (2018) shows that neural machine translation tasks can be greatly improved by adding glossing data to the input mix (We will gloss over the technical details of the implementation here). While there is no direct equivalent to the gloss-sentence relationship, there might be a close analog for words: phonetic transcriptions. Orthography may be conservative and often misleading, but phonetic representations are not.

Meloni et al. (2019) use a phonetic dataset in their experiment, but they map from phonetic representations to phonetic representations, so their input and their target items are represented in IPA. This performs worse than the orthographic task. An interesting further experiment would be to blend orthographic representations and phonetic representations in the input, in the style of Chen (2018), mapping that to an orthographic output. This would be a close analog to the sentence-gloss to sentence mapping that Chen (2018) reports success with.

One thing to consider, is that this may be not ideal for the use-case. Phonetic datasets are not easy to produce and the orthography is often more readily available. While this might improve performance, needing a phonetic as well as an orthographic dataset would likely increase the threshold of reproducability for interested parties.

6 Warning Labels for Interested Linguists

There are some important aspects of this kind of approach that linguists, or community members who are interested in utilizing it for their purposes,

[8]These were trained on an i5-5200 CPU with 2.2GHz, and training took anywhere between 4-7 hours for 10,000 steps.

[9]Since in Figure 2 we observe that Span-Port-Ro and Span-Fre perform quite similarly, and Span-Fre-Port performs similarly to Span-Fre-Port-Fro, to make the graph easier to read, we remove Span-Fre and Span-Fre-Port from this graph.

should be aware of.

There are certain things that this type of approach can and cannot do for a community or project. The model does not so much reconstruct a word for the community, but rather proposes what the word *could be*, according to the data it has been fed. The model will propose these recommendations on the basis of an abstract notion of what the historic phonological and morphological differences are between languages ABC and language D. This does not necessarily mean that the model *learns* or *understands* the historical phonological and morphological processes that separate the input sister languages from the target languages. It has simply learned a way to generalize from the input to the output with some degree of accuracy. What is learned need not necessarily overlap with what linguists believe to have happened.

Therefore, this type of model will *only ever generate cognates of the input*. It cannot generate novel items. This is an important factor to consider for any community or linguist planning on using this approach.

Consider the following case: Imagine we are trying to use this approach to reconstruct English from other Germanic languages. A large part of the English lexicon is not of Germanic ancestry. However, any lexicon we would try to reconstruct using this trained algorithm would give us *approximations of a Germanic derived lexeme* for the word we are trying to reconstruct. This is a potentially undesirable effect of the way the model was trained. Linguists and interested community members need to be aware of this and implement their own quality control.

However, this approach can potentially be useful for any language project where a community and or linguists are working with an incomplete lexicon for a language. The prerequisite for this being a useful tool in such a scenario is the assumption that the *sister languages* to the target language are somewhat well documented and have at least dictionaries available from which data can be extracted. A final prerequisite is the presence of minimally a small dictionary of the target language.

The model would then be trained using the sister languages as input, and the target language list as a target output. After training confirms a reasonable accuracy, the model can then be fed with other known words in the sister language to get a prediction of those words in the target language.

After producing said output, the linguist, or language community, needs to subject the output to a quality control and decide on a series of questions: Do the output patterns match what we know of the target language? Can we assume that these words are cognates in the target language, or is there some evidence that other forms were present? Finally, if this is used by a community to fill in empty patterns in their language, the community needs to decide whether the output is something that the community wants in their language. The algorithm is not infallible, and only proposes. Ultimately, a language community using this tool must make a decision whether to accept or reject the algorithm's recommendations.

7 Conclusions

In this paper, we have shown that NMT frameworks can be used to predict cognates of a target language from cognates of its sister languages. We have further shown that adding or removing input languages has interesting effects on the accuracy of the model. This indicates that we can use additional sister languages to compensate the lack of data in a given situation, though, as demonstrated in the case of Romanian, we cannot blindly add sister languages, nor assume that all additions are equally useful. This might be a promising method for situations where not a lot of data is present, but there are multiple well-documented related languages of the target language.

The next step for this line of research is to move from a proof of concept to an implementation in an actual language revitalization scenario. This is something we are currently working on. A further question that need to be addressed as well, is how well this approach performs with languages that exhibit a different morphology from the Romance languages, such as agglutinative and polysynthetic languages.

All code and data used for this project are open-source and can be found here, in order to reproduce these results.

Something we would like to address in this final paragraphs is that machine learning is a potential *tool*. Like every tool, it has its uses and cases where it is not useful. The decision of using such a tool to expand the lexicon of a language is a decision of that language community, and not of a linguist.

Acknowledgements

The author would like to thank the anonymous reviewers for their comments and give special thanks to Becky Sharp for helping with last minute edits.

References

Yuan Lu Chen. 2018. *Improving Neural Net Machine Translation Systems with Linguistic Information*. Phd thesis, University of Arizona.

KyungHyun Cho, Bart van Merrienboer, Dzmitry Bahdanau, and Yoshua Bengio. 2014. On the properties of neural machine translation: Encoder-decoder approaches. *CoRR*, abs/1409.1259.

Alina Maria Ciobanu and Liviu P. Dinu. 2014. Automatic detection of cognates using orthographic alignment. In *Proceedings of the 52nd Annual Meeting of the Association for Computational Linguistics (Volume 2: Short Papers)*, pages 99–105, Baltimore, Maryland. Association for Computational Linguistics.

Alina Maria Ciobanu and Liviu P. Dinu. 2018. Ab initio: Automatic Latin proto-word reconstruction. In *Proceedings of the 27th International Conference on Computational Linguistics*, pages 1604–1614, Santa Fe, New Mexico, USA. Association for Computational Linguistics.

Leighton Delgado, Irene Navas, Conor Quinn, Tina Tarrant, Wunetu Tarrant, and Harry Wallace. 2019. Digital documentation training for long island algonquian community language researchers: a new paradigm for community linguistics. Presented at: 51st Algonquian Conference, McGill University, Montréal, QC, 24-27 October.

Harald Hammarström, Robert Forkel, Martin Haspelmath, and Sebastian Bank. 2020. *Glottolog 4.3*. Jena.

Fabian Hirschmann, Jinseok Nam, and Johannes Fürnkranz. 2016. What makes word-level neural machine translation hard: A case study on English-German translation. In *Proceedings of COLING 2016, the 26th International Conference on Computational Linguistics: Technical Papers*, pages 3199–3208, Osaka, Japan. The COLING 2016 Organizing Committee.

Sepp Hochreiter and Jürgen Schmidhuber. 1997. Long short-term memory. *Neural Computation*, 9.

Siva Kaylan and Alexandre François. 2019. Freeing the comparative method from the tree model: A framework for historical glottometry. In *Let's talk about trees: Genetic relationships of languages and their phylogenetic representation*. Cambridge University Press, online.

Guillaume Klein, Yoon Kim, Yuntian Deng, Jean Senellart, and Alexander M. Rush. 2017a. Opennmt: Open-source toolkit for neural machine translation. In *Proc. ACL*.

Jared Klein, Brian Joseph, and Matthias Fritz. 2017b. *Handbook of Comparative and Historical Indo-European Linguistics : An International Handbook*. De Gruyter, Berlin.

Wesley Y. Leonhard. 2007. *Miami Language Reclamation in the Home: A Case Study*. Phd thesis, University of California, Berkeley.

Johann-Mattis List, Philippe Lopez, and Eric Bapteste. 2016. Using sequence similarity networks to identify partial cognates in multilingual wordlists. In *Proceedings of the 54th Annual Meeting of the Association for Computational Linguistics (Volume 2: Short Papers)*, pages 599–605.

M. Maiden, J. Smith, and A. Ledgeway, editors. 2013. *The Cambridge History of the Romance Languages*, volume 2. Cambridge University Press, Cambridge.

Teresa L. McCarty and Sheilah E. Nicholas. 2014. Reclaiming indigenous languages: A reconsideration of the roles and responsibilities of schools. *Review of Research in Education*, 31.

Antoine Meillet. 1967. *The comparative method in historical linguistics*. Librairie Honoré Champion, Paris.

Carlo Meloni, Shauli Ravfogel, and Yoav Goldberg. 2019. Ab antiquo: Proto-language reconstruction with rnns.

Graham Neubig. 2017. Neural machine translation and sequence-to-sequence models: A tutorial. *CoRR*, abs/1703.01619.

Kishore Papineni, Salim Roukos, Todd Ward, and Wei-Jing Zhu. 2002. Bleu: a method for automatic evaluation of machine translation. In *Proceedings of the 40th Annual Meeting of the Association for Computational Linguistics*, pages 311–318, Philadelphia, Pennsylvania, USA. Association for Computational Linguistics.

Taraka Rama, Johann-Mattis List, Johannes Wahle, and Gerhard Jäger. 2018. Are automatic methods for cognate detection good enough for phylogenetic reconstruction in historical linguistics? *CoRR*, abs/1804.05416.

Expanding Universal Dependencies for Polysynthetic Languages: A Case of St. Lawrence Island Yupik

Hyunji Hayley Park
Department of Linguistics
University of Illinois
hpark129@illinois.edu

Lane Schwartz
Department of Linguistics
University of Illinois
lanes@illinois.edu

Francis M. Tyers
Department of Linguistics
Indiana University
ftyers@iu.edu

Abstract

This paper describes the development of the first Universal Dependencies (UD, Nivre et al., 2016, 2020) treebank for St. Lawrence Island Yupik, an endangered language spoken in the Bering Strait region. While the UD guidelines provided a general framework for our annotations, language-specific decisions were made necessary by the rich morphology of the polysynthetic language. Most notably, we annotated a corpus at the morpheme level as well as the word level. The morpheme level annotation was conducted using an existing morphological analyzer (Chen et al., 2020) and manual disambiguation. By comparing the two resulting annotation schemes, we argue that morpheme-level annotation is essential for polysynthetic languages like St. Lawrence Island Yupik. Word-level annotation results in *degenerate* trees for some Yupik sentences and often fails to capture syntactic relations that can be manifested at the morpheme level. Dependency parsing experiments provide further support for morpheme-level annotation. Implications for UD annotation of other polysynthetic languages are discussed.

1 Introduction

The Universal Dependencies (UD) project (Nivre et al., 2016, 2020) provides a cross-lingual syntactic dependency annotation scheme for many languages. The most recent release of the UD treebanks (version 2.7) contains 183 treebanks in 104 languages. However, polysynthetic languages, known for words synthesizing multiple morphemes, are still much under-represented in the UD treebanks. To our knowledge, Abaza[1] and Chukchi (Tyers and Mishchenkova, 2020), are the only polysynthetic languages included in UD version 2.7.

In this paper, we describe how we annotated a corpus of St. Lawrence Island Yupik (also known as Central Siberian Yupik), a polysynthetic language spoken in parts of Alaska and Chukotka, Russia, within the framework of the UD guidelines. While UD is a framework for word-level annotations, we argue that morpheme-level annotations are more meaningful for polysynthetic languages. We provide morpheme-level annotations for Yupik in addition to word-level annotations.[2] We believe that subword-level annotations can help better capture morphosyntactic relations for polysynthetic languages and assist further dependency annotations and morphosyntactic research for polysynthetic languages.

Previously Tyers and Mishchenkova (2020) called for the need to annotate parts of words in regard to noun incorporation in Chukchi. They proposed annotating a noun incorporated into a verb via morphology as a separate token available in the enhanced dependency structure. While our approach is motivated by a similar need to annotate subword units for another polysynthetic language, our paper focuses on morpheme-level annotations, which may be applied to other types of multi-morphemic words than just noun incorporation.

In what follows, we describe the characteristics of the Yupik language (§2) and show how we annotated a corpus at the morpheme level as well as the word level (§3 and §4). Then we present some language-specific decisions we made for morpheme-level annotations and illustrate Yupik constructs captured by the new annotation scheme (§5 and §6). We also compare the performance of the two annotation schemes in automatic parsing experiments (§7). Based on our findings, we conclude that the morpheme-level annotation is essential and effective for polysynthetic languages and discuss implications of the study for other polysyn-

[1] The Abaza treebank, as released in UD v2.7, contains 33 sentences and does not provide any language-specific documentation.

[2] The UD_Yupik-SLI treebank is scheduled to be released in UD v2.8 on May 15, 2021. See https://universaldependencies.org for details.

Proceedings of the First Workshop on Natural Language Processing for Indigenous Languages of the Americas, pages 131–142
June 11, 2021.

thetic languages and the UD framework (§8 and §9).

2 St. Lawrence Island Yupik

St. Lawrence Island Yupik (ISO 639-3 *ess*; Yupik hereafter) is a polysynthetic language in the Inuit-Yupik language family, spoken in parts of Alaska and Chukotka, Russia. Like other polysynthetic languages, Yupik is characterized by its rich morphology. Jacobson (2001) provides the most thorough descriptions of the Yupik grammar with an emphasis on the morphology. Yupik is strictly suffixing with the exception of one prefix. Yupik words typically have the following form:

root (+ derivational morphemes)*
+ inflectional morpheme (+ enclitic)

That is, a typical Yupik word has a root, followed by zero or more derivational morphemes (thus forming a stem), followed by obligatory inflectional morpheme(s), finally followed by an optional enclitic. Most roots are nominal or verbal, such as *mangteghagh-* 'house' and *negh-* 'to eat' respectively. The language also includes a set of non-inflecting particles, such as *quunpeng* 'always' or *unaami* 'tomorrow'.

Yupik derivational morphology is highly productive; words with up to seven derivational morphemes have been attested (de Reuse, 1994, p.53), and words with 1-3 derivational morphemes are very common. The Badten et al. (2008) Yupik-English dictionary and the Chen et al. (2020) Yupik finite-state morphological analyzer document about 400 derivational suffixes:

- 81 noun-elaborating suffixes (N→N) that attach to nominal roots and yield nominal bases
- 61 verbalizing suffixes (N→V) that attach to nominal roots and yield verbal bases
- 218 verb-elaborating suffixes (V→V) that attach to verbal roots and yield verbal bases
- 36 nominalizing suffixes (V→N) that attach to verbal roots and yield nominal bases

We now provide two example Yupik sentences involving the Yupik nominal base *mangteghagh-* 'house'.

(1)
Taghnughhaat *aanut* ***mangteghameng***
Taghnughha-at aan-u-t mangtegha-meng
child-ABS.PL to.go.out-IND.INTR-3PL house-ABL_MOD.SG
'The children went out of the house.'
(Jacobson, 2001, p.22)

In (1), the Yupik nominal base *mangteghagh-* 'house' forms the word *mangteghameng* 'from the house' by taking the inflectional suffix *-meng* to mark ablative-modalis case.

(2)
Mangteghaghllangllaghyugtukut.
Mangtegha-ghlla-ngllagh-yug-tu-kut
house-big-to.make-to.want.to-IND.INTR-1PL
'We want to make a big house.'
(Jacobson, 2001, p.47)

In (2), the same nominal base takes multiple derivational morphemes, forming the sentence-length word *Mangteghaghllangllaghyugtukut*. To form this multi-morphemic word, the nominal base *mangteghagh-* first combines with the noun-elaborating derivational suffix *-ghlla-* (N→N), yielding an extended nominal base *mangteghaghlla-* 'big house'. This extended nominal base then combines with the verbalizing derivational suffix *-ngllagh-* (N→V) to create an extended verbal base *mangteghaghllangllagh-* 'to make a big house'. Next, this extended verbal base combines with the verb-elaborating suffix *-yug-* (V→V) to yield the extended verbal stem *mangteghaghllangllaghyug-* 'to want to build a big house'. Finally, the inflectional suffix *-tu-* attaches to the extended verbal stem to mark the verb's valency as intransitive and its mood as indicative, while the inflectional suffix *-kut* marks the person and number of the verb's subject as first person plural; the final result is the fully inflected word *mangteghaghllangllaghyugtukut* 'we want to make a big house'.

(3)
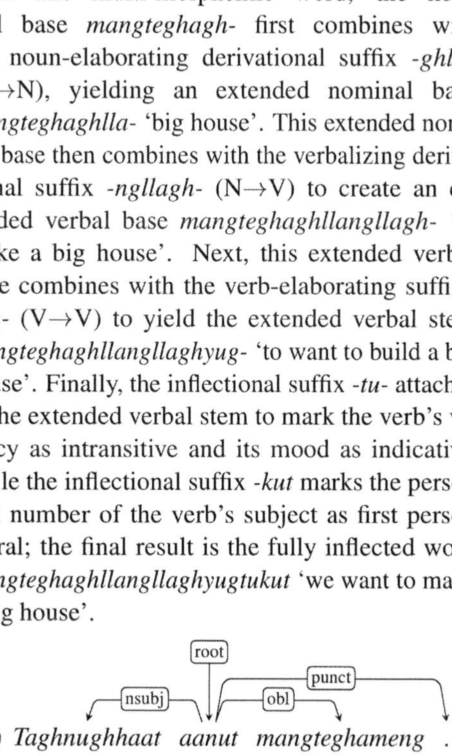

(4)
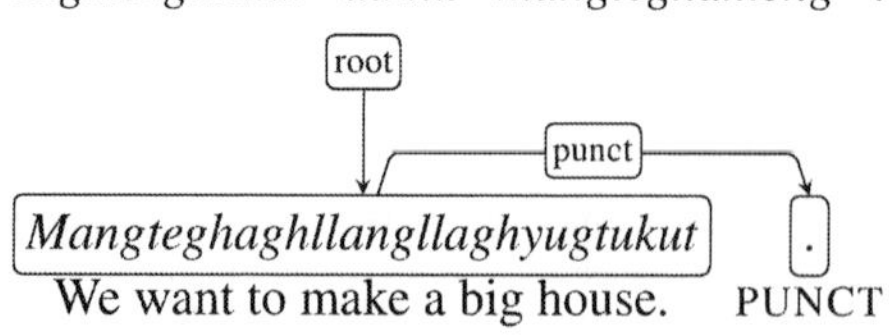

(5) 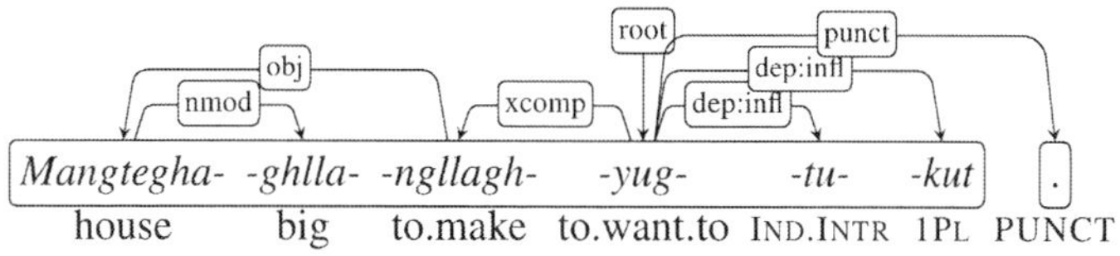

(6) Taaghta-m aghna-mun qayu-nghite-sq-a-a kufi-∅
doctor-REL.SG woman-ALL.SG to.drink-not.to-to.tell.one.to-IND.TRNS-3SG.3SG coffee-ABS.SG
'The doctor prevented the woman from drinking the coffee.' (Jacobson, 2001, p.67)

(7) 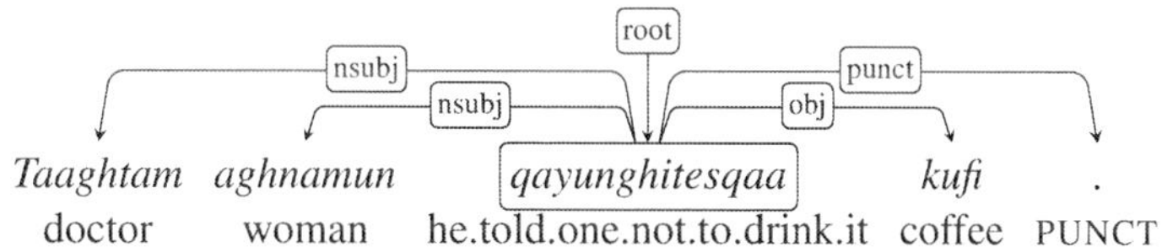

(8) 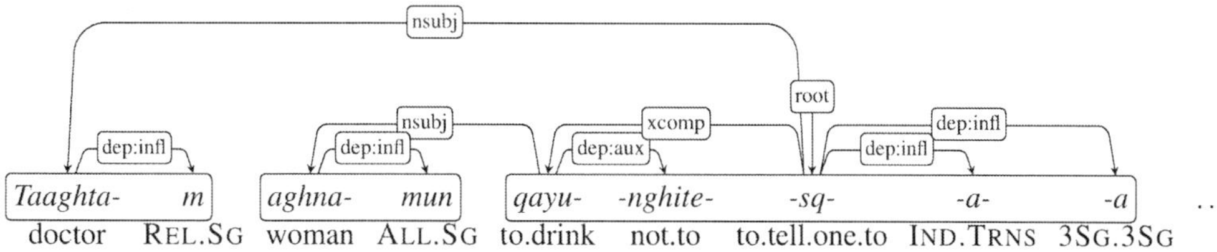

3 Morpheme-level dependency relations

The UD annotation guidelines are lexicalist (Chomsky, 1970; Bresnan and Mchombo, 1995) in nature, specifying that syntax dependencies should be annotated at the word level, such that both the head and the child of each dependency relation are words (Nivre et al., 2016).

In (3), we see the Yupik sentence from (1) with dependency relations annotated at the word level, following the UD guidelines. The resulting dependency tree successfully depicts the core syntactic information in the Yupik sentence, with the intransitive verb *aanut* at the root of the dependency tree, with a nominal subject and an oblique argument as children. However, when we annotate the single-word Yupik sentence from (2) according to the UD annotation guidelines, the result is a degenerate tree that completely fails to capture any syntactic information about the Yupik sentence.

In order to adequately represent the syntactic relations in (2), it is necessary to discard the lexicalist hypothesis and annotate relations between morphemes rather than between words. When we contrast (4) with (5), we observe that annotating relations at the morpheme level results in a meaningful linguistic analysis for this Yupik sentence. It is clear from these two dependency trees that treating morphemes as the basic unit of syntactic dependency relations is necessary in order to adequately encode the syntax of the Yupik sentence in (2). By doing so, we move from a degenerate tree devoid of syntactic information to a tree that successfully encodes a main verb *-yug-* ('to want to') with a complement *-ngllagh-* ('to make'), and an object *mangtegha-* ('house') with a nominal modifier *-ghlla-* ('big'); the inflectional suffixes encode the number and person of the subject (1PL, 'we') and the main verb's mood and valency (IND.INTR).

In (6) we observe a more complex Yupik sentence; we see the sentence *Taaghtam aghnamun qayunghitesqaa kufi* ('The doctor prevented the woman from drinking the coffee') annotated in (7) with dependency relations between words. The resulting dependency tree fails to illustrate the complex verbal structure of the multi-morphemic third word *qayunghitesqaa* ('he told one not to drink it'); it is only in (8) when we annotate (6) with syntactic relations between morphemes that we are able to observe that *aghnamun* ('the woman') is the subject of the embedded verb *qayu-* ('to drink') while *Taaghtam* ('the doctor') is the subject of the main verb *-sq-* ('to tell'). That is, parts of the Yupik word, the main verb *-sq-* ('to tell') and the embedded verb *qayu-* ('to drink'), participate in different syntactic relations, which cannot be annotated at the word level. The necessity for this type of sub-word annotation is not unique to Yupik; see Çöltekin (2016) for a discussion of subword syntactic units in Turkish.

If sentences that required morpheme-level dependency relations were rare, it might be reasonable to accept the inclusion of a few degenerate and under-annotated trees such as (4) and (7) in a Yupik dependency treebank. However, Yupik is polysynthetic, and multi-morphemic words involving complex derivation are very common; the same is true of all of the languages in the Inuit-Yupik language family. For the polysynthetic languages in this language family, there are simply too many sentences that require morpheme-level dependency annotations to annotate only dependency relations between words. In particular, essentially all words formed with derivational suffixes require morpheme-level dependency relations in order to satisfactorily encode the syntax of the sentence.

In annotating Yupik sentences with dependency relations, we therefore treat each Yupik morpheme as a token rather than treating each Yupik word as a token. This necessarily requires that Yupik words be analyzed and segmented into morphemes prior to dependency annotation; this task was performed using the existing Yupik finite-state morphological analyzer (Chen et al., 2020). In cases of ambiguity when the analyzer provided multiple possible analyses for a given word, we selected the gold analysis via manual disambiguation.

We chose to represent all Yupik morphemes as independent syntactic tokens, including inflectional morphemes. An alternative approach would be to instead not tokenize inflectional morphemes, but rather annotate inflectional information using feature values. A major benefit of our choice is greater compatibility with the existing Yupik morphological analyzer (Chen et al., 2020), which treats inflectional morphemes as independent tokens in the underlying lexical form.

Because the UD annotation guidelines were not designed for morpheme-level annotation, some minor adaptations were required; we discuss these adaptations in §5 and §6 as we discuss the POS tags and dependency relations used in our corpus along with sample sentences. In order to enable the use of morphemes as tokens, we adapted the existing "multiword expressions" annotation mechanism. The UD annotation guidelines recognize that syntactic words do not always align perfectly with orthographic word boundaries; this can occur even in analytic languages such as English, for example, in words involving a clitic or a contraction. For example, in Spanish, the word *dámelo* ('give it to me') may be broken down into *dá me lo* ('give me it') for the purpose of UD annotations; the annotation scheme records that the single orthographic token (*dámelo*) is annotated as multiple syntactic words, and that information can be used to collapse the annotations to the single orthographic token when needed. In our case, we treat each multi-morphemic Yupik word as a UD "multiword expression," with Yupik morphemes serving as the tokens within the "multiword expression."

Unit	Word-level	Morph-level
Sentences	309	309
Words	1,221	1,221
Segments	1,221	2,568
Fused	–	773

Table 1: Number of annotations per annotation level for the Jacobson corpus. **Words** mean the number of word tokens while **Segments** count any sub-word tokens instead of word tokens if applicable. **Fused** counts the number of word tokens that are split into subword units.

Recognizing the UD project's lexicalist view of syntax, we provide a script to convert our morpheme-level annotations into word-level annotations. This script deterministically merges each multi-morphemic word into a single word token using Udapi (Popel et al., 2017). Because our morpheme-level annotation does not strictly follow the entirety of the UD guidelines, a small number of sentences had to be manually corrected after the conversion. We plan to release our morpheme-level annotation in UD version 2.8 along with descriptions of the conversion process from the morpheme-level annotations to the word-level annotations.

4 Corpus

The annotated corpus is comprised of exercise sentences from the Yupik reference grammar (Jacobson, 2001, as released in Schwartz et al., 2021). The grammar book, designed to teach Yupik at the college level, provides end-of-chapter exercises with sample Yupik sentences. Morphological segmentation and analyses were performed using the Chen et al. (2020) Yupik morphological analyzer and manually verified when needed.

The number of annotations for the final version of the Yupik treebank is summarized in Table 1. A total of 309 sentences with 1,221 word tokens

UPOS	Word-level	Morph-level
ADV	62	65
CCONJ	-	4
DET	5	5
NOUN	426	486
NUM	1	1
PART	16	16
PRON	19	23
PUNCT	310	310
VERB	382	556
X	-	1,102

Table 2: Frequencies of Part of Speech (POS) tags in the word-level and morpheme-level annotations for the Jacobson corpus.

were annotated. For the morpheme-level annotation, about 63% of the words (773 words) were further analyzed into the subword units, with a total of 2,568 segments (i.e. morphemes, particles and punctuation marks) annotated.

5 POS Tags

We annotated our Yupik corpus using the tags shown in Table 2.[3] Our morpheme-level annotations make use of ten POS tags; when these annotations are converted into word-level annotations, only eight POS tags are utilized.

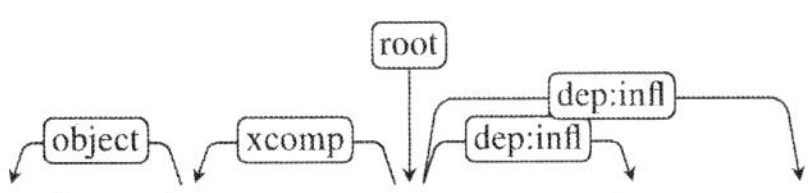

	Qikmi-	-lgu-	-yug-	-tu-	-nga
(9)	NOUN	VERB	VERB	X	X
	dog	to.have	to.want.to	IND.INTR	1SG

We tagged nominals and nominal bases as NOUN and verbals and verbal bases as VERB. We tagged derivational suffixes that yield nominal stems (N→N, V→N) as NOUN and those that yield verbal stems (N→V, V→V) as VERB. For example, (9) shows the morpheme-level annotation for the word *Qikmilguyugtunga* 'I want to have a dog'. In the annotation, the nominal root *Qikmi-* 'dog' combines with a verbalizing derivational suffix (*-lgu-* 'to have', N→V) to yield a verbal base (*Qikmilgu-* 'to have a dog'). Then this extended base combines with the verb-elaborating suffix (*-yug-* 'to want to', V→V) to yield a complex verbal stem (*Qikmilguyug-* 'to want to have a dog'), which is followed by inflection. The two verb-yielding derivational suffixes are tagged as VERB.

Uninflected words or particles were given the particle tag (PART). Many Yupik particles are borrowed from Chukchi, a geographically neighboring language, and are mostly adverbial or connective in meaning (de Reuse, 1994, p.14). Examples include *ighivgaq* 'yesterday' and *qayughllak* 'because'.

The two additional POS tags available only at the morpheme level were X and CCONJ . The POS tag X is reserved for words that are outside of POS tags defined within the UD framework. We used the X tag for inflectional suffixes such as *-tu-* and *-nga* as in (9). Coordinating conjunctions (CCONJ) were only found at the morpheme level because they are only expressed as an enclitic in the language: *=llu* 'and' as in (10).

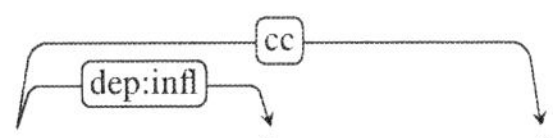

	naa-	*-ka*	*=llu*	
(10)	NOUN	X	CCONJ	...
	mother	ABS.1SGPOSS.SG	and	

6 Dependency relations

Our morpheme annotation scheme makes use of 25 types of dependency relations while our word annotation scheme makes use of 14 dependency relations. In general, we followed the UD annotation guidelines, except in cases where polysynthetic nature of Yupik made divergence from the guidelines necessary. The full documentation on POS tags, morphological features, and dependency relations used in the treebank is available at the language's UD documentation page.[4]

The most notable difference between the two annotation schemes is the dep relation. Within the UD framework, the dep relation is reserved for unspecified relations. Because morpheme-level annotations require multiple dependency relations specified for subword units, we created a few dependency relations under the dep relation for the morpheme-level annotation only. Note that some relations that are commonly annotated at the word level for other languages (e.g. auxiliary, copula) are only available at the morpheme level in Yupik. When we can, we expanded existing relations, defined at the word level, to morphemes (e.g. nmod

[3]The primary descriptions of Yupik are de Reuse (1994), which provides a description of Yupik syntax within the framework of autolexical syntax, and Jacobson (2001), which provides a description of Yupik grammar focusing on morphology and phonology in the context of a college-level Yupik class.

[4]More details are provided in Appendix A. See https://universaldependencies.org/ess/index.html for the full documentation.

for nominal modifier). Whenever that was not possible, we created a version of the corresponding dependency relation in our morpheme annotation scheme.

For example, we used `dep:aux` for verb-elaborating (V→V) derivational morphemes that modify the base verb's tense and aspect information. For example, the V→V derivational morpheme (as manifested as *-aq-* in the context) adds the present tense and progressive aspect to the base *gaagh-* 'to cook' in (11).

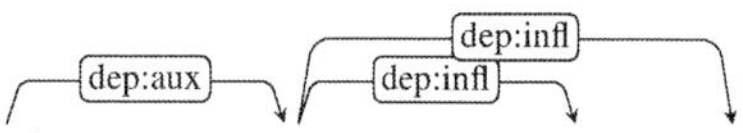

(11) *gaagh-* *-aq-* *-u-* *-q*
to.cook to.be.currently.V IND.INTR 3SG
Aspect=Prog
Tense=Pres

This relation would fit the descriptions of the auxiliary (`aux`) relation if it were annotated at the word level. We created a new relation as `dep:aux` to describe the dependency relation at the morpheme level because there were UD limitations to applying the existing `aux` relation to morphemes. First, the `aux` relation requires a short list of possible word forms while morphemes with the `dep:aux` relation may take many different forms depending on the context as they undergo morphophonological processes. Second, the word with the `aux` relation cannot have any children while corresponding morphemes often have inflections as their children.

Similarly, we included the `dep:mark` relation to represent the marker (`mark`) relation at the morpheme level. In (12) we observe a word that acts as a subordinate clause in a sentence and is roughly translated as 'in order to see them'. The second morpheme of the word *-na-* marks the word as a subordinate clause to the main verb, a `mark` relation in the word level UD annotation.[5] Again, because of some limitations of using this relation at the morpheme level, we created the `dep:mark` relation for morpheme-level anntoations.

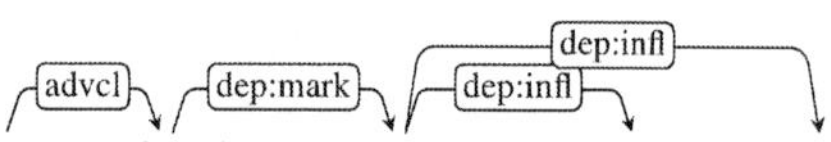

(12) ... *esghagh-* *-na-* *-lu-* *-ki*
... to.see in.order.to SBRD.INTR _.3PL

On a similar note, the `dep:cop` relation was added to represent the copula (`cop`) relation at the morpheme level. In (13), the verbalizing (N→V) derivational suffix *-ngu-* acts as a copula, turning the nominal base as a verbal stem, which combines with the inflection to form a verbal word meaning 'it is a land' in the sentence meaning 'Chaplino is a land'.

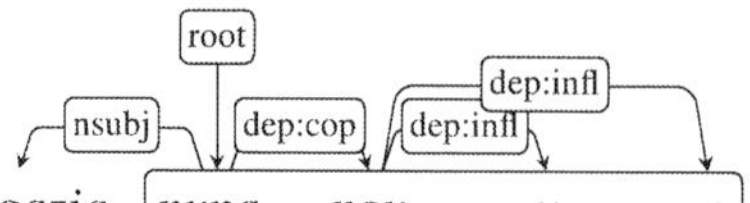

(13) *Ungaziq* *nuna-* *-ngu-* *-u-* *-q* ...
Chaplino land to.be IND.INTR 3SG

The `dep:infl` was used for the relation between the stem and its inflectional suffix as shown in (13). Because all Yupik words other than particles require one or more inflectional morphemes, the `dep:infl` relation was the most frequently used in the morpheme-level annotation.

In general, morpheme-level annotation was needed to capture some of important morphosyntactic relations present in Yupik words. The `aux` and `cop` relations are only available at the morpheme level in Yupik. While a small number of particles act as marker, the `mark` relation was also primarily attributed to derivational suffixes. When annotating Yupik sentences at the word level, such dependency relations are lost. Only when we annotate at the morpheme level can we find such constructions, which may be invaluable in subsequent linguistic inquiries or computational applications alike.

7 Parsing experiments

In order to investigate the practical usage of the annotations, we conducted automatic parsing experiments using UDPipe 1.2 (Straka and Straková, 2017) and UDPipe 2.0 (Straka, 2018). The UDPipe project[6] provides a trainable pipeline for any UD treebanks in the CoNLL-U format.

7.1 Data

We made use of two sets of data: the Jacobson corpus and a separate test corpus annotated using the same word-level and morpheme-level annotation schemes. A text extracted from Nagai (2001) was annotated to provide an out-of-domain test set. The Nagai corpus was smaller than the entire Jacobson corpus with 360 word tokens or 834 tokens when including morphemes. The Nagai corpus is quite distinct from the Jacobson corpus. The former is a collection of an elder Yupik speaker's speech while the latter is a college-level grammar book. Therefore, the former has more disfluencies, repetitions,

[5] The inflection also shows that the word is in subordinative mood, where the subject of the verb is the same as the subject of the main verb.

[6] `https://ufal.mff.cuni.cz/udpipe`

	Word-level (Automatic segmentation)		Morph-level (Automatic segmentation)		Morph-level (Gold segmentation)	
Corpus	Jacobson (2001)	Nagai (2001)	Jacobson (2001)	Nagai (2001)	Jacobson (2001)	Nagai (2001)
Words	100	100	100	100	100	100
Segments	100	100	71.56 ± 3.68	42.39	100	100
UPOS	93.01 ± 2.08	71.59	69.82 ± 3.69	34.16	97.22 ± 1.40	80.79
Lemmas	71.47 ± 3.14	40.39	71.05 ± 3.67	39.51	99.19 ± 0.79	92.32
Features	78.17 ± 3.32	46.24	67.14 ± 2.65	34.02	94.17 ± 2.29	78.03
UAS	88.86 ± 1.64	60.72	45.82 ± 7.77	9.33	91.82 ± 2.98	67.95
LAS	81.52 ± 2.91	43.45	45.13 ± 7.69	9.33	89.30 ± 3.06	61.46

Table 3: Automatic parsing results using UDPipe 2.0 (Straka, 2018) for the word-level and morpheme-level annotation schemes. A test set was either 1) automatically segmented or 2) manually verified to have gold segmentation. The annotations on Jacobson (2001) was trained and tested using ten-fold cross validation. A sample text from Nagai (2001) was annotated to provide an out-of-domain test set. The columns show F_1 score: **Words** word tokenization; **Segments** splitting words into morphemes when applicable; **Lemmas** lemmatization; **UPOS** universal part-of-speech tags; **Feats** morphological features; **UAS** unlabelled attachment score (dependency heads); **LAS** labelled attachment score (dependency heads and relations).

and some code-switching with English words while the latter contains sample sentences in the literary language without any foreign words.[7]

7.2 Tokenization

At annotation time, the process of tokenizing sentences into syntactic tokens is performed manually as part of the annotation process. When annotating relations between morphemes, each morpheme serves as a token. When annotating relations between words, each word (delimited by whitespace or punctuation) serves as a token.

At test time, it is also necessary to tokenize each sentence. In our experiments, we consider three mechanisms for doing so.

In the first experimental condition, we follow standard dependency parsing practice and rely on the dependency parser to tokenize each sentence into word tokens. To do so, we used a UDPipe 1.2 (Straka and Straková, 2017) model to automatically tokenize each test sentence into word tokens. In Table 3, we refer to this tokenization method as *Word-level (Automatic segmentation)*.

In the second experimental condition, we used a UDPipe 1.2 (Straka and Straková, 2017) model to automatically tokenize each test sentence into morpheme tokens. In Table 3, we refer to this tokenization method as *Morpheme-level (Automatic segmentation)*.

In the third experimental condition, we assume that tokenization of words into morphemes is handled as a separate pre-process (for example, by a finite-state morphological analyzer). In this condition, we provide a test file in which words have already been correctly segmented into morpheme tokens. In Table 3, we refer to this tokenization method as *Morpheme-level (Gold segmentation)*.

We observe the results of tokenization in the first two rows of Table 3. The first row shows that all methods were able to identify word boundaries without error. In the second row of Table 3, we observe that using a dependency parser to segment Yupik words into morphemes is only 72% effective. This is problematic, as this places an upper bound on the potential dependency parsing performance of this condition. By definition, the third condition results in perfect morpheme tokenization.

7.3 Methods

We trained separate UDPipe 2.0 (Straka, 2018) parsers for the word-level annotations and the morpheme-level annotations, using the default UDPipe settings. UDPipe 1.2 (Straka and Straková, 2017) models were trained for tokenizing the test sets only, also using the default settings. To test in-domain performance, we trained and tested a parser on the original Jacobson corpus using ten-fold cross validation for each annotation scheme. For out-of-domain performance, we trained a parser on the entire Jacobson corpus and tested it on the Nagai corpus for each annotation scheme. The evaluation was conducted based on the official evaluation script from the *CoNLL 2018 UD Shared Task* (Zeman et al., 2018).

[7] More details about the Nagai corpus are available in Appendix B.

7.4 Results

Parsing results (unlabelled and labelled attachment scores) are shown in the final two rows of Table 3. In all cases, we observe that parsing accuracy for the in-domain data from Jacobson is substantially higher than in the out-of-domain data from Nagai.

When we compare the word-level and morpheme-level parsing given automatically segmented test sets (left and middle columns), the word-level parsing outperforms the morpheme-level parsing due to many segmentation errors present in the latter. Segmentation errors create an effective upper limit for any subsequent parsing efforts at the morpheme level, and all results in the second column are substantially worse than those in the first column.

In contrast, morpheme-level parsing outperforms word-level parsing across the board when correct morpheme tokenization is provided (right-most column). This shows that morpheme-level parsing (the second column) performed poorly on the automatically segmented test set mostly because of the poor quality morpheme segmentation. We observe that the morpheme-level dependency parser (the third column) outperforms the word-level parser (the first column) across the board, and even with the more challenging out-of-domain test set.

The task of analyzing and segmenting a word into its underlying component morphemes is a well-studied task for which robust finite-state solutions are well known. For polysynthetic languages especially, the development of such a finite-state morphological analyzer is nearly always the very first element of language technology developed. It is therefore realistic to assume that tokenization of words into morphemes can be effectively handled by in a pre-processing step prior to dependency parsing.

8 Discussion

The Universal Dependencies project is intended as a de-facto standard for consistent dependency syntax annotations across all of the world's languages (Nivre et al., 2016, 2020). Our attempt to construct a UD corpus of Yupik can be viewed as a kind of stress test for the UD annotation project. If the UD guidelines truly are universal in nature, then it should be possible to construct dependency trees for Yupik while fully following the UD guidelines; to the extent that this is not possible, any such disconnect may serve to illuminate ways in which the UD guidelines might be improved upon in order to be more language universal.

One of the core assumptions of the UD guidelines is lexicalism, the assumption that the fundamental token of syntax should be the word. This assumption has been widely adopted in many syntactic formalisms, including the Lexical-Functional Grammar theory of syntax that UD in part draws upon. It has, however, been widely debated (for a thorough recent critique of lexicalism, see Bruening, 2018), and other theories such as Distributed Morphology (Halle and Marantz, 1993) explicitly reject the lexicalist hypothesis, asserting that large parts of morphology and syntax operate using a common hierarchical mechanism.

The UD guidelines already explicitly recognize that phonological and orthographic boundaries do not always coincide with *syntactic words*. Nivre et al. (2016) recognize that clitics act as words from the viewpoint of syntax, even though phonologically (and orthographically) they must attach to a host word; as such in UD annotations clitics are treated as independent syntactic tokens. Similarly, the UD annotation guidelines recognize that contractions should be treated as the combination of two independent syntactic tokens. Finally, the UD guidelines recognize that some larger units such the English expression *in spite of* act syntactically as a single token.

However, the existing UD guidelines indicate that derivational morphemes should not be treated as syntactic words for the purposes of dependency annotation. For example, in an English dependency tree, the word *dancer* would be treated as a single syntactic token, rather than as two (verbal root *dance-* + nominalizing suffix *-er*). In this paper, we have observed that this approach to derivational morphology fails when applied to Yupik.

The languages in the Inuit-Yupik language family are polysynthetic and rely heavily on productive derivational morphology. St. Lawrence Island Yupik has around 400 derivational suffixes, around half of which are verb-elaborating (V $\rightarrow$ V) derivational suffixes. It is essentially impossible to adequately annotate the syntax of Yupik sentences without recognizing that significant parts of Yupik grammar are handled by Yupik derivational morphology.

In this paper, we have chosen to treat every Yupik morpheme (both derivational and inflectional) as a syntactic token. In future work, it may be beneficial to build upon work by Çöltekin (2016) and treat only some derivational morphemes as syntactic tokens, while not tokenizing other derivational morphemes and perhaps all inflectional morphemes. At a minimum, this work shows that in order to be universal, the UD project must acknowledge that at least some derivational morphemes must be treated as syntactic tokens.

9 Conclusion

This paper presents the first UD treebank for St. Lawrence Island Yupik, the first UD treebank to be annotated at the morpheme level as well as the word level to our knowledge. The polysynthetic language has rich morphology, characterized by a theoretically unlimited number of possible derivations and multimorphemic words. In order to capture the morphosyntactic relations among morphemes, we annotated a corpus (Jacobson, 2001) at the morpheme level and converted the morpheme-level annotations into word-level annotations. While the morpheme-level annotation may require more linguistic resources (e.g. morphological analyzer, morphological segmentation), it provides a deeper insight into the language and better automatic parsing performance. Morpheme-level syntactic dependency annotation may be a better way to represent polysynthetic languages within the framework of UD.

References

Linda Womkon Badten, Vera Oovi Kaneshiro, Marie Oovi, and Christopher Koonooka. 2008. *St. Lawrence Island / Siberian Yupik Eskimo Dictionary*. Alaska Native Language Center, University of Alaska Fairbanks.

Joan Bresnan and Sam A. Mchombo. 1995. The lexical integrity principle: Evidence from Bantu. *Natural Language and Linguistic Theory*, 13(2):181–254.

Benjamin Bruening. 2018. The lexicalist hypothesis: Both wrong and superfluous. *Language*, 94(1):1–42.

Emily Chen, Hyunji Hayley Park, and Lane Schwartz. 2020. Improved finite-state morphological analysis for St. Lawrence Island Yupik using paradigm function morphology. In *Proceedings of the 12th Language Resources and Evaluation Conference*, pages 2676–2684, Marseille, France. European Language Resources Association.

Noam Chomsky. 1970. Remarks on nominalization. In Roderick A. Jacobs and Peter S. Rosenbaum, editors, *Readings in English Transformational Grammar*, pages 184–221. Ginn, Waltham, MA.

Çağrı Çöltekin. 2016. (When) do we need inflectional groups? In *Proceedings of the First International Conference on Turkic Computational Linguistics*.

Willem J. de Reuse. 1994. *Siberian Yupik Eskimo — The Language and Its Contacts with Chukchi*. Studies in Indigenous Languages of the Americas. University of Utah Press, Salt Lake City, Utah.

Morris Halle and Alec Marantz. 1993. Distributed morphology and the pieces of inflection. In Kenneth Hale and S. Jay Keyser, editors, *In The View from Building 20*, pages 111–176. MIT Press, Cambridge, MA.

Steven A. Jacobson. 2001. *A Practical Grammar of the St. Lawrence Island / Siberian Yupik Eskimo Language, Preliminary Edition*, 2nd edition. Alaska Native Language Center, Fairbanks, Alaska.

Kayo Nagai. 2001. *Mrs. Della Waghiyi's St. Lawrence Island Yupik Texts with Grammatical Analysis*. Number A2-006 in Endangered Languages of the Pacific Rim. Nakanishi Printing, Kyoto, Japan.

Joakim Nivre, Marie-Catherine de Marneffe, Filip Ginter, Yoav Goldberg, Jan Hajič, Christopher D. Manning, Ryan McDonald, Slav Petrov, Sampo Pyysalo, Natalia Silveira, Reut Tsarfaty, and Daniel Zeman. 2016. Universal Dependencies v1: A multilingual treebank collection. In *Proceedings of the Tenth International Conference on Language Resources and Evaluation (LREC'16)*, pages 1659–1666, Portorož, Slovenia. European Language Resources Association (ELRA).

Joakim Nivre, Marie-Catherine de Marneffe, Filip Ginter, Jan Hajič, Christopher D. Manning, Sampo Pyysalo, Sebastian Schuster, Francis Tyers, and Daniel Zeman. 2020. Universal Dependencies v2: An evergrowing multilingual treebank collection. In *Proceedings of the 12th Language Resources and Evaluation Conference*, pages 4034–4043, Marseille, France. European Language Resources Association.

Martin Popel, Zdeněk Žabokrtský, and Martin Vojtek. 2017. Udapi: Universal API for Universal Dependencies. In *Proceedings of the NoDaLiDa 2017 Workshop on Universal Dependencies (UDW 2017)*, pages 96–101, Gothenburg, Sweden. Association for Computational Linguistics.

Lane Schwartz, Emily Chen, Hyunji Hayley Park, Edward Jahn, and Sylvia Schreiner. 2021. A digital corpus of St. Lawrence Island Yupik. *ArXiv*, abs/2101.10496.

Milan Straka. 2018. UDPipe 2.0 prototype at CoNLL 2018 UD shared task. In *Proceedings of the CoNLL 2018 Shared Task: Multilingual Parsing from Raw Text to Universal Dependencies*, pages 197–207, Brussels, Belgium. Association for Computational Linguistics.

Milan Straka and Jana Straková. 2017. Tokenizing, POS Tagging, Lemmatizing and Parsing UD 2.0 with UDPipe. In *Proceedings of the CoNLL 2017 Shared Task: Multilingual Parsing from Raw Text to Universal Dependencies*, pages 88–99, Vancouver, Canada. Association for Computational Linguistics.

Francis M. Tyers and Karina Mishchenkova. 2020. Dependency annotation of noun incorporation in polysynthetic languages. In *Proceedings of the Fourth Workshop on Universal Dependencies (UDW 2020)*, pages 195–204.

Daniel Zeman, Jan Hajič, Martin Popel, Martin Potthast, Milan Straka, Filip Ginter, Joakim Nivre, and Slav Petrov. 2018. CoNLL 2018 shared task: Multilingual parsing from raw text to universal dependencies. In *Proceedings of the CoNLL 2018 Shared Task: Multilingual Parsing from Raw Text to Universal Dependencies*, pages 1–21, Brussels, Belgium. Association for Computational Linguistics.

A Overview of dependency relations used in the Jacobson treebank

Table 4 summarizes dependency relations used in the word-level and morpheme-level annotations for the Jacobson corpus. In this section, we provide additional descriptions of the dependency relations that we added for Yupik but were not introduced in the main text due to limited space.

We added a sub-relation (`obl:mod`) to the existing `obl` relation to specify a special usage of a noun in ablative-modalis case. The existing `obl` relation is used for an oblique nominal or as a non-core argument of the corresponding verb. For example, a noun in ablative-modalis case is annotated as an oblique nominal (`obl`) when used to express motion away from somewhere as in *mangteghameng* (house-ABL_MOD.SG, 'from the house') in (14).

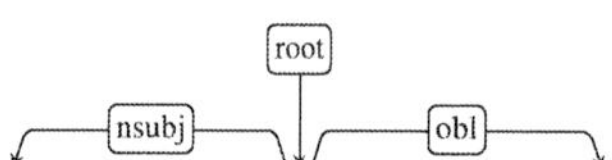

(14) *Taghnughhaat* *aanut* *mangteghameng*
children they.went.out from.house

In contrast, a noun in ablative-modalis case can also be used as "indefinite object" of an intransitive verb (Jacobson, 2001, p.20). For example, *pagunghaghmeng* (crowberry-ABL_MOD.SG) in (15) is understood as the object of an intransitive verb as an indefinite form of the noun (e.g. "crowberries" instead of "the crowberries"). Because an indefinite object in ablative-modalis case is not encoded in the verb, we annotated such nouns as an oblique noun, but distinguished it with the rest of oblique

Dependency	Word-level	Morph-level
acl	-	17
advcl	73	73
advmod	73	76
appos	21	21
cc	–	4
conj	2	2
dep:ana	–	7
dep:aux	–	120
dep:cop	–	12
dep:emo	–	1
dep:infl	–	1,087
dep:mark	–	5
dep:pos	–	3
det	5	5
mark	3	3
nmod	46	68
nmod:arg	-	3
nsubj	173	173
nummod	1	1
obj	94	121
obl	67	69
obl:mod	44	44
punct	310	310
root	309	309
xcomp	-	34

Table 4: Frequencies of dependency relations in the word-level and morpheme-level annotations for the Jacobson corpus.

nouns by specifying the sub-relation, `obl:mod`, dedicated to those indefinite objects.

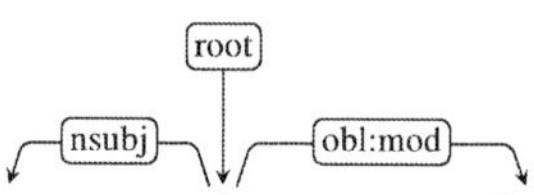

(15) *Afsengaq* *neghtuq* *pagunghaghmeng*
mouse it.ate crowberries

This is different from the `obj` relation for a noun in absolutive case used as the object of a transitive verb. The nominal base (*pagungha-* 'crowberry') takes the absolutive case inflection in (16) when used as the object of a transitive verb.

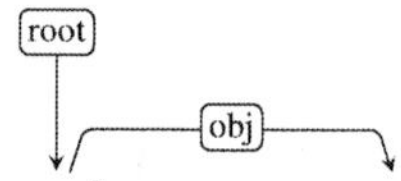

(16) *Pagunghaat* *aavgii*
crowberries she.divided.them

We also added the `nmod:arg` sub-relation to the existing `nmod` (nominal modifier) relation to specify when a nominal base is used as the argument of a noun-elaborating (N→N) derivational suffix. In (17), the nominal base (*aqavzi-* 'cloudberry') modifies the derivational suffix as the argument (*aqavzileg-* 'the one with cloudberry'). The extended base then combines with the inflection to yield the noun in ablative-modalis case (*aqavzilegmeng* 'from the one with cloudberry').

nmod:arg dep:infl

(17) *aqavzi-* *-leg-* *-meng*
cloudberry one.with.N ABL_MOD.SG

The `dep:pos` relation was used for the relation between a postural root and its postbase. A postural root takes a postbase to yield a verbal stem as in (18). The postural root (*ingagh-* 'lying down') combines with the postbase (*-nga-*) to yield a stative form of the root (*ingaghnga* 'to be lying down'), which combines with the inflection to form the word (*ingaghngaghpek*, 'you are lying down'). A postural root is different from nominal or verbal bases as it can only take one of two postbases that turn the root into a stative or active form to be followed by inflection.

dep:pos dep:infl

(18) *ingagh-* *-nga-* *-gpek*
lying.down to.be.in.R.posture 2SG

Similarly, the `dep:emo` relation was used for emotional roots. Emotional roots can take one of a select number of postbases to yield nominal or verbal stems. In (19), the emotional root (*qugina-* 'spooked') takes the postbase (*-k-*) to yield a verbal stem (*quginak* 'to be spooked'), which combines with the inflection to form a verbal (*quginakanka* 'I am spooked by them').

dep:infl
dep:emo dep:infl

(19) *qugina-* *-k-* *-a-* *-nka*
spooked to.feel.R.toward IND.TRNS 1SG.3PL

The `dep:ana` relation is used for the only prefix in Yupik, the anaphoric prefix. In general, the prefix is used for anaphora, emphasis or specificity. The prefix is also used in demonstratives to provide reference to person spoken to or situation spoken about (Jacobson, 2001, p.109).

dep:ana

(20) *taaku-* *-m*
ANAPHOR DEM.PRO.REL.SG

In (20), the anophoric prefix (*taaku-*) combines with the inflection to result in the demonstrative pronoun (*taakum* 'this one').

Unit	Word-level	Morph-level
Sentences	66	66
Words	360	360
Segments	360	834
Fused	–	225

Table 5: Number of annotations in a sample of Nagai (2001). **Words** mean the number of word tokens while **Segments** count any sub-word tokens instead of word tokens if applicable. **Fused** counts the number of word tokens that are split into subword units.

UPOS	Word-level	Morph-level
ADJ	1	1
ADP	1	1
ADV	11	16
NOUN	78	105
NUM	2	2
PART	43	43
PRON	9	9
PUNCT	81	81
VERB	134	214
X	-	362

Table 6: Frequencies of Part of Speech (POS) tags in the word-level and morpheme-level annotations for the Nagai corpus.

B Overview of the Nagai treebank

This section provides additional information about the Nagai annotations, used for the parsing experiments in §7. Table 5 summarizes the number of annotations for the new corpus. As introduced in the main text, this corpus was smaller than the Jacobson corpus, but was bigger than a test set in the ten-fold cross-validation setting.

In general, the new corpus provides a more realistic and challenging test set for an automatic parser. The Nagai corpus records a Yupik elder's speech and presents some code-switching with English words. For example, the Nagai corpus included an English word 'electric beater' inflected in Yupik *electric beater-meng*. For this, we used an additional feature 'Foreign=Yes' in annotating the corpus.

Because of such foreign words, the distribution of the POS tags were slightly different from the Jacobson treebank. Table 6 summarizes the POS tags used to annotate the Nagai corpus, and shows the presence of some tags used only for English words: For example, the Nagai annotations included an adposition (`ADP`), which was an English word, 'on'.

Because the new corpus was smaller than the original treebank, there were some POS tags in the original Jacobson corpus that were missing in the new corpus. No `DET` or `CCONJ` tags were used in the new corpus. Similarly, some dependency relations that were present in the Jacobson corpus were not present in the new corpus: `cc`, `dep:emo`, and `det`.

The More Detail, the Better? – Investigating the Effects of Semantic Ontology Specificity on Vector Semantic Classification with a Plains Cree / *nêhiyawêwin* Dictionary

Daniel Benedict Dacanay (dacanay@ualberta.ca)
Atticus Harrigan (galvin@ualberta.ca)
Arok Wolvengrey (awolvengrey@firstnationsuniversity.ca)
Antti Arppe (arppe@ualberta.ca)

University of Alberta
4-32 Assiniboia Hall,
Edmonton, Alberta, Canada T6G 2E7

Abstract

One problem in the task of automatic semantic classification is the problem of determining the level on which to group lexical items. This is often accomplished using already existing, hierarchical semantic ontologies. The following investigation explores the computational assignment of semantic classifications on the contents of a dictionary of *nêhiyawêwin* / Plains Cree (ISO: crk, Algonquian, Western Canada and United States), using a semantic vector space model, and following two semantic ontologies, WordNet and SIL's Rapid Words, and compares how these computational results compare to manual classifications with the same two ontologies.

1 Introduction

Despite the benefits and usages of semantically organised lexical resources such as dictionaries, ranging from uses as pedagogical tools (Lemnitzer and Kunze 2003) to aids for machine translation (Klyueva 2007), fully elaborated semantic dictionaries remain less common than those assembled with more routine alphabetical ordering systems. Aside from the reason of convention, one prominent dissuasive factor towards creating semantic dictionaries is the sheer amount of effort necessary to create them if their lexical content is not already organised along some ontologically principled semantic lines; the manual semantic classification of even relatively small dictionaries of this nature frequently takes months. This may be a prohibitively costly procedure in situations where resources for linguistic analysis, be they temporal or economic, are limited. Thus, a dilemma faced by the prospective compiler of a semantic dictionary is that of selecting an ontology, that is, a principled system of semantic categories, typically (but not universally) arranged hierarchically, into which lexical items may be grouped. The following investigation aims to address potential remedies to both of these limitations, with vector semantics as a first-pass alternative to manual semantic classification, and with Princeton WordNet and SIL's Rapid Words as two practical contenders for pre-existing semantic ontologies. In practice, these methods are to be demonstrated on an existing bilingual dictionary of Plains Cree (*nêhiyawêwin*), with results compared against human-made semantic classifications in both ontologies.

2 Vector Semantics

The first, and perhaps most daunting, obstacle in the process of creating a semantic dictionary (or indeed any semantically organised lexical resource) is the issue of time; even with a well-defined ontology and ample resources, manual semantic classification is a lengthy and expensive process, with teams of linguists and native speakers often requiring years to produce fully annotated semantic dictionaries (Bosch and Griesl 2017). Even with a more reduced ontology, semantically classifying an already existing full dictionary by hand takes months, and requires a thorough understanding of the chosen ontology (Dacanay et al. 2021). Although the process of manually assigning semantic categories or correspondences to

Proceedings of the First Workshop on Natural Language Processing for Indigenous Languages of the Americas, pages 143–152
June 11, 2021.

dictionary entries is generally not an exceptionally difficult task for a human annotator (Basile et al. 2012), the length of dictionaries, and the existence of highly polysemous lexical items, both complicate and lengthen the process of manual classification. As such, the mechanisation of the process of semantic classification assignment (or semantic annotation) appears to be one of the most direct routes to increasing overall efficiency with respect to time and resources, and to that end, the method of vector semantic classification is an alluring and well-attested alternative (Turney and Pantel 2010).

In short, vector semantic classification is a method of computationally determining the semantic similarity between any two given lexical units based on commonalities in the usage contexts of those units in large corpora. This is accomplished by representing the meaning of a lexical unit (primarily a word) as a vector in multidimensional space, which is based on the co-occurrences of this lexical unit with other lexical units in its context, followed by a reduction of dimensionality using some heuristic to result in a compact, dense vector space (typically with several hundred dimensions). Since this vector space is based on common contextual features, one may compare the multidimensional vector of one word with that of another, calculating their cosine distance to determine similarity; the closer this value is to 1, the more similar the average contexts of those two words are, and thus the more similar those words are semantically. In this way, the model functions largely on the assumptions of the Distributional Hypothesis as put forth by Firth and Harris in the 1950s (Jurafsky and Martin 2019; Firth 1957; Harris 1954), that semantic similarity begets distributional similarity, and vice versa. Vector generation is not monolithic, and various tools using various methods exist in common use, including frequency-weighted techniques such as tf-idf and Latent Semantic Analysis. In the context of this investigation, *word2vec*, a tool which makes use of prediction-based models rather than concurrence matrices to generate clusterable vector sets, has been used to generate all vectors; this decision was motivated chiefly by word2vec being readily available, easily applicable without lengthy training, and being able to leverage extensive, pre-existing pretraining on large English corpora, all advantages which largely offset the primary disadvantage of word2vec, being that it is a purely word-level vector generation tool, lacking the ability to model polysemy and contextual variances, a shortcoming which may possibly be addressed by using a sentence-level model such as BERT (see Section 5 and 7).

The vector method is not a novelty, and its utility as a practical method of semantic classification assignment has been demonstrated on numerous occasions (Brixey et al. 2020; Vecchi et al. 2017). However, useful as the method may be, in order to use vector semantics to classify entries in a dictionary, one requires a principled structure of semantic relationships into which to classify them. To this end, pre-existing semantic ontologies are a widespread and convenient solution.

3 Semantic Ontologies

Although it is possible to computationally generate sets of semantic hierarchies, the results of such attempts generally indicate that human-made, preset ontologies are preferable (Koper et. al 2015). Many such premade ontologies exist, serving a wide variety of different classificational purposes; however, we will compare here only two, being a slightly modified version of the Princeton WordNet and SIL's Rapid Word Collection Method, both popular, general-purpose ontologies intended to cover the breadth of most semantic reference in a largely language-neutral fashion. A visual representation of the structures of both is detailed in Figure 1 (see next page).

3.1 Princeton WordNet

The Princeton WordNet is one of the oldest and most widely-used semantic classification systems, originating in the 1990s at Princeton University as a hierarchically organised structure wherein contextually synonymous word-senses (or individual word-senses) are grouped into 'synsets', each of which has a hypernymic

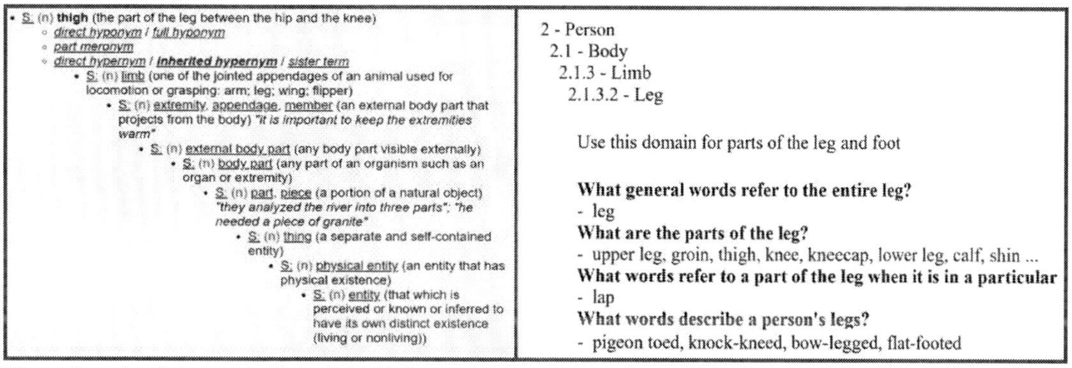

Figure 1, a visual demonstration of the differences in structure and specificity between WordNet (left) and Rapid Words (right).

synset above it in the hierarchy and possibly one or several hyponymic synsets below it (for example, the words *(n) cod#2* and *(n) codfish#1* form a synset with the definition "lean white flesh of important North Atlantic food fish; usually baked or poached"; this synset is a hyponym of the synset *(n) saltwater fish#1*, and is hypernymic to the synset *(n) salt cod#1*.). In this way, WordNet is essentially a hierarchy of hypernyms and hyponyms, with each level of hypernym and hyponym being populated by various contextually synonymous words. Although other semantic relations such as antonymy are also modelled in a 'full' WordNet, the three relations of hypernymy, hyponymy, and synonymy form the "central organizing principle" of WordNet as a whole (Miller 1993), and a structurally complete, albeit semantically basic, WordNet can be constructed using only these three relationships; in Dacanay et al. (2021) we referred to this core-level WordNet as a 'skeletal WordNet'.

3.2 Rapid Words

An alternative semantic classification scheme is the Rapid Word Collection Method of SIL, created as a framework for collecting native speaker vocabulary elicitations for dictionary creation, rather than the organisation of finished dictionaries (Moe 2003). Despite this, the structure of Rapid Words is broadly similar to that of WordNet, consisting of various numbered, hierarchically organised, roughly hyper/hyponymic semantic domains, each of which is populated by highly semantically related (although in Rapid Words, not necessarily contextually synonymous) sets of words, which may be spread across various parts of speech. Broadly speaking, these domains are less specific than WordNet synsets. There are five 'tiers' of domains in RW, with the highest being the most general (e.g. *5 Daily Life*, *7 Physical Actions*, etc) and the lowest being the most specific (e.g. *5.2.3.3.3 Spice*, *7.2.1.1.1 Run*); for our purposes, only domains on the fourth tier (or level) were used for the vector classifications (see Section 5). These semantic domains are sub-organised into specific elicitation questions, each of which has a set of potential vocabulary items in English; for example, the domain *2.1.1.5 Tooth* contains the elicitation question 'What are the parts of a tooth?', which would have with it the list of potential English answers as prompts 'enamel, root, crown, ivory'. Although not explicitly designed for it, Rapid Words has been used successfully for after-the-fact dictionary classification in the past (Reule 2018).

4 Plains Cree / *nêhiyawêwin*

Plains Cree (*nēhiyawēwin*) is an Indigenous language of the Algonquian family, spoken by ~30 000 throughout Saskatchewan, Alberta, and Northern Montana. Although slightly less critically endangered in comparison with other Canadian Indigenous languages, the majority of speakers are elderly, and intergenerational transmission remains low. Various revitalisation efforts have been undertaken in Cree communities, including bilingual education and the creation of online lexical resources (Arppe et al. 2018); however, digital resources for Cree remain limited overall. Like most Algonquian languages, Plains Cree is highly polysynthetic, with extensive morphology, particularly on verbs, which make up the bulk of the lexicon (e.g., Wolfart 1973).

The lexical resource used for this investigation was a fully digitised copy of the database underlying *nêhiyawêwin: itwêwina*/Cree: Words (CW), a continually-updated bilingual Cree-English dictionary compiled by Arok Wolvengrey across the late 20th and early 21st centuries (Wolvengrey 2001). Consisting currently of 21,347 words with morphological notes and PoS-tagging, CW is the most extensive modern dictionary of Plains Cree, and its contents may be accessed through the University of Alberta's online Cree dictionary, *itwêwina*.

5 Method

Word vectors were obtained for every Cree entry in CW using *word2vec*, a popular off-the-shelf vector generation tool (Mikolov et al. 2013). We used the pretrained Google News Corpus, which contains 3 million word embeddings trained on 3 billion tokens. Cree word (or rather, dictionary entry) vectors were obtained as a simple, dimension-wise average of the individual English word vectors as extracted from the English definition phrases/sentences (glosses) of their respective entries, rather than the Cree words themselves, as existing Cree corpora (Arppe 2020) are too small for meaningful dimensional vectors to be obtained (Harrigan and Arppe 2019). For example, the vector for the Cree noun *mahkahk* (glossed in CW as 'tub, barrel; box') would be generated by averaging the vectors for the English words 'tub', 'barrel', and 'box', treated as a bag of words. Similarly, for the Cree verb *nâtwânam* (glossed as 's/he breaks s.t. apart; s/he breaks s.t. off by hand'), the vector would be derived from the average of the vectors for 's/he', 'breaks', 's.t.', 'apart', 'off', and 'hand'. CW noun glosses tend to be either single words or extremely curt noun phrases, and verb glosses are usually brief, utilitarian verb phrases, with no grammatical or derivational information included in the gloss itself; this fact is a further justification for using a word-level vector generation tool such as word2vec rather than a sentence-level tool like BERT, as the pieces of linguistic information on which the CW vectors are based are typically either non-sentential or highly simplistic and formulaic, seemingly making the context-sensitivity of tools such as BERT much less useful.

The Google News Corpus and word2vec were similarly used to generate the vectors for the WordNet synsets, using the head words and synset description (definitions and example sentences) as context to create the vectors, and the head word(s) of the synset as labels (Dacanay et al. 2021). For example, the vector for the synset *(n) barrel#2* (glossed as "barrel, cask (a cylindrical container that holds liquids)") would be the average of the vectors for the words 'barrel', 'cask', 'cylindrical', 'container', 'holds', and 'liquids'. The vectors for Rapid Words were created using the semantic domain levels as labels, with all example words and elicitation questions contained therein as context. For example, for the word 'barrel' in Rapid Words, which is contained in the semantic domain *6.7.7 Container*, the vector would be the average of the vectors for all of the English words in each elicitation question (i.e. "What words refer to a container", "What words refer to what is in a container", etc.), as well as all of the words listed as possible examples (such as 'container', 'vessel', 'bowl', 'pot', 'contents' etc.).

These sets of vectors were then compared against the CW vectors using cosine distance, and for every CW entry, two lists were created. For each entry on the first list (the WordNet list), all WordNet synsets were listed, ordered by cosine similarity to that entry. On the second list (the four-level Rapid Words list), for each CW entry, all Rapid Words semantic domains at the fourth tier of the hierarchy were ordered by similarity. To provide an example for the second list, even if the manually-selected RW domain for the Cree word *acihkos* ('caribou calf, fawn') was *1.6.1.1.3 Hoofed Animal*, because, on this list, the vector method would only have access to the fourth hierarchy level, the ideal, most 'human-like' vector classification would instead be *1.6.1.1 Mammal*, as this domain is at the fourth level of the hierarchy and is identical to the manual classification up to the fourth level (*1.6.1.1*). The reasoning behind limiting the RW domains to the fourth level of the hierarchy in the vector method was threefold; firstly, tests in which the vector method was allowed to select domain classifications from any of the five levels returned notably poorer results than those which limited the choice to only one tier. (see Table 1 Any-Level (AL) columns), secondly, the fourth level of the hierarchy had the largest number of domains (at 983 compared to the fifth level with 311 and the second level with 68), and thirdly, RW did not always provide fifth level domains throughout the hierarchy. Additionally, the fourth level of the hierarchy provided a useful middleground in terms of specificity compared with the other RW levels; fourth level domains are moderately, rather than highly, specific, and thus allow for a more informative comparison with WordNet's highly specific and complex synset structure. Still, investigating whether using the most specific Rapid Words domains as labels would provide more or less accurate results than the moderately specific four-level domains would be a worthwhile avenue of future study, as would be using the individual elicitation questions as labels instead of domains.

In total, applying the vector semantic method to this end requires access to a fully digitised copy of the target dictionary (with entries and their glosses clearly delineated), access to WordNet, Rapid Words, and word2vec (all of which are freely available online), and a computer capable of both generating vectors for the dictionary entries and comparing those vectors with the pre-existing ontology vectors. To this end, a 2-core laptop with 8gb RAM is able to complete the cosine comparisons for the ~16k CW entries with the ~117k WordNet synsets in 4-5 days, and the same entries with the Rapid Words domains in no more than one and half days. On a highly parallelised computing cluster, such as ComputeCanada's Cedar (using 64 cores, each having 4-8gb RAM), performing all of the cosine comparisons takes less than 90 minutes. The computational cost of the actual vector cosine comparisons is fairly negligible, and the lengthy runtime of this operation on more basic machines is likely due to the inefficiency of retrieving each vector from large matrices.

To assess their quality, these vector classifications were compared against a gold standard of manual classifications for each entry in CW. These manual classifications were done following both WordNet and Rapid Words, with one or several synsets or RW elicitation questions assigned to each CW entry based on the meaning of the Cree word. For the WordNet classifications, the part of speech of the English WN synset was ignored; for example, the manual classification of the Cree verb *mihkwâw* ("it is red") was given in WordNet as the adjectival synset *(adj) red#1*. For Rapid Words classifications, given that RW elicitation questions do not have hard-coded parts of speech, whichever domain-internal elicitation question(s) were most semantically related to the target Cree word were used, regardless of their domain level in the hierarchy. For example, for *mihkwâw*, the question *8.3.3.3.4.3 What are the shades of red?* in the domain *8.3.3.3.4 Colors of the Spectrum* was used. More information on the manual classification method used is detailed in Dacanay et al. (2021).

	Verbs, 4L-RW top	Verbs, 4L-RW median	Nouns 4L-RW top	Nouns 4L-RW median	Verbs, AL-RW, top	Nouns, AL-RW, top	Verbs, WN, top	Verbs, WN, median	Nouns, WN, top	Nouns, WN, median
0%	1	1	1	1	1	1	1	1	1	1
10%	1	1	1	1	6	3	5	11	1	2
20%	1	2	1	1	19	7	18	51.7	2	4

30%	3	5	1	1	59	14	51.6	166.3	4	8
40%	6	15	1	2	118	23	136.8	448.8	7	16.1
50%	**15**	**36**	**2**	**3**	**222**	**36.5**	**333**	**1045**	**15**	**30.5**
60%	38	73	4	6.5	354	66	762.2	2057.3	28	60
70%	80	130.5	10	14	519	126	1633.9	4096.4	59	139
80%	161	225	24	33	717	256	3553.8	8036.9	164	375.4
90%	327	369	69	102.1	993	501	9553.8	17488.6	864.2	1670.4
100%	983	983	976	976	1739	1760	137352	137352	121883	121883

Table 1, the vector assigned ranks of manual WN and RW classifications in percentiles, for both the top-ranked manual classification and the median if there were several. '4L' indicates four-level domains, and 'AL' indicates any level of domain. Medians are written in bold.

6 Comparison of WordNet and Rapid Words Results

Statistics: Overall, although the results of both ontologies are comparable, semantic classifications using Rapid Words appear noticeably more human-like than those with WordNet, with 'human-like' here referring to how high the rank of the manual classification(s) is among the total vector classifications for each entry on average. For the vector classifications of Cree nouns, the median position of the top manual classification was 2 for four-level RW domains (with 983 possible classes) and 36.5 when the vector method was allowed to choose from any level of domain (with 1789 possible classes). For Cree verbs, the median position of the top manual classification was 15 for the four-level domains and 222 for any-level domains. In cases where there was more than one manual RW classification, the median position of the median of the multiple classes for CW nouns was 3 for four-levels, and for CW verbs, the median of the medians of multiple classes was 36 for four-levels. For the WordNet vector classifications, the median computationally selected position for the top manual classification was 15th for Cree nouns and 333rd for verbs, and the median position of the manual classifications when there were several was 30.5 for the nouns and 1045 for the verbs.

From this, it is clear that vector classifications with Rapid Words domains are, on average, much more human-like than their WordNet counterparts, being up to 22 times more accurate in the case of Cree verbs, and that limiting the vector methods' potential selections to a single, moderately specific RW hierarchy level provides much more human-like results than allowing it to select from all domains at all levels. However, it is prudent to keep in mind that even with all of its domains, Rapid Words still has far fewer potential correspondences than WordNet (1789 total RW domains (with 983 four-levels) compared to 117,659 WN synsets), and in relative terms, relevant manual classifications occur on average in a higher position proportionate to the total number of possible choices in WN vector classifications than in those with RW; with four-level RW vector classifications, the median position of the top manual classification is in the top 0.203% for the nouns (2nd out of 983) and in the top 1.53% for the verbs (15th out of 983), compared with the top 0.0127% (15th out of 117659) and 0.283% (333rd out of 117659) respectively for WN.

In general, the reduced specificity of Rapid Words, by virtue of both its inherently less detailed structure and its restriction here to a single hierarchical level of specificity, seemed to lend itself well to resolving a particular ill in the vector method, being its propensity to preferentially assign overly specific classifications to the high ranks of 'umbrella-terms', rather than the more appropriate general vocabulary. In this sense, Rapid Words semantic domains often represent concepts several steps higher in the hypernymic hierarchy than their WordNet equivalents. For example, with the WordNet classifications, the top classification for *môhkomân* (glossed as 'knife') was *(n) knife blade#1*, and the top 15 classifications consisted almost entirely of either specific types of knives or parts of knives, with the more appropriate generic term *(n) knife#1* not appearing until 18th place. By contrast, in Rapid Words, in which such specific classifications are by nature impossible at the domain-level, the top ranking classifications are more appropriately general, with the any-level list, for example, having the appropriate *6.7.1 Cutting Tool* as the top classification, and the similarly relevant *4.8.3.7 Weapon, Shoot* in second place.

The 'regift' problem: The in-built simplicity of Rapid Words also seems to have partially remedied, if not entirely solved, the so-called 'regift problem' which was prevalent in WordNet classifications; we discuss this problem in more detail in Dacanay et al. (2021), but simply put, a small number of extremely low frequency WordNet synsets occurred disproportionately frequently in the high-ranking classifications of target Cree words. The problem was so named due to such one low-frequency synset, *(v) regift#1*, being present in the top 1000 computational classifications of 65% of all Cree verbs, despite almost always being entirely unrelated semantically to the target Cree word. *(v) regift#1* is not the only WordNet entry to exhibit this behaviour, and other words, such as *(n) Rumpelstiltskin#1* occurred in as many as 72% of the top 1000 vector classifications of Cree verbs; other common regift words include *(n) Dido#1*, *(n) gumption#1*, and *(n) dingbat#1*. As a rule, these 'regift' words were both low frequency in corpora and highly specific, often being proper nouns, however, there did not appear to be any pattern in the formatting or content of these entries' glosses. The Rapid Words vector classifications also exhibited this problem to an extent; for example, subdomains of the domain *4.1.9 Kinship* occurred in the top 1000 vector classifications of CW nouns and verbs an average of ~12 times, and appeared in the top 10 classifications 33.9% and 35.7% of the time for CW nouns and verbs respectively. However, as a whole, the regift problem was markedly less notable with RW classifications of both types than with WN classifications, with both fewer different regift words (or domains) and fewer occurrences of these words/domains overall. This broadly supported our initial theory that the 'regift' problem was at least partially caused by the excessive degree of specificity in WordNet synsets overwhelming the vector method and providing it with a large number of potential classification choices with poorly defined vectors (due the low frequency of 'regift' words in the Google News Corpus) which muddy the optimal, human-like choices.

By contrast, since Rapid Words generally lacks highly specific vocabulary and is instead structured by more generic categories or 'domains', fewer of these low-frequency words are factored into the Rapid Words vectors, and these vectors are thus, in general, based on higher frequency, more contextually attested vocabulary, and are therefore (in theory) more accurate. In general, the lack of highly specific vocabulary in Rapid Words seems to contribute both to diminishing the number of semantically-related, but overly specific correspondences in the computational classifications, as well as to reducing the prominence of semantically-unrelated, overly specific 'regift' words (or in the case of Rapid Words, domains). One potential method to imitate this degree of simplicity in WordNet could involve using the hypernymic synsets of the current WordNet correspondences as labels, in essence, shifting all classifications one or more levels up in the WordNet hierarchy. This would appear to at least partially resolve the over-specificity issue (although it would do nothing to reduce the number of outright irrelevant classifications), despite incurring an obvious cost in terms of semantic richness.

Vector Content: Broadly speaking, the improved results with Rapid Words seem to be due not only to its simpler hierarchical structure and reduced level of specificity, but also due to its domain internal structure, in which domains generally include fewer irrelevant content words than WordNet synsets do. WordNet synsets frequently include example sentences in their glosses; although useful for human clarification, these inclusions inevitably lead to large amounts of semantically unrelated vocabulary influencing the respective synset vectors. As an example, the gloss for the synset *(v) drive#2* (defined as "travel or be transported in a vehicle") includes the example sentences "We drove to the university every morning" and "They motored to London for the theater". As such, the semantically irrelevant words "university", "morning", "London", and "theater" are all factored equally into the vector for *(v) drive#2* as the semantically relevant terms "drive", "motor", "vehicle". While the inclusion of these less relevant words may more accurately simulate natural linguistic contexts, the otherwise terse nature of WordNet synset glosses means that they introduce a potentially significant amount of distracting information, possibly skewing synset vectors towards the contexts of their irrelevant example sentence vocabulary rather than their relevant gloss vocabulary. By contrast, with the exception of infrequent descriptions of lexicalisation patterns, Rapid Words domains and questions contain only semantically related vocabulary, lessening potential 'distractions' for their vectors.

6.1 Utility of Results

Given the state of current results, it remains unfeasible to fully replace manual semantic annotators using the vector method; even with the best possible RW results, the vector method still only selects the most human-like classification as the top classification less than 50% of the time for Cree nouns, and less than 30% of the time for Cree verbs. Rather, the vector method in its present state seems most immediately usable as an accessory to manual classification, with the method being applied on dictionary resources as a preparatory step for manual annotators, who would then select the best classification for each entry based on the pre-generated vector classification lists. Using only the top 15 vector selected four-level RW classifications, the most human-like classification would be present on this list 50% of the time for Cree verbs, and over 70% of the time for nouns, preventing the annotator from needing to search through the entire ontology every time they wished to classify a word. In this way, present vector results are best suited as a time-saving addition to manual semantic annotation, rather than as a replacement for it.

7 Conclusion

The vector semantic method is a significantly faster and cheaper alternative to manual semantic annotation for tasks of semantic classification. However, the method is not yet capable of producing reliably human-like results across target-language parts of speech, and struggles to match natural levels of semantic specificity. To this end, using a consistent hierarchical level of a simpler, more generalistic semantic ontology, such as Rapid Words, seems to make vector semantic classifications appear more human-like, as restricting the breadth of choices available to the method as labels for correspondences seems to both reduce the number of potentially unrelated classifications and make the remaining classifications general enough that a less precise vector is necessary to generate a human-like correspondence.

Future avenues of research into dictionary vector semantics include the use of sentence-based vector generation tools such as BERT which can more accurately model polysemy, although it should be kept in mind that even a model like BERT cannot be expected to generate human-like results for dictionary glosses if those glosses are non-sentential or otherwise overly brief. It may also prove productive to experiment with the further modification of existing semantic ontologies such as WordNet and Rapid Words (such as reducing the specificity of WN by using only synsets one or several levels higher in the hypernym hierarchy as correspondences), with one of the ultimate goals of this being the integration of the results of automatic vector classifications into online dictionaries in a form which is easily navigable and understandable to an untrained user.

Acknowledgements

We would like to thank the Roger S. Smith Undergraduate Researcher Award for the generous funding they provided for the manual classification process and the early stages of this study.

References

Arppe, Antti, Atticus Harrigan, Katherine Schmirler & Arok Wolvengrey. 2018. A morphologically intelligent online dictionary for Plains Cree, Presentation conducted at the meeting of Stabilizing Indigenous Languages Symposium (SILS), University of Lethbridge, Lethbridge, Alberta.

Arppe, Antti, Katherine Schmirler, Atticus G. Harrigan & Arok Wolvengrey. 2020. A Morphosyntactically Tagged Corpus for Plains Cree**. In M. Macaulay & M. Noodin (eds), Papers of the 49th Algonquian Conference (PAC49), 49: 1-16. East Lansing, Michigan: MSU Press.

Basile, Valerio, Johan Bos, Kilian Evang & Noortje J. Venhuizen. 2012. "Developing a large semantically annotated corpus." *Proceedings of the Eighth International Conference on Language Resources and Evaluation (LREC'12)*, May 2012, 3196-200, doi:http://www.lrec-conf.org/proceedings/lrec2012/pdf/534_Paper.pdf.

Boerger, Brenda H. 2017. "Rapid Word Collection, dictionary production, and community well-being." *5th International Conference on Language Documentation & Conservation*, Mar. 2017, doi:https://scholarspace.manoa.hawaii.edu/bitstream/10125/41988/41988-b.pdf.

Bosch, Sonja E & Marissa Griesel. 2017. "Strategies for building wordnets for underresourced languages: The case of African languages." Literator - Journal of Literary Criticism, Comparative Linguistics and Literary Studies, vol. 38, no. 1, 31, 8, doi:https://literator.org.za/index.php/literator/article/view/1351/2294. Accessed 12 Sept. 2020.

Brixey, Jacqueline, David Sides, Timothy Vizthum, David Traum & Khalil Iskarous. 2020. "Exploring a Choctaw Language Corpus with Word Vectors and Minimum Distance Length." *Proceedings of the 12th Conference on Language Resources and Evaluation (LREC 2020)*, May 2020, 2746-53.

Dacanay, Daniel, Atticus Harrigan & Antti Arppe. 2021. "Computational Analysis versus Human Intuition: A Critical Comparison of Vector Semantics with Manual Semantic Classification in the Context of Plains Cree." *Proceedings of the 4th Workshop on the Use of Computational Methods in the Study of Endangered Languages*, doi:https://computel-workshop.org/wpcontent/uploads/2021/02/2021.computel-1.5.pdf

Fellbaum, Christiane. 1998, ed. WordNet: *An Electronic Lexical Database*. Cambridge, MA: MIT Press.

Firth, J. R. A Synopsis of Linguistic Theory, 1930–1955. 1957. In: Firth, J. R. 1968. Selected Papers of J. R. Firth 1952-1959. London: Logmans, 168-205.

Harrigan, Atticus & Antti Arppe. 2019. Automatic Semantic Classification of Plains Cree Verbs. Paper presented at the 51st Algonquian Conference in Montreal, Canada, 24–27 October.

Harris, Zellig S. 1954. "Distributional Structure." *Word*, vol. 10, no. 2-3, 146-62, doi:https://www.tandfonline.com/doi/pdf/10.1080/00437956.1954.11659520.

Jurafsky, Dan & James H. Martin. 2019. *Speech and Language Processing: An Introduction to Natural Language Processing, Computational Linguistics, and Speech Recognition*. 3rd ed., 94-119

Klyueva, Natalia. "Semantics in Machine Translation." *WDS'07 Proceedings of Contributed Papers, Part I*, 2007, pp. 141-44, doi:https://www.mff.cuni.cz/veda/konference/wds/proc/pdf07/WDS07_123_i3_Klyueva.pdf.

Koper, Maximilian, Christian Scheible & Sabine Schulte im Walde. 2015. "Multilingual Reliability and "Semantic" Structure of Continuous Word Spaces." *Proceedings of the 11th International Conference on Computational Semantics*, 15 Apr. 2015, doi:https://www.aclweb.org/anthology/W15-0105.pdf.

Lemnitzer, Lothar & Claudia Kunze. 2003. "Using WordNets in Teaching Virtual Courses of Computational Linguistics." *Seminar für Sprachwissenschaft, Universität Tübingen*, Jan. 2003

Li, Wei, Yunfang Wu & Xucqiang Lv. 2018. *Improving Word Vector with Prior Knowledge in Semantic Dictionary*. Beijing, Key Laboratory of Computational Linguistics, Peking University.

Mikolov, Tomas, Kai Chen, Greg Corrado & Jeffrey Dean. 2013. *Efficient Estimation of Word Representations in Vector Space*. arxiv.org/pdf/1301.3781.pdf.

Mikolov, Tomas, Ilya Sutskever, Kai Chen, Greg Corrado & Jeffrey Dean. 2013. "Distributed representations of words and phrases and their compositionality." *Advances in Neural Information Processing Systems*, https://arxiv.org/pdf/1310.4546.pdf.

Miller, George A. 1995. "WordNet: A Lexical Database for English".Communications of the ACM, vol. 38, no. 11: 39-41.

Miller, George, Richard Beckwith, Christiane Fellbaum, Derek Gross & Katherine Miller. 1993. *Introduction to WordNet: An On-line Lexical Database*. Princeton University, 1-9

Moe, Ronald. 2003. Compiling dictionaries using semantic domains. *Lexikos* 13, 215-223, doi:http://lexikos.journals.ac.za/pub/article/view/731

Reule, Tanzi. 2018. *Elicitation and Speech Acts in the Maskwacîs Spoken Cree Dictionary Project*. Department of Linguistics, University of Alberta.

Tous, Ruben & Jaime Delgado. 2006. "A vector space model for semantic similarity calculation and OWL ontology alignment." *Proceedings of the 17th International Conference on Database and Expert Systems Applications*, Sept. 2006, 307-16, doi:https://citeseerx.ist.psu.edu/viewdoc/download?doi=10.1.1.61.9727&rep=rep1&type=pdf.

Turney, Peter D. & Patrick Pantel. 2010. "From Frequency to Meaning:Vector Space Models of Semantics." *Journal of Artificial Intelligence Research*, vol. 37, 141-1888, doi:https://www.jair.org/index.php/jair/article/view/10640/25440.

Vecchi EM, Marelli M, Zamparelli R & Baroni M. 2017. "Spicy Adjectives and Nominal Donkeys: Capturing Semantic Deviance Using Compositionality in Distributional Spaces. " *Cognitive Science* 41, 102–136

Wolfart, H. Christoph. 1973. "Plains Cree: A Grammatical Study." *Transactions of the American Philosophical Society, New Series*, vol.63, no. 5, Nov. 1973, 1-90.

Wolvengrey, Arok. 2001. *nêhiyawêwin: itwêwina - Cree: Words*. 11th ed., University of Regina Press.

Experiments on a Guarani Corpus of News and Social Media

Santiago Góngora, Nicolás Giossa, Luis Chiruzzo
Facultad de Ingeniería
Universidad de la República
Montevideo, Uruguay
{sgongora,nicolas.giossa,luischir}@fing.edu.uy

Abstract

While Guarani is widely spoken in South America, obtaining a large amount of Guarani text from the web is hard. We present the building process of a Guarani corpus composed of a parallel Guarani-Spanish set of news articles, and a monolingual set of tweets. We perform some word embeddings experiments aiming at evaluating the quality of the Guarani split of the corpus, finding encouraging results but noticing that more diversity in text domains might be needed for further improvements.

1 Introduction

Guarani is a South American language spoken mainly in Paraguay, but also in some regions of Argentina, Bolivia and Brazil. Despite being an official language of Mercosur and Paraguay, research and resources for Guarani are limited. Our work focuses on the current dialect of Guarani spoken in Paraguay, called Jopara. The Jopara Guarani dialect presents different levels of mixture between Guarani and Spanish, using mainly the Guarani grammar but incorporating many Spanish loanwords (Lustig, 2010).

In this work, we present a Guarani corpus that tries to reflect the nature of this mixed dialect. On the one hand the corpus contains a set of sentences written in a more formal style, composed of news articles, where each sentence also has a Spanish counterpart. On the other hand the corpus has a more informal set of texts extracted from social media; we analyzed them and noticed the different levels of mixture between Guarani and other languages.

This is a work in progress with the aim of creating resources for Guarani that could aid in NLP tasks such as machine translation, so our objective is to make this resource as large as possible but at the same time trying to keep the content quality high. We also show an initial analysis of the corpus based on word embeddings analogies tests and visualization.

2 Related work

Although Guarani remains a little explored language within the NLP community, throughout the years there have been some attempts at creating resources or corpora for this language. COREGUAPA (Secretaría de Políticas Lingüísticas del Paraguay, 2019) is the reference corpus of current Paraguayan Guarani, it can be queried online but it cannot be downloaded in its entirety. Other works have focused on trying to develop machine translation systems or computer aided translation systems for the Guarani-Spanish pair considering the scarcity of NLP resources for the language (Alcaraz and Alcaraz, 2020; Gasser, 2018; Rudnick et al., 2014; Abdelali et al., 2006). Besides the resources focused on the Jopara Guarani dialect, there is a small Universal Dependencies corpus (around a thousand sentences) of the Guarani dialect spoken by the Mbya Guarani people (Thomas, 2019; Dooley, 2006). The work of Chiruzzo et al. (2020) describes the construction of a parallel corpus of Guarani and Spanish sentences built by downloading pages in both languages from web sources and using an automatic process (with manual correction) to align the sentence pairs. We follow a similar approach in the parallel set of our corpus, although we also add a second set of monolingual text extracted from social media. Currently, Guarani is included as one of the target languages in the machine translation Shared Task of the AmericasNLP workshop, which indicates interest in developing resources for this language is on the rise.

3 Construction of the corpus

This section presents the construction of the parallel and the monolingual sets of the corpus.

Proceedings of the First Workshop on Natural Language Processing for Indigenous Languages of the Americas, pages 153–158
June 11, 2021.

3.1 Parallel news set

The parallel corpus was built by crawling a set of pages restricted to the Paraguayan top level domain (.py). As a starting point, we took a set of frequent Guarani words from the Chiruzzo et al. (2020) corpus and queried different permutations of this set into a search engine, creating a set of URL seeds. Our crawler started with these seeds and downloaded, processed and cleaned each text, then used the internal links to collect more content. Although Guarani is widely spoken in Paraguay, it is a minority language with respect to the amount of text one can find in the web, where most of the Paraguayan pages are written mainly in Spanish. As noticed in Jauhiainen et al. (2020), it is very difficult to build resources for languages that are under-represented on the web, even if there is a top level domain where it is more likely to find content in that language, as the pages generally point back to content in the majority language rather than the language we are looking for. We manually inspected the early results of this experiment and found that most of the downloaded content was in Spanish. However, we also noticed that there were some Paraguayan websites which regularly publish content in both Guarani and Spanish.

We noticed two main strategies that were used by the websites to present versions of their content both in Guarani and Spanish: links within the pages to the Spanish version, and publishing the page in both languages in a short time frame. The first strategy is easy to deal with: the scraper collects the Guarani versions of the files and extracts the corresponding Spanish version following the link. This link is present in most articles, but not in all of them. If it is not found, the scraper still downloads the Guarani version[1].

For the second strategy, we designed a heuristic process for matching Guarani and Spanish files based on their timestamps. The heuristic clusters the articles by its creation date, pairing up each Guarani article to the Spanish one with the closest creation time in the group. This simple heuristic solved most of the cases, although we found two types of problematic situations:

- On occasions, the number of Guarani articles published on a given date did not match the number of Spanish ones on the same date.
- Some Guarani articles were paired with the same Spanish article due to sharing the same closest article in time in the group.

Since the number of articles affected by these issues were only a small percentage of the total, we used the heuristic for the general case and manually solved these outliers. We evaluated the heuristic results by sampling 100 random pairs and manually inspecting them, resulting in 100% correct pairs.

The parallel set is composed of 2580 news articles published in Paraguayan websites. These articles are aligned at sentence level, following the n-gram overlap heuristic described in Chiruzzo et al. (2020).

It contains a total of 14,792 Guarani-Spanish sentence pairs; including 334,501 Guarani word tokens and 635,226 Spanish word tokens. Table 1 shows a comparison between our parallel set and the one presented in Chiruzzo et al. (2020)

	Chiruzzo et al. (2020)	Parallel set
Documents	1,858	2,580
Sentences	14,531	14,792
Guarani tokens	268,684	334,501
Spanish tokens	380,275	635,226

Table 1: Size comparison between Chiruzzo et al. (2020) and our parallel set.

3.2 Tweets set

We first tried to extract tweets in Guarani using the Twitter API. The first issue was finding which of the texts contained at least some content in Guarani. The API has a language detection option that includes the Guarani language. However, this language detector API is not perfect, as we empirically found that none of the tweets was ever getting the Guarani label, even it they were written entirely in Guarani. We then trained our own language detector with the aim of telling apart between Spanish and Guarani texts, using a Naïve Bayes classifier with 5-gram character features, trained over the Chiruzzo et al. (2020) corpus. The language detector was very good for detecting Guarani in this corpus (99.6% in our test partition), but it proved to be not good enough for the noisy texts found in tweets.

Finally, we decided to use a frequent words based approach. We created two lists of frequent words: a *long list* (314 words) composed of words that appear in the corpus, filtering out dates, numbers, punctuation symbols, words with less than 3

[1]However, since they only represented 2% of the total, these articles were not included in the corpus.

	Chiruzzo et al. (2020)	Reliable text
Total Tokens	268,684	391,102
Unique tokens	31,456	41,813
Exclusive count	18,056	28,413
Overlap	13,400	

Table 2: Size comparison of the monolingual split. *Exclusive count* shows the number of tokens that are not on the other set. *Overlap* is the number of tokens that are on both sets.

characters and words that could be mistaken with other languages in the region such as Spanish and Portuguese; and a more restrictive *short list* (48 words) containing words that appear over 10 times in the corpus. We periodically collected tweets that contained at least some of the words from the short list, which includes the stop-words and many other very frequent Guarani words, both from Paraguay (*local*) and from anywhere in the world (*global*). Then we counted the number of Guarani tokens present in each tweet using the long list, and manually analyzed the extracted sets of tweets based on location and Guarani tokens. During the manual inspection we marked a tweet as a hit if it had at least some Guarani content, and a miss if all the text was in another language and was a false positive. Paraguayan (*local*) tweets with at least two of the frequent words seem to all have reliable Guarani content. However, for the *global* tweets this threshold seems to be at four words, and precision drops to around 85% with fewer words. We defined three categories:

- A (very reliable): *local* tweets with three or more frequent words and *global* tweets with four or more frequent words. (532 tweets; 7,706 tokens)
- B (reliable): *local* tweets with two frequent words. In this case, although usually containing Guarani content, there are also cases of tweets mainly in Spanish with some Guarani expression. (4,199 tweets; 48,895 tokens)
- C (unreliable): *local* tweets with just one frequent word and *global* tweets with three frequent words. This category contains many tweets in Guarani, but other languages may be present as well, such as Portuguese or Filipino. (46,197 tweets; 453,996 tokens)

We define the monolingual split of the corpus as the reliable tweets (categories A and B) plus the Guarani sentences from the parallel set. Table 2 compares the size of our monolingual split with the Guarani data from Chiruzzo et al. (2020).

4 Experiments

We carried on some experiments to try to analyze the quality of the monolingual split of the corpus built so far. We followed the approach described in Etcheverry and Wonsever (2016), where they trained a word embeddings collection for Spanish from Wikipedia text and analyzed its quality based on intrinsic tests and visualization. We trained several variants of 150-dimensional *word2vec* embeddings collections using the Gensim library (Řehůřek and Sojka, 2010). The different variants we trained correspond to using different sets of data. Besides the text collected in this work, in our experiments we also used the Guarani Wikipedia text[2], and the Guarani data from Chiruzzo et al. (2020). All models reported here were trained on some combination of those sets, a summary of the sizes of the sets is shown in table 3.

Corpus	Token count
Wikipedia	582,122
Chiruzzo et al. (2020)	268,684
Parallel news set	334,501
Reliable tweets set	56,601
Unreliable tweets set	453,996
Total (*reliable* tokens)	1,241,908
Total (*all* tokens)	1,695,904

Table 3: Guarani tokens on each set used in the experiments, tokenized using NLTK (Bird et al., 2009).

4.1 Word clustering visualization

Category	Example	Color (legend)
Years	1975	Black (k)
Months	jasyteĩ (*january*)	Black (k)
Days	arakõi (*monday*)	Black (k)
Countries	hyãsia (*France*)	Magenta (m)
Attributes	vai (*bad*)	Red (r)
Colors	hovy (*blue*)	Cyan (c)
Animals	mbarakaja (*cat*)	Green (g)
People	Romina	Yellow (y)

Table 4: Categories for the visualization experiment.

Following Etcheverry and Wonsever (2016), we selected a subset of words and created a visualization by reducing the dimensionality of the vectors. The aim of this visualization is to show that related words tend to cluster together and form regions in the vector space. The set of words contains

[2]Wikipedia dump from February 20, 2021: `https://dumps.wikimedia.org/gnwiki/20210220/`.

Wiki	Chiruzzo et al. 2020	Parallel News Set	Reliable Tweets	Unreliable Tweets	familiy		ccc	
					Exact	Top 5	Exact	Top 5
X					29.97%	38.89%	4.41%	10.01%
X	X				**41.27%**	**48.41%**	5.27%	11.53%
X	X	X			32.54%	34.92%	**5.53%**	**13.37%**
X	X	X	X		28.57%	36.51%	5.27%	13.04%
X	X	X	X	X	26.98%	35.71%	4.55%	12.25%

Table 5: Results for the analogies tests for the different experiments. For those words that are not in the corpus (and therefore were not trained for the word embeddings) the analogy answer is counted as wrong.

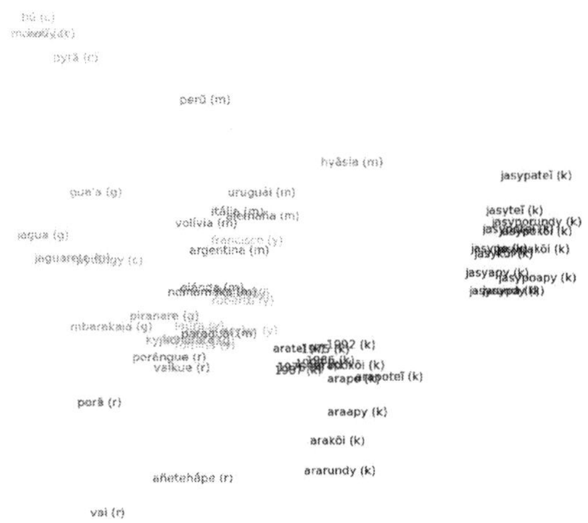

Figure 1: Embeddings visualized over a 2-dimensional space using PCA.

examples from different semantic categories (countries, colors, animals, people names, attributes and dates)[3], and are mostly Guarani translations[4] of the words used in Etcheverry and Wonsever (2016) (see table 4 for details). The embeddings used in this experiment are trained using all the available reliable text (detailed in Table 3). As can be seen in figure 1, words that represent countries (magenta), animals (green) and colors (cyan) form different clusters. Something similar happens with other categories, but notice for example that some proper names show other correlations, such as the name "Francisco" is shown close to "Argentina", probably because it is the name of the Argentinian Pope Francis, a name that appears frequently in the corpus.

4.2 Word analogies task

We did some analogies tests (Mikolov et al., 2013a) based on the vector offset method (Mikolov et al., 2013b). We had to make several simplifications in the analogies test collections due to differences in the language[5], and also because the size of the linguistic resources we use is not enough to cover a great number of the original words used in the tests. However, we were able to translate to Guarani the whole *common capital city* (`ccc`) analogies set from Mikolov et al. (2013a)[6], and we also designed a new `family` set inspired in the original one, but considering the most common family relations in Guarani dictionaries. These two analogies test collections will be made available for future reference and comparison.

Table 5 shows the results of the analogies tests for the five configurations used, corresponding to different combinations of the sets described in table 3. In order to ensure the reliability of the experiments, we ran each configuration three times and averaged the evaluation results. We show exact match and top 5 match for each experiment. First of all notice that including the Guarani part of the parallel corpus described in Chiruzzo et al. (2020) is enough to improve on the results of the Wikipedia embeddings on both categories. Using the parallel set created in this work, we can obtain better results for the *ccc* analogies test, but not for the *family* test (although they are still better for exact match than the vectors using only Wikipedia). One possible reason why the *ccc* tests improve is that this corpus includes more news articles, which frequently speak about political regions and geography, so the semantic generalization in these categories could be improved. However, our new corpus does not include a particular type of text found in Chiruzzo et al. (2020) that is text from blog posts, which includes folktales and biographies that could help the vectors improve their generalization capabilities about family members. On the other hand, includ-

[3]This categories were determined by us based on Etcheverry and Wonsever (2016) before performing the experiment.

[4]The only difference is changing the Spanish word *violeta* (purple) to the Guarani *pytãngy* (pink).

[5]For example, some English pairs do not make sense in Guarani, such as words for some family members, or the ones that change the grammatical number, which is used differently in Guarani.

[6]`https://aclweb.org/aclwiki/Google_analogy_test_set_(State_of_the_art)`

ing text from the tweets collections (both reliable and unreliable) seems to hinder the performance for the tests (although they still behave better than plain Wikipedia for *ccc* tests). We consider this is because text from social media tends to be much more noisy than news articles. However, it is possible that extracting a larger collection of this type of text could still help the generalization, so more experiments are needed in this regard.

5 Conclusions

We described the construction of a Guarani corpus that contains a parallel news set and a monolingual set of social media texts. We performed word embeddings experiments over different combinations of the data. The visualization experiment showed that the available text is enough to form clusters of words of the same semantic category. The analogies experiments showed that, in some cases, adding our corpus improved the performance, although results for the *family* test might indicate that more diversity of texts is needed, and text from tweets seems to be too noisy for enhancing the embeddings.

As future work, we plan to perform machine translation experiments (in line with the experiments described in Borges et al. (2021)), which might be a better way of validating the dataset. We think it is important to widen the variety of texts in the corpus: currently the crawling process keeps running daily to collect more text, and it could also be used to collect more data from different sources. Now that we have more text available and partially annotated, we can try some statistical approaches such as training a language detector for tweets instead of our keyword list strategy. We think this type of text is relevant, providing a broader and modern usage of Jopara Guarani, which might aid in other NLP tasks such as sentiment analysis.

References

Ahmed Abdelali, James Cowie, Steve Helmreich, Wanying Jin, Maria Pilar Milagros, Bill Ogden, Hamid Mansouri Rad, and Ron Zacharski. 2006. Guarani: a case study in resource development for quick ramp-up mt. In *Proceedings of the 7th Conference of the Association for Machine Translation in the Americas, "Visions for the Future of Machine Translation*, pages 1–9.

NB Alvarenga Alcaraz and PR Alvarenga Alcaraz. 2020. Aplicación web de análisis y traducción automática guaraní–español/español–guaraní. *Revista Científica de la UCSA*, 7(2):41–69.

Steven Bird, Ewan Klein, and Edward Loper. 2009. *Natural language processing with Python: analyzing text with the natural language toolkit.* " O'Reilly Media, Inc.".

Yanina Borges, Florencia Mercant, and Luis Chiruzzo. 2021. Using guarani verbal morphology on guarani-spanish machine translation experiments. *Procesamiento del Lenguaje Natural*, 66:89–98.

Luis Chiruzzo, Pedro Amarilla, Adolfo Ríos, and Gustavo Giménez Lugo. 2020. Development of a Guarani - Spanish parallel corpus. In *Proceedings of the 12th Language Resources and Evaluation Conference*, pages 2629–2633, Marseille, France. European Language Resources Association.

Robert A Dooley. 2006. Léxico guarani, dialeto mbyá com informações úteis para o ensino médio, a aprendizagem e a pesquisa lingüística. *Cuiabá, MT: Sociedade Internacional de Lingüística*, 143:206.

Mathias Etcheverry and Dina Wonsever. 2016. Spanish word vectors from Wikipedia. In *Proceedings of the Tenth International Conference on Language Resources and Evaluation (LREC'16)*, pages 3681–3685, Portorož, Slovenia. European Language Resources Association (ELRA).

Michael Gasser. 2018. Mainumby: un ayudante para la traducción castellano-guaraní. *arXiv preprint arXiv:1810.08603*.

Heidi Jauhiainen, Tommi Jauhiainen, and Krister Lindén. 2020. Building web corpora for minority languages. In *Proceedings of the 12th Web as Corpus Workshop*, pages 23–32, Marseille, France. European Language Resources Association.

Wolf Lustig. 2010. Mba'éichapa oiko la guarani? guaraní y jopara en el paraguay. *PAPIA-Revista Brasileira de Estudos do Contato Linguístico*, 4(2):19–43.

Tomas Mikolov, Kai Chen, Greg Corrado, and Jeffrey Dean. 2013a. Efficient estimation of word representations in vector space.

Tomas Mikolov, Wen-tau Yih, and Geoffrey Zweig. 2013b. Linguistic regularities in continuous space word representations. In *Proceedings of the 2013 Conference of the North American Chapter of the Association for Computational Linguistics: Human Language Technologies*, pages 746–751, Atlanta, Georgia. Association for Computational Linguistics.

Radim Řehůřek and Petr Sojka. 2010. Software Framework for Topic Modelling with Large Corpora. In *Proceedings of the LREC 2010 Workshop on New Challenges for NLP Frameworks*, pages 45–50, Valletta, Malta. ELRA.

Alex Rudnick, Taylor Skidmore, Alberto Samaniego, and Michael Gasser. 2014. Guampa: a toolkit for collaborative translation. In *LREC*, pages 1659–1663.

Secretaría de Políticas Lingüísticas del Paraguay. 2019. Corpus de Referencia del Guaraní Paraguayo Actual - COREGUAPA. `http://www.spl.gov.py`. Accessed: 2021-03-13.

Guillaume Thomas. 2019. Universal dependencies for mbyá guaraní. In *Proceedings of the Third Workshop on Universal Dependencies (UDW, SyntaxFest 2019)*, pages 70–77.

Towards a First Automatic Unsupervised Morphological Segmentation for Inuinnaqtun

Tan Le Ngoc and **Fatiha Sadat**
Université du Québec à Montréal / Montreal, Quebec, Canada
201, avenue du Président-Kennedy, H2X 3Y7 Montréal
le.ngoc_tan@courrier.uqam.ca, sadat.fatiha@uqam.ca

Abstract

Low-resource polysynthetic languages pose many challenges in NLP tasks, such as morphological analysis and Machine Translation, due to available resources and tools, and the morphologically complex languages. This research focuses on the morphological segmentation while adapting an unsupervised approach based on Adaptor Grammars in low-resource setting. Experiments and evaluations on Inuinnaqtun, one of Inuit language family in Northern Canada, considered a language that will be extinct in less than two generations, have shown promising results.

1 Introduction

NLP has significant achievements when dealing with different types of languages, such as isolating, inflectional or agglutinative language families. However, Indigenous polysynthetic languages still pose several challenges within NLP tasks and applications, such as morphological analysis or machine translation, due to their complex linguistic particularities and due to the scarcity of linguistic resources and reliable tools (Littell et al., 2018; Mager et al., 2018; Micher, 2019; Le Ngoc and Sadat, 2020).

Herein, we propose an unsupervised morphological segmentation approach, which is primarily based on the grammar containing production rules, non-terminal and terminal symbols, and a lexicon using Adaptor Grammars (Johnson, 2008). Our current research investigates Inuinnaqtun - a polysynthetic language spoken in Northern Canada, in the Inuit language family. Inuinnaqtun is considered as a language that will be extinct in less than two generations[1].

Regarding the Eskimo-Aleut language family including the Inuit, unlike words in English, the word structure of Eskimo are very variable in their form (Lowe, 1985; Kudlak and Compton, 2018). Words may be very short, built up of three formative elements such as word base, lexical suffixes, and grammatical ending suffixes, or very long, with up to ten or even fifteen formative morphemes depending on the dialect.

- Eskimo word structure = **Word base** + Lexical suffixes + *Grammatical ending suffixes*

A single word can be used to express a whole sentence in English. The following example, extracted from (Lowe, 1985), illustrates the polysynthesis effect of *umingmakhiuriaqtuqatigitqilimaiqtara*, an Inuinnaqtun sentence-word, split up into several morphemes:

umingmak-hiu-riaqtu-qati-gi-tqi-limaiq-*ta-ra*
muskox - hunt - go in order to - partner - have as - again - will no more - *I-him*
(*Meaning: I* will no more again have *him* as a partner to go hunting **muskox**.)

We observe there is a general tendency to increase the lexical constituents with a word-base by adding more formative elements. A single word can express the meaning of a whole sentence. Moreover, morphology is highly developed and has extensive use of lexical and grammatical ending suffixes. All these linguistic aspects make the morphological segmentation task for polysynthetic languages more challenging. On the other hand, the benefit of this work helps to identify more unknown word bases by deducting from the known affixes, which in turn helps to enrich the Inuinnaqtun lexicon. The global contribution consists of helping to revitalize and preserve low-resource Indigenous languages and the transmission of the related ancestral knowledge and culture.

The structure of this paper is described as follows: Section 2 presents relevant works. Section 3 describes our proposed approach. Then, Section 4 presents experiments and evaluations. Finally,

[1] https://www.kitikmeotheritage.ca/language

Proceedings of the First Workshop on Natural Language Processing for Indigenous Languages of the Americas, pages 159–162
June 11, 2021. ©2021 Association for Computational Linguistics

Section 5 gives some conclusions and perspectives for future research.

2 Related work

Creutz and Lagus (2007) proposed the Morfessor, for the unsupervised discovery of morphemes. This work was based on Hidden Markov Model for learning the unsupervised morphological segmentation, and by using the hierarchical structure of the morphemes. This framework became a benchmark in unsupervised morphological analysis, such as Morfessor 2.0 (Virpioja et al., 2013).

Johnson (2008) proposed Adaptor Grammars approach that was successful for the unsupervised morphological segmentation. This approach used non-parametric Bayesian models generalizing probabilistic context-free grammar (PCFG). In this approach, a PCFG is considered as a morphological grammar of word structures. Then the AG models can be able to induce the segmentation at the morpheme level.

This approach has been extended in several studies (Botha and Blunsom, 2013; Sirts and Goldwater, 2013; Eskander et al., 2018) for learning non-concatenative morphology, or for unsupervised morphological segmentation of unseen languages. Recently, Godard et al. (2018) applied AG approach for the linguists with word segmentation experiments for very low-resource African languages. Eskander et al. (2019) has applied the AG approach in an unsupervised morphological segmentation of the low-resource polysynthetic languages such as Mexicanero, Nahuatl, Yorem Nokki and Wixarika. Their evaluations have shown a significant improvement up to 87.90% in terms of F1-score, compared to the supervised approaches (Kann et al., 2018). Our work examines the efficiency of the AG-based approach on Inuinnaqtun, a polysynthetic low-resource Inuit language.

3 Our approach

Inspired by the work of Eskander et al. (2019), we adapt an unsupervised morphological segmentation with the Adaptor Grammars (AG) approach for the Inuit language family, by completing an empirical study on Inuinnaqtun.

The main process consists of defining (1) the grammar including non-terminal, terminal symbols, a set of production rules, and (2) collecting a large amount of unsegmented word list in order to discover and to learn all possible morphological patterns.

In our work, we consider that word structures are specified in the grammar patterns where a word is constituted as one word base, a sequence of possible lexical suffixes and grammatical ending suffixes (see Table 1). In contrast, as explained in (Eskander et al., 2019), the word structure is composed of a sequence of prefixes, a stem and a sequence of suffixes. Then, in each production rule, a and b are two parameters of Pitman-Yor process (Pitman and Yor, 1997). Setting $a = 1$ and $b = 1$ indicate, to the running learner, the current non-terminals are not adapted and sampled by the general Pitman-Yor process. Otherwise, the current non-terminals are adapted and expanded as in a regular probabilistic context-free grammar.

In order to adapt the AG scholar-seeded setting with linguistic knowledge, we have collected a list of affixes from dictionaries and Websites in the appropriate language.

4 Experiments

4.1 Data Preparation

In order to train the Adaptor Grammars-based unsupervised morphological segmentation model, the two principal inputs consists of the grammar and the lexicon of the language. The lexicon consists of a unique list of unsegmented words, more than $50K$ words, with the sequence length between three letters and 30 letters.

We collected manually a small corpus from several resources such as the Website of Nunavut[2] government for Inuinnaqtun, open source dictionaries and grammar books (Lowe, 1985; Kudlak and Compton, 2018). The experimental corpus contains 190 word bases and 571 affixes. A small golden testing set is manually crafted containing 1,055 unique segmented words.

4.2 Training Settings

We used the MorphAGram toolkit (Eskander et al., 2020) to train our unsupervised morphological segmentation model. Following (Eskander et al., 2019), we set up the same configuration with adaptation of the best learning settings: the best standard *PrefixStemSuffix+SuffixMorph* grammar and the best scholar-seeded grammar, that become here an adaptation of the standard grammar *WordBase+LexicalSuffix+GrammaticalSuffix* pattern for

[2] `https://www.gov.nu.ca/in/cgs-in`

1 1 Word ->WordBase LexicalSuffix GrammaticalSuffix WordBase -> ^^^ WordBase -> ^^^ WordBaseMorphs 1 1 WordBaseMorphs -> WordBaseMorph WordBaseMorph -> SubMorphs LexicalSuffix -> SubMorphs LexicalSuffix -> SuffixMorphs $$$ LexicalSuffix -> $$$	GrammaticalSuffix -> SuffixMorphs $$$ 1 1 SuffixMorphs -> SuffixMorph SuffixMorphs 1 1 SuffixMorphs -> SuffixMorph 1 1 SubMorphs -> SubMorph SubMorphs 1 1 SubMorphs -> SubMorph SubMorph -> Chars 1 1 Chars -> Char 1 1 Chars -> Char Chars

Table 1: Adaptation of the standard grammar WordBase+LexicalSuffix+GrammaticalSuffix pattern for Inuinnaqtun. The symbols ^^^ and $$$ mean the beginning and the end of the word sequence, respectively. Source: see the standard PrefixStemSuffix+SuffixMorph grammar pattern (Eskander et al., 2019).

Word	Ground Truth	Morfessor	AG-Standard	AG-Scholar
aullarnatin	aullar na tin	aulla rn at in	a ulla rna tin	aullar nati n
havangnatik	havang na tik	hav ang na tik	hav a ngna tik	havang na tik
iaqluktinnagu	iqaluk tinna gu	iqalu k ti nna gu	iqa luk tinna gu	iaqluk tinna gu
nirihuiqtunga	niri huiq tunga	niri huiq tu ng a	niri huiq tu ng a	niri huiq tunga
niritinnagit	niri tinna git	niri ti nna gi t	niri tinna git	niri tinna git
umiarmi	umiar mi	umi a rmi	umi armi	umia r mi
umiaq	umiaq	umi aq	u mi aq	umiaq
tikinnanuk	tikin na nuk	tikinnanuk	t iki nna nuk	tikin na nuk

Table 2: Illustrations of morpheme segmentation predictions on the test set using the different settings such as Standard (AG-Standard), Scholar seeded (AG-Scholar) and Morfessor.

Inuinnaqtun (see Table 1). We evaluate our different models against the baseline, based on Morfessor (Virpioja et al., 2013).

4.3 Evaluations

All the model performances are calculated using common evaluation metrics, such as Precision (P), Recall (R) and F1 score.

$$P = \frac{|\{relevant\ tokens\} \cap \{found\ tokens\}|}{\{found\ tokens\}} \quad (1)$$

$$R = \frac{|\{relevant\ tokens\} \cap \{found\ tokens\}|}{\{relevant\ tokens\}} \quad (2)$$

$$F1 = \frac{2 \times P \times R}{P + R} \quad (3)$$

where $\{found\ tokens\}$ means the amount of predicted *tokens*; and $\{relevant\ tokens\}$ indicates the amount of *tokens* which are correctly segmented.

Tables 2 and 3 show some illustrations of prediction by all the models and the performance of our models versus Morfessor as baseline on the test set. The AG-standard model is better than the baseline, with a gain of +2.47%, +4.9% in terms of precision and recall, on the test set, respectively. Both baseline and AG-Standard models obtained low precision between 48.29% and 50.76%. We observed an over-segmentation in both models.Furthermore, we noticed that the scholar-seeded learning outperformed all the baseline and the standard setting, with performances of 71.06%, 82.83%, 76.49% in terms of Precision, Recall and F1 score, respectively. Our models tend to over-segment more complex morphemes due to the linguistic irregularities and the morphophonological phenomena, to detect common lexical suffixes such as *at*, *aq*, *iq*, *na*, *ng* or grammatical ending suffixes such as *a*, *k*, *q*, *t*, *n*, *it*, *mi* or *uk*.

	Precision	Recall	F1
Morfessor	48.29	75.40	58.87
AG-Standard	50.76	80.30	62.20
AG-Scholar	**71.06**	**82.83**	**76.49**

Table 3: The results on the test set using the different settings such as Standard (AG-Standard), Scholar seeded (AG-Scholar) and Morfessor.

5 Conclusion

In this research paper, we presented how to build the unsupervised morphological segmentation with Adaptor Grammars approach for Inuinnaqtun, an Inuit language, considered as an extremely low-resource polysynthetic language, that will be extinct in less than two generations, as described and referenced above. This Adaptor Grammars-based approach showed promising results, when using a set of grammar rules, that can be collected from grammar books; and a lexicon extracted from very little data. As a perspective, we intend to develop more efficient unsupervised morphological segmentation methods and to extend our research to other Indigenous languages and dialects, especially the very endangered ones; with applications on Machine Translation and Information Retrieval.

Acknowledgments

The authors wish to express their thanks for professor Richard Compton, Canada Research Chair in Knowledge and Transmission of the Inuit Language, and the reviewers, for their constructive feedbacks.

References

Jan A Botha and Phil Blunsom. 2013. Adaptor grammars for learning non- concatenative morphology. Association for Computational Linguistics.

Mathias Creutz and Krista Lagus. 2007. Unsupervised models for morpheme segmentation and morphology learning. *ACM Transactions on Speech and Language Processing (TSLP)*, 4(1):1–34.

Ramy Eskander, Francesca Callejas, Elizabeth Nichols, Judith L Klavans, and Smaranda Muresan. 2020. Morphagram, evaluation and framework for unsupervised morphological segmentation. In *Proceedings of The 12th Language Resources and Evaluation Conference*, pages 7112–7122.

Ramy Eskander, Judith L Klavans, and Smaranda Muresan. 2019. Unsupervised morphological segmentation for low-resource polysynthetic languages. In *Proceedings of the 16th Workshop on Computational Research in Phonetics, Phonology, and Morphology*, pages 189–195.

Ramy Eskander, Owen Rambow, and Smaranda Muresan. 2018. Automatically tailoring unsupervised morphological segmentation to the language. In *Proceedings of the Fifteenth Workshop on Computational Research in Phonetics, Phonology, and Morphology*, pages 78–83.

Pierre Godard, Laurent Besacier, François Yvon, Martine Adda-Decker, Gilles Adda, Hélène Maynard, and Annie Rialland. 2018. Adaptor grammars for the linguist: Word segmentation experiments for very low-resource languages. In *Workshop on Computational Research in Phonetics, Phonology, and Morphology*, pages 32–42.

Mark Johnson. 2008. Unsupervised word segmentation for sesotho using adaptor grammars. In *Proceedings of the Tenth Meeting of ACL Special Interest Group on Computational Morphology and Phonology*, pages 20–27.

Katharina Kann, Manuel Mager, Ivan Meza-Ruiz, and Hinrich Schütze. 2018. Fortification of neural morphological segmentation models for polysynthetic minimal-resource languages. *arXiv preprint arXiv:1804.06024*.

Emily Kudlak and Richard Compton. 2018. *Kangiryuarmiut Inuinnaqtun Uqauhiitaa Numiktitirutait — Kangiryuarmiut Inuinnaqtun Dictionary*, volume 1. Nunavut Arctic College: Iqaluit, Nunavut.

Tan Le Ngoc and Fatiha Sadat. 2020. Revitalization of indigenous languages through pre-processing and neural machine translation: The case of Inuktitut. In *Proceedings of the 28th International Conference on Computational Linguistics*, pages 4661–4666.

Patrick Littell, Anna Kazantseva, Roland Kuhn, Aidan Pine, Antti Arppe, Christopher Cox, and Marie-Odile Junker. 2018. Indigenous language technologies in canada: Assessment, challenges, and successes. In *Proceedings of the 27th International Conference on Computational Linguistics*, pages 2620–2632.

Ronald Lowe. 1985. *Basic Siglit Inuvialuit Eskimo Grammar*, volume 6. Inuvik, NWT: Committee for Original Peoples Entitlement.

Manuel Mager, Ximena Gutierrez-Vasques, Gerardo Sierra, and Ivan Meza-Ruiz. 2018. Challenges of language technologies for the indigenous languages of the Americas. In *Proceedings of the 27th International Conference on Computational Linguistics*, pages 55–69, Santa Fe, New Mexico, USA. Association for Computational Linguistics.

Jeffrey Micher. 2019. Bootstrapping a neural morphological generator from morphological analyzer output for inuktitut. In *Proceedings of the Workshop on Computational Methods for Endangered Languages*, volume 2, page 7.

Jim Pitman and Marc Yor. 1997. The two-parameter poisson-dirichlet distribution derived from a stable subordinator. *The Annals of Probability*, pages 855–900.

Kairit Sirts and Sharon Goldwater. 2013. Minimally-supervised morphological segmentation using adaptor grammars. *Transactions of the Association for Computational Linguistics*, 1:255–266.

Sami Virpioja, Peter Smit, Stig-Arne Grönroos, Mikko Kurimo, et al. 2013. Morfessor 2.0: Python implementation and extensions for morfessor baseline.

Toward Creation of Ancash Quechua Lexical Resources from OCR

Anonymous NAACL-HLT 2021 submission

Abstract

The Quechua linguistic family has a limited number of NLP resources, most of them being dedicated to Southern Quechua, whereas the varieties of Central Quechua have, to the best of our knowledge, no specific resources (software, lexicon or corpus). Our work addresses this issue by producing two resources for the Ancash Quechua: a full digital version of a dictionary, and an OCR model adapted to the considered variety. In this paper, we describe the steps towards this goal: we first measure performances of existing models for the task of digitising a Quechua dictionary, then adapt a model for the Ancash variety, and finally create a reliable resource for NLP in XML-TEI format. We hope that this work will be a basis for initiating NLP projects for Central Quechua, and that it will encourage digitisation initiatives for under-resourced languages.

1 Introduction

In recent years, Quechua has become more visible in the countries where it is spoken, partly as a result of measures to strengthen its use in institutions, but also of a growing interest in these languages as a cultural element among citizens. At the same time, Quechua languages are gradually handled by NLP software. For Southern Quechua (variety of Quechua II, the most widespread linguistic family), resources already exist and many projects are experimenting large corpus digitisation to create Deep Learning models[1]. However, Quechua varieties are heterogeneous and available resources for the aforementioned variety are hardly usable for others, because of important differences in both morphology and lexicon. The present work aims at laying foundations for the development of NLP tools for another variety, the Ancash Quechua (variety of Quechua I).

[1]As the OSCAR corpus `https://oscar-corpus.com`

The main steps describes in this paper are as follows:

- We compare 3 OCR software on the task of digitising a Quechua dictionary : ABBYY Finereader, a commercial proprietary OCR; Tesseract Open Source OCR (Smith, 2007), (Smith, 2013); and GoogleDocs OCR.
- On the basis of this comparison, we use Tesseract to retrain a Quechua model to adapt it to the Ancash variety and to the specific typography of the book.
- The dictionary is fully digitised using this new model; lexical information is then gathered in a XML-TEI format.

2 State Of The Art

2.1 Ancash language and resources

Ancash is a Peruvian department located in the Central Andes, with over 30% native speakers of Quechua[2]. In this area, the Quechua varieties are relatively homogeneous and mutually intelligible, which justifies grouping them under the name Ancash Quechua. This variety is the most widely spoken of the Central Quechua linguistic branch (Q.I). However, very little data is available in digital format, and to the best our knowledge, there are none specifically prepared for NLP development.

2.1.1 Lexical resources

Since Quechua is an agglutinative language, having a lexicon would greatly facilitate the development of morphological analysis systems, which would in turn make it possible to develop useful tools for Quechuan users and the NLP community: spell checker, POS-tagger, automatic alignment of parallel corpora, etc.

Some resources are freely available in electronic format. The most widely used is probably

[2]According to the 2017 census.

Proceedings of the First Workshop on Natural Language Processing for Indigenous Languages of the Americas, pages 163–167
June 11, 2021.

the Quechua-Spanish dictionary (Menacho López, 2005), published by the Ministry of Education, which contains 971 entries and can be queried through the online platform Qichwa 2.0[3].

An online cross-dialectal lexicon (Jacobs, 2006), featuring about 1,800 entries for Ancash, is downloadable in spreadsheet format. This format can be easily used for NLP, but the lexicon contains some redundancies, discrepancies and formatting irregularities.

The largest Ancash Quechua-Spanish dictionaries are either not officially digitised or have been published under restrictive copyright that prevent their use for NLP purposes. The main dictionaries for our variety are: Swisshelm, 1972, 399 pages, Parker et al., 1976, 311 pages; Carranza Romero, 2013, about 8,000 entries, also available as an ebook.

2.1.2 Corpora

The main corpus is in paper format only. It consists of two volumes of narratives in both Quechua and Spanish (*Cuentos y relatos en el Quechua de Huaraz*, Ramos and Ripkens, 1974), with a total of 698 pages. A digitised dictionary would be useful to automatically post-edit the OCR of this corpus (Poncelas et al., 2020).

2.2 OCR of dictionaries

The importance of digitising lexical resources for under-resourced languages has been repeatedly expressed. For the languages of the Americas, two projects are particularly similar to ours.

A off-the-shelf use of Tesseract is reported (Maxwell and Bills, 2017) to digitise 3 bilingual dictionaries (Tzeltal-English, Muinane-Spanish, Cubeo-Spanish). More specifically, authors used Tesseract's hOCR function to preserve entry's structure and infer lexical entries with associated linguistic information. A finite state transducer was used to create the lexicon from this hOCR file.

Tesseract can also be (re)trained to create dedicated models. This has been experimented for an almost extinct Canadian language (Northern Haida) (Hubert et al., 2016) for a large written corpus (100,000 words). Optimal settings discovery was conducted by training 12 models with distinct parameters. This work also experimented training the model with images generated from text using a font similar to the targeted documents, which did not prove to be efficient. The best model, trained on the original source, obtained 96.47% character rate accuracy (CRA) and a 89.03% word rate accuracy (WRA).

2.3 Quechua in OCR tools

Both Tesseract[4] and ABBYY include a pretrained Quechua model for OCR. ABBYY's model is trained on Bolivian Quechua (Q.II). The training corpus for Tesseract's model is not documented.

3 OCR of the Ancash Quechua Dictionary

3.1 Source Document

The document we digitised is a working document by the linguist Gary J. Parker, resulting from his fieldwork (Parker, 1975). It is an unpublished draft of the Ancash Quechua to Spanish dictionary mentioned above (Parker et al., 1976) This book is a list of Ancash lexemes along with their area of use (division by province), their POS, translation or gloss in Spanish, and a set of internal cross-references indicating synonyms, related terms or lectal variants. The overall structure is relatively homogeneous. The elements mentioned above are separated by blanks, but are not vertically aligned. The typography is that of the old typewriters; some typing errors remain in the document.

3.2 Typography

Ancash Quechua is written using Latin script. In the particular case of our document, the author used a phonemic spelling to represent characters whose official modern spelling is a digraph. The Table 1 shows the special characters used by Parker (in first column), their corresponding phonemes, and the graphemes commonly used today.

3.3 Methodology

3.4 Source preprocessing

After scanning the entire document in PDF format, we applied a series of pre-processing operations in order to facilitate the OCR task:

1. Cropping: cutting the file to eliminate everything that comes out of the pages. We used Gimp tool and checked for each page that the cropping did not affect the text;

[3]https://dic.qichwa.net/#/

[4]https://github.com/tesseract-ocr/tesseract

Ancash Quechua phonemes		
Character	Phoneme	Grapheme
ā	/aː/	aa
ī	/iː/	ii
ū	/uː/	uu
l̄	/ʎ/	ll
č	/t͡ʃ/	ch
ĉ	/t͡ʂ/	tr
š	/ʃ/	sh
Spanish loans		
ē, ō	/e/, /o/ (stressed)	e, o
ř	/ʐ/	rr

Table 1: Special characters in the dictionary

2. Conversion to greyscale and increasing contrast;

3. Conversion to high definition PNG (between 350 and 390 dpi).

The last two steps are automatically applied to the whole document thanks to a bash script, using gegl[5] and convert[6] commands.

3.5 OCR selection

In order to determine which OCR is best suited to process our document, we conducted a series of preliminary tests. We selected three of the best performing OCR software (Tafti et al., 2016), and compared their output on a set of 5 pages of the document, randomly extracted. For Tesseract's OCR, we used both Quechua and Spanish pre-trained models. For ABBYY's OCR, we used the Bolivian Quechua model. GoogleDocs OCR does not allow to control any parameter. Table 2 shows the error rates for each of them.

	Tesseract	ABBYY	GoogleDocs
CER	6.64	6.43	5.26
WER	25.5	27.5	20.7

Table 2: OCR comparison on our dictionary

This evaluation shows that GoogleDocs OCR is the best performing. Many of the diacritics described in Section 3.2 are recognised, but the structure of the document is not preserved. The opposite situation occurs in the case of ABBYY. It is worth noting that the output of the latter could be greatly improved by using the numerous settings the software offers.

In addition to performances, we also took in consideration the possibility to distribute the trained model with an open licence. According to these considerations, we chose Tesseract, which gives satisfying results and allows the model to be shared.

3.5.1 Preliminary tests with Tesseract OCR

In order to have a better view of Tesseract's performance, we applied OCR on 10 PNG files, randomly extracted from the pre-processed (Section 3.4) document, using: Spanish model alone (spa FAST); Quechua model alone (que FAST); Spanish and Quechua models together (que+spa) in their compressed (FAST) and uncompressed (BEST) versions.

OCR outputs per page are concatenated into a single file, as well as corresponding gold standards. Resulting files are compared to measure Character Error Rate (CER) and Word Error Rate (WER) with the ocrevalUAtion tool[7]. Table 3 reports those evaluations.

The results show that OCR performance is relatively poor, with a word recognition accuracy (WRA) of less than 80%. The characters with diacritics presented in Section 3.2, which are absent from the character set of Quechua and Spanish models, are not recognised, making manual correction tedious. However, Tesseract offers the possibility to adapt a pre-trained model to additional fonts and characters. In the next section, we describe the training of a model specific to our book, based on Tesseract's Quechua model.

	CER	WER
spa FAST	6.23	23.20
que FAST	7.40	27.55
que+spa FAST	**5.89**	21.82
que+spa BEST	6.05	**21.29**

Table 3: Tesseract performance with pretrained models

3.6 Model training

A training corpus was built from 30 pages of the document (5,676 words, 33,687 characters).

[5]https://gegl.org/

[6]https://imagemagick.org/script/convert.php

[7]https://github.com/impactcentre/ocrevalUAtion

These pages are segmented by lines with the Tesseract hOCR tool, producing a total of 1,544 segments; each segment is then OCRised and the output is manually corrected to constitute the gold standard. The training process is done from the Quechua model. A threshold is reached at 4.379% error rate, after 4200 epochs.

3.7 Evaluation

Previous work showed that the evaluation of an OCR output depends both on the quality of the segmentation of the document and on the quality of text recognition (Karpinski et al., 2018). For this evaluation, we discarded OCR outputs whose segmentation problems affect the global structure of the page; only character recognition is thus evaluated.

Our model is evaluated on 50 randomly selected pages of the dictionary, pre-processed as described in Section 3.4. Table 4 shows CER and WER (Raw). The second score (Corr.) is computed after correction of one-off segmentation problems. The scores show an improvement of more than 3% over the Quechua+Spanish model (see Table 2 of Tesseract for the character recognition accuracy, and of 13% for the word recognition accuracy.

	Raw	Corr.
CER	**2.57**	2.42
WER	**8.19**	7.51
WER (order indep.)	6.69	5.96

Table 4: CER and WER of the Ancash Quechua model

To get a better idea of the impact of the training, we also evaluated the error rate on the characters with diacritics. Table 5 shows their volume in the training corpus (ū, ř and ĉ having only one or two occurrences, they are considered negligible) and corresponding error rates.

	Nb_{train}	Vol_{train} (%)	CER (%)
š	167	0.50	4.04
ł	157	0.47	7.83
č	148	0.44	5.11
ā	130	0.39	63.7
ī, ē, ō		<0,1	100

Table 5: Training volume and CER for special characters

Empirically, manual correction of OCR output is easier with the new model: the most frequent characters with diacritic are well recognised, and the errors are more regular, allowing in some case their automatic detection and correction. For 10 pages, we estimated an average correction time per page of 3'40.

4 Lexical Resource

During the manual correction of the OCRed text, each entry was copied into an ODS file in order to preserve the structure. The resulting file is composed of 5 columns containing the elements described in Section 3.1. Having been reviewed several times, this resource is already available online[8].

In order to distribute this resource in a format suitable for a large variety of tools, the ODS file (previously converted to CSV) is automatically converted to an XML-TEI[9] format, following the guidelines for XML encoding of dictionaries (Budin et al., 2012). The markup structure is built with the following rules :

- Spanish loans, marked in the dictionary by an asterisk before the word, are indicated by insertion of the tag `<etym>`;
- Homographs are grouped in a `<superEntry>`;
- Cross-references are marked with `<xr>`;
- Easily retrievable examples within the column corresponding to the translation or gloss are tagged with `<cit>`.

Our XML-TEI lexicon contains **3626 entries**, and is to date the largest digital resource for Ancash Quechua available for NLP and lexicometry.

5 Conclusion

The present work shows that it is relatively easy to train a new Tesseract model from an existing one, with very little data. The tests carried out on several OCRs show many that alternatives are available for this task depending on the desired output. Based on this work, we started the digitisation of a second dictionary and a corpus with the same characteristics.

[8]https://github.com/rumiwarmi/qishwar/blob/main/Diccionario%20polilectal%20-%20PARKER.ods

[9]https://tei-c.org/

Acknowledgements

We warmly thank César Itier for providing his copy of Parker's dictionary and allowing us to digitise it.

References

Gerhard Budin, Stefan Majewski, and Karlheinz Mörth. 2012. Creating lexical resources in tei p5. a schema for multi-purpose digital dictionaries. *Journal of the Text Encoding Initiative*, (3).

Francisco Carranza Romero. 2013. *Diccionario del Quechua Ancashino*. Iberoamericana Editorial Vervuert.

Isabell Hubert, Antti Arppe, Jordan Lachler, and Eddie Antonio Santos. 2016. Training & quality assessment of an optical character recognition model for Northern Haida. In *Proceedings of the Tenth International Conference on Language Resources and Evaluation (LREC'16)*, pages 3227–3234, Portorož, Slovenia. European Language Resources Association (ELRA).

Philip Jacobs. 2006. Vocabulary. `http://www.runasimi.de/runaengl.htm`.

Romain Karpinski, Devashish Lohani, and Abdel Belaid. 2018. Metrics for complete evaluation of ocr performance. In *IPCV'18-The 22nd Int'l Conf on Image Processing, Computer Vision, & Pattern Recognition*.

Michael Maxwell and Aric Bills. 2017. Endangered data for endangered languages: Digitizing print dictionaries. In *Proceedings of the 2nd Workshop on the Use of Computational Methods in the Study of Endangered Languages*, pages 85–91, Honolulu. Association for Computational Linguistics.

Leonel Alexander Menacho López. 2005. *Yachakuqkunapa Shimi Qullqa, Anqash Qichwa Shimichaw*. Ministerio de Educación, Lima, Perú.

Gary J. Parker. 1975. *Diccionario Polilectal del Quechua de Ancash*. Universidad Nacional Mayor de San Marcos.

G.J. Parker, A.C. Reyes, and A. Chávez. 1976. *Diccionario quechua, Ancash-Huailas*. Ministerio de Educación.

Alberto Poncelas, Mohammad Aboomar, Jan Buts, James Hadley, and Andy Way. 2020. A tool for facilitating ocr postediting in historical documents. *arXiv preprint arXiv:2004.11471*.

S.P. Ramos and J. Ripkens. 1974. *Cuentos y relatos en el quechua de Huaraz*. Estudios culturales benedictinos.

Christian Reul, Uwe Springmann, Christoph Wick, and Frank Puppe. 2018. Improving ocr accuracy on early printed books by utilizing cross fold training and voting. In *2018 13th IAPR International Workshop on Document Analysis Systems (DAS)*, pages 423–428.

Ray Smith. 2007. An overview of the tesseract ocr engine. In *Ninth international conference on document analysis and recognition (ICDAR 2007)*, volume 2, pages 629–633. IEEE.

Ray Smith. 2013. History of the tesseract ocr engine: what worked and what didn't. In *Document Recognition and Retrieval XX*, volume 8658, page 865802. International Society for Optics and Photonics.

G. Swisshelm. 1972. *Un diccionario del quechua de Huaraz: quechua-castellano, castellano-quechua*. Estudios culturales benedictinos.

Ahmad P. Tafti, Ahmadreza Baghaie, Mehdi Assefi, Hamid R. Arabnia, Zeyun Yu, and Peggy Peissig. 2016. Ocr as a service: An experimental evaluation of google docs ocr, tesseract, abbyy finereader, and transym. In *Advances in Visual Computing*, pages 735–746, Cham. Springer International Publishing.

Ayuuk-Spanish Neural Machine Translator

Delfino Zacarías
Facultad de Estudios Superiores Acatlán,
Universidad Nacional Autónoma de México
delfino.zacarias@comunidad.unam.mx

Ivan Meza
Instituto de Investigaciones en Matemáticas Aplicadas y en Sistemas,
Universidad Nacional Autónoma de México
ivanvladimir@turing.iimas.unam.mx

Abstract

This paper presents the first neural machine translator system for the *Ayuuk* language. In our experiments we translate from *Ayuuk* to Spanish, and from *Spanish* to *Ayuuk*. *Ayuuk* is a language spoken in the Oaxaca state of Mexico by the *Ayuukjä'äy* people (in Spanish commonly known as *Mixes*). We use different sources to create a low-resource parallel corpus, more than 6,000 phrases. For some of these resources we rely on automatic alignment. The proposed system is based on the Transformer neural architecture and it uses sub-word level tokenization as the input. We show the current performance given the resources we have collected for the San Juan Güichicovi variant, they are promising, up to 5 BLEU. We based our development on the Masakhane project for African languages.

1 Introduction

In recent years the efforts to preserve and promote the creation of NLP tools for the native languages of the Americas have increased, particularly addressing the challenges that this endeavour requires (Mager et al., 2018). Machine Translation (MT) has become one of the main goals to pursue since in the long term it might offer benefits to the communities that speak such languages. For instance, it might provide access to knowledge in their native language and facilitate access to services such legal, medical and finance assistance. In this work, we explore this avenue for the San Juan Güichicovi variant of the *Ayuuk* language, mainly because one of the authors is a native speaker of this variant. To our knowledge there has not been a construction of such a system for the *Ayuuk* although other variants[1] are available in the JW300 Corpus (Agić and Vulić, 2019).

In this work we rely in multiple previous work. At the core of our proposal we follow the steps from the Masakhane project[2] which focuses on African Languages (Nekoto et al., 2020). We also rely on the following libraries:

- For the automatic alignment of our resources we use the YASA alignment (Lamraoui and Langlais)[3]
- For the tokenization we use *subword-nmt* library[4] (Sennrich et al., 2016)
- For the training of our models we use *JoeyNMT*[5] (Kreutzer et al., 2019).

With these tools we developed our code base that can be consulted online together with the part of the corpus which is freely available [6].

2 *Ayuuk* from San Juan Güichicovi

Ayuukjä'äy can be translated as *people of the mountains*, most them can be located in 24 municipalities of the Oaxaca state. They are the native speakers of the *Ayuuk* language with approximately 139,760 speakers in Mexico. The *Ayuuk* language, which has an ISO 639-3 code *mir*, belongs to the *mixe-zoqueana* linguistic family. This linguistic family is composed by the *Mixe* and *Zoque* subfamilies [7]. In particular, the *Mixe* subfamily also includes *Mixe of Oaxaca*, *Sayula Popoluca* and *Oluta Popoluca* languages. For *Ayuuk* there are six main variants of the language, among these the *Mixe bajo* to which the San Juan Güichicovi variant belongs to. At

[1] Coatlán Mixe (ISO 639-3 *mco*), *Ayuuk* of the Coatlán region.

[2] https://www.masakhane.io/ (last visited march 2021)

[3] https://github.com/anoidgit/yasa (last visited march 2021)

[4] https://github.com/rsennrich/subword-nmt (last visited march 2021).

[5] https://github.com/joeynmt/joeynmt (last visited march 2021)

[6] https://github.com/DelfinoAyuuk/corpora_ayuuk-spanish_nmt

[7] For further information visit about the *mixe-zoqueana* family https://glottolog.org/resource/languoid/id/mixe1284

Proceedings of the First Workshop on Natural Language Processing for Indigenous Languages of the Americas, pages 168–172
June 11, 2021.

this municipality it can be estimated there is approximately 18,298 speakers of the variant. It is important to notice that it is estimated that only 3,205 are monolinguist.

The San Juan Güichicovi's Ayuuk variant does not has a normalized orthography, there are efforts to agree on orthographic conventions however there are strong positions related to number of consonants. One of these positions, it is known as the "bodegeros" position which proposes 20 consonants (see 1b.a) (Willett et al., 2018) vs "petakeros" which proposes a reduction to 13 (see 1b.b) (Reyes Gómez, 2005). In terms of vowels, this variant has six (see 2) which contrast with the other variants of *Ayuuk* which can have up to nine vowels.

(1) a. b ch d ds g j k l m n ñ p r s t ts w x y '
    b. p t k x ts m n wy j l r s '

(2) a e ë i o u

The following are examples of San Juan Güichicovi's*Ayuuk* these were taken from short stories recollected and written by Albino Pedro Juan a native speaker and preserver of the language.

(3) Jantim xyondaak ja koy jadu'un.
The bunny become happy.
El conejo se puso feliz.

(4) Kabëk je'e ti y'ok ëjy y'ok nójnë.
When everything become silence.
Cuando todo se silencia.

2.1 Spanish

In the case of Spanish, our system produces translations in Mexican Spanish which belongs to the American Spanish variant [8], we identify the language by the *es* ISO-639-1 code.

3 The parallel corpus

For the creation of the parallel corpus we collected samples from different sources for which there was a available translation between *Ayuuk* and *Spanish*, see Table 1.

Since we have a diverse source of linguistic sources it was necessary to normalize the orthography. For this we follow the proposal from Sagi-Vela González (2019) who has followed the unification of the *Ayuuk* language avoiding taking sides on the controversy about the number of consonants.

[8] https://glottolog.org/resource/languoid/id/amer1254 (visited, last visited march 2021)

Resource	es	mir
The bible	Open	No open
Songs and poems	No open	No open
The Mexican constitution	Open	No open
Personal colection of Albino Pedro Juan	No open	No open
Esopo Fables	Open	No open
National archive of indigenous languages[a]	No open	Open
Social network[a]	Open	Open
The dragon and the rabbit[a]	Open	Open[b]
Phrases translated by author[a]	Open[c]	Open

[a] https://github.com/DelfinoAyuuk/corpora_ayuuk-spanish_nmt (visited March 18th)
[b] https://mexico.sil.org/es/resources/archives/55868 (visited March 18th)
[c] https://www.manythings.org/anki/ (visited March 18th)

Table 1: Source of data collected

Mainly we made two replacements: *ñ*/*ny* and *ch*/*tsy* Some of the works were already aligned, others not. For those not aligned we created automatic alignments using the YASA tool (Lamraoui and Langlais). We discarded all empty and double alignments. Normalization and automatic alignments were manually verified by one of the authors. The corpus keep differences among both normalization variants: *petakeros* and *bodegeros*.

Finally, we randomly split the sentences into training, development and testing sets. For our experimentation we created two split versions, one *strict* and one *random*. In the *strict* version we use all the phrases from the *National archive of indigenous languages* (Lyon, 1980) as a test. Since these sentences are linguistically motivated and aim to show linguistic aspects of the language they tend to be harder to translate; This split resulted in 5,847/700/912 (train/dev/test). In the *random* split we randomly sample sentences from our sources, the final split resulted in 5,941/700/912 (train/dev/test). Notice that amount of phrases among splits changes, this is because after separating the test phrases, we remove repeated or similar phrases for the train/dev sets. Our intuition was to have a more uniform training/validation for the *random* split while the test follows the distribution of the original sources. We mimic this procedure for the *strict* sample.

4 Neural Architecture

Our translation model is based on the Transformer architecture (Vaswani et al., 2017). We use an *encoder-decoder* setting. For our experiments we

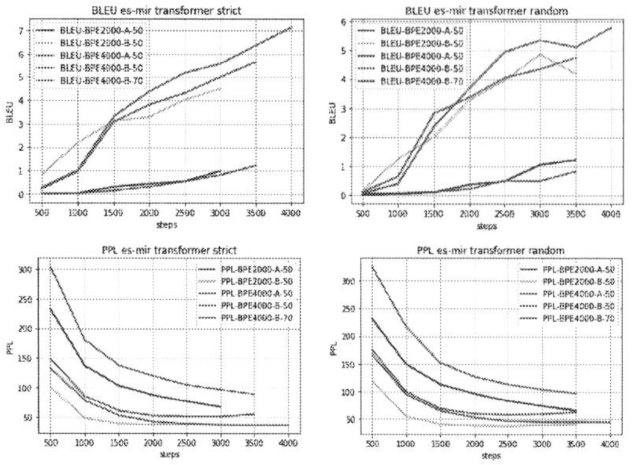

Figure 1: Perplexity and BLEU of *es-mir* in development set.

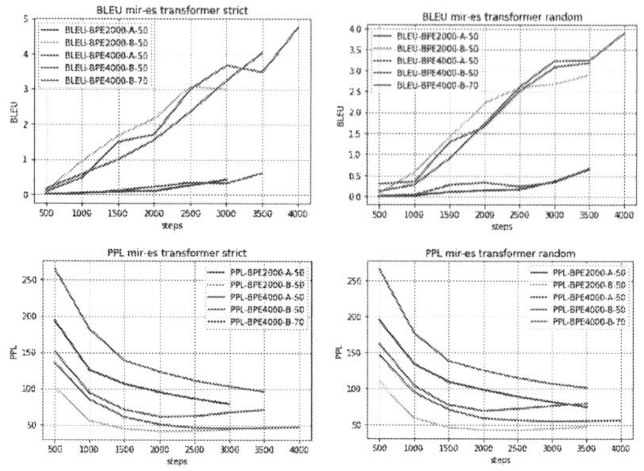

Figure 2: Perplexity and BLEU of *mir-es* in development set.

have two configurations for both encoder and decoder:

A Number of layers: 3, number of heads: 4, Input embedding dimensionality: 64, embedding dimensionality: 64, batch size: 128.

B Number of layers: 6, number of heads: 4, input embedding dimensionality: 256, embedding dimensionality: 256, batch size: 128.

These models were trained in a server with two Tesla V100 GPUs. To obtain a model it usually take us around $2h$ for a 100 epochs. We also were able to reproduce the experiments in the *Colaboratory* platform.

5 Experiments and results

As described in the previous section we have two different versions of our splits, *strict* and *random*. Per split we performed five experiments, two for configuration with fewer layers (*A*), and three for the configuration with more layers (*B*). We also modified: *a)* the maximum length of the phrase (50 or 70) *b)* the vocabulary of the BPE sub-word algorithm (we tested 2000 or 4000). Figure 1 shows the perplexity and the BLEU score in the development set during training for the direction Spanish (*es*) to *Ayuuk* (*mir*). The first part of the Table 2, columns two to five, presents the results on the development and test sets.

Figure 2 shows the lerning curve on the direction of translation *Ayuuk* (*mir*) to Spanish (*es*). The second part of the table 2, columns six to nine, presents the results on the development and test for this translation direction.

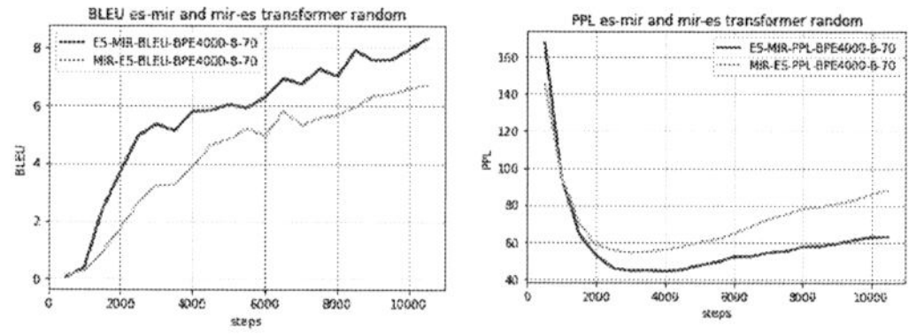

Figure 3: Perplexity and BLEU of *es-mir* and *mir-es* training with 250 epochs.

As we can appreciate these sets of experiments show that the translation is possible. We have some gains on the model with more layers (*B*), this is not trivial since we have a small amount of training data. On the other hand, the *strict* split as expected shows to be very difficult to translate, the BLEU scores are minimal. However with the random splits the BLEU scores are more promising. We also observe there that in the current setting it is more "easy" to translate from Spanish to *Ayuuk* than the other direction. Finally, we perform a larger experimentation with 250 epochs using the *B* configuration, following the intuition we haven reach the right performance with 100. Figure 3 shows the learning curve on the development set, the bottom part of Table 2 shows our final results using the *random* split.

6 Conclusions and Further work

Previous experiences on MT based on deep learning architecture, particularly on *seq2seq* settings, for native languages of the Americas have not been promising (Mager and Meza, 2018). In particular, because there is little to none training data. However, our work shows that a standard model based on the Transformer architecture and under

Configuration A 100 **epochs**	**Strict** ***es-mir***		**Random** ***es-mir***		**Strict** ***mir-es***		**Random** ***mir-es***	
BLEU	**dev**	**test**	**dev**	**test**	**dev**	**test**	**dev**	**test**
Max lenght 50 BPE 2000	1.72	0.05	1.66	1.71	0.64	0.10	0.91	0.66
Max lenght 50 BPE 4000	2.03	0.10	1.21	1.24	1.02	0.16	0.93	0.83
Configuration B 100 **epochs**	**Strict es-mir**		**Random** ***es-mir***		**Strict** ***mir-es***		**Random** ***mir-es***	
BLEU	**dev**	**test**	**dev**	**test**	**dev**	**test**	**dev**	**test**
Max lenght 50 BPE 2000	3.91	0.10	3.59	3.70	2.21	0.41	2.49	2.72
Max lenght 50 BPE 4000	5.02	0.13	4.17	4.20	2.33	0.28	2.13	2.23
Max lenght 70 BPE 4000	7.58	0.10	5.83	5.56	4.03	0.27	3.64	3.52
Configuration B 250 **epochs**	**Random** ***es-mir***				**Random** ***mir-es***			
BLEU	**dev**		**test**		**dev**		**test**	
Max lenght 70 BPE 4000	5.83		5.56		3.64		3.52	

Table 2: BLEU scores of *es-mir* and *mir-es*.

extremely low resource setting can produce some results. They are still low for normal standards of the MT field however they are promising for the future.

In order to improve the performance of the system future work will focus on:

1. Collecting more data, paying attention to other variants of the *Ayuuk* language.

2. Although the *strict* setting strongly penalizes the evaluation, we will continue using linguistic motivated phrases as a good bar to evaluate our progress.

3. At this moment we rely on sub-word of the phrases, however our approach could benefit from a deeper morphology analysis (Kann et al., 2018).

4. Our normalization will continue respecting the *petakeros* and *bodegeros* positions, and for other variants we also incorporate positions regarding the number of vowels.

Acknowledgements

The authors thank CONACYT for the computer resources provided through the INAOE Supercomputing Laboratory's Deep Learning Platform for Language Technologies. We also thank the project "Traducción automática para lenguas indígenas de México" PAPIIT-IA104420, UNAM.

References

Željko Agić and Ivan Vulić. 2019. JW300: A wide-coverage parallel corpus for low-resource languages. In *Proceedings of the 57th Annual Meeting of the Association for Computational Linguistics*, pages 3204–3210, Florence, Italy. Association for Computational Linguistics.

Katharina Kann, Jesus Manuel Mager Hois, Ivan Vladimir Meza-Ruiz, and Hinrich Schütze. 2018. Fortification of neural morphological segmentation models for polysynthetic minimal-resource languages. In *Proceedings of the 2018 Conference of the North American Chapter of the Association for Computational Linguistics: Human Language Technologies, Volume 1 (Long Papers)*, pages 47–57, New Orleans, Louisiana. Association for Computational Linguistics.

Julia Kreutzer, Jasmijn Bastings, and Stefan Riezler. 2019. Joey NMT: A minimalist NMT toolkit for novices. In *Proceedings of the 2019 Conference on Empirical Methods in Natural Language Processing and the 9th International Joint Conference on Natural Language Processing (EMNLP-IJCNLP): System Demonstrations*, pages 109–114, Hong Kong, China. Association for Computational Linguistics.

Fethi Lamraoui and Philippe Langlais. Yet another fast, robust and open source sentence aligner. time to reconsider sentence alignment. *XIV Machine Translation Summit*.

Don D. Lyon. 1980. *Mixe de Tlahuitoltepec, Oaxaca, Archivo de Lenguas Indígenas de México*. Colegio de México, México.

Manuel Mager, Ximena Gutierrez-Vasques, Gerardo Sierra, and Ivan Meza-Ruiz. 2018. Challenges of language technologies for the indigenous languages of the Americas. In *Proceedings of the 27th International Conference on Computational Linguistics*, pages 55–69, Santa Fe, New Mexico, USA. Association for Computational Linguistics.

Manuel Mager and Ivan Meza. 2018. Hacia la traducción automática de las lenguas indıgenas de méxico. *Proceedings of the DH*.

Wilhelmina Nekoto, Vukosi Marivate, Tshinondiwa Matsila, Timi Fasubaa, Taiwo Fagbohungbe, Solomon Oluwole Akinola, Shamsuddeen Muhammad, Salomon Kabongo Kabenamualu, Salomey Osei, Freshia Sackey, Rubungo Andre Niyongabo, Ricky Macharm, Perez Ogayo, Orevaoghene Ahia, Musie Meressa Berhe, Mofetoluwa Adeyemi, Masabata Mokgesi-Selinga, Lawrence Okegbemi, Laura Martinus, Kolawole Tajudeen, Kevin Degila, Kelechi Ogueji, Kathleen Siminyu, Julia Kreutzer, Jason Webster, Jamiil Toure Ali, Jade Abbott, Iroro Orife, Ignatius Ezeani, Idris Abdulkadir Dangana, Herman Kamper, Hady Elsahar, Goodness Duru, Ghollah Kioko, Murhabazi Espoir, Elan van Biljon, Daniel Whitenack, Christopher Onyefuluchi, Chris Chinenye Emezue, Bonaventure F. P. Dossou, Blessing Sibanda, Blessing Bassey, Ayodele Olabiyi, Arshath Ramkilowan, Alp Öktem, Adewale Akinfaderin, and Abdallah Bashir. 2020. Participatory research for low-resourced machine translation: A case study in African languages. In *Findings of the Association for Computational Linguistics: EMNLP 2020*, pages 2144–2160, Online. Association for Computational Linguistics.

J. Carlos Reyes Gómez. 2005. *Aportes al proceso de enseñanza aprendizaje de la lectura y la escritura de la lengua ayuuk*. Centro de Estudios Ayuuk–Universidad Indígena Intercultural Ayuuk, Oaxaca, México.

Ana Sagi-Vela González. 2019. El mixe escrito y el espejismo del buen alfabeto. *Revista de Llengua i Dret*, (71).

Rico Sennrich, Barry Haddow, and Alexandra Birch. 2016. Neural machine translation of rare words with subword units. In *Proceedings of the 54th Annual Meeting of the Association for Computational Linguistics (Volume 1: Long Papers)*, pages 1715–1725, Berlin, Germany. Association for Computational Linguistics.

Ashish Vaswani, Noam Shazeer, Niki Parmar, Jakob Uszkoreit, Llion Jones, Aidan N Gomez, Ł ukasz Kaiser, and Illia Polosukhin. 2017. Attention is all you need. In *Advances in Neural Information Processing Systems*, volume 30. Curran Associates, Inc.

Thomas Willett, Susan Graham, Valerie Hillman, Judith Williams, Miriam Becerra Bautista, Miriam Pérez Luría, Vivian Eberle-Cruz, Karina Araiza Riquer, Julia Dieterman, James Michael McCarty Jr, Victoriano Castañón López, and María Dolores Castañón Eugenio. 2018. *Breve diccionario del mixe del Istmo Mogoñé Viejo, Oaxaca*, primera edition. Instituto Linguistico de Verano, México, D.F.

Explicit Tone Transcription Improves ASR Performance in Extremely Low-Resource Languages: A Case Study in Bribri

Rolando Coto-Solano
Dartmouth College
rolando.a.coto.solano@dartmouth.edu

Abstract

Linguistic tone is transcribed for input into ASR systems in numerous ways. This paper shows a systematic test of several transcription styles, using as an example the Chibchan language Bribri, an extremely low-resource language from Costa Rica. The most successful models separate the tone from the vowel, so that the ASR algorithms learn tone patterns independently. These models showed improvements ranging from 4% to 25% in character error rate (CER), and between 3% and 23% in word error rate (WER). This is true for both traditional GMM/HMM and end-to-end CTC algorithms. This paper also presents the first attempt to train ASR models for Bribri. The best performing models had a CER of 33% and a WER of 50%. Despite the disadvantage of using hand-engineered representations, these models were trained on only 68 minutes of data, and therefore show the potential of ASR to generate further training materials and aid in the documentation and revitalization of the language.

Resumen

Transcribir el tono de forma explícita mejora el rendimiento del reconocimiento de voz en idiomas extremadamente bajos en recursos: Un estudio de caso en bribri. Hay numerosas maneras de transcribir el tono lingüístico a la hora de proveer los datos de entrenamiento a los sistemas de reconocimiento de voz. Este artículo presenta un experimento sistemático de varias formas de transcripción usando como ejemplo la lengua chibcha bribri, una lengua de Costa Rica extremadamente baja en recursos. Los modelos más exitosos fueron aquellos en que el tono aparece separado de la vocal de tal forma que los algoritmos pudieran aprender los patrones tonales por separado. Estos modelos mostraron mejoras de entre 4% y 26% en el error de caracteres (CER), y de entre 3% y 25% en el error de palabras (WER). Esto se observó tanto en los algoritmos GMM/HMM como en los algoritmos CTC de secuencia-a-secuencia. Este artículo también presenta el primer intento de entrenar modelos de reconocimiento de voz en bribri. Los mejores modelos tuvieron un CER de 33% y un WER de 50%. A pesar de la desventaja de usar representaciones diseñadas a mano, estos modelos se entrenaron con solo 68 minutos de datos y muestran el potencial para generar más materiales de entrenamiento, así como de ayudar con la documentación y revitalización de la lengua.

1 Introduction

The documentation and revitalization of Indigenous languages relies on the transcription of speech recordings, which contain vital information about a community and its culture. However, the transcription of these recordings constitutes a major bottleneck in the process of making this information usable for researchers and practitioners. It typically takes up to 50 hours of an expert's time to transcribe each hour of audio in an Indigenous language (Shi et al., 2021). Moreover, there are usually few community members who have the expertise to transcribe this data and who have the time to do so. Because of this, extending automated speech recognition (ASR) to these languages and incorporating it into their documentation and revitalization workflows would alleviate the workload of linguists and community members and help accelerate their efforts.

Indigenous and other minority languages usually have few transcribed audio recordings, and so adapting data-hungry ASR algorithms to assist in their documentation is an active area of research (Besacier et al., 2014; Jimerson and Prud'hommeaux, 2018; Michaud et al., 2019; Adams et al., 2019; Foley et al., 2018; Gupta and Boulianne, 2020b,a; Zahrer et al., 2020; Thai et al., 2019; Li et al., 2020; Partanen et al., 2020; Zevallos et al., 2019; Matsuura et al., 2020; Levow et al., 2021). This paper will examine an element that

Proceedings of the First Workshop on Natural Language Processing for Indigenous Languages of the Americas, pages 173–184
June 11, 2021.

might appear obvious at first, but one where the literature is "inconclusive" (Adams, 2018), and which can have major consequences in performance: How should tones be transcribed when dealing with extremely low-resource languages? This will be examined by building ASR models for the language Bribri from Costa Rica. The results show that simple changes in the orthographic transcription, in the form of explicit tonal markings that are separate from the vowel information, can dramatically improve accuracy.

1.1 Tonal languages and ASR

A tonal language is a language where differences in pitch can change the meaning of a word, even if the consonants and vowels are the same (Yip, 2002). The best-known example of a tonal language is Mandarin Chinese. In Mandarin, the syllable [ma] means "mother" if it is produced with a high pitch. The same syllable means "horse" when pronounced with a dipping-rising pitch, but if it is pronounced with a falling pitch, it means "to scold". Between 40% and 70% of the languages of the world are tonal (Yip, 2002; Maddieson, 2013), including numerous Indigenous languages of the Americas. Because tone is expressed as pitch variations, and those variations can only occur during the pronunciation of consonants and vowels, tonal cues overlap with those of the consonants and vowels in the word. Therefore, it is useful to distinguish between segments - consonants and vowels - and the information that is *suprasegmental*, such as tone, which occurs co-temporally with segments (Lehiste and Lass, 1976).

Precisely because of large tonal languages like Mandarin, there has been research into how tone can play a role in ASR. Many systems treat pitch (the main phonetic cue of tone) as a completely separate feature. In such systems, the traditional ASR algorithm learns the segments, and a separate machine learning module learns the pitch patterns and offers its inference of the tone (Kaur et al., 2020). This has been used for languages like Mandarin (Niu et al., 2013; Shan et al., 2010), Thai (Kertkeidkachorn et al., 2014) and Yoruba (Ọdélọbí, 2008; Yusof et al., 2013). On the other hand, there is research that suggests that, given that the tone and vowel information are co-temporal, these are best learned together. For example, an ASR system would be asked to learn a vowel and its tone as a single unit (e.g. a+highTone). Fusing the representation for vowel and tone, or *embedded tone modeling* (Lee et al., 2002), has been shown to be effective for larger languages like Mandarin (Chang et al., 2000), Vietnamese and Cantonese (Metze et al., 2013; Nguyen et al., 2018), as well as smaller languages like Yoloxóchitl Mixtec from Mexico (Shi et al., 2021) and Anyi from Côte d'Ivoire (Koffi, 2020). Finally, in some tonal languages like Hausa, in which the orthography does not mark any tone, the tone is not included at all in ASR models (Gauthier et al., 2016).

Representations where the tone is marked explicitly but is kept separate from the vowel (i.e. *explicit tone recognition* (Lee et al., 2002)) are not often used for larger languages, but they are very common in low-resource ASR. This is often done using phonetic representations, where the output of the algorithm is in the form of the International Phonetic Alphabet (IPA), which is then converted to the language's orthographic convention. For languages like Na from China and Chatino from Mexico (Ćavar et al., 2016; Adams et al., 2018), the characters representing the tone are separated from the vowel. Wisniewski et al. (2020) argue that it is the transparency of the representation (either orthographic or phonetic) that helps ASR to learn these tonal representations, and this transparency includes having characters that the algorithm can use to generalize the phonetic cues of the tones separate from those of the vowels.

Given the review above, there appears to be more than one way to represent tone effectively as input for ASR. In this paper several different methods will be tested using a language (and indeed, a language family) in which no ASR models have been trained before.

1.2 Chibchan Languages and Bribri

The Bribri language (Glottocode `brib1243`) is spoken by about 7000 people in Southern Costa Rica (INEC, 2011). It belongs to the Chibchan language family, which includes languages such as Cabécar and Malecu from Costa Rica, Kuna and Naso from Panama, and Kogi from Colombia. Bribri is a vulnerable language (Moseley, 2010; Sánchez Avendaño, 2013). This means that there are still children who speak it with their families but there are few circumstances when it is written, and indeed there are very few books published in the language. Bribri has four tones: high, falling, rising, and low tone. The first three are marked in the orthography using diacritics (respectively: *à*, *á*, *â*), while the low tone is left unmarked: *a*. Bribri tone can create differences in meaning: the word *alà* means 'child'; its first syllable is low and the second syllable is high. Contrast this with *alá* 'thunder', where the second syllable has a falling tone.

Bribri has an additional suprasegmental feature: Nasality. Like in French, vowels in Bribri can be oral or nasal. Therefore, *ù* with an oral vowel means 'house', but *ù̱* with a nasal vowel, marked with a line underneath the vowel,[1] means 'pot'.

Bribri orthographies are relatively transparent due to their recent invention, the oldest of which is from the 1970s (Constenla et al., 2004; Jara Murillo and García Segura, 2013; Margery, 2005). This works to our advantage, in that there is almost no difference between an orthographic and a phonetic representation for the input of Bribri ASR.

There has been some work on Bribri NLP, including the creation of digital dictionaries (Krohn, 2020) and morphological analyzers used for documentation (Flores Solórzano, 2019, 2017b). There have also been some experiments with untrained forced alignment (Coto-Solano and Flores Solórzano, 2016, 2017), and with neural machine translation (Feldman and Coto-Solano, 2020). However, there is a need to accelerate the documentation of Bribri and produce more written materials out of existing recordings, and here we face the bottleneck problem mentioned above. One of the main goals of this paper is to build a first ASR system for Bribri in order to alleviate the problems of transcription.

[1]There are two main orthographic systems for Bribri. In the Constenla et al. (2004) system, the nasal is marked with a line under the vowel. In the Jara Murillo and García Segura (2013) system, the nasal is marked with a tilde over the vowel: *ũ̀* 'house'.

2 Transcription Methodology

The first step towards training an ASR model in Bribri was the selection of the training materials. The spontaneous speech corpus of Flores Solórzano (2017a) was used because of its public availability (it is available under a Creative Commons license) and because of its consistent transcription. This corpus contains 1571 utterances from 28 speakers (14 male and 14 female), for a total of 68 minutes of transcribed speech. These utterances contain a total of 13586 words, with 2221 unique words.

The main question in this paper is: How can we easily reformat Bribri text into the best possible input for ASR? Let's take the word *dikì̱* /di˩ˈki˥/ 'underneath' as an example. This word has two syllables, the first one with a low tone and the second one with a high tone, indicated by a grave accent. In addition to the tone, the second syllable is also nasal, and this is marked with a line underneath the vowel. One possible representation of this word would be to interpret it as four different characters, as is shown in condition 1 of table 1. Here, the character for the last vowel would carry in it the information that it is the vowel /i/, that the vowel is nasal, and that the vowel is produced with a high tone. This condition will be called AllFeats, or "all features together", because each character in the ASR alphabet carries with it all the suprasegmental features of the vowel. In this transcription, the Bribri ASR alphabet would have 48 separate vowel symbols: `A-HIGH`, `A-HIGH-NAS`, `A-LOW`, `A-LOW-NAS`, etc.

There are many other ways in which the word

Condition	Example transcription	Length	Symbols for vowels + feats
1. **AllFeats**: All features together	`D I-LOW K I-NAS-HIGH`	4	48
2. **NasSep**: Nasal as separate character	`D I-LOW K I-HIGH NAS`	5	28 + 1 = 29
3. **ToneNasSepWL**: Both tone and nasal separate; explicit indication of low tone	`D I LOW K I HIGH NAS`	7	7 + 5 = 12
4. **ToneNasSep**: Both tone and nasal separate; low tone as implicit default	`D I K I HIGH NAS`	6	7 + 4 = 11
5. **ToneSepWL**: Tone is separate; explicit indication of low tone	`D I LOW K I-NAS HIGH`	6	12 + 4 = 16
6. **ToneSep**: Tone is separate; low tone as implicit default	`D I K I-NAS HIGH`	5	12 + 3 = 15

Table 1: Different ways to transcribe the Bribri word *dikì̱* /di˩ˈki˥/ 'underneath'

could be transcribed. For example, as shown in the second condition, NasSep, the nasality could be written as a separate character and the tone and vowel could be represented together. In this transcription, the final vowel would be made up of two separate alphabetic symbols: `I-HIGH` and `NAS`. This idea of separating features could be taken further, and both the tone and the nasality could be represented as separate characters. This is represented in the third condition, TonesNasSepWL. Here, both the tones and the nasal feature follow the vowel as separate characters, and the final vowel of *diki̱* 'underneath' would be expressed using three alphabetic symbols: `I HIGH NAS`. Notice that, in this condition, the low tone of the first syllable would be represented explicitly after the first vowel, `I LOW`, hence the condition includes the 'WL', "with low [tone]". However, this low tone is the most frequent tone in Bribri, and as a matter of fact it has no explicit diacritic in the Bribri writing system. Because of this, another option for the transcription could be to keep marking the tones and nasals separately from the vowels, but to only represent the three salient tones (high, falling, rising) and leave the low tone as a default, unwritten option in the transcription. This is shown in condition 4, ToneNasSep.

There are some combinations where the nasal marking stays with the vowel, but the tone is separate. In condition 5, ToneSepWL, the tones are indicated separately but the nasality is written jointly with the vowel. The final vowel of *diki̱* 'underneath' would then be represented using two symbols: `I-NAS HIGH`. This means that there would be twelve vowel symbols[2] in the Bribri ASR alphabet (e.g. `A`, `A-NAS`, `E`, `E-NAS`, etc.), and separate indicators for the four tones: `HIGH`, `FALL`, `RISE`, `LOW`. But, given that the low tone is again the most frequent, we could assume it as a default tone and leave the `LOW` marking out. This is done in condition 6, ToneSep. In ToneSep, the second vowel has a high tone, and so it gets a separate `HIGH` tone marker. The first vowel, on the other hand, has a low tone, and therefore gets no marking.

In order to test the different performance of these conditions, two different ASR systems were used. First, the Bribri data was trained using a traditional Gaussian Mixture Models based Hidden Markov Model algorithm (GMM/HMM), implemented in the Kaldi ASR program (Povey et al., 2011). Given the paucity of data, this is likely the best option for training. However, end-to-end systems are also available, and while they are known not to perform well with small datasets (Goodfellow et al., 2016; Glasmachers, 2017), they were still tested to see if the differences in transcription caused any variation in performance. A Connectionist Temporal Classification (CTC) loss algorithm (Graves et al., 2006) with bidirectional recursive neural networks (RNNs) was used, implemented in the DeepSpeech program (Hannun et al., 2014).

3 Traditional ASR Results

Kaldi was used to train models for each of the transcription conditions described above. Two parameters were varied in the experiment: The number of phones in the acoustic model (monophone or triphone), and the number of words in a KenLM based language model (unigrams, bigrams and trigrams) (Heafield, 2011). All other hyperparameters were identical to those in the default Kaldi installation. Thirty models were trained for each of the six transcription conditions, using the six parameter combinations (phones x ngrams), for a total of 1080 models.[3] To train these models utterances were randomly shuffled for every model and then split so that 90% of the utterances were used for training (1571 utterances) and 10% were used for validation (174 utterances). Each of the models had two measures of error: the median character error rate (CER) and the median word error rate (WER), calculated over the input transcription for each condition. The results reported below correspond to the median of the 30 medians in each condition.

Figure 1 shows the summary of the training results. The condition with the best performance is ToneSep, where the tone symbol is kept separate (`HIGH`, `FALL`, `RISE`), the low tone is left out as a default, and the nasal feature remains connected to the vowel symbol (i.e.: `A` versus `A-NAS`).

Table 2 shows the summary of results for three conditions: ToneSep and AllFeats, which had the best performance, and ToneNasSepWL, which had the worst performance. The best performing of all conditions is ToneSep trained with triphones and with a trigram language model. This combination of factors produces models with a median of

[2]There are five vowels that can be both oral and nasal: /a, e, i, o, u/. There are two vowels, /ɪ, ʊ/, written 'ë' and 'ö', which can never be nasal.

[3]The models were trained using an Intel i7-10750H CPU, and each took approximately 5 minutes to train, for a total of 90 hours of processing. The electricity came from the ICE electric grid in Costa Rica, which uses 98% renewable energy.

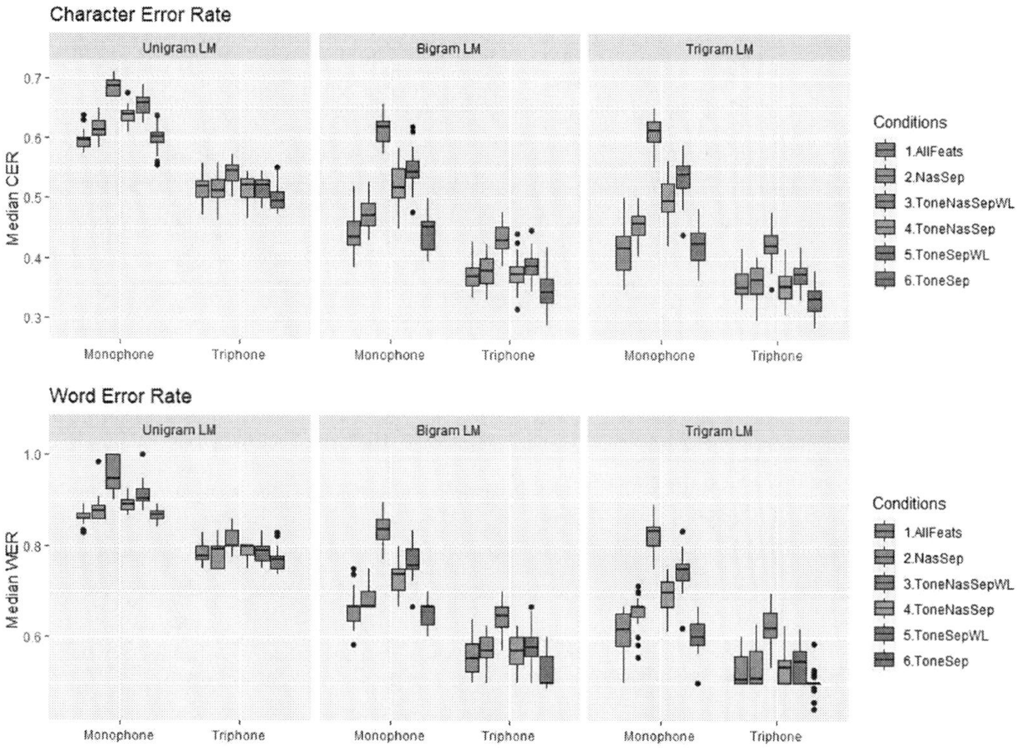

Figure 1: Medians for character error rate (CER) and word error rate (WER) for Kaldi training, using different phone (monophone, triphone) and language models (unigrams, bigrams, trigrams).

	ToneSep	AllFeats	ToneNasSepWL	MaxΔ
CER Mono	60 - 45 - 42	60 - 44 - 42	69 - 62 - 61	9 - 18 - 19
CER Tri	50 - 34 - **33**	52 - 37 - 35	54 - 43 - 42	4 - 9 - 9
WER Mono	87 - 67 - 60	86 - 67 - 62	95 - 84 - 83	9 - 17 - 23
WER Tri	77 - 50 - **50**	78 - 55 - 51	80 - 65 - 62	3 - 15 - 12

Table 2: Median character error rate (CER) and word error rate (WER) for the best conditions (ToneSep and AllFeats) and the worst condition (ToneNasSepWL). The three numbers indicate the error for unigram, bigram and trigram language models. MaxΔ indicates the difference between the worst and the best models.

33% CER and 50% WER. Very close is AllFeats with triphones and trigrams, with 35% CER and 51% WER. These two perform substantially better than ToneNasSepWL, with CER 42% and WER 62% using the same parameters. This means that the ToneSep transcription is associated with an improvement of 9% in CER and 12% in WER. The biggest improvements between conditions are seen with the monophone+trigram models, where ToneSep has a 19% lower CER and a 23% lower WER than ToneNasSepWL.

ToneSep is not the condition with the least vowel symbols, but it is the one with the best performance. This could be due to two reasons. First, what ToneSep appears to be doing is changing the behavior of the triphone window. Kaldi's acoustic model has states with three symbols in them. In a writing system that only has graphemes for segments, the triphone window would, indeed, look at the consonant or vowel in question and to its preceding and following segments. With ToneSep, the tone symbols are surrounded by the vowel the tone belongs to and the following consonant or vowel (or at the nasal symbol). This means that, in practice, when the triphone window looks at the tone, it is looking at two actual phones (the vowel, its tonal cues, and the following consonant/vowel), or even one actual phone (the vowel with its tonal and nasal cues). There are well known effects of tones in their preceding and following segments (Tang, 2008; DiCanio, 2012; Hanson, 2009), so this reduced window might be helping the computer generalize the relatively stable tone patterns of Bribri and their effect on the surrounding segments. The training chops the duration of the vowel into two segments; the first chunk is used to identify the vowel itself, and the second chunk is used to identify the tonal trajectory.[4]

A second reason for the advantage of ToneSep might be the phonetics of the low tone itself. It is not only the most frequent tone in Bribri, but it also the least stable phonetically. The low tone can actually appear as low or mid, depending on its surrounding tones (Coto-Solano, 2015). What Kaldi might be doing is simply learn the more stable patterns of the other tones and label all other pitch patterns as "low".

The reason why ToneNasSepWL is the worst performing transcription is unclear. It might be the case that the addition of the low tone creates an explosion in the number of HMM states, given that the low tone is the most frequent one. Another reason might be the separation of the nasal feature. It is possible that the nasal vowels of Bribri are different enough from their oral equivalents that trying to decouple the vowels from their nasality makes generalization more difficult. As can be seen in figure 1, the NasSep condition also performs poorly. This pattern matches results in languages like Portuguese (Meinedo et al., 2003) and Hindi (Jyothi and Hasegawa-Johnson, 2015), where the best results are obtained by keeping the nasal feature bound to the vowel representations.

Table 3 below shows examples of the transcriptions generated by Kaldi for the validation utterances. In this particular example, the transcription from ToneSep is only off by one space (it doesn't separate the words *e' ta̱* 'so'). The transcription from AllFeats is also fairly good in terms of CER, but it is missing the pronoun *be'* 'you'. Finally, the ToneNasSepWL transcription misses several words. For example, it transcribed the word *tsítsir* 'young, small' as the phonetically similar *chìchi* 'dog', and the adverb *wake'* 'right, anyways' as *wa* 'with'.

4 End-to-End Results

End-to-end algorithms need massive amounts of data to train properly (Goodfellow et al., 2016; Glasmachers, 2017), so they are not the most appropriate way to train the small datasets characteristic of extremely low-resource languages. However, it would be useful to test whether the differences detected in the traditional ASR training are also visible in end-to-end training. A CTC loss algorithm with bidirectional RNNs was used, specifically that implemented in DeepSpeech. Two types of end-to-end learning were studied: First, models were trained using only the available Bribri data. This style of training will be called Just Bribri. Second, the Bribri data was incorporated into transfer learning models (Wang and Zheng, 2015; Kunze et al., 2017; Wang et al., 2020). DeepSpeech has existing English language models,[5] trained with 6-layer RNNs. The final two layers were removed and two new layers were grafted onto the RNN. The first four layers would, in theory, use their English model to encode the phonetic information, and the final two layers would receive that information and produce Bribri text as output. Removing two layers was found to be the optimal point of transfer learning, which matches previous results in literature

[4]No experiment was conducted to test the effect of placing the tone indicator before the vowel (e.g. `d LOW i k HIGH i NAS` for *dikì̱* 'underneath'). In theory, the performance would be worse given that, in the early milliseconds of a vowel, tones can be phonetically co-articulated with their preceding tone and these two cues would blend together (Xu, 1997; Nguyễn and Trần, 2012; DiCanio, 2014). This effect, called *carryover*, causes greater deformations in pitch than the effect of anticipating the following tone, or *anticipatory assimilation* (Gandour et al., 1993; Coto-Solano, 2017, 93-99). Therefore, the second part of the vowel would provide a clearer tonal cue.

[5]A short experiment was run with the Mandarin DeepSpeech models as the base for transfer training, given that both languages are tonal. However, these models had worse performance than with transfer from the English model.

Utterance meaning:	'So you were young then, right?'						
Target utterance:	e' ta̱ be' bák i̱a̱ tsítsir wake'						
ToneSep	e'ta̱	be'	bák	i̱a̱	tsítsir	wake'	CER: 3%
AllFeats	e'ta		bák	i̱a̱	tsítsir	wake'	CER: 16%
ToneNasSepWL	e' ta̱		wake'	chìchi	wa		CER: 61%

Table 3: Example of Kaldi transcriptions for three of the experimental conditions, trained with triphone-trigram models. More examples are shown in Appendix A.

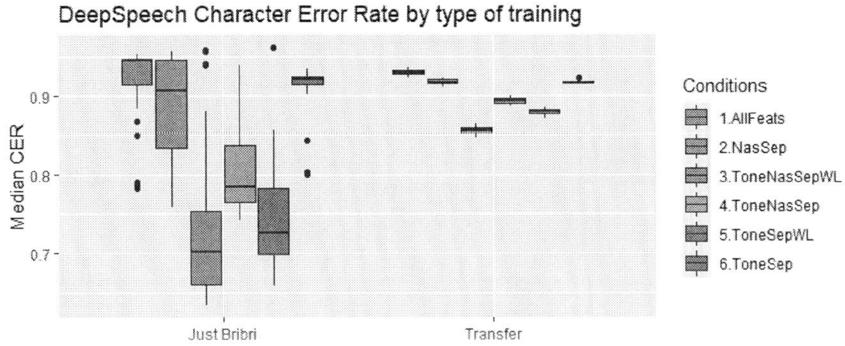

Figure 2: Medians for character error rate (CER) for DeepSpeech models.

(Meyer, 2019; Hjortnaes et al., 2020). This training style will be called Transfer. Both the Just Bribri and Transfer models were trained for 20 epochs, and all other hyperparameters were the same as in the default installation of DeepSpeech.

	Just Bribri	Transfer
AllFeats	95	93
NasSep	91	92
ToneNasSepWL	**70**	**86**
ToneNasSep	78	89
ToneSepWL	73	88
ToneSep	92	91
MaxΔ	25	7

Table 4: Median character error rate (CER) for models trained with CTC (DeepSpeech). MaxΔ indicates the difference between the worst and the best models.

The six transcription conditions were used to train models in both training styles. Same as before, thirty models were trained for each condition. The utterances were randomly shuffled before preparing each model, and then 80% of the utterances were used in the training set (1397 utterances), 10% of the utterances were used for validation (174 utterances), and the final 10% were used for testing. After the training was complete, the median CER and WER were extracted for each model. The median CER for the thirty models in each condition are shown in figure 2.[6]

In the CTC training, the tables have completely turned: ToneSep and AllFeats are the worst performing conditions, and ToneNasSepWL has the best performance. Table 4 shows the median of the 30 medians for each transcription condition. The ToneNasSepWL models trained with Just Bribri have a median of 70% CER, whereas the AllFeats models have a median of 95%, a full 25% worse. As a matter of fact, both WL conditions now have the best performance. This pattern is also visible in the Transfer models: The ToneNasSepWL transcription has a CER of 86%, 7% better than the AllFeats transcription. The median WER is not shown because, for all conditions, the median of the thirty medians was WER=1.

There might be several reasons why the situation has reversed in the CTC models. First, providing an explicit symbol for the low tone might force DeepSpeech to look for more words in the transcription. As can be seen in table 5, the ToneNasSepWL transcription uses the character *4* for the explicit indication of the low tone, which is then eliminated in post-processing to produce a human readable form. The explicit symbol for the low tone appears to force the CTC algorithm to keep looking for tones, and therefore words, whereas, in the other conditions, the CTC algorithm gives up on the search sooner. A second reason why WL performs better is that it provides a clear indication of where a syllable ends, and therefore makes the traverse through the CTC trellis simpler to navigate. Without an explicit low tone, any vowel could be followed by tones, vowels or consonants. On the other hand, when all tones have explicit marking, vowels can only be followed by a tone, which potentially simplifies the path to finding the word.

A third reason for this improvement might have to do with the size of the alphabet: The WL conditions have relatively few symbols for the vowels (12 symbols for ToneNasSepWL versus 48 for

[6]The models were trained using the HPC infrastructure at Dartmouth College in New Hampshire. Each model used 16 CPUs and took approximately 65 minutes to train, for an approximate total of 78 hours of processing.

Utterance meaning:	'So you were young then, right?'		
Target utterance:	*e' t<u>a</u> be' bák <u>ia</u> tsítsir wake'*		
Condition	DeepSpeech output	Human-readable output	CER
ToneNasSepWL	`e4' tax4 i4e4' i4`	`e' ta ie' i`	65%
ToneSep	`e'`	`e'`	91%
AllFeats	`i`	`i`	93%

Table 5: Example of DeepSpeech transcriptions for three of the experimental conditions

AllFeats), which would result in a smaller output layer for the RNNs. Notice that, as with the triphones in Kaldi, the RNNs might be splitting the vowel into separate chunks. It would then proceed to identify the type of vowel from the first chunk, the tone in the second and the nasality in the final part. It would also benefit from the bidirectionality of the neural networks, finding tonal cues in the surrounding segments without the disadvantages of GMM/HMM systems.

Finally, it should be noted that the Transfer models did not provide an improvement in performance. This is somewhat surprising; this might indicate that the Bribri dataset is too small to benefit from the transfer, or that the knowledge of English phones does not overlap sufficiently with the Bribri sound system to produce a boost. Even then, the Transfer models also show effects due to the different transcription conditions, and they also benefited from separating the tone and nasal features from the vowel. This effects will have to be confirmed in the future with other end-to-end techniques, such as *Listen, Attend and Spell* algorithms (Chan et al., 2016) and wav2vec pretraining (Baevski et al., 2020).

5 Conclusions

While hand-engineered representations are suboptimal for high-resource languages, these can still be helpful in low-resource environments, where they can help set up a virtuous cycle of creating imperfect but rapid transcriptions, which can then be improved to create more training materials, improve ASR algorithms, and start helping documentation and revitalization projects right away.

The results above show that performing relatively easy transformations in the input (e.g. not marking the most common tone, separating the tonal markings from the vowel) can lead to major improvements in performance. It also shows that NLP practitioners and linguists can fruitfully combine their knowledge to understand the different features involved in the writing system of a language. Additionally, it provides evidence that the benefits of phonetic transcription can also be gained using semi-orthographic representations. The following recommendations provide a short summary of the results: (i) Separate the tones from the vowels. This will help ASR systems learn their regularities. (ii) Experiment with other features, such as nasality; if they modify the formants of the vowel, they should probably be grouped with the vowel.

Finally, this work is the first attempt at training speech recognition for a Chibchan language. As shown in table 3 and Appendix A, it is feasible to transcribe these languages automatically, and these methods will be refined in the future to incorporate ASR into the documentation pipelines for this language family.

Acknowledgements

The author would like to thank Dr. Sofía Flores for her work on the Bribri corpus, the personnel of Research Computing Department at Dartmouth College for their support with processing resources, and Dr. Samantha Wray and three anonymous reviewers for their work in reviewing and offering helpful suggestions to improve this paper.

References

Oliver Adams. 2018. Persephone Quickstart. `https://persephone.readthedocs.io/en/stable/quickstart.html#using-your-own-data`.

Oliver Adams, Trevor Cohn, Graham Neubig, Hilaria Cruz, Steven Bird, and Alexis Michaud. 2018. Evaluating Phonemic Transcription of Low-resource Tonal languages for Language Documentation. In *LREC 2018 (Language Resources and Evaluation Conference)*, pages 3356–3365.

Oliver Adams, Matthew Wiesner, Shinji Watanabe, and David Yarowsky. 2019. Massively Multilingual Adversarial Speech Recognition. *arXiv preprint arXiv:1904.02210*.

Alexei Baevski, Henry Zhou, Abdelrahman Mohamed, and Michael Auli. 2020. wav2vec 2.0: A framework for self-supervised learning of speech representations. *arXiv preprint arXiv:2006.11477*.

Laurent Besacier, Etienne Barnard, Alexey Karpov, and Tanja Schultz. 2014. Automatic Speech Recognition for Under-resourced Languages: A Survey. *Speech communication*, 56:85–100.

Malgorzata Ćavar, Damir Ćavar, and Hilaria Cruz. 2016. Endangered Language Documentation: Bootstrapping a Chatino speech corpus, Forced Aligner, ASR. In *Proceedings of the Tenth International Conference on Language Resources and Evaluation (LREC'16)*, pages 4004–4011.

William Chan, Navdeep Jaitly, Quoc Le, and Oriol Vinyals. 2016. Listen, attend and spell: A neural network for large vocabulary conversational speech recognition. In *2016 IEEE International Conference on Acoustics, Speech and Signal Processing (ICASSP)*, pages 4960–4964. IEEE.

Eric Chang, Jianlai Zhou, Shuo Di, Chao Huang, and Kai-Fu Lee. 2000. Large Vocabulary Mandarin Speech Recognition with Different Approaches in Modeling Tones. In *Sixth International Conference on Spoken Language Processing*.

Adolfo Constenla, Feliciano Elizondo, and Francisco Pereira. 2004. *Curso Básico de Bribri*. Editorial de la Universidad de Costa Rica.

Rolando Coto-Solano. 2015. The Phonetics, Phonology and Phonotactics of the Bribri Language. In *2nd International Conference on Mesoamerican Linguistics*, volume 25. Los Angeles: California State University.

Rolando Coto-Solano and Sofía Flores Solórzano. 2016. Alineación forzada sin entrenamiento para la anotación automática de corpus orales de las lenguas indígenas de Costa Rica. *Kánina*, 40(4):175–199.

Rolando Coto-Solano and Sofía Flores Solórzano. 2017. Comparison of Two Forced Alignment Systems for Aligning Bribri Speech. *CLEI Electron. J.*, 20(1):2–1.

Rolando Alberto Coto-Solano. 2017. *Tonal Reduction and Literacy in Me̱'pha̱a̱ Vátháá*. Ph.D. thesis, University of Arizona.

Christian DiCanio. 2014. Triqui Tonal Coarticulation and Contrast Preservation in Tonal Phonology. In *Proceedings of the Workshop on the Sound Systems of Mexico and Central America*, New Haven, CT: Department of Linguistics, Yale University.

Christian T DiCanio. 2012. Coarticulation between Tone and Glottal Consonants in Itunyoso Trique. *Journal of Phonetics*, 40(1):162–176.

Ọdétúnjí Àjàdí Ọdélọbí. 2008. Recognition of Tones in Yorùbá Speech: Experiments with Artificial Neural Networks. In *Speech, Audio, Image and Biomedical Signal Processing using Neural Networks*, pages 23–47. Springer.

Isaac Feldman and Rolando Coto-Solano. 2020. Neural Machine Translation Models with Back-Translation for the Extremely Low-Resource Indigenous Language Bribri. In *Proceedings of the 28th International Conference on Computational Linguistics*, pages 3965–3976.

Sofía Flores Solórzano. 2017a. Corpus oral pandialectal de la lengua bribri. `http://bribri.net`.

Sofía Flores Solórzano. 2019. La modelización de la morfología verbal bribri - Modeling the Verbal Morphology of Bribri. *Revista de Procesamiento del Lenguaje Natural*, 62:85–92.

Sofía Margarita Flores Solórzano. 2017b. *Un primer corpus pandialectal oral de la lengua bribri y su anotación morfológica con base en el modelo de estados finitos*. Ph.D. thesis, Universidad Autónoma de Madrid.

Ben Foley, Josh Arnold, Rolando Coto-Solano, Gautier Durantin, T. Mark Ellison, Daan van Esch, Scott Heath, Frantisek Kratochvil, Zara Maxwell-Smith, David Nash, Ola Olsson, Mark Richards, Nay San, Hywel Stoakes, Nick Thieberger, and Janet Wiles. 2018. Building Speech Recognition Systems for Language Documentation: The CoEDL Endangered Language Pipeline and Inference System (ELPIS). In *Proc. The 6th Intl. Workshop on Spoken Language Technologies for Under-Resourced Languages*, pages 205–209.

Jack Gandour, Suvit Ponglorpisit, Sumalee Dechongkit, Fuangfa Khunadorn, Prasert Boongird, and Siripong Potisuk. 1993. Anticipatory tonal coarticulation in thai noun compounds after unilateral brain damage. *Brain and language*, 45(1):1–20.

Elodie Gauthier, Laurent Besacier, and Sylvie Voisin. 2016. Automatic Speech Recognition for African Languages with Vowel Length Contrast. *Procedia Computer Science*, 81:136–143.

Tobias Glasmachers. 2017. Limits of End-to-end Learning. In *Asian Conference on Machine Learning*, pages 17–32. PMLR.

Ian Goodfellow, Yoshua Bengio, and Aaron Courville. 2016. *Deep Learning*. MIT Press. `http://www.deeplearningbook.org`.

Alex Graves, Santiago Fernández, Faustino Gomez, and Jürgen Schmidhuber. 2006. Connectionist Temporal Classification: Labelling Unsegmented Sequence Data with Recurrent Neural Networks. In *Proceedings of the 23rd international conference on Machine learning*, pages 369–376.

Vishwa Gupta and Gilles Boulianne. 2020a. Automatic transcription challenges for Inuktitut, a low-resource polysynthetic language. In *Proceedings of the 12th Language Resources and Evaluation Conference*, pages 2521–2527.

Vishwa Gupta and Gilles Boulianne. 2020b. Speech Transcription Challenges for Resource Constrained Indigenous Language Cree. In *Proceedings of the 1st Joint Workshop on Spoken Language Technologies for Under-resourced languages (SLTU) and Collaboration and Computing for Under-Resourced Languages (CCURL)*, pages 362–367.

Awni Hannun, Carl Case, Jared Casper, Bryan Catanzaro, Greg Diamos, Erich Elsen, Ryan Prenger, Sanjeev Satheesh, Shubho Sengupta, Adam Coates, et al. 2014. Deep Speech: Scaling up End-to-End Speech Recognition. *arXiv preprint arXiv:1412.5567.*

Helen M Hanson. 2009. Effects of Obstruent Consonants on Fundamental Frequency at Vowel Onset in English. *The Journal of the Acoustical Society of America*, 125(1):425–441.

Kenneth Heafield. 2011. KenLM: Faster and smaller language model queries. In *Proceedings of the Sixth Workshop on Statistical Machine Translation*, pages 187–197.

Nils Hjortnaes, Niko Partanen, Michael Rießler, and Francis M Tyers. 2020. Towards a speech recognizer for Komi, an endangered and low-resource Uralic language. In *Proceedings of the Sixth International Workshop on Computational Linguistics of Uralic Languages*, pages 31–37.

INEC. 2011. Población total en territorios indígenas por autoidentificación a la etnia indígena y habla de alguna lengua indígena, según pueblo y territorio indígena. In Instituto Nacional de Estadística y Censos, editor, *Censo 2011.*

Carla Victoria Jara Murillo and Alí García Segura. 2013. *Se' ttö̃ bribri ie Hablemos en bribri.* EDigital.

Robbie Jimerson and Emily Prud'hommeaux. 2018. ASR for Documenting Acutely Under-resourced Indigenous Languages. In *Proceedings of the Eleventh International Conference on Language Resources and Evaluation (LREC 2018).*

Preethi Jyothi and Mark Hasegawa-Johnson. 2015. Improved Hindi broadcast ASR by adapting the language model and pronunciation model using a priori syntactic and morphophonemic knowledge. In *Sixteenth Annual Conference of the International Speech Communication Association.*

Jaspreet Kaur, Amitoj Singh, and Virender Kadyan. 2020. Automatic Speech Recognition System for Tonal Languages: State-of-the-Art Survey. *Archives of Computational Methods in Engineering*, pages 1–30.

Natthawut Kertkeidkachorn, Proadpran Punyabukkana, and Atiwong Suchato. 2014. Using tone information in Thai spelling speech recognition. In *Proceedings of the 28th Pacific Asia Conference on Language, Information and Computing*, pages 178–184.

Ettien Koffi. 2020. A Tutorial on Acoustic Phonetic Feature Extraction for Automatic Speech Recognition (ASR) and Text-to-Speech (TTS) Applications in African Languages. *Linguistic Portfolios*, 9(1):11.

Haakon S. Krohn. 2020. Diccionario digital bilingüe bribri. `http://www.haakonkrohn.com/bribri`.

Julius Kunze, Louis Kirsch, Ilia Kurenkov, Andreas Krug, Jens Johannsmeier, and Sebastian Stober. 2017. Transfer Learning for Speech Recognition on a Budget. *arXiv preprint arXiv:1706.00290.*

Tan Lee, Wai Lau, Yiu Wing Wong, and PC Ching. 2002. Using tone information in Cantonese continuous speech recognition. *ACM Transactions on Asian Language Information Processing (TALIP)*, 1(1):83–102.

Ilse Lehiste and Norman J Lass. 1976. Suprasegmental Features of Speech. *Contemporary issues in experimental phonetics*, 225:239.

Gina-Anne Levow, Emily P Ahn, and Emily M Bender. 2021. Developing a Shared Task for Speech Processing on Endangered Languages. In *Proceedings of the Workshop on Computational Methods for Endangered Languages*, volume 1, pages 96–106.

Xinjian Li, Siddharth Dalmia, Juncheng Li, Matthew Lee, Patrick Littell, Jiali Yao, Antonios Anastasopoulos, David R Mortensen, Graham Neubig, Alan W Black, et al. 2020. Universal phone recognition with a multilingual allophone system. In *ICASSP 2020-2020 IEEE International Conference on Acoustics, Speech and Signal Processing (ICASSP)*, pages 8249–8253. IEEE.

Ian Maddieson. 2013. Tone. In Matthew S. Dryer and Martin Haspelmath, editors, *The World Atlas of Language Structures Online.* Max Planck Institute for Evolutionary Anthropology, Leipzig.

Enrique Margery. 2005. *Diccionario Fraseológico Bribri-Español Español-Bribri*, second edition. Editorial de la Universidad de Costa Rica.

Kohei Matsuura, Sei Ueno, Masato Mimura, Shinsuke Sakai, and Tatsuya Kawahara. 2020. Speech corpus of Ainu folklore and end-to-end speech recognition for Ainu language. *arXiv preprint arXiv:2002.06675.*

Hugo Meinedo, Diamantino Caseiro, Joao Neto, and Isabel Trancoso. 2003. AUDIMUS. media: a Broadcast News speech recognition system for the European Portuguese language. In *International Workshop on Computational Processing of the Portuguese Language*, pages 9–17. Springer.

Florian Metze, Zaid AW Sheikh, Alex Waibel, Jonas Gehring, Kevin Kilgour, Quoc Bao Nguyen, et al. 2013. Models of tone for tonal and non-tonal languages. In *2013 IEEE Workshop on Automatic Speech Recognition and Understanding*, pages 261–266. IEEE.

Josh Meyer. 2019. *Multi-task and transfer learning in low-resource speech recognition*. Ph.D. thesis, The University of Arizona.

Alexis Michaud, Oliver Adams, Christopher Cox, and Séverine Guillaume. 2019. Phonetic lessons from automatic phonemic transcription: preliminary reflections on Na (Sino-Tibetan) and Tsuut'ina (Dene) data. In *ICPhS XIX (19th International Congress of Phonetic Sciences)*.

Christopher Moseley. 2010. *Atlas of the World's Languages in Danger*. Unesco.

Quoc Bao Nguyen, Van Tuan Mai, Quang Trung Le, Ba Quyen Dam, and Van Hai Do. 2018. Development of a Vietnamese Large Vocabulary Continuous Speech Recognition System under Noisy Conditions. In *Proceedings of the Ninth International Symposium on Information and Communication Technology*, pages 222–226.

Thị Lan Nguyễn and Đỗ Đạt Trần. 2012. Tonal Coarticulation on Particles in Vietnamese Language. In *International Conference on Asian Language Processing*, pages 221–224.

Jianwei Niu, Lei Xie, Lei Jia, and Na Hu. 2013. Context-dependent deep neural networks for commercial Mandarin speech recognition applications. In *2013 Asia-Pacific Signal and Information Processing Association Annual Summit and Conference*, pages 1–5. IEEE.

Niko Partanen, Mika Hämäläinen, and Tiina Klooster. 2020. Speech Recognition for Endangered and Extinct Samoyedic languages. *arXiv preprint arXiv:2012.05331*.

Daniel Povey, Arnab Ghoshal, Gilles Boulianne, Lukas Burget, Ondrej Glembek, Nagendra Goel, Mirko Hannemann, Petr Motlicek, Yanmin Qian, Petr Schwarz, et al. 2011. The Kaldi Speech Recognition Toolkit. In *IEEE 2011 workshop on automatic speech recognition and understanding*, CONF. IEEE Signal Processing Society.

Carlos Sánchez Avendaño. 2013. Lenguas en peligro en Costa Rica: vitalidad, documentación y descripción. *Revista Káñina*, 37(1):219–250.

Jiulong Shan, Genqing Wu, Zhihong Hu, Xiliu Tang, Martin Jansche, and Pedro J Moreno. 2010. Search by Voice in Mandarin Chinese. In *Eleventh Annual Conference of the International Speech Communication Association*.

Jiatong Shi, Jonathan Amith, Rey Castillo García, Esteban Guadalupe Sierra, Kevin Duh, and Shinji Watanabe. 2021. Leveraging End-to-End ASR for Endangered Language Documentation: An Empirical Study on Yoloxóchitl Mixtec. *arXiv preprint arXiv:2101.10877*.

Katrina Elizabeth Tang. 2008. *The Phonology and Phonetics of Consonant-Tone Interaction*. Ph.D. thesis.

Bao Thai, Robert Jimerson, Dominic Arcoraci, Emily Prud'hommeaux, and Raymond Ptucha. 2019. Synthetic data augmentation for improving low-resource ASR. In *2019 IEEE Western New York Image and Signal Processing Workshop (WNYISPW)*, pages 1–9. IEEE.

Changhan Wang, Juan Pino, and Jiatao Gu. 2020. Improving Cross-Lingual Transfer Learning for End-to-End Speech Recognition with Speech Translation. *arXiv preprint arXiv:2006.05474*.

Dong Wang and Thomas Fang Zheng. 2015. Transfer learning for speech and language processing. In *2015 Asia-Pacific Signal and Information Processing Association Annual Summit and Conference (APSIPA)*, pages 1225–1237. IEEE.

Guillaume Wisniewski, Alexis Michaud, and Séverine Guillaume. 2020. Phonemic transcription of low-resource languages: To what extent can preprocessing be automated? In *1st Joint SLTU (Spoken Language Technologies for Under-resourced languages) and CCURL (Collaboration and Computing for Under-Resourced Languages) Workshop*, pages 306–315. European Language Resources Association (ELRA).

Yi Xu. 1997. Contextual Tonal Variations in Mandarin. *Journal of phonetics*, 25(1):61–83.

Moira Yip. 2002. *Tone. Cambridge Textbooks in Linguistics*. Cambridge University Press.

Shahrul Azmi Mohd Yusof, Abdulwahab Funsho Atanda, and M Hariharan. 2013. A Review of Yorùbá Automatic Speech Recognition. In *2013 IEEE 3rd International Conference on System Engineering and Technology*, pages 242–247. IEEE.

Alexander Zahrer, Andrej Zgank, and Barbara Schuppler. 2020. Towards building an automatic transcription system for language documentation: Experiences from Muyu. In *Proceedings of The 12th Language Resources and Evaluation Conference*, pages 2893–2900.

Rodolfo Zevallos, Johanna Cordova, and Luis Camacho. 2019. Automatic Speech Recognition of Quechua Language Using HMM Toolkit. In *Annual International Symposium on Information Management and Big Data*, pages 61–68. Springer.

Appendix A: Additional Transcription Examples

Target	ToneSep	AllFeats	ToneNasSepWL	Meaning
dawáska e' ta̱ be' mi̱'ke̱ sulë̀ wa i wéblök	dawáska e' ta̱ wa̱ e' mi̱'ke̱ sulë̀ wa wéblö 14%	dawáska e' ta̱ ma̱ mi̱'ke̱ sulë̀ wa wéblö 14%	dawáska ta̱ mi̱'ke̱ sulë̀ wa wé̱rö 28%	'during the summer then, you go with your arrow to see them'
dùala tso'i̱a̱ kàl a̱	dùla tso'i̱a̱ kàl a̱ 5%	dùala tso'i̱a̱ kàl ta̱ 5%	dúla tso' akàla 42%	'There are birds on the trees.'
iku̱á̱ki̱ iku̱á̱ki̱ sa' é̱n a̱ i̱à̱ne̱ bua'ë	iku̱á̱ki̱ iku̱á̱ki̱ sa' i̱à̱ne̱ bua'ë 14%	iku̱á̱ki̱ iku̱á̱ki̱ se' mí̱a̱ irir bua'ë 26%	wè̱k iku̱á̱ki̱ sa' i̱à̱ne̱ bua'ë 30%	'the others, the others, we understand them well'
sìkua i kiè setenta años	sìkua i kiè setenta años 0%	sìkua i kiè setenta a̱ṉ̃ì̱ 13%	síkwa kë̀ se' kë̀ ta̱' 63%	'[in the] Spanish [language] they say *seventy years* [old]'

Table 6: Additional examples of Kaldi transcriptions for three of the experimental conditions, trained with triphone-trigram models. The numbers represent the character error rate (CER) between the transcription and the target sentence. The fourth example includes code-switching into Spanish.

Towards a morphological transducer and orthography converter for Western Tlacolula Valley Zapotec

Jonathan N. Washington
Swarthmore College
500 College Ave.
Swarthmore, PA 19081 USA
jonathan.washington@swarthmore.edu

Felipe H. Lopez
Pueblo of San Lucas Quiaviní &
Haverford College Libraries
370 Lancaster Ave.
Haverford, PA 19072
lieb@ucla.edu

Brook Danielle Lillehaugen
Haverford College
370 Lancaster Ave.
Haverford, PA 19072
blilleha@haverford.edu

Abstract

This paper presents work towards a morphological transducer and orthography converter for Dizhsa, or San Lucas Quiaviní Zapotec, an endangered Western Tlacolula Valley Zapotec language. The implementation of various aspects of the language's morphology is presented, as well as the transducer's ability to perform analysis in two orthographies and convert between them. Potential uses of the transducer for language maintenance and issues of licensing are also discussed. Evaluation of the transducer shows that it is fairly robust although incomplete, and evaluation of orthographic conversion shows that this method is strongly affected by the coverage of the transducer.

1 Introduction

In this paper, we present work towards a morphological transducer and orthography converter for Dizhsa, also known in the academic literature as San Lucas Quiaviní Zapotec (SLQZ), an endangered language variety of Western Tlacolula Valley Zapotec [zab].[1] To our knowledge, this is the first computational implementation of the morphology of a Zapotec language. (Throughout the paper we use the term "language variety" in place of "dialect" because of the pejorative force of the word *dialecto* in Spanish.)

A morphological transducer, implemented as a finite-state transducer (FST), is a tool that performs morphological analysis (converts between a word form and a morphological analysis) and morphological generation (the reverse). For example, a form like *gunydirëng* 'they won't do' can be quickly converted to an analysis like `uny<v><tv><irre><neg>+ëng<prn><pers><p3><prox><pl>` (read as the negative irrealis form of the transitive verb whose stem is "uny", followed by a 3rd person proximal plural personal pronominal enclitic); similarly, the analysis can be quickly converted to the form.

Not all speakers of SLQZ write their language, though more and more are doing so (Lillehaugen, 2016). There are published proposals for two orthographies, which we refer to as the phonemic orthography (Munro & Lopez et al., 1999) and the simple orthography (Munro et al., 2021). An orthography converter between these two orthographies based on the morphological transducer has been developed as part of this work.

Both tools have the potential to support language maintenance efforts. A morphological transducer can be used in various types of computer-assisted language learning software, such as for learning vocabulary (Katinskaia et al., 2018) and complex inflectional systems (Antonsen et al., 2013). FSTs are also used in electronic corpora (Saykhunov et al., 2019), paradigm generators,[2] text-reading tools,[3] and form-lookup dictionaries (Johnson et al., 2013). FSTs may be trivially converted to spell checkers (Washington et al., 2021) and can also be used in other types of text-proofing and language-learning tools (e.g., Antonsen, 2012); they can further serve as core elements of machine translation systems (Khanna et al., 2021).

Morphological transducers are being developed for languages globally (Khanna et al., 2021), including for entire language families, such as Turkic (Washington et al., 2021). Some of these FSTs are developed for languages with large corpora, such as the national languages of Western Europe (Khanna et al., 2021). One advantage of FSTs is that they can be created for a language without a large quantity of existing text. For example, a morphological trans-

[1] The tools presented in this paper are available publicly under a free/open-source license `https://github.com/apertium/apertium-zab`, and can be used online at `https://beta.apertium.org`.

The three authors recognise that we live and work on the homeland of the Lenape, and pay respect and honor to the caretakers of this land, from time immemorial until now, and into the future.

[2] Such as the prototype at `https://apertium.github.io/apertium-paradigmatrix`

[3] Such as `https://sanit.oahpa.no/read/`.

Proceedings of the First Workshop on Natural Language Processing for Indigenous Languages of the Americas, pages 185–193
June 11, 2021. ©2021 Association for Computational Linguistics

ducer has been developed for Zacatlán-Ahuacatlán-Tepetzintla Nahuatl (Pugh et al., 2021), a threatened language of Central Mexico with a relatively small corpus of texts. The fact that a morphological transducer can be developed with small corpora creates an entry point especially for threatened languages into the potential benefits of the types of language technology described above.

This paper is structured as follows. Section 2 situates SLQZ and overviews its socio-political context and basic morphological properties. Section 3 describes the morphological transducer and demonstrates several of the challenges which were overcome in its implementation. Section 4 presents a basic evaluation, including naïve coverage and accuracy of orthographic conversion. Section 5 overviews some issues related to licensing of the tools and section 6 concludes.

2 San Lucas Quiaviní Zapotec

San Lucas Quiaviní Zapotec is spoken by 98% of the population in San Lucas Quiaviní, Oaxaca, Mexico (DIEGPO, 2015) and by diaspora communities elsewhere in Mexico and the United States, especially the greater Los Angeles area (Lopez and Munro, 1999), with approximately 3500 total speakers. While children are still acquiring the variety as their first language, it should be considered endangered as the community is shifting to Spanish in more and more contexts (Munro, 2003; Pérez Báez, 2009).

Western Tlacolula Valley Zapotec encompasses a number of related varieties, with varying degrees of mutual intelligibility. In the present work we focus on the variety of San Lucas Quiaviní (SLQZ), but we also evaluate the transducer on the variety of San Juan Guelavía (SJGZ), also classified as Western Tlacolula Valley Zapotec. The two pueblos are separated by no more than 10km, but the two varieties of Zapotec differ in many relevant aspects of their grammar, including tone and phonation contrasts, verbal morphophonology, and pronominal systems.

Understanding the morphotactics of SLQZ is essential to developing a morphological transducer. A verb form in SLQZ includes at minimum an aspect marker followed by a verb stem, with very few exceptions. Additionally, a negative-marking enclitic, various other adverbial enclitics (Lee, 2006, 26–27), and pronominal enclitcs may follow. Nouns generally may be marked as possessed using a prefix—with some suppletive forms and a class of "essentially possessed" nouns which are always interpreted as possessed. Possessors follow possessed nouns, either as independent noun phrases or as pronominal enclitics. Pronominal enclitics also appear after predicate adjectives.

The morphophonology of verb forms in SLQZ is complex. Aspectual prefixes often have multiple realisations. Additionally, there is a large number of verbs whose stems alternate irregularly or are synchronically suppletive depending on aspect, subject, and any following enclitics. Some aspect markers have irregular realisations in these forms. There may also be changes in phonation type before certain enclitics.

San Lucas Quiaviní Zapotec has a very complicated system of tone and phonation with over 23 potential contrasts in a stressed syllable (although see Chávez Peón, 2010 for a different count). Representing all of these contrasts results in an orthography that is complicated. Members of the speech community have directly and indirectly expressed preference for a practical orthography that underrepresents these contrasts. Hence a phonemic orthography (described first in Munro & Lopez et al., 1999) is used in dictionaries and linguistic work, and a simplified orthography (described in Munro et al., 2021) which collapses many phonemic distinctions, is preferred by speakers of the language. Being able to convert the simplified practical orthography to the phonemic orthography would allow linguists and speech scientists to recover the phonemic contrasts from text written in the practical orthography.

3 Implementation

The transducer was implemented manually using the two-level approach (Koskenniemi, 1983) and is designed for use with HFST (Lindén et al., 2011), an open-source toolkit for finite-state morphology. In the two-level approach to morphology, the lexicon and morphotactics of a language are implemented in one finite-state transducer (FST), the morphophonology is implemented in another, and they two are intersected into a single FST with an analysis side and a form side. For the Dizsha transducer described here, both the morphotactics and morphophonology compile from hand-written patterns, lexicons, and rules. The `lexd` compiler (Swanson and Howell, 2021) was used to implement the morphotactics, and `twol` (part of HFST) was used to implement the morphophonology.

The grammatical patterns of SLQZ were implemented in these formalisms by the first author in part while receiving classroom instruction in the language from the second author and based largely on patterns observed in the first volume of a Dizhsa textbook (Munro et al., 2021). Later the transducer was expanded and revised in consultation with additional volumes of the textbook and other sources cited here, and under the guidance of the second and third authors, the former of whom is a native speaker and teacher of Dizhsa, and the latter of whom is a linguist with expertise in the language.

In section 3.1, the size and shape of the transducer's lexicon is presented. Section 3.2 discusses some design decisions and how some spelling variants were handled. We explain how some aspects of the language's morphotactics (section 3.3) and morphophonology (section 3.4) were implemented. Section 3.5 presents how orthography conversion was implemented.

3.1 Lexicon

The lexical entries of the transducer are divided by stem type based on morphological patterning. Table 1 shows the number of stems of various types in the transducer, and the overall number of stems.

Category	№ stems
Proper nouns	289
Nouns	133
Verbs	92
Pronouns	46
Complex verb elements	28
Adverbs	26
Punctuation	22
Numbers	31
Prepositions	17
Adjectives & determiners	10
Interjections & modal particles	10
Conjunctions	7
total	711

Table 1: The size of the transducer's entire lexicon, broken down by individual lexicons, corresponding to lexical category.

Several of these categories span multiple lexicons. For example, under "verbs" are counted regular verb stems, irregular verb stems (currently spanning two lexd lexicons), and the copula. Additionally, verbs are subcategorised as intransitive (`<iv>`), transitive (`<tv>`), and ditransitive (`<dtv>`). "Pronouns" include both bound and free forms, which must be in separate lexicons due to their different morphological distribution.

3.2 Design decisions

Despite being the best studied variety of Western Tlacolula Valley Zapotec, many aspects of the grammar of SLQZ are not fully documented or described. Even when the patterns are understood, it is not clear whether particular phenomena are best accounted for through morphology or syntax.

For this reason, in many cases during the construction of the transducer, more than one implementation option seemed reasonable. For example, we chose to analyse verb stems followed by the negative marker ⟨di⟩~⟨dy⟩ as an inflected form of the verb stem, as in `uny<v><tv><irre><neg>+ëng<prn><pers><p3><prox><pl>` for *gunydirëng*. We could also have chosen to analyse it as a verb stem followed by an adverbial enclitic, e.g. `uny<v><tv><irre>+di<adv>+ëng<prn><pers><p3><prox><pl>`.

Another such decision is the choice to use verb stems as the lemma for all forms of a verb, and in the case of suppletive stems, the stem that patterns with the habitual aspect. Dictionaries for speakers and learners, such as the glossary in Munro et al. (2021), use the habitual form (prefix+stem) as the headword for entries. The transducer could just as easily use the habitual form as the lemma.

We made similar decisions regarding the lexicon. Some words in SLQZ have common variant pronunciations and corresponding spellings. For example, the word for 'fish' may be spelled *bel* or *beld*. In this case the lemma was chosen to be *beld*, but the generated form was chosen to be *bel*. The form *beld* is still analysed to the same lemma. This was implemented by adding the entry to the transducer with both spellings, and including a comment on the analyse-only variant that triggers the compiler to remove that line while creating the generator, but not the analyser. The lines corresponding to these entries are shown in Code Block 1.

```
beld:bel  behlld:behll   # "fish"
beld:beld behlld:behlld  # "fish" ! Dir/LR
```

Code Block 1: The entries in the `lexd` file for the word for 'fish'. All material after the # symbol is ignored by the compiler, but a preprocessing command strips all lines containing `Dir/LR` before compiling the generator transducer (but not the analyser transducer).

These analyses reflect our best current understanding of the grammar, but it would be trivial to change the implementation in the future.

3.3 Verbal morphotactics

A verb in SLQZ includes an obligatory prefix that signals aspect, optional endings that include a verbal extender (adding politeness) and a negative morpheme, and optional pronominal clitics. This was implemented fairly straightforwardly by defining a general pattern in lexd, shown in Code Block 2.

```
( :Aspect ( V-Stems(1) [<v>:] V-Stems(3):
) V-Extender(1)? Aspect: ) V-Neg(1)?
Prn-Bound(1)
```

Code Block 2: The pattern used for regular verbs in the SLQZ transducer. The numbers in parentheses after each element reference "components", described in section 3.5. The `:` character indicates separation of analysis and form. The `?` character represents optionality. The parentheses after lexicon names indicate column numbers within lexicons. The parentheses grouping parts of the pattern are not strictly necessary, but speed up compilation due to how matching works (described below).

The reason `lexd` was used instead of HFST's `lexc` or Lttoolbox's `dix` formats—the most common choices for implementing a transducer of this type—is because `dix` is not ideal for agglutinative patterns and `lexc` requires complicated tricks (flag diacritics or filter transducers) to implement prefixational morphology. The conventional structure of tag-based morphological analyses is a lemma followed by a part of speech tag, followed by any subcategory tags, followed by any grammatical tags. In an example like *runy* (form) `uny<v><tv><hab>` (analysis), the analysis presents that `uny` is the lemma (in this case a verb stem), `<v>` (verb) is the category of the word, `<tv>` (transitive) is the subcategory of the word, and `<hab>` (habitual) is a grammatical property of the form. Thus in a transducer we can define the form-analysis pairs `<hab>:r` and `uny<v><tv>:uny`, but if combined in that order, the result would be unconventional `<hab>uny<v><tv>:runy`.

The solution to this is lexicon matching, a feature unique to `lexd`. For SLQZ, we can create an `Aspect` lexicon (containing prefixes paired to their analyses, e.g. `<hab>:r`) and a `V-Stems` lexicon (which lists regular verbs). In the pattern that combines these lexicons shown in Code Block 2, the `lexd` compiler keeps track of multiple mentions of a lexicon and matches them. That is, instead of producing forms with all combinations of aspectual prefixes and tags, only the elements of pairs on the same line are used, despite the fact that the elements are referenced at different places in the pattern.

Another lexd-specific feature employed is columns within lexicons. In the pattern, columns 1 and 3 of the `V-Stems` lexicon are referenced. These contain the simple-orthography form of verbs and the subcategory (transitivity) tag, respectively.

Some SLQZ verbs have irregular alternations in their stems when combined with perfective aspect prefixes or a first person plural (1PL) subject. This was implemented using filters in lexd, which allows for entries in a given lexicon which are tagged a certain way to be referenced from patterns, to the exclusion of other entries in that lexicon. In this way, separate patterns can be constructed that pull, e.g., (1) only the 1PL stems and pronoun forms, and (2) only the non-1PL stems and pronoun forms.

3.4 Verbal morphophonology

Many of the phonological alternations in SLQZ verb forms are regular. For example, the negative marker is written before a vowel as ⟨dy⟩, as in *queity runydyai / que'ity ruhnydya'ih* 'I don't do it' and elsewhere as ⟨di⟩ (simplified orthography) ⟨di'⟩ (phonemic orthography), as in *queity runydi Jwanyi / que'ity ruhnydi' Jwaanyih* 'Juan doesn't do it'.

This alternation is implemented by specifying the morpheme with a special character in the morphotactic transducer (`lexd`), as `<neg>:d{I}` and `<neg>:d{I}'` (depending on orthography), and then controlling the alternation of the `{I}` character using a morphophonology transducer (written in `twol`).

The `twol` formalism allows for symbol mappings to be restricted based on context. The mappings needed to condition the correct forms of the ⟨di(')⟩/⟨dy⟩ alternation are presented in Code Block 3. The compiled FST is intersected with the morphotactic transducer to produce correct forms.

```
"di' → dy before vowels: {I}"
%{I%}:y <=> _ (':) %>:* :0* :Vow ;

"di' → dy before vowels: '"
':0 <=> %{I%}:y _ ;
```

Code Block 3: Morphophonological mapping restrictions specified in the `twol` formalism to condition the alternation of `d{I}(')` as ⟨dy⟩ before vowels. In other contexts, `{I}` is realised as ⟨i⟩.[4]

In the transducer's `twol` file, there are currently 10 characters like `{I}` defined, and 20 mapping restrictions specified.

3.5 Orthography

This section outlines both the orthographic support of the transducer and how it is able to be used to convert between orthographies.

The morphological transducer is compiled into two generators: one for each of the simple and phonemic orthographies. A single analyser is compiled that supports both. This is made possible through a combination of the lexd features of lexicon matching and columns in lexicons, both discussed in section 3.3. For example the phonemic-orthography pattern for regular verbs is shown in Code Block 4, and can be compared to the pattern used for simple-orthography regular verbs shown in Code Block 2. The difference between these patterns lies in which column of the lexicons are referenced on the form side. For example, the verb stem lexicon is referenced using `V-Stems(1):V-Stems(2)` instead of `V-Stems(1)` (equivalent to `V-Stems(1):V-Stems(1)`). The second column of the `V-Stem` lexicon (and most lexicons in the transducer, cf. Code Block 1) is the phonemic-orthography form of each stem. The two sides of the lexicon are matched, as opposed to all elements of the first column being paired with all elements of the second column.

```
( :Aspect ( V-Stems(1):V-Stems(2) [<v>:]
V-Stems(3): ) V-Extender(2)? Aspect: )
V-Neg(2)? Prn-Bound(1):Prn-Bound(2)
```

Code Block 4: The pattern used for phonemic-orthography regular verbs used in the SLQZ transducer.

The other crucial part of this approach is control symbols in comments at the end of patterns for each orthography. Specifically, `Orth/Simp` is added to the end of lines containing simple-orthography patterns and `Orth/Dict` is added to the end of lines containing phonemic-orthography patterns. Then, as part of the compilation process for the transducer in each orthography, lines containing the control symbols for the other orthography are removed. This ensures that each transducer contains only forms in a single orthography. The respective analysers and generators are compiled from these pared-down `lexd` files, and the two analysers are unioned, resulting in an analyser that supports both orthographies.

The simple orthography, as discussed in section 2, collapses many of the distinctions made by the phonemic orthography. Because of this, it is mostly trivial to convert from the phonemic orthography to the simple orthography, but not vice versa.

For example, a word like *xyecwa* (simple) / *x:yèe'cwa'* (phonemic) 'my dog' can be converted from phonemic to simple orthography by simply removing the diacritics ⟨:⟩, ⟨`⟩, and ⟨'⟩, and simplifying sequences of repeated vowels. The only other changes needed for most words is the simplification of doubled consonant letters ⟨ll⟩, ⟨mm⟩, and ⟨nn⟩, and the removal of ⟨h⟩ after vowels, e.g. *behlld* → *beld* 'fish'; *rille'eh* → *rile* 'knows how to'. However, as these examples show, conversion in the other direction is non-deterministic.

To convert between the orthographies, then, two transducers which share an interface are intersected along that interface. Specifically, the analyser in one orthography is intersected with the generator in the other orthography along the analysis side of each. This is possible because the analysis side is the same regardless of the orthography. An example of this method applied to one word is shown in Figure 1.

(simplified orthography analyser)

xyecwa

↕

`becw<n><px>+a<prn><pers><pl><sg>`

∩

`becw<n><px>+a<prn><pers><pl><sg>`

↕

x:yèe'cwa'

(phonemic orthography generator)

Figure 1: Demonstration of the intersection of two transducers to create an orthographic converter. In this example, an analysis in the simplified orthography analyser is matched to an analysis in the phonemic orthography generator, so that when a simplified orthography form is input to the resulting transducer, the corresponding phonemic orthography form is generated.

This approach provides fairly deterministic output, although as discussed in section 4.3, it does not solve the issue of simple-orthography homography.

One additional approach was used to handle orthographic variants, such as any of the apostrophe characters which might be used and the orthography of the Universal Declaration of Human Rights (UDHR) translation, which is like the phonemic or-

[4]For more on the `twol` formalism and its application, see `https://github.com/hfst/hfst/wiki/HfstTwolc`.

thography but uses a colon after a vowel to indicate creaky voice, represent by a grave accent over the vowel in the modern version of the phonemic orthography and in the `lexd` file. A "spellrelax" file, containing a series of regular expressions like those shown in Code Block 5, is compiled to an FST and intersected with an analyser. This allows it to accept forms with any of the specified variants used.

```
[ ?* [ ’ (->) [ %' | %’ | %` | %´ | %ʻ | %‘
] ] ?* ] .o.
[ ?* ( à (->) [ a [ %: | ː ] ] ) ?* ]
```

Code Block 5: Two of the regular expressions contained in the spellrelax file. The first one allows any number of apostrophe characters to be used in place of ⟨’⟩, and the second one allows for ⟨a⟩ followed by one of two colon characters to be used in place of ⟨à⟩. The `.o.` symbol conjoins the patterns.

4 Evaluation

The transducer was evaluated over available texts (4.1) for naïve coverage (4.2) and accuracy of orthographic conversion (4.3).

4.1 Texts used for evaluation

The transducer was evaluated against a number of available texts, including a number of genres in both the simple and phonemic orthographies.

The first two parts of the story *Blal xte Tiu Pamyël* (BxTP) are part of Munro et al. (2021), which is also the source for nearly all of the material in the transducer. A preliminary version of the transducer was evaluated using BxTP parts 1–2, whereafter the transducer was expanded to include unrecognised forms. Hence, BxTP parts 1–2 are treated as development data, and the remaining texts are treated as previously unseen data. Evaluating the transducer over BxTP parts 1–2 also allowed us to observe and correct mismatches between the phonemic and simplified orthographic versions.

A number of poems and stories were also used for evaluation. Those from Tlalocan are in individualised orthographies inspired by the phonemic orthography (Munro, 2014). There is also a blog post from the Ticha blog entirely in Dizhsa. The Universal Declaration of Human Rights (UDHR) is in an older version of the phonemic orthography, which is easily handled by the transducer due to the addition of some spellrelax mappings.

We also evaluated a translation of the New Testament in SJGZ, a language variety closely related to SLQZ which uses a distinct orthography.

The complete list of texts is presented in Table 2, along with naïve coverage results (see section 4.2). The sources for each set of texts are described in footnotes to the table.[5]

4.2 Naïve coverage

Naïve coverage was calculated as the percentage of tokens in a given corpus that received an analysis from the transducer, whether correct or not. Results are shown in Table 2.

The results show that the development text has good coverage, at over 90%—higher, not unexpectedly, than coverage over the remaining sources. Unseen texts vary, but average around two thirds coverage, as does the coverage over all available material. This indicates that the transducer has a solid base, but has many opportunities for expansion. It should also be noted that the development text, besides functioning as a graded reader in an introductory textbook for the language, is relatively short, and so lacks a wide range of vocabulary and morphological patterns.

The lower overall coverage on texts in the phonemic orthography is due primarily to the lack of phonological mappings accounting for all diacritic changes in verb forms, and the homography of the simple orthography. In the simple orthography many words are written the same that are written distinctly in the phonemic orthography. Words that are not in the transducer may receive an incorrect analysis, thus inflating the apparent coverage of texts in the simple orthography.

The individualised orthographies found in the Tlalocan texts are inspired by, but not the same as, the phonemic orthography, yielding much lower coverage results.

The translation of the New Testament in the related language variety of SJGZ, totalling 217K tokens, was also evaluated to test whether the SLQZ transducer could be applied to Western Tlacolula

[5]The entire set of texts is currently available at `https://github.com/jonorthwash/apertium-zab-corpus`. All testing was done on the contents of the transducer repository at revision `0866ec3` and the corpus repository at revision `85fda5c`.

[6]Munro et al. (2021)

[7]Drawn from Lopez and Lillehaugen (2018), Lopez and Lillehaugen (2017), and `https://felipehlopez.weebly.com/`.

[8]Chávez Peón and López Reyes (2009)

[9]Lopez (2018)

[10]`https://ticha.haverford.edu/updates/`

[11]`https://www.ohchr.org/EN/UDHR/Pages/Language.aspx?LangID=ztu1`

Use	Text	Orthography	Tokens	Coverage (%)
development	*Blal xte Tiu Pamyël* 1–2[6]	Simple	625	93.92
		Phonemic	628	91.40
testing	*Blal xte Tiu Pamyël* 3–7	Simple	1532	73.56
	Blal xte Tiu Pamyël 3–4	Phonemic	601	66.89
	Felipe H. Lopez poetry[7]	Simple	514	57.39
	Tlalocan poems & story[8]	Simple	635	57.95
		Individualised	788	47.72
	Niny Bac[6]	Simple	366	73.77
	Liaza Chaa[9]	Simple	963	58.67
	Ticha post 2020-07-17[10]	Simple	1026	60.04
	UDHR (9 articles)[6]	Simple	433	69.98
	UDHR (complete)[11]	Phonemic	1641	65.63
total	all	mixed	9934	67.47

Table 2: Naïve coverage results. BxTP 1–2 was used for development, and the remaining texts were used for testing. Tokens is the number of lexical units according to the transducer, and coverage is the percentage of tokens that received at least one analysis from the transducer.

Valley Zapotec more broadly. Even with a dedicated spellrelax transducer to account for a number of orthographic differences, the coverage was only a little over 34%. This suggests that perhaps a single transducer for Western Tlacolula Valley Zapotec may not be able to be applied to all varieties.

4.3 Orthographic conversion

The first four sections of *Blal xte Tiu Pamyël* are available in both the simple and phonemic orthography. To test orthographic conversion, we created two groups of texts, the first group consisting of sections 1 and 2 of BxTP and the second group consisting of sections 3 and 4.

The conversion of phonemic to simple orthography is almost entirely deterministic. We set up a simple regular expression (regex) replacement conversion system, which removed diacritics and ⟨h⟩ after vowels and also merged adjacent characters which were identical. The performance of this method provides a baseline measure of similarity between the two texts.

Performance was measured using Word Error Rate (WER), or the percentage of words that are different between the converted text and the "gold standard" of the text in the destination orthography. The results of both the regex-based method and the transducer-based method described in section 3.5 are presented in table 3.

The performance of the transducer-based approach has a ceiling defined by the level of coverage and the similarity of the two texts. For example, for phonemic→simple conversion of the first text, it would be impossible to get better (lower) than 8.6% WER, since the text has naïve coverage of 91.4%. None of the words which do not have an analysis in the transducer are able to be converted—although there is a possibility that some of those words would be "free rides", or words that are the same in both orthographies. The result of 11.78% WER should be taken in the context of this ceiling.

In the first group (BxTP 1–2), the simple-to-phonemic conversion performed worse than phonemic-to-simple, despite higher coverage of the source version. This is largely due to homography. While performing disambiguation between available analyses before orthography conversion might improve this result, there are some simple-orthography homographs that may never be possible to accurately decide between (without wider context), such as *re*, corresponding to both phonemic-orthography *rèe* 'that' and *rèe'* 'this'.

The second group of texts (BxTP 3–4) has much lower correspondence between the two orthographies than the first group due to slight differences between the texts, such as words or sentences that seem to be present in one version but absent in the other. That together with the lower coverage over the second group to start with compound for much worse performance.

While phonemic→simple orthography conversion is deterministic (and hence possible to perform

Text	Direction	Method	Tokens	Coverage (%)	WER (%)
Blal xte Tiu Pamyël 1–2	Simple→Phonemic	transducer	625	93.92	20.10
	Phonemic→Simple	transducer	628	91.40	11.78
	Phonemic→Simple	regex	"	"	1.63
Blal xte Tiu Pamyël 3–4	Simple→Phonemic	transducer	574	77.53	46.75
	Phonemic→Simple	transducer	601	66.89	46.79
	Phonemic→Simple	regex	"	"	10.35

Table 3: Orthographic conversion accuracy. Tokens is the number of lexical units according to the transducer, coverage is the percentage of tokens that received at least one analysis from the transducer, and WER is word error rate, or the percentage of tokens after orthography conversion that do not correspond to the text in the other orthography.

accurately with a series of regular expressions), simple→phonemic conversion is not, and hence must be done in some other way. These initial experiments in using a lexical approach show that it is a viable method, although it currently suffers from the low overall coverage of the transducer.

5 Licensing

We have chosen to license this work under the GNU Affero General Public License (AGPL) because we want it to be available for others to use and build on. This work is also part of a long-term commitment to collaboration with Zapotec communities and community members. The AGPL license allows for uses of our work that would be inconsistent with our commitment to the community.

Reciprocity is a defining Zapotec cultural value and practice. Zapotec speakers have shared their knowledge and language in the creation of these resources. Others are allowed to use the tools and in doing so enter into a reciprocal commitment with the Zapotec community that we define in what we call the Guelaguetza clause, shown below:

> While licensed under a free/open-source license that permits commercial uses, it is expected that anything created using this resource be made available to the community of San Lucas Quiaviní free of charge. This is consistent with the community's practice of guelaguetza, a complex system of reciprocity and exchange of goods and labor.

This context reminds us that the more broadly available licenses could use refinements in particular cultural contexts, particularly Indigenous contexts, and that the field should be open to discussions of how culturally specific practices may interact with open source licensing.

6 Conclusion

This paper has overviewed the development of a morphological transducer and orthography converter for San Lucas Quiaviní Zapotec.

An evaluation of the analyser over available texts demonstrates that despite being incomplete, it is fairly robust. Future work to improve the transducer will focus on expanding the lexicon, adding missing morphological patterns, refining the morphophonological patterns, and finding better ways to deal with the nuances of SLQZ verb morphology.

Text in another variety of Western Tlacolula Valley Zapotec was evaluated using the morphological transducer, and the results suggest that a separate transducer might be needed.

An evaluation of the orthography converter shows that this method of orthography conversion has potential, but is affected heavily by the coverage of the transducer.

It is our hope that this resource will be useful to the SLQZ community. In particular, we are excited about the many roles it could play in language maintenance efforts. This work also impacts conversations on language technology for under-resourced languages and open licensing in Indigenous contexts.

Acknowledgements

The authors are grateful to the anonymous reviewers and editors of this volume. We also thank Daniel Swanson for his assistance with lexd. Felipe and Brook express their gratitude to Pamela Munro, who was integral in their understanding of Zapotec grammar. Runybia ra xauzanën, ra Bunyza ni za Quiabni, bsan Dizhsa ni zezaneën nazhi.

References

Lene Antonsen. 2012. Improving feedback on L2 misspellings – an FST approach. In *Proceedings of the SLTC 2012 workshop on NLP for CALL*, pages 1–10.

Lene Antonsen, Ryan Johnson, Trond Trosterud, and Heli Uibo. 2013. Generating modular grammar exercises with finite-state transducers. In *Proceedings of the second workshop on NLP for computer-assisted language learning at NODALIDA 2013*, pages 27–38.

Mario E. Chávez Peón. 2010. *The interaction of metrical structure, tone, and phonation types in Quiaviní Zapotec*. Ph.D. thesis, The University of British Columbia.

Mario E. Chávez Peón and Román López Reyes. 2009. Zidgyni zyala rnalaza liu 'Vengo de la luz del amanecer, recordándote'. Cuatro poemas y un cuento del zapoteco del Valle. *Tlalocan*, 16:17–49.

DIEGPO. 2015. San Lucas Quiaviní. libro demográfico.

Ryan Johnson, Lene Antonsen, and Trond Trosterud. 2013. Using finite state transducers for making efficient reading comprehension dictionaries. In *Proceedings of the 19th Nordic Conference of Computational Linguistics (NODALIDA 2013)*, pages 59–71. Linköping University Electronic Press, Sweden.

Anisia Katinskaia, Javad Nouri, and Roman Yangarber. 2018. Revita: a language-learning platform at the intersection of ITS and CALL. In *Proceedings of LREC: 11th International Conference on Language Resources and Evaluation*, Miyazaki, Japan.

Tanmai Khanna, Jonathan N. Washington, Francis M. Tyers, Sevilay Bayatlı, Daniel G. Swanson, Tommi A. Pirinen, Irene Tang, and Hèctor Alòs i Font. 2021. Recent advances in Apertium, a free / open-source rule-based machine translation platform for low-resource languages. *Machine Translation*.

Kimmo Koskenniemi. 1983. *Two-level Morphology: A General Computational Model for Word-Form Recognition and Production*. Ph.D. thesis, University of Helsinki.

Felicia Lee. 2006. *Remnant Raising and VSO Clausal Architecture: A Case Study of San Lucas Quiaviní Zapotec*. Springer, Dordrecht.

Brook Danielle Lillehaugen. 2016. Why write in a language that (almost) no one can read? twitter and the development of written literature. *Language Documentation and Conservation*, 10:356–392.

Krister Lindén, Erik Axelson, Sam Hardwick, Tommi A. Pirinen, and Miikka Silfverberg. 2011. HFST—framework for compiling and applying morphologies. *Communications in Computer and Information Science*, 100:67–85.

Felipe H. Lopez. 2018. Liaza chaa / I'm going home. *Latin American Literature Today*, 1(7). With Brook Danielle Lillehaugen, translator.

Felipe H. Lopez and Brook Danielle Lillehaugen. 2017. Mam and Guepy: Two Valley Zapotec poems. *Latin America Literary Review*, 44(88):83–84.

Felipe H. Lopez and Brook Danielle Lillehaugen, translator. 2018. Seven poems. *Latin American Literature Today*, 1(7).

Felipe H. Lopez and Pamela Munro. 1999. Zapotec immigration: The San Lucas Quiaviní experience. *Aztlán*, 24:129–49.

Pamela Munro. 2003. Preserving the language of the Valley Zapotecs: The orthography question. Presented at Conference on Language and Immigration in France and the United States: Sociolinguistic Perspectives.

Pamela Munro. 2014. Breaking rules for orthography development. In Michael Cahill and Keren Rice, editors, *Developing orthographies for unwritten languages*, pages 169–189. SIL International Publications, Dallas.

Pamela Munro, Brook Danielle Lillehaugen, and Felipe H. Lopez with Benjamin Paul. 2021. *Cali Chiu? A Course in Valley Zapotec*, 2nd edition. Haverford College Libraries Open Educational Resources.

Pamela Munro and Felipe H. Lopez with Rodrigo Garcia & Olivia Mendez. 1999. *Di'csyonaary X:tèe'n Dìi'zh Sah Sann Luu'c (San Lucas Quiaviní Zapotec Dictionary / Diccionario Zapoteco de San Lucas Quiaviní)*. UCLA Chicano Studies Research Center.

Robert Pugh, Francis M. Tyers, and Marivel Huerta Mendez. 2021. Towards an open source finite-state morphological analyzer for Zacatlán-Ahuacatlán-Tepetzintla Nahuatl. In *Proceedings of the 4th Workshop on Computational Methods for Endangered Languages*, volume 1, pages 80–85.

Gabriela Pérez Báez. 2009. *Endangerment of a transnational language: the case of San Lucas Quiaviní Zapotec*. Ph.D. thesis, State University of New York at Buffalo.

M.R. Saykhunov, R.R. Khusainov, and T.I. Ibragimov. 2019. Сложности при создании текстового корпуса объемом более 400 млн токенов. In *Финно-угорский мир в полиэтничном пространстве России: культурное наследие и новые вызовы*, pages 548–554. UdmFITS UrO RAN.

Daniel Swanson and Nick Howell. 2021. Lexd: A finite-state lexicon compiler for non-suffixational morphologies. In Mika Hämäläinen, Niko Partanen, and Khalid Alnajjar, editors, *Multilingual Facilitation*, pages 133–146. Helsingin yliopisto.

Jonathan N. Washington, Ilnar Salimzianov, Francis M. Tyers, Memduh Gökırmak, Sardana Ivanova, and Oğuzhan Kuyrukçu. 2021. Free/open-source technologies for Turkic languages developed in the Apertium project. In *Proceedings of the Seventh International Conference on Computer Processing of Turkic Languages (TurkLang 2019)*.

Peru is Multilingual, Its Machine Translation Should Be Too?

Arturo Oncevay
School of Informatics, ILCC
University of Edinburgh
a.oncevay@ed.ac.uk

Abstract

Peru is a multilingual country with a long history of contact between the indigenous languages and Spanish. Taking advantage of this context for machine translation is possible with multilingual approaches for learning both unsupervised subword segmentation and neural machine translation models. The study proposes the first multilingual translation models for four languages spoken in Peru: Aymara, Ashaninka, Quechua and Shipibo-Konibo, providing both many-to-Spanish and Spanish-to-many models and outperforming pairwise baselines in most of them. The task exploited a large English-Spanish dataset for pre-training, monolingual texts with tagged back-translation, and parallel corpora aligned with English. Finally, by fine-tuning the best models, we also assessed the out-of-domain capabilities in two evaluation datasets for Quechua and a new one for Shipibo-Konibo[1].

1 Introduction

Neural Machine Translation (NMT) has opened several research directions to exploit as many and diverse data as possible. Massive multilingual NMT models, for instance, take advantage of several language-pair datasets in a single system (Johnson et al., 2017). This offers several advantages, such as a simple training process and enhanced performance of the language-pairs with little data (although sometimes detrimental to the high-resource language-pairs). However, massive models of dozens of languages are not necessarily the best outcome, as it is demonstrated that smaller clusters still offer the same benefits (Tan et al., 2019; Oncevay et al., 2020).

Peru offers a rich diversity context for machine translation research with 47 native languages (Simons and Fenning, 2019). All of them are highly distinguishing from Castilian Spanish, the primary official language in the country and the one spoken by the majority of the population. However, from the computational perspective, all of these languages do not have enough resources, such as monolingual or parallel texts, and most of them are considered endangered (Zariquiey et al., 2019).

In this context, the main question then arises: shouldn't machine translation be multilingual for languages spoken in a multilingual country like Peru? By taking advantage of few resources, and other strategies such as multilingual unsupervised subword segmentation models (Kudo, 2018), pre-training with high resource language-pairs (Kocmi and Bojar, 2018), back-translation (Sennrich et al., 2016a), and fine-tuning (Neubig and Hu, 2018), we deployed the first many-to-one and one-to-many multilingual NMT models (paired with Spanish) for four indigenous languages: Aymara, Ashaninka, Quechua and Shipibo-Konibo.

2 Related work

In Peru, before NMT, there were studies in rule-based MT, based on the Apertium platform (Forcada et al., 2011), for Quechua Eastern Apurimac (*qve*) and Quechua Cuzco (*quz*) (Cavero and Madariaga, 2007). Furthermore, Ortega and Pillaipakkamnatt (2018) improved alignments for *quz* by using an agglutinative language as Finnish as a pivot. Apart from the Quechua variants, only Aymara (Coler and Homola, 2014) and Shipibo-Konibo (Galarreta et al., 2017) have been addressed with rule-based and statistical MT, respectively.

Ortega et al. (2020b) for Southern Quechua, and Gómez Montoya et al. (2019) for Shipibo-Konibo, are the only studies that employed sequence-to-sequence NMT models. They also performed transfer learning experiments with potentially related language pairs (e.g. Finnish or Turkish, which are agglutinative languages). However, as far as we know, this is the first study that trains a multilingual model for some language spoken in Peru. For

[1] Available in: https://github.com/aoncevay/mt-peru

Proceedings of the First Workshop on Natural Language Processing for Indigenous Languages of the Americas, pages 194–201
June 11, 2021.

related work on multilingual NMT, we refer the readers to the survey of Dabre et al. (2020).

3 Languages and datasets

To enhance replicability, we only used the datasets provided in the AmericasNLP Shared Task[2].

- **Southern Quechua**: with 6+ millions of speakers and several variants, it is the most widespread indigenous language in Peru. AmericasNLP provides evaluation sets in the standard Southern Quechua, which is based mostly on the Quechua Ayacucho (quy) variant. There is parallel data from dictionaries and Jehovah Witnesses (Agić and Vulić, 2019). There is parallel corpus aligned with English too. We also include the close variant of Quechua Cusco (quz) to support the multilingual learning.
- **Aymara** (aym): with 1.7 million of speakers (mostly in Bolivia). The parallel and monolingual data is extracted from a news website (Global Voices) and distributed by OPUS (Tiedemann, 2012). There are aligned data with English too.
- **Shipibo-Konibo** (shp): a Panoan language with almost 30,000 speakers in the Amazonian region. There are parallel data from dictionaries, educational material (Galarreta et al., 2017), language learning flashcards (Gómez Montoya et al., 2019), plus monolingual data from educational books (Bustamante et al., 2020).
- **Ashaninka** (cni): an Arawakan language with 45,000 speakers in the Amazon. There is parallel data from dictionaries, laws and books (Ortega et al., 2020a), plus monolingual corpus (Bustamante et al., 2020).

The four languages are highly agglutinative or polysynthetic, meaning that they usually express a large amount of information in just one word with several joint morphemes. This is a real challenge for MT and subword segmentation methods, given the high probability of addressing a "rare word" for the system. We also note that each language belongs to a different language family, but that is not a problem for multilingual models, as usually the family-based clusters are not the most effective ones (Oncevay et al., 2020).

[2]https://github.com/AmericasNLP/americasnlp2021

Language	Mono.	es	en
aym - Aymara	8,680	5,475	5,045
cni - Ashaninka	13,193	3,753	
quy - Quechua		104,101	14,465
shp - Shipibo-Konibo	23,593	14,437	
quz - Quechua Cusco		97,836	21,760

Table 1: Number of sentences in monolingual and parallel corpora aligned with Spanish (es) or English (en). The latter are used for en→es translation and we only noted non-duplicated sentences w.r.t. the *–es corpora.

Pre-processing The datasets were noisy and not cleaned. Lines are reduced according to several heuristics: Arabic numbers or punctuation do not match in the parallel sentences, there are more symbols or numbers than words in a sentence, the ratio of words from one side is five times larger or shorter than the other, among others. Table 5 in the Appendix includes the original and cleaned data size per language-pair, whereas Table 1 presents the final sizes.

English-Spanish datasets We consider the EuroParl (1.7M sentences) (Koehn, 2005) and the NewsCommentary-v8 (174k sentences) corpora for pre-training.

4 Methodology

4.1 Evaluation

The train data have been extracted from different domains and sources, which are not necessarily the same as the evaluation sets provided for the Shared Task. Therefore, the official development set (995 sentences per language) is split into three parts: 25%-25%-50%. The first two parts are our custom dev and devtest sets[3]. We add the 50% section to the training set with a sampling distribution of 20%, to reduce the domain gap in the training data. Likewise, we extract a sample of the training and double the size of the development set. The mixed data in the validation set is relevant, as it allows to evaluate how the model fits with all the domains. We used the same multi-text sentences for evaluation, and avoid any overlapping of the Spanish side with the training set, this is also important as we are going to evaluate multilingual models. Evaluation for all the models used BLEU (Papineni et al., 2002) and chrF (Popović, 2015) metrics.

[3]We are also reporting the results on the official test sets after the finalisation of the Shared Task.

BLEU	Aymara			Ashaninka			Quechua			Shipibo-Konibo		
→Spanish	dev	devtest	test	dev	devtest	test	dev	devtest	test	dev	devtest	test
(a) Multilingual	**11.11**	**9.95**	3.70	**8.40**	**9.37**	**5.21**	12.46	11.03	8.04	**10.34**	**12.72**	**10.07**
(b) Multi+BT	10.76	8.39	2.87	7.30	5.34	3.44	11.48	8.85	7.51	9.13	10.77	7.58
(c) Multi+BT[t]	10.72	8.42	2.86	7.45	5.69	3.15	11.37	10.02	7.12	8.81	10.73	7.18
(d) Pairwise	9.46	7.66	2.04	4.23	3.96	2.38	**15.21**	**14.00**	**8.20**	7.72	9.48	4.44
Spanish→	dev	devtest	test	dev	devtest	test	dev	devtest	test	dev	devtest	test
(e) Multilingual	8.67	6.28	2.19	6.74	11.72	**5.54**	10.04	5.37	**4.51**	10.82	10.44	6.69
(f) Multi+BT	3.31	2.59	0.79	1.29	3.38	2.82	1.36	2.02	1.73	1.63	3.76	2.98
(g) Multi+BT[t]	**10.55**	**6.54**	**2.31**	**7.36**	**13.17**	5.40	**10.77**	5.29	4.23	**11.98**	**11.12**	**7.45**
(h) Pairwise	7.08	4.96	1.65	4.12	8.40	3.82	10.67	**6.11**	3.96	8.76	7.89	6.15

Table 2: BLEU scores for the dev and devtest custom partitions and the official test set, including all the multilingual and pairwise MT systems into and from Spanish. BT = Back-translation. BT[t] = Tagged back-translation.

chrF	Aymara			Ashaninka			Quechua			Shipibo-Konibo		
→Spanish	dev	devtest	test	dev	devtest	test	dev	devtest	test	dev	devtest	test
(a) Multilingual	**31.73**	**28.82**	**22.01**	**26.78**	**26.82**	**22.27**	32.92	32.99	29.45	**31.41**	**33.49**	**31.26**
(d) Pairwise	28.77	25.03	19.79	20.43	20.40	18.83	**36.01**	**36.06**	**30.90**	27.25	29.91	25.31
Spanish→	dev	devtest	test	dev	devtest	test	dev	devtest	test	dev	devtest	test
(g) Multi+BT[t]	**37.32**	**35.17**	**26.70**	**38.94**	**38.44**	**30.81**	44.60	38.94	**37.80**	**40.67**	**39.47**	**33.43**
(h) Pairwise	28.89	28.23	21.13	32.55	32.29	27.10	**45.77**	**39.68**	36.86	34.97	34.96	27.09

Table 3: chrF scores for the dev and devtest custom partitions and the official test sets for the best multilingual setting and the pairwise baseline in each direction.

4.2 Multilingual subword segmentation

Ortega et al. (2020b) used morphological information, such as affixes, to guide the Byte-Pair-Encoding (BPE) segmentation algorithm (Sennrich et al., 2016b) for Quechua. However, their improvement is not significant, and according to Bostrom and Durrett (2020), BPE tends to oversplit roots of infrequent words. They showed that a unigram language model (Kudo, 2018) seems like a better alternative to split affixes and preserve roots (in English and Japanese).

To take advantage of the potential lexical sharing of the languages (e.g. loanwords) and address the polysynthetic nature of the indigenous languages, we trained a unique multilingual segmentation model by sampling all languages with a uniform distribution. We used the unigram model implementation in SentencePiece (Kudo and Richardson, 2018) with a vocabulary size of 32,000.

4.3 Procedure

For the experiments, we used a Transformer-base model (Vaswani et al., 2017) with the default configuration in Marian NMT (Junczys-Dowmunt et al., 2018). The steps are as follows:

Pre-training We pre-trained two MT models with the Spanish–English language-pair in both directions. We did not include an agglutinative language like Finnish (Ortega et al., 2020b) for two reasons: it is not a must to consider highly related languages for effective transfer learning (e.g. English–German to English–Tamil (Bawden et al., 2020)), and we wanted to translate the English side of en–aym, en–quy and en–quz to augment their correspondent Spanish-paired datasets. The en→es and es→en models achieved 34.4 and 32.3 BLEU points, respectively, in the newsdev2013 set.

Multilingual fine-tuning Using the pre-trained en→es model, we fine-tuned the first multilingual model many-to-Spanish. Following established practices, we used a uniform sampling for all the datasets (quz–es included) to avoid under-fitting the low-resource language-pairs[4]. Results are in Table 2, row (a). We replicated this to the es→many direction (row (e)), using the es→en model.

Back-translation With model (a), we back-translated (BT) the monolingual data of the indigenous languages and train models (b) and (f): original plus BT data. However, the results with BT data underperformed or did not converge. Potential reasons are the noisy translation outputs of model (a) and the larger amount of BT than human-translated sentences for all languages, even though

[4]Temperature-based sampling or automatically learned data scorers are more advanced strategies (Wang et al., 2020). However, we left that analysis for further work.

we sampled BT and human translations uniformly.

Tagged back-translation (BT[t]) To alleviate the issue, we add a special tag for the BT data (Caswell et al., 2019). With BT[t], we send a signal to the model that it is processing synthetic data, and thus, it may not hurt the learning over the real data. Table 2 (rows (c,g)) shows the results.

Pairwise baselines We obtained pairwise systems by fine-tuning the same pre-trained models (without any back-translated data). For a straightforward comparison, they used the same multilingual SentencePiece model.

5 Analysis and discussion

One of the most exciting outcomes is the deteriorated performance of the multilingual models using BT data, as we usually expect that added back-translated texts would benefit performance. Using tags (BT[t]) to differentiate which data is synthetic or not is only a simple step to address this issue; however, there could be evaluated more informed strategies for denoising or performing online data selection (Wang et al., 2018).

Besides, in the translation into Spanish, the multilingual model without BT data outperforms the rest models in all languages but Quechua, where the pairwise system achieved the best translation accuracy. Quechua is the "highest"-resource language-pair in the experiment, and its performance is deteriorated in the multilingual setting[5]. A similar scenario is shown in the other translation direction from Spanish, where the best multilingual setting (+BT[t]) cannot overcome the es→quy model in the devtest set.

Nevertheless, the gains for Aymara, Ashaninka and Shipibo-Konibo are outstanding. Moreover, we note that the models are not totally overfitted to any of the evaluation sets. Exceptions are es→aym and es→quy, with a significant performance dropping from dev to devtest, meaning that it started to overfit to the training data. However, for Spanish→Ashaninka, we observe that the model achieved a better performance in the devtest set. This is due to oversampling of the same-domain dev partition for training (§4.1) and the small original training set.

[5] In multilingual training, this behaviour is usually observed, and other approaches, such as injecting adapter layers (Bapna and Firat, 2019), might help to mitigate the issue. We left the analysis for further work.

Stories (shp)	shp→es			es→shp		
	full	half	Δt	full	half	Δt
BestMulti	1.90	1.43	0	0.56	0.68	0
BestMulti+FT	-	**5.73**	-1.66	-	**5.82**	-1.93
Magazine (quy)	quy→es			es→quy		
	full	half	Δt	full	half	Δt
Pairwise	2.96	2.32	0	2.17	1.59	0
Pairwise+FT	-	**9.14**	-0.83	-	**2.92**	+0.78
Apertium	5.82			-	-	
Ortega et al.	0.70			-	-	

Table 4: Out-of-domain BLEU scores. Best model is fine-tuned (+FT) with half of the dataset and evaluated in the other half. Δt = original test score variation.

Concerning the results on the official test set, the performance is lower than the results with the custom evaluation sets. The main potential reason is that the official test is four times bigger than the custom devtest, and therefore, offers more diversity and challenge for the evaluation. Another point to highlight is that the best result in the Spanish–Quechua language-pair is obtained by a multilingual model (the scores between the model (e) and (g) are not significantly different) instead of the pairwise baseline.

Decoding an indigenous language is still a challenging task, and the relatively low BLEU scores cannot suggest a translation with proper adequacy or fluency. However, BLEU works at the word-level, and other character-level metrics should be considered to better assess the highly agglutinative nature of the languages. For reference, we also report the chrF scores in Table 3 for the best multilingual setting and the pairwise baseline. As for the Spanish decoding, fluency is preserved from the English→Spanish pre-trained model[6], but more adequacy is needed.

6 Out-of-domain evaluation

It is relevant to assess out-of-domain capabilities, but more important to evaluate whether the models are still capable to fine-tune without overfitting. We use a small evaluation set for Quechua (*Kallpa*, with 100 sentences), which contains sentences extracted from a magazine (Ortega et al., 2020b). Likewise, we introduce a new evaluation set for Shipibo-Konibo (*Kirika*, 200 sentences), which contains short traditional stories.

We tested our best model for each language-pair, fine-tune it (+FT) with half of the out-of-domain

[6] This might be confirmed by a proper human evaluation

dataset, and evaluate it in the other half. To avoid overfitting, we controlled cross-entropy loss and considered very few updates for validation steps. Results are shown in Table 3, where we observe that it is possible to fine-tune the multilingual or pairwise models to the new domains without loosing too much performance in the original test.

The Quechua translations rapidly improved with the fine-tuning step, and there is a small gain in the original test for es→quy, although the scores are relatively low in general. Nevertheless, our model could outperform others (by extrapolation, we can assume that the scores for the rule-based Apertium system (Cavero and Madariaga, 2007) and Ortega et al. (2020b)'s NMT system are similar in half of the dataset).

For Shipibo-Konibo, we also observe some small gains in both directions without hurting the previous performance, but the scores are far from being robust. *Kirika* is challenging given its *old style*: the translations are extracted from an old book written by missionaries, and even when the spelling has been modernised, there are differences in the use of some auxiliary verbs for instance (extra words that affect the evaluation metric)[7].

7 Conclusion and future work

Peru is multilingual, *ergo*, its machine translation should be too! We conclude that multilingual machine translation models can enhance the performance in truly low-resource languages like Aymara, Ashaninka and Shipibo-Konibo, in translation from and into Spanish. For Quechua, even when the pairwise system performed better in this study, there is a simple step to give a multilingual setting another opportunity: to include a higher-resource language-pair that may support the multilingual learning process. This could be related in some aspect like morphology (another agglutinative language) or the discourse (domain). Other approaches focused on more advanced sampling or adding specific layers to restore the performance of the higher-resource languages might be considered as well. Besides, tagged back-translation allowed to take some advantage of the monolingual data; however, one of the most critical following steps is to obtain a more robust many-to-Spanish model to generate back-translated data with more quality. Furthermore, to address the multi-domain nature of these datasets, we could use domain tags to send more signals to the model and support further fine-tuning steps. Finally, after addressing the presented issues in this study, and to enable zero-shot translation, we plan to train the first many-to-many multilingual model for indigenous languages spoken in Peru.

[7]The dataset, with further analysis, is available at: https://github.com/aoncevay/mt-peru

Acknowledgements

The author is supported by funding from the European Union's Horizon 2020 research and innovation programme under grant agreements No 825299 (GoURMET) and the EPSRC fellowship grant EP/S001271/1 (MTStretch). The author is also thankful to the insightful feedback of the anonymous reviewers.

References

Željko Agić and Ivan Vulić. 2019. JW300: A wide-coverage parallel corpus for low-resource languages. In *Proceedings of the 57th Annual Meeting of the Association for Computational Linguistics*, pages 3204–3210, Florence, Italy. Association for Computational Linguistics.

Ankur Bapna and Orhan Firat. 2019. Simple, scalable adaptation for neural machine translation. In *Proceedings of the 2019 Conference on Empirical Methods in Natural Language Processing and the 9th International Joint Conference on Natural Language Processing (EMNLP-IJCNLP)*, pages 1538–1548, Hong Kong, China. Association for Computational Linguistics.

Rachel Bawden, Alexandra Birch, Radina Dobreva, Arturo Oncevay, Antonio Valerio Miceli Barone, and Philip Williams. 2020. The University of Edinburgh's English-Tamil and English-Inuktitut submissions to the WMT20 news translation task. In *Proceedings of the Fifth Conference on Machine Translation*, pages 92–99, Online. Association for Computational Linguistics.

Kaj Bostrom and Greg Durrett. 2020. Byte pair encoding is suboptimal for language model pretraining. In *Findings of the Association for Computational Linguistics: EMNLP 2020*, pages 4617–4624, Online. Association for Computational Linguistics.

Gina Bustamante, Arturo Oncevay, and Roberto Zariquiey. 2020. No data to crawl? monolingual corpus creation from PDF files of truly low-resource languages in Peru. In *Proceedings of the 12th Language Resources and Evaluation Conference*, pages 2914–2923, Marseille, France. European Language Resources Association.

Isaac Caswell, Ciprian Chelba, and David Grangier. 2019. Tagged back-translation. In *Proceedings of the Fourth Conference on Machine Translation (Volume 1: Research Papers)*, pages 53–63, Florence, Italy. Association for Computational Linguistics.

Indhira Castro Cavero and Jaime Farfán Madariaga. 2007. Traductor morfológico del castellano y quechua (Morphological translator of Castilian Spanish and Quechua). *Revista I+ i*, 1(1).

Matthew Coler and Petr Homola. 2014. *Rule-based machine translation for Aymara*, pages 67–80. Cambridge University Press.

Raj Dabre, Chenhui Chu, and Anoop Kunchukuttan. 2020. A comprehensive survey of multilingual neural machine translation.

Mikel L Forcada, Mireia Ginestí-Rosell, Jacob Nordfalk, Jim O'Regan, Sergio Ortiz-Rojas, Juan Antonio Pérez-Ortiz, Felipe Sánchez-Martínez, Gema Ramírez-Sánchez, and Francis M Tyers. 2011. Apertium: a free/open-source platform for rule-based machine translation. *Machine translation*, 25(2):127–144.

Ana-Paula Galarreta, Andrés Melgar, and Arturo Oncevay. 2017. Corpus creation and initial SMT experiments between Spanish and Shipibo-konibo. In *Proceedings of the International Conference Recent Advances in Natural Language Processing, RANLP 2017*, pages 238–244, Varna, Bulgaria. INCOMA Ltd.

Héctor Erasmo Gómez Montoya, Kervy Dante Rivas Rojas, and Arturo Oncevay. 2019. A continuous improvement framework of machine translation for Shipibo-konibo. In *Proceedings of the 2nd Workshop on Technologies for MT of Low Resource Languages*, pages 17–23, Dublin, Ireland. European Association for Machine Translation.

Melvin Johnson, Mike Schuster, Quoc V. Le, Maxim Krikun, Yonghui Wu, Zhifeng Chen, Nikhil Thorat, Fernanda Viégas, Martin Wattenberg, Greg Corrado, Macduff Hughes, and Jeffrey Dean. 2017. Google's multilingual neural machine translation system: Enabling zero-shot translation. *Transactions of the Association for Computational Linguistics*, 5:339–351.

Marcin Junczys-Dowmunt, Roman Grundkiewicz, Tomasz Dwojak, Hieu Hoang, Kenneth Heafield, Tom Neckermann, Frank Seide, Ulrich Germann, Alham Fikri Aji, Nikolay Bogoychev, André F. T. Martins, and Alexandra Birch. 2018. Marian: Fast neural machine translation in C++. In *Proceedings of ACL 2018, System Demonstrations*, pages 116–121, Melbourne, Australia. Association for Computational Linguistics.

Tom Kocmi and Ondřej Bojar. 2018. Trivial transfer learning for low-resource neural machine translation. In *Proceedings of the Third Conference on Machine Translation: Research Papers*, pages 244–252, Belgium, Brussels. Association for Computational Linguistics.

Philipp Koehn. 2005. Europarl: A parallel corpus for statistical machine translation. In *MT summit*, volume 5, pages 79–86. Citeseer.

Taku Kudo. 2018. Subword regularization: Improving neural network translation models with multiple subword candidates. In *Proceedings of the 56th Annual Meeting of the Association for Computational Linguistics (Volume 1: Long Papers)*, pages 66–75, Melbourne, Australia. Association for Computational Linguistics.

Taku Kudo and John Richardson. 2018. SentencePiece: A simple and language independent subword tokenizer and detokenizer for neural text processing. In *Proceedings of the 2018 Conference on Empirical Methods in Natural Language Processing: System Demonstrations*, pages 66–71, Brussels, Belgium. Association for Computational Linguistics.

Graham Neubig and Junjie Hu. 2018. Rapid adaptation of neural machine translation to new languages. In *Proceedings of the 2018 Conference on Empirical Methods in Natural Language Processing*, pages 875–880, Brussels, Belgium. Association for Computational Linguistics.

Arturo Oncevay, Barry Haddow, and Alexandra Birch. 2020. Bridging linguistic typology and multilingual machine translation with multi-view language representations. In *Proceedings of the 2020 Conference on Empirical Methods in Natural Language Processing (EMNLP)*, pages 2391–2406, Online. Association for Computational Linguistics.

John Ortega, Richard Alexander Castro-Mamani, and Jaime Rafael Montoya Samame. 2020a. Overcoming resistance: The normalization of an Amazonian tribal language. In *Proceedings of the 3rd Workshop on Technologies for MT of Low Resource Languages*, pages 1–13, Suzhou, China. Association for Computational Linguistics.

John Ortega and Krishnan Pillaipakkamnatt. 2018. Using morphemes from agglutinative languages like Quechua and Finnish to aid in low-resource translation. In *Proceedings of the AMTA 2018 Workshop on Technologies for MT of Low Resource Languages (LoResMT 2018)*, pages 1–11.

John E Ortega, Richard Castro Mamani, and Kyunghyun Cho. 2020b. Neural machine translation with a polysynthetic low resource language. *Machine Translation*, 34(4):325–346.

Kishore Papineni, Salim Roukos, Todd Ward, and Wei-Jing Zhu. 2002. Bleu: a method for automatic evaluation of machine translation. In *Proceedings of the 40th Annual Meeting of the Association for Computational Linguistics*, pages 311–318, Philadelphia, Pennsylvania, USA. Association for Computational Linguistics.

Maja Popović. 2015. chrF: character n-gram F-score for automatic MT evaluation. In *Proceedings of the*

Tenth Workshop on Statistical Machine Translation, pages 392–395, Lisbon, Portugal. Association for Computational Linguistics.

Rico Sennrich, Barry Haddow, and Alexandra Birch. 2016a. Improving neural machine translation models with monolingual data. In *Proceedings of the 54th Annual Meeting of the Association for Computational Linguistics (Volume 1: Long Papers)*, pages 86–96, Berlin, Germany. Association for Computational Linguistics.

Rico Sennrich, Barry Haddow, and Alexandra Birch. 2016b. Neural machine translation of rare words with subword units. In *Proceedings of the 54th Annual Meeting of the Association for Computational Linguistics (Volume 1: Long Papers)*, pages 1715–1725, Berlin, Germany. Association for Computational Linguistics.

Gary F. Simons and Charles D. Fenning, editors. 2019. *Ethnologue: Languages of the World. Twenty-second edition.* Dallas Texas: SIL international. Online version: http://www.ethnologue.com.

Xu Tan, Jiale Chen, Di He, Yingce Xia, Tao Qin, and Tie-Yan Liu. 2019. Multilingual neural machine translation with language clustering. In *Proceedings of the 2019 Conference on Empirical Methods in Natural Language Processing and the 9th International Joint Conference on Natural Language Processing (EMNLP-IJCNLP)*, pages 963–973, Hong Kong, China. Association for Computational Linguistics.

Jörg Tiedemann. 2012. Parallel data, tools and interfaces in opus. In *Proceedings of the Eight International Conference on Language Resources and Evaluation (LREC'12)*, Istanbul, Turkey. European Language Resources Association (ELRA).

Ashish Vaswani, Noam Shazeer, Niki Parmar, Jakob Uszkoreit, Llion Jones, Aidan N Gomez, Ł ukasz Kaiser, and Illia Polosukhin. 2017. Attention is all you need. In I. Guyon, U. V. Luxburg, S. Bengio, H. Wallach, R. Fergus, S. Vishwanathan, and R. Garnett, editors, *Advances in Neural Information Processing Systems 30*, pages 5998–6008. Curran Associates, Inc.

Wei Wang, Taro Watanabe, Macduff Hughes, Tetsuji Nakagawa, and Ciprian Chelba. 2018. Denoising neural machine translation training with trusted data and online data selection. In *Proceedings of the Third Conference on Machine Translation: Research Papers*, pages 133–143, Brussels, Belgium. Association for Computational Linguistics.

Xinyi Wang, Yulia Tsvetkov, and Graham Neubig. 2020. Balancing training for multilingual neural machine translation. In *Proceedings of the 58th Annual Meeting of the Association for Computational Linguistics*, pages 8526–8537, Online. Association for Computational Linguistics.

Roberto Zariquiey, Harald Hammarström, Mónica Arakaki, Arturo Oncevay, John Miller, Aracelli García, and Adriano Ingunza. 2019. Obsolescencia lingüística, descripción gramatical y documentación de lenguas en el perú: hacia un estado de la cuestión. *Lexis*, 43(2):271–337.

Appendix

	S (orig.)	S (clean)	% clean	T/S (src)	T/S (tgt)	ratio T src/tgt
es-aym	6,453	5,475	-15.16%	19.27	13.37	1.44
es-cni	3,860	3,753	-2.77%	12.29	6.52	1.89
es-quy	128,583	104,101	-19.04%	14.2	8.17	1.74
es-shp	14,511	14,437	-0.51%	6.05	4.31	1.4
es-quz	130,757	97,836	-25.18%	15.23	8.62	1.77
en-quy	128,330	91,151	-28.97%	15.03	8.68	1.73
en-quz	144,867	100,126	-30.88%	14.84	8.42	1.76
en-aym	8,886	7,689	-13.47%	19.36	13.32	1.45

Table 5: Statistics and cleaning for all parallel corpora. We observe that the Shipibo-Konibo and Ashaninka corpora are the least noisy ones. S = number of sentences, T = number of tokens. There are sentence alignment issues in the Quechua datasets, which require a more specialised tool to address.

Findings of the AmericasNLP 2021 Shared Task on Open Machine Translation for Indigenous Languages of the Americas

Manuel Mager[♠*] Arturo Oncevay[♡*] Abteen Ebrahimi[◇*] John Ortega[Ω]
Annette Rios[ψ] Angela Fan[∇] Ximena Gutierrez-Vasques[ψ] Luis Chiruzzo[△]
Gustavo A. Giménez-Lugo[♣] Ricardo Ramos[η] Ivan Vladimir Meza Ruiz[♯]
Rolando Coto-Solano[℧] Alexis Palmer[◇] Elisabeth Mager[♯] Vishrav Chaudhary[∇]
Graham Neubig[⋈] Ngoc Thang Vu[♠] Katharina Kann[◇]

[⋈]Carnegie Mellon University [℧]Dartmouth College [∇]Facebook AI Research
[Ω]New York University [△]Universidad de la República, Uruguay
[η]Universidad Tecnológica de Tlaxcala [♯]Universidad Nacional Autónoma de México
[♣]Universidade Tecnológica Federal do Paraná [◇]University of Colorado Boulder
[♡]University of Edinburgh [♠]University of Stuttgart [ψ]University of Zurich

Abstract

This paper presents the results of the 2021 Shared Task on Open Machine Translation for Indigenous Languages of the Americas. The shared task featured two independent tracks, and participants submitted machine translation systems for up to 10 indigenous languages. Overall, 8 teams participated with a total of 214 submissions. We provided training sets consisting of data collected from various sources, as well as manually translated sentences for the development and test sets. An official baseline trained on this data was also provided. Team submissions featured a variety of architectures, including both statistical and neural models, and for the majority of languages, many teams were able to considerably improve over the baseline. The best performing systems achieved 12.97 ChrF higher than baseline, when averaged across languages.

1 Introduction

Many of the world's languages, including languages native to the Americas, receive worryingly little attention from NLP researchers. According to Glottolog (Nordhoff and Hammarström, 2012), 86 language families and 95 language isolates can be found in the Americas, and many of them are labeled as endangered. From an NLP perspective, the development of language technologies has the potential to help language communities and activists in the documentation, promotion and revitalization of their languages (Mager et al., 2018b; Galla, 2016). There have been recent initiatives to promote research on languages of the Americas (Fernández et al., 2013; Coler and Homola, 2014; Gutierrez-Vasques, 2015; Mager and Meza, 2018; Ortega et al., 2020; Zhang et al., 2020; Schwartz et al., 2020; Barrault et al., 2020).

*The first three authors contributed equally.

The AmericasNLP 2021 Shared Task on Open Machine Translation (OMT) aimed at moving research on indigenous and endangered languages more into the focus of the NLP community. As the official shared task training sets, we provided a collection of publicly available parallel corpora (§3). Additionally, all participants were allowed to use other existing datasets or create their own resources for training in order to improve their systems. Each language pair used in the shared task consisted of an indigenous language and a high-resource language (Spanish). The languages belong to a diverse set of language families: Aymaran, Arawak, Chibchan, Tupi-Guarani, Uto-Aztecan, Oto-Manguean, Quechuan, and Panoan. The ten language pairs included in the shared task are: Quechua–Spanish, Wixarika–Spanish, Shipibo-Konibo–Spanish, Asháninka–Spanish, Raramuri–Spanish, Nahuatl–Spanish, Otomí–Spanish, Aymara–Spanish, Guarani–Spanish, and Bribri–Spanish. For development and testing, we used parallel sentences belonging to a new natural language inference dataset for the 10 indigenous languages featured in our shared task, which is a manual translation of the Spanish version of the multilingual XNLI dataset (Conneau et al., 2018). For a complete description of this dataset we refer the reader to Ebrahimi et al. (2021).

Together with the data, we also provided: a simple baseline based on the small transformer architecture (Vaswani et al., 2017) proposed together with the FLORES dataset (Guzmán et al., 2019); and a description of challenges and particular characteristics for all provided resources[1]. We established two tracks: one where training models on the development set after hyperparameter tuning is

[1]https://github.com/AmericasNLP/americasnlp2021/blob/main/data/information_datasets.pdf

Proceedings of the First Workshop on Natural Language Processing for Indigenous Languages of the Americas, pages 202–217
June 11, 2021. ©2021 Association for Computational Linguistics

allowed (Track 1), and one where models cannot be trained directly on the development set (Track 2).

Machine translation for indigenous languages often presents unique challenges. As many indigenous languages do not have a strong written tradition, orthographic rules are not well defined or standardized, and even if they are regulated, often times native speakers do not follow them or create their own adapted versions. Simply normalizing the data is generally not a viable option, as even the definition of what constitutes a morpheme or a orthographic word is frequently ill defined. Furthermore, the huge dialectal variability among those languages, even from one village to the other, adds additional complexity to the task. We describe the particular challenges for each language in Section §3.

Eight teams participated in the AmericasNLP 2021 Shared Task on OMT. Most teams submitted systems in both tracks and for all 10 language pairs, yielding a total of 214 submissions.

2 Task and Evaluation

2.1 Open Machine Translation

Given the limited availability of resources and the important dialectal, orthographic and domain challenges, we designed our task as an unrestrained machine translation shared task: we called it *open* machine translation to emphasize that participants were free to use any resources they could find. Possible resources could, for instance, include existing or newly created parallel data, dictionaries, tools, or pretrained models.

We invited submissions to two different tracks: Systems in Track 1 were allowed to use the development set as part of the training data, since this is a common practice in the machine translation community. Systems in Track 2 were not allowed to be trained directly on the development set, mimicking a more realistic low-resource setting.

2.2 Primary Evaluation

In order to be able to evaluate a large number of systems on all 10 languages, we used automatic metrics for our primary evaluation. Our main metric, which determined the official ranking of systems, was ChrF (Popović, 2015). We made this choice due to certain properties of our languages, such as word boundaries not being standardized for all languages and many languages being polysynthetic, resulting in a small number of words per sentence. We further reported BLEU scores (Papineni et al., 2002) for all systems and languages.

2.3 Supplementary Evaluation

To gain additional insight into the strengths and weaknesses of the top-performing submissions, we further performed a supplementary manual evaluation for two language pairs and a limited number of systems, using a subset of the test set.

We asked our annotators to provide ratings of system outputs using separate 5-point scales for adequacy and fluency. The annotation was performed by the translator who created the test datasets. The expert received the source sentence in Spanish, the reference in the indigenous language, and an anonymized system output. In addition to the baseline, we considered the 3 highest ranked systems according to our main metric, and randomly selected 100 sentences for each language. The following were the descriptions of the ratings as provided to the expert annotator in Spanish (translated into English here for convenience):

Adequacy The output sentence expresses the meaning of the reference.

1. Extremely bad: The original meaning is not contained at all.
2. Bad: Some words or phrases allow to guess the content.
3. Neutral.
4. Sufficiently good: The original meaning is understandable, but some parts are unclear or incorrect.
5. Excellent: The meaning of the output is the same as that of the reference.

Fluency The output sentence is easily readable and looks like a human-produced text.

1. Extremely bad: The output text does not belong to the target language.
2. Bad: The output sentence is hardly readable.
3. Neutral.
4. Sufficiently good: The output seems like a human-produced text in the target language, but contains weird mistakes.
5. Excellent: The output seems like a human-produced text in the target language, and is readable without issues.

Language	ISO	Family	Train	Dev	Test
Asháninka	cni	Arawak	3883	883	1002
Aymara	aym	Aymaran	6531	996	1003
Bribri	bzd	Chibchan	7508	996	1003
Guarani	gn	Tupi-Guarani	26032	995	1003
Nahuatl	nah	Uto-Aztecan	16145	672	996
Otomí	oto	Oto-Manguean	4889	599	1001
Quechua	quy	Quechuan	125008	996	1003
Rarámuri	tar	Uto-Aztecan	14721	995	1002
Shipibo-Konibo	shp	Panoan	14592	996	1002
Wixarika	hch	Uto-Aztecan	8966	994	1003

Table 1: The languages featured in the AmericasNLP 2021 Shared Task on OMT, their ISO codes, language families and dataset statistics. For the origins of the datasets, please refer to the text.

3 Languages and Datasets

In this section, we will present the languages and datasets featured in our shared task. Figure 1 additionally provides an overview of the languages, their linguistic families, and the number of parallel sentences with Spanish.

3.1 Development and Test Sets

For system development and testing, we leveraged individual pairs of parallel sentences from AmericasNLI (Ebrahimi et al., 2021). This dataset is a translation of the Spanish version of XNLI (Conneau et al., 2018) into our 10 indigenous languages. It was not publicly available until after the conclusion of the competition, avoiding an accidental inclusion of the test set into the training data by the participants. For more information regarding the creation of the dataset, we refer the reader to (Ebrahimi et al., 2021).

3.2 Training Data

We collected publicly available datasets in all 10 languages and provided them to the shared task participants as a starting point. We will now introduce the languages and the training datasets, explaining similarities and differences between training sets on the one hand and development and test sets on the other.

Spanish–Wixarika Wixarika (also known as Huichol) with ISO code `hch` is spoken in Mexico and belongs to the Yuto-Aztecan linguistic family. The training, development and test sets all belong to the same dialectal variation, Wixarika of Zoquipan, and use the same orthography. However, word boundaries are not always marked according to the same criteria in development/test and train. The training data (Mager et al., 2018a) is a translation of the fairy tales of Hans Christian Andersen and contains word acquisitions and code-switching.

Spanish–Nahuatl Nahuatl is a Yuto-Aztecan language spoken in Mexico and El Salvador, with a wide dialectal variation (around 30 variants). For each main dialect a specific ISO 639-3 code is available.[2] There is a lack of consensus regarding the orthographic standard. This is very noticeable in the training data: the train corpus (Gutierrez-Vasques et al., 2016) has dialectal, domain, orthographic and diachronic variation (Nahuatl side). However, the majority of entries are closer to a Classical Nahuatl orthographic "standard".

The development and test datasets were translated to modern Nahuatl. In particular, the translations belong to Nahuatl Central/Nahuatl de la Huasteca (Hidalgo y San Luis Potosí) dialects. In order to be closer to the training corpus, an orthographic normalization was applied. A simple rule based approach was used, which was based on the most predictable orthographic changes between modern varieties and Classical Nahuatl.

Spanish—Guarani Guarani is mostly spoken in Paraguay, Bolivia, Argentina and Brazil. It belongs to the Tupian language family (ISO `gnw`, `gun`, `gug`, `gui`, `grn`, `nhd`). The training corpus for Guarani (Chiruzzo et al., 2020) was collected from web sources (blogs and news articles) that contained a mix of dialects, from pure Guarani to more mixed Jopara which combines Guarani with Spanish neologisms. The development and test corpora, on the other hand, are in standard Paraguayan Guarani.

Spanish—Bribri Bribri is a Chibchan language spoken in southern Costa Rica (ISO code `bzd`). The training set for Bribri was extracted from six sources (Feldman and Coto-Solano, 2020; Margery, 2005; Jara Murillo, 2018a; Constenla et al., 2004; Jara Murillo and García Segura, 2013; Jara Murillo, 2018b; Flores Solórzano, 2017), including a dictionary, a grammar, two language learning textbooks, one storybook and the transcribed sentences from

[2]ISO 639-3 for the Nahutal languages: `nci`, `nhn`, `nch`, `ncx`, `naz`, `nln`, `nhe`, `ngu`, `azz`, `nhq`, `nhk`, `nhx`, `nhp`, `ncl`, `nhm`, `nhy`, `ncj`, `nht`, `nlv`, `ppl`, `nhz`, `npl`, `nhc`, `nhv`, `nhi`, `nhg`, `nuz`, `nhw`, `nsu`, `xpo`, `nhn`, `nch`, `ncx`, `naz`, `nln`, `nhe`, `ngu`, `azz`, `nhq`, `nhk`, `nhx`, `nhp`, `ncl`, `nhm`, `nhy`, `ncj`, `nht`, `nlv`, `ppl`, `nhz`, `npl`, `nhc`, `nhv`, `nhi`, `nhg`, `nuz`, `nhw`, `nsu`, and `xpo`.

one spoken corpus. The sentences belong to three major dialects: Amubri, Coroma and Salitre.

There are numerous sources of variation in the Bribri data (Feldman and Coto-Solano, 2020): 1) There are several different orthographies, which use different diacritics for the same words. 2) The Unicode encoding of visually similar diacritics differs among authors. 3) There is phonetic and lexical variation across dialects. 4) There is considerable idiosyncratic variation between writers, including variation in word boundaries (e.g. *ikíe* vrs *i kie* "it is called"). In order to build a standardized training set, an intermediate orthography was used to make these different forms comparable and learning easier. All of the training sentences are comparable in domain; they come from either traditional stories or language learning examples. Because of the nature of the texts, there is very little code-switching into Spanish. This is different from regular Bribri conversation, which would contain more borrowings from Spanish and more code-switching. The development and test sentences were translated by a speaker of the Amubri dialect and transformed into the intermediate orthography.

Spanish—Rarámuri Rarámuri is a Uto-Aztecan language, spoken in northern Mexico (ISO: `tac, twr, tar, tcu, thh`). Training data for Rarámuri consists of a set of extracted phrases from the Rarámuri dictionary Brambila (1976). However, we could not find any description of the dialectal variation to which these examples belong. The development and test set are translations from Spanish into the highlands Rarámuri variant (`tar`), and may differ from the training set. As with many polysynthetic languages, challenges can arise when the boundaries of a morpheme and a word are not clear and have no consensus. Native speakers, even with a standard orthography and from the same dialectal variation, may define words in a different standards to define word boundaries.

Spanish—Quechua Quechua is a family of languages spoken in Argentina, Bolivia, Colombia, Ecuador, Peru, and Chile with many ISO codes for its language (`quh, cqu, qvn, qvc, qur, quy, quk, qvo, qve`, and `quf`). The development and test sets are translated into the standard version of Southern Quechua, specifically the Quechua Chanka (Ayacucho, code: `quy`) variety. This variety is spoken in different regions of Peru, and it can be understood in different areas of other countries, such as Bolivia or Argentina. This is the variant used on Wikipedia Quechua pages, and by Microsoft in its translations of software into Quechua. Southern Quechua includes different Quechua variants, such as Quechua Cuzco (`quz`) and Quechua Ayacucho (`quy`). Training datasets are provided for both variants. These datasets were created from JW300 (Agić and Vulić, 2019), which consists of Jehovah's Witness texts, sentences extracted from the official dictionary of the Minister of Education (MINEDU), and miscellaneous dictionary entries and samples which have been collected and reviewed by Huarcaya Taquiri (2020).

Spanish–Aymara Aymara is a Aymaran language spoken in Bolivia, Peru, and Chile (ISO codes `aym, ayr, ayc`). The development and test sets are translated into the Central Aymara variant (`ayr`), specifically Aymara La Paz jilata, the largest variant. This is similar to the variant of the available training set, which is obtained from Global Voices (Prokopidis et al., 2016) (and published in OPUS (Tiedemann, 2012)), a news portal translated by volunteers. However, the text may have potentially different writing styles that are not necessarily edited.

Spanish-–Shipibo-Konibo Shipibo-Konibo is a Panoan language spoken in Perú (ISO `shp` and `kaq`). The training sets for Shipibo-Konibo have been obtained from different sources and translators: Sources include translations of a sample from the Tatoeba dataset (Gómez Montoya et al., 2019), translated sentences from books for bilingual education (Galarreta et al., 2017), and dictionary entries and examples (Loriot et al., 1993). Translated text was created by a bilingual teacher, and follows the most recent guidelines of the Minister of Education in Peru, however, the third source is an extraction of parallel sentences from an old dictionary. The development and test sets were created following the official convention as in the translated training sets.

Spanish—Asháninka Asháninka is an Arawakan language (ISO: `cni`) spoken in Peru and Brazil. Training data was created by collecting texts from different domains such as traditional stories, educational texts, and environmental laws for the Amazonian region (Ortega et al., 2020; Romano, Rubén and Richer, Sebastián, 2008; Mihas, 2011). The texts belong to domains such as: traditional stories, educational texts, environmental laws for the Amazonian region. Not all the texts are translated into Spanish, there is a small fraction of these that are translated into Portuguese because a dialect of pan-Ashaninka is also spoken in the state of Acre in Brazil. The texts come from different pan-Ashaninka dialects and have been normalized using the AshMorph (Ortega et al., 2020). There are many neologisms that are not spread to the speakers of different communities. The translator of the development and test sets only translated the words and concepts that are well known in the communities, whereas other terms are preserved in Spanish. Moreover, the development and test sets were created following the official writing convention proposed by the Peruvian Government and taught in bilingual schools.

Spanish--Otomí Otomí (also known as Hñähñu, Hñähño, Ñhato, Ñûhmû, depending on the region) is an Oto-Manguean language spoken in Mexico (ISO codes: `ott`, `otn`, `otx`, `ote`, `otq`, `otz`, `otl`, `ots`, `otm`). The training set[3] was collected from a set of different sources, which implies that the text contains more than one dialectal variation and orthographic standard, however, most texts belong to the Valle del Mezquital dialect (`ote`). This was specially challenging for the translation task, since the development and test sets are from the Ñûhmû de Ixtenco, Tlaxcala, variant (`otz`), which also has its own orthographic system. This variant is especially endangered as less than 100 elders still speak it.

3.3 External Data Used by Participants

In addition to the provided datasets, participants also used additional publicly available parallel data, monolingual corpora or newly collected data sets. The most common datasets were JW300 (Agić and Vulić, 2019) and the Bible's New Testament (Mayer and Cysouw, 2014; Christodouloupoulos and Steedman, 2015; McCarthy et al., 2020). Besides those, GlobalVoices (Prokopidis et al., 2016) and datasets available at OPUS (Tiedemann, 2012) were added. New datasets were extracted from constitutions, dictionaries, and educational books. For monolingual text, Wikipedia was most commonly used, assuming one was available in a language.

[3]Otomí online corpus: https://tsunkua.elotl.mx/about/

4 Baseline and Submitted Systems

We will now describe our baseline as well as all submitted systems. An overview of all teams and the main ideas going into their submissions is shown in Table 2.

4.1 Baseline

Our baseline system was a transformer-based sequence to sequence model (Vaswani et al., 2017). We employed the hyperparameters proposed by Guzmán et al. (2019) for a low-resource scenario. We implemented the model using Fairseq (Ott et al., 2019). The implementation of the baseline can be found in the official shared task repository.[4]

4.2 University of British Columbia

The team of the University of British Columbia (`UBC-NLP`; Billah-Nagoudi et al., 2021) participated for all ten language pairs and in both tracks. They used an encoder-decoder transformer model based on T5 (Raffel et al., 2020). This model was pretrained on a dataset consisting of 10 indigenous languages and Spanish, that was collected by the team from different sources such as the Bible and Wikipedia, totaling 1.17 GB of text. However, given that some of the languages have more available data than others, this dataset is unbalanced in favor of languages like Nahuatl, Guarani, and Quechua. The team also proposed a two-stage fine-tuning method: first fine-tuning on the entire dataset, and then only on the target languages.

4.3 Helsinki

The University of Helsinki (`Helsinki`; Vázquez et al., 2021) participated for all ten language pairs in both tracks. This team did an extensive exploration of the existing datasets, and collected additional resources both from commonly used sources such as the Bible and Wikipedia, as well as other minor sources such as constitutions. Monolingual data was used to generate paired sentences through back-translation, and these parallel examples were added to the existing dataset. Then, a normalization process was done using existing tools, and the aligned data was further filtered. The quality of the data was also considered, and each dataset was assigned a weight depending on a noisiness estimation. The team used a transformer sequence-to-sequence model trained via two steps. For their main submission they first trained on data which

[4]https://github.com/AmericasNLP/americasnlp2021

Team	Langs.	Sub.	Data	Models	Multilingual	Pretrained
CoAStaL (Bollmann et al., 2021)	10	20	Bible, JW300, OPUS, Wikipedia, New collected data	PB-SMT, Constrained Random Strings	No	No
Helsinki (Vázquez et al., 2021)	10	50	Bible, OPUS, Constitutions, Normalization, Filtering, Back-Translation	Transformer NMT	Yes, all ST languages + Spanish-English	No
NRC-CNRC (Knowles et al., 2021)	4	17	No external data, preoricessing, BPE Dropout.	Transofrmer NMT	Yes, 4-languages	No
REPUcs (Moreno, 2021)	1	2	JW300, New dataset, Europarl	Transformer NMT.	Yes, with Spanish-English	Spanish-English pretraining
Tamalli (Parida et al., 2021)	10	42	-	WB-SMT. Transformer NMT,	10-languages	No
UBC-NLP (Billah-Nagoudi et al., 2021)	8	29	Bible, Wikipedia	Transformer T5	10-Languages	New T5
UTokyo (Zheng et al., 2021)	10	40	Monolingual from other languages. Data	Transformer	Yes	New mBART
Anonymous	8	14	-	-	-	-

Table 2: Participating team (*Team*) with system description paper, number of languages that system outputs were submitted for (*Langs.*), total number of submissions (*Sub.*), external data (*Data*), models (*Models*), if training was multilingual (*Multilingual*), and if pretraining was done (*Pretrained*). More details can be found in the text.

was 90% Spanish–English and 10% indigenous languages, and then changed the data proportion to 50% Spanish–English and 50% indigenous languages.

4.4 CoAStaL

The team of the University of Copenhagen (CoAStaL) submitted systems for both tracks (Bollmann et al., 2021). They focused on additional data collection and tried to improve the results with low-resource techniques. The team discovered that it was even hard to generate correct words in the output and that phrase-based statistical machine translation (PB-SMT) systems work well when compared to the state-of-the-art neural models. Interestingly, the team introduced a baseline that mimicked the target language using a character-trigram distribution and length constraints without any knowledge of the source sentence. This random text generation achieved even better results than some of the other submitted systems. The team also reported failed experiments, where character-based neural machine translation (NMT), pretrained transformers, language model priors, and graph convolution encoders using UD annotations could not get any meaningful results.

4.5 REPUcs

The system of the Pontificia Universidad Católica del Perú (REPUcs; Moreno, 2021) submitted to the the Spanish–Quechua language pair in both tracks. The team collected external data from 3 different sources and analyzed the domain disparity between this training data and the development set. To solve the problem of domain mismatch, they decided to collect additional data that could be a better match for the target domain. The used data from a handbook (Iter and Ortiz-Cárdenas, 2019), a lexicon,[5] and poems on the web (Duran, 2010).[6] Their model is a transformer encoder-decoder architecture with SentencePiece (Kudo and Richardson, 2018) tokenization. Together with the existing parallel corpora, the new paired data was used for finetuning on top of a pretrained Spanish–English translation model. The team submitted two versions of their system: the first was only finetuned on JW300+ data, while the second one additionally leveraged the newly collected dataset.

4.6 UTokyo

The team of the University of Tokyo (UTokyo; Zheng et al., 2021) submitted systems for all languages and both tracks. A multilingual pretrained encoder-decoder model (mBART; Liu et al., 2020) was used, implemented with the Fairseq toolkit (Ott et al., 2019). The model was first pretrained on a huge amount of data (up to 13GB) from var-

[5] https://www.inkatour.com/dico/

[6] https://lyricstranslate.com/

Lang.	Rank	Team	Sub	BLEU	ChrF
aym	1	Helsinki	2	2.80	**31.0**
	2	Helsinki	1	2.91	30.2
	3	Helsinki	3	2.35	26.1
	4	UTokyo	1	1.17	21.4
	5	CoAStaL	1	1.11	19.1
	6	UBC-NLP	2	0.99	19.0
	7	UBC-NLP	4	0.76	18.6
	8	UTokyo	2	1.18	14.9
	9	Anonym	1	0.01	7.3

	Rank	Team	Sub	BLEU	ChrF
bzd	1	Helsinki	2	5.18	**21.3**
	2	Helsinki	1	4.93	20.4
	3	CoAStaL	1	3.60	19.6
	4	Helsinki	3	3.68	17.7
	5	UTokyo	1	1.70	14.3
	6	UBC-NLP	2	0.94	11.3
	7	UTokyo	2	1.28	11.2
	8	UBC-NLP	4	0.89	11.1
	9	Anonym	1	0.14	6.1

Lang.	Rank	Team	Sub	BLEU	ChrF
cni	1	Helsinki	2	6.09	**33.2**
	2	Helsinki	1	5.87	32.4
	3	Helsinki	3	5.00	30.6
	4	CoAStaL	1	3.02	26.5
	5	UTokyo	1	0.20	21.6
	6	UTokyo	2	0.84	18.9
	7	UBC-NLP	2	0.08	18.3
	8	UBC-NLP	4	0.09	17.8
	9	Anonym	1	0.08	11.4

Lang.	Rank	Team	Sub	BLEU	ChrF
gn	1	Helsinki	2	8.92	**37.6**
	2	Helsinki	1	8.18	36.7
	3	Helsinki	3	5.97	31.1
	4	NRC-CNRC	0	4.73	30.4
	5	NRC-CNRC	4	5.27	30.3
	6	NRC-CNRC	2	4.06	28.8
	7	UTokyo	1	3.21	26.5
	8	CoAStaL	1	2.20	24.1
	9	UTokyo	2	3.18	23.3
	10	NRC-CNRC	3	0.64	16.3
	11	Anonym	1	0.03	8.5

Lang	Rank	Team	Sub	BLEU	ChrF
hch	1	Helsinki	2	15.67	**36.0**
	2	Helsinki	1	14.71	34.8
	3	NRC-CNRC	0	14.90	32.7
	4	NRC-CNRC	2	13.65	31.5
	5	Helsinki	3	13.72	31.1
	6	CoAStaL	1	8.80	25.7
	7	UTokyo	1	7.09	23.8
	8	NRC-CNRC	3	4.62	20.0
	9	UBC-NLP	2	5.52	19.5
	10	UBC-NLP	4	5.09	18.6
	11	UTokyo	2	6.30	18.4
	12	Amonym	1	0.06	8.1

Lang	Rank	Team	Sub	BLEU	ChrF
nah	1	Helsinki	2	3.25	**30.1**
	2	Helsinki	1	2.8	29.4
	3	NRC-CNRC	0	2.13	27.7
	4	NRC-CNRC	2	1.78	27.3
	5	Helsinki	3	2.76	27.3
	6	UTokyo	1	0.55	23.9
	7	CoAStaL	1	2.06	21.4
	8	UTokyo	2	0.98	19.8
	9	UBC-NLP	2	0.16	19.6
	10	NRC-CNRC	3	0.14	18.1
	11	Anonym	2	0.09	10.3
	12	Anonym	3	0.09	9.7
	13	Anonym	4	0.08	9.5
	14	Anonym	1	0.04	8.7

Lang	Rank	Team	Sub	BLEU	ChrF
oto	1	Helsinki	2	5.59	**22.8**
	2	Helsinki	1	3.85	19.1
	3	CoAStaL	1	2.72	18.4
	4	Helsinki	3	2.9	18.1
	5	UTokyo	2	2.45	15.2
	6	UTokyo	1	0.12	12.8
	7	Anonym	1	0.15	10.2
	8	UBC-NLP	2	0.04	8.4
	9	UBC-NLP	4	0.04	8.3

Lang	Rank	Team	Sub	BLEU	ChrF
quy	1	Helsinki	2	5.38	**39.4**
	2	Helsinki	1	5.16	38.3
	3	REPUcs	2	3.1	35.8
	4	UTokyo	1	2.35	33.2
	5	UTokyo	2	2.62	32.8
	6	Helsinki	3	3.56	31.8
	7	CoAStaL	1	1.63	26.9
	8	Anonym	2	0.23	10.3
	9	Anonym	4	0.13	9.8
	10	Anonym	1	0.06	9.0
	11	Anonym	3	0.03	6.6

Lang	Rank	Team	Sub	BLEU	ChrF
shp	1	Helsinki	2	10.49	**39.9**
	2	Helsinki	1	9.06	38.0
	3	CoAStaL	1	3.9	29.7
	4	Helsinki	3	6.76	28.6
	5	UTokyo	1	0.33	16.3
	6	UTokyo	2	0.46	15.5
	7	UBC-NLP	2	0.23	12.4

Lang	Rank	Team	Sub	BLEU	ChrF
tar	1	Helsinki	2	3.56	**25.8**
	2	Helsinki	1	3.24	24.8
	3	NRC-CNRC	0	2.69	24.7
	4	NRC-CNRC	2	2.1	23.9
	5	Helsinki	3	1.8	21.6
	6	NRC-CNRC	3	0.83	16.5
	7	CoAStaL	1	1.05	15.9
	8	UTokyo	1	0.1	12.2
	9	UBC-NLP	2	0.05	10.5
	10	UBC-NLP	4	0.1	10.5
	11	UTokyo	2	0.69	8.4

Table 3: Results of Track 1 (development set used for training) for all systems and language pairs. The results are ranked by the official metric of the shared task: ChrF. One team decided to send a anonymous submission (*Anonym*). Best results are shown in bold, and they are significantly better than the second place team (in each language-pair) according to the Wilcoxon signed-ranked test and Pitman's permutation test with $p<0.05$ (Dror et al., 2018).

ious high-resource languages, and then finetuned for each target language using the official provided data.

4.7 NRC-CNRC

The team of the National Research Council Canada (NRC-CNRC; Knowles et al., 2021) submitted systems for the Spanish to Wixárika, Nahuatl, Rarámuri and Guarani language pairs for both tracks. Due to ethical considerations, the team decided not to use external data, and restricted themselves to the data provided for the shared task. All data was preprocessed with standard Moses tools (Koehn et al., 2007). The submitted systems were based on a Transformer model, and used BPE for tokenization. The team experimented with multilingual models pretrained on either 3 or 4 languages, finding that the 4 language model achieved higher performance. Additionally the team trained a Translation Memory (Simard and Fujita, 2012) using half of the examples of the development set. Surprisingly, even given its small amount of training data, this system outperformed the team's Track 2 submission for Rarámuri.

4.8 Tamalli

The team Tamalli[7] (Parida et al., 2021) participated in Track 1 for all 10 language pairs. The team used an IBM Model 2 for SMT, and a transformer model for NMT. The team's NMT models were trained in two settings: one-to-one, with one model being trained per target language, and one-to-many, where decoder weights were shared across languages and a language embedding layer was added to the decoder. They submitted 5 systems per language, which differed in their hyperparameter choices and training setup.

5 Results

5.1 Track 1

The complete results for all systems submitted to Track 1 are shown in Table 3. Submission 2 of the Helsinki team achieved first place for all language pairs. Interestingly, for all language pairs, the Helsinki team also achieved the second best result with their Submission 1. Submission 3 was less successful, achieving third place on three pairs. The NRC-CNRC team achieved third place for Wixárika, Nahuatl, and Rarámuri, and fourth for Guarani.The lower automatic scores of their systems can also be partly due to the team not using additional datasets. The REPUcs system obtained the third best result for Quechua, the only language they participated in. CoAStaL's first system, a PB-SMT model, achieved third place for Bribri, Otomí, and Shipibo-Konibo, and fourth place for Ashaninka. This suggests that SMT is still competitive for low-resource languages. UTokyo and UBC-NLP were less successful than the other approaches. Finally, we attribute the bad performance of the anonymous submission to a possible bug. Since our baseline system was not trained on the development set, no specific baseline was available for this track.

5.2 Track 2

All results for Track 2, including those of our baseline system, are shown in Table 5.

Most submissions outperformed the baseline by a large margin. As for Track 1, the best system was from the Helsinki team (submission 5), winning 9 out of 10 language pairs. REPUcs achieved the best score for Spanish–Quechua, the only language pair they submitted results for. Their pretraining on Spanish–English and the newly collected dataset proved to be successful.

Second places were more diverse for Track 2 than for Track 1. The NRC-CNRC team achieved second place for two languages (Wixarika and Guarani), UTokyo achieved second place for three languages (Aymara, Nahuatl and Otomí), and the Helsinki team came in second for Quechua. Tamalli only participated in Track 2, with 4 systems per language. Their most successful one was submission 1, a word-based SMT system. An interesting submission for this track was the CoAStaL submission 2, which created a random generated output that mimics the target language distribution. This system consistently outperformed the official baseline and even outperformed other approaches for most languages.

5.3 Supplementary Evaluation Results

As explained in §2, we also conducted a small human evaluation of system outputs based on adequacy and fluency on a 5-points scale, which was performed by a professional translator for two language-pairs: Spanish to Shipibo-Konibo and

[7]Participating universities: Idiap Research Institute, City University of New York, BITS-India, Universidad Autónoma Metropolitana-México, Ghent University, and Universidad Politécnica de Tulancingo-México

System	aym	bzd	cni	gn	hch	nah	oto	quy	shp	tar	Avg.
Baseline	49.33	**52.00**	42.80	55.87	41.07	54.07	36.50	59.87	52.00	43.73	48.72
Helsinki-5	**57.60**	48.93	**55.33**	**62.40**	**55.33**	**62.33**	**49.33**	**60.80**	**65.07**	**58.80**	57.59
NRC-CNRC-1	-	-	-	57.20	50.40	58.94	-	-	-	53.47	55.00*

Table 4: Results of the NLI analysis. * indicates that the average score is not directly comparable as the number of languages differs for the given system.

Otomí.[8] This evaluation was performed given the extremely low automatic evaluation scores, and the natural question about the usefulness of the outputs of MT systems at the current state-of-the-art. While we selected two languages as a sample to get a better approximation to this question, further studies are needed to draw stronger conclusions.

Figure 1 shows the adequacy and fluency scores annotated for Spanish–Shipibo-Konibo and Spanish–Otomí language-pairs. considering the baseline and the three highest ranked systems according to ChrF. For both languages, we observe that the adequacy scores are similar between all systems except for `Helsinki`, the best ranked submission given the automatic evaluation metric, which has more variance than the others. However, the average score is low, around 2, which means that only few words or phrases express the meaning of the reference.

Looking at fluency, there is less similarity between the Shipibo-Konibo and Otomí annotations. For Shipibo-Konibo, there is no clear difference between the systems in terms of their average scores. We note that `Tamalli`'s system obtained the larger group with the relatively highest score. For Otomí, the three submitted systems are at least slightly better than the baseline on average, but only in 1 level of the scale. The scores for fluency are similar to adequacy in this case. Besides, according to the annotations, the output translations in Shipibo-Konibo were closer to human-produced texts than in Otomí.

We also show the relationship between ChrF and the adequacy and fluency scores in Figure 2. However, there does not seem to be a correlation between the automatic metric and the manually assigned scores.

[8]In the WMT campaigns, it is common to perform a crowd-sourced evaluation with several annotators. However, we cannot follow that procedure given the low chance to find native speakers of indigenous languages as users in crowd-sourcing platforms.

5.4 Analysis: NLI

One approach for zero-shot transfer learning of a sequence classification task is the translate-train approach, where a translation system is used to translate high-resource labeled training data into the target language. In the case of pretrained multilingual models, these machine translated examples are then used for finetuning. For our analysis, we used various shared task submissions to create different sets of translated training data. We then trained a natural language inference (NLI) model using this translated data, and used the downstream NLI performance as an extrinsic evaluation of translation quality.

Our experimental setup was identical to Ebrahimi et al. (2021). We focused only on submissions from Track 2, and analyzed the `Helsinki-5` and the `NRC-CNRC-1` system. We present results in Table 4. Performance from using the `Helsinki` system far outperforms the baseline on average, and using the `NRC-CNRC` system also improves over the baseline. For the four languages covered by all systems, we can see that the ranking of NLI performance matches that of the automatic ChrF evaluation. Between the Helsinki and Baseline systems, this ranking also holds for every other language except for Bribri, where the Baseline achieves around 3 percentage points higher accuracy. Overall, this evaluation both confirms the ranking created by the ChrF scores and provides strong evidence supporting the use of translation-based approaches for zero-shot tasks.

6 Error Analysis

To extend the analysis in the previous sections, Tables 6 and 7 show output samples using the best ranked system (`Helsinki-5`) for Shipibo-Konibo and Otomí, respectively. In each table, we present the top-3 outputs ranked by ChrF and the top-3 ranked by Adequacy and Fluency.

For Shipibo-Konibo, in Table 6, we observe that the first three outputs (with the highest ChrF) are quite close to the reference. Surprisingly, the ad-

Lang.	Rank	Team	Sub	BLEU	ChrF
aym	1	Helsinki	5	2.29	**28.3**
	2	Helsinki	4	1.41	21.6
	3	UTokyo	3	1.03	20.9
	4	Tamalli	1	0.03	20.2
	5	Tamalli	3	0.39	19.4
	6	UBC-NLP	3	0.82	18.2
	7	UBC-NLP	1	1.01	17.8
	8	UTokyo 4		1.34	17.2
	9	CoAStaL	2	0.05	16.8
	10	Tamalli	2	0.07	16.6
	11	Baseline	1	0.01	15.7
	12	Tamalli	5	0.12	15.1

Lang.	Rank	Team	Sub	BLEU	ChrF
bzd	1	Helsinki	5	2.39	**16.5**
	2	Tamalli	3	1.09	13.2
	3	UTokyo	3	1.29	13.1
	4	Helsinki	4	1.98	13.0
	5	Tamalli	1	0.03	11.3
	6	UBC-NLP	1	0.99	11.2
	7	UBC-NLP	3	0.86	11.0
	8	CoAStaL	2	0.06	10.7
	9	Tamalli	5	0.36	10.6
	10	UTokyo	4	1.13	10.4
	11	Baseline	1	0.01	6.8
	12	Tamalli	2	0.25	3.7

Lang.	Rank	Team	Sub	BLEU	ChrF
cni	1	Helsinki	5	3.05	**25.8**
	2	Tamalli	1	0.01	25.3
	3	Helsinki	4	3.01	23.6
	4	UTokyo	3	0.47	21.4
	5	CoAStaL	2	0.03	21.2
	6	Tamalli	3	0.18	18.6
	7	UTokyo	4	0.76	18.4
	8	UBC-NLP	1	0.07	17.8
	9	UBC-NLP	3	0.09	17.6
	10	Tamalli	5	0.07	17.4
	11	Tamalli	2	0.06	13.0
	12	Baseline	1	0.01	10.2

Lang.	Rank	Team	Sub	BLEU	ChrF
gn	1	Helsinki	5	6.13	**33.6**
	2	Helsinki	4	4.10	27.6
	3	NRC-CNRC	1	2.86	26.1
	4	UTokyo	3	3.16	25.4
	5	UTokyo	4	2.97	25.1
	6	Tamalli	5	1.90	20.7
	7	Baseline	1	0.12	19.3
	8	Tamalli	3	1.03	18.7
	9	Tamalli	1	0.05	17.2
	10	CoAStaL	2	0.03	12.8
	11	Tamalli	2	0.13	10.8

Lang.	Rank	Team	Sub	BLEU	ChrF
hch	1	Helsinki	5	9.63	**30.4**
	2	NRC CNRC	1	7.96	26.4
	3	Helsinki	4	9.13	25.4
	4	UTokyo	3	6.74	22.9
	5	UTokyo	4	6.74	21.6
	6	Tamalli	1	0.01	21.4
	7	Tamalli	3	5.02	20.6
	8	UBC-NLP	1	5.10	19.4
	9	CoAStaL	2	2.07	19.1
	10	UBC-NLP	3	4.95	18.6
	11	Tamalli	5	4.71	16.9
	12	Baseline	1	2.20	12.6
	13	Tamalli	2	3.29	9.4

Lang	Rank	Team	Sub	BLEU	ChrF
nah	1	Helsinki	5	2.38	**26.6**
	2	Helsinki	4	2.02	24.3
	3	UTokyo	4	1.2	23.8
	4	NRC-CNRC	1	0.83	23.7
	5	UTokyo	3	0.29	23.6
	6	Tamalli	1	0.03	21.8
	7	UBC-NLP	1	0.12	19.5
	8	UBC-NLP	3	0.15	18.8
	9	CoAStaL	2	0.03	18.4
	10	Tamalli	3	0.11	17.4
	11	Tamalli	5	0.10	16.6
	12	Baseline	1	0.01	15.7
	13	Tamalli	4	0.08	14.5
	14	Tamalli	2	0.03	11.2

Lang	Rank	Team	Sub	BLEU	ChrF
oto	1	Helsinki	5	1.69	**14.7**
	2	Helsinki	4	1.37	14.1
	3	UTokyo	4	1.28	13.3
	4	UTokyo	3	0.05	12.5
	5	Tamalli	1	0.01	11.8
	6	Tamalli	3	0.12	11.0
	7	CoAStaL	2	0.03	10.1
	8	UBC-NLP	1	0.03	8.2
	9	UBC-NLP	3	0.03	8.1
	10	Tamalli	5	0.01	7.4
	11	Baseline	1	0.00	5.4
	12	Tamalli	2	0.00	1.4

Lang	Rank	Team	Sub	BLEU	ChrF
quy	1	REPUcs	1	2.91	34.6
	2	Helsinki	5	3.63	34.3
	3	UTokyo	4	2.47	33.0
	4	UTokyo	3	2.1	32.8
	5	Baseline	1	0.05	30.4
	6	Tamalli	5	0.96	27.3
	7	Tamalli	3	0.64	26.3
	8	Helsinki	4	2.67	25.2
	9	Tamalli	1	0.22	24.4
	10	Tamalli	2	0.69	23.2
	11	CoAStaL	2	0.02	23.2

Lang	Rank	Team	Sub	BLEU	ChrF
shp	1	Helsinki	5	5.43	**32.9**
	2	Helsinki	4	4.53	29.4
	3	Tamalli	1	0.06	20.4
	4	UTokyo	3	0.71	17.5
	5	CoAStaL	2	0.04	17.3
	6	UTokyo	4	0.64	16.4
	7	Tamalli	3	0.31	14.9
	8	Tamalli	5	0.28	12.5
	9	UBC-NLP	1	0.16	12.4
	10	Baseline	1	0.01	12.1
	11	Tamalli	2	0.09	8.9

Lang	Rank	Team	Sub	BLEU	ChrF
tar	1	Helsinki	5	1.07	**18.4**
	2	Tamalli	1	0.04	15.5
	3	Helsinki	4	0.81	15.5
	4	NRC-CNRC	1	0.27	14.3
	5	UTokyo	3	0.06	12.3
	6	UTokyo	4	0.06	11.9
	7	CoAStaL	2	0.06	11.3
	8	UBC-NLP	1	0.08	10.2
	9	UBC-NLP	3	0.06	10.2
	10	Tamalli	4	0.05	8.9
	11	Tamalli	3	0.04	8.4
	12	Tamalli	5	0.02	7.3
	13	Baseline	1	0.00	3.9
	14	Tamalli	2	0.01	2.8

Table 5: Results of Track 2 (development set *not* used for training) for all systems and language pairs. The results are ranked by the official metric of the shared task: ChrF. Best results per language pair are shown in bold, and they are significantly better than the second place team (in each language-pair) according to the Wilcoxon signed-ranked test and Pitman's permutation test with $p<0.05$ (Dror et al., 2018).

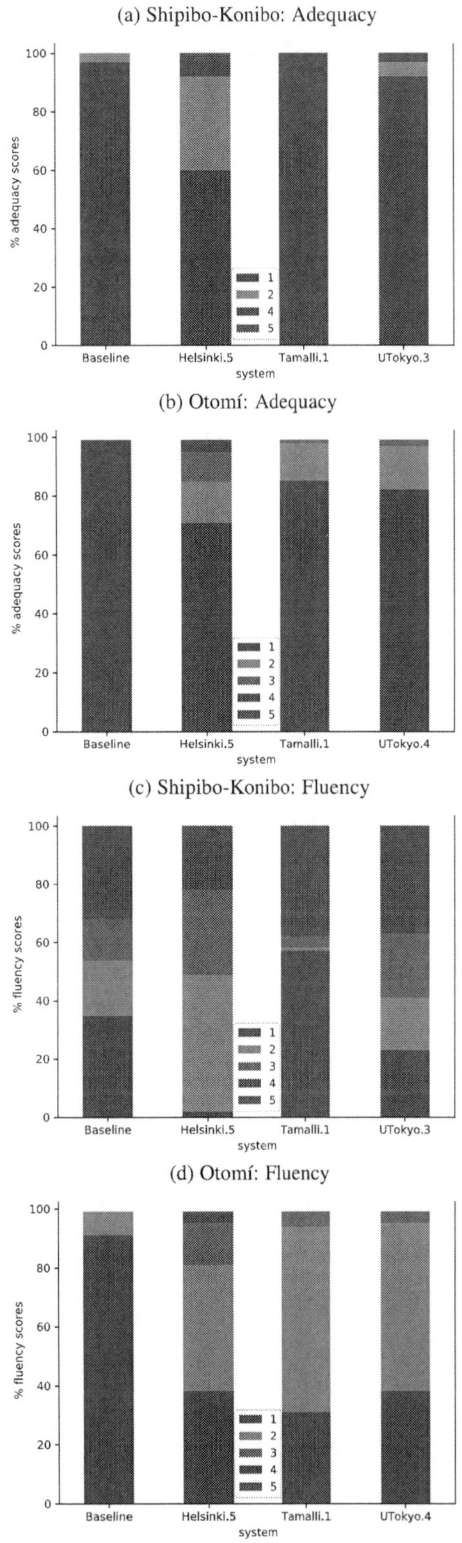

Figure 1: Adequacy and fluency distribution scores for Shipibo-Konibo and Otomí.

equacy annotation of the first sample is relatively low. We can also observe that many subwords are presented in both the reference and the system's output, but not entire words, which shows why BLEU may not be a useful metric to evaluate performance. However, the subwords are still located in different order, and concatenated with different morphemes, which impacts the fluency. Concerning the most adequate and fluent samples, we still observe a high presence of correct subwords in the output, and we can infer that the different order or concatenation of different morphemes did not affect the original meaning of the sentence.

For Otomí, in Table 7, the scenario was less positive, as the ChrF scores are lower than for Shipibo-Konibo, on average. This was echoed in the top-3 outputs, which are very short and contain words or phrases that are preserved in Spanish for the reference translation. Concerning the most adequate and fluent outputs, we observed a very low overlapping of subwords (less than in Shipibo-Konibo), which could only indicate that the outputs preserve part of the meaning of the source but they are expressed differently than the reference. Moreover, we noticed some inconsistencies in the punctuation, which impacts in the ChrF overall score.

In summary, there are some elements to explore further in the rest of the outputs: How many loanwords or how much code-switched text from Spanish is presented in the reference translation? Is there consistency in the punctuation, e.g., period at the end of a segment, between all the source and reference sentences?

7 Conclusion

This paper presents the results of the AmericasNLP 2021 Shared Task on OMT. We received 214 submissions of machine translation systems by 8 teams. All systems suffered from the minimal amount of data and the challenging orthographic, dialectal and domain mismatches of the training and test set. However, most teams achieved huge improvements over the official baseline. We found that text cleaning and normalization, as well as domain adaptation played large roles in the best performing systems. The best NMT systems were multilingual approaches with a limited size (over massive multilingual). Additionally, SMT models also performed well, outperforming larger pretrained submissions.

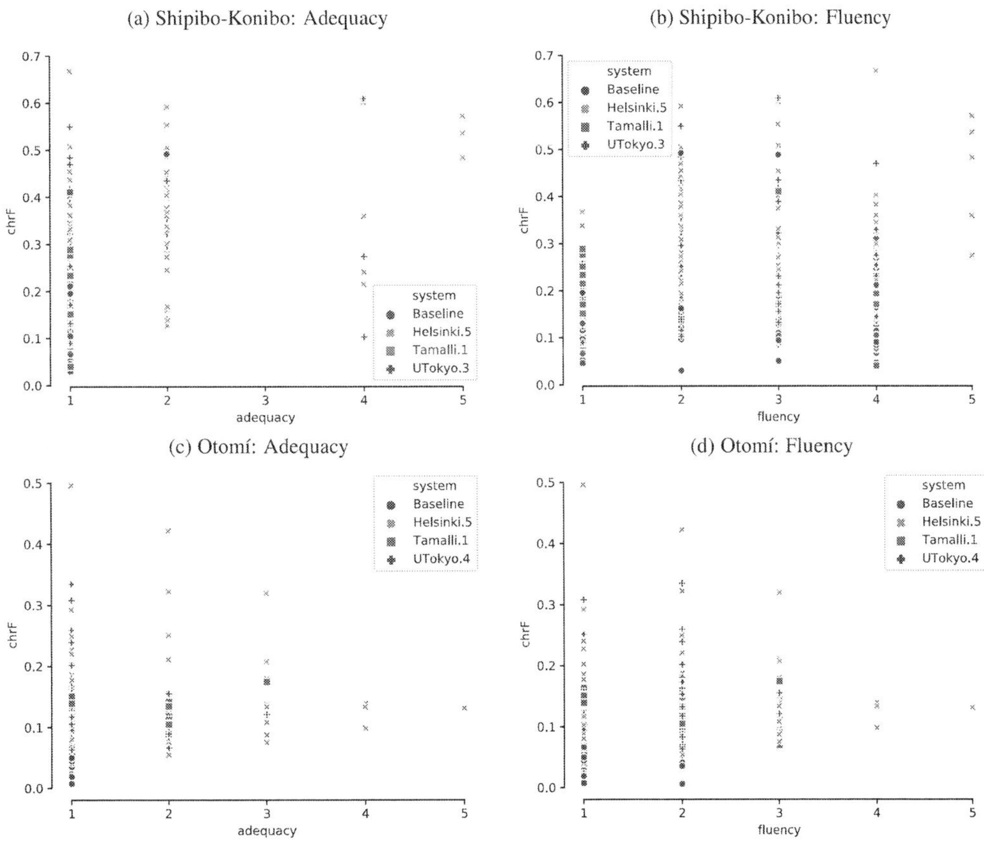

Figure 2: Relationship between ChrF scores and annotations for adequacy (left) and fluency (right).

Scores	Sentences
C: 66.7	SRC: Un niño murió de los cinco.
A: 1	REF: Westiora bakera mawata iki pichika batiayax.
F: 4	OUT: Westiora bakera pichika mawata iki.
C: 60.9	SRC: Sé que no puedes oírme.
A: 4	REF: Eanra onanke min ea ninkati atipanyama.
F: 3	OUT: Minra ea ninkati atipanyamake.
C: 60.1	SRC: Necesito un minuto para recoger mis pensamientos.
A: 4	REF: Eara westiora minuto kenai nokon shinanbo biti kopi.
F: 3	OUT: Westiora serera ea kenai nokon shinanbo biti.
C: 57.1	SRC: Hoy no he ido, así que no lo he visto.
A: 5	REF: Ramara ea kama iki, jakopira en oinama iki.
F: 5	OUT: Ramara ea kayamake, jaskarakopira en oinyamake
C: 53.6	SRC: El U2 tomó mucha película.
A: 5	REF: Nato U2ninra kikin icha película bike.
F: 5	OUT: U2ninra icha pelicula bike.
C: 48.3	SRC: No teníamos televisión.
A: 5	REF: Noara televisiónma ika iki.
F: 5	OUT: Televisiónmara noa iwanke.

Table 6: Translation outputs of the best system (`Helsinki`) for Shipibo-Konibo. Top-3 samples have the highest ChrF (C) scores, whereas the bottom-3 have the best adequacy (A) and fluency (F) values.

Scores	Sentences
C: 49.6	SRC: Locust Hill oh claro, sí, genial
A: 1	REF: Locust Hill handa hâ
F: 4	OUT: Locust Hill ohbuho jä'i
C: 42.2	SRC: Kennedy habló con los pilotos.
A: 4	REF: Kennedy bi ñama nen ya pilotos.
F: 3	OUT: Kennedy bi ñäui ya pihnyo.
C: 32.2	SRC: ¿Te gustan los libros de Harry Potter o no?
A: 4	REF: ¿ di ho-y ya ynttothoma on Harry Potter a hin?
F: 3	OUT: ¿ Gi pefihu na rä libro ra Harry Potter o hina?
C: 13.1	SRC: Un niño murió de los cinco.
A: 5	REF: nã mehtzi bidû on ya qda
F: 5	OUT: N'a ra bätsi bi du ko ya kut'a.
C: 13.9	SRC: Él recibe ayuda con sus comidas y ropa.
A: 4	REF: na di hiâni mâhte nen ynu ynñuni xi áhxo
F: 4	OUT: Nu'a hä häni ko ya hñuni ne ya dutu.
C: 13.3	SRC: Ni siquiera entendió la ceremonia nupcial, ni siquiera sabía que se había casado, en serio–
A: 4	REF: Hin bi ôccode na nînthadi, hin mipâca guê bin miqha nthâdi,maqhuani ngu -a.
F: 4	OUT: Inbi bädi te ra nge'a bi nthati, bi ot'e ra guenda...

Table 7: Translation outputs of the best system (`Helsinki`) for Otomí. Top-3 samples have the highest ChrF (C) scores, whereas the bottom-3 have the best adequacy (A) and fluency (F) values.

Acknowledgments

We would like to thank translators of the test and development set, that made this shared task possible: Francisco Morales (Bribri), Feliciano Torres Ríos and Esau Zumaeta Rojas (Asháninka), Perla Alvarez Britez (Guarani), Silvino González de la Crúz (Wixarika), Giovany Martínez Sebastián, Pedro Kapoltitan, and José Antonio (Nahuatl), José Mateo Lino Cajero Velázquez (Otomí), Liz Chávez (Shipibo-Konibo), and María del Cármen Sotelo Holguín (Rarámuri). We also thank our sponsors for their financial support: Facebook AI Research, Microsoft Research, Google Research, the Institute of Computational Linguistics at the University of Zurich, the NAACL Emerging Regions Funding, Comunidad Elotl, and Snorkel AI. Additionally we want to thank all participants for their submissions and effort to advance NLP research for the indigenous languages of the Americas. Manuel Mager received financial support by DAAD Doctoral Research Grant for this work.

References

Željko Agić and Ivan Vulić. 2019. JW300: A Wide-Coverage Parallel Corpus for Low-Resource Languages. In *Proceedings of the 57th Annual Meeting of the Association for Computational Linguistics*, pages 3204–3210, Florence, Italy. Association for Computational Linguistics.

Loïc Barrault, Magdalena Biesialska, Ondřej Bojar, Marta R. Costa-jussà, Christian Federmann, Yvette Graham, Roman Grundkiewicz, Barry Haddow, Matthias Huck, Eric Joanis, Tom Kocmi, Philipp Koehn, Chi-kiu Lo, Nikola Ljubešić, Christof Monz, Makoto Morishita, Masaaki Nagata, Toshiaki Nakazawa, Santanu Pal, Matt Post, and Marcos Zampieri. 2020. Findings of the 2020 conference on machine translation (WMT20). In *Proceedings of the Fifth Conference on Machine Translation*, pages 1–55, Online. Association for Computational Linguistics.

El Moatez Billah-Nagoudi, Wei-Rui Chen, Muhammad Abdul-Mageed, and Hasan Cavusoglu. 2021. IndT5: A Text-to-Text Transformer for 10 Indigenous Languages. In *Proceedings of the AmericasNLP 2021 Shared Task on Open Machine Translation for Indigenous Languages of the Americas*, Online. Association for Computational Linguistics.

Marcel Bollmann, Rahul Aralikatte, Héctor Murrieta-Bello, Daniel Hershcovich, Miryam de Lhoneux, and Anders Søgaard. 2021. Moses and the character-based random babbling baseline: CoAStaL at AmericasNLP 2021 shared task. In *Proceedings of the AmericasNLP 2021 Shared Task on Open Machine Translation for Indigenous Languages of the Americas*, Online. Association for Computational Linguistics.

David Brambila. 1976. *Diccionario rarámuri-castellano (tarahumar)*. Obra Nacional de la buena Prensa.

Luis Chiruzzo, Pedro Amarilla, Adolfo Ríos, and Gustavo Giménez Lugo. 2020. Development of a Guarani - Spanish parallel corpus. In *Proceedings of the 12th Language Resources and Evaluation Conference*, pages 2629–2633, Marseille, France. European Language Resources Association.

Christos Christodouloupoulos and Mark Steedman. 2015. A massively parallel corpus: the bible in 100 languages. *Language resources and evaluation*, 49(2):375–395.

Matthew Coler and Petr Homola. 2014. *Rule-based machine translation for Aymara*, pages 67–80. Cambridge University Press.

Alexis Conneau, Ruty Rinott, Guillaume Lample, Adina Williams, Samuel Bowman, Holger Schwenk, and Veselin Stoyanov. 2018. XNLI: Evaluating cross-lingual sentence representations. In *Proceedings of the 2018 Conference on Empirical Methods in Natural Language Processing*, pages 2475–2485, Brussels, Belgium. Association for Computational Linguistics.

Adolfo Constenla, Feliciano Elizondo, and Francisco Pereira. 2004. *Curso Básico de Bribri*. Editorial de la Universidad de Costa Rica.

Rotem Dror, Gili Baumer, Segev Shlomov, and Roi Reichart. 2018. The hitchhiker's guide to testing statistical significance in natural language processing. In *Proceedings of the 56th Annual Meeting of the Association for Computational Linguistics (Volume 1: Long Papers)*, pages 1383–1392, Melbourne, Australia. Association for Computational Linguistics.

Maximiliano Duran. 2010. Lengua general de los incas. http://quechua-ayacucho.org/es/index_es.php. Accessed: 2021-03-15.

Abteen Ebrahimi, Manuel Mager, Arturo Oncevay, Vishrav Chaudhary, Luis Chiruzzo, Angela Fan, John Ortega, Ricardo Ramos, Annette Rios, Ivan Vladimir, Gustavo A. Giménez-Lugo, Elisabeth Mager, Graham Neubig, Alexis Palmer, Rolando A. Coto Solano, Ngoc Thang Vu, and Katharina Kann. 2021. AmericasNLI: Evaluating Zero-shot Natural Language Understanding of Pretrained Multilingual Models in Truly Low-resource Languages.

Isaac Feldman and Rolando Coto-Solano. 2020. Neural machine translation models with back-translation for the extremely low-resource indigenous language Bribri. In *Proceedings of the 28th International Conference on Computational Linguistics*, pages 3965–3976, Barcelona, Spain (Online). International Committee on Computational Linguistics.

Dayana Iguarán Fernández, Ornela Quintero Gamboa, Jose Molina Atencia, and Oscar Elías Herrera Bedoya. 2013. Design and implementation of an "Web API" for the automatic translation Colombia's language pairs: Spanish-Wayuunaiki case. In *Communications and Computing (COLCOM), 2013 IEEE Colombian Conference on*, pages 1–9. IEEE.

Sofía Flores Solórzano. 2017. Corpus oral pandialectal de la lengua bribri. http://bribri.net.

Ana-Paula Galarreta, Andrés Melgar, and Arturo Oncevay. 2017. Corpus creation and initial SMT experiments between Spanish and Shipibo-konibo. In *Proceedings of the International Conference Recent Advances in Natural Language Processing, RANLP 2017*, pages 238–244, Varna, Bulgaria. INCOMA Ltd.

Candace Kaleimamoowahinekapu Galla. 2016. Indigenous language revitalization, promotion, and education: Function of digital technology. *Computer Assisted Language Learning*, 29(7):1137–1151.

Héctor Erasmo Gómez Montoya, Kervy Dante Rivas Rojas, and Arturo Oncevay. 2019. A continuous improvement framework of machine translation for Shipibo-konibo. In *Proceedings of the 2nd Workshop on Technologies for MT of Low Resource Languages*, pages 17–23, Dublin, Ireland. European Association for Machine Translation.

Ximena Gutierrez-Vasques. 2015. Bilingual lexicon extraction for a distant language pair using a small parallel corpus. In *Proceedings of the 2015 Conference of the North American Chapter of the Association for Computational Linguistics: Student Research Workshop*, pages 154–160.

Ximena Gutierrez-Vasques, Gerardo Sierra, and Isaac Hernandez Pompa. 2016. Axolotl: a web accessible parallel corpus for Spanish-Nahuatl. In *Proceedings of the Tenth International Conference on Language Resources and Evaluation (LREC'16)*, pages 4210–4214, Portorož, Slovenia. European Language Resources Association (ELRA).

Francisco Guzmán, Peng-Jen Chen, Myle Ott, Juan Pino, Guillaume Lample, Philipp Koehn, Vishrav Chaudhary, and Marc'Aurelio Ranzato. 2019. The FLORES evaluation datasets for low-resource machine translation: Nepali–English and Sinhala–English. In *Proceedings of the 2019 Conference on Empirical Methods in Natural Language Processing and the 9th International Joint Conference on Natural Language Processing (EMNLP-IJCNLP)*, pages 6098–6111, Hong Kong, China. Association for Computational Linguistics.

Diego Huarcaya Taquiri. 2020. Traducción automática neuronal para lengua nativa peruana. Bachelor's thesis, Universidad Peruana Unión.

Cesar Iter and Zenobio Ortiz-Cárdenas. 2019. *Runasimita yachasun. Método de quechua*, 1 edition. Instituto Francés de Estudios Andinos, Lima.

Carla Victoria Jara Murillo. 2018a. *Gramática de la Lengua Bribri*. EDigital.

Carla Victoria Jara Murillo. 2018b. *I Ttè Historias Bribris*, second edition. Editorial de la Universidad de Costa Rica.

Carla Victoria Jara Murillo and Alí García Segura. 2013. *Se' ttö' bribri ie Hablemos en bribri*. EDigital.

Rebecca Knowles, Darlene Stewart, Samuel Larkin, and Patrick Littell. 2021. NRC-CNRC Machine Translation Systems for the 2021 AmericasNLP Shared Task. In *Proceedings of the AmericasNLP 2021 Shared Task on Open Machine Translation for Indigenous Languages of the Americas*, Online. Association for Computational Linguistics.

Philipp Koehn, Hieu Hoang, Alexandra Birch, Chris Callison-Burch, Marcello Federico, Nicola Bertoldi, Brooke Cowan, Wade Shen, Christine Moran, Richard Zens, et al. 2007. Moses: Open source toolkit for statistical machine translation. In *Proceedings of the 45th annual meeting of the association for computational linguistics companion volume proceedings of the demo and poster sessions*, pages 177–180.

Taku Kudo and John Richardson. 2018. SentencePiece: A simple and language independent subword tokenizer and detokenizer for Neural Text Processing. In *Proceedings of the 2018 Conference on Empirical Methods in Natural Language Processing: System Demonstrations*, pages 66–71, Brussels, Belgium. Association for Computational Linguistics.

Yinhan Liu, Jiatao Gu, Naman Goyal, Xian Li, Sergey Edunov, Marjan Ghazvininejad, Mike Lewis, and Luke Zettlemoyer. 2020. Multilingual Denoising Pre-training for Neural Machine Translation. *Transactions of the Association for Computational Linguistics*, 8:726–742.

James Loriot, Erwin Lauriault, Dwight Day, and Peru. Ministerio de Educación. 1993. *Diccionario Shipibo-Castellano*.

Manuel Mager, Diónico Carrillo, and Ivan Meza. 2018a. Probabilistic finite-state morphological segmenter for wixarika (huichol) language. *Journal of Intelligent & Fuzzy Systems*, 34(5):3081–3087.

Manuel Mager, Ximena Gutierrez-Vasques, Gerardo Sierra, and Ivan Meza-Ruiz. 2018b. Challenges of language technologies for the indigenous languages of the Americas. In *Proceedings of the 27th International Conference on Computational Linguistics*, pages 55–69, Santa Fe, New Mexico, USA. Association for Computational Linguistics.

Manuel Mager and Ivan Meza. 2018. Hacia la traducción automática de las lenguas indígenas de méxico. In *Proceedings of the 2018 Digital Humanities Conference*. The Association of Digital Humanities Organizations.

Enrique Margery. 2005. *Diccionario Fraseológico Bribri-Español Español-Bribri*, second edition. Editorial de la Universidad de Costa Rica.

Thomas Mayer and Michael Cysouw. 2014. Creating a massively parallel bible corpus. *Oceania*, 135(273):40.

Arya D. McCarthy, Rachel Wicks, Dylan Lewis, Aaron Mueller, Winston Wu, Oliver Adams, Garrett Nicolai, Matt Post, and David Yarowsky. 2020. The Johns Hopkins University Bible corpus: 1600+ tongues for typological exploration. In *Proceedings of the 12th Language Resources and Evaluation Conference*, pages 2884–2892, Marseille, France. European Language Resources Association.

Elena Mihas. 2011. *Añaani katonkosatzi parenini, El idioma del alto Perené.* WI:Clarks Graphics.

Oscar Moreno. 2021. The REPU CS' spanish–quechua submission to the AmericasNLP 2021 shared task on open machine translation. In *Proceedings of the AmericasNLP 2021 Shared Task on Open Machine Translation for Indigenous Languages of the Americas*, Online. Association for Computational Linguistics.

Sebastian Nordhoff and Harald Hammarström. 2012. Glottolog/Langdoc:Increasing the visibility of grey literature for low-density languages. In *Proceedings of the Eighth International Conference on Language Resources and Evaluation (LREC'12)*, pages 3289–3294, Istanbul, Turkey. European Language Resources Association (ELRA).

John Ortega, Richard Alexander Castro-Mamani, and Jaime Rafael Montoya Samame. 2020. Overcoming resistance: The normalization of an Amazonian tribal language. In *Proceedings of the 3rd Workshop on Technologies for MT of Low Resource Languages*, pages 1–13, Suzhou, China. Association for Computational Linguistics.

Myle Ott, Sergey Edunov, Alexei Baevski, Angela Fan, Sam Gross, Nathan Ng, David Grangier, and Michael Auli. 2019. fairseq: A Fast, Extensible Toolkit for Sequence Modeling. In *Proceedings of the 2019 Conference of the North American Chapter of the Association for Computational Linguistics (Demonstrations)*, pages 48–53.

Kishore Papineni, Salim Roukos, Todd Ward, and Wei-Jing Zhu. 2002. Bleu: a Method for Automatic Evaluation of Machine Translation. In *Proceedings of the 40th Annual Meeting of the Association for Computational Linguistics*, pages 311–318, Philadelphia, Pennsylvania, USA. Association for Computational Linguistics.

Shantipriya Parida, Subhadarshi Panda, Amulya Dash, Esau Villatoro-Tello, A. Seza Doğruöz, Rosa M. Ortega-Mendoza, Amadeo Hernández, Yashvardhan Sharma, and Petr Motlicek. 2021. Open Machine Translation for Low Resource South American Languages (AmericasNLP 2021 Shared Task Contribution). In *Proceedings of the AmericasNLP 2021 Shared Task on Open Machine Translation for Indigenous Languages of the Americas*, Online. Association for Computational Linguistics.

Maja Popović. 2015. chrF: character n-gram F-score for automatic MT evaluation. In *Proceedings of the Tenth Workshop on Statistical Machine Translation*, pages 392–395, Lisbon, Portugal. Association for Computational Linguistics.

Prokopis Prokopidis, Vassilis Papavassiliou, and Stelios Piperidis. 2016. Parallel Global Voices: a Collection of Multilingual Corpora with Citizen Media Stories. In *Proceedings of the Tenth International Conference on Language Resources and Evaluation (LREC'16)*, pages 900–905, Portorož, Slovenia. European Language Resources Association (ELRA).

Colin Raffel, Noam Shazeer, Adam Roberts, Katherine Lee, Sharan Narang, Michael Matena, Yanqi Zhou, Wei Li, and Peter J Liu. 2020. Exploring the Limits of Transfer Learning with a Unified Text-to-Text Transformer. *Journal of Machine Learning Research*, 21:1–67.

Romano, Rubén and Richer, Sebastián. 2008. Ñaantsipeta asháninkaki birakochaki. www.lengamer.org/publicaciones/diccionarios/.

Lane Schwartz, Francis Tyers, Lori Levin, Christo Kirov, Patrick Littell, Chi-kiu Lo, Emily Prud'hommeaux, Hyunji Hayley Park, Kenneth Steimel, Rebecca Knowles, et al. 2020. Neural polysynthetic language modelling. *arXiv preprint arXiv:2005.05477.*

Michel Simard and Atsushi Fujita. 2012. A poor man's translation memory using machine translation evaluation metrics. In *Proceedings of the 10th Biennial Conference of the Association for Machine Translation in the Americas (AMTA).*

Jörg Tiedemann. 2012. Parallel Data, Tools and Interfaces in OPUS. In *Proceedings of the Eight International Conference on Language Resources and Evaluation (LREC'12)*, Istanbul, Turkey. European Language Resources Association (ELRA).

Ashish Vaswani, Noam Shazeer, Niki Parmar, Jakob Uszkoreit, Llion Jones, Aidan N Gomez, Ł ukasz Kaiser, and Illia Polosukhin. 2017. Attention is All you Need. In I. Guyon, U. V. Luxburg, S. Bengio, H. Wallach, R. Fergus, S. Vishwanathan, and R. Garnett, editors, *Advances in Neural Information Processing Systems 30*, pages 5998–6008. Curran Associates, Inc.

Raúl Vázquez, Yves Scherrer, Sami Virpioja, and Jörg Tiedemann. 2021. The Helsinki submission to the AmericasNLP shared task. In *Proceedings of the AmericasNLP 2021 Shared Task on Open Machine Translation for Indigenous Languages of the Americas*, Online. Association for Computational Linguistics.

Shiyue Zhang, Benjamin Frey, and Mohit Bansal. 2020. ChrEn: Cherokee-English machine translation for endangered language revitalization. In *Proceedings of the 2020 Conference on Empirical Methods in Natural Language Processing (EMNLP)*, pages 577–595, Online. Association for Computational Linguistics.

Zheng, Francis, Machel Reid, Edison Marrese-Taylor, and Yutaka Matsuo. 2021. Low-Resource Machine Translation Using Cross-Lingual Language Model Pretraining. In *Proceedings of the AmericasNLP 2021 Shared Task on Open Machine Translation for Indigenous Languages of the Americas*, Online. Association for Computational Linguistics.

Open Machine Translation for Low Resource South American Languages (AmericasNLP 2021 Shared Task Contribution)

Shantipriya Parida[1], Subhadarshi Panda[2], Amulya Ratna Dash[3], Esaú Villatoro-Tello[1,4], A. Seza Doğruöz[5], Rosa M. Ortega-Mendoza[6], Amadeo Hernández[6], Yashvardhan Sharma[3], Petr Motlicek[1]

[1]Idiap Research Institute, Martigny, Switzerland
{firstname.lastname}@idiap.ch
[2]Graduate Center, City University of New York, USA
spanda@gradcenter.cuny.edu
[3]BITS, Pilani, India
{p20200105,yash}@pilani.bits-pilani.ac.in
[4]Universidad Autónoma Metropolitana Cuajimalpa, Mexico City, Mexico
evillatoro@cua.uam.mx
[5]Ghent University, Belgium
as.dogruoz@ugent.be
[6]Universidad Politécnica de Tulancingo, Hidalgo, Mexico
{rosa.ortega,amadeo.hernandez1911001}@upt.edu.mx

Abstract

This paper describes the team ("Tamalli")'s submission to AmericasNLP2021 shared task on Open Machine Translation for low resource South American languages. Our goal was to evaluate different Machine Translation (MT) techniques, statistical and neural-based, under several configuration settings. We obtained the *second-best* results for the language pairs "Spanish-Bribri", "Spanish-Asháninka", and "Spanish-Rarámuri" in the category "Development set not used for training". Our performed experiments will serve as a point of reference for researchers working on MT with low-resource languages.

1 Introduction

The main challenges in automatic Machine Translation (MT) are the acquisition and curation of parallel data and the allocation of hardware resources for training and inference purposes. This situation has become more evident for Neural Machine Translation (NMT) techniques, where their translation quality depends strongly on the amount of available training data when offering translation for a language pair. However, there is only a handful of languages that have available large-scale parallel corpora, or collections of sentences in both the source language and corresponding translations. Thus, applying recent NMT approaches to low-resource languages represent a challenging scenario.

In this paper, we describe the participation of our team (aka, Tamalli) in the Shared Task on Open Machine Translation held in the First Workshop on NLP for Indigenous Languages of the Americas (AmericasNLP) (Mager et al., 2021).[1] The main goal of the shared task was to encourage the development of machine translation systems for indigenous languages of the Americas, categorized as low-resources languages. This year *8* different teams participated with *214* submissions.

Accordingly, our main goal was to evaluate the performance of traditional statistical MT techniques, as well as some recent NMT techniques under different configuration settings. Overall, our results outperformed the baseline proposed by the shared task organizers, and reach promising results for many of the considered pair languages.

The paper is organized as follows: Section 2 briefly describes some related work; Section 3 depicts the methodology we followed for performing our experiments. Section 4 provides the dataset descriptions. Section 5 provides the details from our different settings, and finally Section 6 depict our main conclusions and future work directions.

2 Related work

Machine Translation (Garg and Agarwal, 2018) is a field in NLP that aims to translate natural lan-

[1]http://turing.iimas.unam.mx/americasnlp/st.html

Proceedings of the First Workshop on Natural Language Processing for Indigenous Languages of the Americas, pages 218–223
June 11, 2021.

guages. Particularly, the development of (MT) systems for indigenous languages in both South and North America, faces different challenges such as a high morphological richness, agglutination, polysynthesis, and orthographic variation (Mager et al., 2018b; Llitjós et al., 2005). In general, MT systems for these languages in the state-of-the-art have been addressed by the sub-fields of machine translation: rule-based (Monson et al., 2006), statistical (Mager Hois et al., 2016) and neural-based approaches (Ortega et al., 2020; Le and Sadat, 2020). Recently, NMT approaches (Stahlberg, 2020) have gained prominence; they commonly are based on sequence-to-sequence models using encoder-decoder architectures and attention mechanisms (Yang et al., 2020). From this perspective, different morphological segmentation techniques have been explored (Kann et al., 2018; Ortega et al., 2020) for Indigenous American languages.

It is known that the NMT approaches are based on big amounts of parallel corpora as source knowledge. To date, important efforts toward creating parallel corpora have been carried out for specific indigenous languages of America. For example, for Spanish-Nahuatl (Gutierrez-Vasques et al., 2016), Wixarika-Spanish (Mager et al., 2020) and Quechua-Spanish (Llitjós et al., 2005) which includes morphological information. Also, the JHU Bible Corpus, a parallel text, has been extended by adding translations in more than 20 Indigenous North American languages (Nicolai et al., 2021). The usability of the corpus was demonstrated by using multilingual NMT systems.

3 Methodology

Since the data sizes are small in most language pairs as shown in Table 1, we used a statistical machine translation model. We also used NMT models. In the following sections, we describe the details of each of these approaches.

3.1 Statistical MT

For statistical MT, we relied on an IBM model 2 (Brown et al., 1993) which comprises a lexical translation model and an alignment model. In addition to the word-level translation probability, it models the absolute distortion in the word positioning between source and the target languages by introducing an alignment probability, which enables to handle word reordering.

3.2 Neural MT

For NMT, we first tokenized the text using sentence piece BPE tokenization (Kudo and Richardson, 2018).[2] The translation model architecture we used for NMT is the transformer model (Vaswani et al., 2017). We trained the model in two different setups as outlined below.

One-to-one: In this setup, we trained the model using the data from one source language and one target language only. In the AmericasNLP2021[3] shared task, the source language is always Spanish (es). We trained the transformer model using Spanish as the source language and one of the indigenous languages as the target language.

One-to-many: Since the source language (Spanish) is constant for all the language pairs, we considered sharing the NMT parameters across language pairs to obtain gains in translation performance as shown in previous work (Dabre et al., 2020). For this, we trained a one-to-many model by sharing the decoder parameters across all the indigenous languages. Since the model needs to generate the translation in the intended target language, we provided that information as a target language tag in the input (Lample and Conneau, 2019). The token level representation is obtained by the sum of token embedding, positional embedding, and language embedding.

4 Dataset

For training and evaluating our different configurations, we used the official datasets provided by the organizers of the shared task. It is worth mentioning that we did not use additional datasets or resources for our experiments.

A brief description of the dataset composition is shown in Table 1. For all the language pairs, the task was to translate from Spanish to some of the following indigenous languages: Hñähñu (oto), Wixarika (wix), Nahuatl (nah), Guaraní (gn), Bribri (bzd), Rarámuri (tar), Quechua (quy), Aymara (aym), Shipibo-Konibo (shp), Asháninka (cni). For the sake of brevity, we do not provide all the characteristics of every pair of languages. The interested reader is referred to (Gutierrez-Vasques et al.,

[2] We also compared the BPE subword tokenization to word-level tokenization using Moses tokenizer and character level tokenization. We found that the best results were obtained using the BPE subword tokenization.

[3] `http://turing.iimas.unam.mx/americasnlp/`

Language-pair	Train(#Tokens)			Dev(#Tokens)			Test(#Tokens)	
	#Sentences	Source	Target	#Sentences	Source	Target	#Sentences	Source
es-aym	6531	128154	97276	996	11129	7080	1003	10044
es-bzd	7508	46820	41141	996	11129	12974	1003	10044
es-cni	3883	48752	26096	883	9605	6070	1003	10044
es-gn	26032	604841	405984	995	11129	7191	1003	10044
es-hch	8966	68683	48919	994	11129	10296	1003	10044
es-nah	16145	470003	351580	672	6329	4300	1003	10044
es-oto	4889	68226	72280	599	5115	5069	1003	10044
es-quy	125008	1898377	1169644	996	11129	7406	1003	10044
es-shp	14592	88447	62850	996	11129	9138	1003	10044
es-tar	14720	141526	103745	995	11129	10377	1003	10044

Table 1: Statistics of the official dataset. The statistics include the number of sentences and tokens (train/dev/test) for each language pair.

Task	Baseline		Tamalli			Best Competitor	
	BLEU	CharF	Submission#	BLEU	CharF	BLEU	CharF
es-aym	0.01	0.157	4	0.03	0.202	2.29	0.283
es-bzd	0.01	0.068	3	1.09	0.132	2.39	0.165
es-cni	0.01	0.102	1	0.01	0.253	3.05	0.258
es-gn	0.12	0.193	5	1.9	0.207	6.13	0.336
es-hch	2.2	0.126	1	0.01	0.214	9.63	0.304
es-nah	0.01	0.157	1	0.03	0.218	2.38	0.266
es-oto	0	0.054	1	0.01	0.118	1.69	0.147
es-quy	0.05	0.304	5	0.96	0.273	2.91	0.346
es-shp	0.01	0.121	1	0.06	0.204	5.43	0.329
es-tar	0	0.039	1	0.04	0.155	1.07	0.184

Table 2: Evaluation Results. All results are from the "Track2: Development Set Not Used for Training". For all the tasks, the source language is Spanish. The table contains the best results of our team against the best score by the competitor in its track.

2016; Mager et al., 2018a; Chiruzzo et al., 2020; Feldman and Coto-Solano, 2020; Agić and Vulić, 2019; Prokopidis et al., 2016; Galarreta et al., 2017; Ebrahimi et al., 2021) for knowing these details.

5 Experimental results

We used 5 settings for all the 10 pair translations. The output of each set is named as version [1-5] and submitted for evaluation (shown under column Submission# in Table 2). Among the 5 versions, version [1] is based on statistical MT, and version [2-5] is based on NMT with different model configurations. For model evaluation, organizers provided a script that uses the metrics *BLEU* and *ChrF* for machine translation evaluation. The versions and their configuration details are explained below. We included the best results only from all the versions [1-5] in Table 2.

Version 1: Version 1 uses the statistical MT. The source and target language text were first tokenized using Moses tokenizer setting the language to Spanish. Then we trained the IBM translation model 2 (Brown et al., 1993) implemented in `nltk.translate` api. After obtaining the translation target tokens, the detokenization was carried out using the Moses Spanish detokenizer.

Version 2: This version uses the one-to-one NMT model. First, we learned sentence piece BPE tokenization (Kudo and Richardson, 2018) by combining the source and target language text. We set the maximum vocabulary size to {8k, 16k, 32k} in different runs and we considered the run that produced the best BLEU score on the dev set. The transformer model (Vaswani et al., 2017) was implemented using PyTorch (Paszke et al., 2019). The number of encoder and decoder layers was set to 3 each and the number of heads in those layers was set to 8. The hidden dimension of the self-attention layer was set to 128 and the position-wise feed-forward layer's dimension was set to 256. We used a dropout of 0.1 in both the encoder and the decoder. The encoder and decoder embedding layers were not tied. We trained the model using early stopping with a patience of 5 epochs, that is, we stop training if the validation loss does not improve for 5 consecutive epochs. We used greedy decoding for generating the translations during inference. The training and translation were done using one GPU.

Version 3: This version uses the one-to-many NMT model. For tokenization, we learned sentence piece BPE tokenization (Kudo and Richardson, 2018) by combining the source and target language text from all the languages (11 languages in total). We set the maximum shared vocabulary size to {8k, 16k, 32k} in different runs and we considered the run that produced the best BLEU score on the dev set. The transformer model's hyperparameters were the same as in version 2. The language embedding dimension in the decoder was set to 128. The encoder and decoder embedding layers were not tied. We first trained the one-to-many model till convergence using early stopping with the patience of 5 epochs, considering the concatenation of the dev data from all the language pairs. Then we fine-tuned the best checkpoint using each language pair's data separately. The fine-tuning process was also done using early stopping with patience of 5 epochs. Finally, we used greedy decoding for generating the translations during inference. The training and translation were done using one GPU.

Version 4: This version is based on one-to-one NMT. We have used the *Transformer* model as implemented in OpenNMT-py (PyTorch version) (Klein et al., 2017).[4]. To train the model, we used a single GPU and followed the standard "Noam" learning rate decay,[5] see (Vaswani et al., 2017; Popel and Bojar, 2018) for more details. Our starting learning rate was 0.2 and we used 8000 warm-up steps. The model *es-nah* trained up to 100K iterations and the model checkpoint at 35K was selected based on the evaluation score (*BLEU*) on the development set.

Version 5: This version is based on One-to-One NMT. We have used the *Transformer* model as implemented in OpenNMT-tf (Tensorflow version) (Klein et al., 2017). To train the model, we used a single GPU and followed the standard "Noam" learning rate decay,[6] see (Vaswani et al., 2017; Popel and Bojar, 2018) for more details. We used 8K shared vocab size for the models and the model checkpoints were saved at an interval of 2500 steps. The starting learning rate was 0.2 and 8000 warm-up steps were used for model training. The early-stopping criterion was 'less than 0.01 improvement in BLEU score' for 5 consecutive saved model checkpoints. The model *es-gn* was trained up to 37.5K iterations and the model checkpoint at 35K was selected based on evaluation scores on the development set. The model *es-quy* was trained up to 40K iterations and the model checkpoint at 32.5K was selected based on evaluation scores on the development set.

We report the official automatic evaluation results in Table 2. The machine translation evaluation matrices BLEU (Papineni et al., 2002) and ChrF (Popović, 2017) used by the organizers to evaluate the submissions. Based on our observation, the statistical approach performed well as compared to NMT for many language pairs as shown in the Table 2 (Parida et al., 2019). Also, among NMT model settings one-to-one and one-to-many perform well based on the language pairs.

6 Conclusions

Our participation aimed at analyzing the performance of recent NMT techniques on translating indigenous languages of the Americas, low-resource languages. Our future work directions include: *i)* investigating corpus filtering and iterative augmentation for performance improvement (Dandapat and Federmann, 2018), *ii)* review already existing extensive analyses of these low-resource languages from a linguistic point of view and adapt our methods for each language accordingly, *iii)* exploring transfer learning approach by training the model on a high resource language and later transfer it to a low resource language (Kocmi et al., 2018).

[4] http://opennmt.net/

[5] https://nvidia.github.io/OpenSeq2Seq/html/api-docs/optimizers.html

[6] https://nvidia.github.io/OpenSeq2Seq/html/api-docs/optimizers.html

Acknowledgements

The authors Shantipriya Parida and Petr Motlicek were supported by the European Union's Horizon 2020 research and innovation program under grant agreement No. 833635 (project ROXANNE: Real-time network, text, and speaker analytics for combating organized crime, 2019-2022). Author Esaú Villatoro-Tello, was supported partially by Idiap Research Institute, SNI-CONACyT, and UAM-Cuajimalpa Mexico during the elaboration of this work. Author Rosa M. Ortega-Mendoza was supported partially by SNI-CONACyT.

The authors do not see any significant ethical or privacy concerns that would prevent the processing of the data used in the study. The datasets do contain personal data, and these are processed in compliance with the GDPR and national law.

References

Željko Agić and Ivan Vulić. 2019. JW300: A wide-coverage parallel corpus for low-resource languages. In *Proceedings of the 57th Annual Meeting of the Association for Computational Linguistics*, pages 3204–3210, Florence, Italy. Association for Computational Linguistics.

Peter F. Brown, Stephen A. Della Pietra, Vincent J. Della Pietra, and Robert L. Mercer. 1993. The mathematics of statistical machine translation: Parameter estimation. *Computational Linguistics*, 19(2):263–311.

Luis Chiruzzo, Pedro Amarilla, Adolfo Ríos, and Gustavo Giménez Lugo. 2020. Development of a Guarani - Spanish parallel corpus. In *Proceedings of the 12th Language Resources and Evaluation Conference*, pages 2629–2633, Marseille, France. European Language Resources Association.

Raj Dabre, Chenhui Chu, and Anoop Kunchukuttan. 2020. A survey of multilingual neural machine translation. *ACM Comput. Surv.*, 53(5).

Sandipan Dandapat and Christian Federmann. 2018. Iterative data augmentation for neural machine translation: a low resource case study for english-telugu. In *Proceedings of the 21st Annual Conference of the European Association for Machine Translation: 28-30 May 2018, Universitat d'Alacant, Alacant, Spain*, pages 287–292. European Association for Machine Translation.

Abteen Ebrahimi, Manuel Mager, Arturo Oncevay, Vishrav Chaudhary, Luis Chiruzzo, Angela Fan, John Ortega, Ricardo Ramos, Annette Rios, Ivan Vladimir, Gustavo A. Giménez-Lugo, Elisabeth Mager, Graham Neubig, Alexis Palmer, Rolando A. Coto Solano, Ngoc Thang Vu, and Katharina Kann. 2021. Americasnli: Evaluating zero-shot natural language understanding of pretrained multilingual models in truly low-resource languages.

Isaac Feldman and Rolando Coto-Solano. 2020. Neural machine translation models with back-translation for the extremely low-resource indigenous language Bribri. In *Proceedings of the 28th International Conference on Computational Linguistics*, pages 3965–3976, Barcelona, Spain (Online). International Committee on Computational Linguistics.

Ana-Paula Galarreta, Andrés Melgar, and Arturo Oncevay. 2017. Corpus creation and initial SMT experiments between Spanish and Shipibo-konibo. In *Proceedings of the International Conference Recent Advances in Natural Language Processing, RANLP 2017*, pages 238–244, Varna, Bulgaria. INCOMA Ltd.

Ankush Garg and Mayank Agarwal. 2018. Machine translation: A literature review. *arXiv*.

Ximena Gutierrez-Vasques, Gerardo Sierra, and Isaac Hernandez. 2016. Axolotl: A web accessible parallel corpus for Spanish-Nahuatl. *Proceedings of the 10th International Conference on Language Resources and Evaluation, LREC 2016*, pages 4210–4214.

Katharina Kann, Manuel Mager, Ivan Meza-Ruiz, and Hinrich Schütze. 2018. Fortification of neural morphological segmentation models for polysynthetic minimal-resource languages. In *NAACL HLT 2018 - 2018 Conference of the North American Chapter of the Association for Computational Linguistics: Human Language Technologies - Proceedings of the Conference*, volume 1, pages 47–57.

Guillaume Klein, Yoon Kim, Yuntian Deng, Jean Senellart, and Alexander M. Rush. 2017. OpenNMT: Open-source toolkit for neural machine translation. In *Proc. ACL*.

Tom Kocmi, Shantipriya Parida, and Ondřej Bojar. 2018. Cuni nmt system for wat 2018 translation tasks. In *Proceedings of the 32nd Pacific Asia Conference on Language, Information and Computation: 5th Workshop on Asian Translation: 5th Workshop on Asian Translation*.

Taku Kudo and John Richardson. 2018. Sentencepiece: A simple and language independent subword tokenizer and detokenizer for neural text processing. *arXiv preprint arXiv:1808.06226*.

Guillaume Lample and Alexis Conneau. 2019. Cross-lingual language model pretraining. *Advances in Neural Information Processing Systems (NeurIPS)*.

Tan Ngoc Le and Fatiha Sadat. 2020. Low-Resource NMT: an Empirical Study on the Effect of Rich Morphological Word Segmentation on Inuktitut. *Proceedings of the 14th Conference of the Association for Machine Translation in the Americas (Volume 1: Research Track)*, 1(2012):165–172.

Ariadna Font Llitjós, Lori Levin, and Roberto Aranovich. 2005. Building Machine translation systems for indigenous languages. *Communities*.

Manuel Mager, Diónico Carrillo, and Ivan Meza. 2018a. Probabilistic finite-state morphological segmenter for wixarika (huichol) language. *Journal of Intelligent & Fuzzy Systems*, 34(5):3081–3087.

Manuel Mager, Carrillo Dionico, and Ivan Meza. 2020. The Wixarika-Spanish Parallel Corpus The Wixarika-Spanish Parallel Corpus. (August 2018).

Manuel Mager, Ximena Gutierrez-Vasques, Gerardo Sierra, and Ivan Meza-Ruiz. 2018b. Challenges of language technologies for the indigenous languages of the Americas. In *Proceedings of the 27th International Conference on Computational Linguistics*, pages 55–69, Santa Fe, New Mexico, USA. Association for Computational Linguistics.

Manuel Mager, Arturo Oncevay, Abteen Ebrahimi, John Ortega, Annette Rios, Angela Fan, Ximena Gutierrez-Vasques, Luis Chiruzzo, Gustavo Giménez-Lugo, Ricardo Ramos, Anna Currey, Vishrav Chaudhary, Ivan Vladimir Meza Ruiz, Rolando Coto-Solano, Alexis Palmer, Elisabeth Mager, Ngoc Thang Vu, Graham Neubig, and Katharina Kann. 2021. Findings of the AmericasNLP 2021 Shared Task on Open Machine Translation for Indigenous Languages of the Americas. In *Proceedings of theThe First Workshop on NLP for Indigenous Languages of the Americas*, Online. Association for Computational Linguistics.

Jesus Manuel Mager Hois, Carlos Barrón Romero, and Ivan Vladimir Meza Ruiz. 2016. Traductor estadístico wixarika-español usando descomposición morfológica. *Comtel*, pages 63–68.

C. Monson, Ariadna Font Llitjós, Roberto Aranovich, Lori S. Levin, R. Brown, E. Peterson, Jaime G. Carbonell, and A. Lavie. 2006. Building nlp systems for two resource-scarce indigenous languages : Mapudungun and quechua.

Garrett Nicolai, Edith Coates, Ming Zhang, and Miikka Silfverberg. 2021. Expanding the JHU Bible Corpus for Machine Translation of the Indigenous Languages of North America. 1:1–5.

John E Ortega, Richard Castro Mamani, and Kyunghyun Cho. 2020. Neural machine translation with a polysynthetic low resource language. *Machine Translation*, 34(4):325–346.

Kishore Papineni, Salim Roukos, Todd Ward, and Wei-Jing Zhu. 2002. Bleu: a method for automatic evaluation of machine translation. In *Proceedings of the 40th annual meeting of the Association for Computational Linguistics*, pages 311–318.

Shantipriya Parida, Ondřej Bojar, and Satya Ranjan Dash. 2019. Odiencorp: Odia–english and odia-only corpus for machine translation. In *Smart Intelligent Computing and Applications: Proceedings of the Third International Conference on Smart Computing and Informatics, Volume 1*, volume 159, page 495. Springer Nature.

Adam Paszke, Sam Gross, Francisco Massa, Adam Lerer, James Bradbury, Gregory Chanan, Trevor Killeen, Zeming Lin, Natalia Gimelshein, Luca Antiga, Alban Desmaison, Andreas Kopf, Edward Yang, Zachary DeVito, Martin Raison, Alykhan Tejani, Sasank Chilamkurthy, Benoit Steiner, Lu Fang, Junjie Bai, and Soumith Chintala. 2019. Pytorch: An imperative style, high-performance deep learning library. In H. Wallach, H. Larochelle, A. Beygelzimer, F. d'Alché-Buc, E. Fox, and R. Garnett, editors, *Advances in Neural Information Processing Systems 32*, pages 8024–8035. Curran Associates, Inc.

Martin Popel and Ondřej Bojar. 2018. Training tips for the transformer model. *The Prague Bulletin of Mathematical Linguistics*, 110(1):43–70.

Maja Popović. 2017. chrf++: words helping character n-grams. In *Proceedings of the second conference on machine translation*, pages 612–618.

Prokopis Prokopidis, Vassilis Papavassiliou, and Stelios Piperidis. 2016. Parallel Global Voices: a collection of multilingual corpora with citizen media stories. In *Proceedings of the Tenth International Conference on Language Resources and Evaluation (LREC'16)*, pages 900–905, Portorož, Slovenia. European Language Resources Association (ELRA).

Felix Stahlberg. 2020. Neural machine translation: A review. *Journal of Artificial Intelligence Research*, 69:343–418.

Ashish Vaswani, Noam Shazeer, Niki Parmar, Jakob Uszkoreit, Llion Jones, Aidan N Gomez, Łukasz Kaiser, and Illia Polosukhin. 2017. Attention is all you need. In *Advances in Neural Information Processing Systems*, pages 5998–6008.

Shuoheng Yang, Yuxin Wang, and Xiaowen Chu. 2020. A Survey of Deep Learning Techniques for Neural Machine Translation. *arXiv e-prints*, page arXiv:2002.07526.

NRC-CNRC Machine Translation Systems for the 2021 AmericasNLP Shared Task

Rebecca Knowles and **Darlene Stewart** and **Samuel Larkin** and **Patrick Littell**
National Research Council Canada
{Rebecca.Knowles, Darlene.Stewart, Samuel.Larkin, Patrick.Littell}@nrc-cnrc.gc.ca

Abstract

We describe the NRC-CNRC systems submitted to the AmericasNLP shared task on machine translation. We submitted systems translating from Spanish into Wixárika, Nahuatl, Rarámuri, and Guaraní. Our best neural machine translation systems used multilingual pretraining, ensembling, finetuning, training on parts of the development data, and subword regularization. We also submitted translation memory systems as a strong baseline.

1 Introduction

This paper describes experiments on translation from Spanish into Wixárika, Nahuatl, Rarámuri, and Guaraní, as part of the First Workshop on Natural Language Processing (NLP) for Indigenous Languages of the Americas (AmericasNLP) 2021 Shared Task on open-ended machine translation. Our approach to this task was to explore the application of simple, known methods of performing neural machine translation (NMT) for low-resource languages to a subset of the task languages. Our initial experiments were primarily focused on the following questions: *(1)* How well does multilingual NMT work in these very low resource settings? *(2)* Is it better to build multilingual NMT systems using only closely-related languages or does it help to add data from additional languages? *(3)* Is applying subword regularization helpful?

As we progressed through the task, it raised questions regarding domain and about use cases for low-resource machine translation. The approaches that we used for this task are not entirely language-agnostic; they might be more appropriately characterized as "language naïve" in that we applied some simple language-specific pre- and post-processing, but did not incorporate any tools that required in-depth knowledge of the language.

We submitted four systems, including ensembles, single systems, and a translation memory baseline. Our best system (S.0) consisted of an ensemble of systems incorporating multilingual training and finetuning (including on development data as pseudo-in-domain data).

Language	Family	Train	Dev
Nahuatl	Uto-Aztecan	16145	672
Rarámuri	Uto-Aztecan	14720	995
Wixárika	Uto-Aztecan	8966	994
Guaraní	Tupian	26032	995

Table 1: Language, language family, and number of lines of training and development data.

2 Data and Preprocessing

The shared task provided data for 10 language pairs, all with the goal of translating from Spanish. We chose to start with Wixárika (hch; Mager et al., 2018), Nahuatl (nah; Gutierrez-Vasques et al., 2016), and Rarámuri (tar; Brambila, 1976) as our main three languages of interest, all of which are languages in the Uto-Aztecan family indigenous to Mexico. We added Guaraní (gn; Chiruzzo et al., 2020) as an unrelated language (as spoken in Paraguay), to explore building multilingual NMT systems within and across language families. Ebrahimi et al. (2021) describes work on collecting development and test sets for the languages in the shared task. The datasets vary in size, dialect and orthographic variation/consistency, and level of domain match to the development and test data. Due to space considerations, we direct readers to the task page and the dataset information page for more information on the languages and on the datasets provided for the task.[1]

Given the size of the data (Table 1), additional data collection (particularly of data in the domain of interest) is likely one of the most effective ways to improve machine translation quality. However,

[1]Task page: `http://turing.iimas.unam.mx/americasnlp/`, Dataset descriptions: `https://github.com/AmericasNLP/americasnlp2021/blob/main/data/information_datasets.pdf`

Proceedings of the First Workshop on Natural Language Processing for Indigenous Languages of the Americas, pages 224–233
June 11, 2021.

noting both ethical (Lewis et al., 2020) and quality (Caswell et al., 2021) concerns when it comes to collecting or using data for Indigenous languages without community collaboration, we limited our experiments to data provided for the shared task.

2.1 Preprocessing and Postprocessing

We used standard preprocessing scripts from Moses (Koehn et al., 2007): `clean-corpus-n.perl` (on training data only), `normalize-punctuation.perl`, and `tokenizer.perl` (applied to all text, regardless of whether it already appeared tokenized).[2] The only language-specific preprocessing we performed was to replace "+" with an alternative character (reverted in postprocessing) for Wixárika text to prevent the tokenizer from oversegmenting the text. We note that the `13a` tokenizer used by `sacrebleu` (Post, 2018) tokenizes "+", meaning that scores that incorporate word n-grams, like BLEU (Papineni et al., 2002), are artificially inflated for Wixárika.

We detokenize (after unBPEing) the text and perform a small amount of language-specific postprocessing, which we found to have minimal effect on CHRF (Popović, 2015) and some effect on BLEU on development data.

2.2 BPE and BPE-Dropout

Following (Ding et al., 2019), we sweep a range of byte-pair encoding (BPE; Sennrich et al., 2016) vocabulary sizes: 500, 1000, 2000, 4000, and 8000 merges (we do not go beyond this, because of sparsity/data size concerns, though some results suggest we should consider larger sizes).

For each language pair or multilingual grouping, we learned a BPE model jointly from the concatenation of the source and target sides of the parallel data using `subword-nmt` (Sennrich et al., 2016), and then extracted separate source- and target-side vocabularies. We then applied the joint BPE model, filtered by the source or target vocabulary, to the corresponding data.

We apply BPE-dropout (Provilkov et al., 2020) in part to assist with data sparsity and in part because it may be an effective way of handing orthographic variation (as a generalization of the spelling errors that it helps systems become more robust to). Usually, BPE-dropout would be performed during training as mini-batches are generated, but we opted to generate 10 BPE-dropout versions of the training corpus using a dropout rate of 0.1 as part of our preprocessing. We then simply concatenate all 10 alternate versions to form the training corpus.

[2]See Appendix B for details.

3 Models and Experiments

We report CHRF (Popović, 2015) scores computed with `sacrebleu` (Post, 2018).

3.1 Models

We trained Transformer (Vaswani et al., 2017) models using Sockeye-1.18.115 (Hieber et al., 2018) and cuda-10.1. We used the default value of 6 encoder/decoder layers, 8 attention heads, the Adam (Kingma and Ba, 2015) optimizer, label smoothing of 0.1, a cross-entropy loss, a model size of 512 units with a FFN size of 2048, and the vocabulary was not shared. We performed early stopping after 32 checkpoints without improvement. We chose custom checkpoint intervals of approximately two checkpoints per epoch. We optimized for CHRF instead of BLEU and used the whole validation set during validation. The batch size was set to 8192 tokens, and the maximum sequence length for both source and target was set to 200 tokens. We did not use weight tying, but we set gradient clipping to absolute and lowered the initial learning rate to 0.0001.

We performed preliminary experiments decreasing the number of encoder and decoder layers in our bilingual systems to 3 each, but did not observe improvements. Nevertheless, a wider search of architecture parameters, as in Araabi and Monz (2020), could yield improvements. After submission, we performed some additional experiments, building multilingual models with a range of numbers of decoder heads (1, 2, 4, 8), finding that a smaller number of decoder heads (e.g., 2) may be a promising avenue to explore in future work. Other approaches from Araabi and Monz (2020) also appear to show promise in our preliminary post-submission experiments, including a 4 layer encoder with a 6 layer decoder and changing layer normalization from pre to post, demonstrating that there are additional ways to improve upon our submitted systems.

3.2 MT Baselines

For each of the four language pairs, we build baseline systems translating out of Spanish. The best baseline systems with their respective BPE sizes

System	gn	hch	nah	tar
Official (Organizer) Baseline	0.220	0.126	0.182	0.046
Baseline	0.222 (4k)	0.201 (2k)	0.201 (1k)	0.141 (2k)
+ Dropout	0.238 (8k)	0.226 (8k)	0.216 (4k)	0.127 (2k)
Multilingual-3	–	0.183 (4k)	0.203 (2k)	0.122 (4k)
Multilingual-4	0.222 (2k)	0.209 (4k)	0.213 (4k)	0.127 (8k)
+ Dropout	0.247 (8k)	0.226 (2k)	0.243 (4k)	0.142 (1k)
Multi.-4 + Dropout; Language Finetune (no dr.)	0.251 (8k)	**0.265** (2k)	0.250 (4k)	**0.149** (8k)
Multi.-4 + Dropout; Language Finetune	**0.258** (8k)	0.262 (2k)	**0.252** (2k)	0.134 (4k)

Table 2: System scores (CHRF) on the development set. Vocabulary size in parentheses.

are shown in Table 2. All of our baseline CHRF scores are higher than the official baselines released during the shared task,[3] likely due in part to more consistent tokenization between training and development/test (see Appendix C for additional discussion of training and development/test mismatch). For all languages except Rarámuri, adding BPE-dropout improved performance.

3.3 Multilingual Systems

Both Johnson et al. (2017) and Rikters et al. (2018) train multilingual systems by prepending a special token at the start of the source sentence to indicate the language into which the text should be translated. For example, the token "<nah>" prepended (space-separated) to a Spanish source sentence indicates that the text should be translated into Nahuatl. To train such a model, we concatenate all training data after adding these special tokens; the development data is similarly the concatenation of all development data. We do not perform any upsampling or downsampling to even out the distribution of languages in our training or development data (rather, we rely on language finetuning, as described in Section 3.4 to improve translation quality).

One of our initial questions was whether language relatedness mattered for building multilingual systems, so we first built a three-language (Wixárika, Nahuatl, Rarámuri) model, *Multiligual-3*, and then built a four-language (Guaraní, Wixárika, Nahuatl, Rarámuri) model, *Multilingual-4*. The Multilingual-4 system had consistently higher scores for all languages than the Multilingual-3 system, so we moved forward with experiments on Multilingual-4. Adding BPE-dropout to Multilingual-4 appeared to improve performance for all languages, but in the case of Wixárika (the language with the smallest amount of data), it was nearly identical to the baseline. Within the scope of this paper, we do not experiment with a wider range of languages (i.e., the remaining 6 languages), though it would not be surprising to find that additional language resources might also be beneficial.

Lang.	1k	2k	4k	8k
gn	889	1737	3299	5936
hch	516	728	1006	1389
nah	817	1502	2513	4033
tar	529	762	1072	1500

Table 3: Number of unique subwords in each language's training corpus (target side) for 1k, 2k, 4k, and 8k BPE merges in a Multilingual-4 scenario.

For the Multilingual-3 and Multilingual-4 models, the vocabulary is trained and extracted from the respective concatenated training corpus, so the target vocabulary is shared by all target languages as a single embedding matrix. Where languages share subwords, these are shared in the vocabulary (i.e., the language-specific tags are applied at the sentence level, not at the token level). The consequence of this is that each particular target language may not use the full multilingual vocabulary; we expect the system to learn which vocabulary items to associate (or not associate) with each language. For example, with a vocabulary produced through 8k merges, the full Multilingual-4 target side training corpus contains 7431 unique subwords, but the language-specific subcorpora that combine to make it only use subsets of that: Guaraní training data contains 5936 unique subwords, while Wixárika contains only 1389 (the overlap between Guaraní and Wixárika subwords is 1089 subwords). Table 3 shows the number of unique subwords in the target language training corpus for the Multilingual-4 setting. Our systems are free to generate any subword from the full combined vocabulary of target subwords since there is no explicit restriction during decoding. Thus, in some cases, our multilingual systems do generate subwords that were not seen in a specific language's training data vocabulary sub-

[3] `https://github.com/AmericasNLP/americasnlp2021/tree/main/baseline_system`

set; while some of these *could* result in translation errors, a preliminary qualitative analysis suggests that many of them may be either source language words (being copied) or numerical tokens, both of which point to potential benefits of having used the larger concatenated multilingual corpus.

3.4 Language Finetuning

We can then finetune[4] the multilingual models to be language-specific models.[5] The intuition here is that the multilingual model may be able to encode useful information about the source language, terms that should be copied (e.g., names/numbers), target grammar, or other useful topics, and can then be specialized for a specific language, while still retaining the most relevant or most general things learned from all languages trained on. We do this finetuning based on continued training on each language's training data, with that language's development data, building a new child system for each language based on the parent Multilingual-4 system (with or without dropout).[6] When we do this, we no longer use the language-specific tags used during multilingual model training.

Language finetuning appears to produce improvements, with some performing better with dropout and some better without, as seen in the final two lines of Table 2. Rarámuri appears to have a drop in performance after language finetuning with dropout. However, all Rarámuri scores are extremely low; it is likely that many of the decisions we make on Rarámuri do not represent real improvements or performance drops, but rather noise, so we have very low confidence in the generalizability of the choices (Mathur et al., 2020).

3.5 Development Finetuning

Noting that the development data was of a different domain, and sometimes even a different dialect or orthography than the training data, we followed an approach used in Knowles et al. (2020): we divided the development set (in this case in half), performing finetuning with half of it and using the remainder for early stopping (and evaluation). We acknowledge that, given the very small sizes of the development sets, minor differences we observe are likely to be noise rather than true improvements (or true drops in performance); while we made choices about what systems to submit based on those, we urge caution in generalizing these results or drawing strong conclusions.

We show performance of models finetuned on the first half of the development set (performance measured on the second half of the development set), both with and without first finetuning for language, in Table 4. We also compare these against the best systems we trained without training on development data, as well as with the translation memory approach (Section 4.3).

4 Submitted Systems

4.1 Systems with Dev. (S.0, S.2, and S.4)

We submitted single systems (not ensembled) that were trained using the first half of the development set (labeled S.2 in submission). They were selected based on highest scores on the second half of the development set (see Table 4 for scores and vocabulary sizes). For Guaraní, Wixárika, and Nahuatl, we selected systems of the type Multi.-4 + BPE Dr.; Lang. finetuning; 1/2 Dev. finetuning. For Rarámuri, we selected a system with only 1/2 dev. finetuning (Multi.-4 + BPE Dr.; 1/2 Dev. Ft.).

Our best systems were ensembles (labeled S.0 in submission) of the systems described above and their corresponding system trained with the second half of the development set. For Guaraní, we also submitted an ensemble of four systems; the two *Multi.-4 + BPE Dr.; Lang. finetuning; 1/2 Dev finetuning* systems and the two *Multi.-4 + BPE Dr.; 1/2 Dev Ft.* systems (S.4). It performed similarly to the two-system ensemble.

4.2 Systems without Dev. (S.1)

We also submitted systems that were not trained on development data. For these, we were able to select the best system from our experiments, based on its CHRF score on the full development set. For Guaraní and Nahuatl, these were *Multi.4 + BPE Dr.; Lang. ft.* systems, for Rarámuri it was the *Multi.4 + BPE Dr.; Lang. ft. (no dr.)* system, and for Wixárika it was an ensemble of the two.

4.3 Translation Memory (S.3)

Noting the very low automatic metric scores across languages and without target language expertise to

[4]In our tables, we use the following notation to indicate finetuning: "[parent model]; [child finetuning]" and this notation stacks, such that "X; Y; Z" indicates a parent model X, finetuned as Y, and then subsequently finetuned as Z.

[5]We note that all finetuning experiments reported in this paper used BPE-dropout unless otherwise noted.

[6]We note that some catastrophic forgetting may occur during this process; it may be worth considering modifying the learning rate for finetuning, but we leave this to future work.

System	gn	hch	nah	tar
Multi.-4 + Dropout	0.249 (8k)	0.228 (2k)	0.247 (8k)	0.145 (1k)
Multi.-4 + Dr.; Lang. Finetune	0.260 (8k)	0.261 (2k)	0.252 (2k)	0.137 (500)
Multi.-4 + Dr.; 1/2 Dev. Finetune	0.331 (4k)	0.367 (4k)	0.368 (8k)	**0.289** (4k)
Multi.-4 + Dr.; Lang. Finetune; 1/2 Dev. Ft.	**0.338** (4k)	**0.368** (8k)	**0.376** (8k)	0.280 (2k)
S.1 (no dev)	0.260 (8k)	0.266 (2k)	0.252 (2k)	0.150 (8k)
S.2 (1/2 dev, single system)	**0.338** (4k)	**0.368** (8k)	**0.376** (8k)	**0.289** (4k)
Translation Memory	0.257 (na)	0.273 (na)	0.285 (na)	0.246 (na)

Table 4: System scores on the second half of the development set.

System	gn	hch	nah	tar
S.0	0.304	0.327	0.277	0.247
S.4	0.303	–	–	–
S.2	0.288	0.315	0.273	0.239
S.3/TM	0.163	0.200	0.181	0.165
S.1/no dev	0.261	0.264	0.237	0.143
Helsinki 2	0.376	0.360	0.301	0.258

Table 5: Submitted systems scores (CHRF) on test data. Final row shows best overall submitted system for each language, Helsinki submission 2.

determine if the output is fluent but not adequate, adequate but not fluent, or neither fluent nor adequate, we decided to build a translation memory submission. In computer aided translation (CAT), a "translation memory" (TM) is a database of prior source-target translation pairs produced by human translators. It can be used in CAT as follows: when a new sentence arrives to be translated, the system finds the closest source-language "fuzzy match" (typically a proprietary measure that determines similarity; could be as simple as Levenshtein distance) and returns its translation (possibly with annotations about the areas where the sentences differed) to the translator for them to "post-edit" (modify until it is a valid translation of the new sentence to be translated).

With the understanding that the development and test sets are closer to one another in terms of domain and dialect than they are to the training data, we treat the development set as a TM. Following Simard and Fujita (2012), we use an MT evaluation metric (CHRF) as the similarity score between the test source sentences and the TM source sentences, with the translation of the closest source development set sentence as the output.[7]

We validated this approach on the two halves of the development set (using the first half as a TM for the second half and vice versa). On half the development set, for all languages except for Guaraní, the TM outperformed the system trained without any development data (S.1), highlighting the differences between the training and development/test data (Table 4), particularly striking because the TM used for these experiments consisted of only half the development set (<500 lines) as compared to the full training set.[8] On the test set, only the Rarámuri TM outperformed the best of our MT systems built without training on development.

5 Results

Our results consistently placed our submissions as the second-ranking team (behind Helsinki's top 2-3 submissions) in the with-development-set group, and second or third ranking team (2nd, 3rd, or 4th submission) within the no-development-set cluster as measured by CHRF. For Wixárika and Rarámuri particularly, our TM submission proved to be a surprisingly strong baseline.

We note that CHRF and BLEU are not strictly correlated, and for all languages, scores are low. This raises questions about goals, metrics, and use cases for very low resource machine translation. We provide a short discussion of this in Appendix A. It will require future work and human evaluation to determine whether such systems are useful or harmful in downstream tasks.

Acknowledgements

We thank the translators who provided their expertise and time to make this work possible:[9] Giovany Martinez Sebastián, Pedro Kapoltitan, José Antonio (Nahuatl), Silvino González de la Crúz (Wixárika), Perla Alvarez Britez (Guaraní), and María del Cármen Sotelo Holguín (Rarámuri). We thank the anonymous reviewers and our colleagues Michel Simard, Gabriel Bernier-Colborne, and Chi-kiu Lo for their comments and suggestions.

[7] In the event of a tie, we chose the first translation.

[8] See Appendix C for additional detail on vocabulary coverage between training, development, and test data.

[9] Full list for all languages available here: `https://github.com/AmericasNLP/americasnlp2021/blob/main/data/information_datasets.pdf`

References

Ali Araabi and Christof Monz. 2020. Optimizing transformer for low-resource neural machine translation. In *Proceedings of the 28th International Conference on Computational Linguistics*, pages 3429–3435, Barcelona, Spain (Online). International Committee on Computational Linguistics.

David Brambila. 1976. *Diccionario Raramuri-Castellano (Tarahumara)*. Obra Nacional de la Buena Prensa, México.

Isaac Caswell, Julia Kreutzer, Lisa Wang, Ahsan Wahab, Daan van Esch, Nasanbayar Ulzii-Orshikh, Allahsera Tapo, Nishant Subramani, Artem Sokolov, Claytone Sikasote, Monang Setyawan, Supheakmungkol Sarin, Sokhar Samb, Benoît Sagot, Clara Rivera, Annette Rios, Isabel Papadimitriou, Salomey Osei, Pedro Javier Ortiz Suárez, Iroro Orife, Kelechi Ogueji, Rubungo Andre Niyongabo, Toan Q. Nguyen, Mathias Müller, André Müller, Shamsuddeen Hassan Muhammad, Nanda Muhammad, Ayanda Mnyakeni, Jamshidbek Mirzakhalov, Tapiwanashe Matangira, Colin Leong, Nze Lawson, Sneha Kudugunta, Yacine Jernite, Mathias Jenny, Orhan Firat, Bonaventure F. P. Dossou, Sakhile Dlamini, Nisansa de Silva, Sakine Çabuk Ballı, Stella Biderman, Alessia Battisti, Ahmed Baruwa, Ankur Bapna, Pallavi Baljekar, Israel Abebe Azime, Ayodele Awokoya, Duygu Ataman, Orevaoghene Ahia, Oghenefego Ahia, Sweta Agrawal, and Mofetoluwa Adeyemi. 2021. Quality at a glance: An audit of web-crawled multilingual datasets.

Luis Chiruzzo, Pedro Amarilla, Adolfo Ríos, and Gustavo Giménez Lugo. 2020. Development of a Guarani - Spanish parallel corpus. In *Proceedings of the 12th Language Resources and Evaluation Conference*, pages 2629–2633, Marseille, France. European Language Resources Association.

Shuoyang Ding, Adithya Renduchintala, and Kevin Duh. 2019. A call for prudent choice of subword merge operations in neural machine translation. In *Proceedings of Machine Translation Summit XVII Volume 1: Research Track*, pages 204–213, Dublin, Ireland. European Association for Machine Translation.

Abteen Ebrahimi, Manuel Mager, Arturo Oncevay, Vishrav Chaudhary, Luis Chiruzzo, Angela Fan, John Ortega, Ricardo Ramos, Annette Rios, Ivan Vladimir, Gustavo A. Giménez-Lugo, Elisabeth Mager, Graham Neubig, Alexis Palmer, Rolando A. Coto Solano, Ngoc Thang Vu, and Katharina Kann. 2021. Americasnli: Evaluating zero-shot natural language understanding of pretrained multilingual models in truly low-resource languages.

Ximena Gutierrez-Vasques, Gerardo Sierra, and Isaac Hernandez Pompa. 2016. Axolotl: a web accessible parallel corpus for Spanish-Nahuatl. In *Proceedings of the Tenth International Conference on Language Resources and Evaluation (LREC'16)*, pages 4210–4214, Portorož, Slovenia. European Language Resources Association (ELRA).

Felix Hieber, Tobias Domhan, Michael Denkowski, David Vilar, Artem Sokolov, Ann Clifton, and Matt Post. 2018. The sockeye neural machine translation toolkit at AMTA 2018. In *Proceedings of the 13th Conference of the Association for Machine Translation in the Americas (Volume 1: Research Track)*, pages 200–207, Boston, MA. Association for Machine Translation in the Americas.

Melvin Johnson, Mike Schuster, Quoc V. Le, Maxim Krikun, Yonghui Wu, Zhifeng Chen, Nikhil Thorat, Fernanda Viégas, Martin Wattenberg, Greg Corrado, Macduff Hughes, and Jeffrey Dean. 2017. Google's multilingual neural machine translation system: Enabling zero-shot translation. *Transactions of the Association for Computational Linguistics*, 5:339–351.

Diederik P. Kingma and Jimmy Ba. 2015. Adam: A method for stochastic optimization. *CoRR*, abs/1412.6980.

Rebecca Knowles, Darlene Stewart, Samuel Larkin, and Patrick Littell. 2020. NRC systems for the 2020 Inuktitut-English news translation task. In *Proceedings of the Fifth Conference on Machine Translation*, pages 156–170, Online. Association for Computational Linguistics.

Philipp Koehn and Ulrich Germann. 2014. The impact of machine translation quality on human post-editing. In *Proceedings of the EACL 2014 Workshop on Humans and Computer-assisted Translation*, pages 38–46, Gothenburg, Sweden. Association for Computational Linguistics.

Philipp Koehn, Hieu Hoang, Alexandra Birch, Chris Callison-Burch, Marcello Federico, Nicola Bertoldi, Brooke Cowan, Wade Shen, Christine Moran, Richard Zens, Chris Dyer, Ondřej Bojar, Alexandra Constantin, and Evan Herbst. 2007. Moses: Open source toolkit for statistical machine translation. In *Proceedings of the 45th Annual Meeting of the Association for Computational Linguistics Companion Volume Proceedings of the Demo and Poster Sessions*, pages 177–180, Prague, Czech Republic. Association for Computational Linguistics.

Jason Edward Lewis, Angie Abdilla, Noelani Arista, Kaipulaumakaniolono Baker, Scott Benesiinaabandan, Michelle Brown, Melanie Cheung, Meredith Coleman, Ashley Cordes, Joel Davison, Kūpono Duncan, Sergio Garzon, D. Fox Harrell, Peter-Lucas Jones, Kekuhi Kealiikanakaoleohaililani, Megan Kelleher, Suzanne Kite, Olin Lagon, Jason Leigh, Maroussia Levesque, Keoni Mahelona, Caleb Moses, Isaac ('Ika'aka) Nahuewai, Kari Noe, Danielle Olson, 'Ōiwi Parker Jones, Caroline Running Wolf, Michael Running Wolf, Marlee Silva, Skawennati Fragnito, and Hēmi Whaanga. 2020. Indigenous protocol and artificial intelligence position paper. Project Report 10.11573/spectrum.library.concordia.ca.00986506, Aboriginal Territories in Cyberspace, Honolulu, HI. Edited by Jason Edward Lewis.

Manuel Mager, Diónico Carrillo, and Ivan Meza. 2018. Probabilistic finite-state morphological segmenter for wixarika (huichol) language. *Journal of Intelligent & Fuzzy Systems*, 34(5):3081–3087.

Nitika Mathur, Timothy Baldwin, and Trevor Cohn. 2020. Tangled up in BLEU: Reevaluating the evaluation of automatic machine translation evaluation metrics. In *Proceedings of the 58th Annual Meeting of the Association for Computational Linguistics*, pages 4984–4997, Online. Association for Computational Linguistics.

Kishore Papineni, Salim Roukos, Todd Ward, and Wei-Jing Zhu. 2002. Bleu: a method for automatic evaluation of machine translation. In *Proceedings of the 40th Annual Meeting of the Association for Computational Linguistics*, pages 311–318, Philadelphia, Pennsylvania, USA. Association for Computational Linguistics.

Maja Popović. 2015. chrF: character n-gram F-score for automatic MT evaluation. In *Proceedings of the Tenth Workshop on Statistical Machine Translation*, pages 392–395, Lisbon, Portugal. Association for Computational Linguistics.

Matt Post. 2018. A call for clarity in reporting BLEU scores. In *Proceedings of the Third Conference on Machine Translation: Research Papers*, pages 186–191, Brussels, Belgium. Association for Computational Linguistics.

Ivan Provilkov, Dmitrii Emelianenko, and Elena Voita. 2020. BPE-dropout: Simple and effective subword regularization. In *Proceedings of the 58th Annual Meeting of the Association for Computational Linguistics*, pages 1882–1892, Online. Association for Computational Linguistics.

Matīss Rikters, Mārcis Pinnis, and Rihards Krišlauks. 2018. Training and adapting multilingual NMT for less-resourced and morphologically rich languages. In *Proceedings of the Eleventh International Conference on Language Resources and Evaluation (LREC 2018)*, Miyazaki, Japan. European Language Resources Association (ELRA).

Rico Sennrich, Barry Haddow, and Alexandra Birch. 2016. Neural machine translation of rare words with subword units. In *Proceedings of the 54th Annual Meeting of the Association for Computational Linguistics (Volume 1: Long Papers)*, pages 1715–1725, Berlin, Germany. Association for Computational Linguistics.

Michel Simard and Atsushi Fujita. 2012. A poor man's translation memory using machine translation evaluation metrics. In *Proceedings of the 10th Bienniall Conference of the Association for Machine Translation in the Americas*. Association for Machine Translation in the Americas.

Ashish Vaswani, Noam Shazeer, Niki Parmar, Jakob Uszkoreit, Llion Jones, Aidan N. Gomez, Lukasz Kaiser, and Illia Polosukhin. 2017. Attention is all you need. In *Advances in Neural Information Processing Systems 30: Annual Conference on Neural Information Processing Systems 2017, 4-9 December 2017, Long Beach, CA, USA*, pages 5998–6008.

A When does it make sense to build MT systems?

Our recent participation in shared tasks has made us consider scenarios and use cases for low-resource MT, which we discuss in this appendix.

At the WMT 2020 News translation task, the Inuktitut-English translation task was arguably mid-resource (over a million lines of parallel legislative text), with the Hansard (legislative assembly) portion of the development and test set being a strong domain match to the training data. The news data in the development and test sets represented a domain mismatch.

In the supervised low-resource task at WMT, there was an arguably low-resource (approximately 60,000 lines of parallel text) language pair of German-Upper Sorbian. However, the test set was extremely well-matched to the training data (though not exact duplicates), resulting in surprisingly high automatic metric scores (BLEU scores in the 50s and 60s).

In this AmericasNLP shared task, we observed perhaps the hardest scenario (outside of zero-shot): low resource with domain/dialect/orthographic mismatch. It should come as no surprise, then, that we observe extremely low automatic metric scores for this task.

	Domain Match	**Mismatch**
Low-Res.	Upper Sorbian	AmericasNLP
Mid-Res.	Inuktitut Hansard	Inuktitut News

Table 6: Comparison of recent shared tasks on low-resource machine translation.

For both the Inuktitut and Upper Sorbian systems, we know of community and/or government organizations that may be interested in using machine translation technology, for example as part of a computer aided translation (CAT) tool.[10] Provided that human evaluation found the quality level of the machine translation output appropriately high (no human evaluation was performed in the Upper Sorbian task, and the Inuktitut human evaluation is ongoing), there appear to be clear suitable use cases here, such as as part of a human translation workflow translating the Hansard as it is produced or translating more of the same domain Upper Sorbian/German text. It is less clear, where there is a domain mismatch, whether the quality is anywhere near high enough for use in a CAT setting. We know that the usefulness of machine translation in CAT tools varies by translator (Koehn and Germann, 2014); some find even relatively low-quality translations useful, while others benefit only from very high-quality translations, and so on. There are also potential concerns that MT may influence the way translators choose to translate text.

But what about this low-resource, domain mismatch setting? While human evaluation would be the real test, we suspect that the output quality may be too low to be beneficial to most translators. As a brief example, we consider the CHRF scores that were generated between two Spanish sentences as a byproduct of the creation of our translation memory submission.

- Washington ha perdi**do todos los** partidos. (Washington has lost all the games.)
- Continuaron visitan**do todos los** días. (They continued visiting every day.)

In part on the basis of the 10-character (spaces ignored) substring "do todos los" (for which "todos los" can be glossed as "every", but the string-initial "do" suffix belongs to two different verbs, one of which is in its past participle form and the other of which is in its present participle form), these sentences have a score of 0.366 CHRF (if we consider the first to be the "system" output and the second to be the "reference").

Here of course both sentences are grammatical, but they are clearly not semantic equivalents. Nevertheless, comparing the two produces a CHRF score comparable to the the highest scores observed in this task.[11] We argue then, that if the goal is CAT, then it may be better to consider a TM-based approach, even though it has lower scores, given that CAT tools are well-equipped to handle TMs, and typically provide some sort of indication about the differences between the sentence to be translated and its fuzzy-match from the TM as a guide for the translator. In an MT-based approach, the translator may be confronted with fluent text that is not semantically related to the source, ungrammatical language, or types of other problematic output.

[10] For example, the presentation of the Upper Sorbian-German machine translation tool *sotra* (`https://soblex.de/sotra/`) encourages users to proofread and correct the output where necessary: `https://www.powtoon.com/online-presentation/cr2llmDWRR9/`

[11] We acknowledge that this is an imperfect comparison, since the scores in this task are of course not on Spanish output and thus should not be compared directly.

If the goal of these MT tools is *not* CAT, but rather for a reader to access text in their preferred language, we expect that neither the MT systems nor the TMs would provide the kind of quality that users of online MT systems have come to expect. This raises questions of how to alert potential users to the potential for low-quality MT.

It is possible that there may be other use cases, in which case a downstream evaluation may be more appropriate than automatic metrics.

B Pre- and Post-processing Details

Training corpora (but not development or test corpora) were processed using the Moses `clean-corpus-n.perl` script (Koehn et al., 2007), with a sentence length ratio of 15:1 and minimum and maximum lengths of 1 and 200, respectively. All corpora were preprocessed with the `normalize-punctuation.perl` script, with the language set to Spanish (since no language-specific rules are available for the other languages in this task), and all instances of U+FEFF ZERO WIDTH NO-BREAK SPACE were removed. The only additional language-specific preprocessing that we performed was to replace "+" with U+0268 LATIN SMALL LETTER I WITH STROKE in the Wixárika text; this prevents the text from being oversegmented by the tokenizer, and is reverted in post-processing.[12] We note that it might be desirable to perform a similar replacement of apostrophes with a modifier letter apostrophe, but because some of the training data was released in tokenized format we were not confident that we could guarantee consistency in such an approach.[13]

All text is then tokenized with the Moses tokenizer `tokenizer.perl`, with aggressive hyphen splitting, language set to Spanish, and no HTML escaping.[14] Note that we apply the tokenization even to already-tokenized training data, in the hopes of making the different datasets as consistent as possible.

Postprocessing consists of unBPEing then detokenizing using Moses' `detokenizer.perl`. An extra step is needed for Wixárika to revert back to the "+" character. We also perform a small amount of extra language-specific postprocessing, which has limited effects on CHRF (it primarily involves tokenization) with some effect on BLEU. For example, for Guaraní, we delete spaces around apostrophes and replace sequences of three periods with U+2026 HORIZONTAL ELLIPSIS. For Wixárika, we add a space after the "¿" and "¡" characters. For Nahuatl, we make sure that "$" is separated from alphabetic characters by a space. For Rarámuri, we replace three periods with the horizontal ellipsis, convert single apostrophes or straight quotation marks before "u" or "U" to U+2018 LEFT SINGLE QUOTATION MARK and remove the space between it and the letter, and then convert any remaining apostrophes or single straight quotes to U+2019 RIGHT SINGLE QUOTATION MARK as well as removing any surrounding spaces. These are all heuristics based on frequencies of those characters in the development data, and we note that their effect on BLEU scores and CHRF scores is minimal (as measured on development data).

C Coverage

The Wixárika and Guaraní data was provided untokenized, but Nahuatl and Rarámuri datasets contained training data that was tokenized while the development and test data was untokenized. Here we briefly illustrate the impact of the mismatch, through token and type coverage. In Table 7, we show what percentage of target language development tokens (and types) were also observed in the training data, before and after applying tokenization. Table 8 shows the same for source language. Table 9 shows source coverage for the test data instead of the development data. Finally, Table 10 shows what percentage of the source test data is contained in the *development set.* Unsurprisingly, coverage is higher across the board for Spanish (source), which is less morphologically complex than the target languages. Spanish-Rarámuri has the lowest coverage in both source and target. Spanish-Nahuatl has the second-highest coverage on the source side, but not on the target side, perhaps due to the historical content in the training data and/or the orthographic conversions applied. Spanish-Guaraní has the highest coverage on both source and target.

Applying BPE results in approximately 100% coverage, but it is still worth noting the low full-word coverage, as novel vocabulary may be hard

[12] Note, however, that the `13a` tokenizer used by `sacrebleu` (Post, 2018) tokenizes "+", meaning that BLEU scores and other scores that incorporate word n-grams are artificially inflated for Wixárika.

[13] With CHRF as the main metric, this is less of a concern than it would be were the main metric BLEU or human evaluation. We note that even the use of CHRF++, with its use of word bigrams, would make this a concern.

[14] `tokenizer.perl -a -l es -no-escape`

	Tokens		Types	
	Raw	Tok.	Raw	Tok.
es-hch	54.4%	65.3%	27.5%	31.7%
es-nah	53.8%	63.9%	25.3%	30.0%
es-tar	32.7%	55.0%	8.1%	14.4%
es-gn	61.4%	81.1%	35.0%	46.4%

Table 7: Target language training data coverage on development set.

	Tokens		Types	
	Raw	Tok.	Raw	Tok.
es-hch	70.5%	78.4%	35.2%	43.7%
es-nah	77.8%	89.1%	51.2%	68.6%
es-tar	66.7%	76.7%	30.4%	41.3%
es-gn	84.5%	90.9%	62.0%	72.8%

Table 8: Source language (Spanish) training data coverage on development set (compared against training data).

for the systems to translate or to generate.

For all languages except Guaraní, the first half of the development set had higher target language coverage on the second half of the development set, as compared to training target language coverage on the full development set (or second half of the development set), which may explain both the improved performance of systems that trained on development data and the quality of the translation memory system.

	Tokens		Types	
	Raw	Tok.	Raw	Tok.
es-hch	74.8%	83.1%	42.0%	51.2%
es-nah	77.6%	89.3%	48.6%	68.0%
es-tar	69.2%	80.9%	34.0%	48.5%
es-gn	83.5%	90.8%	59.5%	71.3%

Table 9: Source language (Spanish) training data coverage on test set (compared against training data).

	Tokens		Types	
	Raw	Tok.	Raw	Tok.
es-hch	73.3%	81.0%	34.1%	40.3%
es-nah	69.8%	78.2%	27.7%	33.3%
es-tar	73.3%	81.0%	34.1%	40.3%
es-gn	73.3%	81.0%	34.1%	40.3%

Table 10: Source language (Spanish) *development data* coverage on test set. Note that Wixárika, Rarámuri, and Guaraní share identical source data for the development set, and all languages share identical source data for the test set.

	Tokens		Types	
	Raw	Tok.	Raw	Tok.
es-hch	72.3%	80.4%	38.3%	45.7%
es-nah	69.0%	77.3%	37.4%	43.8%
es-tar	73.1%	81.1%	37.8%	45.8%
es-gn	72.7%	80.2%	37.2%	44.0%

Table 11: Source language (Spanish) *first half of the development data* coverage on *second half of the development data*. I.e., for raw es-hch data, 72.3% of source language tokens in the second half of the development set appeared somewhere in the first half of the development set.

	Tokens		Types	
	Raw	Tok.	Raw	Tok.
es-hch	66.3%	74.8%	36.8%	41.4%
es-nah	59.1%	67.8%	33.0%	37.4%
es-tar	73.8%	85.1%	39.1%	46.8%
es-gn	56.7%	77.7%	31.9%	40.2%

Table 12: Target language *first half of the development data* coverage on *second half of the development data*. I.e., for raw es-hch data, 66.3% of target language tokens in the second half of the development set appeared somewhere in the first half of the development set.

Low-Resource Machine Translation Using Cross-Lingual Language Model Pretraining

Francis Zheng, Machel Reid, Edison Marrese-Taylor, Yutaka Matsuo
Graduate School of Engineering
The University of Tokyo
{francis, machelreid, emarrese, matsuo}@weblab.t.u-tokyo.ac.jp

Abstract

This paper describes UTokyo's submission to the AmericasNLP 2021 Shared Task on machine translation systems for indigenous languages of the Americas. We present a low-resource machine translation system that improves translation accuracy using cross-lingual language model pretraining. Our system uses an mBART implementation of FAIRSEQ to pretrain on a large set of monolingual data from a diverse set of high-resource languages before finetuning on 10 low-resource indigenous American languages: Aymara, Bribri, Asháninka, Guaraní, Wixarika, Náhuatl, Hñähñu, Quechua, Shipibo-Konibo, and Rarámuri. On average, our system achieved BLEU scores that were 1.64 higher and CHRF scores that were 0.0749 higher than the baseline.

1 Introduction

Neural machine translation (NMT) systems have produced translations of commendable accuracy under large-data training conditions but are data-hungry (Zoph et al., 2016) and perform poorly in low resource languages, where parallel data is lacking (Koehn and Knowles, 2017).

Many of the indigenous languages of the Americas lack adequate amounts of parallel data, so existing NMT systems have difficulty producing accurate translations for these languages. Additionally, many of these indigenous languages exhibit linguistic properties that are uncommon in high-resource languages, such as English or Chinese, that are used to train NMT systems.

One striking feature of many indigenous American languages is their polysynthesis (Brinton, 1885; Payne, 2014). Polysynthetic languages display high levels of inflection and are morphologically complex. However, NMT systems are weak in translating "low-frequency words belonging to highly-inflected categories (e.g. verbs)" (Koehn and Knowles, 2017). Quechua, a low-resource, polysynthetic American language, has on average twice as many morphemes per word compared to English (Ortega et al., 2020b), which makes machine translation difficult. Mager et al. (2018b) shows that information is often lost when translating polysynthetic languages into Spanish due to a misalignment of morphemes. Thus, existing NMT systems are not appropriate for indigenous American languages, which are low-resource, polysynthetic languages.

Despite the scarcity of parallel data for these indigenous languages, some are spoken widely and have a pressing need for improved machine translation. For example, Quechua is spoken by more than 10 million people in South America, but some Quechua speakers are not able to access health care due to a lack of Spanish ability (Freire, 2011).

Other languages lack a large population of speakers and may appear to have relatively low demand for translation, but many of these languages are also crucial in many domains such as health care, the maintenance of cultural history, and international security (Klavans, 2018). Improved translation techniques for low-resource, polysynthetic languages are thus of great value.

In light of this, we participated in the AmericasNLP 2021 Shared Task to help further the development of new approaches to low-resource machine translation of polysynthetic languages, which are not commonly studied in natural language processing. The task consisted of producing translations from Spanish to 10 different indigenous American languages.

In this paper, we describe our system designed for the AmericasNLP 2021 Shared Task, which achieved BLEU scores that were 1.64 higher and CHRF scores that were 0.0749 higher than the baseline on average. Our system improves translation accuracy by using monolingual data to improve understanding of natural language before finetuning

Proceedings of the First Workshop on Natural Language Processing for Indigenous Languages of the Americas, pages 234–240
June 11, 2021. ©2021 Association for Computational Linguistics

for each of the 10 indigenous languages.

2 Methods

2.1 Data

Our model employs two types of data:

1. 13 GB of monolingual data from Bulgarian, English, French, Irish, Korean, Latin, Spanish, Sundanese, Vietnamese, and Yoruba

2. 140 MB of parallel data between Spanish and Aymara, Bribri, Asháninka, Guaraní, Wixarika, Náhuatl, Hñähñu, Quechua, Shipibo-Konibo, and Rarámuri

2.1.1 Monolingual Data

We selected a variety of widely-spoken languages across the Americas, Asia, Europe, Africa, and Oceania for the monolingual data we used during our pretraining, allowing our model to learn from a wide range of language families and linguistic features. These monolingual data were acquired from CC100[1] (Wenzek et al., 2020; Conneau et al., 2020). We use these monolingual data as part of our pretraining, as this has been shown to improve results with smaller parallel datasets (Conneau and Lample, 2019; Liu et al., 2020; Song et al., 2019).

2.1.2 Parallel Data

The parallel data between Spanish and the indigenous American languages were provided by AmericasNLP 2021 (Mager et al., 2021).

We have summarized some important details of the training data and development/test sets (Ebrahimi et al., 2021) below. More details about these data can be found in the AmericasNLP 2021 official repository[2].

Aymara The Aymara–Spanish data came from translations by Global Voices and Facebook AI. The training data came primarily from Global Voices[3] (Prokopidis et al., 2016; Tiedemann, 2012), but because translations were done by volunteers, the texts have potentially different writing styles. The development and test sets came from translations from Spanish texts into Aymara La Paz jilata, a Central Aymara variant.

Bribri The Bribri–Spanish data (Feldman and Coto-Solano, 2020) came from six different sources (a dictionary, a grammar, two language learning textbooks, one storybook, and transcribed sentences from a spoken corpus) and three major dialects (Amubri, Coroma, and Salitre). Two different orthographies are widely used for Bribri, so an intermediate representation was used to facilitate training.

Asháninka The Asháninka–Spanish data[4] were extracted and pre-processed by Richard Castro (Cushimariano Romano and Sebastián Q., 2008; Ortega et al., 2020a; Mihas, 2011). Though the texts came from different pan-Ashaninka dialects, they were normalized using **AshMorph** (Ortega et al., 2020a). The development and test sets came from translations of Spanish texts done by Feliciano Torres Ríos.

Guaraní The Guaraní–Spanish data (Chiruzzo et al., 2020) consisted of training data from web sources (blogs and news articles) written in a mix of dialects and development and test sets written in pure Guaraní. Translations were provided by Perla Alvarez Britez.

Wixarika The Wixarika–Spanish data came from Mager et al. (2018a). The training, development, and test sets all used the same dialect (Wixarika of Zoquipan) and orthography, though word boundaries were not consistent between the development/test and training sets. Translations were provided by Silvino González de la Crúz.

Náhuatl The Náhuatl–Spanish data came from Gutierrez-Vasques et al. (2016). Náhuatl has a wide dialectal variation and no standard orthography, but most of the training data were close to a Classical Náhuatl orthographic "standard." The development and test sets came from translations made from Spanish into modern Náhuatl. An orthographic normalization was applied to these translations to make them closer to the Classical Náhuatl orthography found in the training data. This normalization was done by employing a rule-based approach based on predictable orthographic changes between modern varieties and Classical Náhuatl. Translations were provided by Giovany Martinez Sebastián, José Antonio, and Pedro Kapoltitan.

[1] `http://data.statmt.org/cc-100/`

[2] `https://github.com/AmericasNLP/americasnlp2021/blob/main/data/information_datasets.pdf`

[3] `https://opus.nlpl.eu/GlobalVoices.php`

[4] `https://github.com/hinantin/AshaninkaMT`

Hñähñu The Hñähñu–Spanish training data came from translations into Spanish from Hñähñu text from a set of different sources[5]. Most of these texts are in the Valle del Mezquital dialect. The development and test sets are in the Ñûhmû de Ixtenco, Tlaxcala variant. Translations were done by José Mateo Lino Cajero Velázquez.

Quechua The training set for Quechua–Spanish data (Agić and Vulić, 2019) came from Jehova's Witnesses texts (available in OPUS), sentences extracted from the official dictionary of the Minister of Education (MINEDU) in Peru for Quechua Ayacucho, and dictionary entries and samples collected and reviewed by Diego Huarcaya. Training sets were provided in both the Quchua Cuzco and Quechua Ayacucho variants, but our system only employed Quechua Ayacucho data during training. The development and test sets came from translations of Spanish text into Quechua Ayacucho, a standard version of Southern Quechua. Translations were provided by Facebook AI.

Shipibo-Konibo The training set of the Shipibo-Konibo–Spanish data (Galarreta et al., 2017) was obtained from translations of flashcards and translations of sentences from books for bilingual education done by a bilingual teacher. Additionally, parallel sentences from a dictionary were used as part of the training data. The development and test sets came from translations from Spanish into Shipibo-Konibo done by Liz Chávez.

Rarámuri The training set of the Rarámuri–Spanish data came from a dictionary (Brambila, 1976). The development and tests sets came from translations from Spanish into the highlands Rarámuri by María del Cármen Sotelo Holguín. The training set and development/test sets use different orthographies.

2.2 Preprocessing

We tokenized all of our data together using SentencePiece (Kudo and Richardson, 2018) in preparation for our multilingual model. We used a vocabulary size of 8000 and a character coverage of 0.9995, as the wide variety of languages covered carry a rich character set.

Then, we sharded our data for faster processing. With our SentencePiece model and vocabulary, we used FAIRSEQ[6] (Ott et al., 2019) to build vocabularies and binarize our data.

2.3 Pretraining

We pretrained our model on the 20 languages described in 2.1 with an mBART (Liu et al., 2020) implementation of FAIRSEQ (Ott et al., 2019). We pretrained on 32 NVIDIA V100 GPUs for three hours.

Balancing data across languages

Due to the large variability in text data size between different languages, we used the exponential sampling technique used in Conneau and Lample (2019); Liu et al. (2020), where the text is resampled according to smoothing parameter α as follows:

$$q_i = \frac{p_i^\alpha}{\sum_{j=1}^{N} p_j^\alpha} \quad (1)$$

In equation 1, q_i refers to the resample probability for language i, given multinomial distribution $\{q_i\}_{i=1...N}$ with original sampling probability p_i.

As we want our model to work well with the low-resource languages, we chose a smoothing parameter of $\alpha = 0.25$ (compared with $\alpha = 0.7$ used in mBART (Liu et al., 2020)) to alleviate model bias towards the higher proportion of data from high-resource languages.

Hyperparameters

We used a six-layer Transformer with a hidden dimension of 512 and feed-forward size of 2048. We set the maximum sequence length to 512, with a batch size of 1024. We optimized the model using Adam (Kingma and Ba, 2015) using hyperparameters $\beta = (0.9, 0.98)$ and $\epsilon = 10^{-6}$. We used a learning rate of 6×10^{-4} over 10,000 iterations. For regularization, we used a dropout rate of 0.5 and weight decay of 0.01. We also experimented with lower dropout rates but found that a higher dropout rate gave us a model that produces better translations.

2.4 Finetuning

Using our pretrained model, we performed finetuning on each of the 10 indigenous American languages with the same hyperparameters used during pretraining. For each language, we conducted our finetuning using four NVIDIA V100 GPUs for three hours.

[5] https://tsunkua.elotl.mx/about/

[6] https://github.com/pytorch/fairseq

Language	Baseline[1]		Dev[2]		Test1[3]		Test2[4]	
	BLEU	CHRF	BLEU	CHRF	BLEU	CHRF	BLEU	CHRF
Aymara (aym)	0.01	0.157	2.84	0.2338	1.17	0.214	1.03	0.209
Bribri (bzd)	0.01	0.058	1.22	0.1203	1.7	0.143	1.29	0.131
Asháninka (cni)	0.01	0.102	0.48	0.2188	0.2	0.216	0.45	0.214
Guaraní (gn)	0.12	0.193	3.64	0.2492	3.21	0.265	3.16	0.254
Wixarika (hch)	2.2	0.126	4.89	0.2093	7.09	0.238	6.74	0.229
Náhuatl (nah)	0.01	0.157	0.3	0.253	0.55	0.239	1.2	0.238
Hñähñu (oto)	0	0.054	0.04	0.1035	2.45	0.152	1.28	0.133
Quechua (quy)	0.05	0.304	1.46	0.3155	2.35	0.332	2.47	0.33
Shipibo-Konibo (shp)	0.01	0.121	0.49	0.176	0.33	0.163	0.71	0.175
Rarámuri (tar)	0	0.039	0.12	0.1163	0.1	0.122	0.06	0.123

[1] Baseline test results provided by AmericasNLP 2021, from a system where the development set was not used for training
[2] Our own results on the development set
[3] Our official test results for our system where the development set was used for training
[4] Our official test results for our system where the development set was not used for training

Table 1: Results

2.5 Evaluation

Using the SacreBLEU library[7] (Post, 2018), we evaluated our system outputs with detokenized BLEU (Papineni et al., 2002; Post, 2018). Due to the polysynthetic nature of the languages involved in this task, we also used CHRF (Popović, 2015) to measure performance at the character level and better see how well morphemes or parts of morphemes were translated, rather than whole words. For these reasons, we focused on optimizing the CHRF score.

3 Results

We describe our results in Table 1. Our test results (**Test1** and **Test2**) show considerable improvements over the baseline provided by AmericasNLP 2021. We also included our own results on the development set (**Dev**) for comparison. The trends we saw in the **Dev** results parallel our test results; languages for which our system achieved high scores in **Dev** (e.g. Wixarika and Guaraní) also demonstrated high scores in **Test1** and **Test2**. Likewise, languages for which our system performed relatively poorly in **Dev** (e.g. Rarámuri, whose poor performance may be attributed to the difference in orthographies between the training set and development/test sets) also performed poorly in **Test1** and **Test2**. This matches the trend seen in the baseline scores.

The baseline results and **Test2** results were both produced using the same test set and by systems where the development set was not used for training. Thus, the baseline results and **Test2** results can be directly compared. On average, our system used to produce the **Test2** results achieved BLEU scores that were 1.54 higher and CHRF scores that were 0.0725 higher than the baseline. On the same test set, our **Test1** system produced higher BLEU and CHRF scores for nearly every language. This is expected, as the system used to produce **Test1** was trained on slightly more data; it used the development set of the indigenous American languages provided by AmericasNLP 2021 in addition to the training set.

If we factor in our results from **Test1** to our **Test2** results, we achieved BLEU scores that were 1.64 higher and CHRF scores that were 0.0749 higher than the baseline on average. Overall, we attribute this improvement in scores primarily to the cross-lingual language model pretraining (Conneau and Lample, 2019) we performed, allowing our model to learn about natural language from the monolingual data before finetuning on each of the 10 indigenous languages.

4 Conclusions and Future Work

We described our system to improve low-resource machine translation for the AmericasNLP 2021 Shared Task. We constructed a system using the mBART implementation of FAIRSEQ to translate from Spanish to 10 different low-resource indigenous languages from the Americas. We demon-

[7] `https://github.com/mjpost/sacrebleu`

strated strong improvements over the baseline by pretraining on a large amount of monolingual data before finetuning our model for each of the low-resource languages.

We are interested in using dictionary augmentation techniques and creating pseudo-monolingual data to use during the pretraining process, as we have seen improved results with these two techniques when translating several low-resource African languages. We can also incorporate these two techniques in an iterative pretraining procedure (Tran et al., 2020) to produce more pseudo-monolingual data and further train our pretrained model for potentially better results.

Future research should also explore using probabilistic finite-state morphological segmenters, which may improve translations by exploiting regular agglutinative patterns without the need for much linguistic knowledge (Mager et al., 2018a) and thus may work well with the low-resource, polysynthetic languages dealt with in this paper.

References

Željko Agić and Ivan Vulić. 2019. JW300: A wide-coverage parallel corpus for low-resource languages. In *Proceedings of the 57th Annual Meeting of the Association for Computational Linguistics*, pages 3204–3210, Florence, Italy. Association for Computational Linguistics.

David Brambila. 1976. *Diccionario Raramuri–Castellano (Tarahumara)*. Obra Nacional de la Buena Prensa, México.

D.G. Brinton. 1885. *On Polysynthesis and Incorporation: As Characteristics of American Languages*. McCalla & Stavely.

Luis Chiruzzo, Pedro Amarilla, Adolfo Ríos, and Gustavo Giménez Lugo. 2020. Development of a Guarani - Spanish parallel corpus. In *Proceedings of the 12th Language Resources and Evaluation Conference*, pages 2629–2633, Marseille, France. European Language Resources Association.

Alexis Conneau, Kartikay Khandelwal, Naman Goyal, Vishrav Chaudhary, Guillaume Wenzek, Francisco Guzmán, Edouard Grave, Myle Ott, Luke Zettlemoyer, and Veselin Stoyanov. 2020. Unsupervised cross-lingual representation learning at scale. In *Proceedings of the 58th Annual Meeting of the Association for Computational Linguistics*, pages 8440–8451, Online. Association for Computational Linguistics.

Alexis Conneau and Guillaume Lample. 2019. Cross-lingual language model pretraining. In *Advances in Neural Information Processing Systems 32: Annual Conference on Neural Information Processing Systems 2019, NeurIPS 2019, December 8-14, 2019, Vancouver, BC, Canada*, pages 7057–7067.

Rubén Cushimariano Romano and Richer C. Sebastián Q. 2008. Ñaantsipeta asháninkaki birakochaki. diccionario asháninka-castellano. versión preliminar. `http://www.lengamer.org/publicaciones/diccionarios/`.

Abteen Ebrahimi, Manuel Mager, Arturo Oncevay, Vishrav Chaudhary, Luis Chiruzzo, Angela Fan, John Ortega, Ricardo Ramos, Annette Rios, Ivan Vladimir, Gustavo A. Giménez-Lugo, Elisabeth Mager, Graham Neubig, Alexis Palmer, Rolando A. Coto Solano, Ngoc Thang Vu, and Katharina Kann. 2021. Americasnli: Evaluating zero-shot natural language understanding of pretrained multilingual models in truly low-resource languages.

Isaac Feldman and Rolando Coto-Solano. 2020. Neural machine translation models with back-translation for the extremely low-resource indigenous language Bribri. In *Proceedings of the 28th International Conference on Computational Linguistics*, pages 3965–3976, Barcelona, Spain (Online). International Committee on Computational Linguistics.

Germán Freire. 2011. *Perspectivas en salud indígena: cosmovisión, enfermedad y políticas públicas*. Ediciones Abya-Yala.

Ana-Paula Galarreta, Andrés Melgar, and Arturo Oncevay. 2017. Corpus creation and initial SMT experiments between Spanish and Shipibo-konibo. In *Proceedings of the International Conference Recent Advances in Natural Language Processing, RANLP 2017*, pages 238–244, Varna, Bulgaria. INCOMA Ltd.

Ximena Gutierrez-Vasques, Gerardo Sierra, and Isaac Hernandez Pompa. 2016. Axolotl: a web accessible parallel corpus for Spanish-Nahuatl. In *Proceedings of the Tenth International Conference on Language Resources and Evaluation (LREC'16)*, pages 4210–4214, Portorož, Slovenia. European Language Resources Association (ELRA).

Diederik P. Kingma and Jimmy Ba. 2015. Adam: A method for stochastic optimization. In *3rd International Conference on Learning Representations, ICLR 2015, San Diego, CA, USA, May 7-9, 2015, Conference Track Proceedings*.

Judith L. Klavans. 2018. Computational challenges for polysynthetic languages. In *Proceedings of the Workshop on Computational Modeling of Polysynthetic Languages*, pages 1–11, Santa Fe, New Mexico, USA. Association for Computational Linguistics.

Philipp Koehn and Rebecca Knowles. 2017. Six challenges for neural machine translation. In *Proceedings of the First Workshop on Neural Machine Translation*, pages 28–39, Vancouver. Association for Computational Linguistics.

Taku Kudo and John Richardson. 2018. SentencePiece: A simple and language independent subword tokenizer and detokenizer for neural text processing. In *Proceedings of the 2018 Conference on Empirical Methods in Natural Language Processing: System Demonstrations*, pages 66–71, Brussels, Belgium. Association for Computational Linguistics.

Yinhan Liu, Jiatao Gu, Naman Goyal, Xian Li, Sergey Edunov, Marjan Ghazvininejad, Mike Lewis, and Luke Zettlemoyer. 2020. Multilingual denoising pre-training for neural machine translation. *Transactions of the Association for Computational Linguistics*, 8:726–742.

Manuel Mager, Diónico Carrillo, and Ivan Meza. 2018a. Probabilistic finite-state morphological segmenter for Wixarika (Huichol) language. *Journal of Intelligent & Fuzzy Systems*, 34(5):3081–3087.

Manuel Mager, Elisabeth Mager, Alfonso Medina-Urrea, Ivan Vladimir Meza Ruiz, and Katharina Kann. 2018b. Lost in translation: Analysis of information loss during machine translation between polysynthetic and fusional languages. In *Proceedings of the Workshop on Computational Modeling of Polysynthetic Languages*, pages 73–83, Santa Fe, New Mexico, USA. Association for Computational Linguistics.

Manuel Mager, Arturo Oncevay, Abteen Ebrahimi, John Ortega, Annette Rios, Angela Fan, Ximena Gutierrez-Vasques, Luis Chiruzzo, Gustavo Giménez-Lugo, Ricardo Ramos, Anna Currey, Vishrav Chaudhary, Ivan Vladimir Meza Ruiz, Rolando Coto-Solano, Alexis Palmer, Elisabeth Mager, Ngoc Thang Vu, Graham Neubig, and Katharina Kann. 2021. Findings of the AmericasNLP 2021 Shared Task on Open Machine Translation for Indigenous Languages of the Americas. In *Proceedings of the The First Workshop on NLP for Indigenous Languages of the Americas*, Online. Association for Computational Linguistics.

Elena Mihas. 2011. *Añaani katonkosatzi parenini, El idioma del alto Perené*. Milwaukee, WI: Clarks Graphics.

John Ortega, Richard Alexander Castro-Mamani, and Jaime Rafael Montoya Samame. 2020a. Overcoming resistance: The normalization of an Amazonian tribal language. In *Proceedings of the 3rd Workshop on Technologies for MT of Low Resource Languages*, pages 1–13, Suzhou, China. Association for Computational Linguistics.

John E. Ortega, Richard Castro Mamani, and Kyunghyun Cho. 2020b. Neural machine translation with a polysynthetic low resource language. *Machine Translation*, 34(4):325–346.

Myle Ott, Sergey Edunov, Alexei Baevski, Angela Fan, Sam Gross, Nathan Ng, David Grangier, and Michael Auli. 2019. fairseq: A fast, extensible toolkit for sequence modeling. In *Proceedings of the 2019 Conference of the North American Chapter of the Association for Computational Linguistics (Demonstrations)*, pages 48–53, Minneapolis, Minnesota. Association for Computational Linguistics.

Kishore Papineni, Salim Roukos, Todd Ward, and Wei-Jing Zhu. 2002. Bleu: a method for automatic evaluation of machine translation. In *Proceedings of the 40th Annual Meeting of the Association for Computational Linguistics*, pages 311–318, Philadelphia, Pennsylvania, USA. Association for Computational Linguistics.

D.L. Payne. 2014. *Morphological Characteristics of Lowland South American Languages*. University of Texas Press.

Maja Popović. 2015. chrF: character n-gram F-score for automatic MT evaluation. In *Proceedings of the Tenth Workshop on Statistical Machine Translation*, pages 392–395, Lisbon, Portugal. Association for Computational Linguistics.

Matt Post. 2018. A call for clarity in reporting BLEU scores. In *Proceedings of the Third Conference on Machine Translation: Research Papers*, pages 186–191, Brussels, Belgium. Association for Computational Linguistics.

Prokopis Prokopidis, Vassilis Papavassiliou, and Stelios Piperidis. 2016. Parallel Global Voices: a collection of multilingual corpora with citizen media stories. In *Proceedings of the Tenth International Conference on Language Resources and Evaluation (LREC'16)*, pages 900–905, Portorož, Slovenia. European Language Resources Association (ELRA).

Kaitao Song, Xu Tan, Tao Qin, Jianfeng Lu, and Tie-Yan Liu. 2019. MASS: masked sequence to sequence pre-training for language generation. In *Proceedings of the 36th International Conference on Machine Learning, ICML 2019, 9-15 June 2019, Long Beach, California, USA*, volume 97 of *Proceedings of Machine Learning Research*, pages 5926–5936. PMLR.

Jörg Tiedemann. 2012. Parallel data, tools and interfaces in OPUS. In *Proceedings of the Eighth International Conference on Language Resources and Evaluation (LREC'12)*, pages 2214–2218, Istanbul, Turkey. European Language Resources Association (ELRA).

Chau Tran, Yuqing Tang, Xian Li, and Jiatao Gu. 2020. Cross-lingual retrieval for iterative self-supervised training. *34th Conference on Neural Information Processing Systems (NeurIPS 2020), Vancouver, Canada.*

Guillaume Wenzek, Marie-Anne Lachaux, Alexis Conneau, Vishrav Chaudhary, Francisco Guzmán, Armand Joulin, and Edouard Grave. 2020. CCNet: Extracting high quality monolingual datasets from web crawl data. In *Proceedings of the 12th Language Resources and Evaluation Conference*, pages

4003–4012, Marseille, France. European Language Resources Association.

Barret Zoph, Deniz Yuret, Jonathan May, and Kevin Knight. 2016. Transfer learning for low-resource neural machine translation. In *Proceedings of the 2016 Conference on Empirical Methods in Natural Language Processing*, pages 1568–1575, Austin, Texas. Association for Computational Linguistics.

The REPUcs' Spanish–Quechua Submission to the AmericasNLP 2021 Shared Task on Open Machine Translation

Oscar Moreno Veliz
Pontificia Universidad Católica del Perú
omoreno@pucp.edu.pe

Abstract

We present the submission of REPUcs[1] to the AmericasNLP machine translation shared task for the low resource language pair Spanish–Quechua. Our neural machine translation system ranked first in Track two (development set not used for training) and third in Track one (training includes development data). Our contribution is focused on: (i) the collection of new parallel data from different web sources (poems, lyrics, lexicons, handbooks), and (ii) using large Spanish–English data for pre-training and then fine-tuning the Spanish–Quechua system. This paper describes the new parallel corpora and our approach in detail.

1 Introduction

REPUcs participated in the AmericasNLP 2021 machine translation shared task (Mager et al., 2021) for the Spanish–Quechua language pair. Quechua is one of the most spoken languages in South America (Simons and Fenning, 2019), with several variants, and for this competition, the target language is Southern Quechua. A disadvantage of working with indigenous languages is that there are few documents per language from which to extract parallel or even monolingual corpora. Additionally, most of these languages are traditionally oral, which is the case of Quechua. In order to compensate the lack of data we first obtain a collection of new parallel corpora to augment the available data for the shared task. In addition, we propose to use transfer learning (Zoph et al., 2016) using large Spanish–English data in a neural machine translation (NMT) model. To boost the performance of our transfer learning approach, we follow the work of Kocmi and Bojar (2018), which demonstrated that sharing the source language and a vocabulary of subword units can improve the performance of low resource languages.

[1]"Research Experience for Peruvian Undergraduates - Computer Science" is a program that connects Peruvian students with researchers worldwide. The author was part of the 2021 cohort: https://www.repuprogram.org/repu-cs.

2 Spanish→Quechua

Quechua is the most widespread language family in South America, with more than 6 millions speakers and several variants. For the AmericasNLP Shared Task, the development and test sets were prepared using the Standard Southern Quechua writing system, which is based on the Quechua Ayacucho (quy) variant (for simplification, we will refer to it as Quechua for the rest of the paper). This is an official language in Peru, and according to Zariquiey et al. (2019) it is labelled as endangered. Quechua is essentially a spoken language so there is a lack of written materials. Moreover, it is a polysynthetic language, meaning that it usually express large amount of information using several morphemes in a single word. Hence, subword segmentation methods will have to minimise the problem of addressing "rare words" for an NMT system.

To the best of our knowledge, Ortega et al. (2020b) is one of the few studies that employed a sequence-to-sequence NMT model for Southern Quechua, and they focused on transfer learning with Finnish, an agglutinative language similar to Quechua. Likewise, Huarcaya Taquiri (2020) used the Jehovah Witnesses dataset (Agić and Vulić, 2019), together with additional lexicon data, to train an NMT model that reached up to 39 BLEU points on Quechua. However, the results in both cases were high because the development and test set are split from the same distribution (domain) as the training set. On the other hand, Ortega and Pillaipakkamnatt (2018) improved alignments for Quechua by using Finnish(an agglutinative language) as the pivot language. The corpus source is the parallel treebank of Rios et al. (Rios et al., 2012)., so we deduce that they worked with Quechua Cuzco (quz). (Ortega et al., 2020a)

In the AmericasNLP shared task, new out-of-

Proceedings of the First Workshop on Natural Language Processing for Indigenous Languages of the Americas, pages 241–247
June 11, 2021. ©2021 Association for Computational Linguistics

domain evaluation sets were released, and there were two tracks: using or not the validation set for training the final submission. We addressed both tracks by collecting more data and pre-training the NMT model with large Spanish-English data.

3 Data and pre-processing

In this competition we are going to use the AmericasNLP Shared Task datasets and new corpora extracted from documents and websites in Quechua.

3.1 AmericasNLP datasets

For training, the available parallel data comes from dictionaries and Jehovah Witnesses dataset (JW300; Agić and Vulić, 2019). AmericasNLP also released parallel corpus aligned with English (en) and the close variant of Quechua Cusco (quz) to enhance multilingual learning. For validation, there is a development set made with 994 sentences from Spanish and Quechua (quy) (Ebrahimi et al., 2021).

Detailed information from all the available datasets with their corresponding languages is as follows:

- JW300 (quy, quz, en): texts from the religious domain available in OPUS (Tiedemann, 2012). JW300 has 121k sentences. The problems with this dataset are misaligned sentences, misspelled words and blank translations.
- MINEDU (quy): Sentences extracted from the official dictionary of the Ministry of Education in Peru (MINEDU). This dataset contains open-domain short sentences. A considerable number of sentences are related to the countryside. It only has 650 sentences.
- Dict_misc (quy): Dictionary entries and samples collected and reviewed by Huarcaya Taquiri (2020). This dataset is made from 9k sentences, phrases and word translations.

Furthermore, to examine the domain resemblance, it is important to analyse the similarity between the training and development. Table 1 shows the percentage of the development set tokens that overlap with the tokens in the training datasets on Spanish (es) and Quechua (quy) after deleting all types of symbols.

We observe from Table 1 that the domain of the training and development set are different as the overlapping in Quechua does not even go above 50%. There are two approaches to address this problem: to add part of the development set into the training or to obtain additional data from the same or a more similar domain. In this paper, we focus on the second approach.

Dataset	% Dev overlapping	
	es	quy
JW300	85%	45%
MINEDU	15%	5%
Dict_misc	40%	18%

Table 1: Word overlapping ratio between the development and the available training sets in AmericasNLP

3.2 New parallel corpora

Sources of Quechua documents Even though Quechua is an official language in Peru, official government websites are not translated to Quechua or any other indigenous language, so it is not possible to perform web scrapping (Bustamante et al., 2020). However, the Peruvian Government has published handbooks and lexicons for Quechua Ayacucho and Quechua Cusco, plus other educational resources to support language learning in indigenous communities. In addition, there are official documents such as the Political Constitution of Peru and the Regulation of the Amazon Parliament that are translated to the Quechua Cusco variant.

We have found three unofficial sources to extract parallel corpora from Quechua Ayacucho (quy). The first one is a website, made by Maximiliano Duran (Duran, 2010), that encourages the learning of Quechua Ayacucho. The site contains poems, stories, riddles, songs, phrases and a vocabulary for Quechua. The second one is a website for different lyrics of poems and songs which have available translations for both variants of Quechua (Lyrics translate, 2008). The third source is a Quechua handbook for the Quechua Ayacucho variant elaborated by Iter and Cárdenas (2019).

Sources that were extracted but not used due to time constrains were the Political Constitution of Peru and the Regulation of the Amazon Parliament. Other non-extracted source is a dictionary for Quechua Ayacucho from a website called InkaTour [2]. This source was not used because we already had a dictionary.

Methodology for corpus creation The available vocabulary in Duran (2010) was extracted manually and transformed into parallel corpora using the first

[2] https://www.inkatour.com/dico/

pair of parenthesis as separators. We will call this dataset "Lexicon".

All the additional sentences in Duran (2010) and a few poems from (Lyrics translate, 2008) were manually aligned to obtain the Web Miscellaneous (WebMisc) corpus. Likewise, translations from the Quechua educational handbook (Iter and Cárdenas, 2019) were manually aligned to obtain a parallel corpus (Handbook).[3]

In the case of the official documents for Quechua Cusco, there was a specific format were the Spanish text was followed by the Quechua translation. After manually arranging the line breaks to separate each translation pair, we automatically constructed a parallel corpus for both documents. Paragraphs with more than 2 sentences that had the same number of sentences as their translation were split into small sentences and the unmatched paragraphs were deleted.

Corpora description We perform a large number or rare events (LNRE) modelling to analyse the WebMisc, Lexicon and Handbook datasets[4]. The values are shown in Table 2. The LNRE modelling for the Quechua Cusco datasets are shown in appendix as they are not used for the final submission.

	WebMisc		Lexicon		Handbook	
	es	quy	es	quy	es	quy
S	985		6161		2297	
N	5002	2996	7050	6288	15537	8522
V	1929	2089	3962	3361	4137	5604
V1	1358	1673	2460	1838	2576	4645
V/N	0.38	0.69	0.56	0.53	0.26	0.65
V1/N	0.27	0.55	0.34	0.29	0.16	0.54
mean	2.59	1.43	1.77	1.87	3.75	1.52

Table 2: Corpora description: S = #sentences in corpus; N = number of tokens; V = vocabulary size; V1 = number of tokens occurring once (hapax); V/N = vocabulary growth rate; V1/N = hapax growth rate; mean = word frequency mean

We notice that the vocabulary and hapax growth rate is similar for Quechua (quy) in WebMisc and Handbook even though the latter has more than twice the number of sentences. In addition, it was expected that the word frequency mean and the vocabulary size were lower for Quechua, as this demonstrates its agglutinative property. However, this does not happens in the Lexicon dataset, since is understandable as it is a dictionary that has one or two words for the translation.

Moreover, there is a high presence of tokens occurring only once in both languages. In other words, there is a possibility that our datasets have spelling errors or presence of foreign words (Nagata et al., 2018). However, in this case this could be more related to the vast vocabulary, as the datasets are made of sentences from different domains (poems, songs, teaching, among others).

Furthermore, it is important to examine the similarities between the new datasets and the development set. The percentage of the development set words that overlap with the words of the new datasets on Spanish (es) and Quechua (quy) after eliminating all symbols is shown in Table 3.

Dataset	% Dev overlapping	
	es	quy
WebMisc	18.6%	4%
Lexicon	20%	3.4%
Handbook	28%	10.6%

Table 3: Percentage of word overlapping between the development and the new extracted datasets

Although at first glance the analysis may show that there is not a significant similarity with the development set, we have to take into account that in Table 1, JW300 has 121k sentences and Dict_misc is a dictionary, so it is easy to overlap some of the development set words at least once.However , in the case of WebMisc and Handbook datasets, the quantity of sentences are less than 3k per dataset and even so the percentage of overlapping in Spanish is quite good. This result goes according to the contents of the datasets, as they contain common phrases and open domain sentences, which are the type of sentences that the development set has.

3.3 English-Spanish dataset

For pre-training, we used the EuroParl dataset for Spanish–English (1.9M sentences) (Koehn, 2005) and its development corpora for evaluation.

4 Approach used

4.1 Evaluation

From the Europarl dataset, we extracted 3,000 sentences for validation. For testing we used the devel-

[3]All documents are published in: https://github.com/Ceviche98/REPUcs-AmericasNLP2021

[4]We used the LNRE calculator created by Kyle Gorman: https://gist.github.com/kylebgorman/

opment set from the WMT2006 campaign (Koehn and Monz, 2006).

In the case of Quechua, as the official development set contains only 1,000 sentences there was no split for the testing. Hence, validation results will be taken into account as testing ones.

The main metric in this competition is chrF (Popović, 2017) which evaluates character n-grams and is a useful metric for agglutinative languages such as Quechua. We also reported the BLEU scores (Papineni et al., 2002). We used the implementations of sacreBLEU (Post, 2018).

4.2 Subword segmentation

Subword segmentation is a crucial process for the translation of polysinthetic languages such as Quechua. We used the Byte-Pair-Encoding (BPE; Sennrich et al., 2016) implementation in SentencePiece (Kudo and Richardson, 2018) with a vocabulary size of 32,000. To generate a richer vocabulary, we trained a segmentation model with all three languages (Spanish, English and Quechua), where we upsampled the Quechua data to reach a uniform distribution.

4.3 Procedure

For all experiments, we used a Transformer-based model (Vaswani et al., 2017) with default parameters from the Fairseq toolkit (Ott et al., 2019). The criteria for early stopping was cross-entropy loss for 15 steps.

We first pre-trained a Spanish–English model on the Europarl dataset in order to obtain a good encoding capability on the Spanish side. Using this pre-trained model, we implemented two different versions for fine-tunning. First, with the JW300 dataset, which was the largest Spanish–Quechua corpus, and the second one with all the available datasets (including the ones that we obtained) for Quechua.

5 Results and discussion

The results from the transfer learning models and the baseline are shown in Table 4. We observe that the best result on BLEU and chrF was obtained using the provided datasets together with the extracted datasets. This shows that the new corpora were helpful to improve translation performance.

From Table 4, we observe that using transfer learning showed a considerable improvement in comparison with the baseline (+0.56 in BLEU and +0.007 in chrF). Moreover, using transfer learning with all the available datasets obtained the best BLEU and chrF score. Specially, it had a 0.012 increase in chrF which is quite important as chrF is the metric that best evaluates translation in this case. Overall, the results do not seem to be good in terms of BLEU. However, a manual analysis of the sentences shows that the model is learning to translate a considerable amount of affixes.

Dataset	Size	Direction	BLEU	chrF
Europarl	1.9M	es→en	34.2	0.606
JW300 (baseline)	121k	es→quy	1.49	0.317
JW300 (fine-tuning)	121k	es→quy	2.05	0.324
All datasets (fine-tuning)	133k	es→quy	**2.18**	**0.336**

Table 4: Results of transfer learning experiments

Input (ES)	*El control de armas probablemente no es popular en Texas.*
Input (EN)	*Weapon control is probably not popular in Texas.*
Reference (QUY)	***Texas**piqa sutillapas **arma** controlayqa **mana**chusmi hin**achu** apa**kun***
Output	***Texas** llaqtapi **arma**kuna controlayqa **mana**m runa**kuna**pa run**achu***

Table 5: Subword analysis on translated and reference sentence

For instance, the subwords "arma", "mana", among others, have been correctly translated but are not grouped in the same words as in the reference. In addition, only the word "controlayqa" is translated correctly, which would explain the low results in BLEU. Decoding an agglutinative language is a very difficult task, and the low BLEU scores cannot suggest a translation with proper adequacy and/or fluency (as we can also observe this from the example). Nevertheless, BLEU works at word-level so other character-level metrics should be considered to inspect agglutinative languages. This would be the case of chrF (Popović, 2017) were there is an increase of around 3% when using the AmericasNLP altogether with the new extracted corpora.

Translations using the transfer learning model trained with all available Quechua datasets were submitted for track 2 (Development set not used for Training). For the submission of track 1 (Development set used for Training) we retrained the best transfer learning model adding the validation to the training for 40 epochs. The official results of the competition are shown in Table 6.

	Rank	Team	BLEU	chrF
Track 1	1	Helsinki	5.38	0.394
	3	**REPUcs**	3.1	**0.358**
Track 2	1	**REPUcs**	2.91	**0.346**
	2	Helsinki	3.63	0.343

Table 6: Official results from AmericasNLP 2021 Shared Task competition on the two tracks.Track 1: Development set used for Training, Track 2: Development set not used for Training

6 Conclusion

In this paper, we focused on extracting new datasets for Spanish–Quechua, which helped to improve the performance of our model. Moreover, we found that using transfer learning was beneficial to the results even without the additional data. By combining the new corpora in the fine-tuning step, we managed to obtain the first place on Track 2 and the third place on Track 1 of the AmericasNLP Shared Task. Due to time constrains, the Quechua Cusco data was not used, but it can be beneficial for further work.

In general, we found that the translating Quechua is a challenging task for two reasons. Firstly, there is a lack of data for all the variants of Quechua, and the available documents are hard to extract. In this research, all the new datasets were extracted and aligned mostly manually. Secondly, the agglutinative nature of Quechua motivates more research about effective subword segmentation methods.

Acknowledgements

This work could not be possible without the support of REPU Computer Science (Research Experience for Peruvian Undergraduates), a program that connects Peruvian students with researchers across the world. The author is thankful to the REPU's directors and members, and in particular, to Fernando Alva-Manchego and David Freidenson, who were part of the early discussions for the participation in the Shared Task. Furthermore, the author is grateful to the insightful feedback of Arturo Oncevay, Barry Haddow and Alexandra Birch, from the University of Edinburgh, where the author worked as an intern as part of the REPU's 2021 cohort.

References

Željko Agić and Ivan Vulić. 2019. JW300: A wide-coverage parallel corpus for low-resource languages. In *Proceedings of the 57th Annual Meeting of the Association for Computational Linguistics*, pages 3204–3210, Florence, Italy. Association for Computational Linguistics.

Gina Bustamante, Arturo Oncevay, and Roberto Zariquiey. 2020. No data to crawl? monolingual corpus creation from PDF files of truly low-resource languages in Peru. In *Proceedings of the 12th Language Resources and Evaluation Conference*, pages 2914–2923, Marseille, France. European Language Resources Association.

Maximiliano Duran. 2010. Lengua general de los Incas. http://quechua-ayacucho.org/es/index_es.php. Accessed: 2021-03-15.

Abteen Ebrahimi, Manuel Mager, Arturo Oncevay, Vishrav Chaudhary, Luis Chiruzzo, Angela Fan, John Ortega, Ricardo Ramos, Annette Rios, Ivan Vladimir, Gustavo A. Giménez-Lugo, Elisabeth Mager, Graham Neubig, Alexis Palmer, Rolando A. Coto Solano, Ngoc Thang Vu, and Katharina Kann. 2021. Americasnli: Evaluating zero-shot natural language understanding of pretrained multilingual models in truly low-resource languages.

Diego Huarcaya Taquiri. 2020. Traducción automática neuronal para lengua nativa peruana. Bachelor's thesis, Universidad Peruana Unión.

Cesar Iter and Zenobio Ortiz Cárdenas. 2019. *Runasimita yachasun*.

Tom Kocmi and Ondřej Bojar. 2018. Trivial transfer learning for low-resource neural machine translation. In *Proceedings of the Third Conference on Machine Translation: Research Papers*, pages 244–252, Belgium, Brussels. Association for Computational Linguistics.

Philipp Koehn. 2005. Europarl: A parallel corpus for statistical machine translation. In *MT summit*, volume 5, pages 79–86. Citeseer.

Philipp Koehn and Christof Monz. 2006. Manual and automatic evaluation of machine translation between european languages. In *Proceedings on the Workshop on Statistical Machine Translation*, pages 102–121, New York City. Association for Computational Linguistics.

Taku Kudo and John Richardson. 2018. SentencePiece: A simple and language independent subword tokenizer and detokenizer for neural text processing. In *Proceedings of the 2018 Conference on Empirical Methods in Natural Language Processing: System Demonstrations*, pages 66–71, Brussels, Belgium. Association for Computational Linguistics.

Lyrics translate. 2008. Lyrics translate. https://lyricstranslate.com/. Accessed: 2021-03-15.

Manuel Mager, Arturo Oncevay, Abteen Ebrahimi, John Ortega, Annette Rios, Angela Fan, Ximena Gutierrez-Vasques, Luis Chiruzzo, Gustavo

Giménez-Lugo, Ricardo Ramos, Anna Currey, Vishrav Chaudhary, Ivan Vladimir Meza Ruiz, Rolando Coto-Solano, Alexis Palmer, Elisabeth Mager, Ngoc Thang Vu, Graham Neubig, and Katharina Kann. 2021. Findings of the AmericasNLP 2021 Shared Task on Open Machine Translation for Indigenous Languages of the Americas. In *Proceedings of theThe First Workshop on NLP for Indigenous Languages of the Americas*, Online. Association for Computational Linguistics.

Ryo Nagata, Taisei Sato, and Hiroya Takamura. 2018. Exploring the Influence of Spelling Errors on Lexical Variation Measures. *Proceedings of the 27th International Conference on Computational Linguistics*, (2012):2391–2398.

John Ortega, Richard Alexander Castro-Mamani, and Jaime Rafael Montoya Samame. 2020a. Overcoming resistance: The normalization of an Amazonian tribal language. In *Proceedings of the 3rd Workshop on Technologies for MT of Low Resource Languages*, pages 1–13, Suzhou, China. Association for Computational Linguistics.

John Ortega and Krishnan Pillaipakkamnatt. 2018. Using morphemes from agglutinative languages like Quechua and Finnish to aid in low-resource translation. In *Proceedings of the AMTA 2018 Workshop on Technologies for MT of Low Resource Languages (LoResMT 2018)*, pages 1–11.

John E Ortega, Richard Castro Mamani, and Kyunghyun Cho. 2020b. Neural machine translation with a polysynthetic low resource language. *Machine Translation*, 34(4):325–346.

Myle Ott, Sergey Edunov, Alexei Baevski, Angela Fan, Sam Gross, Nathan Ng, David Grangier, and Michael Auli. 2019. fairseq: A fast, extensible toolkit for sequence modeling. In *Proceedings of the 2019 Conference of the North American Chapter of the Association for Computational Linguistics (Demonstrations)*, pages 48–53, Minneapolis, Minnesota. Association for Computational Linguistics.

Kishore Papineni, Salim Roukos, Todd Ward, and Wei-Jing Zhu. 2002. Bleu: a method for automatic evaluation of machine translation. In *Proceedings of the 40th Annual Meeting of the Association for Computational Linguistics*, pages 311–318, Philadelphia, Pennsylvania, USA. Association for Computational Linguistics.

Maja Popović. 2017. chrF++: words helping character n-grams. In *Proceedings of the Second Conference on Machine Translation*, pages 612–618, Copenhagen, Denmark. Association for Computational Linguistics.

Matt Post. 2018. A call for clarity in reporting BLEU scores. In *Proceedings of the Third Conference on Machine Translation: Research Papers*, pages 186–191, Brussels, Belgium. Association for Computational Linguistics.

Annette Rios, Anne Göhring, and Martin Volk. 2012. Parallel Treebanking Spanish-Quechua: how and how well do they align? *Linguistic Issues in Language Technology*, 7(1).

Rico Sennrich, Barry Haddow, and Alexandra Birch. 2016. Neural machine translation of rare words with subword units. In *Proceedings of the 54th Annual Meeting of the Association for Computational Linguistics (Volume 1: Long Papers)*, pages 1715–1725, Berlin, Germany. Association for Computational Linguistics.

Gary F. Simons and Charles D. Fenning, editors. 2019. *Ethnologue: Languages of the World. Twenty-second edition.* Dallas Texas: SIL international. Online version: http://www.ethnologue.com.

Jörg Tiedemann. 2012. Parallel data, tools and interfaces in opus. In *Proceedings of the Eight International Conference on Language Resources and Evaluation (LREC'12)*, Istanbul, Turkey. European Language Resources Association (ELRA).

Ashish Vaswani, Noam Shazeer, Niki Parmar, Jakob Uszkoreit, Llion Jones, Aidan N Gomez, Ł ukasz Kaiser, and Illia Polosukhin. 2017. Attention is all you need. In I. Guyon, U. V. Luxburg, S. Bengio, H. Wallach, R. Fergus, S. Vishwanathan, and R. Garnett, editors, *Advances in Neural Information Processing Systems 30*, pages 5998–6008. Curran Associates, Inc.

Roberto Zariquiey, Harald Hammarström, Mónica Arakaki, Arturo Oncevay, John Miller, Aracelli García, and Adriano Ingunza. 2019. Obsolescencia lingüística, descripción gramatical y documentación de lenguas en el Perú: hacia un estado de la cuestión. *Lexis*, 43(2):271–337.

Barret Zoph, Deniz Yuret, Jonathan May, and Kevin Knight. 2016. Transfer learning for low-resource neural machine translation. *EMNLP 2016 - Conference on Empirical Methods in Natural Language Processing, Proceedings*, pages 1568–1575.

A Appendix

	Constitution		Regulation	
	es	quz	es	quz
S	999		287	
N	14295	9837	14295	3227
V	3404	4030	3404	1591
V1	2145	3037	2145	1248
V/N	0.2381	0.4097	0.2381	0.493
V1/N	0.1501	0.3087	0.1501	0.3867
mean	4.1995	2.4409	4.1995	2.083

Table 7: Description of the corpora extracted, but not used, for Quechua Cusco (quz). S = #sentences in corpus; N = number of tokens; V = vocabulary size; V1 = number of tokens occurring once (hapax); V/N = vocabulary growth rate; V1/N = hapax growth rate; mean = word frequency mean

Moses and the Character-Based Random Babbling Baseline: CoAStaL at AmericasNLP 2021 Shared Task

Marcel Bollmann **Rahul Aralikatte** **Héctor Ricardo Murrieta Bello**
Daniel Hershcovich **Miryam de Lhoneux** **Anders Søgaard**
Department of Computer Science
University of Copenhagen
{marcel,rahul,dh,ml,soegaard}@di.ku.dk xhd160@alumni.ku.dk

Abstract

We evaluated a range of neural machine translation techniques developed specifically for low-resource scenarios. *Unsuccessfully.* In the end, we submitted two runs: (i) a standard phrase-based model, and (ii) a random babbling baseline using character trigrams. We found that it was surprisingly hard to beat (i), in spite of this model being, in theory, a bad fit for polysynthetic languages; and more interestingly, that (ii) was better than several of the submitted systems, highlighting *how* difficult low-resource machine translation for polysynthetic languages is.

Language		Source(s)
AYM	Aymara	Prokopidis et al. (2016)
BZD	Bribri	Feldman and Coto-Solano (2020)
CNI	Asháninka	Ortega et al. (2020), Cushimariano Romano and Sebastián Q. (2008), Mihas (2011)
GN	Guaraní	Chiruzzo et al. (2020)
HCH	Wixarika	Mager et al. (2018a)
NAH	Nahuatl	Gutierrez-Vasques et al. (2016)
OTO	Hñähñu	Comunidad Elotl (2021)
QUY	Quechua	Agić and Vulić (2019)
SHP	Shipibo-Konibo	Galarreta et al. (2017)
TAR	Rarámuri	Brambila (1976)

Table 1: Languages in the shared task with sources of their training datasets

1 Introduction

Shared tasks on machine translation are often conducted on large parallel training corpora: for example, the majority of datasets used in the WMT20 shared tasks have sentence pairs in the hundred thousands, often even millions (Barrault et al., 2020). In contrast, the AmericasNLP 2021 shared task (Mager et al., 2021) provided us with as little as 3,883 sentence pairs (for Ashaninka), and with the exception of Quechua (125k pairs), all languages had fewer than 30k sentence pairs. Additionally, many of these languages are polysynthetic, which is known to provide additional challenges for machine translation (Klavans et al., 2018; Mager et al., 2018b).

We initially focused our efforts on two areas: (i) obtaining more data, both parallel and monolingual (Sec. 2); and (ii) exploring a range of different neural machine translation techniques, particular those specifically developed for low-resource scenarios, to find a promising system to build on and tweak further. Unfortunately, we were wholly unsuccessful in the latter (Sec. 5). All neural models that we tried performed extremely poorly when compared to a standard statistical phrase-based model (Sec. 3.1). The overall low performance of all our models further prompted us to implement a "random babbling" baseline (Sec. 3.2): a model that outputs plausible-looking n-grams in the target language without any actual relation to the source sentences. This baseline, together with the phrase-based model, were the only two systems we ended up submitting. Our main findings are:

- It was surprisingly hard to beat a standard phrase-based model, as evidenced not only by our own failed attempts, but also by this system taking third place on three languages in the official evaluation (track 1).
- It is apparently challenging for many MT systems to even produce well-formed outputs in the target languages, as our random babbling baseline outperformed *at least* one other system on nine of the languages, and even took fifth place out of 12 on Ashaninka (track 2).

2 Data

We train models for all languages provided by the shared task, using their official training datasets (cf. Table 1). As the shared task allowed for using external datasets, we also tried to find more data sources to use for model training.

Proceedings of the First Workshop on Natural Language Processing for Indigenous Languages of the Americas, pages 248–254
June 11, 2021.

Parallel data We gathered parallel Spanish-to-target datasets for the following languages which should not overlap with the data provided by the shared task organizers: Aymara from JW300 (Agić and Vulić, 2019); Guarani from Tatoeba; and Nahuatl and Quechua from the Bible corpus by Christodouloupoulos and Steedman (2015). We note that for the Bible corpus, the Nahuatl portion is from a narrower dialectal region (NHG "Tetelcingo Nahuatl") than the data in the shared task, and it also covers a different variant of Quechua (QUW "Kichwa" vs. QUY "Ayacucho Quechua"), but we hoped that in this extremely low-resource scenario, this would still prove useful. All datasets were obtained from OPUS[1] (Tiedemann, 2012).

Monolingual data Wikipedias exist for Aymara, Guaraní, Nahuatl, and Quechua. We use WikiExtractor (Attardi, 2015) to obtain text data from their respective dumps,[2] then use a small set of regular expressions to clean them from XML tags and entities. This gives us between 28k and 100k lines of text per language.

We obtain further monolingual data from several online sources in PDF format. For Nahuatl and Hñähñu, we use a book provided by the Mexican government;[3] for Quechua, we use two books: *The Little Prince* (Saint-Exupéry, 2018) and Antonio Raimondi's *Once upon a time.. in Peru* (Villacorta, 2007). The Mexican government also publishes the series *Languages from Mexico* which contains books based on short stories in Nahuatl (Gustavo et al., 2007), Raramuri (Arvizu Castillo, 2002), Hñähñu (Mondragón et al., 2002b), and Wixárika (Mondragón et al., 2002a). Finally, we also use the Bible translated to Quechua, Guarani, and Aymara. We extract the text for all of these resources with the Google OCR API.[4]

3 Models

We first describe the two models we submitted: a standard phrase-based model (CoAStaL-1) and a random babbling baseline (CoAStaL-2). Other models that we experimented with but did not submit for evaluation are discussed later in Sec. 5.

3.1 Phrase-Based MT

We train a statistical phrase-based model with Moses (Koehn et al., 2007) using default settings, following the guidelines for training a baseline.[5] We do minimal preprocessing: we use the provided cleaning script and rely on plain whitespace tokenization, with the only exception that we also insert spaces around square brackets. The language model is trained with 5-grams instead of 3-grams, as this improved the results very slightly on the development sets. We train a separate model for each language and use the respective development set for tuning before translating the test set.

The models we submitted did, mistakenly, *not* make use of the additional parallel data we gathered (cf. Sec. 2). We evaluated the same system trained *with* this additional data after the deadline, but unfortunately did not observe an improvement; we present results for both variants in Sec. 4.

3.2 Random Babbling Baseline

Since we observed very low scores for all the models we tried, we wanted to compare with a baseline that generates text based only on (i) n-gram distributions in the target language, and (ii) lengths of the source sentences. We call this baseline *random babbling* because it is in no way conditioned on the actual words in the source sentences.

Concretely, we "train" our baseline by extracting and counting all *character trigrams* in the training file of the target language. Characters were chosen over words as the official evaluation metric of the shared task, chrF, is character-based. We also calculate the average *length ratio* of the sentence pairs in order to determine the desired length of our "translation" at test time. To generate output, we simply choose the top n most frequent character trigrams, with n chosen so that the desired sentence length is reached.[6]

Lastly, we perform a few tweaks to disguise this babbling as an actual translation: (i) we randomize the order of the chosen trigrams, (ii) reduce multiple consecutive whitespace characters to a single space, (iii) lowercase all characters that are not word-initial and uppercase the sentence-initial

[1] `https://opus.nlpl.eu/`

[2] `https://dumps.wikimedia.org/`

[3] `https://www.gob.mx/inpi/documentos/libros-en-lenguas-indigenas`

[4] `https://cloud.google.com/vision/docs/pdf`

[5] `http://www.statmt.org/moses/?n=Moses.Baseline`

[6] We also tried random baseline models with other n-gram lengths, sampling from the distribution (instead of always picking the most frequent items), and training a simple language model, but found nothing that significantly improved on this approach on the development set.

Set	System	Track	AYM	BZD	CNI	GN	HCH	NAH	OTO	QUY	SHP	TAR
Dev	CoAStaL-1: Phrase-based	1	.225	.213	.253	.235	.261	.204	.160	.276	.276	.174
	CoAStaL-2: Random	2	.178	.113	.214	.132	.195	.189	.094	.234	.182	.116
Test	Helsinki-2 (best)	1	.310	.213	.332	.376	.360	.301	.228	.394	.399	.258
	CoAStaL-1: Phrase-based	1	.191	.196	.265	.241	.257	.214	.184	.269	.297	.159
	+ extra data	1	.188	–	–	.242	–	.216	–	.250	–	–
	CoAStaL-2: Random	2	.168	.107	.212	.128	.191	.184	.101	.232	.173	.113
	Baseline	2	.157	.068	.102	.193	.126	.157	.054	.304	.121	.039

(a) chrF

Set	System	Track	AYM	BZD	CNI	GN	HCH	NAH	OTO	QUY	SHP	TAR
Dev	CoAStaL-1: Phrase-based	1	2.57	3.83	2.79	2.59	6.81	2.33	1.44	1.73	3.70	1.26
	CoAStaL-2: Random	2	0.02	0.03	0.04	0.02	1.14	0.02	0.02	0.02	0.06	0.02
Test	Helsinki-2 (best)	1	2.80	5.18	6.09	8.92	15.67	3.25	5.59	5.38	10.49	3.56
	CoAStaL-1: Phrase-based	1	1.11	3.60	3.02	2.20	8.80	2.06	2.72	1.63	3.90	1.05
	+ extra data	1	1.07	–	–	2.24	–	2.06	–	1.24	–	–
	CoAStaL-2: Random	2	0.05	0.06	0.03	0.03	2.07	0.03	0.03	0.02	0.04	0.06
	Baseline	2	0.01	0.01	0.01	0.12	2.20	0.01	0.00	0.05	0.01	0.00

(b) BLEU

Table 2: Results for our submitted models on Dev and Test sets. All Test results are from the official evaluation except for the "Phrase-based + extra data" setting, which we evaluated after the deadline.

character, and (iv) if the sequence does not end in a punctuation mark but the Spanish source sentence did, we copy and add this punctuation character from the source side.

4 Results

Results of our models are shown in Table 2, both for our own evaluation on the development sets and for the official evaluation on the test sets (Ebrahimi et al., 2021).

Phrase-Based MT Our phrase-based model (Sec. 3.1) was ranked in track 1 of the shared task evaluation as it makes use of the development sets for tuning. Compared to the other systems evaluated in this track, we observe a solid average performance of our model—it usually ranks in the middle of the field, with the best placement being 3rd on Bribri, Hñähñu, and Shipibo-Konibo, and the worst ranking being 8th out of 11 on Guarani. In terms of chrF score, the model ranges between 0.159 (on Raramuri) and 0.297 (on Shipibo-Konibo), but we note that there is a noticeable gap to the best-performing system, Helsinki-2, which outperforms ours by about +0.09 chrF on average.

Random Babbling Our random babbling baseline (Sec. 3.2) did *not* make use of the development sets and was therefore ranked in track 2 of the official evaluation. Amazingly, it almost never ranks last and even takes 5th place out of 12 on Ashaninka. It also outperforms the official baseline on eight of the languages. In terms of BLEU score, on the other hand, this model usually scores close to zero. This is because we based it on character trigrams; if we wanted to optimize for BLEU, we could have chosen word-based babbling instead. Comparing across the tracks with our first, phrase-based system, we observe that the latter scores consistently better, which is reassuring.

4.1 Discussion

We intended our phrase-based Moses system more as a baseline for our experiments with different neural models than as an actual system submission. It was surprising to us how clearly this system outperformed our attempts at building a neural MT system, and that it already did so with its default configuration. In theory, whitespace tokenization should be a bad fit for polysynthetic languages, as a high degree of morphological complexity exacerbates the problem of data sparsity and rarely seen word forms. We experimented with different subword tokenization techniques in combination with Moses, but this always resulted in degraded performance on the development sets.

The random babbling baseline was motivated by two observations: (i) performance was extremely low for all models we tried, and (ii) outputs of the neural models frequently looked very unnatural, to the point that the models had not yet learned how to form plausible-looking sentences in the target languages. This is quite typical behavior for underfitted neural models. As an example, this is an output we observed when running the official baseline system on the development set for Raramuri:

(1) IN: *Realmente no me importa si tengo un lugar para vivir.*
GOLD: *Ke chibi iré mapure ke nirúlisaka kúmi ne betélima.*
PRED: *(2) (a) ké ne ga'rá ne ga'rá ne ga'rá ga'rá ne ga'rá ne ga'rá ne ga'rá ne ga'rá ne ga'rá ne ga'rá ne ga'rá ne ga'rá ne ga'rá ne ga'rá ne ga'rá ne ga'rá ne ga'rá ne ga'rá ne ga'rá ne ga'rá ne ga'rá ne ga'rá ne ga'rá [. . .]*

This prompted us to implement a baseline which, while having *no* relation to the actual input sentence, at least better resembles the typical distribution of character n-grams in the given language. Here is an example from the test set for Ashaninka with outputs from both our phrase-based (SYS-1) and random (SYS-2) model:

(2) IN: *Todavía estoy trabajando para este día.*
GOLD: *Irosatitatsi nantabeeti oka kitaiteriki.*
SYS-1: *Tekirata nosaikaki trabajando inchamenta itovantarori." día.*
SYS-2: *Iritsiri irotakntakanarishiantakiro aka.*

We can see that both system outputs bear very little resemblance to the gold translation or to each other. While Moses (SYS-1) copies a few Spanish words and includes implausibly placed punctuation marks, random babbling (SYS-2) produces output of similar length to the correct translation and overlaps with it in several observable character trigrams (e.g. *iro, tsi, ant*).

Obviously, the random babbling baseline is not meant as an actual suggestion for a translation system—it literally does not "translate" anything. However, as the official shared task evaluation and the examples above show, it can serve as a useful "sanity check" for situations where the performance of actual MT systems is so low that it is unclear whether they even acquired superficial knowledge of character distributions in the target language.

5 Things that did not work

Here we briefly describe other ideas that we pursued, but were unfortunately not successful with, so we did not submit any systems based on these techniques for evaluation.

Pre-trained Transformers Following Rothe et al. (2020), we use an auto-encoding transformer as the encoder and an auto-regressive transformer as the decoder of a sequence-to-sequence model. Out of the several configurations we experimented with, the best performance was observed when the encoder is pre-trained on the Spanish OSCAR corpus (Ortiz Suárez et al., 2020) and the decoders are pre-trained on language-specific monolingual corpora collected from the web (cf. Sec. 2) along with the target files of the training data. However, the results were not on-par with the simpler models; averaging over all languages, we observed a chrF score of 0.12 on the dev sets, compared to 0.23 with the phrase-based model (cf. Sec. 3.1). We postulate that the training data was just not enough to train the cross-attention weights between the encoder and decoders. Note that these weights need to be trained from scratch, as opposed to the other weights which are initialized from language modelling checkpoints.

Back-translation In an attempt to improve the transformer-based models, we used the shared task data to train similar transformer-based models in the reverse direction, i.e. *to* Spanish, in order to back-translate the monolingual corpora (cf. Sec. 2). This would give us automatically translated Spanish outputs to use as the source side for additional training data (Sennrich et al., 2016; Hoang et al., 2018). Since monolingual data in Spanish—which was used to pre-train the decoder's language model for this experiment—is abundant, we expected the machine-translated Spanish text to be of reasonably good quality. However, the models turned out to perform quite badly, with the resulting Spanish text being of very low quality and often very repetitive. We therefore decided to abandon this direction after preliminary experiments.

Character-Level NMT Since many of the languages in the shared task are polysynthetic, a character-level model might be better suited here, as it can better learn morphology (Belinkov et al., 2017). We train fully character-level models following Lee et al. (2017), which are based on combining convolutional and recurrent layers.[7] Finding a good hyperparameter configuration for this model proved very time-consuming; the best configuration we found modifies the original model by using half the number of units in the embedding layer and decoder layers (256 and 512, respectively). For Quechua, which we initially experimented on, this yielded a chrF score of 0.33 on the dev set vs. 0.27 with phrase-based MT, but we ran out of time to train models for the other languages. A post-hoc evaluation on the other languages failed to replicate this success, though. Potentially, the hyperparameter configuration is very sensitive to the language in question, or the amount of training data was not enough for the other languages (Quechua had by far the largest training set of all languages in the shared task).

Language Model Prior We train NMT models using a language model prior, following Baziotis et al. (2020). This method allows us to make use of the additional monolingual data we gathered (cf. Sec. 2) within a neural MT framework, and we hoped that this would help the model to produce valid words in the target languages, i.e., reduce the "babbling" effect we saw in outputs like Example (1) above. We focused our efforts on the LSTM-based models provided by the authors[8] rather than the transformer ones, since we believe that those should be easier to train in this extremely low-resource setting. Despite experimenting with different hyperparameters (including number and size of LSTM layers), we could not exceed an average 0.16 chrF on the dev sets (compared to 0.23 with the phrase-based model).

Graph Convolutional Encoders We experiment with graph convolutional encoders using the framework by Bastings et al. (2017). Thus, we train NMT systems that operate directly over graphs; in our case, syntactic annotations of the source sentences following the Universal Dependencies (UD) scheme (Nivre et al., 2020). We parsed the all the source sentences from training set provided by the task organizer with Stanza (Qi et al., 2020). We were initially motivated to follow this approach because UD annotation can provide extra information to the encoder to generate better translations, ideally with less data. Even though we tested several configurations, not even our best architecture—two layers of GCN encoder with 250 units, and LSTM decoder with 250 units, trained for 5 epochs, with a vocabulary of 5000 words in source and target—was able to outperform the random babbling system. We hypothesize that with this amount of examples, UD's external information is not sufficient to produce an efficient encoder.

6 Conclusion

The (relative) success of our random babbling baseline shows that many MT systems fail to reproduce even superficial characteristics of word formation and character distribution in the target languages; a result that was confirmed by our own failed attempts at training a competitive neural MT model.

Out of the neural models we tried, purely character-level MT was among the more promising ones. We speculate that in the Spanish-to-target setting, a model that combines a strong pre-trained Spanish encoder with a purely character-level decoder might be a promising direction for further experiments.

We also note that there are several language-specific resources, such as morphological segmentation tools,[9] that might be worth using. We focused our efforts here on finding a broadly applicable architecture without any language-specific components, but would be curious to see if including such components can yield significant improvements on individual languages.

Acknowledgements

Marcel Bollmann was funded from the European Union's Horizon 2020 research and innovation programme under the Marie Skłodowska-Curie grant agreement No. 845995. Rahul Aralikatte and Anders Søgaard were funded by a Google Focused Research Award. Miryam de Lhoneux was funded by the Swedish Research Council (grant 2020-00437).

References

Željko Agić and Ivan Vulić. 2019. JW300: A wide-coverage parallel corpus for low-resource languages. In *Proceedings of the 57th Annual Meeting of the Association for Computational Linguistics*, pages 3204–3210, Florence, Italy. Association for Computational Linguistics.

Teresa Arvizu Castillo. 2002. *Relatos tarahumaras = Ki'á ra'ichaala rarámuli*. CNCA-Dirección Gen-

[7] We use our own reimplementation of the authors' code.

[8] `https://github.com/cbaziotis/lm-prior-for-nmt`

[9] e.g. Apertium for Guarani: `https://github.com/apertium/apertium-grn`

eral de Culturas Populares e Indígenas, Ciudad de Mexico.

Giuseppe Attardi. 2015. Wikiextractor. https://github.com/attardi/wikiextractor.

Loïc Barrault, Magdalena Biesialska, Ondřej Bojar, Marta R. Costa-jussà, Christian Federmann, Yvette Graham, Roman Grundkiewicz, Barry Haddow, Matthias Huck, Eric Joanis, Tom Kocmi, Philipp Koehn, Chi-kiu Lo, Nikola Ljubešić, Christof Monz, Makoto Morishita, Masaaki Nagata, Toshiaki Nakazawa, Santanu Pal, Matt Post, and Marcos Zampieri. 2020. Findings of the 2020 conference on machine translation (WMT20). In *Proceedings of the Fifth Conference on Machine Translation*, pages 1–55, Online. Association for Computational Linguistics.

Jasmijn Bastings, Ivan Titov, Wilker Aziz, Diego Marcheggiani, and Khalil Sima'an. 2017. Graph convolutional encoders for syntax-aware neural machine translation. In *Proceedings of the 2017 Conference on Empirical Methods in Natural Language Processing*, pages 1957–1967, Copenhagen, Denmark. Association for Computational Linguistics.

Christos Baziotis, Barry Haddow, and Alexandra Birch. 2020. Language model prior for low-resource neural machine translation. In *Proceedings of the 2020 Conference on Empirical Methods in Natural Language Processing (EMNLP)*, pages 7622–7634, Online. Association for Computational Linguistics.

Yonatan Belinkov, Nadir Durrani, Fahim Dalvi, Hassan Sajjad, and James Glass. 2017. What do neural machine translation models learn about morphology? In *Proceedings of the 55th Annual Meeting of the Association for Computational Linguistics (Volume 1: Long Papers)*, pages 861–872, Vancouver, Canada. Association for Computational Linguistics.

David Brambila. 1976. *Diccionario Raramuri–Castellano (Tarahumara)*. Obra Nacional de la Buena Prensa, Mexico.

Luis Chiruzzo, Pedro Amarilla, Adolfo Ríos, and Gustavo Giménez Lugo. 2020. Development of a Guarani - Spanish parallel corpus. In *Proceedings of the 12th Language Resources and Evaluation Conference*, pages 2629–2633, Marseille, France. European Language Resources Association.

Christos Christodouloupoulos and Mark Steedman. 2015. A massively parallel corpus: the Bible in 100 languages. *Language Resources and Evaluation*, 49(2):375–395.

Comunidad Elotl. 2021. Tsunkua – corpus paralelo otomí-español.

Rubén Cushimariano Romano and Richer C. Sebastián Q. 2008. Ñaantsipeta asháninkaki birakochaki. Diccionario Asháninka-Castellano. Versión preliminar. http://www.lengamer.org/publicaciones/diccionarios/.

Abteen Ebrahimi, Manuel Mager, Arturo Oncevay, Vishrav Chaudhary, Luis Chiruzzo, Angela Fan, John Ortega, Ricardo Ramos, Annette Rios, Ivan Vladimir, Gustavo A. Giménez-Lugo, Elisabeth Mager, Graham Neubig, Alexis Palmer, Rolando A. Coto Solano, Ngoc Thang Vu, and Katharina Kann. 2021. Americasnli: Evaluating zero-shot natural language understanding of pretrained multilingual models in truly low-resource languages.

Isaac Feldman and Rolando Coto-Solano. 2020. Neural machine translation models with back-translation for the extremely low-resource indigenous language Bribri. In *Proceedings of the 28th International Conference on Computational Linguistics*, pages 3965–3976, Barcelona, Spain (Online). International Committee on Computational Linguistics.

Ana-Paula Galarreta, Andrés Melgar, and Arturo Oncevay. 2017. Corpus creation and initial SMT experiments between Spanish and Shipibo-konibo. In *Proceedings of the International Conference Recent Advances in Natural Language Processing, RANLP 2017*, pages 238–244, Varna, Bulgaria. INCOMA Ltd.

Aguilar Gutiérrez Gustavo, Arellano Zamora Rogelio, Conde Reyes Magdaleno, Tepole Rivera Miguel Ángel, and Tzanahua Antonio. 2007. *Relatos nahuas = Nahua zazanilli*. CNCA-Dirección General de Culturas Populares e Indígenas, Ciudad de Mexico.

Ximena Gutierrez-Vasques, Gerardo Sierra, and Isaac Hernandez Pompa. 2016. Axolotl: a web accessible parallel corpus for Spanish-Nahuatl. In *Proceedings of the Tenth International Conference on Language Resources and Evaluation (LREC'16)*, pages 4210–4214, Portorož, Slovenia. European Language Resources Association (ELRA).

Vu Cong Duy Hoang, Philipp Koehn, Gholamreza Haffari, and Trevor Cohn. 2018. Iterative back-translation for neural machine translation. In *Proceedings of the 2nd Workshop on Neural Machine Translation and Generation*, pages 18–24, Melbourne, Australia. Association for Computational Linguistics.

Judith Klavans, John Morgan, Stephen LaRocca, Jeffrey Micher, and Clare Voss. 2018. Challenges in speech recognition and translation of high-value low-density polysynthetic languages. In *Proceedings of the 13th Conference of the Association for Machine Translation in the Americas (Volume 2: User Track)*, pages 283–293, Boston, MA. Association for Machine Translation in the Americas.

Philipp Koehn, Hieu Hoang, Alexandra Birch, Chris Callison-Burch, Marcello Federico, Nicola Bertoldi, Brooke Cowan, Wade Shen, Christine Moran, Richard Zens, Chris Dyer, Ondřej Bojar, Alexandra Constantin, and Evan Herbst. 2007. Moses: Open source toolkit for statistical machine translation. In *Proceedings of the 45th Annual Meeting of the Association for Computational Linguistics Companion*

Volume Proceedings of the Demo and Poster Sessions, pages 177–180, Prague, Czech Republic. Association for Computational Linguistics.

Jason Lee, Kyunghyun Cho, and Thomas Hofmann. 2017. Fully character-level neural machine translation without explicit segmentation. *Transactions of the Association for Computational Linguistics*, 5:365–378.

Manuel Mager, Diónico Carrillo, and Ivan Meza. 2018a. Probabilistic finite-state morphological segmenter for wixarika (huichol) language. *Journal of Intelligent & Fuzzy Systems*, 34(5):3081–3087.

Manuel Mager, Elisabeth Mager, Alfonso Medina-Urrea, Ivan Vladimir Meza Ruiz, and Katharina Kann. 2018b. Lost in translation: Analysis of information loss during machine translation between polysynthetic and fusional languages. In *Proceedings of the Workshop on Computational Modeling of Polysynthetic Languages*, pages 73–83, Santa Fe, New Mexico, USA. Association for Computational Linguistics.

Manuel Mager, Arturo Oncevay, Abteen Ebrahimi, John Ortega, Annette Rios, Angela Fan, Ximena Gutierrez-Vasques, Luis Chiruzzo, Gustavo Giménez-Lugo, Ricardo Ramos, Anna Currey, Vishrav Chaudhary, Ivan Vladimir Meza Ruiz, Rolando Coto-Solano, Alexis Palmer, Elisabeth Mager, Ngoc Thang Vu, Graham Neubig, and Katharina Kann. 2021. Findings of the AmericasNLP 2021 Shared Task on Open Machine Translation for Indigenous Languages of the Americas. In *Proceedings of the First Workshop on NLP for Indigenous Languages of the Americas*, Online. Association for Computational Linguistics.

Elena Mihas. 2011. *Añaani katonkosatzi parenini, El idioma del alto Perené*. Milwaukee, WI: Clarks Graphics.

Lucila Mondragón, Jacqueline Tello, and Argelia Valdez. 2002a. *Relatos huicholes = Wixarika' 'ïxatsikayari*. CNCA-Dirección General de Culturas Populares e Indígenas, Ciudad de Mexico.

Lucila Mondragón, Jacqueline Tello, and Argelia Valdez. 2002b. *Relatos otomíes. Nfini Hñähñu*. CNCA-Dirección General de Culturas Populares e Indígenas, Ciudad de Mexico.

Joakim Nivre, Marie-Catherine de Marneffe, Filip Ginter, Jan Hajič, Christopher D. Manning, Sampo Pyysalo, Sebastian Schuster, Francis Tyers, and Daniel Zeman. 2020. Universal Dependencies v2: An evergrowing multilingual treebank collection. In *Proceedings of the 12th Language Resources and Evaluation Conference*, pages 4034–4043, Marseille, France. European Language Resources Association.

John Ortega, Richard Alexander Castro-Mamani, and Jaime Rafael Montoya Samame. 2020. Overcoming resistance: The normalization of an Amazonian tribal language. In *Proceedings of the 3rd Workshop on Technologies for MT of Low Resource Languages*, pages 1–13, Suzhou, China. Association for Computational Linguistics.

Pedro Javier Ortiz Suárez, Laurent Romary, and Benoît Sagot. 2020. A monolingual approach to contextualized word embeddings for mid-resource languages. In *Proceedings of the 58th Annual Meeting of the Association for Computational Linguistics*, pages 1703–1714, Online. Association for Computational Linguistics.

Prokopis Prokopidis, Vassilis Papavassiliou, and Stelios Piperidis. 2016. Parallel Global Voices: a collection of multilingual corpora with citizen media stories. In *Proceedings of the Tenth International Conference on Language Resources and Evaluation (LREC'16)*, pages 900–905, Portorož, Slovenia. European Language Resources Association (ELRA).

Peng Qi, Yuhao Zhang, Yuhui Zhang, Jason Bolton, and Christopher D. Manning. 2020. Stanza: A Python natural language processing toolkit for many human languages. In *Proceedings of the 58th Annual Meeting of the Association for Computational Linguistics: System Demonstrations*.

Sascha Rothe, Shashi Narayan, and Aliaksei Severyn. 2020. Leveraging pre-trained checkpoints for sequence generation tasks. *Transactions of the Association for Computational Linguistics*, 8:264–280.

Antoine de Saint-Exupéry. 2018. *Quyllur Llaqtayuq Wawamanta*. Ediciones El Lector, Arequipa, Peru. Translated by Lydia Cornejo Endara & César Itier.

Rico Sennrich, Barry Haddow, and Alexandra Birch. 2016. Improving neural machine translation models with monolingual data. In *Proceedings of the 54th Annual Meeting of the Association for Computational Linguistics (Volume 1: Long Papers)*, pages 86–96, Berlin, Germany. Association for Computational Linguistics.

Jörg Tiedemann. 2012. Parallel data, tools and interfaces in OPUS. In *Proceedings of the Eighth International Conference on Language Resources and Evaluation (LREC'12)*, pages 2214–2218, Istanbul, Turkey. European Language Resources Association (ELRA).

Luis Felipe Villacorta. 2007. "Había una vez... El Perú de Antonio Raimondi". Historia y alcances de un cuento para niños creado en el museo. *Illapa Mana Tukukuq*, (4):101–112.

The Helsinki submission to the AmericasNLP shared task

Raúl Vázquez **Yves Scherrer** **Sami Virpioja** **Jörg Tiedemann**

Department of Digital Humanities
University of Helsinki
`firstname.lastname@helsinki.fi`

Abstract

The University of Helsinki participated in the AmericasNLP shared task for all ten language pairs. Our multilingual NMT models reached the first rank on all language pairs in track 1, and first rank on nine out of ten language pairs in track 2. We focused our efforts on three aspects: (1) the collection of additional data from various sources such as Bibles and political constitutions, (2) the cleaning and filtering of training data with the OpusFilter toolkit, and (3) different multilingual training techniques enabled by the latest version of the OpenNMT-py toolkit to make the most efficient use of the scarce data. This paper describes our efforts in detail.

1 Introduction

The University of Helsinki participated in the AmericasNLP 2021 Shared Task on Open Machine Translation for all ten language pairs. The shared task is aimed at developing machine translation (MT) systems for indigenous languages of the Americas, all of them paired with Spanish (Mager et al., 2021). Needless to say, these language pairs pose big challenges since none of them benefits from large quantities of parallel data and there is limited monolingual data. For our participation, we focused our efforts mainly on three aspects: (1) gathering additional parallel and monolingual data for each language, taking advantage in particular of the OPUS corpus collection (Tiedemann, 2012), the JHU Bible corpus (McCarthy et al., 2020) and translations of political constitutions of various Latin American countries, (2) cleaning and filtering the corpora to maximize their quality with the OpusFilter toolbox (Aulamo et al., 2020), and (3) contrasting different training techniques that could take advantage of the scarce data available.

We pre-trained NMT systems to produce back-translations for the monolingual portions of the data. We also trained multilingual systems that make use of language labels on the source sentence to specify the target language (Johnson et al., 2017). This has been shown to leverage the information available data across different language pairs and boosts performance on the low-resource scenarios.

We submitted five runs for each language pair, three in track 1 (development set included in training) and two in track 2 (development set not included in training). The best-performing model is a multilingual Transformer pre-trained on Spanish–English data and fine-tuned to the ten indigenous languages. The (partial or complete) inclusion of the development set during training consistently led to substantial improvements.

The collected data sets and data processing code are available from our fork of the organizers' Git repository.[1]

2 Data preparation

A main part of our effort was directed to finding relevant corpora that could help with the translation tasks, as well as to make the best out of the data provided by the organizers. In order to have an efficient procedure to maintain and process the data sets for all the ten languages, we utilized the OpusFilter toolbox[2] (Aulamo et al., 2020). It provides both ready-made and extensible methods for combining, cleaning, and filtering parallel and monolingual corpora. OpusFilter uses a configuration file that lists all the steps for processing the data; in order to make quick changes and extensions programmatically, we generated the configuration file with a Python script.

Figure 1 shows a part of the applied OpusFilter workflow for a single language pair, Spanish–Raramuri, and restricted to the primary training data. The provided training set and (concatenated)

[1] `https://github.com/Helsinki-NLP/americasnlp2021-st`

[2] `https://github.com/Helsinki-NLP/OpusFilter`, version 2.0.0-beta.

Proceedings of the First Workshop on Natural Language Processing for Indigenous Languages of the Americas, pages 255–264
June 11, 2021.

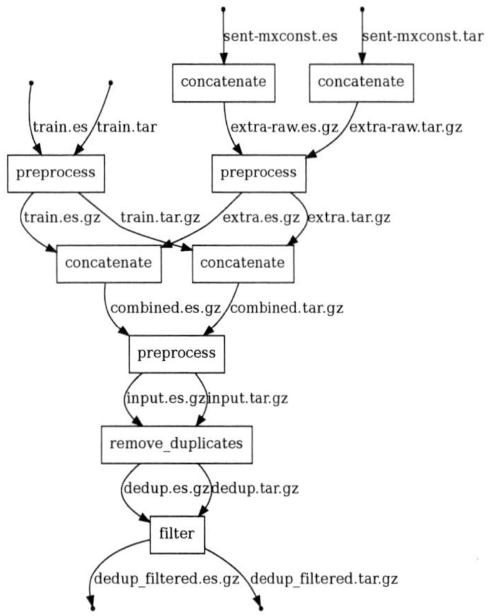

Figure 1: Diagram of the OpusFilter workflow used for Spanish (es) – Raramuri (tar) training data. Boxes are OpusFilter steps and arrows are data files.

additional parallel data are first independently normalized and cleaned (preprocess), then concatenated, preprocessed with common normalizations, filtered from duplicates, and finally filtered from noisy segments.

2.1 Data collection

We collected parallel and monolingual data from several sources. An overview of the resources, including references and URLs, is given in Tables 3 and 4 in the appendix.

Organizer-provided resources The shared task organizers provided parallel datasets for training for all ten languages. These datasets are referred to as *train* in this paper. For some of the languages (Ashaninka, Wixarika and Shipibo-Konibo), the organizers pointed participants to repositories containing additional parallel or monolingual data. We refer to these resources as *extra* and *mono* respectively. Furthermore, the organizers provided development and test sets for all ten language pairs of the shared task (Ebrahimi et al., 2021).

OPUS The OPUS corpus collection (Tiedemann, 2012) provides only few datasets for the relevant languages. Besides the resources for Aymara and Quechua provided by the organizers as official training data, we found an additional parallel dataset for Spanish–Quechua, and monolingual data for Aymara, Guarani, Hñähñu, Nahuatl and Quechua. These resources are also listed under *extra* and *mono*.

Constitutions We found translations of the Mexican constitution into Hñähñu, Nahuatl, Raramuri and Wixarika, of the Bolivian constitution into Aymara and Quechua, and of the Peruvian constitution into Quechua.[3] We extracted the data from the HTML or PDF sources and aligned them with the Spanish version on paragraph and sentence levels. The latter was done using a standard length-based approach with lexical re-alignment, as in hunalign[4] (Varga et al., 2005), using paragraph breaks as hard boundaries. They are part of the *extra* resources.

Bibles The JHU Bible corpus (McCarthy et al., 2020) covers all languages of the shared task with at least one Bible translation. We found that some translations were near-duplicates that only differed in tokenization, and removed them. For those languages for which several dialectal varieties were available, we attempted to select subsets based on the target varieties of the shared task, as specified by the organizers (see Tables 3 and 4 for details). All Spanish Bible translations in the JHUBC are limited to the New Testament. In order to maximize the amount of parallel data, we substituted them by full-coverage Spanish Bible translations from Mayer and Cysouw (2014).[5]

Since we have multiple versions of the Bible in Spanish as well as in some of the target languages, we applied the `product` method in OpusFilter to randomly take at most 5 different versions of the same sentence (skipping empty and duplicate lines).

2.2 Data normalization and cleaning

We noticed that some of the corpora in the same language used different orthographic conventions and had other issues that would hinder NMT model training. We applied various data normalization

[3]Two additional resources, a translation of a Peruvian law into Shipibo-Konibo and a translation of the Paraguayan constitution into Guarani, are provided on our repository, but they became available too late to be included in the translation models. They are listed under *extra** in Tables 3 and 4.

[4]`https://github.com/danielvarga/hunalign`

[5]We would like to thank Garrett Nicolai for helping us with the conversion.

language	code	train	extra	combined	dedup	filtered	bibles	monoling	backtr	dev
Ashaninka	cni	3883	0	3883	3860	3858	38846	13195	17278	883
Aymara	aym	6531	8970	15501	8889	8352	154520	16750	17886	996
Bribri	bzd	7508	0	7508	7303	7303	38502	0	0	996
Guarani	gn	26032	0	26032	14495	14483	39457	40516	62703	995
Hñähñu	oto	4889	2235	7124	7056	7049	39726	537	366	599
Nahuatl	nah	16145	2250	18395	17667	17431	39772	9222	8450	672
Quechua	quy	125008	284517	409525	260680	228624	154825	60399	68503	996
Raramuri	tar	14720	2255	16975	16815	16529	39444	0	0	995
Shipibo-Konibo	shp	14592	28936	43528	28854	28854	79341	23595	38329	996
Wixarika	hch	8966	2654	11620	11541	11525	39756	511	493	994

Table 1: Numbers of segments in the data sets (train: training set provided by the organizers, extra: additional training data collected by the organizers and us, combined: combined training data, dedup: combined training without duplicates, filtered: training data filtered with all filters, bibles: generated Bible data segments after filtering, monoling: monolingual data after filtering, backtr: back-translations created from monolingual data after filtering, dev: development set)

and cleaning steps to improve the quality of the data, with the goal of making the training data more similar to the development data (which we expected to be similar to the test data).

For Bribri, Raramuri and Wixarika, we found normalization scripts or guidelines on the organizers' Github page or sources referenced therein (cf. the *norm* entries in Tables 3 and 4). We reimplemented them as custom OpusFilter preprocessors.

Bribri, Hñähñu, Nahuatl, and Raramuri training sets were originally tokenized. Following our decision to use untokenized input for unsupervised word segmentation, we detokenized the respective corpora with the Moses detokenizer supported by OpusFilter, using the English patterns.

Finally, for all datasets, we applied OpusFilter's WhitespaceNormalizer preprocessor, which replaces all sequences of whitespace characters with a single space.

2.3 Data filtering

The organizer-provided and extra training data sets were concatenated before the filtering phase. Then all exact duplicates were removed from the data using OpusFilter's duplicate removal step. After duplicate removal, we applied some predefined filters from OpusFilter. Not all filters were applied to all languages; instead, we selected the appropriate filters based on manual observation of the data and the proportion of sentences removed by the filter. Appendix A describes the filters in detail.

2.4 Back-translations

We translated all monolingual data to Spanish, using early versions of both Model A and Model B (see Section 3), in order to create additional synthetic parallel training data. A considerable amount of the back-translations produced by Model A ended up in a different language than Spanish, whereas some translations by Model B remained empty. We kept both outputs, but aggressively filtered them (see Appendix A), concatenated them, and removed exact duplicates.

2.5 Data sizes

For most language pairs, the Bibles made up the largest portion of the data. Thus we decided to keep the Bibles separate from the other smaller, but likely more useful, training sources. Table 1 shows the sizes of the training datasets before and after filtering as well as the additional datasets. It can be seen that there is a difference of almost two orders of magnitude between the smallest (cni) and largest (quy) combined training data sets. The addition of the Bibles and back-translations evens out the differences to some extent.

2.6 Spanish–English data

Model B (see below) takes advantage of abundant parallel data for Spanish–English. These resources come exclusively from OPUS (Tiedemann, 2012) and include the following sources: *OpenSubtitles, Europarl, JW300, GlobalVoices, NewsCommentary, TED2020, Tatoeba, bible-uedin*. All corpora are again filtered and deduplicated, yielding 17,5M sentence pairs from OpenSubtitles and 4,4M sentence pairs from the other sources taken together. During training, both parts are assigned the same weight to avoid overfitting on subtitle data. The Spanish–English *WMT-News* corpus, also from OPUS, is used for validation.

Data	Model	Run	aym	bzd	cni	gn	hch	nah	oto	quy	shp	tar	Average
dev	B-50dev	1	0.390	0.392	0.414	0.408	0.409	0.426	0.313	0.457	0.452	0.317	0.398
	A-50dev	3	0.330	0.322	0.385	0.337	0.351	0.359	0.251	0.361	0.352	0.272	0.332
	B-0dev	5	0.327	0.238	0.268	0.311	0.299	0.298	0.147	0.338	0.317	0.196	0.274
	A-0dev	4	0.245	0.188	0.240	0.260	0.255	0.251	0.138	0.245	0.292	0.159	0.227
test	B-100dev	2	0.310	0.213	0.332	0.376	0.360	0.301	0.228	0.394	0.399	0.258	0.317
	B-50dev	1	0.302	0.204	0.324	0.367	0.348	0.294	0.191	0.383	0.380	0.248	0.304
	A-50dev	3	0.261	0.177	0.306	0.311	0.311	0.273	0.181	0.318	0.286	0.216	0.264
	B-0dev	5	0.283	0.165	0.258	0.336	0.304	0.266	0.147	0.343	0.329	0.184	0.262
	A-0dev	4	0.216	0.130	0.236	0.276	0.254	0.243	0.141	0.252	0.294	0.155	0.220

Table 2: chrF2 scores for the five submissions, computed on the development set and test set. Note that only 50% of the development set is used for evaluation for the *50dev* submissions. The chrF2 scores for *B-100dev* on the development set are all above 0.98, but they are not meaningful since it was fully included in training. The Run column provides the numeric IDs with which our submissions are listed in the overview paper.

3 Models

We experimented with two major model setups, which we refer to by A and B below. Both are multilingual NMT models based on the Transformer architecture (Vaswani et al., 2017) and are implemented with OpenNMT-py 2.0 (Klein et al., 2017). All models were trained on a single GPU.

The training data is segmented using SentencePiece (Kudo and Richardson, 2018) subword models with 32k units, trained jointly on all languages. Following our earlier experience (Scherrer et al., 2020), subword regularization (Kudo, 2018) is applied during training. Further details of the configurations are listed in Appendix B.

3.1 Model A

Model A is a multilingual translation model with 11 source languages (10 indigenous languages + Spanish) and the same 11 target languages. It is trained on all available parallel data in both directions as well as all available monolingual data. The target language is specified with a language label on the source sentence (Johnson et al., 2017).

The model was first trained for 200 000 steps, weighting the Bibles data to occur only 0.3 times as much as all the other corpora. We picked the last checkpoint, since it attained the best accuracy and perplexity in the combined development set. This model constitutes submission *A-0dev*.

Then, independently for each of the languages, we fine-tuned this model for another 2 500 steps on language-specific data, including 50% of the development set of the corresponding language. These models, one per language, constitute submission *A-50dev*.

3.2 Model B

Model B is a multilingual translation model with one source language (Spanish) and 11 target languages (10 indigenous languages + English). It is trained on all available parallel data with Spanish on the source side using target language labels.[6]

The training takes place in two phases. In the first phase, the model is trained on 90% of Spanish–English data and 1% of data coming from each of the ten American languages. With this first phase, we aim to take advantage of the large amounts of data to obtain a good Spanish encoder. In the second phase, the proportion of Spanish–English data is reduced to 50%.[7]

We train the first phase for 100k steps and pick the best intermediate savepoint according to the English-only validation set, which occurred after 72k steps. We then initialize two phase 2 models with this savepoint. For model *B-0dev*, we change the proportions of the training data and include the back-translations. For model *B-50dev*, we additionally include a randomly sampled 50% of each language's development set. We train both models until 200 000 steps and pick the best intermediate savepoint according to an eleven-language validation set, consisting of *WMT-News* and the remaining halves of the ten development sets.

Since the inclusion of development data showed massive improvements, we decided to continue training from the best savepoint of *B-50dev* (156k), adding also the remaining half of the development

[6] To generate the back-translations, we used an analogous, but distinct model trained on 11 source languages and one target language.

[7] We experimented also with language-specific second phase training, but ultimately opted for a single run combining all eleven language pairs.

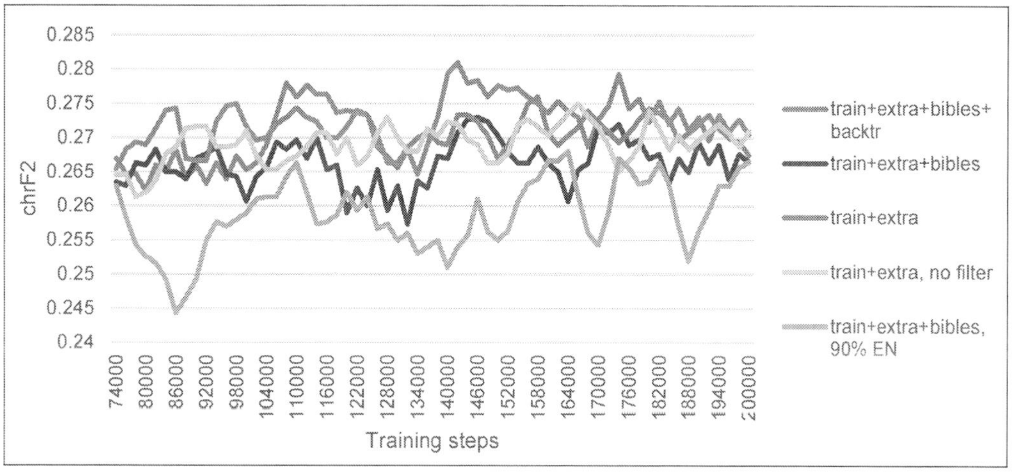

Figure 2: ChrF2 scores obtained with different training configurations of model B. Note: to improve the readability of the graph, the plotted values are smoothed by averaging over three consecutive training steps.

set to the training data. This model, referred to as *B-100dev*, was trained for an additional 14k steps until validation perplexity reached a local minimum.

4 Results

We submitted three systems to track 1 (development set allowed for training), namely *A-50dev*, *B-50dev* and *B-100dev*, and two systems to track 2 (development set not allowed for training), namely *A-0dev* and *B-0dev*. The results are in Table 2.

In track 1, our model *B-100dev* reached first rank and *B-50dev* reached second rank for all ten languages. Model *A-50dev* was ranked third to sixth, depending on the language. This shows that model B consistently outperformed model A, presumably thanks to its Spanish–English pre-training. Including the full development set in training (*B-100dev*) further improves the performance, although this implies that savepoint selection becomes guesswork.

For track 2, the tendency is similar. Model *B-0dev* was ranked first for nine out of ten languages, taking 2nd rank for Spanish–Quechua. *A-0dev* was ranked second to fourth on all except Quechua.[8]

4.1 Ablation study

We investigate the impact of our data selection strategies via an ablation study where we repeat the second training phase of model B with several variants of the *B-0dev* setup. In Figure 2 we show intermediate evaluations on the concatenation of the 10 development sets every 2000 training steps.

[8]After submission, we noticed that the Quechua backtranslations were generated with the wrong model. This may explain the poor performance of our systems on this language.

The green curve, which corresponds to the *B-0dev* model, obtains the highest maximum scores. The impact of the back-translations is considerable (blue vs. green curve) despite their presumed low quality. The addition of Bibles did not improve the chrF2 scores (blue vs. orange curve). We presume that this is due to the mismatch in linguistic varieties, spelling and genre. It would be instructive to break down this effect according to the language.

The application of the OpusFilter pipeline to the *train* and *extra* data (yellow vs. orange curve) shows a positive effect at the beginning of the training, but this effect fades out later.

Finally, and rather unsurprisingly, our corpus weighting strategy (50% English, 50% indigenous languages, blue curve) outperforms the weighting strategy employed during the first training phase (90% English, 10% indigenous languages, grey curve). It could be interesting to experiment with even lower proportions of English data, taking into account the risk of catastrophic forgetting.

5 Conclusions

In this paper, we describe our submissions to the AmericasNLP shared task, where we submitted translations for all ten language pairs in both tracks. Our strongest system is the result of gathering additional relevant data, carefully filtering the data for each language pair and pre-training a Transformer-based multilingual NMT system with large Spanish-English parallel data. Except for Spanish-Quechua in track 2, all our submissions ranked top for both tracks.

Acknowledgments

This work is part of the FoTran project, funded by the European Research Council (ERC) under the European Union's Horizon 2020 research and innovation programme (grant agreement № 771113).

References

Željko Agić and Ivan Vulić. 2019. JW300: A wide-coverage parallel corpus for low-resource languages. In *Proceedings of the 57th Annual Meeting of the Association for Computational Linguistics*, pages 3204–3210, Florence, Italy. Association for Computational Linguistics.

Mikko Aulamo, Sami Virpioja, and Jörg Tiedemann. 2020. OpusFilter: A configurable parallel corpus filtering toolbox. In *Proceedings of the 58th Annual Meeting of the Association for Computational Linguistics: System Demonstrations*, pages 150–156, Online. Association for Computational Linguistics.

David Brambila. 1976. *Diccionario Raramuri – Castellano (Tarahumara)*. Obra Nacional de la Buena Prensa, México.

Gina Bustamante, Arturo Oncevay, and Roberto Zariquiey. 2020. No data to crawl? monolingual corpus creation from PDF files of truly low-resource languages in Peru. In *Proceedings of The 12th Language Resources and Evaluation Conference*, pages 2914–2923, Marseille, France. European Language Resources Association.

Luis Chiruzzo, Pedro Amarilla, Adolfo Ríos, and Gustavo Giménez Lugo. 2020. Development of a Guarani - Spanish parallel corpus. In *Proceedings of the 12th Language Resources and Evaluation Conference*, pages 2629–2633, Marseille, France. European Language Resources Association.

Rubén Cushimariano Romano and Richer C. Sebastián Q. 2008. Ñaantsipeta asháninkaki birakochaki. diccionario asháninka-castellano. versión preliminar. `http://www.lengamer.org/publicaciones/diccionarios/`.

Abteen Ebrahimi, Manuel Mager, Arturo Oncevay, Vishrav Chaudhary, Luis Chiruzzo, Angela Fan, John Ortega, Ricardo Ramos, Annette Rios, Ivan Vladimir, Gustavo A. Giménez-Lugo, Elisabeth Mager, Graham Neubig, Alexis Palmer, Rolando A. Coto Solano, Ngoc Thang Vu, and Katharina Kann. 2021. Americasnli: Evaluating zero-shot natural language understanding of pretrained multilingual models in truly low-resource languages.

Isaac Feldman and Rolando Coto-Solano. 2020. Neural machine translation models with back-translation for the extremely low-resource indigenous language Bribri. In *Proceedings of the 28th International Conference on Computational Linguistics*, pages 3965–3976, Barcelona, Spain (Online). International Committee on Computational Linguistics.

Ana-Paula Galarreta, Andrés Melgar, and Arturo Oncevay. 2017. Corpus creation and initial SMT experiments between Spanish and Shipibo-konibo. In *Proceedings of the International Conference Recent Advances in Natural Language Processing, RANLP 2017*, pages 238–244, Varna, Bulgaria. INCOMA Ltd.

Ximena Gutierrez-Vasques, Gerardo Sierra, and Isaac Hernandez Pompa. 2016. Axolotl: a web accessible parallel corpus for Spanish-Nahuatl. In *Proceedings of the Tenth International Conference on Language Resources and Evaluation (LREC'16)*, pages 4210–4214, Portorož, Slovenia. European Language Resources Association (ELRA).

Melvin Johnson, Mike Schuster, Quoc V. Le, Maxim Krikun, Yonghui Wu, Zhifeng Chen, Nikhil Thorat, Fernanda Viégas, Martin Wattenberg, Greg Corrado, Macduff Hughes, and Jeffrey Dean. 2017. Google's multilingual neural machine translation system: Enabling zero-shot translation. *Transactions of the Association for Computational Linguistics*, 5:339–351.

Guillaume Klein, Yoon Kim, Yuntian Deng, Jean Senellart, and Alexander M. Rush. 2017. Opennmt: Open-source toolkit for neural machine translation. In *Proc. ACL*.

Taku Kudo. 2018. Subword regularization: Improving neural network translation models with multiple subword candidates. In *Proceedings of the 56th Annual Meeting of the Association for Computational Linguistics (Volume 1: Long Papers)*, pages 66–75, Melbourne, Australia. Association for Computational Linguistics.

Taku Kudo and John Richardson. 2018. SentencePiece: A simple and language independent subword tokenizer and detokenizer for neural text processing. In *Proceedings of the 2018 Conference on Empirical Methods in Natural Language Processing: System Demonstrations*, pages 66–71, Brussels, Belgium. Association for Computational Linguistics.

Manuel Mager, Diónico Carrillo, and Ivan Meza. 2018. Probabilistic finite-state morphological segmenter for wixarika (huichol) language. *Journal of Intelligent & Fuzzy Systems*, 34(5):3081–3087.

Manuel Mager, Arturo Oncevay, Abteen Ebrahimi, John Ortega, Annette Rios, Angela Fan, Ximena Gutierrez-Vasques, Luis Chiruzzo, Gustavo Giménez-Lugo, Ricardo Ramos, Anna Currey, Vishrav Chaudhary, Ivan Vladimir Meza Ruiz, Rolando Coto-Solano, Alexis Palmer, Elisabeth Mager, Ngoc Thang Vu, Graham Neubig, and Katharina Kann. 2021. Findings of the AmericasNLP 2021 Shared Task on Open Machine Translation for

Indigenous Languages of the Americas. In *Proceedings of theThe First Workshop on NLP for Indigenous Languages of the Americas*, Online. Association for Computational Linguistics.

Jesús Manuel Mager Hois, Carlos Barron Romero, and Ivan Vladimir Meza Ruíz. 2016. Traductor estadístico wixarika - español usando descomposición morfológica. *COMTEL*, 6.

Thomas Mayer and Michael Cysouw. 2014. Creating a massively parallel Bible corpus. In *Proceedings of the Ninth International Conference on Language Resources and Evaluation (LREC'14)*, pages 3158–3163, Reykjavik, Iceland. European Language Resources Association (ELRA).

Arya D. McCarthy, Rachel Wicks, Dylan Lewis, Aaron Mueller, Winston Wu, Oliver Adams, Garrett Nicolai, Matt Post, and David Yarowsky. 2020. The Johns Hopkins University Bible corpus: 1600+ tongues for typological exploration. In *Proceedings of the 12th Language Resources and Evaluation Conference*, pages 2884–2892, Marseille, France. European Language Resources Association.

Elena Mihas. 2011. *Añaani katonkosatzi parenini, El idioma del alto Perené*. Milwaukee, WI: Clarks Graphics.

Héctor Erasmo Gómez Montoya, Kervy Dante Rivas Rojas, and Arturo Oncevay. 2019. A continuous improvement framework of machine translation for Shipibo-konibo. In *Proceedings of the 2nd Workshop on Technologies for MT of Low Resource Languages*, pages 17–23, Dublin, Ireland. European Association for Machine Translation.

John Ortega, Richard Alexander Castro-Mamani, and Jaime Rafael Montoya Samame. 2020. Overcoming resistance: The normalization of an Amazonian tribal language. In *Proceedings of the 3rd Workshop on Technologies for MT of Low Resource Languages*, pages 1–13, Suzhou, China. Association for Computational Linguistics.

Prokopis Prokopidis, Vassilis Papavassiliou, and Stelios Piperidis. 2016. Parallel Global Voices: a collection of multilingual corpora with citizen media stories. In *Proceedings of the Tenth International Conference on Language Resources and Evaluation (LREC'16)*, pages 900–905, Portorož, Slovenia. European Language Resources Association (ELRA).

Yves Scherrer, Stig-Arne Grönroos, and Sami Virpioja. 2020. The University of Helsinki and aalto university submissions to the WMT 2020 news and low-resource translation tasks. In *Proceedings of the Fifth Conference on Machine Translation*, pages 1129–1138, Online. Association for Computational Linguistics.

Jörg Tiedemann. 2020. The Tatoeba translation challenge – realistic data sets for low resource and multilingual MT. In *Proceedings of the Fifth Conference on Machine Translation*, pages 1174–1182, Online. Association for Computational Linguistics.

Jörg Tiedemann. 2012. Parallel data, tools and interfaces in OPUS. In *Proceedings of the Eight International Conference on Language Resources and Evaluation (LREC'12)*, Istanbul, Turkey. European Language Resources Association (ELRA).

D. Varga, L. Németh, P. Halácsy, A. Kornai, V. Trón, and V. Nagy. 2005. Parallel corpora for medium density languages. In *Proceedings of Recent Advances in Natural Language Processing (RANLP-2005)*, pages 590–596.

Ashish Vaswani, Noam Shazeer, Niki Parmar, Jakob Uszkoreit, Llion Jones, Aidan N Gomez, Łukasz Kaiser, and Illia Polosukhin. 2017. Attention is all you need. In *Advances in Neural Information Processing Systems*, pages 5998–6008, Long Beach, California, USA.

Raúl Vázquez, Umut Sulubacak, and Jörg Tiedemann. 2019. The University of Helsinki submission to the WMT19 parallel corpus filtering task. In *Proceedings of the Fourth Conference on Machine Translation (Volume 3: Shared Task Papers, Day 2)*, pages 294–300, Florence, Italy. Association for Computational Linguistics.

A OpusFilter settings

The following filters were used for the training data except for back-translated data and Bibles:

- LengthFilter: Remove sentences longer than 1000 characters. Applied to Aymara, Nahuatl, Quechua, Raramuri.
- LengthRatioFilter: Remove sentences with character length ratio of 4 or more. Applied to Ashaninka, Aymara, Guarani, Hñähñu, Nahuatl, Quechua, Raramuri, Wixarika.
- CharacterScoreFilter: Remove sentences for which less than 90% characters are from the Latin alphabet. Applied to Aymara, Quechua, Raramuri.
- TerminalPunctuationFilter: Remove sentences with dissimilar punctuation; threshold -2 (Vázquez et al., 2019). Applied to Aymara, Quechua.
- NonZeroNumeralsFilter: Remove sentences with dissimilar numerals; threshold 0.5 (Vázquez et al., 2019). Applied to Aymara, Quechua, Raramuri, Wixarika.

The Bribri and Shipibo-Konibo corpora seemed clean enough that we did not apply any filters for them.

After generating the Bible data, we noticed that some of the lines contained only a single 'BLANK' string. The segments with these lines were removed afterwards.

From the provided monolingual datasets, we filtered out sentences with more than 500 words.

The back-translated data was filtered with the following filters:

- LengthRatioFilter with threshold 2 and word units
- CharacterScoreFilter with Latin script and threshold 0.9 on the Spanish side and 0.7 on the other side
- LanguageIDFilter with a threshold of 0.8 for the Spanish side only.

B Hyperparameters

Model A uses a 6-layered Transformer with 8 heads, 512 dimensions in the embeddings and 1024 dimensions in the feed-forward layers. The batch size is 4096 tokens, with an accumulation count of 8. The Adam optimizer is used with beta1=0.9 and beta2=0.998. The Noam decay method is used with a learning rate of 3.0 and 40000 warm-up steps. Subword sampling is applied during training (20 samples, $\alpha = 0.1$).

Model B uses a 8-layered Transformer with 16 heads, 1024 dimensions in the embeddings and 4096 dimensions in the feed-forward layers. The batch size is 9200 tokens in phase 1 and 4600 tokens in phase 2, with an accumulation count of 4. The Adam optimizer is used with beta1=0.9 and beta2=0.997. The Noam decay method is used with a learning rate of 2.0 and 16000 warm-up steps. Subword sampling is applied during training (20 samples, $\alpha = 0.1$). As a post-processing step, we removed the `<unk>` tokens from the outputs of model B.

Language	Type	Data
Aymara aym	train	GlobalVoices (Tiedemann, 2012; Prokopidis et al., 2016)
	extra	BOconst: `https://www.kas.de/c/document_library/get_file?uuid=8b51d469-63d2-f001-ef6f-9b561eb65ed4&groupId=288373`
	bibles	*ayr-x-bible-2011-v1, ayr-x-bible-1997-v1*
	mono	Wikipedia crawls (Tiedemann, 2020)
Bribri bzd	train	(Feldman and Coto-Solano, 2020)
	bibles	*bzd-x-bible-bzd-v1*
	norm	`https://github.com/AmericasNLP/americasnlp2021/blob/main/data/bribri-spanish/orthographic-conversion.csv`
Ashaninka cni	train	`https://github.com/hinantin/AshaninkaMT` (Ortega et al., 2020; Cushimariano Romano and Sebastián Q., 2008; Mihas, 2011)
	bibles	*cni-x-bible-cni-v1*
	mono	ShaShiYaYi (Bustamante et al., 2020): `https://github.com/iapucp/multilingual-data-peru`
Guarani gn	train	(Chiruzzo et al., 2020)
	extra*	PYconst: `http://ej.org.py/principal/constitucion-nacional-en-guarani/`
	bibles	*gug-x-bible-gug-v1*
	mono	Wikipedia crawls (Tiedemann, 2020)
Wixarika hch	train	`https://github.com/pywirrarika/wixarikacorpora` (Mager et al., 2018)
	extra	MXconst: `https://constitucionenlenguas.inali.gob.mx/`
	bibles	*hch-x-bible-hch-v1*
	mono	`https://github.com/pywirrarika/wixarikacorpora` (Mager et al., 2018)
	norm	`https://github.com/pywirrarika/wixnlp/blob/master/normwix.py` (Mager Hois et al., 2016)
Nahuatl nah	train	Axolotl (Gutierrez-Vasques et al., 2016)
	extra	MXConst: `https://constitucionenlenguas.inali.gob.mx/`
	bibles	*nch-x-bible-nch-v1, ngu-x-bible-ngu-v1, nhe-x-bible-nhe-v1, nhw-x-bible-nhw-v1*
	mono	Wikipedia crawls (Tiedemann, 2020)

Table 3: Data used for training (1). *train* refers to the official training data provided by the organizers, whereas *extra* refers to additional parallel non-Bible data. Corpora marked with *extra** are available on our repository but were not used in the translation experiments.

Language	Type	Source
Hnähñu oto	train	Tsunkua: `https://tsunkua.elotl.mx/about/`
	extra	MXConst: `https://constitucionenlenguas.inali.gob.mx/`
	bibles	*ote-x-bible-ote-v1*
	mono	JW300 (Tiedemann, 2012; Agić and Vulić, 2019)
Quechua quy	train	JW300 (quy+quz) (Agić and Vulić, 2019)
		MINEDU + dict_misc: `https://github.com/AmericasNLP/americasnlp2021/tree/main/data/quechua-spanish`
	extra	Tatoeba (Tiedemann, 2012)
		BOconst: `https://www.kas.de/documents/252038/253252/7_dokument_dok_pdf_33453_4.pdf/9e3dfb1f-0e05-523f-5352-d2f9a44a21de?version=1.0&t=1539656169513`
		PEconst: `https://www.wipo.int/edocs/lexdocs/laws/qu/pe/pe035qu.pdf`
	bibles	*quy-x-bible-quy-v1, quz-x-bible-quz-v1*
	mono	Wikipedia crawls (Tiedemann, 2020)
Shipibo-Konibo shp	train	(Galarreta et al., 2017; Montoya et al., 2019)
	extra	Educational and Religious from `http://chana.inf.pucp.edu.pe/resources/parallel-corpus/`
	extra*	LeyArtesano: `https://cdn.www.gob.pe/uploads/document/file/579690/Ley_Artesano_Shipibo_Konibo_baja__1_.pdf`
	bibles	*shp-SHPTBL*
	mono	ShaShiYaYi (Bustamante et al., 2020): `https://github.com/iapucp/multilingual-data-peru`
Raramuri tar	train	(Brambila, 1976)
	extra	MXConst: `https://constitucionenlenguas.inali.gob.mx/`
	bibles	*tac-x-bible-tac-v1*
	norm	`https://github.com/AmericasNLP/americasnlp2021/pull/5`
Spanish	bibles	*spa-x-bible-americas, spa-x-bible-hablahoi-latina, spa-x-bible-lapalabra, spa-x-bible-newworld, spa-x-bible-nuevadehoi, spa-x-bible-nuevaviviente, spa-x-bible-nuevointernacional, spa-x-bible-reinavaleracontemporanea*

Table 4: Data used for training (2). *train* refers to the official training data provided by the organizers, whereas *extra* refers to additional parallel non-Bible data. Corpora marked with *extra** are available on our repository but were not used in the translation experiments.

IndT5: A Text-to-Text Transformer for 10 Indigenous Languages

El Moatez Billah Nagoudi[1], **Wei-Rui Chen**[1], **Muhammad Abdul-Mageed**[1], **Hasan Cavusoglu**[2]
[1] Natural Language Processing Lab,
[1,2] The University of British Columbia
[1] {moatez.nagoudi,weirui.chen,muhammad.mageed}@ubc.ca, [2] cavusoglu@sauder.ubc.ca

Abstract

Transformer language models have become fundamental components of natural language processing based pipelines. Although several Transformer models have been introduced to serve many languages, there is a shortage of models pre-trained for low-resource and Indigenous languages. In this work, we introduce IndT5, the first Transformer language model for Indigenous languages. To train IndT5, we build IndCorpus–a new dataset for ten Indigenous languages and Spanish. We also present the application of IndT5 to machine translation by investigating different approaches to translate between Spanish and the Indigenous languages as part of our contribution to the AmericasNLP 2021 Shared Task on Open Machine Translation. IndT5 and IndCorpus are publicly available for research.[1]

Figure 1: A map of the ten Indigenous languages covered by IndT5, our text-to-text Transformer model, and our IndCorpus dataset. The languages are mainly spoken in five Latin American countries.

1 Introduction

Indigenous languages are starting to attract attention in the field of natural language processing (NLP), with the number of related publications growing in recent years (Mager et al., 2018). In spite of this interest, there remains a multitude of challenges for handling Indigenous languages. Complexity of the morphological systems of some of these languages and lack of standard orthography for writing them are among these challenges (Mager et al., 2018; Littell et al., 2018). The most fundamental issue facing NLP efforts, however, remains the lack of digital textual data that can be exploited for systems development.

In this work, we describe a scenario usually faced when trying to develop NLP systems for Indigenous languages and we focus on machine translation (MT). We adopt a neural machine translation approach (NMT) (Koehn, 2017) as our method. We show that, in spite of its recent success on many contexts, NMT still struggles in very low-resource settings involving Indigenous languages. This is due to the core difficulty of lack of parallel textual data, but also even monolingual data.

Although our main goal in this work in particular is to develop translation models from Spanish to several Indigenous languages of the Americas, we adopt a transfer learning approach where we offer resources that can be exploited for other downstream tasks. Namely, we build a dataset for ten Indigenous languages and Spanish which we refer to as **IndCorpus**. Figure 1 and Table 1 provide an overview of the ten Indigenous languages in our new dataset (Eberhard et al., 2021). We also exploit **IndCorpus** for pre-training a Transformer language model following the unified approach introduced by (Raffel et al., 2019). Our resulting model,

[1] https://github.com/UBC-NLP/IndT5

Proceedings of the First Workshop on Natural Language Processing for Indigenous Languages of the Americas, pages 265–271
June 11, 2021.

Language	Code	Main location	Speakers
Aymara	aym	Bolivia	1,677,100
Asháninka	cni	Peru	35,200
Bribri	bzd	Costa Rica	7,000
Guarani	gn	Paraguay	6,652,790
Hñähñu	oto	Mexico	88,500
Nahuatl	nah	Mexico	410,000
Quechua	quy	Peru	7,384,920
Rarámuri	tar	Mexico	9,230
Shipibo-Konibo	shp	Peru	22,500
Wixarika	hch	Mexico	52,500

Table 1: Overview of our ten Indigenous languages (Eberhard et al., 2021).

IndT5, treats every text NLP problem as a "text-to-text" problem, i.e. taking text as input and producing new text as output. We apply **IndT5** to the MT task as a way to transfer knowledge acquired by the model to this particular context. Our experiments show the utility of our new language model and the dataset it exploits for the downstream Indigenous MT task but that very large space for improvement still exists.

The rest of the paper is organized as follows: In Section 2, we introduce recent MT work in low-resource and Indigenous languages settings. In Section 3, we describe how we develop our new language model for ten Indigenous languages. In Section 4, we describe our NMT models. We conclude in Section 5.

2 Related Work

2.1 Low-Resource MT

A number of methods and techniques have been proposed to mitigate the effects of having rather small datasets for machine translation. These include data augmentation, transfer learning, hyper-parameter tuning, incorporating linguistic knowledge, and knowledge distillation.

Since the main bottleneck of low-resource MT is the lack of abundant parallel textual data, data augmentation is straightforwardly a potential method to enhance the model performance. Back translation is a way to augment parallel data (Sennrich et al., 2016a). By training a target-to-source translation model with original data and feeding in monolingual data of target language, synthetic parallel data is generated. If the target language is rich in textual data, much synthetic parallel data can be added into training data and may benefit the final translation model.

Transfer learning is another method that can boost the performance of MT on low-resource languages (Zoph et al., 2016; Nguyen and Chiang, 2017; Kocmi and Bojar, 2018). The rationale behind one approach to transfer learning is that knowledge obtained while translating high-resource languages may be transferable to translation of low-resource languages. In Zoph et al. (2016), a parent model is first trained on a high-resource language pair (i.e., French to English) then a child model is trained on a low-resource language pair (i.e., Uzbek to English). The Uzbek-English model has 10.7 BLEU score without parent model and 15.0 with the parent model. It is also shown that the more similar the two source languages, the more performance gain is possible. For example, a Spanish-English MT model has 16.4 BLEU score without parent model and 31.0 with French-English parent model. The performance gain is much more than when transferring French-English parent model to the more distant context of the Uzbek-English child model.

Sennrich and Zhang (2019) argue that instead of using hyperparameters that work in high-resource settings, there should be a set of hyperparameters specific to the low-resource scenario. For example, keeping the vocabulary size small, training a model with relatively small capacity, and having smaller batch size may be beneficial to model performance. When building a vocabulary with BPE, by reducing the the number of merge operations, a smaller vocabulary can be obtained and an inclusion of low-frequency (sub)words can be avoided. Inclusion of inclusion of low-frequency (sub)words could otherwise negatively influencing representation learning effectiveness.

Leveraging linguistic knowledge for data augmentation, Zhou et al. (2019) use a rule-based syntax parser and a dictionary to generate parallel data. By reordering target-language sentences into source-language syntactic structure and then mapping target-language words into source-language words with a dictionary, the size of parallel data is enlarged and translation performance is improved.

Baziotis et al. (2020) leverage a language model to help enhance the performance of the translation model. Similar to the idea of knowledge distillation (Hinton et al., 2015), a teacher model and a student model are trained where the language model plays the role of teacher and translation model plays the role of student. With this design, the teacher model needs only monolingual data and does not have to rely on large parallel data.

2.2 MT of Indigenous Languages

Unlike high-resource languages such as English and French, Indigenous languages are often low-resource. Due to this, it is common that researchers of Indigenous languages adopt methods that can fare well in low-resource scenarios. This includes using the Transformer architecture and its variants in both low-resource (Adebara et al., 2021, 2020; Przystupa and Abdul-Mageed, 2019) and Indigenous language (Feldman and Coto-Solano, 2020; Orife, 2020; Le and Sadat, 2020) settings.

Despite the fact that Indigenous languages face difficulties similar to most low-resource languages, there are some challenges specific to Indigenous languages. As Mager et al. (2018) point out, some Indigenous languages have complex morphological systems and some have various non-standardized orthographic conventions. For example, Micher (2018) shows that in Inuktitut, an Indigineous language in North America with a complex morphological system, a corpus of one million tokens, there are about 225K different types for Inuktitut while about 30K types for English. Also, Micher (2018) shows that there can be lack of standardized spelling for some words. For example, the word *Haammalat* in Inuktitut has another seven different forms.

To cope with the issue of complex morphology, Ortega et al. (2020) build a translation model for Qeuchua, an Indigenous language of South America, with an integrated morphological segmentation method. To treat orthographic variation, Feldman and Coto-Solano (2020) standardize text with a rule-based system which converts diacritics and letters to contemporary orthographic convention.

3 IndT5

We train an Indigenous language model adopting the unified and flexible text-to-text transfer Transformer (T5) approach (Raffel et al., 2019). T5 treats every text-based language task as a "text-to-text" problem, taking text format as input and producing new text format as output. T5 is essentially an encoder-decoder Transformer (Vaswani et al., 2017), with the encoder and decoder similar in configuration and size to a $\text{BERT}_{\text{Base}}$(Devlin et al., 2019) but with some architectural modifications. Modifications include applying a normalization layer before a sub-block and adding a pre-norm (i.e., initial input to the sub-block output). We call our resulting model **`IndT5`**. We now describe our dataset, vocabulary, and pre-training method for developing **`IndT5`**.

3.1 Training Data

We build **`IndCorpus`**, a collection of ten Indigenous languages and Spanish comprising 1.17 GB of text ($\sim$5.37M sentences), to pre-train **`IndT5`**. **`IndCorpus`** is collected from both Wikipedia and the Bible. Table 2 provides the size and number of sentences for each language in our dataset.

3.2 IndT5 Vocabulary

The T5 (Raffel et al., 2019) model is based on a vocabulary acquired by the SentencePiece library[2] using English, French, German, and Romanian web pages from "Colossal Clean Crawled Corpus" (or C4 for short). We use a similar procedure to create our Indigenous languages vocabulary. Namely, we use SentencePiece (Kudo, 2018) to encode text as WordPiece (Sennrich et al., 2016b) tokens with a vocabulary size of 100K WordPieces extracted from **`IndCorpus`**.

3.3 Unsupervised Pre-Training

We leverage our unlabeled Indigenous corpus, **`IndCorpus`**, to pre-train **`IndT5`**. For that, we use a denoising objective (Raffel et al., 2019) that does not require labels. The main idea is feeding the model with corrupted (masked) versions of the original sentence, and training it to reconstruct the original sentence. Inspired by BERT's objective (i.e., masked language model) (Devlin et al., 2019), the denoising objective (Raffel et al., 2019) works by randomly sampling and dropping out 15% of tokens in the input sequence. All consecutive spans of dropped-out tokens are then replaced by a single sentinel token. We pre-train our model for 100K steps on the **`IndCorpus`** using the T5_{Base} architecture.[3] We refer to this model as $\text{IndT5}_{\text{100k}}$. Afterwards, we further pre-train on only the ten Indigenous languages part of our dataset (i.e., without the Spanish data) for 40K steps. We refer to this version of the model as $\text{IndT5}_{\text{140k}}$. For both pre-training steps, we use a learning rate of 0.01,

[2] `https://github.com/google/sentencepiece`

[3] Both encoder and decoder of T5_{Base} model has 12 layers each with 12 attention heads, and 768 hidden units.

Target language	Wikipedia		Bible	
	Size (MB)	Sentences	Size (MB)	Sentences
Hñähñu	-	-	1.4	7.5K
Wixarika	-	-	1.3	7.5K
Nahuatl	5.8	61.1K	1.5	7.5K
Guarani	3.7	28.2K	1.3	7.5K
Bribri	-	-	1.5	7.5K
Rarámuri	-	-	1.9	7.5K
Quechua	5.9	97.3K	4.9	31.1K
Aymara	1.7	32.9K	5	30.7K
Shipibo-Konibo	-	-	1	7.9K
Asháninka	-	-	1.4	7.8K
Spanish	1.13K	5M	-	-
Total	1.15K	5.22M	19.8	125.3K

Table 2: Datasets in IndCorpus by language

Languages	Train	Dev	Test
es-aym	6,531	996	1,003
es-cni	3,883	883	1,003
es-bzd	7,506	996	1,003
es-gn	26,032	995	1,003
es-oto	4,889	599	1,003
es-nah	16,145	672	1,003
es-quy	125,008	996	1,003
es-tar	14,720	995	1,003
es-shp	14,592	996	1,003
es-hch	8,966	994	1,003

Table 3: Distribution of MT data

a batch size of 128 sequences, and a maximum sequence length of 512. We use the original implementation of T5 in the TensorFlow framework. [4]. We train the models on Google Cloud TPU with 8 cores (v3.8) from TensorFlow Research Cloud (TFRC).[5]

4 Our Machine Translation Models

4.1 Parallel Data

As part of the AmericasNLP 2021 Shared Task on Open Machine Translation, the training (Train) and development (Dev) datasets for ten target Indigeneous languages along with the source language Spanish were released. All the datasets are manually translated. Table 3 shows the number of sentences of different language pairs in shared task data. Table 4 provides example sentences extracted from the Dev dataset with their corresponding translations.

[4]https://github.com/google-research/text-to-text-transfer-transformer

[5]https://www.tensorflow.org/tfrc

4.2 Approach

For all languages pairs except *quy* and *gn*, we fine-tune each of the two versions of our language model, i.e., both $\text{IndT5}_{\text{100k}}$ and $\text{IndT5}_{\text{140k}}$, under two conditions: **(A)** we train on Train using 100% of Dev data for validation, for 150 epochs; **(B)** we fine-tune the best epoch from setting A for 50 epochs, adding 80% of Dev data to Train (using the remaining 20% Dev for validation).

4.3 Evaluation

We report the results of both $\text{IndT5}_{\text{100k}}$ and $\text{IndT5}_{\text{140k}}$ models using two metrics: BLEU score (Papineni et al., 2002) and ChrF++ (Popović, 2017). Tables 5 and 6 show the results of both models on Test sets for each of the language pairs using settings A and B described in Section 4.2, respectively.

4.4 Discussion

The results presented in Table 5 and Table 6 show that all our models, with both settings A and B, outperform the respective baselines across all languages. An exception is the languages *aym* and *shp*. As expected, fine-tuning the $\text{IndT5}_{\text{100k}}$ and $\text{IndT5}_{\text{140k}}$ models using the training data and 80% of the Dev data (i.e., setting B) improves the results with a mean of +0.003% and +0.04% in ChrF++ on the Test data, respectively. Interestingly, fur-

Pair	Sentence	Translation
es-aym	Algunos actores usan el teatro comunitario para mejorar.	Yaqhip akturanakax juk'amp yatsuñatakiw ayllunkir tiyatrur mantapxi.
	Los artistas de IRT ayudan a los niños en las escuelas.	IRT artistanakax jisk'a yatiqañ utankir wawanakaruw yanapapxi.
es-cni	Pensé que habías ido al campamento.	Nokenkeshireashitaka pijaiti imabeyetinta.
	Viajar es un beneficio que obtenemos.	Akenayeeterika aparo ayeeti aneakeri.
es-bzd	Fui a un seminario que se hizo vía satélite.	Ye' dë'rö seminario ã wéx yö' satélite kĩ.
	El grupo está interesado en temas ambientales.	E' wakpa kĩ ujtè kiànã e' dör káx ajkóqnũk.
es-gn	Veía a su hermana todos los días.	Ko'êko'êre ohecha heindýpe.
	Ramona nunca ha estado en Concord.	Ramona noîriva Concord-pe.
es-nah	Santo trabajó para Disney y operó las tazas de té.	zanto quitequitilih Disney huan quinpexontih in cafen caxitl
	La hermana de la abuela no era blanca.	ihueltiuh in cihtli ixchipahuac catca
es-quy	De vez en cuando me gusta comer ensalada.	Yananpiqa ensaladatam mikuytam munani
	Ellos vivían en Broad Street.	Broad Streetpi paykuna yacharqaku.
es-tar	Es un hombre griego.	Bilé rejói Griego ju
	Nuestro padre dijo que no los llamaran animales.	Kini onó aniyé mapu ke chuwé namúti anéba ajaré jákami.
es-shp	El Museo se ve afectado por las inversiones.	Ja Museora en oinai inversionesbaon afectana.
	Loren Field es el científico principal de la escuela	Nato Loren Field riki científico rekena axeti xobonko
es-hch	Era una selva tropical.	pe h+k+t+kai metsi+ra+ ye tsie nieka ti+x+kat+.
	Son más económicos porque son realmente buenos en gas.	p+ h+k+ nip+ka raye at+ka aix+ m+ anenek+ ik+ gas.

Table 4: Example sentences of the various language pairs and corresponding translations (from Dev set).

Pair	Baseline		Setting A		Setting B	
	Bleu	ChrF++	Bleu	ChrF++	Bleu	ChrF++
aym	0.3	**0.188**	1.01	0.178	0.76	0.186
cni	0.03	0.104	0.09	0.176	0.09	**0.178**
bzd	0.54	0.077	0.86	0.11	0.89	**0.111**
oto	0.01	0.059	0.03	0.081	0.04	**0.083**
nah	0.33	0.182	-	-	0.16	**0.196**
tar	0.01	0.046	0.06	0.102	-	-
hch	3.18	0.126	4.95	**0.186**	5.09	**0.186**

Table 5: Evaluation results of IndT5_{100k} in BLEU and ChrF++ on the Test sets for the different language pairs.

Pair	Baseline		Setting A		Setting B	
	Bleu	ChrF++	Bleu	ChrF++	Bleu	ChrF++
aym	0.3	0.188	0.820	0.182	0.990	**0.190**
cni	0.03	0.104	0.070	0.178	0.080	**0.183**
bzd	0.54	0.077	0.990	0.112	0.940	**0.113**
oto	0.01	0.059	0.030	0.082	0.040	**0.084**
nah	0.33	0.182	0.150	0.188	0.160	**0.196**
tar	0.01	0.046	0.080	0.102	0.050	**0.105**
shp	0.34	**0.139**	0.160	0.124	0.230	0.124
hch	3.18	0.126	5.100	0.194	5.520	**0.195**

Table 6: Evaluation results of IndT5_{140k} in BLEU and ChrF++ on the Test sets for the different language pairs.

ther pre-training IndT5 on only the ten Indigenous languages (i.e. target languages) produces better results with an average improvement of +0.003% and +0.004% in settings A and B, respectively. Overall, the impact of limited data is clear.

5 Conclusion

In this work, we introduced a new Transformer language model (**IndT5**) and a dataset (**IndCorpus**) for ten Indigenous languages and Spanish. We applied **IndT5** to the MT task on eight languages pairs as part of our submission to the AmericasNLP 2021 Shared Task. While **IndT5** helps improve translation, the task remains hard due to absence of parallel as well as monolingual data. In the future, we plan to integrate statistical MT methods to augment our data as well as investigate best hyperparameters for our neural models.

Acknowledgements

We gratefully acknowledge support from the Natural Sciences and Engineering Research Council of Canada, the Social Sciences and Humanities Research Council of Canada, Canadian Foundation for Innovation, Compute Canada, and UBC ARC-Sockeye. We also thank the Google TFRC program for providing us with free TPU access.

References

Ife Adebara, Muhammad Abdul-Mageed, and Miikka Silfverberg. 2021. Translating the Unseen? Yorùbá-English MT in Low-Resource, Morphologically-Unmarked Settings. *AfricNLP*.

Ife Adebara, El Moatez Billah Nagoudi, and Muhammad Abdul Mageed. 2020. Translating similar languages: Role of mutual intelligibility in multilingual transformers. In *Proceedings of the Fifth Conference on Machine Translation*, pages 381–386, Online. Association for Computational Linguistics.

Christos Baziotis, Barry Haddow, and Alexandra Birch. 2020. Language model prior for low-resource neural machine translation. *arXiv preprint arXiv:2004.14928*.

Jacob Devlin, Ming-Wei Chang, Kenton Lee, and Kristina Toutanova. 2019. BERT: Pre-training of Deep Bidirectional Transformers for Language Understanding. In *Proceedings of the 2019 Conference of the North American Chapter of the Association for Computational Linguistics: Human Language Technologies, Volume 1 (Long and Short Papers)*, pages 4171–4186.

David M. Eberhard, Gary F. Simons, and Charles D. Fennig. 2021. Ethnologue: Languages of the world. twenty-fourth edition. Dallas, Texas. SIL International.

Isaac Feldman and Rolando Coto-Solano. 2020. Neural machine translation models with back-translation for the extremely low-resource indigenous language bribri. In *Proceedings of the 28th International Conference on Computational Linguistics*, pages 3965–3976.

Geoffrey Hinton, Oriol Vinyals, and Jeff Dean. 2015. Distilling the knowledge in a neural network. *arXiv preprint arXiv:1503.02531*.

Tom Kocmi and Ondrej Bojar. 2018. Trivial transfer learning for low-resource neural machine translation. *CoRR*, abs/1809.00357.

Philipp Koehn. 2017. Neural machine translation. *arXiv preprint arXiv:1709.07809*.

Taku Kudo. 2018. Subword regularization: Improving neural network translation models with multiple subword candidates. *arXiv preprint arXiv:1804.10959*.

N. Tan Le and F. Sadat. 2020. Addressing challenges of indigenous languages through neural machine translation: The case of inuktitut-english.

Patrick Littell, Anna Kazantseva, Roland Kuhn, Aidan Pine, Antti Arppe, Christopher Cox, and Marie-Odile Junker. 2018. Indigenous language technologies in Canada: Assessment, challenges, and successes. In *Proceedings of the 27th International Conference on Computational Linguistics*, pages 2620–2632, Santa Fe, New Mexico, USA. Association for Computational Linguistics.

Manuel Mager, Ximena Gutierrez-Vasques, Gerardo Sierra, and Ivan Meza-Ruiz. 2018. Challenges of language technologies for the indigenous languages of the Americas. In *Proceedings of the 27th International Conference on Computational Linguistics*, pages 55–69, Santa Fe, New Mexico, USA. Association for Computational Linguistics.

J.C. Micher. 2018. *Addressing Challenges of Machine Translation of Inuit Language*. ARL-TN. US Army Research Laboratory.

Toan Q. Nguyen and David Chiang. 2017. Transfer learning across low-resource, related languages for neural machine translation. *CoRR*, abs/1708.09803.

Iroro Orife. 2020. Towards neural machine translation for edoid languages. *arXiv preprint arXiv:2003.10704*.

John E. Ortega, Richard Castro Mamani, and Kyunghyun Cho. 2020. Neural machine translation with a polysynthetic low resource language. *Machine Translation*, 34(4):325–346.

Kishore Papineni, Salim Roukos, Todd Ward, and Wei-Jing Zhu. 2002. Bleu: a method for automatic evaluation of machine translation. In *Proceedings of the 40th annual meeting of the Association for Computational Linguistics*, pages 311–318.

Maja Popović. 2017. chrf++: words helping character n-grams. In *Proceedings of the second conference on machine translation*, pages 612–618.

Michael Przystupa and Muhammad Abdul-Mageed. 2019. Neural machine translation of low-resource and similar languages with backtranslation. In *Proceedings of the Fourth Conference on Machine Translation (Volume 3: Shared Task Papers, Day 2)*, pages 224–235.

Colin Raffel, Noam Shazeer, Adam Roberts, Katherine Lee, Sharan Narang, Michael Matena, Yanqi Zhou, Wei Li, and Peter J Liu. 2019. Exploring the limits of transfer learning with a unified text-to-text transformer. *arXiv preprint arXiv:1910.10683*.

Rico Sennrich, Barry Haddow, and Alexandra Birch. 2016a. Improving neural machine translation models with monolingual data. In *Proceedings of the 54th Annual Meeting of the Association for Computational Linguistics (Volume 1: Long Papers)*, pages 86–96, Berlin, Germany. Association for Computational Linguistics.

Rico Sennrich, Barry Haddow, and Alexandra Birch. 2016b. Neural machine translation of rare words with subword units. In *Proceedings of the 54th Annual Meeting of the Association for Computational Linguistics (Volume 1: Long Papers)*, pages 1715–1725, Berlin, Germany. Association for Computational Linguistics.

Rico Sennrich and Biao Zhang. 2019. Revisiting low-resource neural machine translation: A case study. In *Proceedings of the 57th Annual Meeting of the Association for Computational Linguistics*, pages 211–221.

Ashish Vaswani, Noam Shazeer, Niki Parmar, Jakob Uszkoreit, Llion Jones, Aidan N Gomez, Łukasz Kaiser, and Illia Polosukhin. 2017. Attention is all you need. In *Advances in Neural Information Processing Systems*, pages 6000–6010.

Chunting Zhou, Xuezhe Ma, Junjie Hu, and Graham Neubig. 2019. Handling syntactic divergence in low-resource machine translation.

Barret Zoph, Deniz Yuret, Jonathan May, and Kevin Knight. 2016. Transfer learning for low-resource neural machine translation. In *Proceedings of the 2016 Conference on Empirical Methods in Natural Language Processing*, pages 1568–1575.

Author Index

Association for Computational Linguistics
209 N. Eighth Street
Stroudsburg, Pennsylvania 18360

CURRAN ASSOCIATES INC.
proceedings.com

ISBN 978-1-7138-3015-3